Years of Am~~ition~~ European Hi~~story~~ 1815–1914

Contributors

DAVID COOPER, JOHN LAVER
& DAVID WILLIAMSON

Edited by

JOHN LAVER

Hodder & Stoughton

A MEMBER OF THE HODDER HEADLINE GROUP

✎ ACKNOWLEDGEMENTS ✎

The Publishers would like to thank the following for permission to reproduce material in this book:

Addison Wesley Educational Publishers Inc., for an extract from *Francis Joseph* by S. Beller (1996) used on pages 363–4, 378. Addison Wesley Longman Inc., for an extract from *Revolutionary Europe 1780–1850* by J. Sperber (2000) used on pages 228–9. Hodder & Stoughton Educational, for an extract from *The Habsburg Empire 1815–1918* by N. Pelling (1996) used on page 377. John Murray (Publishers) Ltd, for an extract from *Success in European History 1815–1915* by J. B. Watson (1981) used on page 70. Longman, for an extract from *France 1814–1914* by Robert Tombs (1996) used on page 67. Longman (Pearson Education Corporate Communications), for an extract from *The Decline and Fall of Habsburg Empire* by A. Sked (2000) used on pages 187, 231. Longman (Pearson Professional Education), for an extract from *The Ascendancy of Europe* by M. Anderson (1999) used on pages 70, 72, 377. Longman Publishing Group, for an extract from *The Origins of the Wars of German Unification* by W. Carr (1995) used on page 148. Longman Publishing Group, for an extract from *Napoleon III* by James F. McMillan (1995) used on page 155. Orion Publishing Group (Phoenix Press), for an extract from *The Lawful Revolution* by Martin Gilbert, used on page 229. Oxford University Press, for an extract from *Transformation of European Politics 1763–1848* by P. W. Schroeder (1994) used on page 10. Praeger (New York), for an extract from *The Decline of Imperial Russia 1855–1914* by Hugh Seton-Watson, used on page 37. Routledge Historical Collections (Taylor & Francis), for an extract from *The Italian Risorgimento* by Lucy Riall (1994) used on page 119. Orion Books, for an extract from *The Lawful Revolution: Louis Kossuth and the Hungarians 1848–49* by I. Deak (2001) used on page 229. Yale University Press, for an extract from *Mazzini* by Denis Mack Smith (1994) used on page 92.

The Publishers would like to thank the following for permission to reproduce the following copyright illustrations in this book:
Archivo del Lavoro di Milano, page 328 above; Bibliothèque Nationale de France (Paris), pages 55 above, 56, 66, 256, 394; Bildarchive Preussischer Kulturbesitz, pages 171, 184, 293, 404, 431, 434; *Proclamation of the Empire* by Anton Alexander von Werner, Schloss Friedrichsruhe/Bridgeman Art Library, page 198; John Appleton, Atlantic Syndication/Centre for the Study of Cartoons and Caricature, University of Kent, Canterbury, page 277 below; David King Collection, page 343; Edimedia/Snark International, page 276; © Giancarlo Costa, pages 328 below, 329 above, 330 above; Index, Florence, pages 110, 330 below; Istituto Centrale per il Catalogo e la Documentazione, Roma, page 323; Roger-Viollet, Paris, page 257 below; Photothèque des Musées de la ville de Paris, pages 57, 257 above; © Private Collection, page 55 below; Punch, pages 234, 272, 273, 274, 290, 295, 308, 405, 457; Réunion des Musées Nationaux, page 58; Scala/Museo Risorgimento, Milano, pages 91, 117.

Every effort has been made to trace and acknowledge ownership of copyright. The publishers will be glad to make suitable arrangements with any copyright holders whom it has not been possible to contact.

Orders: please contact Bookpoint Ltd, 130 Milton Park, Abingdon, Oxon OX14 4SB. Telephone: (44) 01235 827720. Fax: (44) 01235 400454. Lines are open from 9:00–6.00, Monday to Saturday, with a 24 hour message answering service. Email address: orders@bookpoint.co.uk

British Library Cataloguing in Publication Data
A catalogue record for this title is available from the British Library

ISBN 0 340 72127 8

First published 2001
Impression number   10 9 8 7 6 5 4 3 2 1
Year   2007 2006 2005 2004 2003 2002 2001

Copyright © 2001 David Cooper, John Laver and David Williamson

Cover photo of Liberty guiding the people, celebrating the 28th July 1830 by Eugene Delacroix, the Louvre/Réunion des Musées Nationale.

Produced and typeset by Gray Publishing, Tunbridge Wells, Kent
Printed in Great Britain for Hodder & Stoughton Educational, a division of Hodder Headline Plc, 338 Euston Road, London NW1 3BH by J. W. Arrowsmith Ltd, Bristol

Contents

⤳ LIST OF MAPS ⤳

⤳ LIST OF PICTURES ⤳

Preface: How to use this Book

We approached the preparation and writing of *Years of Ambition* with two main aims. The first was to provide a readable and useful textbook for students, principally in the 16–19-year age range, who were studying the popular area of nineteenth-century European history. Secondly, we wanted to make the book very relevant to the modular history examination syllabuses implemented in 2000. Many textbooks on this period have already been published, but few are specifically written with the demands of AS and A2 modules in mind. While *Years of Ambition* concentrates on these demands, we believe that it also has relevance for other post-16 history courses on the nineteenth century.

The structure of the book is in some ways 'traditional'. The chapter headings and much of the content will seem familiar in that we have retained a traditional structure of having some chapters devoted to domestic developments in some of the major European powers, while others focus on relations between those powers during the nineteenth century. This was a deliberate policy. While it would have been superficially tempting to structure the book in direct relation to the content of specific modules offered by examination boards, this did not seem on more detailed investigation to be a helpful model. Different examination boards offer different options within their overall syllabus structures. Tying chapters to specific modules is very restricting. We believe that teachers and students will find the material in this book adaptable to the demands of all examination syllabuses, especially at AS and A2 level, where they focus on nineteenth-century European history.

Other features of *Years of Ambition* are designed to be of practical use to students. There are advice sections in the tradition of the *Years of ...* books, geared to the expectations of examination syllabuses and also reflecting the teaching and examining experience of the authors.

Continuity with the spirit of the original *Years of ...* series has been maintained in some important respects. This is a book about European history. It seeks to give an appropriate balance to the various geographic regions, topics and themes important in this period of history. However, we recognise that for the purposes of practical study, some subjects should receive fuller treatment or more prominence than others. So for example, although the history of the Habsburg Empire is an important part of European history throughout the nineteenth century, this book has one chapter devoted to it, while Russia has three. This is not to suggest that Russian history is inherently more important than Austrian history, but it is a reflection of the respective popularity of these topics with teachers and students. In some cases the focus on a particular topic reflects what is generally perceived to be its wider significance, for example the origins of World War I. British history does not receive treatment in its own right, but a British perspective is included where it impinges on continental affairs. This is not, of course, to suggest that Britain was not an important part of Europe in the nineteenth century. But, rather it is recognition of the fact that students concentrating on British history modules will require the more detailed treatment of British domestic history that a book of this size could not give.

Years of Ambition concentrates on political, economic and international themes. We do not believe that social and cultural themes are unimportant, but again, the constraints of space require harsh decisions to be made. In some chapters on individual countries, the text is divided into sections on political history, economic history and foreign policy. This is an artificial division: history is a complex web of interwoven themes, even if at certain times particular factors or events seem more prominent than others. However, the structure we have chosen reflects the fact that students generally find books divided into the sections outlined above easier to deal with than a more 'thematic' approach. There will be some overlap of content: for example the sections on the foreign policies of individual countries will sometimes overlap with chapters on international affairs. This is deliberate: it allows the study of a theme from different perspectives – but it should also be an encouragement to use the index and the cross-references.

As stated earlier, we are very conscious of the practical needs of students studying for higher level examinations. Additional material at the end of many chapters is designed to further develop students' knowledge and understanding of the contents and to give opportunities for relevant practice, particularly in meeting examination requirements. There are also bibliographies helpful to further study of the topics, suggested titles for essays and structured questions, sources exercises, and advice on how to write relevant answers to examination questions.

SOURCE ⌐ ANALYSIS AND EVALUATION SKILLS

Students are required to use sources and documentary extracts either as stimulus material when tackling a particular question, or they are asked to directly analyse and evaluate the evidence so as to demonstrate a range of historical skills. This section will highlight important strategies you can use when analysing source material, either as part of the course or when answering an examination question.

It is important not to make *stock responses* to source questions. For example, a statement such as 'All sources are biased' is not helpful unless the source is treated in context; that is, the answer is specifically related to the particular source being considered. Similarly, assumptions about the supposed superiority of one type of source – primary or secondary – over the other, are not helpful. Each source should be treated on its merits.

If a sources question carries a *mark allocation*, use it as a guide: a question carrying two or three marks requires a short response, one carrying six or seven marks probably requires a response of one or two paragraphs; one carrying 9–12 marks may require a 'mini-essay'.

Make sure that you *read* both the sources and any accompanying questions thoroughly before answering them: self-evident perhaps, but many students make errors or miss obvious points, especially in examinations. Sources usually carry their *attribution*, that is, information about when they were produced, who produced them, sometimes for whom they were produced, and perhaps other details. Use this information when available – it is part of the evidence and may help you to answer the questions.

Sources questions often fall into one of the following categories:

- Short introductory questions may ask you to explain a word, phrase or historical reference. Such questions usually test *recall*, and you will either know the answer or you will not, but the topic is not likely to be an obscure one.
- Questions relating to one or more sources may ask you a variety of things – for example, why a source was significant in the history of a particular event. You may be asked to *summarise* the contents. You will probably be required to show *comprehension* of the source; that is, an understanding of what you have read, and possibly the ability to précis or summarise the source. In doing this, you should avoid regurgitating the actual source or quoting large chunks of it wholesale – a fairly meaningless activity.
- You may be asked to *compare and/or contrast* particular sources for a particular reason. Make the comparison or contrast very specific, and write a conclusion, do not just describe each source.
- You may be asked about the *reliability* of a source. This means more than whether it is authentic. Always ask, 'reliable for what?'. Relate your answer to the particular source, do not discuss sources in general.
- You may be asked about the *value*, or *uses and limitations*, of sources. This is not the same thing as reliability: an 'unreliable' source may be useful to an historian; for example, a propaganda source may not be 'truthful', but it may tell you a lot about the person who produced it, or the society in which it appeared.
- Some questions may require a *synthesis*. You may be asked to query a particular statement, making use of the source or sources, and possibly your own knowledge *also*. If you are asked to use both sources and 'own knowledge', ensure that you do so.

Answering sources questions is not necessarily easier than answering structured questions or essay questions. Sources questions may often require shorter answers, but they still need careful thought, preparation and practice.

THE SKILLS OF ANSWERING STRUCTURED QUESTIONS AND ESSAYS

For the purpose of this book, the distinction between essay questions of the type that might be attempted by A2 candidates and structured questions as might be attempted by AS candidates is as follows:

European Relations 1814–56

INTRODUCTION

AN OVERVIEW OF EUROPEAN DIPLOMACY 1814–56: THREE THEMES

A *War and peace*

Between 1792 and 1815, Europe had been the victim of an almost continuous series of devastating wars. These had their origin in the French Revolution of 1789, as Europe's crowned heads tried first to crush, and then to contain, the regime which had had Louis XVI guillotined in 1793. But to the astonishment and dismay of Europe's established rulers, the French Republic more than held its own. With the emergence of Napoleon Bonaparte, a military commander of genius, who proclaimed himself Emperor in 1804, the overwhelming superiority of French forces was confirmed.

Napoleon, however, overreached himself, and his 1812 invasion of Russia was a disaster. He was forced to withdraw, and in a series of campaigns in 1813–14 was forced out of central Europe too. Britain, Russia, Prussia and Austria pooled their resources against him, and Paris was taken in 1814. Napoleon's last throw of the dice ended in defeat at Waterloo in June 1815.

It was one thing to defeat Napoleon; it was another to restore Europe to its pre-Napoleonic state. Two decades of war had threatened to wipe the old order of Europe off the map. At the peak of Napoleon's power, much of Europe had been under France's direct or indirect rule, and he had redrawn the borders of central Europe, largely disregarding the rights of traditional rulers.

In 1814–15, therefore, Europe's peacemakers were faced with a variety of tasks:

- how far could – or should – the old states of Europe be restored?
- how could France – whose size, population and wealth had made it such a formidable enemy – be restrained from future aggression?
- how could international relations as a whole be restructured so as to minimise the risks of future conflict?

B *The Spectre of Revolution*

See page 31

It had proved hard enough to cope with the military threat posed by France after 1792. But perhaps even more dangerous, in the long run, were the ideas unleashed by the Revolution. Liberty, Equality and Fraternity had been the cry of 1789. Together, these ideas meant that the ultimate source of political authority was not the king (claiming to rule by inheritance and grace of God), but the nation and its citizens. Such ideas were clearly incompatible with Europe's old order, which the Revolution had nearly destroyed, and (in most respects) with the order which Europe's peacemakers strove to restore. The peacemakers of Europe were therefore driven by both **ideological** and strategic concerns:

an **ideology** is a system of political ideas which helps to determine policy and mobilize support

absolutism a political system under which the monarchy or government has complete or absolute power, without any checks or balances

liberals in a nineteenth century context, people who believed in the rights of individuals

nationalism a belief that peoples of a particular race, background or culture should be citizens of their own country or nation-state, or a concept vigorously promoting patriotic sentiments

- With the exception of France itself, which was given a constitution in 1814, and a few medium-sized states in Germany, restoration Europe was politically **absolutist**, i.e. the powers of its Emperors, Kings and Dukes were restored unchecked by any representative institutions. But throughout Europe, **liberals** would continue to challenge these arrangements, arguing that the people should be allowed to send representatives to a parliament where, by approving (or rejecting) laws and taxation, they might make an active contribution to government, and counterbalance the power of the executive.
- The revolutionary claim that political authority belonged to the people – i.e. the nation – helped to inspire ideas of **nationalism**. As the map of Europe opposite shows, the peacemakers created a Europe which – again, with the exception of France – simply disregarded the continent's ethnic divisions. Russia, Austria (and the Ottomans) ruled over multinational empires. Equally, the German and Italian peoples were divided amongst literally dozens of independent ministates. Nationalists strove – mostly unsuccessfully for the first half of the nineteenth century – to rectify this situation.

A good deal of the diplomacy of this era revolved around how and how far the liberal/nationalist challenge could be contained. The threat of revolution seemed ever present, with risings in Greece, Italy, Spain, Belgium and Poland calling for an international response. The possibility of another revolution in France was the greatest worry of the major Powers, however, for the precedent of the 1790s suggested that the French saw revolution as a product for export and a means of self-aggrandisement. France was indeed to be convulsed by revolution again, in 1830 and 1848. The fact that neither crisis led to renewed bids for French expansionism or a major European war counts as a considerable success for the strategy of containment promoted by the peacemakers of 1814–15.

C *The Eastern Question*

Paradoxically, the most serious threat to Europe's peace between 1815 and 1848, and indeed the issue which was to engulf Britain, France and Russia in war in 1853, was one which had not been touched by the

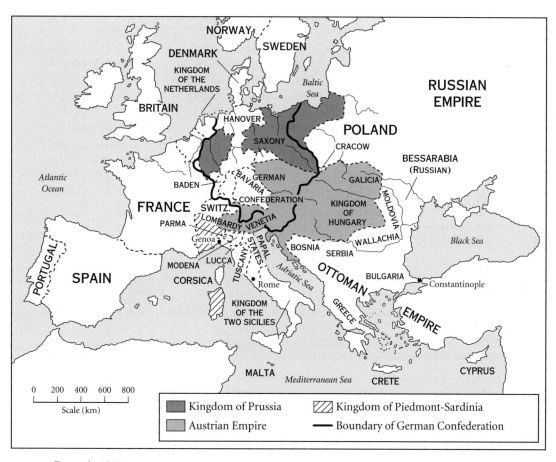

MAP 1 *Europe in 1815*

peacemakers of 1815: the Eastern Question. The Eastern Question was a compound of two problems: the Ottoman Empire appeared to be in interminable decline; and Europe's Great Powers (Russia, Britain, Austria and France, certainly) believed that they had vital interests at stake in this region. Crises in the Near East therefore repeatedly tended to draw in the Powers. Throughout the 1820s, the implications of ongoing struggle for Greek independence (Greece was a part of the Ottoman Empire until 1830) were a major headache for Europe's statesmen. The ambitions of Mehmet Ali, an overmightly subject of the Sultan, precipitated major international crises in 1831–3 and again in 1839–41; whilst the conflicting ambitions of the Russian, French and British – and the Turks – entwined to cause the Crimean War in 1853. A factor in each of the crises was fear of Russian expansionism: the Tsar's massive empire was widely seen as a power capable of exercising a dominance over Europe comparable to that of Napoleonic France at the peak of its power.

See Map 2 on page 4

Nevertheless, between 1815 and 1853, none of Europe's major Powers had been to war with each other. These decades constitute

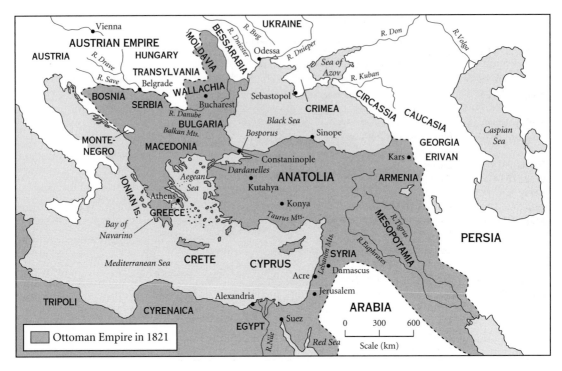

MAP 2 *The Eastern Question*

Europe's 'long peace'. Whatever the failings of the peacemakers of 1815, this period of relative stability suggests that in many ways, they did a good job. Identifying the reasons for that success is one of the most important themes of this chapter.

1 ⌐ EUROPE MAKES PEACE: THE TREATIES OF PARIS AND THE CONGRESS OF VIENNA

As the timeline on page 5 indicates, military and diplomatic activity in Europe immediately before and after the end of the Napoleonic Wars was hectic and complicated.

In April 1814, Emperor Napoleon, facing certain defeat by the allies, was forced to abdicate by the French Senate. After some intrigue and uncertainty, Louis XVIII was installed (with allied approval) as the French King, and his Government accepted the peace terms on offer. By the First Treaty of Paris, France lost some small parcels of territory along its eastern frontier (the Treaty more or less restoring the borders of January 1792). France also committed itself to accepting the broader European settlement as it would emerge from the international congress planned for Vienna.

- the second strategy, however, was pursued more successfully. Metternich was able to convince enough of Europe's other leaders, at crucial moments, that what was good for Austria was good for them and for Europe as a whole. This supplied a mid-term solution to the 'Austrian problem'. But whether Austria's neighbours would be happy to sustain the illusion of Austrian power indefinitely was less likely.

The settlement was more successful in containing France. France was to remain a Great Power, but it was caged and closely guarded:

- the First Treaty of Paris had been relatively generous to the French; but, inspired by Napoleon's escape from the island of Elba, they repudiated it. After Napoleon's final defeat, the peace terms were significantly revised. The Second Treaty of Paris increased France's territorial losses, imposed a heavy **indemnity**, backed up by a temporary army of occupation. It was designed to bring home the painful reality of defeat and thereby discourage further adventures
- the peacemakers at Vienna created a sort of *cordon sanitaire* (protective barrier) on France's eastern border, systematically strengthening those points which, in the past, had proved most vulnerable to French aggression. Accordingly, on her north-eastern frontier, the former Austrian Netherlands were fused with Holland to form the new (larger and supposedly stronger) United Netherlands; French ambitions in the Rhineland were to be checked by Prussian expansion there, whilst France's well-worn path into the Italian peninsula would now be blocked by an expanded Kingdom of Piedmont-Sardinia, and a weightier Austrian presence there too
- although not strictly a part of the Vienna Settlement, the installation of a **constitutional monarchy** in France was also designed to contribute to European stability. This aimed simultaneously to reconcile liberals to the Bourbon restoration, and to ensure that the government of France would be cautious, responsible and anti-revolutionary in outlook. The possibility of re-imposing an absolutist system on France was not seriously considered. The Congress of Vienna, although in most respects reactionary, here showed itself to be flexible.

The Treaty of Chaumont (March 1814) was turned into the Quadruple Alliance (November 1815). By this, the four victorious Powers of the 'Waterloo Coalition' committed themselves for 20 years to uphold the terms of the Second Treaty of Paris and to prevent, by force if necessary, the return of Napoleon. It also provided for the holding of periodic international conferences to consider 'measures which shall be the most salutary for the repose and prosperity of Nations, and for the maintenance of the Peace of Europe'. Metternich's 'Congress System' was to grow out of this idea.

KEY ISSUE

Why did Austria find it difficult to carry out the diplomatic role which it had been given at the Congress of Vienna?

See pages 36–7

---

indemnity payment extracted by a victorious country from another defeated in war

---

constitutional monarchy a system of government in which a monarch governs according to a constitution, usually involving a parliament, which limits the monarch's powers

---

See page 11

KEY ISSUE

How did the peacemakers at Vienna try to neutralise the threat from France?

P. W. Schroeder evaluates The Congress of Vienna

In the *Transformation of Europe Politics 1763–1848*, Professor Schroeder offers a very positive evaluation of The Congress of Vienna, challenging the assumption that it ignored popular demands and insisting that it laid the foundations for long-term peace in Europe:

… one may seriously doubt that there was at this time any wide popular demand in Europe for freedom, and national unity. If people called for anything in 1815, it was for the same thing most princes and élites wanted, and what the congress gave them – peace and order under their traditional rulers.

… how well did it establish peace? Judged on this basis, the Vienna system comes out with a remarkably positive balance sheet. This is immediately apparent simply from its handling of the major persistent areas of conflict in Europe. … it managed the German, French and Near Eastern questions as well as could reasonably be hoped; and even in areas of comparative failure, like Italy and Poland, though it did not prevent future conflict, it at least controlled it for a good while. No other general peace settlement in European history [e.g. the Treaty of Versailles] comes anywhere close to this record. Every one failed this test, [and] led almost immediately to new or continued conflict. Only the Vienna settlement got things right; only it genuinely established peace.

© Paul W. Schroeder 1994. Reprinted from *Transformation of European Politics 1763–1848* by Paul W. Schroeder (1994) by permission of Oxford University Press.

How convincing is Schroeder's assessment?

TIMELINE

1818	Congress of Aix-la-Chapelle
1819	Carlsbad Decrees
1820	Congress of Troppau; Troppau Protocol
1821	Congress of Laibach Greek Revolt began
1822	Congress of Verona
1823	French intervention in Spain

The Concert of Europe is the name given to the ideal – sometimes achieved in practice – according to which Europe's Great Powers would act together in a spirit of trust and mutual goodwill, to preserve peace and defuse crises

There is a profile of Metternich on pages 364–5

2 ⌇ THE AGE OF METTERNICH – 1: 1815–24 – CONDUCTING THE CONCERT OF EUROPE

A *Metternich*

Metternich was Austrian Foreign Minister from 1809, and Chancellor from 1821, only falling from office in the wake of the revolutions of 1848. He was therefore at or near the centre of European diplomacy for almost 40 years. Hence some historians call these decades 'the Age of Metternich'. This phrase implies that, usually behind the scenes, Metternich pulled the strings of European diplomacy for all these years, shaping events to conform to Austria's needs; and secondly, that he was able to impose on most of the continent a political system which – absolutist, aristocratic and repressive – was designed to frustrate the desires of the peoples of Europe for freedom: until his policy finally got its just deserts in 1848. The first claim is only partially true, and the second needs severe qualification.

One of Metternich's undoubted gifts was in the field of personal diplomacy: the art of persuading Europe's rulers and statesmen to see the world through Vienna's eyes. Metternich would achieve his greatest successes in this role in the period between 1815 and 1821.

B *The Holy Alliance*

With the exception of the brief but intense crisis at Vienna in the winter of 1814–15 (see above), the last years of the war had been characterised by close collaboration between Russia, Austria, Britain and Prussia. The leaders of these Powers believed it essential that such co-operation be continued in peace time. Only then could the supposed scourge of revolution be contained, and any future tensions between the Powers resolved.

Alexander I tried to give some reality to these ideals with his plans for a Holy Alliance, proclaimed in the summer of 1815. The Tsar was a religious mystic with a utopian streak who saw himself as on a mission to bring peace and harmony to Europe. This explains the overtly religious language of the Alliance: international relations 'ought to be guided by the sublime truths taught by the eternal religion of God our Saviour' and guided by the objective of 'rendering mutual service and testifying individual goodwill'. Harder-headed politicians like Castlereagh and Metternich did not know what to make of this. The former privately dismissed it as 'a piece of sublime mysticism and nonsense', and Britain declined to become a signatory. Metternich was left in some difficulties, especially as the original version of the Holy Alliance seemed to imply that the best way of establishing a reign of peace and Christian harmony was to bring about liberal political reforms throughout Europe. Yet Austria could hardly risk offending its mighty neighbour by refusing to sign. The final version, partially rewritten by Metternich, stressed that the alliance was a paternalistic brotherhood of Christian sovereigns, whose duty it was to protect their subjects rather than give them political rights. Metternich – not for the last time – had channelled the Tsar's unorthodox impulses down conservative paths. It was in this safer format that Austria, Prussia and Russia signed the treaty in 1815. Before long, the term 'Holy Alliance', stripped of its original elevated connotations was used to identify the common **reactionary** front which the three autocracies of eastern Europe presented against the threat from liberalism and nationalism.

> **KEY ISSUE**
>
> *What was the significance of the Holy Alliance?*

> **reactionary** a belief or policy fundamentally opposed to change or reform

C *The Congresses*

Metternich hoped in 1815 that the Concert of Europe should be as inclusive as possible. At first, this seemed to be one of the principles of the Congress System – the name given to the series of summit meetings held in Europe between 1818 and 1822 (the word 'system' is a little misleading – these meetings followed no pre-planned schedule):

- Aix-la-Chapelle, September–November 1818
- Troppau, October–December 1820
- Laibach, January–May 1821
- Verona, October–December 1822.

The first of these was perhaps the most successful. France, which had speedily paid off its indemnity, was formally welcomed into the Concert as a Great Power equal to the others in dignity and status. But even here, tensions were beneath the surface, with Russia jealous at Britain's expanding role as a world power, and Metternich still anxious at Russia's potential to dominate continental Europe.

ANALYSIS

See page 39

The Congress of Troppau

The Congress of Troppau was probably the most significant of the summits. It took place against a background of revolutionary upheaval in Europe. In Germany, militant nationalists were active; in France, the heir to the throne had been assassinated; and in Spain and Italy, revolution had broken out. How should the Great Powers respond?

● Two very different approaches soon emerged. The Tsar, still longing to bring justice to Europe, argued that the Great Powers should act collectively to enforce settlements on Europe's troubled regions. Some of his advisers even suggested that this might involve imposing constitutions on countries like Spain and the Italian states, regardless of the wishes of their rulers. This, rather than repression, offered the best prospect of securing long term stability. The British, however, disliked any attempt to fix the conduct of foreign policy according to any general principles. According to them the merits, or demerits, of international intervention in the internal affairs of another country should be judged according to the circumstances of each case.

● The Russian and British positions would be hard to reconcile. They also left Austria in a quandary. Metternich was clear that the revolution in Naples had to be crushed: Italy was Austria's 'backyard'. Castlereagh would raise no objection to Austria intervening by itself to restore order. The problem was that such **unilateral** action would risk alienating Russia. On the other hand, if Metternich sought the active collaboration of the continental Great Powers in solving the Italian problem, and thereby established a general principle of international intervention, Austria would alienate Britain.

● The broader implications of the second option were also worrying. Was Russia to be given the green light to intervene with its massive army in the name of peace and justice in any corner of Europe? Was the Congress System to actively sponsor the spread of liberal constitutionalism? Metternich was aghast at either prospect.

● Metternich skilfully manoeuvred out of this tight corner. The key to his success was the personal ascendancy he won over the Tsar. Correctly sensing that Alexander's sympathies with liberalism were waning (the Tsar was becoming preoccupied by signs

unilateral action taken by one country or person without consultation with anybody else

of subversion in Russia, Poland and Germany), Metternich persuaded Alexander that 'the whole of Europe was threatened by [a] revolutionary spirit'. Metternich did not hesitate to identify Paris as the headquarters of this conspiracy.

● Having thus won the Tsar round, the final draft of the Troppau Protocol exhibited none of the liberal sentiments which Metternich had feared. It was an unambiguous statement of anti-revolutionary, monarchical solidarity. And its small-print gave Metternich room for manoeuvre on the crucial questions of when and where – if at all – Russian troops might be deployed in any anti-revolutionary expeditions. Metternich had endorsed the principle of collective action, but in a way which mostly served Austria's Great Power needs.

● Metternich was also pleased to have widened the gap between Russia and France, by labelling the latter as the centre of revolutionary conspiracy (see above). The possibility of a Franco-Russian **entente** or alliance – one of Vienna's worst nightmares – was now remote. But there was a price to be paid for Metternich's successes. Britain followed France in declining to sign the Protocol. Could the Concert of Europe remain harmonious?

entente friendly agreement

KEY ISSUE

What was resolved at the Congress of Troppau?

The Congress of Troppau set the pattern for the last two Congresses. Metternich continued to exploit his personal ascendancy over the Tsar. The Holy Alliance powers drew closer together in their common cause to suppress revolution; and Britain and France, by contrast, found themselves increasingly out of sympathy with this reactionary front, but also – as the pursuit of national interest reasserted itself – out of sympathy with each other:

● at Laibach, Metternich skilfully persuaded the Tsar not to support the Greeks in their struggle against Ottoman rule, claiming that the revolt was a further manifestation of an international revolutionary conspiracy

● he also won the Congress's approval for Austria's 'policing' actions in Italy

See pages 88–9

● but at Verona, it proved impossible to co-ordinate an effective collective response to the Spanish revolution: France, Britain and Russia each had very different ideas about what should be done. After the Congress, the French intervened to restore absolutism without the full consent of the Concert of Europe. Canning, the new British Foreign Secretary (Castlereagh had committed suicide in 1822), summed up the new mood: 'every nation for itself and God for us all'.

See page 40

There would be future European congresses: but any Congress System was dead. What had it achieved? The summits had failed to live up to hopes that they would inaugurate an era of international harmony. Instead, they became a mechanism by which Metternich attempted –

KEY ISSUE

What were the failures and successes of Metternich's Congress System?

TIMELINE

1827	Battle of Navarino
1829	Treaty of Adrianople
1830	Revolution in France (July)
	'Chiffon de Carlsbad'
	Belgian Revolt
	Polish Revolt
1831	Austria crushed revolution in Papal States
	Belgian independence confirmed by Treaty of London
	Mehmet Ali invaded Syria
1833	Treaty of Unkiar Skelessi
	Münchengrätz agreement
1834	Quadruple Alliance
1839	Mehmet Ali at war again with Turkey
1840	Four Power Ultimatum to Mehmet Ali; Thiers threatened war in Europe
1841	Straits Convention

See Map 2 on page 4

with decreasing success – to reconcile the Great Powers' competing or divergent interests and persuade them that what was good for Austria was good for Europe as a whole. As the number of contentious issues to be dealt with piled up, each meeting became a progressively more complicated exercise in manoeuvre, manipulation and diplomatic sleight of hand. By 1823, the tricks of Metternich were wearing thin and his capacity to shape the course of events had passed its peak.

3 ⌁ THE AGE OF METTERNICH – 2: 1825–41 – DECLINE?

The crises which threatened to disturb the peace of Europe between 1825 and 1841 were to be resolved with little or no reference to Metternich. Nicholas I, who succeeded Tsar Alexander in 1825, refused to accept Metternich's diplomatic lead and instead began to assert Russia's national interest, notably with regard to the Eastern Question. The 1830 Revolution in Paris threw Metternich into total despair, and he had little role in containing the crisis over Belgium which followed. Metternich was also largely bypassed whilst the two Near Eastern crises of 1831–33 and 1839–41 were resolved.

Only briefly, at a summit meeting with Nicholas I at Münchengrätz in 1833, did Metternich reclaim centre stage in European affairs; and even then, it was widely assumed that Nicholas I was the effective master of the Austro-Prusso-Russian Holy Alliance which followed.

A *The Eastern Question*

Map 2 might suggest that the Ottoman Empire was one of Europe's Great Powers. In fact, the Sultan's rule had long been a byword for corruption and inefficiency and throughout the nineteenth century, European statesmen were predicting the Empire's imminent collapse. Its internal decay was compounded by three factors:

● the ambitions of Mehmet Ali, Viceroy of Egypt (1805–48), who repeatedly challenged the authority of his supposed masters in Constantinople
● the growth of nationalism amongst the Sultan's Christian subjects in 'Turkey-in-Europe' (e.g. Greece)
● pressure from Russia to acquire Constantinople.

What made the fate of this corner of Europe so internationally sensitive was the fact that most of the Great Powers had important interests at stake there and expected to have a say in sharing out the spoils should the Empire finally collapse:

● Austria was bound to be concerned by a collapse of Ottoman power, for that would surely be followed by Russian expansion towards the Balkans, an unstable border region of the Austrian Empire.

- France, its eastern borders locked tight by the Congress of Vienna, looked to the Mediterranean and its coastline to fulfil its Great Power ambitions. Mehmet Ali, who had transformed Egypt and its army with the help of French advisers and investment, was Paris's tool.
- Britain had vital imperial and naval interests in the eastern Mediterranean. Although it had no ambitions to control Constantinople or annex Ottoman territory itself, Britain wanted to make sure that no other Great Power, Russia especially, did either. Russian control of Constantinople would give its navy access from the Black Sea to the Mediterranean (an access denied by long standing treaty commitments), whilst Russian expansion southward might jeopardise British routes to India through the Near East and the Persian Gulf.
- Russia's role in the Near East was ambiguous. Its minimum objective was to ensure that the vital sea-link from the Black Sea into the Mediterranean was kept open for Russian merchant shipping. Russia could also reasonably aim to close the Black Sea to hostile warships in time of conflict. But at times, Russian policy seemed much more ambitious: patronising the cause of Balkan Christian races so as to accelerate the disintegration of the Empire; opening up the Straits to allow the passage of Russian warships into the Mediterranean; even seizing control of Constantinople itself. Although in reality, Russian policy was often guided by self-restraint, the suspicion of what Russia *might* be aiming at was a major cause of international tension throughout this period.

> **KEY ISSUE**
>
> *Why did the Eastern Question pose such a threat to the harmony of the Concert of Europe?*

The Greek Revolt 1821–30

ANALYSIS

Self-restraint *mostly* characterised Russian policy during the Greek revolt. Inspired by Greek nationalists and fuelled by Christian resentment of Muslim oppression, the revolt got off to a disastrous start. The Greeks had banked on the support of Russia. But to the horror of many of the Tsar's advisors – who saw the revolt as a chance to expand Russian influence and sympathised with the plight of their fellow Christians – Metternich was able at the Congress of Laibach to get Alexander I to join him in denouncing the Greeks as rebels. The revolt therefore seemed doomed.

> See page 13

But on Alexander I's death in 1825, the new Tsar Nicholas I changed Russian policy. Impatient with Metternich, and anxious to assert Russia's interests, he struck a deal with Britain in 1826, the aim of which was to secure Greek **autonomy**. France joined the pact in 1827. Later that year, an unplanned encounter between a combined Anglo-French naval force and the Sultan's fleet at Navarino led to the total destruction of the latter. The Turks, outraged, declared war on Russia.

> **autonomy** self-government/self-rule

They were soon on the defensive, and by August 1829, the Russians were within striking distance of Constantinople. But the Tsar pulled back from a final assault. He had been persuaded, in the words of his advisors, that 'the advantages of the preservation of the Ottoman Empire outweighed its disadvantages'. Better to have Constantinople in the Sultan's hands, as long as the latter was weak and acutely vulnerable to the Tsar's displeasure, than to precipitate the break up of the Ottoman Empire, and, as a consequence of partition, risk the growth in influence of a potentially hostile Power on Russia's borders. Thus, the terms concluded in the Treaty of Adrianople (1829) were quite moderate: some territorial gains for Russia at the mouth of the Danube and in the Caucasus; and a greater role for Russia in the semi-autonomous Ottoman provinces of Serbia, Wallachia and Moldovia. As to Greece itself, the Sultan had to agree to the London Protocol (1830), which established an independent Greek State, with France, Britain and Russia acting as guarantors.

The whole episode had been a nightmare to Metternich. He had been certain that Navarino would lead to a general European war, and that the Ottomans were 'coming to the end of their independent existence'. He was wrong on both counts, but the final resolution of the crisis was almost as bad. In a dramatic reversal of the anti-revolutionary diplomacy of the Congress System, Britain, France and Russia had worked together to establish an independent Greek state – and Metternich himself had been ignored.

B *Further problems*

See page 46

The overthrow of the Bourbon dynasty in the July Revolution of 1830 seemed at first to be an even bigger set-back to Metternich. He collapsed at his desk when he heard the news, moaning 'my whole life's work is destroyed'. It was not just the blow struck against the principle of legitimacy which incapacitated him; it was the danger that the disease of revolution would spread from Paris across Europe like an epidemic. Indeed, inspired (but not assisted) by France, outbreaks of revolution soon occurred in the United Netherlands, Germany, Poland and Italy.

Before long, however, it was clear that Metternich had over-reacted again:

See pages 9 and 46

● Louis-Philippe, the new King of France, was reviled by reactionaries like Metternich (and Nicholas I) as a usurper. But they missed the point. By securing the French *throne*, he had stopped France becoming a *republic*. Furthermore, this cautious man was determined that the French revolution of 1830 was not for export. At first, Metternich had hoped to persuade the Quadruple Alliance to raise an army to restore the Bourbons; in the end, he had to be satisfied with coordinating the dispatch of a diplomatic note to the new Government in Paris (the 'Chiffon de Carlsbad') warning the French to behave themselves. They hardly needed to be told.

● In neither Germany nor Italy did the Revolution make much progress. Public protests in several of the German states demanding constitutional government and an end to press censorship scored some early victories, but by 1832 the conservatives were in the ascendancy again. The Italian Revolution, centred on Papal Bologna, was bloodier, but a combination of internal divisions, Austrian arms and the absence of French support condemned it to defeat too.

See pages 89 and 168

● the Polish revolt was more serious. Nationalist Polish army officers, inspired by events in Paris, and anxious at the possibility of being launched westwards by Tsar Nicholas in an anti-revolutionary crusade, revolted against Russian domination, and in February 1831, the Polish *Diet* proclaimed national independence. But with dreams of French assistance coming to nothing, and the Polish peasantry unmoved by the national cause, defeat by the Russian army was inevitable. The revolt was perhaps not completely futile – it *may* have dissuaded Nicholas I from intervening in Belgium (see below) – but even this is not certain, and the consequence for the Polish people was the imposition of a harsh Russian military dictatorship.

See pages 68–82

● The Belgian Revolution seemed to present the most serious threat to peace in Europe. A complicated mixture of religious and political complaints meshed with economic grievances to produce riots in Brussels in August–September 1830. Dutch troops failed to contain these, and a Belgian Provisional Government declared independence. The King of the United Netherlands called for international assistance to put the Revolution down and thereby to defend the Vienna Settlement and the principle of legitimacy. This was the moment of crisis. If Prussia, for example, intervened to support King William, the French Government would feel compelled to come to the Belgians' rescue. Given the strategic sensitivity of the Low Countries, that in turn would provoke British intervention. The Revolution in Brussels could have precipitated a major European war.

See page 7

● By seizing the initiative, Palmerston, the British Foreign Secretary, ensured that it did not. At the London Conference of November 1830, he proposed a solution: the Great Powers should recognise and mutually guarantee the independence of Belgium. This, he argued, was the best way of bringing to the region both internal stability and international harmony. With a mixture of bluff, brinkmanship and coercion, he got his way, and in 1831, the Great Powers signed the Treaty of London, establishing the existence of Belgium as an independent and neutral state. To Metternich, all this was a mixed blessing. The peace of Europe had been preserved, and the value of Great Power congresses to negotiate the settlement of international crises vindicated. But the concession of independence to the people of Belgium was a victory for revolutionary nationalism; and the settlement had been engineered by his arch rival Palmerston, whose blustering assertion of liberal principles appalled Metternich.

KEY ISSUE

What was the impact of the 1830 revolutions on the European order?

ANALYSIS

The Eastern Question again: the adventures of Mehmet Ali

Whilst Europe's major Powers were preoccupied with the Belgian crisis, a strange episode in the history of the Eastern Question began. It was to pose another serious threat to international peace. Mehmet Ali, Viceroy of Egypt, was its central figure. In theory, Mehmet Ali, was subordinate to the Sultan. But he was a fantastically ambitious man, whose aim was nothing less than to establish his family as the dynastic rulers of Egypt, and Syria as well! Having, with French help, built the Egyptian army and navy into the Near East's most efficient fighting force, there seemed every prospect of him succeeding.

Mehmet Ali's son launched his attack in November 1831. Within barely a year Constantinople itself was within his sights. The Ottoman position seemed hopeless. In desperation, the Sultan turned to the Tsar for help. By April 1833, 14 000 Russian soldiers had landed on the Bosphorous, and Constantinople was saved. There was, however, a price for the Tsar's goodwill: the Treaty of Unkiar-Skelessi (July 1833). Formally this was a mutual defence pact; secret clauses, however, explained that the Sultan's responsibilities would be limited to closing the Dardenelles to foreign warships whenever Russia was at war, thereby sealing off the Black Sea from enemy attack. The Treaty's overall effect was to elevate Russia into the position of chief guarantor and protector of the Ottoman Empire.

Palmerston was horrified at these developments. Turkey seemed on the point of being reduced to a Russian satellite state. He also suspected (incorrectly) that the Russians had forced from Turkey the right to send their warships *through* the Dardenelles – which would potentially destroy British naval supremacy in the Mediterranean.

The second Near Eastern crisis was precipitated by Sultan Mahmud II. Determined to punish his 'overmighty subject', he attacked Mehmet Ali's armies in April 1839. A series of disasters followed. In June, the Ottoman forces were comprehensively defeated; shortly afterwards Mahmud himself died. His successor was a sickly sixteen year old. To cap it all, the Ottoman fleet then deserted *en masse* to the enemy. Constantinople was even more hopelessly vulnerable than it had been in 1832–3. Perhaps surprisingly, Britain and Russia discovered that they would co-operate together in resolving the crisis. Both sides wanted to preserve the power of the Sultan. The Russians, anxious at their empty treasury, doubted if they could afford to do this alone; so, in return for British support, they agreed not to renew the Treaty of Unkiar-Skelessi. Nicholas I also saw the possibility of using the crisis to disrupt Britain's good relations with France. Given Mehmet Ali's close ties to Paris, the French Government would object to the Egyptian ruler being squashed.

See Map 2 on page 4

The complicated negotiations which followed during 1840 re-volved around the question of how much of his Near Eastern con-quests Mehmet Ali would be allowed to retain. Mehmet Ali was determined to keep Syria as an hereditary possession, and the new French Prime Minister, Thiers, supported this. But Russia and Britain, with diplomatic backing from Austria and Prussia, made it clear, in a joint ultimatum (July), that he would have to settle for less. Weeks of brinkmanship followed. Thiers, infuriated that he had been allowed no say about this four power ultimatum and conscious that French honour was at stake, launched a desperate gamble. He banked on Mehmet Ali's forces being able to hold their ground long enough for Palmerston's position in the British Cabinet to unravel – his colleagues were indeed anxious at the damage his unyielding stance was doing to Anglo-French rela-tions. Thiers even raised the spectre of French intervention in the Rhineland, thinking that Prussia and Austria might be bullied into revising their anti-French stance.

See page 53

He lost on every count: Mehmet Ali's army was defeated at Beirut and Acre (September and November) with the British fleet playing a key role; Palmerston outmanoeuvred his rivals in Lon-don; and in Paris, Louis Philippe, horrified at the prospect of a European war which France seemed certain to lose, withdrew his support for Thiers, who therefore resigned. It was now possible to restore stability to the Near East. Mehmet Ali abandoned his grandiose dreams and settled for the establishment of his own purely Egyptian dynasty, whilst the London Straits Convention of 1841 restored 'the ancient rule of the Ottoman Empire' according to which no foreign naval ships could enter the Straits while Turkey was at peace. Although in practical terms this retreat cost Russia little, the form of the Convention – underwritten by all the five Great Powers – was in marked contrast to the unilateral Russ-ian diplomacy of the 1830s. Russia was not going to be allowed to dictate policy to Constantinople: the Eastern Question was recog-nised as a matter of interest for all the Great Powers.

According to Rich 'the peaceful coercion of France, and the Straits Convention of 1841, were among the more notable achieve-ments of the Concert of Europe in the nineteenth century'. But other aspects of the crisis and its resolution and settlement should be noted:

See the bibliography section on page 29

- Thiers' threats of war on the Rhine had a dramatic impact on the growth of German nationalism
- the thwarting of French ambitions was a major blow to the popularity of Louis-Philippe
- Palmerston's show-down with Thiers did lasting damage to Anglo-French relations, helping to set at odds the two liberal Great Powers of Europe
- the temporary success of Anglo-Russian co-operation led the Tsar to underestimate the full depth of Britain's suspicions of his long-term intentions towards the Ottoman Empire.

C East-v-West: ideology or self-interest in European diplomacy?

Metternich's greatest personal success of the 1830s was the Austro-Russian summit meeting at Münchengrätz in 1833. It was designed to co-ordinate the two Great Powers' policies on three points: the Polish problem; the threat of revolution in Europe; and the Eastern Question:

See pages 68–82

- Metternich and the Emperor agreed to support each other in the eventuality of any further insurrections in Poland. The Austrians as well as the Russians had many Polish subjects within their Empire, and the Polish rising had demonstrated the need for a common front against Polish nationalism.
- This anti-revolutionary alliance, later joined by Prussia, was extended so as to commit each Power to come to the assistance of fellow monarchs, in the event of *any* liberal or nationalist challenges to their authority. This was effectively a renewal of the principles of Troppau and of the Holy Alliance.

See page 12

- The Tsar reassured Metternich – who had been bewildered by the Tsar's support for Greek independence and worried about the implications of the Treaty of Unkiar-Skelassi – that Russia had no plans to dismember the Ottoman Empire. The two Powers now proclaimed their joint desire to uphold the Sultan's power. Privately, they made plans for close co-operation if and when it became necessary to partition the Ottoman Empire.

To liberals in the west, all this looked very sinister. Palmerston responded in 1834 by engineering his own Quadruple Alliance, according to which Britain and France committed themselves to restoring and nurturing liberal monarchies in Portugal and Spain. This alliance was presented as a counter balance to the 'triple league of the despotic powers' of the east; the latter were indeed supplying arms and money to anti-liberal forces in Spain. But Palmerston's public statements were really designed to enhance his domestic reputation as a crusading progressive whilst hiding his real agenda of securing and extending Britain's national self-interest. In fact, in this case, Palmerston's main concern was to keep *French* influence in the Iberian peninsula to a minimum. Palmerston imagined that – with France otherwise isolated in Europe, and anxious for someone's friendship – the Anglo-French partnership would be conducted on London's terms. Not surprisingly, Paris was reluctant to accept a subordinate role, and Anglo-French relations deteriorated in the 1840s. Indeed, on the eve of the 1848 revolutions the French chief minister and leading liberal, Guizot, had embarked on serious negotiations with Metternich to attempt to establish a Franco-Austrian *entente*. European diplomacy had failed to polarise along ideological lines.

See page 59

KEY ISSUE

How fair is it to characterise European diplomacy between 1833 and 1847 as being shaped by a conflict between reactionary and liberal fronts?

But by March 1848, neither Guizot nor Metternich were any longer in power as France and Austria succumbed to revolution.

4 ∽ THE AGE OF METTERNICH – 3: 1848 – FALL

A *Interpretations of Metternich*

In this section the focus will be an assessment of Metternich's responsibility for the outbreak of the 1848 revolutions.

Generations of historians came to regard the 1848 Revolution as the verdict of the peoples of Europe on the Austrian Chancellor and his reviled international system. It is easy to see why. The Vienna Settlement of 1815, which Metternich had taken a major role in devising, was in part a conscious attempt to frustrate the aspirations of German and Italian nationalists, and to stifle those voices calling for a greater share in government for the people of Europe. And thereafter, whether with policies of political censorship and repression in Germany (e.g. the Carlsbad Decrees of 1819), or the despatch of Austrian armies to put down recurrent revolts in Italy (e.g. 1821, 1831), Metternich seemed to have made it his life's mission to crush the life out of liberalism and nationalism.

According to Metternich's critics, this strategy was doomed to failure. Nineteenth century German and Italian historians, writing in the era immediately after unification, regarded the ultimate triumph of nationalism as inevitable: it was a manifestation of the popular will, guided to success by Bismarck and Cavour, statesmen who combined genius with a sense of destiny. Twentieth century historians offered a different emphasis, identifying the 'rise of the middle class' as the key to the story, as industrialisation dramatically increased the wealth and self-confidence of manufacturers and merchants, and accordingly the power of the liberal case for constitutional government. Either way, Metternich stood accused of defending the indefensible. Politically, economically, and socially – even morally – it was argued that the hierarchies of Restoration Europe had hardly been re-established before they were past their 'sell-by' dates.

Such sweeping judgements are now out of favour. Historians question the popularity of the appeal of nationalism in societies where local affiliations (municipal, dynastic or religious) remained strong, and where levels of literacy (and therefore receptivity to nationalist propaganda) were sometimes very low. The strength of liberalism too, has been questioned. The industrial revolution seems to have arrived across Europe later and in a more piecemeal fashion than previously suggested. With industrialisation's more hesitant advance, the rise of the middle class seems less significant too. In brief, Metternich can no longer be dismissed as a living **anachronism** who foolishly tried to stand in the way of the march of history.

Nevertheless, Restoration Europe was not socially or economically static. Cities grew, railways spread, and the middle classes – despite censorship – read their newspapers and periodicals in ever increasing numbers. Metternich's response to these changes was essentially hostile and counter productive. The mixture of paranoia, prejudice and almost ludicrous misjudgement which afflicted Metternich whenever liberalism

An analysis of the 1848 revolutions will be found in Chapter 7

See pages 88–9

See pages 211–12

anachronism transferring the expectations or values of one era to an earlier (or later) one is to be guilty of anachronism

reared its ugly head is best indicated by his response to political reform in Britain in the 1830s. Britain had more than its fair share of pushy middle-class newspaper-readers, and by 1830, they were expressing increasingly vocal discontent with the aristocratic – dominated political system. The British Government's response was flexible: anxious about the possibility of revolution, it decided to extend the franchise, giving many of the middle class the vote. Most contemporaries came to regard this as a stroke of genius, which in fact helped to *prolong* aristocratic predominance in British politics for decades. But to Metternich, it seemed like a disaster, and he repeatedly and mistakenly predicted that the British aristocracy would be swept away by revolution.

Metternich's loathing of liberalism and contempt for the middle classes are not difficult to understand. The French Revolution had driven young Metternich and his father into exile. But these experiences warped his political judgement. Metternich viewed the world as an arena of perpetual struggle between two great principles: of order and good versus anarchy and evil. In Metternich's eyes, as Schroeder puts it, 'every existing right was not merely legitimate but holy; every call for change or attempt at change made by anyone except a legitimate sovereign was not merely illegitimate but wickedly presumptuous. All the good men of right principles, sound reasoning, loyalty, and courage were on Metternich's side; only knaves, malcontents, and fools were on the other. All liberals, however moderate, were really revolutionaries; all demands for a constitution or for reforms, however limited, were really steps toward anarchy and revolution'.

This was the great weakness of Metternich's statesmanship. In theory, Metternich was in favour of efficient, paternalistic government. But in practice, he was incapable of devising or implementing genuinely constructive policies. His negative attitudes meant stifling innovation, deriding reform, or crushing revolution. Conservatism should be intelligently flexible, preserving where it can, but accepting change – so as to restrain and guide it – where change cannot be avoided. But change was something Metternich could never accept: this imaginative deficiency, suggests Schroeder, means Metternich should be characterised, not as a thoughtful conservative, but as a backward-looking reactionary.

> **KEY ISSUE**
>
> *What (unwitting) contribution did Metternich make to the outbreak of revolutions in Europe 1848?*

B *The Long Peace and the Great Powers*

See the bibliography of P.W. Schroeder on page 29

The almost unbroken peace in Europe between 1815 and 1853 is not easily explained. The American diplomatic historian P.W. Schroeder argued that the peace was a consequence of a collective change in the attitude of Europe's Great Powers towards each other. Schroeder suggests that this change was a sort of 'repentence'.

The Schroeder thesis on the Long Peace

After the anarchy and devastation of Napoleon's wars, the outlook of Europe's leaders was dramatically transformed. They abandoned the habits of relentless competition and unprincipled aggression which had characterised international relations for most of the eighteenth century. Instead, building on the spirit of co-operation and trust which had proved essential for final victory over France, they created a diplomatic culture based on self-restraint and mutual respect. In this new climate, crises which in earlier decades would have precipitated large scale conflict, provoked by the major Powers making grabs for territory and prestige, were contained and peacefully resolved.

One test of Schroeder's thesis would be to analyse some of the crises between 1815 and 1848. Try this in a class-based discussion exercise. Identify the four or five most potentially explosive 'flare-ups' of these years, e.g. the Belgian Revolution of 1830, and the Mehmet Ali affair of 1840. Then, work out the intentions and objectives of the Great Powers' leading statesmen, as these problems emerged and were defused. You should always bear in mind the following question: how important in causing or resolving each crisis was an old-fashioned readiness to assert or to defend national self-interest, including the threatened or actual use of force, and how important was a new spirit of trust and self-restraint? How far was the behaviour of the great powers over the period as a whole characterised by a spirit of 'repentence'?

● **Prussian foreign policy** as conducted up to 1840 was **timid**, and thereafter increasingly **eccentric**. As such it reflected the personalities of Frederick William III (1797–1840) and Frederick William IV (1840–62). The former was quite colourless: overawed by Russia, and manipulated by Metternich. His successor was too much of a dreamer to make any effective intervention in European affairs. Anyway, until the 1850s and its industrial take-off, Prussia was clearly the least of the Great Powers.

● The watch words of **French foreign policy** in this era were **prudence** and **caution**. *La grande nation* chafed at the constraints upon it, as occasional adventures and/or temptations revealed (Spain 1823; Algeria 1830; Belgium 1831–2; Thiers and Mehmet Ali 1840). But rulers as diverse in temperament as Louis XVIII (1814–24), Charles X (1824–30) and Louis-Philippe (1830–48) each recognised that any serious French aggression would bring back to life the dreaded 'Waterloo Coalition' of Britain, Austria, Russia and Prussia. The reign of Napoleon III, however, and the disasters which accompanied it, were to strongly suggest that the French had not yet 'repented' of the pursuit of *la gloire*.

See page 149–50

● The **Austrian Empire**, under Metternich's guidance, was just as anxious to maintain peace and stability in Europe as France or Prussia, if for rather different reasons. Austria's watchword was

As long as the two 'Super Powers', Britain and Russia, accepted each other's respective spheres of dominance – Britain with its colonies and on the high seas, Russia in much of central Asia and eastern Europe – a true Great Power conflict was unlikely. The one region where their interests were in potential collision was the Near East. Europe's long peace only came to an end when, essentially as a result of accidents and misunderstandings, Russia and Britain, the latter in alliance with France and Turkey, went to war in an attempt to impose their own respective solutions to the Eastern Question.

The extent to which the preceding predominance of Russia and Britain over Europe had contributed to the 'long peace' is indicated by the aftermath of the Crimean War. As the two world Powers retreated into semi-isolationism, as if to lick their respective wounds, Prussia, Austria and France seemed to be freed from their moorings. Their resulting collisions in the 15 years which followed the Crimean Wars were to transform the map of Europe almost beyond recognition.

ANALYSIS

The Crimean War

The Crimean War (1853–6) was by far the bloodiest eruption of the Eastern Question during the whole of the nineteenth century. It was fought in and around the Black Sea, and pitted Ottoman, French and British forces against the Russians: total casualties neared one million. Its causes were ostensibly trivial, and the territorial adjustments made in the Congress of Paris which brought the war to an end were microscopic. But the diplomatic consequences of the war were highly significant. Indeed, for Austria (whose own forces had not been engaged in the war, but which had given much practical support to the anti-Russian cause), the consequences were disastrous.

The conflict originated in – and in some respects continued as – a question of prestige. The Ottomans controlled the Christian Holy Places in Bethlehem and Jerusalem, allowing Christian pilgrims generous access. But the sites themselves were supervised by two separate orders of monks, who were bitter rivals. One order – the 'Latins' – owed their allegiance to the Pope, the other – the 'Orthodox' – looked to the protection of the Tsar.

In 1852, Napoleon III – hoping to impress a domestic Catholic audience – adopted the Latin monks' cause and bullied the Sultan into restoring French precedence over their Orthodox enemies. Tsar Nicholas I felt this as a personal humiliation. He loathed Napoleon III as a usurper, and decided to teach him and the Sultan a lesson. In February 1853, he dispatched General Menshikov to

Constantinople with instructions not merely to force the Sultan to reverse all the concessions he had just made, but also claiming for Russia a sort of protectorate over all of the Ottoman Empire's thirteen million Christian subjects. Menshikov made it clear that, if these terms were not accepted, war would follow.

The Menshikov mission was a disaster in every respect:

- The British, for reasons of national self-interest, were determined to protect the integrity of the Ottoman Empire, and were appalled by Menshikov's bullying, fearing that it was designed to lead to Turkey's dismemberment. But the Tsar mistakenly believed that, during the course of a visit to Britain in 1844, and in discussions with the British ambassador to Russia early in 1853, he had convinced London that the break-up of the Ottoman Empire was inevitable, and that Russia, Austria and Britain would happily share in the spoils.
- The Tsar was equally mistaken in his reading of Austrian intentions. He had convinced himself that there was 'a complete conformity of views and interests in the Orient between ourselves and Vienna'. In fact, Austria regarded Russian expansionism in the Balkans with considerable alarm.
- Finally, the Tsar was absolutely certain that what Menshikov was demanding was no more than Russia's right – indeed, that the most important points had already been conceded by the Turks in previous treaties. In fact, as contemporaries recognised, and modern historians agree, the Russian interpretation of these treaties was 'extravagantly broad'. The Turks, in rejecting the Tsar's demands, were not trying to wriggle out of their commitments – they were trying desperately to protect their independence.

In short, Nicholas I, in his combination of bullying, self-righteousness, incomprehension and sheer misjudgement, was the individual with most responsibility for the outbreak of the Crimean War.

A last-minute compromise, called the 'Vienna Note', was negotiated between Austria, Britain, France and Russia. But the Turks had not been a party to these talks, and when they demanded some modification of the terms, the Russians refused – and went on to give their own interpretation of the Note in way which offended Britain. War was inevitable.

The first clash saw the total destruction of the Turkish fleet at Sinope (November 1853). It was reported in the British press as a massacre, thereby further inflaming public opinion. Some British politicians believed they were being dragged into the war by the Turks ('cunning barbarians', wrote the Prime Minister in private). Certainly the Sultan saw an alliance with Britain and France as Turkey's only chance of checking the Russians and recovering some of the losses the Ottoman Empire had suffered at Russia's hands. But others in Britain, like Foreign Minister Palmerston and the British Ambassador in Constantinople, believed that a *British* reckoning with Russia was itself overdue.

The war, which came to focus on the siege of the Russian port of Sebastapol, dragged on for over two years, both sides suffering terrible casualties and displaying incompetent leadership. But the Anglo-French forces were better armed, and better supplied, and Russia became increasingly diplomatically isolated. Piedmont, Austria, Prussia and Sweden all supported the Anglo-French-Ottoman alliance (the Italians actually supplied 13 000 troops). The fall of Sebastopol (September 1855) was the key to allied victory, but by the end, all the combatants approached peace negotiations in Paris in a spirit of exhaustion.

Minor territorial readjustments apart, the main terms of the treaty were:

- Russia abandoned any special claims to a protectorate over the principalities of Moldavia and Wallachia, or over the Sultan's Christian subjects in general.
- the Black Sea was **demilitarised**. This clause was felt by Russia to be a particular humiliation. The main objective of Russian diplomacy, successfully completed in 1870, was to renegotiate it.

But there was not much pleasure to be had in victory, either. Britain had gained much less from the war than Palmerston had hoped, and the poor performance of its army encouraged a period of national self-criticism, and a spirit of isolationism. Napoleon III was pleased with his prestige victory, and the diplomatic gain of friendship with Britain. However, this friendship would prove to be transitory, and it remained unclear how the French Emperor would advance either his territorial claims in Europe or his *politique des nationalitiés*.

The big loser of the Crimean War was arguably not Russia, but Austria. Austria had lost no troops or territory, but it had lost the Tsar's friendship. Nicholas I, having counted on Austria's support, had regarded its 'betrayal' as 'unbelievable and indescribable'. Austro-Russian friendship, which had been at the heart of the Holy Alliance since at least the Treaty of Münchengrätz, was at an end. Vienna would look in vain to St Petersburg when it was confronted by French and Piedmontese aggression in Italy, and by Prussian aggression in Germany. The Crimean War did not, of course, *cause* Italian or German unification. But it helped to create the international power alignments that made the unifications possible, and it inaugurated an era in international affairs where the only guiding principle seemed to be 'every man for himself'.

demilitarisation
the removal of armed forces or military equipment from a region

See pages 136–7

5 ⇌ BIBLIOGRAPHY

An excellent place to start is *The Concert of Europe: International Relations 1814–70* by J. Lowe (Hodder and Stoughton 'Access', 1990). A useful modern overview of the foundations of the topic is *The Congress of Vienna* by T. Chapman (Routledge Lancaster Pamphlet, 1998). More demanding are *The Great Powers and the European States System 1815–1914* by F. Bridge and R. Bullen (Longman, 1980) and the collection of essays *Europe's Balance of Power 1815–1848* edited by A. Sked (Macmillan, 1979). *Great Power Diplomacy 1814–1914* by N. Rich (McGraw-Hill, 1992) is an excellent synthesis. Rich has also written provocatively on the Crimean War: *Why the Crimean War? A Cautionary Tale* (Hanover University Press, 1985). The Crimean War is also covered in *The Origins of the Crimean War* by D. Goldfrank (Longman, 1994) and – particularly suitable for students in the 16–19 age range – *The Eastern Question* by M. Anderson (Macmillan, 1966), which is helpful on Greece and Mehmet Ali too.

The Transformation of European Politics 1763–48* by P.W. Schroeder (Oxford, 1994) is demanding but important. Particularly useful is his re-appraisal of the Congress of Vienna on pages 575–82. *Metternich's Diplomacy at its Zenith 1820–23*, also by Schroeder (University of Texas, 1962) is useful for its conclusion. *The Foreign Policy of Victorian England 1830–1902* by K. Bourne (Oxford, 1970) will help in an understanding of the Belgian and Eastern Questions.

6 ⇌ STRUCTURED QUESTIONS AND ESSAYS

1. (a) Outline the measures taken to contain France following the defeat of Napoleon in 1814–15; (10 marks)
    (b) How successfully did the European Congresses maintain European peace between 1815 and 1830? (15 marks)
2. (a) Outline the main the terms of Treaty of Vienna; (10 marks)
    (b) To what extent were the Great Powers at Vienna motivated by principle or self-interest? (15 marks)
3. To what extent did the 'Concert of Europe' succeed in averting revolution between 1820 and 1848? (25 marks)
4. (a) Outline the main causes of the Crimean War; (10 marks)
    (b) Why was the 'Eastern Question' so important in European affairs in the period 1815–1856? (25 marks)

France 1814–48

THE FRENCH MONARCHY

Why did a constitutional monarchy fail to take root in France between 1814 and 1848?

The return of Louis XVIII from exile in 1814 signalled the restoration of the Bourbon dynasty to the French throne. The Bourbons had ruled France since the sixteenth century, but the Revolution of 1789 had led to the creation of a Republic, the execution of Louis XVI and his wife, and the exile of the King's brothers.

Everyone wondered if the new King would be capable of making the monarchy a success. After a bad start, the signs seemed good. The moderate and pragmatic policies of Louis XVIII and his ministers suggested that political stability might be achieved, and the bitter divisions which had rent France in the Revolutionary and Napoleonic eras be healed. But from 1820 onwards the increasing influence of Charles, the King's brother and heir, and of Charles' hard-line aristocratic followers, the *Ultras*, provoked increasing anxieties amongst many Frenchmen. They feared that an attempt would be made to return France to the ways of the pre-Revolutionary **Ancien Régime** (Old Regime).

When Charles X became king in 1824, the *Ultras*' political ambitions grew, and the gap between the king and his ministers on the one hand, and the rest of French society on the other, widened. In the end, Charles X attempted to mount a royalist **coup d'état** to neutralise his critics, but his plan was hopelessly ill-conceived. Instead, it precipitated the July Revolution of 1830, which swept Charles X himself into exile and finally brought the Bourbon dynasty to an end.

The July Revolution did not, however, abolish the monarchy. A new king was installed: Louis-Philippe, head of the House of Orléans and himself a descendant of Louis XIV. The 'July Monarchy' promised to inaugurate a new style of politics. Louis-Philippe was capable and forward-looking, and was committed to making constitutional monarchy work. Although Louis-Philippe had violent enemies on the left and the right – the King survived no fewer than eight assassination attempts – by 1835, the dynasty seemed firmly established.

Appearances were deceptive. A lacklustre foreign policy, faltering economic growth and growing public cynicism about political 'sleaze'

Ancien Régime is the term used to characterise the political and social order of pre-Revolutionary France and Europe. To its critics, the **Ancien Régime**'s main features included aristocratic privilege (the nobles paid few taxes and kept the best jobs for themselves), unchecked royal power (no constitution or representative assembly), and an excessively wealthy and influential Church, spreading superstition and stifling intellectual debate

coup d'état an armed seizure of power involving the suspension or abolition of the constitution.

made Louis-Philippe vulnerable. A well organised campaign demanding an extension of the franchise ended in public disorder – which, to most people's surprise, turned into a revolution. In 1848, Louis-Philippe was overthrown, and a Republic established.

What was it about French political culture which made monarchies so vulnerable and revolution a habit? To understand some of the answers to these questions, it is necessary to examine the legacy of the French Revolution.

1 ⌐ THE LEGACY OF REVOLUTION

Both the French Revolution and the Napoleonic era left a legacy of bitter and lasting division. The Revolution had produced 'winners' (most of the middle classes and some of the peasantry) but also 'losers' (the monarchy and some of the aristocracy). After 1814 each group wanted respectively to consolidate its gains or recoup its losses. The Revolution and its aftermath confronted all French citizens with a series of inescapable political choices. For or against the principles of 1789? For or against the Republic? For or against Napoleon? The answers to these questions would go a long way to determining whether any individual was for or against the restoration of the Bourbons, for or against the July Revolution, or for or against 'monarchy' itself.

A *The Principles of 1789*

Liberty was the guiding principle of the Revolution of 1789. It transformed the French *Ancien Régime* into a constitutional monarchy. The Declaration of the Rights of Man guaranteed basic freedoms of speech, assembly and religious belief. Alongside Liberty came Equality and Fraternity. The Revolution abolished feudalism, that is, the privileges enjoyed by the nobility by which, for example, they were exempt from most taxation themselves but could impose various taxes and duties on their own peasants. An era of *fraternity* was inaugurated in its place, one in which every individual would extend to every other equal consideration and respect.

To many Frenchmen the principles of 1789 seemed to promise a new era, not just in French politics, but for European civilisation. Throughout the nineteenth century, liberal-minded members of the aristocracy and middle classes believed that the political and social reforms based on the spirit of 1789 offered the best prospects for the nation's future prosperity, political stability and social harmony. But, unfortunately for French liberals, the Revolution did not stop in 1789.

B *1792: The Republic, the Terror and the 'Mob'*

The constitutional monarchy collapsed in 1792. Louis XVI was suspected of treasonable dealings with France's enemies, and of wanting to restore the *Ancien Régime*. France was made into a Republic in September 1792; and the king was executed in January 1793. The advance of Austrian and Prussian armies towards Paris in 1792 and 1793 spread fear and paranoia amongst its citizens. An era of something like mob rule began. Some three thousand aristocrats and royalists, regarded as potential traitors, were guillotined during 'the Terror' of 1793–4. Others fled into exile, where they joined the ranks of aristocrats (led by the King's brothers, the future Louis XVIII and Charles X) who had already left out of disgust at the liberal and **egalitarian** principles of the 1789 revolution. All of these *émigrés*, who often joined the armies of France's enemies, were punished by the confiscation and resale of their estates in France. This resale gave their new owners – the urban middle classes and peasants – a sizeable vested interest in the defence of the Revolutionary order, and an understandable fear that a restored monarchy would confiscate these lands and return them to their original owners.

> **egalitarian** believing in equality

The Terror left an indelible imprint on nineteenth-century French politics. It associated republicanism with blood, social upheaval and mob rule. All men of property, not just the nobility, feared what the masses, especially the Parisian masses, could do. These experiences help to explain why liberals were so afraid of a republic in 1830 and why the authorities turned with such savagery on the Parisian lower classes in June 1848 and in May 1871.

See pages 47 and 252–3

C *The Revolution and the Catholic Church*

France was an overwhelmingly Catholic country, but the Catholic Church had suffered as badly in the course of the Revolution as the aristocracy. The leaders of the Revolution were fundamentally anti-clerical, i.e. they were opposed to the political power, wealth and privileges of the Church. After 1789, the Church was attacked at every level. Its property, amounting to almost one-tenth of the surface area of France, was 'nationalised' and then sold off. Over 2000 clergymen were killed and over 30 000 driven into exile. Although Napoleon restored a working relationship with the Papacy in 1801, a generation of French people grew up outside the faith. In 1815, the Church, as an institution, was shattered: the clergy, decimated; the Church's physical fabric either sold off or in disrepair; and its claims to the spiritual and moral leadership of society, widely disregarded.

Given such experiences, it is hardly surprising that the Catholic Church rejected the principles of 1789. Instead, faced with an awesome task of reconstruction, the Church turned to the aristocracy and monarchy for protection and support. The so-called 'alliance of throne and altar', in which monarchists and clericalists invested so much hope, was born out of this experience of joint persecution.

Education was a particularly important issue for the future of the Church. Napoleon had created a network of *élite* schools to train leaders of French society. The Church – against all precedent – had no influence over these schools. Its attempts after 1815 to set up its own colleges and/or gain some control over the state system were to provoke a fierce reaction from liberals, who feared that the Church aimed to capture the minds of young Frenchmen for the cause of royalism, superstition and reaction. The battle offers another example of how the revolution created conflicts of interests and beliefs which lasted for decades.

D *Glory and grandeur*

The Revolution left a deeply divided nation. But, paradoxically, perhaps its most subversive legacy was a dream of dominating the rest of Europe. This dream came close to uniting the French nation in the nineteenth century. The gigantic 'people's armies' raised during the Terror had driven France's invaders back across the Rhine and gone on to inflict repeated and crushing defeats on its traditional enemies, Austria and Prussia. At its peak, Napoleonic France dominated almost as much of Europe as Hitler's Germany did in 1942.

In retrospect, although the campaigns are reckoned to have cost 1.5 million French lives alone, and ended in the disasters of Moscow and Waterloo, these years came to be seen as an era of unparalleled glory for the French nation. Old soldiers kept memories alive, and popular ballads extolled the genius of 'the little corporal' and the triumphs of the tricolour flag. On the left, liberals and republicans alike could celebrate the triumph of France's mission to bring freedom and civilisation (as they saw it) to the oppressed peoples of Europe. Patriots of the right were stirred by the sheer grandeur of France's achievements as a European power in the revolutionary era.

As a consequence, any government after 1815 which was perceived as failing to defend the honour of France was liable to be rejected by the French people. Wiser heads, like Louis-Philippe, knew all too well that any attempt to renew France's days of glory and conquest would lead to humiliation. His overthrow in 1848 was in part a reward for his caution. But Napoleon III, who ruled France over the next two decades, was made to pay the price for attempting to live up to the image of imperial greatness: crushing defeat at the hands of its enemies. In foreign affairs at least, what the French people wanted was not in the real interests of France.

> *The Bourbons*
> The Bourbons restored their predominantly white 'fleur-de-lys' flag, banning the red, white and blue revolutionary tricolour. So potent were these symbols that some royalists wanted the possession of the tricolour to be classed as treason.

E *Learning and forgetting*

It is often said of the Bourbons that they learnt nothing and forgot nothing: that is, when the monarchy was restored in 1814, they hoped to recreate the privileged world of the *Ancien Régime*, and to humiliate those who had cast them down, all the while oblivious to the fact that such reactionary attitudes had cost them the French throne in the first place. This may be partly true of Charles X; it is less true of Louis XVIII, who preached, and tried to practise, 'the duty to forget'. But what is striking about nineteenth century France is how far the nation *as a whole* was trapped in history – incapable of forgetting. Property owners could not forget the Terror, nor patriots the glories of conquest – whilst

Paris could not forget the possibility of revolution. This helps to explain why no government seemed to enjoy real stability. Unable to forget, France found itself on a long, slow and painful collective learning curve.

2 ↩ THE BOURBON RESTORATION: LIBERALISM OR REACTION?

A *The new king*

By 1814, it was clear even to those closest to Napoleon that his reign was coming to an end. The catastrophic French retreat from Moscow (1812), had been followed by defeats in Germany and the invasion of France, with Paris capitulating in March 1814. Desperate for peace, the French Senate and Legislative Body voted to depose Napoleon, and a provisional government was set up. What form should the post-Napoleonic constitution take? The country could hardly turn itself back into a Republic: memories of the Terror ruled that out. So France would have to be a monarchy again. Although the Bourbons enjoyed little genuine popularity, Louis XVIII (who had spent the years between 1791 and 1814 in exile) was the only really serious candidate. His claims were strengthened by behind-the-scenes intrigue, carefully stage-managed demonstrations of popular enthusiasm, the support of the British Government and his own promise to give France a liberal constitution.

PROFILE

KEY ISSUE

How did Louis XVIII approach his responsibilities as King of France?

LOUIS XVIII (1755–1824)

Louis XVIII was determined not to be a mere figurehead. He loved power, although perhaps more for the opportunities for intrigue and display it provided, than for any desire to serve his country. He was not an attractive figure. Although Louis XVIII had about him a certain imposing grandeur, and he was unmistakably conscious of the supreme dignity of his station, as a person, he was cold, unsympathetic and calculating. Obese and gouty from his years of lazy exile, he often needed to be ferried around in a sort of wheelchair. Although his courtiers were in awe of him, the French people contemptuously nicknamed him 'the fat pig'.

However, Louis XVIII was no fool. Although his instincts and tastes were those of *Ancien Régime* France, he had the good sense to realise that it would be folly to attempt to turn back the clock: counter-revolution was not on his political agenda. To many royalists, this realistic approach looked like unprincipled selfishness: 'long live the king', they cried, 'in spite of himself'. However, Louis XVIII's moderation and flexibility proved much wiser than the stubbornness of his successor Charles X.

B *The Constitution*

Perhaps reluctantly, the king kept his promise to reign as a constitutional monarch. The Charter was issued in June 1814 and spelt out his powers and their limits. Most of the practical benefits which ordinary French people had derived from the Revolution were preserved in the Charter. These included: equality before the law, the career 'open to talents', religious freedom, and (with some qualifications) freedom of the press. It was also guaranteed that the new owners of former Church or *émigré* land were to be allowed to keep these properties.

Nevertheless, the Constitution conferred extensive powers on the King:

- he could make war or peace, direct the armed forces, and 'make such rules and ordinances as are necessary for the safety of the state'. (This was the provision – Article XIV – which Charles X was to try to exploit with such disastrous effect in 1830)
- **legislative power** could only be exercised collectively by the King in conjunction with a Chamber of Peers and a Chamber of Deputies. However, the Chamber of Peers was appointed by the King, with no limit on their number
- the Chamber of Deputies was elected, but on a highly selective franchise. Electors had to be over 30 years old and pay 300 francs a year in direct tax; would-be deputies had to be over 40, and pay over 1000 francs tax. Thus out of a total population of 29 million, only 100 000 men – mainly landowners – had the right to vote, whilst their representatives were drawn from an even narrower *élite*.

To its critics, government in Restoration France was by the few, for the few. But this cautiously liberal constitution was hardly meant to be democratic. To most nineteenth century liberals as well as conservatives, wealth, education and political 'good sense' were believed to go hand in hand. In particular, the French *élites*, with experience of the Terror, had reason to fear the passions of 'the mob'.

But some aspects of Louis XVIII's proclamation caused the liberals a degree of unease. The Charter's preamble had an old-fashioned flavour to it, recalling memories of the *Ancien Régime* and royal absolutism:

> We have recognised that in desiring a constitutional charter our subjects were expressing a real need; but in granting their desire we have taken every precaution to ensure that the charter was worthy of us and of the people we are proud to command ... our first duty to our people was to maintain, in their own interests, the rights and prerogatives of the crown.
>
> In seeking thus to re-forge the links of time, which fatal departures have broken, we have effaced from our memory all the evils which have afflicted our country during our absence, as we would wish that they could be erased from the pages of history.

KEY ISSUE

What were the main features of the constitutional settlement proclaimed by Louis XVIII?

See page 45

---

legislative power the power to make laws

Ancien Régime
In *Ancien Régime* France, appointment to public positions, e.g. in the army or the legal system – depended much less on 'what you knew' than 'who you knew'. Many jobs were reserved for aristocrats. The ideal of 'the career open to talents' aimed to break up these cosy networks. Merit, intelligence and hard-work were to get their due rewards at last. Restoration France was full of young men working hard to pass exams and hoping for glorious careers in Paris.

Q

In what respect might Louis XVIII be said to have deceived himself, or his audience, by presenting the Charter as a voluntary concession?

What other aspects of the preamble might have caused concern to liberals and other veterans of the Revolution?

> For these reasons, we have voluntarily, and through the free exercise of our royal authority, granted and do hereby grant, concede and bestow upon our subjects, on behalf of ourselves and our successors for ever, the following constitutional charter …

Even with these reservations, the Charter was a significant achievement. It might have marked the start of that process of national reconciliation which Louis XVIII recognised as his greatest priority. 'All the efforts of my government', he stated 'are directed to the effort to fuse the two peoples, who exist only too much in fact, into a single one'. Over the next 16 years, it was the acts of the Bourbons' friends, at least as much as those of their enemies, which would make this task so difficult.

However, the first blow against Louis XVIII would come from a surprising quarter.

3 ⌐ THE HUNDRED DAYS AND THEIR SIGNIFICANCE

A *The Hundred Days*

On 26 February 1815, Napoleon escaped from exile on the Mediterranean island of Elba. He landed on the French coast near Cannes with 700 followers. His return marked the beginning of the Hundred Days – his last, all or nothing bid for glory. Napoleon believed, probably correctly, that few Frenchmen had any real affection for the Bourbons, and knew that the new Government's acceptance of what was seen as a humiliating peace treaty and its imposition of cutbacks on the army had made it more unpopular.

Current disaffections and shared memories of glory help to explain the popularity of Napoleon's crusade. He made his way northwards, winning over the forces sent against him by the power of his charisma and the rekindling of old loyalties. By 20 March, he was in Paris. Louis XVIII resigned himself to a second period of exile, and fled to Ghent.

Napoleon's defeat at Waterloo, on 18 June, ensured that Louis' exile was brief. However, the 'Hundred Days' were to have profound repercussions:

KEY ISSUE

What was the long term significance of the Hundred Days?

● The French were punished for rallying to Napoleon by having a much more severe peace treaty imposed on them. France was now reduced to the borders of 1789, losing all of Savoy and strategically sensitive enclaves along her north-eastern frontier too. Furthermore, an indemnity of 700 million francs was levied, adding massively to an already severe tax burden. To complete its humiliation, two-thirds of France was to be occupied by a million foreign soldiers, who would be paid for, fed, clothed and housed at French expense until the indemnity was paid. In short, France was to be reduced to the status of a second-class Power.

Curiously, the intense feelings of resentment engendered by the Second Treaty did not rebound upon the head of Napoleon, but on Louis XVIII. He returned, his critics jeered, 'in the baggage train of foreign powers', and it was his Government which actually signed the second treaty. However unfairly, 'the association with defeat and humiliation, and dependence on the hated foreign enemy, was an affliction that the Bourbons were never able to shake off' (Tombs).

● The ecstasy of the Hundred Days, and the supposed martyrdom inflicted on Napoleon through his imprisonment on the tiny mid-Atlantic island of St Helena (where he died in 1821), became essential elements of the Napoleonic myth. Waterloo had been a defeat, but it had been a glorious one, and a reminder of the great nation's martial valour. Furthermore, however despotic and power-crazed Napoleon had been in real life, he presented himself during the Hundred Days and thereafter as a friend of freedom. This image encouraged many French nationalists, republicans and even some liberals to identify themselves with the Bonapartist cause. The domestic appeal of Bonapartism undermined the stability of both the Bourbon and Orleanist monarchies, and helps to explain the accession to power of Napoleon's nephew, Louis Napoleon, in 1848.

See the bibliography section on page 64

See page 124

● The Hundred Days severely undermined the policy of national reconciliation which Louis XVIII had undertaken in 1814. The *Ultras*, eager for vengeance and for jobs, had despaired when Louis XVIII had at first declined to purge the old Napoleonic political élite. But most of Napoleon's old friends had returned to his service in the Hundred Days, betraying their new king. Now they would have to pay the price of treachery. Accordingly, some 250 special courts were set up, presided over by royalist officers, with no rights of appeal. 6000 sentences were passed, and up to 80 000 officials and 5000 army officers dismissed. These purges created irreconcilable enemies for the Bourbons. The victims of 1815–16 would take **their** revenge in 1830.

The bitter divisions which the Hundred Days had reopened were compounded by a 'White Terror' which swept large tracts of the south and west of France. Catholic 'death squads' went on the rampage, targeting liberals and Protestants. Up to three hundred were killed. The local authorities either turned a blind eye, or actively encouraged the mobs. In the Chamber, the *ultra* royalist La Bourdonnaye called for a regime of 'irons, executioners and torture' to teach the enemies of the Bourbons a lesson. The spirit of counter-revolution was bloody, vengeful and dangerous.

B *Domestic policy*

The general election of August 1815 was held in this atmosphere. It produced a Chamber in which royalists had an overwhelming majority. Between October 1815 and January 1816 a series of laws were passed aiming to strengthen the Restoration. In addition to the establishment of the special courts already described, a strict regime of press censorship was imposed, and provision made for the imprisonment without trial of individuals who were considered a threat to state security. There was a triumphalist mood amongst the royalists: a leading nobleman recorded, 'after 25 years of rule by wretches who despise us, one is rather pleased to be back at the top, in the position from which we should never have been toppled'. They loathed anything that recalled the Revolution; by contrast, Louise XVIII remained committed to a policy of conciliation, and there were soon tensions between the King and the Chamber.

Given the aggression with which the *Ultras* were pressing their case, civil war in France was a real possibility. The Duke of Richelieu was the leading member of Louis XVIII's cabinet which had to confront the emerging crisis, worsened by a severe harvest failure and famine. He succeeded. His complete integrity and sense of honour won wide respect, and his policies combined firmness and moderation. In particular, he was able to persuade Louis XVIII to confront the *Ultras*, who were blocking the Government's financial policies – essential for the payment of the indemnity and thus the evacuation of foreign troops from France.

In September 1816, to the shock and dismay of his brother, Louis XVIII dissolved the ultra-royalist chamber, and called new elections. A sustained campaign in the liberal newspapers against the threat of reaction and the return of feudalism, combined with arm-twisting and government bribery for the voters – a characteristic of all elections in nineteenth century France – to secure a government majority of 146 seats to the *Ultras'* 92.

King Louis XVIII, his ministers and parliament could now work more constructively with each other. They achieved a lot:

- the massive indemnity was soon paid off, and at the diplomatic conference of Aix-la-Chapelle (1818) France was formally treated as an equal by the other Great Powers: a striking recovery of prestige barely three years after Waterloo
- the new Press Law of 1819, drawn up with the assistance of the leading liberal intellectual and politician Guizot, re-established the principle of a free press
- the army reforms of 1818, stressing that promotion would be determined by merit, were an explicit rebuttal of the *Ultras*, who had hoped to make the army's officer class into a royalist-aristocratic monopoly.

Had Restoration politics continued along this track, France might well have become a stable constitutional monarchy. However, intrigue, assassination and a disastrous succession re-opened the door first to reaction, and ultimately to the abortive **coup d'état** and revolution of 1830.

4 ∽ REACTION RESURGENT

A *Decazes and Villèle*

The role of constitutional monarch did not come readily to Louis XVIII, as the rise of Elie Decazes, the King's favourite, as Chief Minister in 1818 indicates. Unscrupulous and insinuating, Decazes ousted Richelieu from office and lent his opportunistic support to the Parliament's liberal-leaning legislation. But he had no political convictions of his own: his only objective was to please his master, the King. Widely loathed though he was, as long as Decazes could keep Louis XVIII amused with scandalous gossip, he seemed invulnerable. The presence of such a figure at the centre of French politics showed that even at its most 'liberal' the regime was far from becoming a parliamentary monarchy (that is a system in which the King could only govern with the sustained approval of a parliamentary majority).

However, even Louis XVIII could not protect Decazes from the reactionary storm which swept French politics in 1820. This was unleashed by the assassination of the Duke of Berry, Louis XVIII's nephew, and the only Bourbon capable of producing an heir. This event was perhaps the turning point of the Restoration era. The resulting outrage provoked an *Ultra* political counter-attack which made the *ultras* the dominant force in French politics for the rest of the decade. Yet the policies the *Ultras* pursued widened the acute divisions within the nation so seriously that, in the end, the Bourbon dynasty itself was fatally undermined.

The first and least lamented victim of the *Ultras* was Decazes. His right-wing enemies argued that liberal ideas had inspired the assassination. Despite Louis XVIII's pathetic pleas, Decazes was forced to resign. More ominous was the sustained barrage of anti-liberal legislation which followed: detention without trial for those suspected of conspiracy; a dramatic tightening of the censorship regulations; and, in June 1820, the 'law of the double vote'. This last innovation gave the wealthiest 25 per cent of all electors a second vote, with two-fifths of the places in the Chamber reserved for the selected candidates of this electoral *élite*. The *Ultras'* calculation was brazen: the richer the voter, the more conservative his views were likely to be. Not surprisingly, the election which followed in November saw a dramatic swing to the *Ultras*, the liberals winning only 80 of the 450 seats.

Republicans, Bonapartists and conspiracy

ANALYSIS

See page 88

The right-wards shift of the Bourbon regime after 1820 stimulated conspiracies in the Republican and Bonapartist underground. The vague ideals and secrecy of societies like the *Charbonnerie* (directly inspired by the Italian *Carbonari*) make it hard to be certain about their members' motivation. However, nostalgia for the glory days of Napoleon, anger at the threat to liberty posed by the *Ultras*, family traditions of republicanism and, amongst army officers, the sheer boredom of life in provincial garrison towns, all seem to have played their part.

A series of plots culminated in the 'conspiracy of the four sergeants of La Rochelle' in 1822: its discovery – spies and informers were everywhere – led to the sergeants' execution.

Although abortive, such episodes were significant. They indicate an undercurrent of republican opposition to Bourbon rule, which was to re-surface in 1830. Lafayette, for example, who played a vital role in the installation of Louis-Philippe, was an important patron of the anti-Bourbon underground. And a tradition of militant republicanism was to continue into the 1830s and beyond, with risings and riots in Lyons and Paris. For some Frenchmen, revolution was never off the agenda – as Louis-Philippe himself was to discover in 1848.

See page 48

The *Ultras* were also working hard behind the scenes to consolidate their power. These years saw the greatest influence of the top secret catholic-aristocratic organisation, the Knights of the Faith. Founded in 1810 with the aim of subverting Napoleon's regime, they remained dedicated to the defence of all that was monarchic, aristocratic, Catholic and anti-revolutionary in France. Even the Countess of Cayla, the King's new 'companion' – impotent, he had no need of a mistress – was a sympathiser: she used her influence to promote the political career of the Count of Villèle. A Knight of the Faith, and leader of the *Ultras* in the Chamber, Villèle prospered under the Countess' patronage. In 1820, he was appointed Minister of Finance; by the end of 1821, he was effectively Prime Minister. He was to prove a better servant of the state than this dubious background suggests.

See page 41

Villèle's rise was not the *Ultras'* only genuine success. In 1823, a French army was despatched to Spain to reverse the liberal revolution of 1820 and restore the deeply reactionary King Ferdinand VII to his full powers. This blow for absolutism not only satisfied the *Ultras'* ideological agenda; the speedy success of the campaign raised French prestige in Europe, with 'glory' reflecting on the Bourbons themselves. As Foreign Minister Chateaubriand remarked, 20 days of war had done more to strengthen the French monarchy than eight years of peace.

However, Louis XVIII did not live long to enjoy the fruits of this triumph. Bloated and increasingly infirm, he died in September 1824. His achievements should not be underestimated. Until the tragedy of 1820, he had been able to keep the *Ultras* at arm's length, believing that their spirit of blind reaction was a danger to France's tranquillity and prosperity. Perhaps Louis XVIII was a liberal of necessity rather than choice, but he gave France its first real experience of constitutional monarchy. Above all, he was able to work towards the future rather than remaining trapped in the past. And in this respect, he was the very opposite of his brother, Charles X, whose disastrous reign has tended to obscure a proper appreciation of the achievements of the Bourbon Restoration.

B *Charles X*

Superficially, Charles X appeared to show much promise. The new King was personally a much more attractive figure than his brother: he was kindly, loyal, generous, and despite his years (he had been born in 1757), elegant and still handsome. But all the King's grace and splendour counted for nothing against his sadly mediocre intellect, his breath-taking political insensitivity, and his extraordinary stubbornness. These were to prove a fatal combination, for Charles X was a king determined not merely to reign but actually to rule.

Not every aspect of his reign was a disaster. Villèle continued as chief minister, and enjoyed some success. 'The least *Ultra* of the *Ultras*', Villèle did not exhibit the rigid idealism or religious fervour which characterised many of the far right. Instead, he was distinguished by a tremendous capacity for hard work and a penetrating intellect which could find a path through the most complicated of problems. He reorganised the various departments of the exchequer, increasing centralisation, tightening procedures and stamping out dishonesty, and his budgets were clear, carefully itemised and usually balanced. The creation of a sound and stable system of public finance was arguably the Restoration era's most important legacy to France.

Even before the accession of Charles X, however, Villèle had made a political blunder which would come to haunt them both. Exasperated by the size of the bill for Chateaubriand's Spanish adventure and jealous of his colleague's fame, Villèle had his Foreign Minister dismissed, in the most peremptory and humiliating way. Chateaubriand was to prove a deadly enemy. One of the most brilliant writers of his day, he launched a series of savage attacks on the 'timidity' and 'corruption' of the 'Villèle system' in the press. Combined with criticism from the liberal left, the effect was devastating: the Prime Minister found himself losing the battle for public opinion.

The Government certainly offered easy targets for caricature and attack. Liberals claimed that Villèle had embarked on a fully fledged programme of feudal reaction. They pointed, first, to the Prime Minister's attack on press freedom; secondly, to his attempt to increase the wealth and power of the aristocracy; and thirdly, to his partisan support of the Catholic Church.

Villèle's attack on press freedom had begun in March 1822. The 'Law of Tendency' made newspapers or journals liable to temporary or permanent closure if the royal courts (trial was *not* to be by jury) detected a persistent 'tendency' to undermine 'the respect due to ... religion [or] the authority of the king'. Villèle further exploited the reactionary climate of these years by calling a general election in 1824. The new chamber was overwhelmingly *Ultra* in composition: only 19 out of 430 deputies were liberals.

In reality, these triumphs proved a mixed blessing. A celebrated censorship case in 1825 revealed that the courts were unwilling to convict journalists for anti-clericalism, whilst the 'Ultra-royalist' chamber was so reactionary as to prove unmanageable – Villèle was too *moderate* for many of its deputies' liking!

Villèle's fortunes in his attempts to consolidate and expand aristo-cratic influence were equally mixed. He worked out an ingenious plan to compensate the *émigré* noblemen for the loss of their confiscated estates (the Law on Indemnity, 1825) without adding to the tax burden. This should have defused one of the most explosive issues in Restoration politics. But the Chamber of Peers rejected the package as prejudicial to the interests of the Government's stockholders. A modified scheme, implemented the following year, left Villèle vulnerable to the charge that the *émigré élite* was being enriched at the nation's expense. Their windfall was popularly known as the '*émigrés*' billion'.

See page 32

The Peers completely rejected another of Villèle's measures to strength-en the aristocracy. The proposed 'Right of the Eldest' bill (1826) aimed to encourage primogeniture, that is, the principle by which the bulk of property descends to the first-born male heir. Villèle had feared that the progressive breaking up of the great estates through 'partible inheritance' was weakening the land-owning class, but liberals denounced the scheme as opening the door to the restoration of feudalism, and it was defeated.

However the government's most controversial policy was the backing it gave to the militant campaign of the Church to reclaim a dominant role for Catholicism in public life. The first move – one about which Villèle himself had serious doubts – was the Law on Sacrilege (April 1825). This made punishable, by beheading, any malicious tampering with the consecrated host (that is, the holy wafer which, according to Catholic belief became, during the Mass, the very body of Christ). No-one, neither the framers of the law, nor its liberal critics, expected it ever to be implemented. But its symbolic significance was profound, and, to some disturbing. It gave the Catholic faith privileged protection, by creating a uniquely awful punishment for anyone who desecrated its most holy of rituals. As one of the *Ultras*' apologists exulted, the law was designed to be a negation of the spirit of 1789: 'the Revolution which began by a declaration of the rights of man will end with a decla-ration of the rights of God'.

The reinvigorated alliance of Church and State was nowhere more explicit than at the Coronation of Charles X at Rheims Cathedrals in 1825. The climax of the ceremony was the King's consecration. This fea-tured the Archbishop of Rheims anointing Charles (as he lay prostrate at the Archbishop's feet) with drops from a phial of holy oil which, true believers insisted, had first been sent from heaven in the beak of a dove in 496 AD, for the coronation of Clovis, the very first King of France. To the liberal heirs of the Revolution, it was grotesque evidence of the profound-ly reactionary – and superstitious – mentality of their new monarch.

5 ⌐ CLERICALISM, ANTI-CLERICALISM AND THE LIBERAL RECOVERY

The Law on Sacrilege and the coronation of Charles X touched some of the most sensitive of all political nerves for nineteenth century French-men. 'Clericalism' – the name given to identify the priesthood's claim to special privileges and increased political power – was regarded by liberals with intense suspicion. The Bourbon Restoration had given anti-clericalists a lot to be suspicious about.

Education was perhaps the Church's most important battlefield. The Church had already been working to re-establish its traditional role as the teacher of the sons of the French land-owning classes, by opening the doors of its 'little seminaries' to them (even if they had no intention to enter the priesthood, as the name 'seminary' would otherwise imply). The creation of the Ministry of Public Education and Religious Affairs in 1822 and the appointment as its head a royalist bishop seemed to indicate the Catholics' ambition to take control of higher education, and the Government's support for its plans. Supposedly subversive university lecturers, like Guizot, were suspended, and replaced with 'good Catholics'. Across the 'learned professions' (medicine and law, as well as higher education), 'good Catholics' prospered, whilst liberals' careers stalled. The Revolution of 1830 would in part be the work of a generation of 'alienated intellectuals', their prospects derailed by the forces of reaction.

The anti-clerical response in turn was fierce, and ultimately successful. 'Anti-clericalism' drew on many currents in French political and cultural life, and offered a banner around which all those who were uneasy or resentful at the course taken by Charles X could gather. Its appeal was increased when Catholic militants took to burning 'irreligious' or 'subversive' books by great French writers like Voltaire. The liberals' fear of a new 'Inquisition' sometimes combined with frustrated career expectations (see above) to produce outpourings of vitriolic anti-Catholic journalism. In newspaper columns, reports of high-minded speeches by liberal deputies defending the freedom of the press rubbed shoulders with scandalous stories hinting at the sexual proclivities of monkish choirmasters. Popular songs were also very important in spreading the anti-clerical message. The Jesuits, supposedly the most sinister of the Catholic religious orders, were a particular target.

Anti-clericalism was supported by many good Catholics as well as radicals. These Catholics were worried that their Church's increasingly *Ultra* leadership was linking their faith far too closely with political extremism. They also feared that a faction within the hierarchy of the Catholic Church was trying to make the state subservient to the Pope in Rome. The anti-clerical campaign had destroyed the unity of the right-wing: good Catholics could freely attack the politics of the Church, and loyal monarchists could denounce Villèle.

The opposition began an impressive organisational counter-attack, masterminded by Guizot. In 1827 he founded *Aide-toi, le ciel t'aidera* ('Heaven helps those who help themselves'). This organisation's main purpose was to counter the trickery of local government officials who, under instructions from the Ministry of the Interior, had become skilled in methods designed to keep known liberals off the electoral registers (and so unable to vote); whilst enrolling as many convinced royalists as possible, whether they were really qualified or not. *Aide-toi* had soon established a network of committees in over 60 *Departments*

KEY ISSUE

How effective was the liberals' counter-attack?

(counties) of France. The results of this organisation's work were dramatic. Simply by making the officials play by the rules, over 20 000 liberals secured their rights as voters, a significant number given the small electorate. In some *departments*, the electoral lists grew by 40 per cent.

The 1827 elections were a crushing victory for the liberals, quite reversing the catastrophe of 1824. They won between 180 and 200 seats. Given his problems with political divisions on the right, Villèle reluctantly accepted that he could not win the support of a majority in the Chamber, and in January 1828 he resigned. The great question he left behind was whether Charles X would accept the logic of the parliamentary situation and adopt more moderate policies which reflected the new balance of power in the Chamber.

6 ⌐ THE JULY REVOLUTION AND THE STRAITJACKET OF HISTORY

Louis XVIII had not loved the Charter, but he accepted that he had to live with it and work within its provisions. However, Charles X loathed the French Revolution: although he had sworn as part of his coronation oath to govern as a constitutional monarch, his interpretation of the constitution was absolutist.

Charles X was quite determined that the French monarch should never become a mere figurehead. The Charter had created a constitutional monarchy, he insisted, not a parliamentary one. He explicitly rejected the English political model, in which the Lords and the Commons were ultimately supreme. 'In England', he said, 'the Houses defined the role of King ... here, the King defines the role of the Houses'.

Charles X lacked the necessary political sensitivity and flexibility to make his interpretation work. 'Concession' and 'compromise' were not in his vocabulary. His experience of revolution led him to declare 'the first retreat that my unfortunate brother made was the signal for his downfall'. To Charles X, behind every liberal, there hid a **regicide**.

regicide murderer of a king

The real choice facing Charles X on the eve of the July Revolution was not between the unyielding defence of royal authority or the guillotine: it was between compromise or exile. Like so many other French people in the nineteenth century, Charles X was trapped by, and ultimately the victim of, his own interpretation of the past.

In August 1829, the full extent of Charles X's political insensitivity and misjudgement revealed itself. For some time, he had been unhappy with the moderate course pursued by Villèle's successor. After lengthy intrigues, Count Polignac – his long-standing friend, fellow *émigré* and Knight of the Faith – was installed as Charles' new chief minister. La Bourdonnaye was Minister of the Interior and Bourmont Minister of War.

The appointment of this trio provoked dismay and astonishment. Polignac had the mentality of an *Ancien Régime* courtier-aristocrat and

KEY ISSUE

How and why did the political crisis escalate after the appointment of Polignac in August 1829?

was incapable of formulating any realistic policies. He was also stubborn and unshakeably self-confident. La Bourdonnaye had first won notoriety with his blood-curdling endorsement of the White Terror of 1815–16. General de Bourmont was perhaps the most hated of the three: he had supposedly betrayed Napoleon's battle plan to the allies on the eve of Waterloo.

See page 37

A collision between Charles X's brazenly *Ultra* ministry and the liberal-dominated Chamber of Deputies was inevitable. Charles X made a menacing speech to Parliament in March 1830, in which he reminded his audience of the emergency powers vested in the crown by Article 14 of the Charter. The Chamber replied that the Charter required the King's Government to respect the wishes of the nation, and warned the King that his people were 'distressed' and 'alarmed' by his government's attitudes.

See page 35

Few, if any, of the liberal deputies were yet thinking of revolution. They saw themselves as defenders of the constitution. As men of substantial wealth, they would be loath to jeopardise the social order by calling 'the mob' out onto the streets. Equally, Charles X and his advisors had not yet begun to think seriously about a *coup d'état*. However, an absolutely central constitutional issue was at stake, on which the Charter was ambiguous. Could the King choose whoever he wanted as his ministers, or did the King's Government have to be constructed so as to enjoy the support of a majority in parliament? Charles X believed just as firmly as the Chamber that he was defending his legitimate rights. In these circumstances, retreat for either side would be very difficult.

Charles X had one last card to play before he resorted to force. In May 1830, he dissolved the Chamber and called new elections. This manoeuvre only made his position worse. Charles X put his authority at grave risk by giving his full personal endorsement to Polignac's ministry in the campaign: 'Harken to the advice of your King ... ', he announced, 'it is a father who calls you. Fulfil your duties. I will know how to fulfil mine'.

The electors of France did not respond to their 'father's' command. 270 of the 428 deputies returned were liberals. Government supporters numbered only 145. Even the top 25 per cent of the electorate, with their 'double vote', was unsympathetic. The political isolation of the Court was complete; France had voted against the King.

Charles X and his ministers had manoeuvred themselves into the tightest of corners. So, invoking Article 14 of the Charter, Charles launched his royalist 'coup'.

Charles X's 'Four Ordinances' (emergency decrees) were published in the 26th July's edition of *Le Moniteur* – the government's mouthpiece. The Ordinances were a systematic attempt to put the monarchy and its ministers beyond the reach of public criticism. Freedom of the press was suspended and extremely restrictive censorship regulations were introduced, designed to silence the liberal press permanently: only government authorised newspapers were to be printed. New elections were called, on a franchise limited to 25 000 voters.

See page 35

KEY ISSUE

Why did Charles X's attempted coup provoke a revolution, and why was the revolution successful?

Liberal politicians were caught by surprise. Leading deputies agreed that the Ordinances were illegal, but these cautious men would not go beyond recommending tax strikes and making statements of condemnation. However, the working classes responded more strongly, having suffered several years of unemployment and high bread prices. They also feared that the Government was destroying the Charter and wished to restore the *Ancien Régime.*

Revolution was initially sparked by the journalists and printers of the liberal press. The rigorous censorship laws threatened their livelihoods as well as their principles. Police raids on newspapers which had gone to press with denunciations of the *coup* provoked rioting. Shots were fired and the Revolution had its first martyrs: crowds which had begun by shouting 'Long live the Charter', were now shouting 'Death to Polignac', and began breaking into gun shops to arm themselves. Barricades were built.

Charles X and his ministers were bumbling and complacent. No serious resistance to the Ordinances had been anticipated, and so no plans had been made to contain any! Many of the King's best troops were in Algeria. (Charles X hoped that a successful imperial crusade would increase his prestige, but news of the capture of Algiers had come too late to affect the June elections.) The 9000 troops who were sent into the centre of Paris had little taste for shooting fellow Frenchmen, and anyway clearing the barricades from the warrens of narrow medieval streets was difficult. The 'three glorious days' of the July Revolution are largely the story of the progressive demoralisation of Charles X's troops, of repeated breakdowns in the army's system of command and communication, and of Charles X's refusal to make any concessions to the revolutionaries until it was too late. When he finally agreed to abdicate, on condition that his grandson be crowned king, his opponents simply ignored the claims of 'Henry V'. Soon the Bourbons were on their way to exile in England.

Charles X had played his hand extraordinarily badly. On Louis XVIII's death, the Bourbons had seemed well established. The opposition was on the defensive, the exchequer was healthy, and the prestige of the dynasty had been boosted by the army's successful intervention in Spain. Louis XVIII was no political genius, but he had shown the pragmatism needed to make the liberal constitutional system work. By contrast, Charles X had made the *Ultras'* programme his own. He then stuck to an inflexible political strategy which inevitably led to grave conflict with the Chamber of Deputies – a conflict which he mishandled at every point. As Alfred Cobban wrote, 'the fall of the last Bourbon king of France was so little determined by the nature of things that it took almost inconceivable imbecility on the part of Charles X and [Polignac] to bring it about'.

See the bibliography on page 64

7 ⌐ THE JULY MONARCHY: ESTABLISHING THE NEW REGIME

The liberal politicians had not made the July Revolution: it was the work of the people of Paris. Could the politicians now control it? In 1830, the liberals' great worry was that Republicans would fill the power vacuum unexpectedly created in Paris, and push France down the path of social revolution and international conflict.

In fact, the Revolution was quickly over. To the liberals, this was what was so 'glorious' about the Three Glorious Days. Louis-Philippe was skilfully eased towards the political centre stage, largely due to Adolphe Thiers.

ADOLPHE THIERS (1797–1877)

Adolphe Thiers became the leading figure of a generation of Frenchmen whose political attitudes and expectations had been transformed by the Revolution – and who had therefore found the era of the Bourbon Restoration deeply frustrating. After 1815, there were no top jobs for people of his liberal views. But, determined to make his mark, he made his way to Paris. There, the combination of his powerful intelligence and sheer hard work won him considerable influence as a journalist and historian and as a society figure: he was soon one of the key figures in opposition politics. From the pages of *Le Constitutionnel* and *Le National* (which he part-owned and edited), he attacked Charles X and urged the creation of a political system where 'the king reigns but does not rule'. The Government's attempt to close down *Le National* in late July 1830 helped to spark the July Revolution, and gave Thiers an opportunity to promote Louis-Phillipe's claims to the throne. Thiers was twice to become the new regime's Prime Minister. He was active in French politics until his death in 1877, remaining throughout his career committed to the defence of liberal, representative institutions, social order and the rights of property.

In a newspaper campaign, Thiers had for some time been suggesting that what France needed was a change of dynasty. Using *Le National* as his platform, he denounced the Ordinances. On 29 July, he and a friend composed the following poster, advertising the merits of Louis-Philippe, and the demerits of Charles X.

KEY ISSUE

How did Louis-Philippe emerge from the chaos of revolution to become 'King of the French'?

Charles X can never again enter Paris: he caused the blood of the people to be shed.
The Republic would expose us to frightful divisions: it would embroil us with Europe.
The Duc d'Orléans is a prince devoted to the cause of the revolution.
The Duc d'Orléans was at Jemappes (an important early [1792] victory against France's enemies in the Revolutionary Wars).
The Duc d'Orléans is a Citizen King.
The Duc d'Orléans has carried the tricolour under the enemy's fire.
The Duc d'Orléans has declared himself: he accepts the Charter as we have always wanted it. It is from the French people that he will hold his crown.

KEY ISSUE

How did Thiers try to maximise support for the Duc d'Orléans as King and minimise support for the alternatives?

Legitimists
The Legitimists upheld the legally superior, i.e. legitimate, claims of the House of Bourbon to the French throne, and considered the Duke of Orleans an illegitimate usurper. This division in the royalist ranks gravely weakened the monarchist cause, especially in the 1870s.

See page 39

KEY ISSUE

What problems faced the new Government when it tried to define the nature of Louis-Philippe's authority?

Thiers candidly explained his objectives to the duke's sister: 'We need a new dynasty which owes the crown to us and which, because it owes it to us, is ready to accept the role assured to it by the representative system. Thrones belong to those who first take possession.'

Louis-Philippe probably needed little persuading. He had little love for his Bourbon relatives, and ignored Charles X's desperate plea to proclaim the accession of Henry V and safeguard the interests of the boy-king. The Legitimists never forgave Louis-Philippe for his betrayal. But the new King always claimed that he had only accepted the liberals' summons reluctantly, as a way to save France from civil war and/or a republic.

On 31 July, these outcomes could still not be ruled out. For although Louis-Philippe enjoyed liberal support, there was no certainty that he would be able to win over the people of Paris. After all, the people had driven Charles X off the throne, they still ruled the streets, and many of them had Republican or Bonapartist sympathies. At this point, the imposing and revered figure of Lafayette, a popular hero from the early days of the 1789 revolution, played a key role. Although a Republican, Lafayette did not believe that the French people were ready for the responsibilities of a more democratic style of politics. Accordingly, in a dramatic scene in the centre of Paris, surrounded by thousands of revolutionaries, he endorsed Louis-Philippe's claim to power by draping him in the tricolour and embracing him. The best thing for France in 1830, Lafayette later told the King, was ' a popular throne surrounded by republican institutions'.

What did this mean in practice? The 1814 Charter was revised. Louis-Philippe's accession to the throne was made explicitly *conditional* on his acceptance of the restrictions on a *constitutional* monarch. Article 14 of the Charter, under which Charles X had proclaimed a state of emergency, was completely rewritten. Louis-Philippe's coronation was held in the Houses of Parliament, and there was not a clergyman, a bible, a crucifix – or a phial of holy oil – in sight.

The fact that the origins of the new Regime were revolutionary, however, was something Louis-Philippe and most of his supporters preferred to forget. The chequered early career of the painting on the cover of this book, Delacroix's *The 28th July: Liberty Leading the People*, indicates some of this queasiness. Now generally recognised as one of the masterpieces of nineteenth Century French art, it spent most of the July Monarchy 'in store'. Art historians believe that the Ministry of the Interior preferred to keep it out of the public eye because it unashamedly celebrated the fighting heroism of the people of Paris in July and recognised that blood had had to be shed in the Revolution. Louis-Philippe had no desire to be reminded that he owed his power to 'the nomination of the streets'. He probably agreed with Casimir Périer, a leading supporter of the July Monarchy but a conservative-leaning politician, who denied that there had been any revolution, but only 'a change in the person of the King'.

What was at stake was the very legitimacy – and therefore the stability – of the regime. Louis-Philippe fell between two stools. He was the head of a great dynasty, and had royal blood in his veins: but he was not the legitimate hereditary King of France. He could also claim to be the heir of revolution – he had fought on the side of the nation in 1792 – but he could not acknowledge his debts to the people of Paris, whose potential for destructive radicalism frightened him and his supporters. To paraphrase the French historian Francois Furet, the July Monarchy was a risky compromise between the sovereignty of kings and the sovereignty of the people. When it fell in 1848, it was despised by many on the right and left alike.

KEY ISSUE

In what ways did the origins of the July Monarchy compromise its authority?

8 ∽ CRISES CONTAINED

In its first few years, Louis-Philippe's regime seemed in perpetual turmoil. Repeated challenges to its authority and very existence were proof that some Frenchmen completely rejected its legitimacy. That the monarchy survived tells us much about the inner toughness of Louis-Philippe and most of his leading ministers. It also perhaps indicates that most Frenchmen were prepared to tolerate the new regime: whatever the Government's apprehensions, none of the challenges received significant popular support.

ANALYSIS

The early crises of the July Monarchy

- December 1830. Massive demonstrations accompanied the trial of Polignac for treason. When the Paris 'mob' was denied the death sentence it was demanding, a republican insurrection was widely feared.
- February 1831. A religious service to commemorate the death of the Duke of Berry, organised by embittered *Ultras*, provoked widespread anti-clerical rioting. The National Guard stood by and watched as the Archbishop of Paris' palace was looted and then demolished.
- October–November 1831. There were serious disturbances in Lyons, where silk weavers were demonstrating against wage cuts. The weavers defeated the royal troops who fired on them, and they held on to control of the city for three days.
- April–November 1832. The Duchess of Berry, mother of 'Henry V', operating via an underground *Ultra*-network, tried to instigate risings in the royalist south and west. Although the forces she raised were easily defeated (May–June), she herself evaded capture for many months, causing the Government much anxiety.
- June 1832. The funeral of a republican hero, General Lamarque, was the occasion for another insurrection in Paris. A total of 800 were killed or wounded before it was put down.

● April 1834. The trial of some workers' leaders in Lyons being prosecuted for organising a trades union (illegal in France until 1864) led to rioting. This developed into a full-scale rising, with local Republicans to the fore. The latter, members of a nationwide network of clubs called *The Society of the Rights of Man*, had hoped to spark simultaneous insurrections in Paris and elsewhere. In the end, the revolt in Lyons was crushed after bloody fighting (over 300 killed, and 800 wounded) and the planned rising in Paris proved largely abortive when the Government arrested up to 150 known Republican militants.

● 28 July 1835. In the most bloody of the eight attempted assassinations of Louis-Philippe, a Republican extremist named Fieschi unleashed a hail of bullets at a royal procession from an 'infernal machine' consisting of 25 rifles. Eighteen were killed, 22 wounded. The King escaped with minor wounds.

Good fortune accounts partly for the survival of the July Monarchy over these years. Fieschi could easily have killed Louis-Philippe. The Legitimist cause was done grave damage, less by the capture of the Duchess of Berry than by the discovery that the Duchess had got herself pregnant while on the run after the failure of her rising. The Government also probably benefited from the end to the economic depression from which France had been suffering between 1827 and 1832. There was now less discontent.

But much of the credit for the survival of the regime should go to the Government itself. It was ruthless in holding on to power. Seventy-nine of France's 86 **Prefects** were purged, so as to ensure the loyalty of these vital officials to the new regime. Spies infiltrated the royalist and republican underground making it possible, in Paris in 1834, and in the royalist south in 1832, to snuff out insurrection almost before it had begun. The ministers who had mishandled the violent outbreak of anti-clericalism of 1831 were dismissed as being too soft-hearted towards the left. By contrast, Casimir Périer, the new Prime Minister, knew which side of the barricades he was on. Newspapers were confiscated for **sedition**, unreliable state officials were sacked and demonstrations banned.

The September Laws of 1835 which followed Fieschi's assassination attempt marked an even fiercer period of repression. Legal procedures against political offenders and censorship of newspapers were tightened up. The July Monarchy placed a higher priority on the preservation of order than on the preservation of liberty.

The Government was also ready to use the army and the National Guard against actual or potential insurrection. The December 1830 crisis had been defused by flooding the centre of Paris with 30 000 troops, before any real trouble could start. After the first rising in Lyons, a garrison of 10 000 troops was established there; in the bloody battle of 1834, artillery was used to bombard working class strongholds. Thiers,

---

The **Prefects** were not just the government's eyes and ears in the Departments of France; they were responsible for law and order and the distribution of patronage. It was therefore essential that they be loyal to the Government

sedition the publication of anti-government, treasonable literature

Minister of the Interior in 1834, was clearly taking no half measures –
as the massacre in Paris in the Rue Transnonian, which occurred as his
troops were mopping up in the aftermath of the 14 April insurrection,
also indicated.

See the exercise on
page 66

9 ⌐ ORLEANISM: IDEOLOGY AND SOCIAL BASIS

The Government's repression of dissent might suggest that **Orleanism**
was an essentially reactionary ideology. In fact, as Robert Tombs has
pointed out, many of its objectives were modern and progressive. It
aimed to 'protect the individual, maintain international peace, and
foster economic growth'. Orleanists believed that a parliamentary
monarchy – such as that established in Britain – was the key to success
in these respects. King and nation could unite around the compromise
of the Charter. Louis-Philippe and his advisers were determined that
militant Republicans would not wreck the work of July. Thiers summed
up their fighting spirit: 'Behind the July Government there is the
counter-revolution, in front of it is anarchy'. They had found 'a middle
way' (*juste milieu*) which they would fight to defend.

Orleanism is the name
given to the political
beliefs of the defenders
of the July Monarchy

See the bibliography
section on page 64

This made Orleanism rather exclusive. The franchise was lowered in
the revised Charter, but was still restricted to those who paid more than
200 francs a year in tax. The electorate of 170 000 (5 per 1000 inhabitants) was soon seen as dangerously restrictive. But the Orleanists'
political caution was understandable. The experience of mass politics
during The Terror had left deep scars. The Orleanists, like all other
European liberals, feared democracy. Electors needed to be men of
wealth and education because, it was believed, this was the precondition
of political maturity and stability.

However, it would be misleading to characterise the July Monarchy as
a 'bourgeois' monarchy, as Karl Marx did in 1853. 'Under the Bourbons,
the big landowners controlled politics; under the Orleanists, large scale
industry, big capital and trade. The July Monarchy was simply the political expression of the usurpation of power by the upstart bourgeoisie'.

Marx implies that, in 1830, a social and political system dominated
by aristocratic landowners was overthrown and replaced by a system in
which the bourgeoisie [that is, middle-class financiers, merchants and
manufacturers] were in control. Yet historians now argue that 1830 was
not a *social* revolution. After 1830, deputies came from the same sort of
social background as before, with landowners and civil servants still
predominating. Land was still the main source of wealth. Most modern
historians believe that the French industrial revolution and with it, the
rise of a big, thrusting bourgeoisie, did not get off the ground before
the 1850s. Indeed, to its critics, the July Monarchy seemed to be run not
by the middle classes, but by a greedy and self-perpetuating *élite*. After
all, had it been a bourgeois monarchy, the bourgeoisie would hardly
have campaigned so vigorously against it in 1847–8 in an attempt to
persuade it to give them a share of power.

KEY ISSUE

*Why is the July
Monarchy sometimes
referred to as 'bourgeois
monarchy', and with
what justification?*

See page 59

10 ⌐ ORLEANIST FOREIGN POLICY AND THE TEMPTATION OF GRANDEUR

KEY ISSUE

What did many Frenchmen believe to be the international mission of France, and why did their visions disturb Louis-Philippe?

See pages 17 and 89

The Orleanist *élite* feared a Republic not merely because they thought it would be anti-aristocratic; but also because of the reckless foreign policies many republicans wanted to pursue. Republicans believed that 1789 had inaugurated a new era in world civilisation. It was France's mission to spread the gospel of liberty, equality and fraternity throughout Europe and beyond. The oppressed peoples of the German Confederation and the Italian peninsula (both largely under Habsburg control) and Poland especially (Russian dominated), were supposedly merely waiting for a sign from Paris to throw off their tyrants' shackles. It was France's duty to come to their assistance.

These heroic ideals also had a selfish side. A bold foreign policy might result in the expansion of France to her 'natural frontiers', along the Rhine. *La Grande Nation* would overturn the verdict of Waterloo and the Vienna Settlement.

As saner Frenchmen realised, this was a fantasy. The peoples of Europe did not wish to be liberated by Frenchmen. For example, German nationalism was largely a response to fears of French aggression. Also, any French expansionism would be vigorously resisted by Europe's other Great Powers, Prussia, Austria, Russia and Great Britain, which had defeated France twice, in 1814 and 1815.

This was the nightmare haunting Louis-Philippe in 1830. Partly in response to the July Revolution in Paris, revolts had broken out in Brussels (August) and Warsaw (November), followed by risings in Italy in 1831. To republicans, this was the moment of destiny: to Louis-Philippe, it was the moment for Casimir Périer. Périer, leader of 'the Party of Resistance' gave an emphatic 'no' to the 'Party of Movement' abroad as well as at home. France did not aid Polish or Italian nationalists, and Louis-Philippe's intervention in Belgium was effectively limited to an international peace-keeping role.

ANALYSIS

Party politics in France

Political parties as we understand them today, did not emerge in nineteenth century France, at least until the 1880s. The Chamber of Deputies was split up into half a dozen factions, from Republicans on the Left to Legitimists on the Right. The votes of many deputies could effectively be bought by ministerial promises of favours for their constituencies. 'Party of Resistance' or 'Party of Order' is shorthand for the fluctuating body of conservative-minded liberals who thought that the revolutions of 1789–1830 had gone far enough; the 'Party of Movement', consisting of left-leaning liberals, believed that the mission of the Revolution had yet to be completed.

Peace would have to take priority over honour abroad, as was the case throughout the July Monarchy. Louis-Philippe's opponents derided his supposed 'passion for peace' and believed that it had betrayed the true spirit of France. Only once, in 1840, in what Robert Tombs describes as the 'turning point of the reign', did his Government come near to favouring war over his own instincts, and the episode ended in a disaster for French diplomacy.

See the bibliography section on page 64

THE MEHMET ALI CRISIS

Since Napoleon's adventures in the Middle East, the French had claimed an interest in the affairs of the Ottoman Empire in general, and Egypt in particular. Mehmet Ali, the Sultan's governor in Egypt, had established himself as an independent ruler in his own right, and was busy extending his 'empire' into Syria, even hoping to found his own dynasty. He looked to France to support his ambitions. Thiers' Government agreed to back him, seeing in Ali a powerful counterweight to Russian and British influence in the region. Thiers was also well aware that success abroad would consolidate his position at home, especially on the left, where criticisms of the Government's refusal to take up parliamentary reform were mounting.

See pages 18–19

KEY ISSUES

How did Thiers hope to exploit the Near Eastern Crisis of 1840, and how, and with what consequences, did he fail?

Thiers' bold support for Mehmet Ali was a mixture of a bluff and a gamble. When in July 1840, all the other Great Powers delivered an ultimatum to Mehmet Ali to withdraw from Syria, Thiers' position became precarious. The French Government had not even been consulted about the ultimatum, a diplomatic snub which provoked the Republican *Le National* to declare in October 1840:

> France, noble France, awake! Resume your task, the task of '89 and 1830 ... The time has come. Think of your supreme mission and the grandeur of your destiny ... March on the Rhine, tear up the treaties of 1815, tell Germany, Italy, Spain and Poland that you carry the magnet of civilisation at the tip of your weapons – whether France will retain its rank in the world or not is at stake.

Q

1. Explain 'March on the Rhine ... The tip of your weapons'
2. Why might Louis-Philippe's government have been annoyed at Le National's comments?

Thiers pressed on with a rearmament programme, and seemed ready for conflict, but when a joint Anglo-Austrian-Turkish military operation led to the capture of Beirut and the full scale retreat of Mehmet's army, the game was up, as Louis-Philippe knew. Thiers resigned, leaving the king to take much of the blame for France's humiliation.

Lasting damage was done to the legitimacy of the July Monarchy. De Tocqueville, an independent-minded Deputy, had warned that to allow France to be treated as a second rate power 'would be more fatal to us than the loss of 20 battles and would lead to the burial of the monarchy itself beneath the ruins of our national honour'. But Louis-Philippe was convinced – probably rightly – that war would have resulted in total defeat for France. The whole episode increased his general contempt for politicians as a class. Only Guizot was excepted. Moreover, it convinced the King that any further extension of the franchise would be against the national interest, and would create a more ignorant and belligerent electorate. The roots of the political immobility and stagnation which came to characterise the July Monarchy in its last years can be found here.

France could not satisfy her quest for grandeur abroad; could Louis-Philippe contrive to supply it at home? He recognised the potential of political theatre and symbolism in strengthening popular attachment to his government, reconciling the French people to their past, and to each other. In 1833, the Palace of Versailles was reopened as a museum dedicated 'to all the glories of France', whilst in 1840, the remains of Napoleon were brought back to lie in a great mausoleum in the centre of Paris. However, popular comparisons between Louis-Philippe and Napoleon could only be to the latter's favour.

Louis-Philippe had considerable personal and political virtues. He was hard-working, vastly experienced and often shrewd in his judgements. But he was something of a pen-pusher, whose self-conscious adoption of bourgeois manners and dress, made him seem simply grey and dull. His facial likeness to a pear proved irresistible to hostile cartoonists. If France looked for *grandeur*, the nation would not find it in the person of Louis-Philippe.

ANALYSIS

Louis-Philippe and the caricaturists

The first five years of Louis-Philippe's reign saw an unparalleled growth in the impact of the political caricature. This is partly explained by a (temporary) relaxation of censorship, cheaper reproductive techniques, and the emergence of the leading caricaturists Philipon and Daumier. The genius and savage wit of these two artists made them popular heroes on the left of French politics. But it also provoked the sustained opposition of the authorities who were outraged at the insults being hurled at them, and who were conscious of how effective this form of satire was at stirring up the semi-literate masses. By 1835, political cartoons had effectively been banned.

Gargantua (Picture 1) was Daumier's first great cartoon. It was prompted by the size of the civil list (that is, the contribution made to the King's income from tax payers) and the way Louis-Philippe and his Government used that money to buy political favours and reward their cronies. 'Gargantua' earned Daumier a six-month goal sentence for the indignity it inflicted on the King, who was revealed enthroned on the royal toilet, doing his business.

The single most effective symbolic attack on the July Monarchy came via the conversion of Louis-Philippe's head into a pear. Philipon sketched Picture 2 in court, in an attempt to convince the judges that there was nothing malicious or perverse about this transformation.

PICTURE 1
Gargantua, caricature by Daumier

PICTURE 2
Metamorphosis of the Pear
by Philipon

PICTURE 3
Caricature by Philipon

It was a stroke of genius. Representing the monarch as a fruit was not simply to inflict a further indignity on France's Head of State (especially as in French slang pear means fool). It also gave the caricaturist vital room for manoeuvre. When Philipon produced a cartoon hinting at the guillotining of a pear, he was able to defend himself in court against the charge of inciting assassination with the quip that his cartoon 'would be at most a provocation to make marmalade'.

Louis-Philippe and the pear became synonymous.

Fieschi's bloody assassination attempt on Louis-Philippe in 1835 gave the authorities an excuse for a strict tightening of political censorship. The September Laws effectively banned the political cartoon. In the words of the Minister of Justice, it was vital to bring an end to 'this torrent of immorality and seduction … to obscene engravings … and insolent lithographs which bring derision, ridicule and scorn … on the authority of the King'.

Philipon went out in style. He published the new law in his satirical weekly – but in the format shown in Picture 4: the September Laws were described as 'another fruit of the July Revolution'.

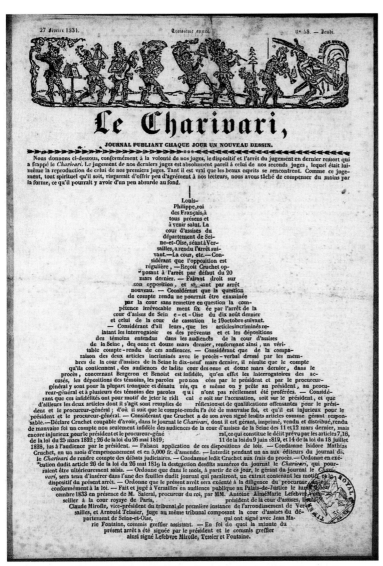

PICTURE 4 *The last edition of Philipon's satirical journal Le Charivari*

11 ⌐ LOUIS-PHILIPPE, GUIZOT AND THE PRELUDE TO REVOLUTION

The July Monarchy's first five years had been a struggle for survival. The following five years, by contrast, were characterised by a prolonged, sordid and undignified squabble for power between the leaders of the various factions in the Chamber of Deputies, further complicated

KEY ISSUE

What did Guizot achieve as a politician and statesman between 1840 and 1847?

by Louis-Philippe's determination to play a central role in decision making. The public reputation of politics and politicians sank: principle and policy seemed to matter for nothing besides the backstairs deals and clash of personalities, according to which ministries rose or fell. Thiers might have had the energy and personality to stamp his authority on the proceedings, but the failure of his over-ambitious foreign policy ended his attempt to construct a broader based coalition of forces in the Chamber and left him, discredited, in the political wilderness.

Guizot headed Louis-Philippe's Government from 1840. Despite their excellent working relationship and Guizot's great gifts, its legislative record disappointed. The Railway Law of 1842 was its only significant achievement. This began an era of state/private enterprise partnership (the state designed the network and built the lines, leasing them out to private companies) which enabled the construction of 1900 kilometres of track by 1848. Investment in this economic sector underpinned the boom of the 1840s with tens of thousands employed in associated works in construction, iron and steel, and engineering. But Guizot's free-market philosophy did not solve the emerging 'social question' – the crises of rural overpopulation and the growing prominence of an

PROFILE

PICTURE 5 *Sketch of Guizot*

See page 43

FRANCOIS GUIZOT (1787–1874)

Thiers' fall opened the door to his great rival: Francois Guizot. Guizot was one of the most intellectually gifted politicians ever to lead a French administration. His (conservative-leaning) liberal principles were derived from his study of history. He cherished the French revolution of 1789; by contrast, he hated the unreason of the Terror, which had cost his father his life. A doer as well as a thinker, the defence of the 'middle way' represented by constitutional monarchy was the theme of his long political career. He had been an influential figure amongst those trying to steer Louis XVIII's government away from reaction; and when the *Ultras* finally seized control he emerged as the brains behind '*Aide toi, le ciel t'aidera*', which was to be instrumental in organising the successful electoral opposition to Charles X. Guizot combined deep conviction, piercing intelligence and practical experience.

Guizot was neither popular nor ultimately successful. He was an outsider in French political life. A Protestant amongst Catholics, a politician of honour and integrity amongst self-serving careerists, a man of stubborn principle at a time of expediency and compromise – this was, at least, how he saw himself. Others saw arrogance and self-deception, especially in view of his electoral manipulation. Guizot and Louis-Philippe were to pay a high price for this isolation and unpopularity in 1848.

urban underclass. Above all, the Government continued to oppose the increasing clamour for parliamentary reform.

Critics labelled the Government's inactivity as 'immobilism'. It had several causes:

See page 62

- both Guizot and Louis-Philippe were cautious by nature. The King – 70 years old in 1843, and much affected by the death of his brilliant son and heir in an accident the year earlier – had lost much of his former energy
- Guizot's position in the Chamber was difficult. Only in 1846 did he achieve a clear majority, and even then most Deputies remained primarily concerned with local rather than national issues, and Guizot always had to be careful not to offend vested interests. But the members of the opposition were not impressed by excuses: one critic, asking what the Government had achieved, gave the following damning answer to his own question – 'Nothing! Nothing! Nothing!'
- the growing mood of public disenchantment was summarised by the poet-turned politician, Lamartine, who warned Louis-Philippe in 1839 that 'France is bored', denouncing the prevalent 'spirit of materialism and trafficking'; and predicting a 'revolution of contempt'.

Contempt was certainly provoked by Louis-Philippe's foreign policy in the 1840s. A row over the maltreatment of an English missionary on a French island in the Pacific blew up into an international incident, and when Guizot backed down (1844), apologising to London, the press was furious at this new betrayal of national honour. The marriage in 1846 of one of Louis-Philippe's surviving sons to the younger sister of the Spanish queen was also derided by the opposition. It now complained that the British – whose own candidate for the hand of the Queen's sister had been outmanoeuvred – had been alienated by Guizot's intrigues. Guizot had supposedly put service to the family of Louis-Philippe before the interests of the nation.

See page 52 for the context.

France was hit by scandal in the mid-1840s. Two former ministers were found guilty of corruption. The Duke of Choiseul-Praslin, one of France's grandest noblemen, killed himself while awaiting trial for the bludgeoning to death of his wife. Here was more evidence of the rottenness at the heart of France's social *élite*. Its end was closer than almost anyone expected.

12 ᕽ FEBRUARY 1848: THE ACCIDENTAL REVOLUTION

The revolution which broke out in Paris in February 1848, toppling Louis-Philippe from his throne, caught most contemporaries by surprise. The 1846 election results had suggested that Guizot and Louis-Philippe were safer than ever. Furthermore, most of the Government's opponents were aiming at the reform, not the overthrow, of the Orleanist political system. But in retrospect, it can be seen that the July

Monarchy was far less stable than either its supporters or opponents imagined.

Revolutions are dramatic and highly complex events, and historians sometimes construct models to help identify the most important features. One useful approach is to distinguish between three different levels of causation: long-term causes or **preconditions**; medium-term causes or **precipitants**: and short-term causes or **triggers**. The **preconditions** will usually be found deep in the social and political structure of a country: the tensions and internal contradictions which make a state potentially unstable. The **precipitants** are the events – typically an economic recession – which bring such contradictions to the surface. The **triggers** – often matters of chance or miscalculation, such as soldiers panicking and firing into a crowd of protestors – are needed to spark the revolution.

A *Social and economic preconditions of revolution*

French society had undergone profound changes over the first half of the nineteenth century. Its population had increased from around 27 million in 1800 to almost 36 million in 1850. Economic growth, however, had failed to keep pace. Agricultural production was sluggish, so the price of food rose. Equally, the expanding work force, with too few factories to absorb it, threatened to swamp the already overcrowded traditional crafts, depressing wages and restricting job opportunities. In some sectors, the plight of skilled workers was made worse by the introduction of new technologies and labour practices, undermining their cherished independence and driving them towards poverty. Such were the causes of the bloody risings of the Lyons silk-workers in 1831 and 1834, with their desperate cry: 'to live working or die fighting'.

See page 49

Paris itself had seen the greatest changes. Its population had exploded from barely 860 000 in 1831 to almost 1.3 million in 1846. Some of this increase was absorbed in the suburbs, where the railway and factories were beginning to make their mark. But most of it gravitated towards the ancient centre of the city, with its narrow winding streets (ideal for barricades), overcrowded slums and tiny workshops, where too many craftsmen chased too little business.

Paris was the nerve centre of French political life, and the presence there of this potentially volatile mass of workers was ominous – especially since Parisians were prone to violent protest (1830, 1832, 1834, 1839, 1848). A Government which lost control of Paris usually lost control of France.

KEY ISSUE

How did social problems contribute to political instability in the years before 1848?

B *Ideological preconditions of revolution*

The July Monarchy was not ideologically well equipped to meet these growing social tensions. The ultimate source of Louis-Philippe's authority was unclear and ambiguous. France was a monarchy, yet its ruler owed his throne to the people of Paris and the Revolution of

1830. Unable to lay claim to the sanction of divine right or dynastic inheritance, Louis Philippe styled himself 'King of the French'. But to old-fashioned monarchists, this was a sham, and Louis-Philippe a usurper. These 'Legitimists' regarded the exiled Bourbons as the true royal family: even in the 1870s, they still looked hopefully to the restoration of '**Henry V**', the 'miracle child' of 1820. Accordingly, when revolution came, they did not lift a finger to save a monarchy which they despised.

Louis-Philippe also lacked support on the left. Many of the Parisians who rebelled in July 1830 had been Republicans. Not surprisingly, they felt cheated when, as if by sleight of hand, the institution of the monarchy survived. A republican 'underground' lived on after 1830 and its leaders played a crucial role in February 1848. Furthermore in the 1840s, pro-republican sentiment began to influence mainstream politics. Novels, plays, and Thiers' and Lamartine's best-selling histories of the Revolution made some of the revolutionaries of the 1790s into popular heroes again. Republican newspapers like *Le National* and *La Réforme* exposed incidents of electoral corruption and damned the supposed feebleness of Orleanist foreign policy. On the far left, there were demands for universal manhood suffrage and progressive social legislation. 'Socialism' was becoming increasingly significant. Writers like Louis Blanc preached the 'rights of labour' and the ideals of co-operation and fraternity at the work place. Hard-pressed craftsmen were attracted by such ideas.

The July Monarchy had no answer to their grievances. Its prevailing economic philosophy of *laissez-faire* individualism seemed merely to confirm the widespread perception that France was being run in the interests of an *élite* of ruthless 'spivs' whose only creed was 'get rich quick'. Few French kings can have been so little loved as Louis-Philippe. The relative ease and bloodlessness of the Revolution of February 1848 can only be understood when we appreciate the shallowness of the roots which the Orleans dynasty had established in the nation. When Paris spat him out, the rest of France turned its back on him.

C *Precipitants*

The main precipitants of the crisis which brought the July Monarchy to the brink of disaster in February 1848 were economic and political.

The French economy was successively hit, first by a disastrous harvest in 1846 (the worst for 25 years) and then by a major industrial and financial slump. In 1846–7, food was unbearably expensive in many regions of France: in some places there was near famine. Worse was to come, for what turned out to be the last major subsistence crisis of French history coincided with the first major economic recession of the industrial era. In 1847 French investors had begun to worry about over-production in general and the profitability of railway companies in particular. Guizot had offered Government backing to a programme of railway expansion in 1842, and railway construction had become the most dynamic sector of the economy. But speculation got out

Henry V's mother, the wife of the Duke of Berry, had been pregnant at the time of the latter's assassination in 1820 (see page 39). Thus the Bourbon line lived on

laissez-faire a belief that the state should interfere in the workings of the economy as little as possible, trusting instead to market forces and the energy and ambition of individuals to create general prosperity

KEY ISSUE

What were the ideological weaknesses of the Orleanist regime?

of control and the bubble burst. The end of 'railway mania' caused unemployment to rocket in the engineering, metallurgy and construction sectors With the average cost of some basic food stuffs rising fourfold, consumer spending on non-essentials was badly hit. Even when food prices returned to normal levels, business confidence remained very low.

This sharp downturn left Guizot's ministry extremely vulnerable. Previously Guizot had been able to reply to those who complained about repression that political stability had made property owners feel secure and had thereby encouraged investment. Economic growth was also the answer to demands for a lowering of the franchise: if voters went out and made money, they would qualify for a share of political power.

National prosperity would also make France great again. Guizot's slogan was '*enrichissez-vous!*' [make yourselves rich]. This phrase embodied a programme which had seemed to satisfy simultaneously the pursuit of individual self-interest, internal political stability, and international prestige. But in the slump of 1846–7, the command 'enrich yourself' had become a bad joke.

KEY ISSUE
Why was the economic crisis of 1847 so damaging to the government?

Resentment and despair gave added impetus to a campaign for electoral reform, which ultimately led to the collapse of the monarchy. The campaign took the form of a series of banquets. These got round the government's ban on political meetings – after the meal, the diners, sometimes over a thousand in number, would hear anti-government speeches from opposition deputies, demanding parliamentary reform.

There were four main aspects to these demands:

● the franchise had to be widened – France had an electorate of barely 250 000 in 1846, and 84 per cent of deputies had been returned with less than 400 votes
● the reformers called for an end to electoral corruption – individual votes were commonly bought with the promise of a job (e.g. as a local tax collector), and whole communities could be bribed with the promise of a new primary school or a railway branch-line
● the rights of civil servants and other state officials to sit in the Chamber were to be closely regulated – according to the opposition, two-fifths of all deputies were on the Government payroll – and not surprisingly these men were loyal followers of Guizot
● constituency boundaries needed to be redrawn, so as to end the over-representation of relatively thinly populated and easily manipulated rural communities.

Similar demands for reform had often been made in the Chamber, but had always been defeated. Guizot and his followers were hardly likely to vote for their own extinction; furthermore, both the King and his Prime Minister genuinely feared that lowering the franchise would unleash dangerous passions into French politics, especially into the conduct of foreign affairs. But, by bringing extra-parliamentary pressure on the Government, the reformers calculated that its isolation would be exposed, and Louis-Philippe might be forced into concessions.

Originally, the campaign had been led by moderate reformers like Barrot, essentially sympathetic to the July Monarchy. However, Socialists and hard line Republicans like Ledru-Rollin infiltrated the movement. Their after-dinner toasts proclaimed 'the right to work', called for universal manhood suffrage, and an end to the monarchy. This was too radical for many reformers. When the Government banned a Republican banquet planned for 22 February 1848, the moderates were secretly relieved. But a demonstration of the unemployed, planned to coincide with the banquet, went ahead.

D *Triggers*

To the shock and disbelief of all of France's political *élite*, from Guizot to opposition leaders like Thiers and Barrot, within two days this demonstration had grown into a revolution; Louis-Philippe had abdicated; and Paris was in the hands of the people and their republican and socialist tribunes.

No single spark detonated this revolution. Instead, an unpredictable series of events, blunders and misfortunes gave the initiative to the militants on the streets of Paris. Louis-Philippe's Government proved unexpectedly vulnerable and confused in the face of the crisis.

The King had been unperturbed by the demonstration of 22 February, even keeping troops in their barracks to avoid provocative incidents. However, the demonstrations did not disperse. Instead, the Republican underground took control of the protest on the night of 22–23, distributing weapons. This had to be stopped, so Louis-Philippe called out the National Guard, but it refused to rally to the monarchy. Too many of its members were disaffected from the regime: denied the vote, and badly hit by the recession, they were not eager to risk their lives for Guizot. Those Guardsmen who bothered to turn out either interposed themselves between the rioters and the troops (now deployed), or even joined in the cries of 'Down with Guizot' and 'Up with Reform'.

This was a great psychological and practical blow to Louis-Phillippe. For the first time, it brought home to him how isolated and unpopular the Orleanist regime had become. How could authority be restored? Some advised the ruthless use of the army; but could its loyalty be guaranteed? Louis-Philippe lacked stomach for the fight. 'I have seen enough blood', he declared. Having stubbornly resisted earlier advice to sack Guizot and agree to moderate reforms, his self-confidence now utterly collapsed, to be replaced by exhaustion and despair. Helplessness and paralysis, alternating with sheer panic, spread throughout the King's court and beyond.

Louis-Philippe dismissed Guizot on 23 February, but none of the three chief ministers who replaced him in quick succession over the next hours (first Molé, then Thiers and finally Barrot) could stabilise the situation. Events on the streets were soon out of control. A crucial incident happened around 5.00 pm on the 23rd. Panicking soldiers in front of the Foreign Ministry fired on demonstrators celebrating Guizot's fall. Over 50 civilians were killed. The enraged crowd called 'To the barricades! To arms!' Confused and demoralised soldiers began to fraternise with the people, handing over their weapons. Their commanders, under the King's instruction to avoid bloodshed, failed to protect the Chamber of Deputies from the insurgent Republicans.

This failure was crucial. Louis-Philippe had decided, around midday on 24 February, that his best chance of preserving the monarchy was to abdicate in favour of his nine-year-old grandson. This boy and his courageous mother went to the Chamber, which had begun a chaotic debate on the terms of the regency. However, discussion was cut short when armed republicans broke into the Chamber. The royal party managed to escape – but only to join Louis-Philippe in exile.

Lamartine and Ledru-Rollin, the leading Republicans present, led the victorious crowds to the Hotel de Ville (by tradition, the centre of popular revolution). A provisional government was proclaimed from here The new ministers included the editors of *Le Nation* and *La Reforme*, and the socialist writer and theorist Louis Blanc. The Government's leader was Lamartine: Romantic poet and, popular historian. The following day, France was proclaimed a Republic. Not just Louis-Philippe and Guizot, but Thiers and Barrot seemed to have been swept into oblivion. The people of Paris had revolutionised the political institutions and the political *élite* of France. Would they now be able to revolutionise French society as well?

> ### KEY ISSUE
>
> *'A chapter of accidents'.
> How fair is this analysis
> of the fall of the July
> Monarchy?*

13 ∽ BIBLIOGRAPHY

France 1814–70 by K. Randall (Hodder and Stoughton, 1986) provides a very clear introduction. *The Constitutional Monarchy in France 1814–48* by P. Pilbeam (Longman Seminar Studies, 2000) is a more demanding survey, but includes a selection of documents. *The 1830 Revolution in France* (Macmillan, 1991) and *Republicanism in Nineteenth Century France,* (Macmillan, 1995), both also by P. Pilbeam, are more specialised. *France 1814–1914* by R. Tombs (Longman, 1996), *Restoration and Reaction 1815–48* by A. Jardin and A. Tudesq (Cambridge, 1983), and *Revolutionary France 1770–1880* by F. Furet (Basil Blackwell, 1992) are demanding but also useful. *The Bourbon Restoration* by G. de Bertier de Sauvigny (University of Pennsylvania Press, 1966) is a rare example of work by a French historian sympathetic to the Restoration.

Documents on the French Revolution of 1848 by R. Price (Macmillan, 1996) and *Recollections by* A. de Tocqueville, trans. G. Lawrence (Anchor Books, 1971) cover the Revolution and its aftermath.

14 ⌐ STRUCTURED QUESTIONS AND ESSAYS

1. (a) Outline the policies of Louis XVIII and his Governments between 1815 and 1824; (10 marks)
   (b) To what extent did Charles X continue these policies, and with what success? (15 marks)
2. (a) Outline the causes of the 1830 Revolution in France; (10 marks)
   (b) To what extent did Louis Philippe fulfil the hopes of the revolutionaries? (15 marks)
3. (a) Outline the domestic policies of Louis Philippe and his Governments between 1830 and 1848; (10 marks)
   (b) Why was Louis Philippe overthrown in 1848? (15 marks)
4. 'France is bored.' Is this an adequate explanation for the overthrow of the Orleanist monarchy in 1848? (25 marks)
5. To what extent was France politically unstable between 1815 and 1848? (25 marks)

15 ⌐ THE JULY MONARCHY: A SOURCES EXERCISE

Study Sources A–E and answer the questions which follow.

The principle behind the July Revolution, and consequently behind the government which derives from it, is not insurrection. The principle behind the July Revolution is resistance to aggression by the authorities. France was provoked; she was defied. She defended herself and her victory was that of justice, unworthily outraged. Respect for vows sworn; respect for law – that is the principle behind the July Revolution; that is the principle behind the government which it founded.

For it founded a government: it did not inaugurate anarchy. It did not overturn the social order; it affected only the political order. It had for its aim the establishment of a government which was free but orderly … Society needs impartial order and authority …

SOURCE A
From a speech by Casimir Périer, Louis-Philippe's Chief Minister, to the Chamber of Deputies, 18 March 1831

On 4th April 1834, troops went on the rampage along Rue Transonian. Mopping up in the aftermath of a failed Republican uprising, they had been provoked when a sniper opened fire on a soldier on a stretcher, killing him. The search for the sniper descended into a murderous assault on innocent householders, during which several of them were bludgeoned or bayoneted to death. Thiers, who had been personally involved in the military operation, tried to cover up these events, dramatised by Daumier in this picture. The government responded to the publication of Daumier's lithography by attempting to seize and destroy as many of the prints as it could find.

SOURCE B
This describes the scene in Picture 6

PICTURE 6
Rue Transonian, 14 April 1834,
a lithograph by Daumier,
printed in 1834

President of the Court: On the 25th of June last, at a quarter past six in the evening, just as the King, accompanied by the Queen and Her Royal Highness Princess Adelaide, was getting into the coach to drive to Neuilly, was it you who, from a position in the courtyard of the Tuileries on the side nearest the gateway from the Pont Royal, fired upon the king almost at point-blank range a bullet which was later found inside the coach?

Alibaud: Yes, my lord.

President: Was not your object, in committing this horrible crime, to bring about an upheaval which would lead to the establishment of a republic?

Alibaud (in a loud clear voice): Yes, sir.

President: In other words, it was that which made you conceive the idea of an attempt on the king's life?

Alibaud: Yes, sir.

President: How long have you harboured this deadly plan?

Alibaud: Ever since Philippe I (i.e. Louis-Philippe) put Paris in a state of siege; ever since Philippe I wanted to rule instead of reign; ever since the king caused citizens to be massacred in the streets of Lyon and in the cloister of Saint-Mery (i.e. at the funeral of General Lamarque, June 1832). His reign is a reign of blood; the reign of Philippe I is an infamous reign. I wanted to smite the king.

SOURCE C

The cross-examination of Alibaud, a would-be assassin of Louis-Philippe, 9 July 1836

The July Monarchy has few friends among historians, and ever since its own day has been caricatured contemptuously as a 'bourgeoisie monarchy'. Yet its leaders had high-minded intentions: to safeguard liberty and peace, and set France on the high road of progress, a road marked out by the working models of Britain and America. Few regimes have been run by such remarkably intelligent men. No other nineteenth century French regime had perspectives that seem, from the end of the twentieth century, so 'modern': to protect the individual, to maintain international peace and to foster economic growth. But a system similar to that which prevailed in most of north-western Europe failed in France, politically, intellectually and morally.

SOURCE D
From France 1814–1914 *by Robert Tombs, 1996*

The bourgeoisie was triumphant. It had placed a prince on the throne, who owed his authority to its gift alone. The ministers were men whose power and reputation it had created. ... The bourgeoisie, all powerful in society by its possession of the soil, of capital, and of credit, had now only to provide for the establishment of its political supremacy. The people, on the other hand, too ignorant as yet to desire any share of the civil power, writhed under the yoke of a social system that brought it nothing but oppression.

SOURCE E
From The History of Ten Years 1830–40 *(published 1841–4) by Louis Blanc, a socialist, revolutionary and journalist*

Q

(a)   Study Source A. Using this source and your own knowledge, explain what was meant by 'the principle behind the July Revolution is resistance to aggression by the authorities'. *(5 marks)*

(b)   (i) Study Source B. How useful is this source as evidence about the nature of the July Monarchy? *(6 marks)*
      (ii) How useful is Source C as evidence of the Republican threat to the July Monarchy? *(6 marks)*

(c)   Account for the differences between Sources D and E in their interpretations of the reign of Louis-Philippe. *(10 marks)*

(d)   'A selfish and repressive regime'. Using your own knowledge and the evidence of this collection of Sources A–E, explain how far you would agree with this interpretation of the reign of Louis-Philippe. *(13 marks)*

Russia 1815–55

INTRODUCTION

THE EMERGENCE OF RUSSIA

The emergence of Muscovy had led to a Russia based on serfdom and absolute rule. By the nineteenth century the Russian state was socially, economically and politically backward by the standards of Western Europe. Peter the Great (1682–1725) and Catherine the Great (1762–96) had extended and strengthened Russia's borders and begun a series of reforms designed to make Russia a great European Power. Some of these reforms had overlaid an essentially inward-looking state with a veneer of Western European culture. Some industrialisation was begun. At the same time the Tsars increased their power. They wanted to tie the nobility more closely to the regime, although the nobility was freed from compulsory service by Catherine. A bureaucratic class emerged to administer the Tsars' power. Periodic revolts by the serfs, the bulk of the Russian population, failed to significantly better their lot. Russia emerged into the nineteenth century as a Power increasingly to be taken seriously on the European stage, but one which was very reactionary and backward at least by prevailing Western European standards.

This chapter will consider developments under Alexander I and Nicholas I. Their reigns were marked by limited reform but also reaction and a determination to maintain the autocracy – so much so that Russia became one of the bulwarks against political change throughout Europe. Russia was increasingly drawn into the mainstream of European politics. Yet by the end of this period, the Crimean War showed that without fundamental reforms affecting important areas like serfdom and the army, Russian pretensions to Great Power status would be seriously undermined.

1 ～ POLITICAL HISTORY

A *Alexander I*

Despite the Europanisation of Russia's ruling *élite*, the Russian political, administrative and social structure retained many distinctive features which marked it off from other European Great Powers. During the

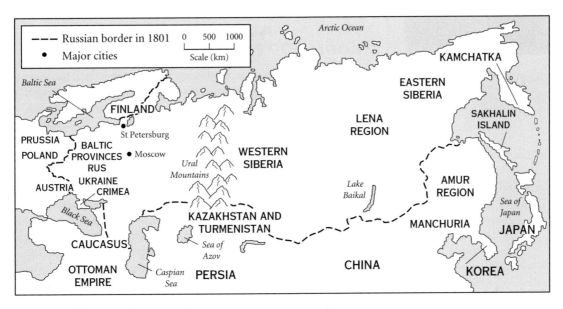

MAP 3 *Russia in the early nineteenth century*

eighteenth century the Russian nobility gradually freed itself from compulsory service to the state, and increased its powers over the land and the serfs. Professional administrators increasingly replaced the nobility in the bureaucracy. The mass of the Russian people, mostly serfs, was relatively unaffected by these changes.

Catherine's short-lived successor Paul I (1796–1801) was weak and unstable. He was succeeded after his murder by his son Alexander. Alexander I proved a powerful ruler. He made Russia one of the mainstays of the alliance against Napoleon, and in the process of ensuring that France would not dominate the continent, Russia was brought irretrievably into the mainstream of European affairs. Thereafter the Great Powers of Europe always had to include Russia in their political calculations, whether as an ally or as a potential enemy.

Alexander made liberal concessions early in his reign:

- political prisoners and exiles were granted an amnesty
- in 1807 Alexander asked his adviser Michael Speransky to draw up a programme of constitutional government. He was briefly interested in the American constitution
- Alexander showed an interest in education, founding schools and universities
- Poland was allowed a constitution and *diet* (parliament), and Finland was given some autonomy after its annexation in 1809.

Whilst in 1803 landowners were given the power to free their serfs they were under no compulsion to do so, although serfdom was abolished in Estonia, Livonia and some other non-Russian provinces. Alexander could not afford to antagonise the nobility. For the same reason, Speransky's proposals for representative central and local assemblies

KEY ISSUE

Was Alexander I a reformer or a reactionary?

| PROFILE | ALEXANDER I (BORN 1777; REIGNED 1801–1825) |

ALEXANDER I (BORN 1777; REIGNED 1801–1825)

Alexander was a man of contradictory impulses, groomed for leadership by his grandmother Catherine II. He was influenced early on by his liberal Swiss tutor, Cesar Laharpe, but also enjoyed the military training he received from his father, Tsar Paul. Alexander knew of the plot to oust his father Paul, but probably not of the decision to then murder him. He inherited the most autocratic empire in Europe, one with traditions of strong government, and so he was also influenced by conservative advisers. Alexander was pulled in both directions. He frequently changed tack, partly because he could be indecisive as well as stubborn, and partly because he rarely stayed interested in a particular course of action for long, preferring grand gestures to the routine of government. Alexander had the pretensions but not the stamina of an enlightened despot. His adviser Speransky claimed that Alexander was 'too weak to rule and too strong to be ruled'.

Alexander's occasional liberal impulses have not convinced most historians. A typical judgement is that of M. Anderson: 'from 1811–12 onwards the real interests and needs of the empire – social change, administrative reform and economic development – were consistently sacrificed to the tsar's grandiose and often erratic idealism. By the time of Alexander's death the social and economic gap between Russia and much of Western Europe was wider than ever before.' (M. Anderson *The Ascendancy of Europe* (Longman, 1972)). Similarly, from J. Watson: 'Alexander ... settled for stagnation ... When he died he left Russia much as he had found it, with a tottering economy, a creaking administration, a feudal society and a Church sunk in medieval ritual and superstition.' (J. Watson, *Success in European History 1815–1941* (John Murray, 1981)). Perhaps a more balanced view is that Alexander did not suddenly change from being a liberal autocrat to a reactionary: both impulses were present throughout his reign, each coming to the fore at different times. He wanted both change and stability at the same time. Alexander's enigmatic reputation was enhanced by rumours that he had only faked his death in 1825.

were shelved. The only constitutional amendment made was the creation in 1810 of a council of state to assist the Tsar in drafting legislation. Even these limited reforms provoked opposition from the conservative nobility on whom Alexander depended, and he had to sack Speransky in 1812.

Alexander's desire to maintain his power was bolstered by the fears of revolutionary change which haunted all established regimes in the Napoleonic era. He became convinced of the existence of an international conspiracy against monarchy and Christianity: his reactionary impulses were reinforced by events such as the mutiny of the Semyonovsky guards against harsh discipline in 1820, and by the promptings of Metternich, who actually believed that Alexander was *too* liberal. Discussion of further reform died away. The well-meaning but ineffectual Prince Golitsyn failed to make the effective educational reforms with which he was charged. The formation of secret opposition societies prompted new restrictions: earlier measures to relax censorship were reversed, and Russians were forbidden to study abroad. In the last years of his reign Alexander was much influenced by General Arakcheyev: his harsh reputation was based mainly on his establishment of 'military colonies' in which army regiments were quartered in villages alongside state serfs, both to assist them in their farmwork and to retain their military readiness. The serfs in turn were subject to brutal discipline, which was increased when they rebelled.

B *The Decembrist Revolt, 1825*

Alexander's death in December 1825 created uncertainty. In 1822 the childless Alexander had persuaded his brother Constantine, a supposed liberal and commander of the Polish Army, to renounce his own claim to the throne in a secret deal. Alexander secretly decreed that his younger brother Nicholas should succeed him. Nicholas was not aware of this arrangement, and in 1825 he would not accept the crown until Constantine gave further confirmation of his renunciation. Uncertainty reigned as both brothers proclaimed the other Tsar, and Nicholas had to suppress the poorly planned and organised revolts known collectively as the Decembrist conspiracy. This comprised two groups:

- the Northern Society was based in St. Petersburg and included army officers who favoured a constitutional monarchy under Constantine
- the better organised Southern Society comprised radicals led by Colonel Paul Pestel. They favoured a republic and an end to serfdom.

Pestel and four other Decembrist leaders were hanged, and over 200 rebels exiled.

The Decembrist conspiracy was unusual in being led by usually loyal army officers. Some of the conspirators were educated and westernised, and had political aims, and as such the conspiracy was very different from the frequent peasant uprisings against poor conditions or brutal treatment. Although Republicans, the leaders also wanted strong government.

The rebellion had a marked effect on Nicholas I, who was left mistrustful of the aristocracy, many of whom he tried to keep out of office. The Decembrist Rising was the first internal revolution against a Great Power in the nineteenth century, and its suppression helped to establish Russia's reputation as a bulwark against revolution generally. However, it also led Nicholas I to consider the causes of dissatisfaction, without convincing him that there was anything essentially wrong with the system of autocracy.

TIMELINE

Principal events in Russia
1801–55

1801	Alexander I became Tsar
1807	Speransky drew up new constitution
1810	Creation of Council of State
1815	Defeat of Napoleon Creation of Kingdom of Poland
1820	Semyonovsky mutiny
1825	Death of Alexander I Decembrist Revolt Accession of Nicholas I
1826	Creation of Third Section
1828–9	Russo-Turkish War
1830–1	Polish Revolt
1833	Treaty of Unkiar Skelessi
1841	Straits Act
1849	Intervention in Hungary
1853–6	Crimean War
1855	Death of Nicholas I

KEY ISSUE

What was the significance of the Decembrist Conspiracy?

C *Nicholas I*

Once in power, Nicholas I faced a similar dilemma as Alexander had confronted: reform or reaction? Nicholas was a religious man who took his duties seriously, although an army background had not prepared him for the role of Tsar. He believed he had a duty to maintain the aristocracy. There must be unswerving obedience to the Tsar and his Government, reinforced by alliance with the Orthodox Church and supported by the bureaucracy and army. The secret police, disbanded by Alexander but now reinstated by Nicholas, was known as the Third Section from 1826. Under its leader Alexander von Benckendorff it rooted out perceived threats to the autocracy.

At the start of his reign Nicholas set up a committee which reported on inefficiency, outdated laws, and increasing economic burdens on both nobility and serfs. The Tsar took control of policy, establishing the Imperial Chancery to help him, and using some able non-Russian advisers like Nesselrode. Various bodies were set up: the Second Section in 1826 to codify the laws; the Fourth Section in 1828 to monitor and control education and charitable organisations; the Fifth Section in 1836 to reorganise the administration of state peasants. Nicholas re-called Speransky in place of Arakcheyev. There was limited reform:

- the laws were codified although not modified
- the first Factory Acts were passed
- punishment by the *knout* (a form of whip) was abolished. The auctioning of serfs was outlawed in 1841, and state serfs were granted personal freedom in 1838.

However, entry to the provincial gymnasium schools was mostly restricted to the nobility. There was rigid censorship, and from 1848 the censors themselves were censored by a higher committee. The Polish constitution was revoked and Poland was incorporated into the Russian Empire following the failed revolt of 1830–1.

See page 17

Despite its fearsome reputation, Nicholas' regime failed to eradicate the bribery and corruption endemic in Russia's large and unwieldy bureaucracy. This bureaucracy expanded considerably during his reign and earned the description of this period as 'thirty years of black frost.' The basis of the aristocratic system remained intact. In the words of M. Anderson, the 'Russian Empire was therefore left to stagger through the nineteenth century at the hands of a bureaucracy which had no standardised recruitment procedures and no common educational tradition or specialised training, which was underpaid, often corrupt and, at least in its lower ranks, bitterly hostile to any suggestion of new methods' (M. Anderson, *The Ascendancy of Europe 1815–1914* (Longman, 1972)). The national debt continued to rise, mostly as the result of military expenditure.

Nicholas based his rule on three key principles:

- *orthodoxy* meant emphasising his divine right to rule, supported by a close alliance with the Church

KEY ISSUE

What principles underlay Nicholas I's domestic policies, and how effective were these policies?

NICHOLAS I (REIGNED 1825–55)

Nicholas, as the third son of Tsar Paul, was destined for a military career, which suited his orderly, rather narrow character. However, thrust into the limelight in 1825, he took his duties as an autocratic ruler very seriously – so much so that he damaged his health by his incessant work in both domestic and foreign affairs. Nicholas was a stickler for detail, and was obsessed with order and planning. Like his brother Alexander, he was a contradictory character, paternalist in nature, wanting to better the lot of ordinary Russians, but at the same time suspicious and repressive, both at home and abroad – hence his nickname, the 'Gendarme of Europe'. It was a time of repression in Russia, but also a period in which cultural life flourished: for example it was the era of Russia's most famous writer, Alexander Pushkin.

Most historians have been as hard on Nicholas as on Alexander I, although recognising his conscientiousness and sense of duty, characterised in pronouncements like 'Revolution is at the gates of Russia, but I swear that it shall not enter as long as I have a breath of life left within me.' He was in a genuine dilemma over reform: Nicholas conceded that 'There is no question that serfdom in its present state in our country is an evil, palpable and obvious to everyone. However, to attack it now would be, of course, an even more disastrous evil'.

Some contemporary observers were not sympathetic to Nicholas' dilemma, believing that Russian society was not even standing still, but going backwards in terms of efficiency and justice. For example, the Russian historian Granovski wrote in 1849, 'Russia is nothing but a living pyramid of crimes, frauds and abuses, full of spies, policemen, rascally governors, drunken magistrates and cowardly aristocrats, all united in their desire for theft and pillage and supported by 600 000 automata with bayonets.' Most historians have conceded Nicholas' good intentions, but agree that he left to his successors an increasingly stagnant and bankrupt economy, a growing but inefficient bureaucracy, and a social structure that was increasingly outmoded and losing the respect of more enlightened and educated Russians.

- *autocracy* meant the traditional Russian concept of the all-powerful father figure who would protect his people and isolate them from unsettling ideas
- *nationality* meant the promotion of Russian culture, which increasingly came to mean **Russification** of subject peoples.

Russification forcing Russian culture and language on to subject peoples

It proved impossible to keep all ideas of change at the frontier, despite the censorship exercised by Minister of Education Uvarov between 1833 and 1849. There were educated Russians, nobles and others, inevitably interested in the liberal ideas discussed in some Western European

KEY ISSUE

What were the aims of reformers and opponents of the regime in Russia in the first half of the nineteenth century?

circles since the French Revolution. Some believed that political, economic and social changes were interdependent, and should be influenced by events outside Russia. Intellectuals following this line were influenced by Chaadayev, whose *Philosophical Letter* of 1836 had highlighted Russia's backwardness. Other radicals rejected the West as inferior, and believed that Russia should carve out its own road to reform. They were sometimes called Slavophiles. Some wanted to go further and unite all Slavs outside the Empire with their Russian cousins.

Reformers also disagreed on other matters. Some wanted an overhaul of serfdom, thereby striking at the whole basis of Russian society. The Russian exile Alexander Herzen favoured agrarian reform leading to peasant communes replacing the power of landlords. Ideas for a constitutional monarchy were equally radical. Some reformers had specific objectives like an uncensored press. Radicals and more moderate reformers disagreed on tactics: some put their faith in the free spread of ideas; some believed that terror, including the assassination of the Tsar, was the only way to combat autocracy.

Internal dissatisfaction became a major threat to Nicholas. Continuing social unrest culminated in over 400 peasant risings during his reign, three quarters of them occurring after 1840. The Fifth Section was headed by Kiselev, Ministry of State Domains between 1837 and 1856. His ministry surveyed the land and gave loans to peasants for improvements. But the rural population was still expanding and did not become more productive, and so land hunger and discontent continued. Disaffected intellectuals and peasant rebels made up many of the 150 000 exiles sent to Siberia under Nicholas. Repression became more rigid after the 1848 Revolutions in Europe, but the resulting discontent did not go away. Nicholas had not solved Russia's problems, but nevertheless his death in December 1855, with the Crimean War in progress, came at an inopportune time for the regime.

2 ∾ ECONOMIC HISTORY

A *Productive and unproductive classes*

The nineteenth-century Russian sociologist K.I. Arsenev used the tax returns of 1812 and 1816 to analyse Russia's social and economic structure after the Napoleonic Wars (see Table 1). He divided the Russian population into two classes:

- *the productive classes* – mainly merchants, serfs and peasants – made up almost 90 per cent of the population
- *the unproductive classes*, 'who live at the expense of the first class' – principally the nobility, clergy, military and officials – made up about 10 per cent.

This was a crude classification, but nevertheless illustrated a basic truth about Russian society down to the 1917 Revolution, that there

	1000s	(%)	
			TABLE 1 *Arsenev's analysis of Russian* *society, 1812–16*
Unproductive classes			
Nobility	450	(1.1)	
Clergy	430	(1.1)	
Military	2 000	(5.0)	
Officials and 'mixed' ranks	1 500	(3.7)	
Total	4 380	(10.9)	
Productive classes			
Merchants	204	(0.5)	
Small town-dwellers	1 490	(3.7)	
State peasants	13 100	(32.7)	
Landlords' serfs	20 300	(50.7)	
'Free people'	234	(0.6)	
'Other' peasants	360	(0.9)	
Total	35 688	(89.1)	

was a great gulf between classes, at least in terms of legal status, which was difficult to change. There were many obstacles, for example, to a serf acquiring his freedom.

RURAL RUSSIA

Early nineteenth-century Russia was essentially a pre-industrial society in which over 90 per cent of the population lived for most of the time off the land. Unlike rural communities in Western Europe, village life was dominated by the *mir*, or commune. This was an organisation of households in which senior members determined when agricultural tasks in the locality should be carried out, and how taxes should be allocated. It also allocated strips of land to families in order to make viable farming units, and adjusted them as the population changed. This made the basis of strip farming very different from the medieval English practice with which the Russian system is sometimes compared. It was described in some quarters as a form of primitive socialism, which gave some measure of security to the peasants. It was a self-sufficient economy in which peasants produced almost everything they needed, although the smallness of most farming units did not encourage progressive farming. Russian peasants seeking cash during slacker periods of the farming year practised crafts or sought work in the nearest town, usually returning to the village for the sowing of crops or harvesting.

The most populated areas were those centring on the old heartland of Muscovy and the Southern steppes. The most fertile area was the black soil region of the South and the Ukraine, increasingly intensively farmed in the eighteenth and nineteenth centuries. Productive farming outside the black earth area was hampered by poor soil fertility and the waste involved in crop rotation.

> **KEY ISSUE**
>
> *How did the institution of serfdom affect Russia's economy and society?*

SERFDOM

The majority of peasants were landlords' serfs or state peasants. Those in the former category had to perform labour service, pay cash, make payments in kind, or contribute any combination of the three, to their landlords. Some serfs were household serfs who performed household duties in return for board and lodging. Serfs were not slaves, but although it was not in landlords' interests to badly mistreat serfs, they did exercise a wide range of rights, for example giving permission for their serfs to marry. Most importantly, landlords could repossess their serfs' land. Peasants paid up to 40 per cent of their income, or its equivalent in terms of labour, to their lords, although in theory they could keep any extra profits once they had paid their dues.

State peasants were subject to similar burdens, although they were responsible to Government officials rather than landlords. All peasants faced additional pressures: they were liable to be conscripted into the army, often effectively for life; they had to pay a direct tax called the *obrok*; and they were subject to heavy indirect taxes on vodka and salt, which together made up 35 per cent of the state's revenue.

The institution of serfdom was under investigation in Nicholas I's reign. In 1827 there were limitations on the rights of landlords to exile serfs. In 1833 the public auctioneering of serfs was banned. In 1842 and 1847 it was made easier for serfs to buy their freedom. However, the essentials of the system remained in place, because entrenched interests were fearful of the economic and social consequences of fundamental change.

THE NOBILITY

The nobility was a diverse group. By the 1850s there were about one million nobles, but only about 90 000 were serf owners, and only about 18 000 or 0.02 per cent of the total population owned over 100 serfs each. This latter group was very powerful: its members voted in provincial assemblies and occupied dominant positions in the army and bureaucracy. It was also Europeanised in its culture, and identified itself closely with the interests of the Tsar, although this was to change. In contrast, many of the nobles outside this small group were poor and had more in common with the peasantry than with their richer cousins. The 1815 Table of Ranks confirmed the duty of the nobility to serve the state, but service was no longer for life.

OTHER CLASSES

In addition to the peasantry and the nobility there were other identifiable groups in Russian society. One comprised government officials, who were not all nobles and so depended upon salaries. They became increasingly important to the Government during the nineteenth century, and the nobility, which had once dominated the bureaucracy, less so.

There were also the merchants, who were not serf owners but might be wealthy, and the clergy. However, members of the 'non-productive' classes were not united in their attitudes. Some nobles resented the growing powers of bureaucrats; merchants resented the special privileges of the nobility; intellectuals from all classes felt alienated from a system which appeared to underuse their talents. Another divisive factor was that the upper ranks of the nobility were far more Europeanised in their outlook than the rest, even to the extent of despising their native Russian language. Nevertheless, there was a clear distinction between the 'productive' and 'non-productive' classes. An important distinction was cultural: over 90 per cent of the population was illiterate. Another distinction was legal: a clearly defined Table of Ranks carefully outlined everyone's place in society, and hierarchy was all-important in Russia. Most Russians accepted the idea of hierarchy and autocracy, particularly the latter, since it was seen as providing strong government and preventing corrupt or powerful interest groups coming to power.

B *Industry*

Industrialisation was not well-advanced in early nineteenth-century Russia except perhaps in iron production, of which Russia provided one third of the world's output. The backwardness of Russia's economy was partly due to geography and climate. Vast distances made communications difficult. Navigable rivers frequently froze and there was limited access to markets, which remained localised. Small industries were protected from foreign competition, and an abundance of serf labour reduced the need to search for more efficient methods of production. Manufacturing was mostly on a small-scale local basis. What technological progress there was, was largely dependent on foreign technology and enterprise.

Under Peter the Great substantial industrial growth was begun to meet Government requirements, for example in iron and wool. Serfs made up an industrial workforce. Commercial restrictions had been relaxed and so there had been steady if not spectacular industrial progress by the early nineteenth century, although this progress was retarded by the disruption of the Napoleonic Wars and growing competition from Western Europe. However, Soviet historians claimed that there was evidence of a small-scale industrial revolution from about the 1830s onwards. There was an increase in the volume of internal trade; there were improvements in communications – canals and railways were built; and there was an increase in manufacturing, particularly of consumer goods. Mining was developed in the Urals, the textile industry grew in the area around Moscow, and metal and textiles developed in St. Petersburg. Manufacturing also developed in Poland. Not all this activity was state-generated, and indeed many tsarist advisers were suspicious of industrial growth and the accompanying urban conurbations which might breed working class discontent. However, protectionist policies aided expansion, particularly in the cotton industry, centred in Moscow and St. Petersburg. A notable feature of industrial change was that by the 1860s over four-fifths of the industrial workforce were wage earners rather than serfs.

KEY ISSUE

To what extent was there significant industrial progress in Russia in the first half of the nineteenth century?

TABLE 2
Russian industrial development – enterprises and workers

	1804	1830	1860
No. of enterprises			
Woollen textiles	157	389	706
Cotton textiles	199	538	1 200
Linen textiles	285	190	117
Silk	365	234	393
Leather	843	1 619	2 515
Iron and steel	28	198	693
No. of workers			
Woollen textiles	28 689	67 241	120 025
Cotton textiles	8 181	76 228	152 236
Linen textiles	23 711	26 845	17 284
Silk	9 161	14 019	14 287
Leather	6 304	10 547	14 151
Iron and steel	4 121	19 889	54 832

Year	Population (millions)	Urban population (millions)
1811	41.8	2.8
1838	48.8	4.5
1863	61.2	6.1

TABLE 3
Rise in population in European Russia, 1811–63

It would be an exaggeration to describe industrial progress in Russia between the 1830s and the 1860s as a significant revolution:

● some industries like coal mining were still relatively undeveloped
● capital for investment was limited
● the majority of industry was still small scale.

Russia was falling behind other Great Powers. The institution of serfdom still inhibited major economic change. Nevertheless the developments outlined above should qualify the views of some Western historians who tended to ignore or downplay Russian industrial development before the late nineteenth century.

3 ↜ FOREIGN POLICY

A *European Involvement*

ALEXANDER I AND THE HOLY ALLIANCE

Russian involvement in European affairs before the 1850s is covered in Chapter 1. This section will look at foreign affairs purely from a Russian perspective. Russia became a major player on the European stage during the Napoleonic Wars. Following the Treaty of Tilsit in 1807 Alexander I and Napoleon effectively divided the continent into two spheres of influence. The Russian Empire expanded territorially, absorbing Finland and Bessarabia. Following the break with France in 1812 and repulsion of the French invasion, Russia became more involved in Western Europe as one of the driving forces of the Allied coalition which defeated Napoleon. Alexander then projected the notion of a Christian alliance embracing rulers and their peoples. Although Metternich turned this 'Holy Alliance' into a more pragmatic instrument of conservatism, Alexander also had more practical motives. Whilst revelling in his status as 'Liberator', he also proposed disarmament and a Europe-wide system of collective security. He personally represented Russian interests at European Congresses, assisted by his foreign minister Count Karl von Nesselrode, who conducted Russian foreign policy for 40 years.

KEY ISSUE

What principles underlay Alexander I's foreign policy?

NICHOLAS I, 'THE GENDARME OF EUROPE'

Nicholas I felt it to be his God-given duty to defend Europe against the threat of revolution, and therefore he wished to preserve the Holy Alliance and cooperate with his fellow conservative monarchs in Austria and Prussia. However, he also wished to expand Russian influence if the opportunity arose. If there was a turning point in his foreign policy, it was prompted by the 1848 Revolutions: although Russia was not directly affected, Nicholas I's repugnance for revolution caused him to intervene in Hungary, and he was suspicious of those like Louis Philippe in France who came to power as the result of the overthrow of a previous regime.

Nicholas I became Tsar during the Greek Revolt. Although he had a conservative's repugnance for assisting rebels, he thought it in Russia's interests to support the Greeks against the Turkish Empire, which he thought to be on the verge of dissolution. Having failed to persuade the British and French Governments to take stronger action against Turkey, Russia itself attacked Turkey in 1828. The Russo-Turkish War of 1828–9 was ended by the Treaty of Adrianople in September 1829. Apart from losses to Greece, Turkey had to cede land in Asia to the Russians. Although it was a moderate settlement, Russian gains at the expense of Turkey were bound to alarm other Great Powers, particularly Austria and Britain, who feared Russian expansion in the Middle East. Their fears were not completely unfounded, since despite joining Britain and France in recognising Greek independence in the 1832 Treaty of London, Russia had every intention of capitalising on any Turkish weakness.

KEY ISSUE

Did Nicholas I deserve the title of 'Gendarme of Europe'?

A further opportunity arose with Mehmet Ali's revolt against the Sultan in 1831. The Turks had to appeal to Nicholas for assistance and were forced into the Treaty of Unkiar Skelessi of July 1833. The Treaty obliged Turkey to close the Straits to foreign warships should Russia be attacked. From Russia's standpoint this was a defensive provision, but it inevitably fuelled British and French fears of Russian expansionism. Therefore Russia turned to Austria: at Munchengratz in September 1833 the two countries agreed to help preserve the Turkish Empire. Nicholas' cautious approach was also demonstrated in 1840: following a renewal of the Mehmet Ali-Turkish conflict in 1839, Russia joined Austria, Britain and France in a Quadruple Alliance which forced Mehmet Ali to return his territorial gains to Turkey in the 1841 Treaty of London. In 1842 the Straits Convention closed the Straits to *all* foreign warships. This was a setback for Nicholas I. He would have welcomed an alliance with Britain, but the British were averse to the prospect of Russian expansion at the expense of the Turkish Empire, whose demise the Tsar still expected.

KEY ISSUE

How successful was Nicholas I's foreign policy?

Russian foreign policy was both strengthened and weakened by the 1848 revolutions:

- it was strengthened because the revolutions did not directly threaten the Russian regime in contrast to other continental Powers, which were weakened by internal rebellion
- on the other hand, Russia's increased power and ruthlessness, demonstrated by its suppression of the Hungarian rebels and its repression in Poland. made it an object of suspicion especially to some British politicians like Palmerston.

Austrian and Prussian preoccupations in Europe increased the opportunities for Russian expansion in the Near East, and fed Nicholas' misconception that he could dismember Turkey's Empire with either British compliance or cooperation. His failure to divide Britain and France and his intervention in the 'Holy Places' affair in Palestine helped to bring on the Crimean War. War was not desired by Nicholas, but his mistaken belief that he could get away with bullying Turkey made the over-confident Tsar reject efforts at compromise beforehand. Whilst some historians have interpreted the Tsar's policies in the Near East as defensive, his overconfidence, his occupation of the Danubian Principalities, and possibly the expansionist ambitions of some of his advisers, were certainly major causes of the war. The outcome of the war reduced Russia's prestige and influence in Europe and was a serious setback for Nicholas' successor, Alexander II.

See pages 26–8

B *Poland*

Poland had been partitioned in the eighteenth century, and effectively disappeared again in 1815 when the Congress of Vienna gave most of Poland's territory to Russia. Alexander I became king of 'Congress Poland'. Poland was given a constitution in 1816, allowing for the election of a parliament or *sejm* – ironically something which Russia itself did not have. Civil rights and the freedom of the press were guaranteed and the Catholic Church and the Polish language were recognised. There was also a Polish army. Although the *sejm* had limited powers – real authority was exercised by an executive council and viceroy responsible to the Tsar – Poland was treated remarkably generously by contemporary standards.

Alexander regarded himself as Poland's only friend, and was genuinely hurt when Polish nationalists conspired against Russian domination. Polish resentment against Russia was still very strong, especially in the army, universities and amongst many noblemen. At first Alexander made little attempt to suppress conspiracies, but steps were being taken in that direction at the time of his death.

Nicholas I adopted a hardline attitude towards Poland. The Third Section was active there, the press was censored and Russian officials replaced Polish ones. The *sejm* was not allowed to meet after 1828. Polish officers objected to the possibility of Polish troops being used against revolutionaries in 1830 and rebelled. Many of the nobility and urban dwellers supported the rebels. However, Polish nationalists were divided between radicals and moderate reformers, whilst the peasantry had no interest in joining a nationalist revolt. Nicholas I refused to make concessions and the Russian army invaded Poland in 1831. The *sejm* declared its independence, but the Polish revolt stood no chance of success without foreign intervention, which was not forthcoming. The rebels caved in. Nicholas instituted a new constitution. Although some civil rights remained on paper, the *sejm* was abolished and rule was by military decree. An accelerated policy of Russification ensured the teaching of Russian in Polish schools. A separate Polish army was abolished, there was an increase in the number of Russian officials and 10 per cent of Polish land was confiscated to Russians. Many Poles were exiled to Siberia or fled the country.

Nicholas I governed Poland ruthlessly, despite foreign protests. In the short term his policy was successful: Poland was not involved in the 1848 Revolutions. However, simmering Polish resentment remained as a concern to the Tsars who followed Nicholas.

> **KEY ISSUE**
>
> *What caused the Polish rebellion and why did it fail?*

4 ∽ BIBLIOGRAPHY

A general introduction to Russian history in this period is *Russia in the Age of Reaction and Reform, 1801–1881* by D. Saunders (Longman, 1992). Also useful is *Russia, 1815–81* by R. Sherman (Hodder & Stoughton, 1991), a book written for the 16–19 age group and containing advice on study skills. Biographies of Alexander I include *Alexander I, Tsar of War and Peace* by A. Palmer (Phoenix, 1997). Biographies of Nicholas I include *Nicholas I* by W. Bruce Lincoln (1978). There is some useful background material on economic development in *The Industrialisation of Russia 1700–1914* by M.E. Falkus (Macmillan, 1988). Russia's foreign policy in this period is covered in the bibliography for Chapter 1

5 ∽ STRUCTURED QUESTIONS AND ESSAYS

1. (a) Outline Alexander I's policies inside Russia between 1815 and 1825; (10 marks)
   (b) 'A flawed reformer.' To what extent is this a valid judgement on Alexander's rule inside Russia? (15 marks)
2. (a) Outline Nicholas I's domestic policies; (10 marks)
   (b) How valid is the assessment of Nicholas I's domestic policy that it was 'a triumph of conservatism over reform'? (15 marks)
3. 'A period of missed opportunity.' To what extent is this an accurate assessment of the reigns of Alexander I and Nicholas I inside Russia between 1815 and 1855? (25 marks)
4. (a) What objectives did Alexander I and Nicholas I have in their foreign policies? (10 marks)

(b)   To what extent did they succeed in extending Russian influence in Europe? (15 marks)

5. (a)   Outline the objectives of Russian regimes, in the period 1815–55, towards any **two** of the following: Poland; the Turkish Empire; the serfs; internal opposition; (10 marks)

(b)   To what extent did Alexander I and Nicholas I succeed in carrying out their objectives in the two areas you have selected? (15 marks)

6. (a)   Outline the main strengths and weaknesses of Russia's economy in the period 1815–55; (10 marks)

(b)   To what extent was there economic progress in Russia during this period? (15 marks)

Italy
1815–70

See Map 4 on page 84

INTRODUCTION

THE UNIFICATION OF ITALY

In 1815, the obstacles to the fulfilment of the hopes of Italian nationalists seemed massive. The Congress of Vienna (1815) had for the most part restored the rulers of *Ancien Régime* Italy to their thrones, thereby dividing the peninsula into nine assorted duchies and kingdoms. Austria was also given a special role in Italian affairs. Lombardy and Venetia, two of Italy's wealthiest regions, were placed directly under Habsburg control. The rulers of Modena, Parma, Tuscany and the Kingdom of the Two Sicilies were either descended from the Habsburgs themselves, or had married into the dynasty. Relying on Austrian troops to uphold their authority in any crisis, these states were practically satellites of Vienna. Only the state of Piedmont – Sardinia, ruled by the House of Savoy since 1559, was outside the Austrian sphere of influence – but its restored King, Victor Emmanuel I, was the most reactionary ruler of all.

It was against this background that the *Risorgimento* emerged. This was an artistic, cultural and political movement which aimed to remind Italians of their glorious past and to instill in them a longing for freedom and independence in the future. Giuseppe Mazzini was its most prominent figure, and his fervent republican and nationalist beliefs, and taste for revolution and conspiracy, made him a much feared and hunted figure. But when, in 1848, revolutions did break out in the peninsula, they probably owed more to economic problems than to nationalist propaganda. The revolutionaries anyway failed to co-ordinate their efforts, and by 1849 – everywhere but in Piedmont – the old order was restored.

Piedmont was to prove a vital exception. Building on its new liberal constitution, unique in Italy, Prime Minister Count Camillo di Cavour embarked on a programme of modernisation, aiming to make Piedmont the dominant state in Italy. Cavour was an immensely ambitious, energetic man. His overriding aim was less to unite Italy than to drive out the Austrians. To do this, foreign help was necessary, and at Plombières in 1858, he secured the backing of Napoleon III and France.

War against Austria was finally declared in April 1859. After less than three months, however, the French pulled out, limiting Piedmont's gains to the annexation of Lombardy. More skilful diplomacy from Cavour was required before he could recover the initiative. But his achievements seemed to be put in jeopardy when, in 1860, Giuseppe

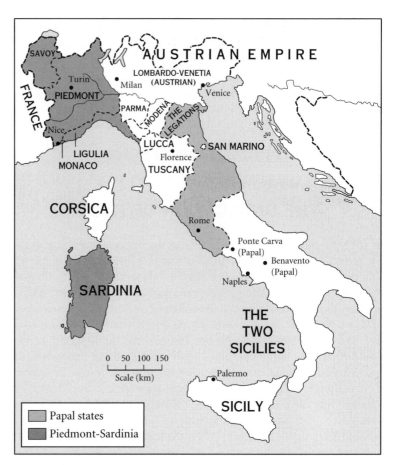

MAP 4 *The Italian states in 1815*

Garibaldi – a former Mazzinian – amazed Europe by conquering Sicily and most of southern Italy with a tiny guerrilla army. He intended to go on to take Rome from the Pope.

Cavour seemed to have totally lost control. He decided to intercept Garibaldi by sending the Piedmontese army into southern Italy. This high risk strategy was successfully completed by October – and plebiscites soon sanctioned the annexation of Sicily, Naples and most of the Papal states to Piedmont. (Venetia and Rome were finally added in 1866 and 1870 respectively). Between them, Cavour, Garibaldi and Napoleon III had united Italy. Victor Emmanuel, ruler of Piedmont, was to be its king.

But difficult tasks remained The number of Italian nationalists had grown considerably since 1815, but they were still a tiny minority of the population, concentrated in the *élite* of Italian society. The peasants of Sicily and Naples especially proved resentful of their masters from the north, and the new state only asserted its authority after great difficulty and considerable bloodshed. It would be many years before most of the citizens of Italy came to think of themselves as Italians.

1 ～ 'BEAUTIFUL LEGENDS': THE HISTORIOGRAPHY OF THE RISORGIMENTO

The rulers of the new state soon appreciated that it would be at least as difficult to make Italians as it had been to make Italy. They knew that the teaching and writing of history had a major contribution to make to this task of national propaganda. Thus the myth of national unification was born. Its main features included:

- the cruel oppression suffered by the Italian people under Austrian and absolutist rule
- the people's deep and widespread longing for freedom, independence and national unity
- the extraordinary genius of Italy's statesmen and warriors – Cavour, Garibaldi and Victor Emmanuel (Mazzini, too revolutionary for some tastes, was only added later to this heroic *élite*), whose complementary talents made unification possible.

This myth dominated perceptions of the *Risorgimento* for the best part of a century, obscuring the complexity of the unification process, and covering up its internal contradictions and accidental nature. Vital archives were closed to scholars, and published editions of key documents, like Cavour's letters, were doctored to eliminate embarrassing passages. An Italian Prime Minister declared on the eve of World War I that 'it would not be right to let beautiful legends be discredited by historical criticism'. But in the late 1940s, the British historian Denis Mack Smith gained full access to the archives. His findings transformed perspectives on the process of unification. He summarised his work thus:

> Its theme is the conflict between Cavour and Garibaldi, that is to say between moderate and radical Italian patriots. Everyone [in 1985] now accepts that this conflict was of crucial importance in the process which led to Italian unification, and indeed it helped to determine the kind of nation that emerged. The year 1860 saw the birth of a united Italy as the product of a clash between quite different ideas about ends and means. During six months of this year there existed two conflicting centres of policy-making in what was still a disunited country, one of them being at Turin where Cavour was Prime Minister of Piedmont, the other at Palermo and Naples where Garibaldi ruled as a revolutionary dictator. Cavour was eventually able to impose his own solution, but he succeeded only because his radical opponents first broke free from his leadership and then forced him into actions that he had neither intended nor even foreseen.

Q

In what respects does Mack Smith's interpretation of the unification process differ from the 'official' story?

Some more recent studies of the *Risorgimento* – for example. the ideas of John Breuilly – are even more radical. He has argued that the

Italian state was foisted on an essentially unwilling 'Italian' people by a self-interested *élite*, and that nationalism, far from being a cause of unification, was, first, the ideology used to legitimise this take over, and secondly, the historical myth by which this *élite* tried, in many ways unsuccessfully, to bind the ramshackle nation together.

Bear these views in mind as you read the following account of the unification story.

2 ⌒ RESTORATION ITALY AND ITS ENEMIES

A *A divided Italy*

To have restored these old **republics** to their former status would have given out the wrong signals – 'republic' sounded radical, and Metternich could hardly endorse that But note that the disappearance of these two states ignored the principle of 'restoration' which supposedly guided the peacemakers at Vienna – by no means the only example of them breaking their own rules when it suited them.

Metternich described Italy as 'a geographical expression'. The Alps and the Mediterranean Sea unmistakably constituted Italy's natural borders, but it was absurd to imagine that Italy could aspire to the status of a single political, cultural or economic unit. Italy **was** divided, and the Austrian Emperor and Italy's other rulers intended to keep things that way. The Congress of Vienna had restored Italy's eight pre-Napoleonic dynasties and the Papacy to their rightful places. It had also transferred the formerly independent **republics** of Genoa and Venice to Piedmont and Austria, respectively.

Italy was at least as divided culturally as she was politically. To most nationalists, linguistic unity was an essential part of national identity, but Italy contained perhaps a score of often mutually incomprehensible dialects. Overwhelming illiteracy posed grave difficulties for propagandists of Italian nationalism like Mazzini: how were they to instil a sense of nationhood into the Italian people if the latter could not read nationalist propaganda? Italian society was also very regionalised. The peninsula's geography, with its mountain ranges, made communications difficult, but poor roads and tardy railway construction made them worse.

Inevitably, regionalism shaped the political loyalties and hopes of most Italians. Local affiliations – and animosities – were notoriously intense. The town or the village were all that mattered: the world beyond was inhabited by foreigners who often spoke a different language. Nationalists complained bitterly about this spirit of *campanilismo* – 'the cult of the parish'. Rivalries between adjacent towns and cities, and between regions (for example, Sicily versus Naples), were damaging to the nationalist cause:

Italian nationalists not only had to confront both the overwhelming indifference (at best) of the majority of the peninsula's inhabitants and the hostility of its established rulers. They also had to somehow transform a distinctly unfavourable international context for their ambitions. Italy was a **European** issue. Any attempts at unification seemed likely to be opposed by the Papacy, which might reasonably hope that either Austria or France (both overwhelmingly Catholic countries) would come to its rescue in any crisis. The Congress of Vienna itself

KEY ISSUE

What obstacles would nationalists have to confront in the efforts to create an Italian sense of identity?

TIMELINE

1820/1	Revolutions in Naples, Sicily and Piedmont were repressed
1831	Austrians defeated revolutions
1834	Founding of Mazzini's 'Young Italy'
1846	Election of Pope Pius IX
1848 Jan	Revolution in Kingdom of Naples and Sicily
March	Piedmontese Constitution
	Revolutions in Lombardy and Venice
	Piedmont declared war on Austria
July	Defeat of Piedmont at Custozza
1849 Feb	Roman Republic
March	Piedmont defeated at Novara
	Accession of Victor Emmanuel II
June	Restoration of Pope
1852	Cavour becomes Prime Minister of Piedmont
1855	Piedmont joins Anglo-French alliance against Russia in Crimea
1857	Founding of National Society
1858	Cavour and Napoleon III meet at Plombieres
1859 April	War between France and Austria
May	Revolutions in Parma, Modena and Romagna
June	French victories at Magenta and Solferino
July	Peace at Villafranca
1860 April	Garibaldi's expedition to Sicily
Sept	Garibaldi's entry into Naples
	Piedmontese invasion of Papal States
Nov	Victor Emmanuel King of Italy
1861	Death of Cavour
1866	Italy acquired Venice
1870	Rome became capital of Italy

had given Austria a large stake in Italy's future in the form of the provinces of Lombardy and Venetia, as well as extensive 'policing' responsibilities over the rest of the peninsula.

In these circumstances, the failure of every attempt to overthrow the political order of restoration Italy between 1820 and 1848 was not surprising. Only one factor was in the Italian nationalists' favour: Austria – the keystone of restoration Italy – was also the most overextended and potentially the most vulnerable of the Great Powers. If Austria could somehow be neutralised, the whole reactionary structure might come tumbling down. This happened – tantalisingly briefly – in 1848. It would only be definitively achieved in 1859–60.

There were frequent and apparently diverse political uprisings in the Italian peninsula between 1815 and 1848. The unpredictability of Italian society and politics in this period was due to:

● Italy was in the throes of a long-term economic crisis. A combination of factors brought grinding poverty to the peasants who made up 80 per cent of the population. The population rose from about 18 million in 1800 to about 22 million in 1840, predominantly in the countryside, depressing wages and worsening an already severe land hunger. This problem was worsened by the increasing tendency of middle class landowners to enclose 'common land' or forest areas, hitting the traditional rights of poorer peasants, who often depended on occasional grazing or wood-collection to make ends meet. Hence

> **KEY ISSUE**
>
> *What was the significance of the role of Austria in Restoration Italy?*

'*Dangerous classes*'
The 'dangerous classes' were a social category invented by anxious property owners and government officials to identify a social group whose main characteristics included (i) drifting in and out of casual, unskilled labour; (ii) criminality; and (iii) political radicalism and/or disrespect for their betters. The invention of the term probably tells us more about the fears of the nineteenth-century middle classes than about the objective existence of any such class.

the growth of rural brigandage, and the swelling numbers of the unemployed and underemployed thronging the streets of Italy's towns and cities, where they joined the ranks of the 'dangerous classes'

● Italy's intellectuals were also dissatisfied. The eighteenth-century Enlightenment had brought an expansion in higher education, but there were too few jobs to absorb this small army of would-be bureaucrats, lawyers, doctors and engineers. Reactionary governments anyway looked with suspicion on such types: they had too often picked up liberal ideas at university. In the Papal States, government jobs were monopolised by clerics, whilst in Lombardy and Venetia, preference was given to (German speaking) Austrians and Hungarians. With so few careers open to their talents, many young Italians took to radical and/or nationalist politics to express their frustrations. Mazzini and his followers can be seen as a sort of alienated intelligentsia

● the Governments of nearly all of Italy's Restoration states offered tempting targets for these alienated intellectuals to attack. The Governments were unrepresentative and generally slow moving. Lombardy was probably the least backward, but even here, Austrian financial policies, which included high taxes and restrictive trade regulations, bred resentment.

These difficulties were fertile ground for the growth of a variety of underground revolutionary societies. Their very nature, characterised by secret oaths, elaborate rituals and complex hierarchies, make their extent and impact hard to evaluate. Even Metternich, with his network of informers, found it hard to keep track of them; 'in design and principle divided among themselves, these sects change every day and on the morrow may be ready to fight against one another'.

Two societies were significant: the *Carbonari* (or charcoal-burners) and the Perfect Sublime Masters. Most of the *Carbonari* were to be found in the south. Possibly they numbered 300 000. They attracted a mixture of ex-Napoleonic officers and officials, professionals, small landowners and artisans. The *Carbonari* had links with the Republican movement in France: their single most famous member was Louis Napoleon, later Napoleon III. Their objectives, however, were vague, and their impact slight. Even more mysterious were the Perfect Sublime Masters. Their mastermind was Buonarroti, a veteran of the most militant wing of the French Revolution. Based in Geneva for most of these years, Buonarroti seems to have had a widespread network of agents throughout Italy, especially in the north. However, his political impact was also negligible.

KEY ISSUE

What social and political factors made Restoration Italy inherently unstable?

B *Political instability in Italy 1820–30*

● **Naples** (July 1820–March 1821). The Neapolitan *Carbonari* (spearheaded by its members inside the royal army) launched a *coup*, aiming not to unite Italy but to impose a constitution on Ferdinand VII. The King gave in to these demands, but was naively allowed to travel to the Congress of Laibach – where he had no difficulty in persuading the leaders of the Holy Alliance that the revolution should be put down. By March 1821, an Austrian army had done just this. The revolutionaries' cause was not helped by increasing divisions in their ranks between moderates and democrats, and the fact that many of their best troops were engaged in putting down a separatist revolt in Sicily

See page 13

● **Piedmont** (March–April 1821). An army-led *coup*, with links to the *Carbonari* and the 'Sublime Perfect Masters', aimed at constitutional reform, a 'national' war to drive out the Austrians, and the annexation of Lombardy. But the plot depended too much for its success on Charles Albert, second in line to the throne and the supposed ally of the liberals. Although King Victor Emmanuel abdicated, he did so in favour of his reactionary brother (Charles Felix), who refused to grant a constitution – and Charles Albert ultimately backed the new regime rather than put himself at the head of the revolution, as many had hoped. Charles Felix's loyalist troops, helped by Austrian contingents (and by divisions amongst the revolutionaries between moderates and democrats), soon put the rising down

● **Central Italy** (February–March 1831). The 1830 Revolution in Paris inspired liberals in Modena, Parma and Bologna to demand 'the independence, unity and liberty of all Italy' and 'a representative monarchy to be elected by a national assembly'. But France's rather cautious Government disappointed the revolutionaries by declining to come to their assistance, leaving the way free for Austrian forces to reimpose control. Regional rivalries anyway undermined any prospects of revolutionary success. The Bolognese Government actually warned its citizens against going to the assistance of the 'foreigners' of Modena, even though the latter were less than 40 miles away and under assault by Austrian troops! As Duggan concludes: 'the 1831 risings exposed in the most painful manner the inadequacy of the secret societies and their leadership; and more alarmingly, they again demonstrated just how politically unreliable 'the people' in Italy were'.

See pages 47–8

See the bibliography section on page 119

By the 1830s, a sort of political stalemate had been reached: underground conspiracy had been tried and had failed, with Austrian troops seemingly always on hand to restore the old order. The Governments of the Italian states had shown themselves incapable of responding to the threat of revolution and the underlying social problems except by increasing repression. The refusal of the Papal Government to implement a series of modest reforms recommended by an international conference in 1832 – plans even endorsed by Metternich – is characteristic of the backwardness and negativity of reaction at its worst. Italy seemed in danger of stagnation.

> **KEY ISSUE**
>
> *Why had Italian liberals and nationalists made so little progress between 1820 and 1831?*

C *The Risorgimento: visions of a New Italy*

'*Risorgimento*' is an Italian word meaning renewal, rebirth or regeneration, and it identifies the cultural and political movement which culminated in the unification of Italy. In particular, it designates the work of the intellectuals and artists (painters and composers as well as writers) who self-consciously took up the mission of awakening 'Italy'.

The *Risorgimento* is at the heart of the 'beautiful legend' of unification. The first historians of Italian nationalism – convinced nationalists themselves – wrote as if the spirit of '*Italianatà*' was merely laying dormant in the people of the peninsula and waiting to be summoned back to life by the *Risorgimento*. Having rekindled this longing for freedom and nationhood, it was left to the genius of Italy's soldiers and statesmen – Garibaldi and Cavour to the fore – to make Italy a political reality. But just as historians have exposed the personal antagonism between Garibaldi and Cavour and their divergent objectives, so it has exploded the myth of 'national awakening'. It seems less and less likely that the mass of 'Italians' were inspired by the *Risorgimento's* ideals. The mass of Italians could not read; indeed to many the concept of 'Italy' itself was meaningless. It is tempting, therefore, to reduce the heroes of the *Risorgimento* to a self-promoting and self-admiring clique, whose message was only received by a narrow *élite* and merely served, in the end, to justify the conquest of the rest of the peninsula by Piedmont. Just as an official, single Italian language was only defined and imposed **after** unification, it is argued that, Italy's sense of nationhood was much more the **consequence** than the **cause** of unification.

See pages 111–12

See page 85

Nevertheless, the *Risorgimento* was important. Although the ideas were confined to an *élite*, the *Risorgimento* gave the opinion-makers of Italy a new vocabulary in which to think about politics, and common points of reference – even a common agenda. Literally and metaphorically, Italy's *élite* eventually began to speak the same language. Foreign oppression, the call of liberty and the duty of self-sacrifice were the themes of paintings, novels and operas alike.

THE *RISORGIMENTO* AS HIGH CULTURE

Painters, composers and artists had a political mission in nineteenth century Italy. It was to awaken the Italian people to their current plight, and remind them of the greatness of their past. The nation would therefore be inspired to claim for itself a glorious free and independent future. So, d'Azeglio's paintings, Manzoni's great novel *The Betrothed* and many of Verdi's operas took as their themes the overthrow of foreign oppression and the duty of self-sacrifice. Censorship meant that contemporary political issues could not be explicitly addressed. But, for example, the real meaning of one of Verdi's greatest choruses – 'Oh! My country, so beautiful and lost' – could hardly have been lost on its audience, even if the opera concerned was set in biblical times.

THE PRACTICAL *RISORGIMENTO*

The *Risorgimento* did not merely appeal to patriotic idealism; it promoted a range of practical improvements. The Napoleonic era (1796–1814) had already brought advances to Italy: a more rational legal system, the abolition of feudalism, better roads. But by the 1830s, at the same time as Britain and France were increasingly modernising, with widening franchises, industrialisation [at least in Britain], dramatic improvements in public health and education, and so on Italy seemed at best to be stagnating, and at worst going backwards. It seemed all too typical that Pope Gregory XIV had denounced railway engines as 'infernal machines' and banned them from the Papal States!

The most powerful voice of the practical *Risorgimento* was the Milanese intellectual Carlo Cattaneo (1801–69). He wrote about economics, statistics, engineering, agricultural reform, railway schemes, popular education, science and history, and insisted that knowledge had to be useful and that progress was best served by freedom: the freedom to debate and criticise. His ideas were discussed in the growing number of scientific and philosophical societies and agrarian associations, which themselves often established national networks and congresses. Such links helped to erode the regionalism prevalent in Italian politics. Cavour's first (1845) major public statement, for example, was a call for an Italian railway network to break down local patriotisms and integrate Italy into the European economy. Just as in Germany, the down-to-earth imperatives of business and improvement made would-be reformers into political liberals and political liberals into Italian nationalists.

THE POLITICAL PROGRAMMES OF THE RISORGIMENTO:
MAZZINI, BALBO AND GIOBERTI

Three political theorists in particular were important to the intellectual background of the *Risorgimento*: Giuseppe Mazzini; Cesare Balbo; and Vincenzo Gioberti.

Mazzini (1805–72) was the most significant of the three and the most controversial. His passionate conviction that Italy would be reborn as a unitary republic naturally won him the enmity of Metternich. Cavour also detested him: Cavour's opportunism and preference for the political middle ground was the very opposite of Mazzini's principled extremism. But even fellow revolutionaries could become exasperated by his stubborn insistence – in the face of all experience – that one day his strategy of launching brave bands of patriots into Italy to spark a popular revolution would succeed. Mazzini's practical record was indeed one of complete failure, with a string of abortive risings between 1833 and 1857 costing the lives of dozens of young patriotic idealists to no apparent effect. Garibaldi broke with Mazzini in the 1850s, commenting pointedly that 'wishful thinking and ignorance are a fatal combination in a would-be revolutionary'.

PICTURE 7
Giuseppe Mazzini

Mazzini himself took a chilling view of how patriotic self-sacrifice would strengthen the nationalist cause. 'Ideas ripen quickly when nourished by the blood of martyrs', he wrote. Italy, Mazzini insisted, would 'make herself', rising as one people to form one nation. He rejected Cavour's ultimately successful strategy of foreign intervention. Equally, to the despair of Marx, Mazzini refused to take up the cause of social equality, which might have mobilised peasants and artisans behind the national movement, thereby creating the possibility of a genuinely popular revolution. E.J. Hobsbawm, a Marxist historian writing in 1977, denounced Mazzini for his detestation of socialism and 'unfailing instinct for the politically futile'.

See page 96

But there are counter arguments. Some of Mazzini's judgements were very shrewd. For example, he was justified in his fears that Cavour's negotiations with Napoleon III entailed the risk that Austrian domination of Italy would be replaced by French domination. He could be pragmatic: his brief rule over the Roman Republic in 1849 won considerable praise for its moderation and practical good sense. He was even prepared to suspend his (entirely justifiable) suspicions of Piedmont's selfish ambitions, and his own republicanism, if the House of Savoy would subordinate itself to the national mission.

Mazzini is best remembered as the founder of Young Italy (1831) and as the inspiration of a whole generation of Italian nationalists. His overpowering charisma, and his pure and passionate devotion to the cause – held with an almost religious intensity – won him converts and admirers wherever he went. Although in exile for almost all his life, he nevertheless established in Young Italy a network of collaborators who, through the movement's newspaper, spread the gospel of Italian nationalism. Young Italy marked a clear break from the conspiratorial tradition of Buonarroti or the *Carbonari*, with their elaborate rituals and hierarchies, and their confused or secret objectives. Although its risings invariably failed, its objectives were clear and its public profile high. Young Italy was eventually replaced by the National Society – very different in its programme and methods – as the vanguard of Italian nationalism, but many of the National Society's leading figures had begun their political careers as Mazzini's disciples. And in many ways, the gloriously successful expedition of Garibaldi and the Thousand to Sicily was a Mazzinian venture, a passionate band of brothers rekindling popular revolt and freeing the people of the south from their oppressors.

See pages 109–11

In his book *Mazzini* (1994), Mack Smith assessed Mazzini positively:

> Most of his conspiracies failed and could hardly help but fail, yet they exerted a constant pressure which in the long run was highly effective … Hard though it might be to quantify, successive generations of Italian youth were inspired by his vision, perseverance, honesty and enthusiasm. His personal magnetism and humanity attracted disciples in each generation and persuaded them to risk their lives under his inspiration. He was an intrepid agitator and effective pamphleteer whose designs were feared by the leading politicians of Europe … Above all he was a great educator who did more than anyone to formulate the idea of Italian patriotism and stimulate a growing number of people to bring a new nation into being.

KEY ISSUE

What was Mazzini's contribution to the Risorgimento?

However, Mazzini's programme was too militant for those upper- and middle-class Italians, whom the *Risorgimento* had been encouraging to think in Italian terms. Such people turned instead to Cesare Balbo's *Of the Hopes of Italy* (1844) and Vincenzo Gioberto's *Of the Moral and Civil Primacy of Italians* (1843).

Both were reassuringly moderate. Balbo envisaged a federal Italy under the leadership of the House of Savoy, with Piedmont annexing

Lombardy, and Austria being compensated for its loss by expansion in the Balkans at the expense of the Ottoman Empire. All this could supposedly be fixed at a diplomatic congress, without the unpleasant upheaval of war or revolution.

Gioberti's vision seemed even more fanciful. He was a priest, and a disillusioned Mazzinian. He proposed the creation of an Italian federation under the presidency of the Pope. The book presented the Pope as the historic defender of Italy's liberty, and the Catholic Church as Italy's gift to European civilisation – hence 'Italian primacy'. However, central problems such as how Austria was to be accommodated within (or expelled from) the new order were simply ignored. Nevertheless, it became a best-seller, because it told cautious, respectable Catholic Italian nationalists what they wanted to hear: that nationhood could be achieved with a minimum of pain.

In the end, unification was only to be completed after war and revolution, and in the teeth of Papal opposition. Balbo and Gioberti were wishful thinkers; but their work was, nevertheless, significant. Balbo (later briefly Piedmont's Prime Minister) helped to put into people's minds the idea that Turin could and should take the lead in unification. Gioberti confirmed for his readership that it was possible to be a good nationalist and a good Catholic at the same time.

> **KEY ISSUE**
>
> *What did Balbo and Gioberti contribute to the Risorgimento?*

3 ⌐ ITALY IN REVOLUTION, 1848–9

The chain reaction of revolutions which had, by the end of March 1848, transformed political life in every state and region of the Italian peninsula, began in Sicily on 12 January. The Sicilian revolution was driven by a combination of peasant grievances about taxation and the loss of land rights, and liberal demands for freedom from Bourbon absolutism. The revolt spread to Naples, where on 27 January, Ferdinand II was forced to grant a constitution. Thereafter, a crisis of confidence undermined the rest of Italy's rulers. In Florence (11 February), Turin (4 March) and Rome (14 March), they gave up their absolutist powers and accepted the need for political reform.

> See pages 87–8 for the social and economic background to the revolution

The fall of Metternich in Vienna on 13 March gave the revolutionary spiral another twist. Lombardy and Venetia – Austria's two Italian provinces – were soon in turmoil. The garrison in Venice gave up without a fight. In Milan, however, General Radetzky tried to crush the rebels. It took five days of bitter street fighting to drive the beleaguered Austrians out – striking evidence that civilians could, with courage and determination, take on and defeat a professional army.

> See pages 218–19

This was to prove the Italian revolution's greatest victory, and it seemed to open the prospect of the peninsula's unification. But Radetzky had retreated successfully to the Quadrilateral – Austria's strategic strong point in the north-east. Nationalists failed to act quickly to stop him receiving reinforcements and counter-attacking and thus missed a key opportunity.

A *Missed Opportunities: the liberal Catholics*

Pius IX had been elected pope in 1846. His predecessor Gregory XVI had run such a cruel, corrupt and inefficient Government in the Papal States that even Metternich had complained. Pius IX was greeted enthusiastically and commenced his reign with a series of progressive actions that delighted his subjects. There was an amnesty for all prisoners, including the many political ones. Censorship was relaxed; plans for railways (refused by Gregory XVI) were made; and lay representatives were invited into the Government in a consultative capacity. Austria climbed down in a row over its right to garrison the Papal town of Ferrara, and made the Pope look like a hero of Italian nationalism. Liberal Catholics had prayed for such a Pope; and God had given them one.

This was an illusion. Pius IX was a man of presence, charm and piety. But he was no politician; and the idea that he could assume the leadership of the liberal/national cause was tragically mistaken. The nature of his God-given authority, and his duty to all the Catholic faithful (beyond as well as within Italy) made this impossible. Liberals believed that the ultimate source of political authority lay with the nation's citizens; the Catholic Church taught that the source of the Pope's authority was God. It would be hard to design a constitution which accommodated two such contradictory principles. Neither could the Pope use his worldly power to promote unification. This would mean turning the Papal army on the Austrians – who were just as much his 'children in Christ' as his 'beloved' Italians. So, when in March 1848, acting without the Pope's permission, the general commanding the Papal army on the Lombardy border proclaimed a crusade of 'divine vengeance' to 'exterminate the enemies of God and Italy', Pius had to act. On 29 April, he declared his revulsion at the idea that he could ever launch a war against Austria. He repudiated any idea that he might become president of any future Italian state – a key element of the liberal Catholic programme. Instead, he instructed all Italians to obey their current rulers.

This announcement shattered the hopes of liberal Catholics who had believed that the Pope was leading them to freedom and unity. It also began a summer of increasing political instability in Rome itself. The Pope's cabinet, which had supported the idea of war, resigned; on the streets, the talk now was of the Pope's treason towards the Italian cause. The Austrian army's successful fightback in July and August further weakened his position. The crisis came with the appointment of Pelligrino Rossi as Prime Minister in September. This tough-minded liberal set about restoring law and order in Rome and clamping down on revolutionary militants. He was assassinated by some followers of Mazzini in November. This effectively left Rome in the hands of the radicals and the Pope their prisoner. But on 24 November, Pius IX managed to escape from the city. From his (temporary) exile in southern Italy he denounced the Roman revolution. Pius IX would never again be mistaken for a political progressive. Until his death in 1878, he did all in his power to frustrate the advance of liberalism and nationalism in Italy.

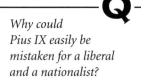

Why could Pius IX easily be mistaken for a liberal and a nationalist?

KEY ISSUE

How did the Pope's action in March disappoint liberal Catholics?

B *Missed Opportunities: Charles Albert and Piedmont*

The collapse of liberal Catholic hopes left the field clear for Charles Albert, King of Piedmont. This cold and morbidly introspective man was an unlikely hero for Italian nationalists. Many believed he had betrayed the attempted revolution of 1821; and he had savagely persecuted Young Italy in the 1830s. But on 4 March, he granted his citizens a constitution – and on 24 March he put himself at the head of the national cause by declaring war against Austria.

His motives were probably a mixture of prudence and opportunism. The constitution pleased liberals and isolated democrats, thereby strengthening the foundations of the monarchy, whilst war opened the possibility of major territorial gains. Acting in the name of Italy and freedom, Piedmont could annex Lombardy, and perhaps Venetia. Not for the last time, dynastic self-aggrandisement could disguise itself beneath the cloak of nationalism.

Charles Albert's war, however, did not go according to plan:

- suspicious of his nationalist credentials, the new liberal Governments in Naples and Florence were reluctant to commit their forces to Charles Albert's anti-Austrian crusade: the forces of Italian nationalism were therefore regionally divided
- radicals in Milan and Venice also distrusted Charles Albert, who in turn rejected an offer of help from Garibaldi (see below) with aristocratic contempt: the Italian nationalists were therefore socially divided too
- the campaign itself was a military disaster: not only was Radetzky allowed to complete his retreat into the Quadrilateral; no serious attempt was made to stop him receiving reinforcements. So, although Charles Albert easily won the plebiscites he had organised to secure popular approval for Piedmont's annexation of Lombardy and Venetia, he lost the battle of Custozza (25 July) and simply abandoned Milan – which he had promised to defend – to the advancing Austrians.

Charles Albert's 'rule' over Lombardy and Venice had barely lasted a month. Faith in the monarchist leadership of the national cause collapsed overnight. There were further misadventures. Early in 1849, Republican successes in Florence and Rome rekindled nationalist hopes, and again the stability of the monarchy seemed threatened. Charles Albert renewed war against Austria (12 March) in an attempt to outmanoeuvre his Republican critics. But the Piedmontese were defeated once more, at the Battle of Novara (23 March). Charles Albert decided to abdicate as the only way of saving his dynasty. His son, Victor Emmanuel, ascended the throne; Charles Albert died in exile in Portugal in July 1849.

See page 96

KEY ISSUE

Why did Charles Albert fail?

C *Missed opportunities: the Republicans*

'The royal war is over; the war of the people begins'. Mazzini's reaction to Charles Albert's defeat at Custozza was a call for a national uprising. Instead, republican nationalism found itself confined to isolated pockets of resistance, notably in Venice, Florence and Rome. The geographical divisions were to be compounded by political ones, ultimately enabling the republican centres to be picked off one by one:

- Daniel Manin was leader of the Venetian revolution. Adored by the Venetian people, he managed to maintain widespread support until almost the bitter end. But he was not a skilful military commander, and anyway the double defeat of Piedmont by Austria at Custozza and Novara left the city facing impossible odds. It was besieged, bombarded, and finally surrendered in August 1849
- Florence, the capital of Tuscany, was the scene of complicated in-fighting within the revolutionary ranks between moderates and democrats, which culminated in the flight of its ruler Leopold II (February 1849) and the brief establishment of a Republic. But moderates continued to resist plans for fusion with Mazzini in Rome, and the Austrian army, fresh from its victory at Novara, was able to restore Leopold in May 1849
- the Roman Republic achieved much between February and July 1849, despite being confronted by armies sent from Austria, Naples and France. Mazzini – effectively Rome's dictator – governed with 'wisdom, moderation and unexpected administrative capacity' (Mack Smith, 1994). His policies – the abolition of the death penalty; tax-cuts for poor citizens; the introduction of religious toleration – were both progressive and practical. Even more impressive was the defence of Rome, organised by Garibaldi. His volunteers beat off the first French assault. Louis Napoleon, facing humiliation, sent massive reinforcements, and so Garibaldi – rather than risk the city's destruction in hopeless street fighting – led a bold retreat, eventually escaping into exile.

See the bibliography details on page 119

See page 125

KEY ISSUE

Why did the Republicans fail?

The heroic defence of the Roman Republic was a lasting inspiration for patriots. But, by the autumn of 1849, Republicans, monarchists and liberal Catholics alike had to accept the reality of total defeat.

D *The failure of the revolutions*

City-republics
In the fifteenth and sixteenth centuries, Florence and Venice had been completely self-governing and two of the richest cities in the world.

The isolation and defeat of these three city-republics reflected a broader weakness of the *Risorgimento*: political loyalties in Italy were more often regional or even municipal than national. The revolutions in Venice and Florence had drawn much of their inspiration from these cities' proud, independent histories.

Manin had no desire to be subordinated to a Roman Republic, and had refused to send delegates to a Constituent Assembly proposed by Mazzini, whom he regarded as a fanatic. Similarly, the object of Sicily's revolution had been independence for the island – not to exchange rule by Turin or Rome for rule by Naples. Arguably, Italy's '1848' was a regional revolution first, a liberal revolution second, and a nationalist revolution only third.

Social tensions inhibited thoughts of 'unity'. Men of property feared 'the mob': hence Milan's notables welcomed Charles Albert. As a monarch, he would put the local Republicans and democrats in their place. In Venice, Manin's supporters instructed the people as to the limits of the revolution in leaflets and posters such as this:

> No communism – No social subversion – No government in the streets – Respect for property – Equality of all before the law – Full freedom of thought and speech – Free discussion without rioting – Improvement of the condition of the poor who wish to live off their own work.

They also warned against inciting the people of the city, or the peasants of the countryside, for fear of their 'blood thirsty enthusiasm', even though such a mass mobilisation would probably have strengthened the revolution's chances of success. But where the poor did slip the leash of middle and upper class control, the old order exploited the resulting divisions. In Naples, Ferdinand II had staged a successful counter-revolution as early as May 1848, partly because of the fears provoked amongst property owners by peasants taking over and occupying noble estates. When the choice seemed to be between 'revolution and anarchy' or 'absolutism and order', men of property invariably sided with the forces of reaction.

> **KEY ISSUE**
>
> *How important are social divisions in the ranks of the revolutionaries in explaining their defeat?*

E *Italy will make itself?*

To Mazzinians, the slogan 'Italy will make herself' had meant that through struggle and sacrifice, the Italian people might prove themselves worthy and capable of achieving nationhood. To Charles Albert, it had expressed his refusal to seek help from Republican France – help which might undermine the Piedmontese monarchy and limit its self-aggrandisement. But the defeat of revolution had exposed the hollowness of Mazzini's and Charles Albert's dreams alike. Italy was too divided geographically, socially and politically to make itself, or to defeat Austria.

The reassertion of Austria's military power was the key factor in the revolution's collapse. Within a month of Radetzky's victory at Custozza in July 1848, all of Lombardy and Venetia (with the exception of Venice) had been subdued. By the end of 1849, Habsburg control – either direct or indirect – seemed to be back in place throughout northern and central Italy.

However, the restoration was temporary. More than ever, Austrian rule in Lombardy and Venetia relied solely on force of arms; Tuscany, Parma and Modena were completely reduced to the status of Austrian satellites; and after 1848 'reform' became a very dirty word in Rome and Naples. Paradoxically, Piedmont and the House of Savoy, which had acquitted themselves so badly in the revolutionary crisis, were left as the only hope of Italian nationalism, with the Piedmontese constitution the single positive gain of 1848.

1848 has been described as a vital lesson for Italian nationalists; it was arguably more of a painful process of elimination. Liberal Catholicism, Republicanism and Charles Albert had all been found wanting. If Italy were to be made, it would have to forget the Pope, turn its back on Mazzini, and find a Great Power to fight for its cause. In Cavour, Italy – and Piedmont – were to find a statesman equal to this task.

4 ∽ CAVOUR AND THE MODERNISATION OF PIEDMONT

Piedmont's defeat at Novara was not a complete disaster. Its position as a buffer state between France and Austria effectively guaranteed its territorial integrity and independence: France would not have tolerated its dismemberment or conversion into an Austrian satellite. Piedmont was allowed to keep its constitution: Radetzky calculated that a moderate constitutional government would be more stable and better able to resist nationalistic and republican tendencies.

This was a decision which many in Austria would come to regret. Limited though the constitution was, its survival meant that Piedmont was left as the only state in the peninsula with a representative government, and was therefore a beacon of hope for liberals throughout Italy. Piedmont also became a refuge for thousands of political activists fleeing persecution by repressive regimes elsewhere. Their presence in Piedmont helped to give political debate there a truly 'national' perspective. It was one of the Government of Piedmont's greatest successes in the 1850s to consolidate and project this progressive image. Cavour, Prime Minister between 1852 and 1861, masterminded this strategy, and, more than any other individual, made unification possible.

Cavour was determined to make Piedmont the dominant state in Italy. There were two distinct stages to his plan: the modernisation of Piedmont internally; and a diplomatic and military campaign to isolate *and defeat Austria*, and so drive her out of the peninsula.

Cavour's programme of modernisation was designed to accelerate Piedmont's political, social and economic development. In particular, he was determined to consolidate parliamentary government; to tame the power and privileges of the (backwards looking) Catholic Church; and to create the conditions for rapid economic growth, not least so that Piedmont could afford an army and navy to match its ambitions. Modernisation would also help to convince liberals and nationalists within Italy, and sympathisers of the Italian cause abroad, that Piedmont was fit and proper to take the leading role there. Cavour knew that an ally would be needed if the Austrians were to be defeated. France was the only candidate for the role, so Napoleon III would need to be convinced that Piedmont was a serious and responsible player in the game of Great Power diplomacy. But Cavour's objectives were realistic. Despite the myths of *Risorgimento* historiography, it seems unlikely that he was initially aiming at unification. Austrian ascendancy over

COUNT CAMILLO DI CAVOUR (1810–61)

Cavour's background was privileged. His family had long served the House of Savoy and his father was Chief of Police in Turin. Cavour could have had a glittering career as an army officer and courtier. But he was determined to be his own man. Confident of his abilities, sometimes arrogant, he knew he was quicker, sharper and clever than anyone around him. But Cavour's ideas – unusually progressive for a man of his background – also made him stand out. In part, he was influenced by his mother's family, freethinking Protestants who had settled in Geneva. He also immersed himself in the writers of the **Enlightenment**, developing sceptical and anti-clerical ideas at odds with traditional Catholicism. He read economists such as Adam Smith, whose arguments for free trade were to have a powerful influence on his economic policies in the 1850s. Lengthy spells in Paris and England in the 1830s left a powerful impression too. The survival of the French King Louis Philippe, despite assaults from enemies on the left and the right, meant that Cavour became a keen defender of what he called *le juste milieu* – a middle way between reaction and revolution. Cavour thus became an advocate of conservative reform: as he himself explained, 'reforms, carried out in time, instead of weakening authority, strengthen it; instead of increasing the strength of the revolutionary spirit, reduce it to impotence'.

Cavour was an immensely practical man. To him, the Britain of the 1830s – with its factories, railways, docks, hospitals and workhouses – offered a glimpse of the future. When he returned from his travels, he was determined to apply some of the lessons he had learnt. He became a modernising farmer, and a banker and investor in railways and industry. But his passion for progress, his ambition, and his sheer energy made him determined to get to the top of Piedmontese politics.

Elected a member of parliament in 1848, he soon made his mark, striking out against both the left (denouncing revolutionary nationalism) and the right (attacking clerical privileges). His strength in defending the *juste milieu* in debate, combined with his mastery of detail, ensured his rapid advancement into the cabinet, and Cavour was appointed Minister of Trade and Agriculture in 1850. Ambitious and unscrupulous, he was soon conspiring behind the back of D'Azeglio, his Prime Minister. Cavour aimed to broaden the Government's fragile political base by forming an alliance with a parliamentary group on the moderate left, and making himself Prime Minister. By December 1852, Cavour had succeeded.

The **Enlightenment** was the greatest intellectual movement of the eighteenth century. Its leading authors, such as Voltaire, stressed the power of human reason to uncover the laws governing nature and society, and opposed the forces of tradition, prejudice and superstition – which they often associated with the Catholic Church – as obstacles to mankind's freedom and progress.

the peninsula was to be replaced by Piedmont's: but Piedmont could dominate Italy without uniting it.

Cavour's programme of internal modernisation was controversial, but mostly successful:

● Cavour's record as a parliamentarian was, by modern liberal/democratic standards, less than perfect. He ensured the return of his own supporters through the distribution of bribes and favours and manipulated the rules to deny opponents their seats. He would blur any lines of division in parliament by his so-called 'see-saw' style of politics, continually playing off right against left (and vice-versa) and neutralising critics by buying them off with government posts. Such tactics gave parliamentary politics a bad name, to the long-term damage of Italian liberalism. However, the practical alternative to Cavour was not a purer version of liberalism but the resurgence of monarchical authority under an incompetent, belligerent and autocratic Victor Emmanuel. Cavour kept the clericalist and absolutist forces around the king in check, and thus preserved the institutions of Piedmontese liberalism beyond their first decade.

● Cavour's attack on the Catholic Church was an important aspect of his liberal crusade, but they aroused the bitter hostility of Piedmontese conservatives. Although nominally a Catholic, Cavour was essentially a free thinker. He had little respect for the Papacy and the privileges of the Church. He had happily supported the Siccardi laws of 1850, which abolished separate courts for ecclesiastics (liberals strongly believed that all citizens should be equal before the law). He stepped up the attack in 1855, dissolving hundreds of monasteries, describing them as 'impediments to social progress'. Their wealthy endowments were confiscated. Pope Pius IX understandably became a fierce opponent of Cavour. But the dissolution of the monasteries provided money for the state and advertised to liberals throughout Italy, and in Protestant England too, that Piedmont had dedicated itself to the cause of progress and was not afraid even to take on the might of the Catholic Church.

● Cavour's economic policies aimed to develop Piedmont's infrastructure and military capacity. His approach was a characteristically pragmatic mixture of free trade liberalism and state intervention. Customs duties were reduced in bilateral deals with France, with the *Zollverein* and with Britain. Cavour was keen to cultivate Britain, for it opened up 'the richest market in the world to [our] foodstuffs'. Piedmont's deepening economic ties with France and Britain made these countries more sympathetic to his diplomatic objectives; whilst at home, the increasing profitability of agriculture encouraged Piedmont's influential land-owning class to give Cavour their political support.

Overall, the volume of Piedmont's imports and exports more than doubled over the course of the 1850s: a triumph for free trade. But Cavour recognised the limits of non-intervention: in the absence of private capital, the state, through subsidies and guarantees, became the patron of massive infrastructural projects. Piedmont had only eight kilometres of railway back in 1849; by 1859 some 850 kilometres had been built – about half the total mileage in the peninsula. All this had to be paid for; and Cavour helped to negotiate large-scale foreign investment (notably from France) and he also encouraged the founding of savings banks in Piedmont. State revenue rose about two-fold between 1850 and 1859, but the public debt increased by a factor of six. All of Cavour's technical skill was needed in parliament to explain away this alarming deficit, the burden of which was eventually and painfully assumed by the Italian state as a whole in 1860.

- Considerable sums had also been spent on the army and navy. In some respects, the military returns from these investments were disappointing. Piedmontese forces fell well short of the 100 000 strong army which Cavour was to promise Napoleon III, and their actual performance – under-provisioned, poorly-prepared and incompetently led – was poor. But Cavour did derive diplomatic dividends. Piedmont's new fortresses and battalions were essential counters in his negotiations. They helped to persuade Napoleon III in 1858, and Bismarck in 1866, that Cavour and his successors were worth doing business with.

KEY ISSUES

How did Cavour's programme of modernisation strengthen:
(i) Cavour's position within Piedmont; and
(ii) Piedmont's position within Italy?

5 ◠ CAVOUR AS DIPLOMAT: INTRIGUE, CONSPIRACY AND THE AGGRANDISEMENT OF PIEDMONT

Historical interpretations of the *Risorgimento* were for a long time influenced by the new Italian state's need for a national myth. This was particularly true of Cavour's contribution to the unification process. In reality, the heroes of the *Risorgimento* were not a happy band of brothers with the same objectives. Cavour loathed and feared Mazzini; he was deeply (and unreasonably) suspicious of Garibaldi; and his relationship with Victor Emmanuel was often fraught. Cavour's main aim was not the unification of Italy but the self-aggrandisement of Piedmont.

Piedmont's intervention on the side of Britain and France in the Crimean War (although it had no strategic interests at stake in the region) used to be presented as a diplomatic masterstroke by which Cavour won the gratitude of these two Great Powers and thus paved the way for their support for Italian unification in 1858–60. However, the main reason why Cavour joined in was because, if he had not, Victor Emmanuel (who saw war as a means to add glory to his dynasty) would have sacked him. Cavour's diplomacy at the peace congress at Paris resulted in no real benefits for Piedmont. However, Cavour did brilliantly exploit the following rupture in Austrian/Russian relations.

See page 28

Cavour's greatest objective was an alliance with the French. A bizarre incident brought Cavour and Napoleon III together. On 14 January 1858, Felice Orsini, a militant Italian nationalist, attempted to assassinate Napoleon III. Orsini seems to have regarded the failure of the Emperor (a *Carbonari* in his youth) to advance the cause of Italian nationalism as a betrayal. Eight bystanders were killed but the Emperor was unscathed. Before his execution, Orsini wrote to Napoleon III, repenting of his crime, and begging the French leader to take up the claims of Italian nationalism again. Extraordinarily, Napoleon III arranged for Cavour to have the letter published. This turned Orsini into a nationalist hero, but was also a sign that the Emperor was preparing to move on the Italian question. How far Napoleon III was anxious to pre-empt future assassination attempts, or how far the incident had pricked his *Carbonari's* conscience, is impossible to say. Four months later, the French Emperor and Cavour met at Plombières, to plan a war against Austria.

The meeting was kept secret even from the French and Italian cabinets. The agreement in its cynicism and blatant pursuit of national self-aggrandisement, is a good example of *Realpolitik*.

Napoleon III and Cavour agreed to make war on Austria. The main objective was the total expulsion of Austria from the peninsula, and the annexation by Piedmont of Lombardy and Venetia (provinces directly under Austrian rule) and of Parma and Modena (effectively Austrian satellite states).

But the arrangements made at Plombières for the rest of Italy were surprisingly indistinct. The future of the Papal States, for example, was left ambiguous. Cavour expected to be allowed to take the Romagna, with its important towns of Bologna and Ferrara, and perhaps most of the province of the Marche too. But this was not made definite.

The benefits which France was to derive from its sponsorship of Piedmontese expansion were also unclear. France would receive some territorial rewards: **Savoy** certainly; **Nice** probably. But thereafter the plan got more vague. The future of the Kingdom of the Two Sicilies was of interest to the Emperor. Cavour and Napoleon agreed that King Ferdinand might well lose his throne, with Napoleon expressing the hope that the kingdom be given to Lucien Murat, the son of one of Napoleon I's greatest generals, who had been King of Naples from 1808 to 1815. Later, Napoleon III also seems to have toyed with the idea of making his cousin King of Central Italy, a new state incorporating Tuscany (whose duke would be overthrown too) and Papal Umbria. These moves would have dramatically increased French influence in Italy. The Pope would receive some compensation for the loss of most of his territories by being made the head of a new Italian Confederation. Overall, Napoleon III's thinking seems to have been shaped by a confusing blend of sentiment, ideology, national self-interest and a sheer love of conspiracy. Napoleon also wanted to gain prestige for the House of Bonaparte by marrying off his cousin, Prince Napoleon, to Victor Emmanuel's fifteen-year old daughter Clothide, who came from a much older dynasty.

The negotiations at Plombières were not a victory for Italian nationalism. Italy was not to be united, but carved up in the interests of the French Emperor and the King of Piedmont. Napoleon III expected that the new kingdom of Upper Italy would be little more than a client state of France, and with luck, rulers sympathetic to France could be installed in Florence and Naples. The Confederation of Italy would arguably be more completely under French control than the peninsula

See the definition of *Realpolitik* on page 181

See Map 5 on page 105

Savoy and **Nice** These were the two most westerly provinces of Piedmont. Geographically and linguistically, the loss of Savoy – on the north side of the Alps and French speaking – would make sense. The annexation of Nice could not be so easily justified, as Cavour pointed out. Napoleon's ultimately successful demand for **both** provinces sheds interesting light on his supposed *politique des nationalités* (see page 149)

ever had been during Austria's ascendancy. But Cavour was nobody's dupe. As he pointed out to Victor Emmanuel, Piedmont's annexation of Lombardy, Venetia, Parma and Modena would make the King 'sovereign in law over the richest and most powerful part of Italy, [and] sovereign in fact over the whole peninsula'. *Realpolitik* had no place for sentiment, honour or trust even amongst fellow conspirators, and sure enough Cavour would soon be intriguing against Napoleon III, just as he had intrigued with him against the Austrians.

KEY ISSUE

What benefits did Cavour hope to derive from his deal with Napoleon III at Plombières?

6 ⌁ WAR: PRELUDE, VICTORY AND BETRAYAL

The terms of the Treaty of Plombières were renegotiated with great secrecy in January 1859 in Turin. Napoleon insisted on the cession of both Savoy and Nice as the price of the alliance, a fact which Cavour brazenly denied to a secret parliamentary committee only a few days later.

European opinion had to be prepared for the conflict. Victor Emmanuel's declared publically on 10 January: 'we cannot remain insensible to the cry of pain which comes to us from so many parts of Italy'. But Britain and Russia put great pressure on France, Piedmont and Austria to settle their differences at a congress. On 17 April, Napoleon III gave way, and instructed his ally to demobilise. Cavour was devastated: 'we have lost everything and Napoleon had abandoned us', he cried. Close friends feared that Cavour was on the point of suicide.

Only an extraordinary Austrian blunder saved the day. Their Foreign Minister, concluding that Napoleon III's apparent climbdown left Piedmont hopelessly isolated, and Austria unable to afford to keep its army fully mobilised for much longer, decided that the time had come to teach Turin a lesson. Austria sent an ultimatum to Cavour, insisting on immediate disarmament. This bullying aggression made the Piedmontese the injured party in the eyes of the other Great Powers, so Napoleon III could renew his full support for them. Cavour would get his war after all.

The French-dominated army (Napoleon III supplied 200 000 troops; Cavour only 63 000) won two bloody victories over the Austrians at Magenta (4 June) and Solferino (24 June), but in early July Napoleon III shocked Cavour by signing a truce at Villafranca. The peace terms, negotiated behind Cavour's back, gave Piedmont less than half it had wanted: it would gain Lombardy, but not Venetia, let alone Modena or Parma. An Italian Confederation was to be set up – but with **Austria** as a member. The French Emperor declined to press his claim for Savoy or Nice, but this was small compensation.

The reasons for Napoleon III's change of stance are discussed on pages 137–8

In addition to international complications, Napoleon III did not care for the way Cavour was running his side of the war. Barely three-fifths of the 100 000 troops he had promised had materialised, but Cavour's agents were busy in the Papal Legations and Tuscany, preparing the ground for their ultimate annexation by Piedmont. Napoleon must have wondered how much of Italy Cavour was planning to swallow. As Napoleon III explained, 'I will not have [Italian] unity … France would not be pleased to see rise beside her a great nation that might diminish her preponderance'.

Cavour felt betrayed by Napoleon, and was furious that Victor Emmanuel seemed content with Piedmont's limited gains. He insisted that Piedmont should fight on alone. When Victor Emmanuel (with rare prudence) refused, Cavour resigned and stormed out, denouncing the King as a 'traitor'. Victor Emmanuel parted with him with mixed feelings: '[Cavour] is a muddle-head who is always pushing me into some wasp's nest or other… He did a good job, but he is finished'. The affair could, indeed, have marked the end of Cavour's political career.

KEY ISSUE

Why was the truce of Villafranca such a set-back for Cavour?

7 ⌐ CAVOUR REGAINS THE INITIATIVE

Cavour soon made an extraordinary comeback. Between April 1859 and March 1860 Piedmont, thanks to the annexation of Tuscany, Modena, Parma and Romagna, almost doubled the size of its territories, as shown in Map 5 on the opposite page.

During the spring of 1859, the pro-Austrian regimes of Tuscany, Parma and Modena had collapsed. The old order (either anticipating Austrian defeat or as a consequence of it) lost the will or the capacity to exercise authority, and the rulers fled. Moderate representative assemblies promptly constituted themselves, often with the local leaders of the National Society to the fore, and over August and September, they called for annexation by Piedmont. Initially, Napoleon III had tried to block this, and the armistice of Villafranca called for the restoration of these states' former rulers. However, they could only have been restored by force, and the British Government made it plain that this would be unacceptable, whilst Napoleon III himself, on reflection, could not stomach it either. Meanwhile, in January, Cavour had returned to power – even Victor Emmanuel could see that only this man was a match for the tasks ahead. Cavour worked out a deal to appease the French: in return for Napoleon III's approval of the annexations, Piedmont would finally cede Savoy and Nice to France. In March, carefully managed plebiscites gave the necessary popular approval for these plans. As Cavour had promised in 1858, Piedmont now controlled north-central Italy – and seemed set to exercise a massive influence over the rest of the peninsula too.

See pages 106–8

How did Cavour manage this feat? The problem of the rulers of central Italy in the 1850s was that none of them enjoyed legitimacy – their Governments were both unrepresentative and ineffective. They were over-reliant on Austrian troops for protection. Many of their citizens were desperate for reform. Banditry and brigandage were rife in the countryside, and widespread urban poverty increasingly made city streets unsafe too. Many citizens looked to the well-ordered affairs of Turin with envy. Piedmont seemed to offer order and security.

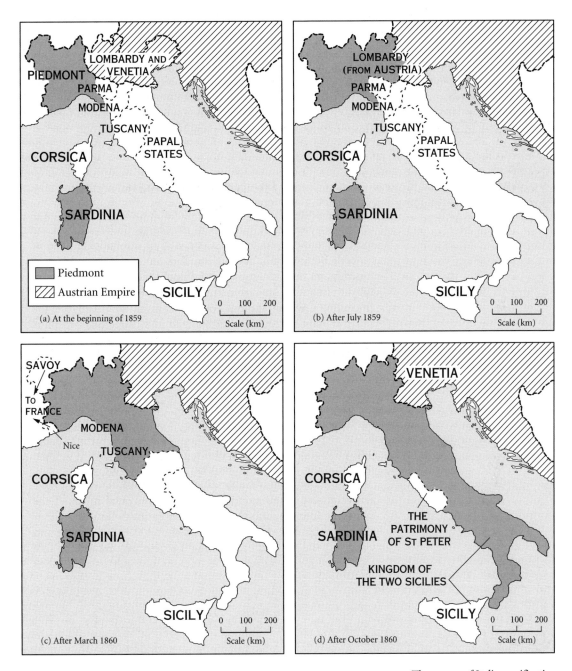

MAP 5 *The process of Italian unification*

In this context, the crisis of 1859 was both a golden opportunity and a potential catastrophe. The Franco-Piedmontese campaign against the Austrians clearly sounded the death-knell for the absolutist regimes of central Italy. But what would fill the resulting power vacuum? If radicals and democrats attempted to take control, as had sometimes

KEY ISSUE

Why were most of the notables of the central regions of Italy anxious to be taken over by Piedmont?

happened in 1848–9, it was feared that social anarchy would follow. Instead, conservative-minded moderates moved in: Baron Ricasoli in Tuscany, Farini in Modena and Parma, and Cipriani in Romagna. Either out of conviction (the last two were leading members of the National Society) or pragmatism, these provisional leaders recognised Turin as the only realistic source of authority after the collapse of (Austrian) power. Cavour could do for them what he had done for Piedmont: he could make these regions liberal and orderly.

ANALYSIS

The National Society

Officially founded in 1857, the National Society had taken a key role in persuading the 'notables' of the central Italian states of the merits of annexation by Piedmont, and of the national ideal in general. Before 1857, nationalism had too often been compromised by its association with republicanism and revolution to be fully welcome in the mainstream of Italian politics. To many (including Cavour) Mazzini was 'an assassin', who damaged the cause of Italian freedom with his wild and dangerous conspiracies. It was the achievement of the National Society to make nationalism respectable.

Many former collaborators of Mazzini were growing disillusioned with him anyway. In 1855 one of them, Daniel Manin (the hero of the Venetian revolution of 1848) publicly broke away. Rejecting Mazzini's republicanism, he proclaimed: 'Convinced that above all Italy must be made, that this is the first and most important question, we say to the Monarchy of Savoy [i.e. Piedmont]: "Make Italy and we are with you – if not, not"'.

Manin was soon collaborating with Pallavicino, a Lombard aristocrat and fellow ex-republican, who provided much of the necessary funding, and the Sicilian La Farina, who was a hard-working organiser. They soon established links with Cavour and Garibaldi, the last two being brought together by Pallavicino in a secret meeting in August 1856. Cavour was still regarded with some suspicion. Pallavicino, for example, insisted that, 'what [he] wants, and I am sure of it, is just for Piedmont to be enlarged by a few square miles of Italian soil'. But by the mid 1850s, Piedmont seemed the last, best hope for Italian nationalism. The failure of 1848, confirmed by the disasters which regularly overtook Mazzinian-inspired insurgencies, suggested that the national cause would only prosper if it could be harnessed to a state and an army – which meant harnessing it to Piedmont. Furthermore, although Piedmont was a monarchy, Cavour was hard at work transforming it into a progressive, liberal state: a model of what a united Italy, purged of oppressive clericalism and Austrian-style absolutism, might become. To moderate nationalists, unity was a means to efficient and responsible government, law and order, and economic growth. In these respects, whether or not Cavour can himself be called a nationalist, he was clearly on the nationalists' wavelength.

The National Society's manifesto issued in February 1858 reflected its moderate style of nationalism. Its central theme was that Austrian tyranny and internal division condemned Italy, 'the most fertile and beautiful country in the world', to economic backwardness:

> To recover the prosperity and glory she knew in the Middle Ages, Italy must become not only independent but politically united. Political unity alone can reconcile various interests and laws, can mobilise credit and put our collective energies to speeding up communications. Only thus will we find sufficient capital for large-scale industry. Only thus will we create new markets, suppress internal obstacles to the free flow of commerce, and find the strength and reputation needed for traffic in distant lands.

The National Society also aimed to appeal to all sections of society, and rejected extreme radicalism: 'we will not repudiate the aristocracy if they recognise our present needs, as we also embrace the common people so long as their pretensions do not go beyond justice or equity'. The manifesto concluded with a declaration of support for the Piedmontese Government, 'for it has a warlike army, money, credit, reputation, and an organised administration'.

The National Society was never a mass movement: its membership is estimated at between four and eight thousand. Neither was it an effective *revolutionary* organisation: Cavour was to be disappointed by its failure to mobilise demonstrations in the Central Duchies and the Papal Legations in 1859, even after Austria's reversals in June. But these expectations were unrealistic. The Society's most effective work was done through education, not agitation. The respectable citizens of Parma and Modena, had no intention of raising the streets: disorder was precisely what they strove to avoid. However, with careful guidance from National Society officials, the provisional assemblies of Modena, Parma, the Papal Legations and even Tuscany (where regional feeling remained strong) called for annexation by Piedmont. The plebiscites which followed have been called 'triumphs of creative electioneering … arguably the National Society's finest hour' (Clark). In Tuscany, 'yes' votes outnumbered 'no' votes by 25:1; in Modena, Parma, Bologna and the Legations, only 756 electors dared to vote 'no': less than 0.002 per cent of the total electorate. Without a secret ballot, and with local notables unanimous as to the merits of unification, it would be dangerous for dissenters to register a protest vote. The festival atmosphere in which the plebiscites were conducted, with plenty of free wine, helped to ease the doubts of oth-

See the bibliography on page 119

ers. But, however dubious the exercise was by twentieth century standards of liberal democracy, Cavour and his King could claim that an overwhelming majority of citizens had voted for 'annexation to the constitutional monarchy of King Victor Emmanuel II'. The voice of the nation had been heard.

Cavour's initial sponsorship of the Society had been conditional on its moderation and respectability. Outside Italy as much as inside, it was essential to demonstrate that nationalism had been decoupled from fanatics, insurgents and the mob: in a word, from Mazzini. Cavour presented himself as simultaneously the alternative to, and enemy of, Mazzinianism.

Napoleon III the survivor of Orsini's assassination attempt, needed little persuading of the merits of Cavour's stance. Cavour also enjoyed significant support in Britain, where the cause of Italian freedom was popular at many levels. But practical factors also came into play. Britain was suspicious of French ambitions in the peninsula, and supported an enlarged Piedmont in the expectation that it was then less likely to become a French satellite. Accordingly, London made clear its objections to any attempt to re-impose the old order on the central Italian states against the wishes of their inhabitants. In January 1860, Napoleon III, sweetened by Cavour's secret promise of Savoy and Nice, reluctantly agreed to developments.

It is important to remember the skills Cavour showed in his dealings with the British and French, at times almost playing them off against each other. He exploited British fears of French expansion; he sensed in Napoleon III the sentimental pull of his *Carbonari* past which would make him loath to become a collaborator in the restoration of Austrian power; and he lied through his teeth to the British Ambassador in Turin about the ultimate fate of Nice and Savoy. Trusting to his gambler's instinct, and aided by the National Society of which he was the unofficial patron, Cavour's role in the months after Villafranca was crucial to the successful consolidation of Piedmont's position in central-north Italy.

> **KEY ISSUE**
>
> *How did Cavour win the backing of both Britain and France for Piedmont's programme of expansion in central Italy?*

8 ⌐ GARIBALDI AND THE MIRACLE OF THE 'THOUSAND'

Garibaldi did not appreciate such diplomatic niceties and manoeuvres. He was outraged by the loss of Savoy and Nice (his birthplace) to France. Since breaking with Mazzini in 1854, Garibaldi had dedicated himself to the cause of Italy through service to King Victor Emmanuel. He had been made a major general in the Sardinian army, and in 1859 led his brigade of volunteers with distinction in the Italian Alps. But Garibaldi's unorthodox approach and republican past meant that he was never trusted by the army high-command, and he had been deeply frustrated by the last minute cancellation of a planned invasion of the Papal states (one of Victor Emmanuel's wilder schemes). He resigned his rank in the army, and decided to go freelance again – a heroic, almost mythological figure, with his own private army, recognising no authority but his duty to serve Italy and (perhaps) Victor Emmanuel.

Garibaldi was uncertain where he should strike. But in the end, having received (mostly faulty) intelligence that Mazzinian conspirators had detonated a successful rising in Sicily, he gathered his legendary '**Thousand**' and set sail on 6 May from the Genoese coast for the south.

Garibaldi landed five days later at the port of Marsala on the western side of Sicily. Over the next six weeks, aided by the local peasantry and volunteer reinforcements from Piedmont, he fought a brilliant guerrilla campaign across the island, capturing Palermo en route.

Although the Bourbon army in Sicily was over 20 times larger and much better armed than the Red Shirts, it was led by aged, lethargic, complacent and incompetent commanders. The Italian patriots and their 'general' consistently outwitted, outmanoeuvred and outfought their opponents. Garibaldi's extraordinary charisma and personal courage played a large part in this. He was invariably in the thick of the action, whether leading bayonet charges or defending barricades, yet was seemingly miraculously preserved from injury. He conveyed his self-belief to others. In Sicily, he proved himself to be arguably the greatest guerrilla leader of all time.

TIMELINE

Garibaldi and the 'Thousand'

16 May	Garibaldi and the 'Thousand' set sail
11 May	Garibaldi landed on Sicily. 25 000 Neapolitan troops were stationed on the island, but Garibaldi found the port of Marsala unguarded. He declared himself 'Dictator of Sicily'
15 May	Battle of Calatafimi: the Red Shirts, through sheer courage, defeated a far larger Neapolitan army
22–26 May	Clever guerrilla tactics enabled Garibaldi and his forces (now swollen by Sicilian peasants) to outmanoeuvre another Neapolitan army
27 May	Garibaldi began his attack on Palermo, the regional capital. After bitter street fighting, the Neapolitan garrison asked for an armistice (30 May) and then capitulated (6 June)
Mid-June	New arms and ammunition, and 2500 more Red Shirts, arrived to reinforce Garibaldi's expedition
7 July	La Farina, (an enemy of Garibaldi) was sent by Cavour as an envoy to try and bring Sicily under Turin's control, but was expelled. Cavour's suspicions of Garibaldi's ultimate intentions grew
20 July	Battle of Milazzo. The courage and inspiration of Garibaldi's army resulted in the defeat of superior Neapolitan forces, but the Red Shirts suffered heavy casualties
18–19 Aug	Secretly encouraged by Victor Emmanuel, and with the passive support of the British navy, Garibaldi crossed the Strait of Messina to the Italian mainland; Reggio was captured 21 August
Late Aug/ early Sept	Garibaldi, and the Red Shirts (now about 5000 strong) advanced towards Naples, meeting no effective resistance from the totally demoralised Neapolitan forces
7 Sept	Garibaldi entered Naples in triumph

The composition of the '**Thousand**' – actually a force of 1089 volunteers – is suggestive of the appeal of Italian nationalism. Less than 10 per cent came from Rome, the Papal States or the Kingdom of the Two Sicilies: the geographical origins of the 'Thousand' were overwhelmingly in the north. About half of them were workers from the cities; about half were from the middle classes – lawyers, doctors, and so on – although many of these were only just out of university. To Garibaldi's regret, there was not a single peasant: 'that sturdy and hard working class', he remarked, 'belongs to the priests, who keep them in ignorance'.

Garibaldi's image
One of the curious features of Garibaldi's success is that he bore a striking physical resemblance to traditional representations of Jesus Christ – images with which Sicilian peasants would be familiar in their local church. As the contemporary print (opposite) suggests, Garibaldi himself was happy to exploit this similarity. Peasants reportedly welcomed him as if he were divine, men kneeling down to kiss his feet. He was seen as the Redeemer's brother, or 'our second Jesus Christ'. And he was capable of miracles, too. His charmed life in battle was explained by the belief that rifle balls merely lodged in his red shirt, to be shaken out after the fighting was over!

PICTURE 8 *A lithograph of Garibaldi made to resemble conventional pictures of Christ and circulated in Piedmont in 1850*

This remarkable triumph is the centrepiece of the 'myth' of the *Risorgimento.* The 'miracle of the Thousand' is a story of success against all the odds. But although the patriotic fervour of the original Thousand cannot be doubted, the motivation of the thousands of Sicilians – mostly peasants – who so drastically swelled Garibaldi's ranks was hardly nationalist. Overwhelmingly illiterate, they could have had little concept of an 'Italian nation'. Apparently they understood that Garibaldi's call to fight for '*Victor Emmanuel et L'Italia*' was a reference to the Piedmontese King and – they assumed – his consort! Nineteenth-century Sicily was an ungovernable place, with a reputation for endemic violence. Given such tensions, Garibaldi's arrival was a signal for anarchy. Peasants flocked to him as their redeemer. In return, he promised land reform and the abolition of hated taxes.

But, with the collapse of Bourbon authority, the notables turned to Garibaldi too: 'all roles have been inverted', a French observer wryly noted, 'the good bourgeois, the enemies of revolution, await Garibaldi anxiously, as he alone can save their cash tills'.

In the end, Garibaldi was to disappoint the peasants. He abolished the grist tax, but he introduced conscription, and failed to deliver land reform. When peasants took the law into their own hands, the results could be grisly. At one village, the violence which began with the forced partition of a hated noblewoman's lands, ended with the burning alive of her local agent – but only after his heart and liver had been cut from his body and publicly eaten in a ceremonial act of vendetta! Garibaldi sent in one of his more brutal lieutenants, who rounded up the supposed ringleaders, and summarily executed them. Even more so than in Romagna or the Central Duchies, not the least of the attractions of the struggle for unification was that its leaders brought to disturbed communities the promise of law and order.

Cavour's relationship with Garibaldi remained at best ambiguous and often intensely suspicious and historians still debate its exact nature. The heroic interpretation runs something like this. Cavour's and Garibaldi's talents were contrasting but complementary. Cavour established the diplomatic preconditions for unification, and, with the help of French arms, completed the first stage. But Garibaldi's genius was needed to raise the ardour of the Italian people. With his daring liberation of Sicily and Naples, the south of Italy could be united to the Piedmontese north. In public, not least to appease Napoleon III, Cavour had to condemn Garibaldi's expedition to Sicily as rash and dangerously subversive – he even had to pretend to hinder it – but privately he knew that Garibaldi had a decisive contribution to make to the making of Italy, and gave him secret assistance whenever possible. Therefore, the unification of Italy stands as the joint achievement of two great men, secretly working together to free the peninsula from foreign tyranny.

However, as Denis Mack Smith first pointed out in the 1950s, not all of the facts fit this version of the story. Garibaldi for one disputed it. In a memoir first published in 1908, he asserted: 'every possible obstacle was raised in our path [by Cavour] between the time we left Genoa and we arrived at Naples … It is true that the government put no absolute veto in our way (Garibaldi here wrote in the original manuscript, but then crossed out, 'hoping to be rid forever of a lot of trouble makers like us'); nevertheless they raised every kind of obstacle. I was not allowed to take any of the 15 000 muskets which belonged to our Million Rifle Fund [Garibaldi had launched a highly successful appeal to pay for modern weapons in September 1859] and were kept in storage at Milan. This one fact delayed by several days the sailing of our expedition. La Farina [a colleague of Cavour's] then gave us 1000 bad firearms'.

Ridley summed up Cavour's views of Garibaldi and his expedition as follows: '[he would] not support the revolution until he thought that it was likely to succeed; thereafter he supported it in order to control it and reap the rewards of the revolutionaries' daring'. But just as Cavour's attempt to bring Garibaldi to heel in July via his envoy La Farina was rebuffed, so his conspiracies to prevent Garibaldi from leaving Sicily came to nothing. In mid August, Garibaldi crossed the Straits of Messina and began to move north. On 6 September, Francis II, the King of the Two Sicilies – young, inexperienced and weak-willed – withdrew to the fortress

KEY ISSUE

How can Garibaldi's conquest of Sicily be explained?

See the bibliography on page 119

of Gaeta, leaving Naples open to the Red Shirts. Garibaldi entered the city the following day to a rapturous welcome, and proclaimed himself 'Dictator [i.e. temporary ruler] in the name of Victor Emmanuel'.

Cavour's worst fears had come true. He feared the possibility of his own removal from office. Garibaldi actually demanded this in mid-September, and the fact that he was in secret communication with Victor Emmanuel, has made historians wonder whether there was a high level conspiracy against Cavour. Certainly, neither Victor Emmanuel nor Garibaldi, who were both warriors by instinct, would have been sorry to see the back of Cavour, the scheming, slippery and arrogant diplomat. Cavour's second fear was political. Garibaldi **might** be loyal to Victor Emmanuel. But in his immediate entourage were radicals and Republicans (Mazzini himself had slipped down into Naples in mid-September, and saw Garibaldi regularly) who were no friends of monarchy or aristocracy. They were lobbying hard for Garibaldi to demand a 'national assembly', out of which a democratic 'people's Italy' might be born. Cavour, in most respects a social conservative, was appalled by such revolutionary ideas. Cavour's third fear was diplomatic and strategic. Garibaldi had proved himself a guerrilla leader of genius – but his sense of Great Power realities was non-existent. Cavour feared that Garibaldi was determined to complete the task of unification as soon as possible, even though this would mean war against the Pope to secure Rome and war against Austria for Venetia. Such a course was undoubtedly patriotic and heroic, but to Cavour it seemed insane. If one thing could unite France and Austria, Europe's Catholic Powers against Italy, it would be such a campaign. All Piedmont's gains over the preceding 14 months would be put in jeopardy. But how could Garibaldi be stopped?

> **KEY ISSUE**
>
> *Why was Cavour so suspicious of Garibaldi?*

9 ᕁ CAVOUR TRIUMPHANT

Cavour found himself forced into making the boldest single gamble of his career. The only option left was to place an army between Garibaldi and Rome. But that would mean first having to invade the Papal States Declaring war on the Pope was not something to be done lightly: it would above all be essential to get the agreement of Napoleon III. A secret meeting between the French Emperor and Cavour's representatives was arranged. Nothing was left on record of their exchange but Cavour believed that the Emperor had been very understanding. Piedmontese forces attacked on 7 September.

The Papal army was defeated at the Battle of Castelfidardo on 18 September. Piedmont had effectively conquered the Papal States, although it gave Rome itself a wide berth. Garibaldi, who had himself just held off a determined Neapolitan counter-attack in early October, could now be intercepted. Cavour was still suspicious that Garibaldi was a secret Republican, and feared that force might have to be used. He ordered the commander of the Piedmontese army to 'exterminate' the Red Shirts if necessary But when guerrilla leader and king finally met at Teano on 26 October, Garibaldi warmly welcomed 'the King of Italy'. Refusing all gifts and honours, Garibaldi retired to the tiny island of Caprera. In fact he was only waiting for a suitable opportunity to complete the task of unification: this remarkable man was not ready yet to write himself out of the story.

Cavour himself still had many loose ends to tie up. Most immediately, he had to drive home his victory against the threat of militant democratic nationalism. The Red Shirts, now 30 000 strong, and in Cavour's imagination a hive of Mazzinian conspiracy, were swiftly disbanded. Then there were the plebiscites to arrange, to give popular approval to the annexation of Sicily and Naples. The result was predictable: almost 1¾ million 'yes' votes, to 10 979 saying 'no'. There was no constitutional debate about the union: the men from Turin were in control – at least on paper. In fact, the south was highly unenthusiastic about 'Italy'. Victor Emmanuel was perceived as a foreign King. Here was the genesis of the Southern Question – namely, how was the south to be integrated into the new Italian state? It was a problem which had already begun to preoccupy Cavour before his unexpected death (he had contracted malaria during a visit to the family estates) on 6 June 1861.

> **KEY ISSUE**
>
> *How, in the end, did Cavour outmanoeuvre Garibaldi?*

10 ⌁ EVALUATING CAVOUR

Was Cavour a nationalist? He has more claim than anyone – even Garibaldi – to the title of architect of the Italian nation. But Cavour detested some variants of nationalism. He talked of Mazzini as an 'assassin' who was 'Italy's greatest enemy', and promised to hunt him down and have him hanged. Cavour was disgusted by Mazzini's populism, utopianism, self-righteousness and revolutionary republicanism. Cavour had a fraught relationship with Garibaldi because he believed that the latter possessed a powerful strand of Mazzinianism. As Mack Smith suggests, 'Cavour feared revolution more than he loved Italy'.

Cavour was not preoccupied with **any** vision of national unification. He was extraordinarily ignorant of the south and had surprisingly little interest in Italian history or literature. He was in many ways more French than Italian: French was his first language, Italian only coming to him with difficulty. But more than France or Italy, Cavour's homeland was liberal Europe. He borrowed freely from the culture of the Enlightenment, and the political and economic experience of France and Britain. Cavour's guiding beliefs were freedom, progress and reason. Absolutism was the great enemy: 'rule by priests', he asserted early in 1860, 'is perhaps as damaging for Italy as the Austrian dominion over Venice'. Absolutism suffocated individualism and the possibilities of economic growth alike. The cure for absolutism was emancipation: unification was – at best – an optional extra. The priests had to be put in their place, and northern Italy purged of its Austrian overlords. In order to achieve Cavour's programme, Piedmont had to modernise and expand. The annexation of Rome or Naples seemed to be neither practicable nor even desirable objectives. Many contemporary Italian nationalists rightly suspected that Cavour was ready to use Italian nationalism as an instrument of Piedmontese self-aggrandisement.

See page 103

KEY ISSUE

How accurate is it to describe Cavour as an Italian nationalist?

The Treaty of Plombières revealed Cavour's real priorities. The annexation of Lombardy and Venetia was spelt out clearly enough, but the future of the rest of the peninsula was left hazy. These details were relatively unimportant to Cavour. He explained to Victor Emmanuel that whatever the legal boundaries of the states making up the peninsula a 'greater Piedmont would dominate 'Italy' economically, and morally'. Piedmont came so quickly to dominate 'Italy' militarily and politically as well through a mixture of luck and opportunism. Cavour did not expect to be able to unite all of Italy, preferring (in Mack Smith's words) '[to leave] Naples and Sicily for a future generation to sort out'. He may have been happier to hold the south at arm's length, for he believed it to be 'the weakest and most corrupt region of Italy'. Others in Cavour's circle were even less enthusiastic. Farini, governor of Naples, described the city as a 'hell-pit' run by 'tricksters, lawyers, and professional liars with the consciences of pimps' who ideally should be flogged, have their tongues cut out or be systematically drowned. D'Azeglio, ex-Prime Minister, declared that for the north to have annexed the south was as attractive as 'going to bed with someone with smallpox'. Mazzini dreamed of Italian unification, Garibaldi helped to realise it; but to Cavour's followers, the dream was more like a nightmare.

Why then did Cavour, in September 1860, undertake his extraordinarily risky invasion of the Papal states, thereby uniting northern and southern Italy? The essential answer, as we have seen, is that Garibaldi forced him to. Indeed, to interpret this adventure as if it marked the completion of some national mission is to misunderstand the most characteristic and essential features of Cavour's statecraft – his 'capacity to recover from mistakes and [to] exploit adverse conditions' [Mack Smith]. Cavour had no time for plans. 'All plans, all projects are useless', he wrote: 'everything depends on an accident … [on seizing] fortune by the hair'. With such a philosophy, how *could* Cavour have any 'plan' for the unification of Italy?

There was good reason why Cavour formulated few long-term 'plans' in his diplomatic and strategic thinking: Piedmont was too weak to impose any. Circumstances forced Cavour to be the great improviser: rarely can a statesman have been so fertile in expedients. His endless inventiveness and extraordinary capacity for intrigue made for some breathtakingly bold manoeuvres – and some utterly implausible schemes as well. Circumstances also forced Cavour to be a persistent and utterly shameless liar. A friend was to remark: 'no-one any longer takes Cavour's word seriously because people have learnt to believe almost automatically the very opposite of whatever he says'. Cavour was fully aware of the dubious morality of his behaviour, but he excused himself as follows. 'If we did for ourselves what we are doing for Italy, we should really be scoundrels'. He was, after all, a statesman in the age of *Realpolitik*, and any co-conspirator with Napoleon III had to keep his wits about him.

It is Piedmont's objective weakness which makes Cavour's achievement so great. According to Denis Mack Smith 'no politician of the century – certainly not Bismark – made so much out of so little'. The comparison is an illuminating one. There are striking similarities: two masterly exponents of *Realpolitik* manipulating the men and ideas of their age and at times chancing their all on the fortunes of war, so as to turn their native states into far greater powers. But the contrasts are at least as great. Cavour had no Von Roon or Von Moltke – the military geniuses who organised and led Prussia's superb army. He had no Krupps – the industrial magnate from the Ruhr who equipped the Prussian army with its mighty cannons. Indeed, Piedmont had precious little industry at all! And instead of William I – upright, scrupulous, and solid to a fault – Cavour had Victor Emmanuel – boorish, belligerent and perpetually conspiring to replace his Prime Minister with someone more amenable to his wild schemes. For Cavour to have made Italy out of such limited human and material resources was an achievement indeed.

> **KEY ISSUE**
>
> *What qualities made Cavour one of the great politicians and statesmen of the nineteenth century?*

11 ～ UNITED AT LAST? ITALY 1861–70

Cavour's death was widely lamented in Italy, not least because Italians realised that their fledgling state still faced many urgent and difficult tasks, and that none of Cavour's potential successors were of his stature. The decade which followed Cavour's death saw the geographical completion of unification with the annexation of Venetia (1866) and Rome (1870). But many detected something rotten near the nation's core: the 1860s were also a decade of tragic-comic military blundering, political instability and repression, and at times near civil war.

A *Piedmontisation*

Italian nationalists had long debated the ideal constitution for Italy. Many wanted a devolved, federal structure, with a high degree of regional autonomy which reflected the diversity of the peninsula's political traditions. However, shortly before his death Cavour began to impose a system of rigid legal and political centralisation on the new state. The laws of Piedmont were to be enforced throughout Italy; and Turin would appoint all Italy's prefects and mayors. There good reasons for this. Naples and Sicily in particular were racked by disorder and crime, and there was a real danger that a system of devolved government would be captured by criminal elements and/or supporters of the old regimes. But Cavour, who at the time of his death was simultaneously Prime Minister, Foreign Minister, and Minister of Finance, also seemed to want to concentrate in himself as much power as possible in the new Italy. Likewise his lieutenants tended to view the provinces they governed as if they were imperial viceroys, whose main task was to 'keep the natives down'. Northern Italians literally saw themselves as belonging to a different race to the 'ferocious bedouin' of the south: Africa, it was said, began at Rome.

To many in the south the process of unification must indeed have seemed like the imposition of colonial rule. Few of the citizens of the new Italy were accorded any share of political power. All men could vote in managed plebiscites; but voting in parliamentary elections was restricted to an *élite* of about 2 per cent, with the franchise determined by property and literacy tests. Conscription was introduced throughout the peninsula (Italy's rulers were determined to build an army big enough to justify their pretensions to Great Power status). Piedmont's massive public debt was also redistributed, leading to big rises in taxes, which fell disproportionately heavily on the poor. Perhaps most insensitively of all, Turin extended its war against the wealth and privileges of the Catholic Church across the whole of Italy. Bishops who objected were imprisoned, and over a thousand monasteries were dissolved. Such an attack seemed harsh and sacrilegious. The church still performed a significant educational and charitable role, especially in the south. Any chance of reconciliation between the papacy and the new state was gone. The Pope had already lost almost all his territories to Piedmont in 1860, and had to rely on French troops to preserve his rule in Rome. But he was still powerful. Victor Emmanuel and his ministers were excommunicated, and the *Syllabus of Errors*, published in 1864, mounted a frontal attack on liberal ways of thought. Over 100 000 priests publicised the Pope's opposition to Cavour's successors, and reminded good Catholics that His Holiness had forbidden them from holding public office or even voting in Italian elections. A damaging gap was opened up between Church and state, leaving generations of Italians struggling to reconcile their conflicting duties to their faith and to their country.

B *Brigands and Rebels*

These shocks and disappointments help to explain the serious challenges mounted against the authority of the Italian state during the 1860s:

- **The Brigand's War.** Between 1861 and 1864, the southern provinces were in turmoil. Over 100 000 troops were needed to restore law and order, and in the course of their campaigns over 5000 'brigands' were killed: a higher number of casualties than the total Italian death toll for all of Italy's Wars of Independence between 1848 and 1870. The name 'Brigand's War' is in part Government propaganda: the 'brigand's' were uncoordinated gangs made up of former soldiers, impoverished farm labourers or young men on the run from the police or the recruiting officers. It was as much a war against the new state, its agents and its policies, as against property. The army, fearing the possibility of Bourbon counter-revolution, took no half measures, and was ordered to 'inculcate terror' on the local populations through martial law and summary executions.
- **Sicily in revolt.** A more self-consciously political challenge to the new state's authority was mounted in Palermo in 1866. Sicily found rule from Turin more oppressive than rule from Naples. Conscription was particularly resented. Aristocrats, democrats and peasants all had their grievances, and Palermo was briefly occupied by the revolutionaries. The Italian navy had to shell the city into submission.
- **'Rome or Death': Garibaldi and Victor Emmanuel.** Garibaldi was determined to make Rome Italy's capital city, and Victor Emmanuel, with Cavour's restraining influence removed, offered unofficial support to his schemes. Garibaldi made two disastrous attempts to capture

PICTURE 9 *The meeting of Victor Emmanuel (left) and Garibaldi (right) depicted in a painting by Induno Domenico (1875)*

the city in the 1860s. In 1862 he was shot and wounded by the Italian army in a skirmish at Aspromonte. Victor Emmanuel, bowing to international pressure at the last minute, had treacherously decided that Garibaldi's mission would have to be aborted. The second attempt, in 1867, resulted in 600 of Garibaldi's men being killed by the French troops defending Rome, with the king again playing 'a devious and unheroic role in another national disaster' (Mack Smith).

C *Venice and Rome*

Victor Emmanuel's craving for war found other, hardly more glorious outlets in the 1860s. In April 1866 Victor Emmanuel's Government entered an alliance with Bismarck's Prussia to wage war against Austria. Italy's reward would be the annexation of Venetia, and after the Prussian army's victory at Königgratz, the territorial transfer was made. But it had not been the war of Victor Emmanuel's dreams. The Italian army was defeated at Custozza in June, and the navy was humiliated at the Battle of Lissa in July, losing its flagship and 1000 dead. The King's hopes of adding lustre to his dynasty and cementing the fragile unity of his nation via military triumphs were thus disappointed.

Rome, the final piece of the jigsaw, fell into place in September 1870. Napoleon III, at war with Prussia, had to withdraw the French garrison which had defended the Pope's independence since 1849. The Italian army moved in, facing only token resistance from papal troops. Once again, a plebiscite gave popular approval to the annexation, and Rome became the capital of Italy. But there had been no real fighting and there was no genuine enthusiasm for this final achievement of the

KEY ISSUE

Would it be fair to categorise 1861–70 as a decade of disappointment for Italian nationalists?

Risorgimento. The king decided against making a triumphal entry into the city, fearing a lukewarm response from his new subjects.

All this was far removed from the Mazzinian vision of unification, according to which the people of Italy should have risen as one to throw off their oppressors, Austrians, priests and kings alike. To the end, Italy's destiny had been shaped more by the outcome of great power diplomacy than by the exertions of the Italian people. Not many Italian soldiers gave their lives at Magenta and Solferino, and none at all at Königgratz and Sedan. Italy did not 'make itself'.

D *Italian unification and the Risorgimento: a retrospect*

'Italy' was enmeshed in a net of international power structures: most notably the treaty systems created by the Congress of Vienna, and the powerful friends of the Catholic Church in Vienna and Paris. This made it inevitable that any nationalist solution to 'the Italian question' would require much diplomatic manoeuvring and alliance building if nationalism's enemies within and beyond the peninsula were to be neutralised. The harsh lessons of 1848–9 – and of the abortive Mazzinian insurgencies of the 1830s and 1850s – were that the Italian people alone were too weak, and generally unwilling, to 'make Italy'. Without the slippery statecraft of Cavour, the *Risorgimento* would never have achieved its political objectives.

However, Mazzini, and many historians too, were curiously blind to the contribution made by the spirit of the *Risorgimento* to the success of Cavour's diplomacy. France and Britain were not entirely self-interested in their support for Piedmont. They approved of Cavour's economically progressive, cautiously liberal, moderately nationalist approach to the *Risorgimento*. Although Cavour was interested above all in Piedmont, he made its growth seem synonymous with the forward march of European civilisation and thus won the support of France and Britain.

Within Italian domestic politics the idea of the *Risorgimento* helped to create and sustain a broad political front, diverse in its nature, but able to work towards one clear objective. For most nationalists, the nation was not an end in itself, but a means to a variety of ends: good government, law and order, and economic growth. Progressive-minded Italians in Palermo, Bologna or Milan believed that things were managed much better in Turin. And even Garibaldi – for whom the rebirth of Italy probably **was** a self-sufficient objective – could be co-opted to this cause. Cavour, Victor Emmanuel and Garibaldi were very different men, with very different ideals, riven by clashes of personality and ideology. But they all believed in 'Italy', whatever the word really meant to them.

The new state faced the problem that few outside the political *élite*, an educated urban minority, shared the language of nationalism, or even a common language at all. Marxist analysts like Antonio Gramsci, detected in this *élitism* the seeds of many of Italy's later discontents. The process of unification, he complained in his writings of the 1930s, was purposely decoupled from any genuine mass mobilisation: land reform for the peasantry, or social welfare for the urban working classes, were neglected. The overwhelming majority of the people entered the new state socially and politically disenfranchised. Lacking a vigorous democratic political culture, Italy the more easily fell prey to the temptations of Fascism in the 1920s.

Certainly the 'moderate' *élite* of aristocrats and landowners gained most from the 1846–61 struggles. Rule from Turin was good for law and order, and the landed classes added to their wealth (not least through the resale of monastic lands). The 'losers' were the rural poor, hit by heavier taxes, conscription and the continuing loss of grazing rights and common lands. But could it have been different? A more radically-based campaign for unification would have faced the hostility and not the patronage of Cavour, Napoleon III or Italy's upper classes.

'We have made Italy; now we must make Italians'. D'Azeglio's comment would seem to give powerful support to those historians like John Breuilly who have argued that 'nationalism was more important as a product than a cause of unification'. With 17 million out of a total population of 23 million unable to read or write, and less than 10 per cent of the population even able to *speak* the Italian language, the task of national education required to 'make Italians' was enormous. No wonder history books stressing the united purpose of the *Risorgimento's* heroes were required.

However, nationalism did serve a useful function. As Lucy Riall explained:

> It is clear that nationalist movements did not 'create' a united Italy, and that Piedmont did. Yet, nationalism mobilised public opinion against the Restoration states and in favour of Piedmont. The increasing popularity of nationalism (even if only among educated élites) made national unity the obvious political solution after the Restoration states collapsed. Thus, without reference to nationalism, the great battle to mobilise public opinion, it is impossible to explain why Cavour was able, or was forced, to unite Italy in 1860.

> **KEY ISSUE**
>
> *What was the contribution of the* Risorgimento *to Italian Unification?*

12 ⌐ BIBLIOGRAPHY

Short introductory surveys include: *The Unification of Italy 1815–70* by A. Styles (Hodder Access to History, 1986); *The Making of Modern Italy 1800–71* by V. Brendon (Hodder History at Source, 1998) – a documentary collection; *The Unification of Italy* by J. Gooch (Lancaster Pamphlets); *The Italian Risorgimento* by M. Clark (Longman Seminar Studies, 1998), which is relatively demanding, but contains documents; and *The Italian Risorgimento* by L. Riall (Routledge Historical Collections). Amongst longer general surveys, *The Risorgimento and the Unification of Italy* by D. Beales (Longman, 1981) is outstanding. Also useful are the last 100 pages of *A History of Italy 1700–1860* by S. Woolf (Methuen, 1979) and C. Duggan *A Concise History of Italy* (Cambridge, 2000).

Denis Mack Smith has redefined the study of the unification era and its personalities. His *The Making of Italy 1796–1870* (Macmillan,1988) is an extensive collection of documents. His interpretation of unification can also be pursued through his biographies: *Garibaldi* (1957); *Cavour* (Methuen 1985); *Mazzini* (Yale, 1994) and a most unflattering portrait of Victor Emmanuel in *Italy and its Monarchy* (Yale, 1989).

Other biographical approaches to the *Risorgimento* include *Cavour* by H. Hearder (Historical Association, 1972) and *Garibaldi* by J. Ridley (Constable, 1974).

Pio Nono by E. Hales (Eyre and Spottiswoode, 1954) offers a sympathetic portrait to be supplemented by *A History of the Popes 1830 to 1914* by O. Chadwick (Oxford, 1998).

A provocative analysis of the contribution of nationalism can be found in *Nationalism and the State* by J. Breuilly (Manchester University Press, 1995), chapter 4.

The Leopard by G. di Lampedusa (Collins, 1960) is a classic novel about the impact of Garibaldi on Sicily.

13 ⌐ STRUCTURED QUESTIONS AND ESSAYS

1. (a) Outline the factors which hindered Italian unification between 1815 and 1849; (10 marks)
   (b) Which of these factors were most important, and why? (15 marks)

2. (a) Outline the ways in which the 1848 Revolutions affected Italy; (10 marks)
   (b) What influence did Mazzini have on the Risorgimento to 1848? (15 marks)

3. (a) Outline the stages by which Cavour secured Napoleon III's support for his policies within Italy; (10 marks)
   (b) How successfully did Cavour fulfil his hopes for Piedmont and Italy? (15 marks)

4. (a) Outline Garibaldi's contribution to the unification of Italy; (10 marks)
   (b) Was Garibaldi's contribution to unification more significant than that of Cavour? Explain your answer. (15 marks)

5. How valid is the judgement that 'Italy was united by accident rather than design'? (25 marks)

6. (a) Outline the stages in the unification of Italy between 1859 and 1870; (10 marks)
   (b) To what extent was the unification of Italy complete by 1870? (15 marks)

7. How significant was foreign intervention to the success of the Risorgimento? (25 marks)

France 1848–70: From Republic to Empire

INTRODUCTION

THE AFTERMATH OF REVOLUTION AND THE PRICE OF STABILISATION

The Provisional Government was in a very vulnerable position at the end of February 1848. It owed what authority it had to the streets of Paris, and although contemporaries were optimistic, their high expectations of political and social change were to prove hard to satisfy. Paris would be difficult to control. But the introduction of universal manhood suffrage and the forthcoming elections for a Constitutional Assembly meant that – for once – the rest of France would have a major share in shaping the nation's affairs too. The resulting tension between the capital and its provinces, and its bloody resolution, offer a key to understanding the events of 1848 in France.

Widespread poverty and a sense of social injustice had fuelled the revolution. Therefore many radicals saw the 'organisation of work' as a priority. Louis Blanc – one of the fathers of socialism – and '**Albert**' were brought into the Provisional Government to appease militants. 'National Workshops' were set up, supposedly not merely guaranteeing employment to the jobless of Paris, but standing as models of a new co-operative way of organising production. In reality, they soon became a demoralising exercise in state charity: the mechanism for delivering the dole to over 100 000 of the unemployed. Inevitably they were soon being criticised by tax-payers.

'**Albert**' was the pseudonym of Alexandre Martin, a key figure of the revolutionary underground and a genuine member of the working class – one of the first people from such a background to take a share in the government of a European state.

TIMELINE

(Foreign affairs in italics)

1848	Revolution in Paris
	June Days
	Election of Louis Napoleon as President of Second Republic
1851	Napoleon's coup
1852	Declaration of Second Empire
1854–6	*Crimean War*
1858	Orsini plot
1859	*War against Austria*
1860	*Annexation of Nice and Savoy.* First stage of liberalisation
1862–7	*Expedition to Mexico*
1866	Prussia defeats Austria at Sadowa: no gains for France
1870	Ollivier Government
	Franco-Prussian War

See page 1

Political parties
These terms help to
identify general political
tendencies in mid-
nineteenth century
Europe at a time when
formal political party
organisations were rare.
'The Party of Progress'
would be made up of
more radical minded
liberals, probably
favouring a generous
franchise and an adven-
turous foreign policy;
'the Party of Order'
designates conservatives
and conservative-
minded liberals, who
wanted to defend the
interests of property
owners and were suspi-
cious of the passions of
'the mob'.

KEY ISSUE

*What problems con-
fronted France's new
Government?*

Other problems facing the new Republic proved almost as divisive. Some of the fiercest disputes focused on foreign policy. Militant republicans believed that France had a duty to liberate the oppressed peoples of Europe; especially the Poles. But Lamartine, the Republic's Foreign Minister, knew that the time was not right for crusades. Any foreign adventurism might provoke a renewal of the Waterloo coalition, embroiling France in a war against Austria, Prussia, Russia and perhaps even Britain, which France would certainly lose. There were major protests against this cautious stance, and on 15 May extremists made a half-hearted attempt at a *coup*. The defeat of the *coup* and imprisonment of its leaders seriously weakened the political left.

A final reckoning between 'the Party of Progress' and 'the Party of Order' was perhaps inevitable. Paris had made the February Revolution, but the French nation had to determine what precise form the new Republic was to take. Elections for the Constituent Assembly (whose main responsibility would be to work out France's new constitution) were held on 23 April (Easter Sunday).

The result was a victory for the 'Party of Order'. Less than 10 per cent of the Constituent Assembly were from the militant Left, whilst crypto-monarchists and moderate Republicans each took about one-third of the 900 seats. Radicals had feared and predicted this outcome, but their calls for the elections to be postponed until their propaganda could 'educate' the electorate had been ignored. Peasants marched behind priest and landowner to the polling booth on Easter Sunday. Provincial suspicions of Paris and its dangerous, advanced opinions, and resentment of central government taxation (the Provisional Government had just imposed a 45 per cent tax increase to balance the books and pay for the National Workshops), came to the fore. These considerations help to explain a paradox: the profoundly conservative results of the first election ever held in France under the rules of universal manhood suffrage. The Assembly was soon to come into confrontation with the workers of Paris. There could only be one winner.

A showdown was precipitated between the Constituent Assembly and the Parisian socialists by a Government announcement on 21 June that the workshops were to be closed, and that the unemployed should either enlist in the army or find work in the provinces. The Left had been progressively weakened over the preceding month, with the imprisonment of Blanqui (a revolutionary Socialist) and other militants after the 15 May 'uprising' and the removal of Blanc and Albert from the Government. Provoked beyond endurance, barricades went up in the working class quarters of Paris on 23 June. Three days of bitter fighting followed. The National Guard and the newly formed Mobile Guard, as well as the regular army, led by a convinced Republican, General Cavaignac, were unleashed on the 40 000 insurgents.

The Government lost about 800 troops in the fighting, the workers perhaps three or four times as many. Afterwards, there were 15 000 arrests and 5000 prisoners were deported to Algeria. The writer Victor Hugo, an impassioned Republican, lamented that in the June Days, 'civilisation had defended itself with methods of barbarism'.

The events of June confirmed the suspicions of conservatives that they had to be ready to face down the mob. The respectable press dwelt on such incidents as the cruel murder by the Reds of would-be peacemakers like the Archbishop of Paris, and glossed over the summary executions, arbitrary imprisonments and deportations which followed their own side's victory. 'Social fear' re-emerged as one of the great themes of French politics – a psychological factor which does much to explain the rise of Louis Napoleon.

The June Days weakened the Republic in another way. As Price suggests, it created bitter and lasting division between moderate Republicans, 'the only republicans most of France could accept in power', and the workers, 'who alone might have provided mass support for republican institutions'. In December 1851, when Louis Napoleon destroyed the Republic in his *coup*, few barricades were raised in protest in Paris. Why, the workers demanded, should they risk their lives to defend a Republic of the bourgeoisie, which had so cruelly turned its forces on them in June 1848?

See bibliography on page 152

See pages 126–7

The June Days closed a long chapter in French history. Since 1789, the people of Paris had got into the habit of dictating the direction of events to the rest of the country. July 1830 and February 1848 continued the pattern. But the April elections had shown how isolated the Parisian militants were, and the June Days had destroyed their pretensions to power. Now, for the first time since the French Revolution 'France was governing Paris' [Furet].

With the defeat of the militant Left, the Constituent Assembly could at last devote its attention to the task of determining the constitutional framework of the new Republic. Its main features were finally agreed in early November:

- the Legislative Assembly would consist of 750 members elected by universal manhood suffrage
- a President would be directly elected by the French people. He would be responsible for the executive functions of government.

> **KEY ISSUE**
>
> *What was the significance of the June Days?*

These arrangements contained inbuilt ambiguities and tensions which were to lead directly to the constitutional crisis of 1851 and Louis Napoleon's *coup d'état*. Conservatives were anxious to build up the powers of the presidency so as to restrain the single chamber legislature (note that there was no Upper House to revise or delay legislation): by having the President directly elected they hoped to increase his authority and independence. But they carelessly provided no mechanism for resolving possible conflicts between the Assembly and the President.

The Presidency was to be limited to a four-year term, to prevent any President becoming an elected dictator. But the possibility that an unscrupulous and ambitious individual might use the President's control over the army and police to smash the constitution was ignored. The political stabilisation achieved by the Republic at such bloody cost in June 1848 was to be short-lived.

1 ⌐ THE EMERGENCE OF LOUIS NAPOLEON

A *The presidential election*

Louis Napoleon Bonaparte was elected President of the Republic in December 1848, by universal manhood suffrage.

PROFILE

See page 88

LOUIS NAPOLEON

When Louis Napoleon was born in 1808, his uncle, Emperor Napoleon I, was one of the most powerful men in Europe. The Emperor's defeat, exile and death in 1821, and the death of the Emperor's son in 1832 (he had been styled Napoleon II, even though he had never reigned), left Louis Napoleon the heir to the Bonapartist legacy. But before the events of 1848, Louis Napoleon had done little to suggest that he would ever be able to mount a serious challenge for political power. His early manhood was spent in exile from France, and he lived the life of a romantic adventurer whose dreams of greatness were hopelessly compromised by his insignificance and lack of judgement. An early involvement with the Italian *Carbonari* (1831 was followed by two attempted *coups* against Louis Philippe, both of which (Strasbourg 1836; Boulogne 1840) ended in farcical failure). Sentenced to life imprisonment for treason after the second, he managed to escape from prison in 1846, and was living in London when the February 1848 Revolution broke out. He had played no role in bringing about the downfall of the July Monarchy – but he was to be the greatest beneficiary of its collapse.

Napoleon returned to France in September. With the backing of a skilful publicity campaign which exploited the powerful memory of his name, he manoeuvred his way into the position where the 'Party of Order' came to adopt him as their candidate in the presidential election of December 1848.

Louis Napoleon scored an astonishing triumph. His 5.4 million votes – representing 74 per cent of the poll – left his nearest challenger General Cavaignac (to some voters the hero of the June Days, but to many others, its villain) trailing 4 million votes behind. The other candidates (Ledru-Rollin 400 000 votes; Raspail 37 000; Lamartine 8000) were left nowhere. The electorate of 9 million in 1848 represented a 36-fold increase on that of the Orleanist era.

Three principal factors account for this landslide:

● Louis Napoleon's name and the memories of glory and order associated with it
● the Bonapartist electoral campaign was perfectly judged to appeal to French peasant culture. Songs, pictures and medals extolled the virtues of France's coming saviour. Given that some three-quarters of the electorate were peasants, and most of these would be illiterate,

such propaganda was infinitely more effective than the newsprint favoured by Louis Napoleon's rivals
● the many faces of Bonapartist ideology were carefully deployed, each to its appropriate audience. Louis Napoleon's book, *The Extinction of Pauperism* – distributed free of charge – told the workers that in their president-to-be they had a friend who cared about their plight. But the 'Party of Order' knew that they could trust Louis Napoleon too – for Bonapartism was the very opposite of anarchy. And to the peasants, 'Napoleon' was a guarantor of their property against the depredations of 'feudal' nobles and Parisian socialists alike. There were long-term difficulties for Louis Napoleon here – the President could not remain all things to all men indefinitely – but the democratic mandate which the newly elected President had received from the people of France truly made it seem as if he embodied the national will.

The old Orleanist political *élite*, however, refused to be overawed. Thiers and Barrot had swung their support behind Louis Napoleon in the weeks before the election, believing that they had found in the President a figurehead – someone to reign but not rule. They were certain that this inarticulate, uneducated dreamer – a man with no experience of administration, but a well-developed taste for life's fleshier pleasures – would be easily enough managed. To Thiers, Louis Napoleon seemed to be 'a cretin' – 'We'll supply him with the women', he sneered. But this proved to be a monumental misjudgement.

> **KEY ISSUE**
>
> *Why was Louis Napoleon elected President of France in 1848?*

B *The presidency*

At first, all seemed to go according to Thiers' plan. The old gang, led by Barrot, filled Louis Napoleon's first cabinet. The Government's policies also suggested that the Party of Order was in command:

● *Foreign policy.* Turning the expectations of republican internationalism upside down, Louis Napoleon's Government sent an army to Rome in June 1849 to crush the recently established Republic and restore the Pope.

See page 96

● *Education.* The Falloux Law (March 1850) removed almost all obstacles which had been placed in the way of the Church opening its own secondary schools, whilst accompanying legislation for primary schools opened what had been a predominantly lay profession to monks and nuns with few or no teaching qualifications. The local authorities were also instructed to keep a careful eye on the political involvement of primary school teachers. Several hundred of these were sacked, suspected of being socialist agitators.
● *The Franchise.* The electoral law of May 1850 reduced the number of voters from 9.6 million to 6.8 million. To keep their place on the electoral register, voters now had to be: (i) personal taxpayers, (ii) without a criminal record, and (iii) to have been living in one place for three years. These requirements hit the Left and the poor disproportionately hard, for they were the class of voters most likely to be: (i) out of work, (ii) suffering police harassment, or (iii) mov-

ing around looking for work. Thiers explained that the Bill was designed to disenfranchise 'the dangerous part' of the population, which he called – *'la vile multitude'*. This notorious phrase showed that the 'Party of Order' was still driven by the psychology of social fear which helps to explain the brutal aftermath of the June Days.

C *The December coup*

Louis Napoleon soon realised that the Right's fears gave him an opportunity. He wanted to remain President for (at least) another four-year term: his destiny, and his creditors (he was heavily in debt) demanded it. He could only be re-elected President for a second term if the constitution were changed. But this would require a three-quarters majority in the Assembly – which proved unattainable. Louis Napoleon was left with only one option: a *coup d'état*.

The President had begun manoeuvring against his would-be 'keepers' as early as October 1849, when a ministerial reshuffle replaced prominent and forceful figures like Barrot with politicians easier for Louis Napoleon to control. He publicly distanced himself from the electoral law of May 1850, and his extensive tours of the provinces and patronage of the armed forces showed that Louis Napoleon was hard at work building up his personal support. By the summer of 1851, the question was less whether he would attempt a *coup*, but when?

Republicans had enough time to organise resistance to the President's plans, but failed to establish a common front. In fact, the Republic had few loyal friends. Many 'Republicans' were really monarchists, and the latter were divided between Orleanists and Legitimists. On the left of the Assembly, there was no love for the President, but even less for the Party of Order. Such divisions clearly worked to the advantage of Louis Napoleon and continued to weaken potential opposition to him for many years.

The *coup* of 1–2 December 1851 had been carefully prepared and was brilliantly executed. Over the preceding months, Louis Napoleon had appointed personal followers to vital positions in the Government, the police and the army. In a precisely targeted sweep, 20 key opposition deputies, like Cavaignac and Thiers, were arrested, along with some 80 Parisian militants (possible 'leaders of the barricades'). Paris awoke to placards announcing the dissolution of the Legislative Assembly, the promise of a new constitution and – a clever touch – the restoration of universal manhood suffrage. There was little resistance to the *coup* in the capital. Some barricades went up, but the *coup*'s leaders took decisive action, deploying some 30 000 troops against the 200 insurgents. In reality, working class militants could summon little enthusiasm to risk death for a 'bourgeois' Republic.

plebiscite a vote by all the people on a particular issue

In December 1852, Louis Napoleon held a **plebiscite** to seek retrospective approval for his *coup*. The massive majority in his favour (7 439 000 votes for, 641 000 against) was no real surprise. One-third of the country was still under martial law, and it was impossible for the opposition to organise. France's property owners, by contrast, still

The rise and fall of the Démoc-Socs

To conservatives, a particularly worrying feature of electoral politics in the Second Republic was the growing attraction of socialist ideas in the countryside. The *Démoc-Socs* were responsible for this trend. To the Republic's slogans of Liberty, Equality and Fraternity, the *Démoc-Socs* added the words 'Progress' and 'Solidarity'. Built around the leadership of key local figures – perhaps a radical doctor or teacher, or a 'Red' cafe-owner – their programme included making the wealthy pay more tax and the poor less, free education, and state control of railways, mines and canals. All of this terrified middle class conservatives, who clung to Louis Napoleon as the friend of order and property.

The *Démoc-Socs* had hoped that the 1852 elections would bring them to power: as such, the electoral 'reform' of 1850 had been a major blow to them. But the *coup d'état* launched by Louis Napoleon himself in November 1851 threatened to rob them of the Republic itself. A spontaneous rising, involving at its peak 70 000 leftists, swept whole regions of rural France. But it was uncoordinated, and army units were able to pick off peasant columns one by one. About 100 rebels were killed, and 26 000 were arrested.

In the aftermath of the rising, the magistrates and police had their final reckoning with the Reds. The activists were mercilessly targeted, especially any class-traitors from the bourgeoisie. Often on the flimsiest of evidence, a total of 9000 were transported to Algeria, and 239 to the notorious penal colony of Cayenne.

Louis Napoleon ruthlessly exploited the rising for ideological purposes too. By highlighting and exaggerating a (very) few cases of looting and violence, the *Démoc-Socs* could be presented as inhuman savages. As in the June Days, the forces of order could claim to have rescued France from anarchy and barbarism. And so, perversely, this rural rebellion was turned into a sort of justification for the *coup* which had in fact provoked it.

shaken by their narrow escape from the supposed clutches of Red anarchy, were grateful to the bringer of social order.

Louis Napoleon remarked that his conscience had been eased by the result of the plebiscite. But his political situation was uncomfortable. His reputation was blackened in the eyes of Republicans by the events of December 1851, and his room for political manoeuvre was decisively curtailed. Despite the brutal authoritarianism of which he was capable, many of Louis Napoleon's political instincts were unorthodox and radical. Some of his ideas for social and economic reform, for example, and many aspects of his foreign policy disturbed the established *élites*. But where, now, would he find radical political

Why was Louis Napoleon's coup d'état successful?

allies? It would be 1869 before any leading ex-Republican was ready to throw his weight behind Louis Napoleon. Although he appeared to emerge from his *coup* as a figure of near dictatorial authority, much of the domestic politics of the next two decades would revolve around how and how far Louis Napoleon would be free to pursue his vision of what France should be; and how far France's conservative minded social and political *élites* would be able to restrain him.

2 ⌐ AN OVERVIEW OF THE EMPIRE

Louis Napoleon was proclaimed Emperor Napoleon III in December 1852. This move was ratified by another plebiscite (7.8 million votes for, 350 000 against), which was intended to establish the Bonapartes as the ruling dynasty of France and its 'Second Empire' (the First Empire, proclaimed by Napoleon I in 1804, had collapsed in 1814). However, Napoleon III's reign and his dynastic ambitions were to come to an abrupt end in 1870.

Domestically, the regime was authoritarian until 1860. Then, a series of constitutional innovations began to give it a more liberal appearance. This process was much accelerated in 1870 with the establishment of the Liberal Empire, in which Napoleon III seemed to embrace a more truly parliamentary style of government. But the Liberal Empire was not to last long.

See pages 26–8

Foreign affairs had been progressing towards disaster. France, in alliance with Britain, won an early victory over Russia in the Crimean War (1854–56), but the Emperor's war against Austria in Italy (1859), although militarily successful enough, had unforeseen and largely unwelcome consequences – notably the formation of an independent and united Italy on France's borders. The rise of Prussia under Bismarck posed a greater problem, especially as its first stages coincided with the humiliating collapse of a French colonial adventure in Mexico. Prussia's defeat of Austria in 1866 established its hegemony over Germany, and effectively frustrated French hopes for influence and territorial expansion along the Rhine. An attempt to slap down Prussian pretensions in 1870 was grossly mishandled, and led instead to a war. Grotesquely over-confident of victory, the French in fact found themselves diplomatically isolated and militarily unprepared, and the Prussians inflicted a crushing defeat at Sedan in September. The Second Empire collapsed under the blow, the Emperor departing to exile in Britain. He left behind a refashioned Republic struggling to come to terms with both the scale of the Prussian victory and the perennial conflict in French politics between Left and Right which Napoleon III had attempted to transcend but seemed in retrospect merely to have papered over.

3 ~ THE ENIGMA OF BONAPARTISM

Two key questions are:

- did the Second Empire leave any positive mark on French history?
- is there any pattern or purpose behind these events to help us make sense of this roller-coaster ride over two decades?

For many years, French historians in particular thought that the answer to both questions was 'no'. These historians' political loyalties were often Republican: for them, Napoleon III had begun his reign in betrayal, sustained it by oppression and ended it with disaster. The Emperor himself was seen as an adventurer and opportunist, driven by expediency at home, completely out of his depth in foreign affairs, and without a serious idea in his head: hence the shuddering lurches from crisis to crisis, culminating in disaster, which characterised the Second Empire.

Such a damning verdict is harsh. It makes it hard to understand how such a supposedly second rate figure as Louis Napoleon could not only seize power in the first place but then hang on to it for almost two decades. It also glosses over difficult questions. Why, perhaps uniquely, did this authoritarian state reform itself along liberal lines? Can the responsibility for the defeat of 1870 be rested so squarely on the Emperor's shoulders? Above all, by reducing the Second Empire to an historical black hole, it obscures the extent to which it was in reality a crucial era of transition in French history. In politics, it saw the (irreversible) growth of democracy; in economics, a revolution in transport, with far reaching implications for industry, agriculture and popular culture; whilst in social history, these decades constituted 'the golden age of the peasant'. Any analysis of Napoleon III must recognise these positive aspects and evaluate his contribution to them. It must also take into account how far the Emperor tried to pursue his vision for France.

Napoleonic ideas

ANALYSIS

Louis Napoleon's rise from near obscurity to the leadership of France convinced him that he was a man of destiny, whose mission was to complete the work which his uncle had been forced to abandon in 1815.

There were four main aspects to this:

- Louis Napoleon would restore order to French life and rescue the nation from the cycle of revolution and counter-revolution which had afflicted it for over half a century
- as the embodiment of the will of the French people – his name and his overwhelming popularity enabled him to make this claim – he aimed to dispense with parliamentary government. Political parties, he believed, only worsened the divisions in society: politicians themselves were self-serving careerists. But ultimately, with order consolidated, liberty could be restored to the people

See page 125

- order would help to create prosperity; and in a virtuous circle, prosperity would encourage political maturity and calm. Satisfying the legitimate material needs of the people was one of Louis Napoleon's priorities – as advertised in a booklet he had published in 1844, *The Extinction of Pauperism*. This work's widespread distribution in 1848 had done his electoral prospects no harm, and the large role which the President/Emperor accorded to state intervention in the economy in an attempt to promote growth and prosperity suggests that the work was more than mere propaganda
- it was also Louis Napoleon's mission to satisfy the expectations of his people for 'glory' abroad. This helps to explain Napoleon III's role as the patron of European nationalisms – his so-called *politique des nationalités*. Supporting moderate nationalists (like Cavour) would spare Europe from convulsions at the hands of revolutionary militants (like Mazzini). And if, as a reward for his help, the borders of France were to expand a little, encompassing the Rhine perhaps, the Emperor would hardly complain.

See the bibliography on page 152

As Plessis notes, Napoleon III 'manoeuvred with immense skill to maintain himself in power and ... to shape events in accordance with his convictions'. But, in the end, as Thiers famously remarked, he too often confused the verb 'to dream' with the verb 'to think'. He sometimes seemed to be pursuing all of his objectives simultaneously, oblivious either to the need to identify priorities amongst them or to be aware of the possibility that they might in some respects be mutually contradictory. Was it really in France's national interest to promote the growth of Italian nationalism? Or German nationalism ...? Domestically, how could the power of universal manhood suffrage be reconciled to the project of founding an imperial dynasty? And how could the Emperor remain a friend to both the poor and the rich?

Napoleon III claimed to have distilled the political wisdom of the political era through which he lived with the following watchwords:

> March at the head of your century, and its ideas will follow and support you. March behind them and they will drag you along. March against them and they will overthrow you.

The ideas at whose head Napoleon III found himself marching included nationalism, liberalism, conservatism, democracy and even socialism. He should not have been surprised to discover that they often pushed him in different directions.

4 ✑ AUTHORITARIANISM AND ITS LIMITS

The constitution of the Second Empire, published in January 1852, looked for inspiration to Napoleon I. Around Napoleon III, and each clearly subordinated him, were three key institutions: the Senate, the Council of State, and the Legislative Body:

● as the Constitution spelt out, the Emperor had immense formal powers: 'he commands the army and navy, declares war, concludes peace treaties, alliances and commercial treaties, [and] makes all appointments ... He alone can initiate laws [and], approves and promulgates [them]'. All major domestic and foreign policy decisions depended on him

● the Senate was to act as the guardian of the constitution, with a duty to oppose any laws that violated its basic principles (for example freedom of worship and the equality of citizens before the law). But the Senate was appointed by the Emperor, and he was responsible for convening it and approving its decisions

● the Council of State supervised the drafting of legislation, and accepted or rejected amendments proposed by the Legislative Body. Its members too, were appointed by the Emperor, who presided over its meetings

● the Legislative Body could debate the merits of bills and taxes, which could not be enforced or levied without its consent. It members – some 270 deputies – were elected by universal manhood suffrage. But it was, in important respects, unlike a parliament: the Legislative Body could not vote the Government out of office, nor determine Government policy. Furthermore, in the national elections (held every six years), the Government blatantly gave its backing to 'official candidates'. So effective, indeed, was the Government's deployment of 'sticks and carrots' that very few opposition voices were heard in the Legislative Body until the 1860s

● ministers were appointed by the Emperor: they were not meant to have policies of their own, but were instruments of the Emperor's will. There was no question either of collective decision-making in cabinet. At ministerial meetings a minister would make his report, and a discussion might follow, but the Emperor would usually conclude with a comment like 'we shall see', and settle the matter in private later.

Napoleon III appeared to control all the levers of power. It is not surprising that many Republicans regarded him as a dictator. But a mixture of formal and informal constraints on the Emperor in fact limited his freedom of action.

Napoleon III was always conscious that the ultimate source of authority in the Second Empire was the nation, and he attached great importance to the nation's voice. Plebiscites overwhelmingly legitimised his *coup* of 1851, the inauguration of the Empire itself (1852), and the creation of the Liberal Empire (1870). National elections, although less than 'free and fair', were not rigged, as the growing opposition vote

See page 146

See page 143

demonstrated (1852 – 810 000; 1857 – 665 000; 1863 – 1 954 000; 1869 – 3 355 000). Napoleon III and his advisers were genuinely concerned by the Empire's failure to win over the urban working class to the Bonapartist cause. Major policy decisions were partly shaped by the public mood (as reported by the Prefects and others), even including matters of war or peace, as in 1866 and 1870. It was one of the great objectives of Bonapartism to reconcile the principles of authority and democracy, and this could not be achieved by ignoring or trying to crush the public will.

Napoleon III anyway lacked two of the main instruments by which dictators impose their will on society: a police force large enough to tyrannise the population, and an official Bonapartist party to mobilise popular support for the Emperor. The 'official' candidates at elections subscribed to no national manifesto, nor were they members of any party 'slate'. Bonapartism was, after all, much more than a party ideology: it was the will of the nation, and the Emperor a statesman above politics. But the absence of a Bonapartist party made it hard for Napoleon III to get his policies implemented. France had very few convinced Bonapartists eager to do his bidding. Napoleon III had spent most of his life in exile or prison, and as such had been unable to cultivate a following amongst the French political *élite*, who furthermore regarded his idiosyncratic ideas with a good deal of scepticism. The Emperor's weakness was clearly identified by Guizot:

> Risings are put down with soldiers, elections are won with peasants, but soldiers and peasants are not enough to govern; one also needs the assistance of the upper classes, who are by nature governing classes. The latter, however, are generally hostile to the president.

Napoleon III
In 1853 Napoleon had married Eugénie de Montijo, a Spanish noblewoman and a considerable beauty with whom the Emperor had become infatuated. She gave birth to a son in 1856, thereby helping to establish (or so Napoleon III hoped) an imperial dynasty, but her political instincts were fiercely reactionary, and her increasing interference in politics (especially in 1870) weakened the Emperor.

Napoleon III had rely on politicians and administrators who had first made their mark in Orleanist days, and who often remained Orleanist in their political outlook. Sometimes they used their positions – especially on the Council of State – to slow down things down or dilute some of the Emperor's more idiosyncratic schemes. Furthermore, their hold on power was strengthened by the liberalisation of the Empire after 1860, with its increase in the influence of the Legislative Body, and decrease in the prerogatives of the Emperor.

Similar constraints were evident in the *Departments*. Although the Prefect might be regarded as a 'little Emperor', it was a brave man who took on the local *élites*. The wealth, standing and influence of the 'notables' made it much easier to govern with them than against them. The prefects were mostly notables themselves, and the notables provided most of the deputies for the Legislative Assembly.

Finally, there was the Emperor himself. No one after December 1851 was likely to mistake him for a 'cretin'. But neither was he a Gladstone, a Cavour or a Bismarck. Napoleon III had vision – but too rarely the drive, determination and attention to detail see a project through. By 1860, he seemed prematurely old. A taste for wine and women, as well as the pressures of office, had taken their toll, and illness (he suffered agonisingly from gout and gallstones) debilitated him further. He began to lose his grip, and his misjudgements piled up. By the summer of 1870, he was losing control: of the Legislative Assembly; of his politically interfering wife; of his ministers; and of the army.

KEY ISSUE

To what extent can Napoleon III be described as a dictator?

5 ➷ ECONOMIC TRENDS IN THE SECOND EMPIRE

Napoleon III was very interested in 'the social question'. He believed that economic expansion and prosperity were the keys to breaking out of the cycle of revolution and repression which had afflicted France since 1789. He spelled out part of his programme in a famous speech at Bordeaux (October 1852), in which his schemes for road, railway and canal building became a list of 'conquests to make'. Guizot had already preached *enrichissez-vous*. But far more than Guizot, the Emperor believed that the state had a major role to play in the economy. There was no question of 'nationalisation' or adopting a centralised economic plan. But Napoleon III did believe that the state should stimulate and facilitate economic growth. Possibly the Emperor was influenced in his social thinking by Saint-Simon, an early French socialist.

Certainly some of the most dynamic and innovative figures in the Second Empire – financiers like the Pèreire brothers, the influential economist Michel Chevalier, and Baron Haussmann, Prefect of the Seine – were Saint-Simonians. Much of the expansion of credit, railways, industry, trade, and the rebuilding of Paris in this period – arguably the most significant achievements of the Second Empire – derived from them:

See the exercise on page 153

Saint-Simon Saint-Simon (1760–1824) was a social theorist who believed that the state should be controlled by scientists and entrepreneurs. His ideas were mixed up with eccentric religious teachings, and Saint-Simon himself spent some time in a lunatic asylum But he had practical ideas too – for example, massive state investment in public works – and his meritocratic vision of society inspired many Frenchmen.

● *Railways.* The most successful example of state intervention was the dramatic expansion of France's railway network: a mere 3248 kilometres in 1851; 16 465 kilometres by 1869. The state played a vital role by extending operating leases (thereby increasing profitability), promoting mergers and guaranteeing shareholders dividends when the companies began to build the potentially less profitable branch-line networks in the early 1860s. The 'knock-on' effects were spectacular. The demands made on engineering, iron and steel, and coal production led to growth rates in these sectors of over 6 per cent a year. Transport costs were slashed by 80 per cent, and the regionalism characteristic of the French economy was shattered. This enabled many French peasants to abandon near-subsistence types of agriculture and – for example, like the wine-makers of the Languedoc – begin to produce for urban markets, including Paris. Equally, the outside world could now more readily penetrate rural France, whether to deliver fertiliser (thereby increasing yields and profitability) or to distribute books and journals, thus making the peasantry, perhaps for the first time, part of a national culture.
● *Banking.* The Second Empire saw a partially successful revolution in the French banking system. For the first time, banks were set up

which aimed to attract the small investor and channel savings towards enterprises such as railway building and urban redevelopment. The most famous of these was *Crédit Mobilier*, founded by the Pèreire brothers.

● *Free Trade.* The boldest single economic initiative undertaken by Napoleon III was his backing for the free trade treaty between Britain and France negotiated by Michael Chevalier in 1860. It was designed to lower the cost of food (cheaper imports), and increase exports (France was particularly competitive in the luxury goods sector) as well as to improve Anglo-French diplomatic relations at a time of near crisis.

● *Haussmann and Paris.* Napoleon III also gave his full support to the plans of Baron Haussmann, the dynamic but rather unscrupulous Prefect of the Seine, for the redevelopment of Paris. Much of the ancient centre, with its dirty, winding streets, was knocked down, and replaced by grand boulevards, which served to connect the new railway stations. The gigantic project served diverse purposes: (i) job creation – at its peak, the process of 'Haussmannisation' directly employed about 20 per cent of all Paris' workers; (ii) public health – central Paris was at last given a proper sewage system (so impressive, it even became a tourist attraction!); (iii) public order – the new wider streets, impossible to barricade, would be easier to control in the event of riot; (iv) prestige – Paris was to be made into Europe's most magnificent capital, a fitting stage for the diplomatic triumphs by which Napoleon III expected to raise France to the standing of Europe's greatest Power.

See page 137

KEY ISSUE

Why and how did Napoleon III aim to promote economic growth?

Together, this was an ambitious programme, and it was initially successful. It helped that the world economy was buoyant, spurred on by major gold finds in California and Australia. But perhaps the most important single cause of the economic growth of the 1850s was the surge of business confidence that sprang from the establishment and consolidation of the Second Empire itself: Napoleon III had made property safe from the Reds!

In the 1860s, the economic scene started to cloud over. The railway boom ended in 1864. *Crédit Moblier*, having overstretched itself and facing fierce competition from traditional bankers like the Rothschilds, had to be rescued, practically bankrupt, by the *Banque de France* in 1867. The free trade treaty of 1860 proved immensely controversial, with old-fashioned producers in the textiles and metal sectors badly hit by British competition. They found effective spokesmen like Thiers to put the case for protectionism and thus damage Napoleon III politically. The high levels of state borrowing produced such anxiety in the financial world that the Emperor had to agree to rein himself in. Finally in 1869, an investigative journalist revealed just how vast and irregularly managed Paris' debts were, and Haussmann was forced to resign.

By the late 1860s, the Saint Simonian dream was looking a little ragged. The social policy associated with Saint-Simonianism seemed to be failing too. The Emperor in 1864 gave workers the right to strike. But he was rewarded by a disturbing wave of industrial disputes, culminating in 1869–70 with bloody clashes between strikers and troops.

Neither had Haussmann's schemes done much for the poor of Paris. Haussmann had merely dispatched them from slums in the centre to slums in the suburbs, where they now faced higher rents and a long walk to and from work. The eruption of the Commune in 1871 would demonstrate that the so-called 'dangerous classes' had not been tamed (one of the Communards' favourite targets was the grasping landlord). Napoleon III's hopes of creating social harmony in Paris and in France's other great cities were to be gravely disappointed.

See page 252

But the failure of the Emperor's social vision was not total. The Second Empire can be divided into two halves: success in the 1850s; mounting difficulties, leading to catastrophe, in the 1860s. Napoleon III's contrasting political fortunes correlate with the Emperor's changing economic fortunes. Average annual industrial growth, for example, was almost 4 per cent between 1850 and 1854; between 1860–5, it was barely 2 per cent; between 1865–70, it was down to 1 per cent. Economic expansion in the 1850s meant that all might share in the Emperor's prosperity. To a remarkable extent, Napoleon III could be all things to all men. However, many businessmen, bankers and workers voiced their discontent in the 1860s. As the opposition vote mounted in general elections; so the Government was forced into political concessions.

Yet a bedrock of political support remained. In the 1863 general elections, 5 308 000 voters supported official candidates – more than had done so in 1852. And the plebiscite endorsing the creation of the Liberal Empire in 1870 was a triumph. It remained vitally important that the Emperor retained the backing of rural France. The Second Empire had been good to the peasant. Railways, political stability, and a Government that guaranteed respect for property all helped. Napoleon III was lucky too: a sustained pattern of emigration to the towns eased pressure for land, allowing wealthier peasants to expand their holdings, whilst a series of bumper crops coincided with high prices. The Emperor, it seemed, made the sun shine.

See pages 145–6

The political implications of this were significant. Although Napoleon III could rarely rely on the support of urban workers, and his command of the notables and the bourgeoisie depended on how badly these easily frightened classes feared the peril of red anarchy, he seemed to be able to retain the loyalty of most of the French peasants. Their sheer numbers made this crucial in elections. As an old Republican exclaimed, 'The Peasants! That's where every government must get its greatest support! The peasants will defend Napoleon less out of sympathy than out of self-interest. They form a mass of 20 or 22 million individuals. That's a formidable army, and it would be a fine thing to command it'.

The Emperor's programme of political and economic 'conquests' were therefore far from complete; but he seemed safe as long as he retained peasant support.

KEY ISSUE

To what extent did Napoleon III fulfil the objectives of his economic policy?

6 ⌒ 1852–61: FROM TRIUMPH TO UNCERTAINTY

Between 1852 and 1856, Napoleon III appeared invulnerable. The plebiscites of 1851 and 1852 had given massive endorsement to the *coup* and to the foundation of the Empire itself. Political opposition was cowed and seemingly broken, with over 6000 Republicans either in jail or exile. Thousands more were kept under surveillance; radical teachers faced the sack; and newspaper editors experienced strict censorship and the ever present threat of closure. But to most French people, the Second Empire had positive aspects too. Increasing prosperity and – at last! – political stability, made the Government widely popular. The Duke of Morny, a central figure in imperial politics until his death in 1865, quipped: 'this country is so tired of revolutionaries that all it wants today is a good despotism – and that's just what it's got'.

A *The foreign policy of Napoleon III and the Crimean War*

Napoleon III first turned his attention to foreign policy. Despite his promise that 'the Empire means peace', France was soon at war. It seemed to have least at stake, strategically speaking, in the Eastern Question. Nevertheless, fighting Russia in the Crimean War fitted in well with the main objectives of Napoleon's foreign policy.

See pages 26–8

THE PRINCIPLES OF NAPOLEONIC FOREIGN POLICY

The Emperor's guiding obsession was the overturning of the detested Vienna Settlement. It was bad enough that it was built on the ruins of the work of Napoleon I. But the territorial settlement it imposed on Europe was itself intolerable. It put France in a straightjacket. It had been forced to give up strategically vital frontier regions, and was also confronted by a *cordon sanitaire* (from Piedmont in the south to Belgium in the north) designed to make it impossible for France to expand its 'natural frontiers' – that is the Rhine and the Alps. Napoleon III repeatedly made moves for territories along this sensitive corridor (successfully so with regard to Savoy, but ultimately disappointed in his bids for Luxembourg and Belgium). In addition to hopes of territorial expansion, the French saw themselves ideologically as in the vanguard of civilisation with a mission to liberate the oppressed peoples of Europe. The causes of 'Poland' and 'Italy' were especially close to Napoleon's heart. He seemed to believe that a Europe of peoples constituting their own nation states would be a Europe of freedom and harmony. French diplomacy (or, if necessary, French arms) could ease the continent's transition to this new era, whilst by-passing the bloodshed of revolution and terror.

See page 195

Together, territorial expansion and *la politique des nationalités* would win *la gloire* for the new Emperor and his France, thereby satisfying an image of national greatness which (to his considerable cost) Louis Philippe had neglected. Napoleon's destiny – and his nation – demanded it.

Napoleon III was convinced that the key to success was to break up the Holy Alliance and forge a friendship with Britain. France had been defeated in 1814–15 because it had had to fight a Great Power coalition of Russia, Austria, Prussia and Britain. Over the following decades, Britain – more liberal than her central and eastern European allies – had drifted out of 'the Waterloo Coalition' into near isolation, leaving the Holy Alliance of Russia, Austria and Prussia to defend the cause of legitimacy. But there were tensions between these three conservative powers – Austria and Prussia were increasingly rivals for influence in Germany, whilst Austria and Russia made uneasy neighbours in the Balkans. Napoleon III exploited these tensions. Austria was his particular target as the most vulnerable of the three Powers. As for Britain, the Emperor argued that one of Napoleon I's few mistakes had been to force this great sea power into remorseless opposition to France. He hoped instead that the success of the foreign policy of the Second Empire would be founded on the friendship of, or even an alliance with, Great Britain.

THE CRIMEAN WAR

Napoleon III managed his first adventure in European diplomacy reasonably well. Just when public opinion was beginning to grow restive at the cost of the expedition (it is estimated that the French army suffered 100 000 casualties), the dramatic capture of Sebastapol had simultaneously brought French troops a share of long-expected glory, and the Russians to the negotiating table. Although France gained no territory from the Peace of Paris, French influence in the Near East had been defended, and French prestige more widely asserted still. Napoleon could project himself as the arbiter of Europe. More importantly, the war had helped precipitate a revolution in European diplomacy. Russia was now hostile to Austria. On the other hand, France's relations with Britain and, perhaps surprisingly, Russia, were cordial (the Russians were grateful to Napoleon III because the latter had pursued the peace settlement in Paris much more energetically than had the British delegation). Old enemies had been divided from each other; new friends had been made. The scene was set for further foreign policy adventures, this time in Italy.

Q

Read the account of the cause, course and consequences of the Crimean War on pages 26–8. Focusing on France's relationships with Britain, Austria and Russia, assess how successfully Napoleon III followed his 'guiding principles' between 1853 and 1856.

B *The Italian adventure*

The disappointing results of the 1857 election for the Legislative Assembly, and Orsini's assassination attempt of January 1858, both probably increased Napoleon III's belief that he needed to do something for the Italian people. Nearly 3.4 million had abstained from voting, and Republican candidates won five of the ten Parisian constituencies. The Orsini bomb outrage which left eight dead and 150 injured, dramatically reminded the Emperor that many old friends felt

See pages 101–2

See pages 96 and 125

See page 102

KEY ISSUE

What does Plombières reveal about the methods and objectives of Napoleon III's foreign policy?

See pages 102–3

deeply betrayed by his political conduct since 1848. Just as French Republicans could not forget the 1851 coup, Italian nationalists felt betrayed by the events of June 1849, when French troops had intervened to restore the Pope.

Intervening on behalf of the cause of nationalism – the moderate nationalism sponsored by Cavour in Piedmont – would pay one debt of honour. It would also align French foreign policy with the internationalist traditions of the Republican Left, and thus give the workers of Paris something patriotic to shout about. This was probably in the mind of Napoleon III, who was conspiratorial by nature, when he made his secret rendezvous with Cavour at the Plombières. The deal satisfied Napoleon's hopes of material gain as well as his sentimental attachment to 'Italy'.

The Pact of Plombières was designed to enlarge Piedmont, through a joint French – Piedmontese campaign against Austria. France was to receive Savoy and Nice for its troubles, ceded from Piedmont. The annexation of Savoy could be justified culturally and geographically – the province was predominantly French speaking and lay to the north of the Alps, thereby arguably falling within France's 'natural frontiers'. No such arguments could justify the annexation of Nice, which Cavour and the Piedmontese King only reluctantly agreed to at the Treaty of Turin (January 1859), whereby the terms negotiated months earlier were ratified.

Napoleon was determined that the alliance be cemented by the marriage of Prince Napoleon to King Victor Emmanuel's daughter. They were to prove an unhappy and singularly ill-matched couple, but the Emperor believed that this close association with the House of Savoy – one of Europe's oldest royal dynasties – would increase the standing of his own family, whose pedigree was rather more recent. But perhaps the most important benefit Napoleon III anticipated from the promotion of the Piedmontese cause was the gratitude of the Government in Turin, which would instinctively turn to France as its friend and protector. The new 'Kingdom of Northern Italy' would be a sort of French satellite. But Napoleon did not want Italian unity. He explained: 'unity would bring danger to me and France itself, because of the Roman question, and France would not see with pleasure a great nation armed on her flank which might diminish her preponderance'.

Plombières began a painful series of lessons for Napoleon III. The business of dismantling the 1815 settlement was fraught with danger. The months between the meeting at Plombières and March 1861, when Victor Emmanuel was proclaimed King of Italy, were marked by hesitations and u-turns on Napoleon's part, and his manifest inability to shape events to his liking. Napoleon III had struck his deal with Cavour without informing his ministers. When details of the alliance emerged, there was widespread dismay – neither France's businessmen nor the Emperor's ministers had much taste for the expense and uncertainties of war, especially one which served a left-wing agenda. Napoleon III seemed to pull back from the idea of conflict, proposing a European Congress instead to explore 'the Italian Question'. But the spectacular blunders of Austrian diplomacy forced the issue. The patriotic fervour in Paris as the

Emperor left for the front on 10 May suggested that he might achieve his aim of securing working class support for the Bonapartist cause.

Only two months later, the Emperor's strategy had been derailed. The victories of Magenta and Solferino had given the French and Piedmontese the upper hand, but on 12 July Napoleon III unilaterally negotiated an armistice with the Austrians. Cavour regarded this as a shameless betrayal. But Napoleon III recognised that the Austrian army was still far from beaten, that Cavour had ambitions to expand Piedmontese territory at the expense of the Pope, and that Prussia was mobilising its army on the Rhine, thereby constituting a possible threat to Paris. The Piedmontese would have to make do with the secession of Lombardy from Austria. With the job only half done, Napoleon III waived any claims to Nice and Savoy.

Had it finished here, Napoleon III could have claimed a partial success for his adventure. But the Italian nationalists were not finished yet:

- The Central Duchies, Papal Romagna and even Tuscany, were clamouring for annexation by Piedmont, even though the truce of Villafranca called for the restoration of these regions' former rulers. A clash seemed inevitable. Instead, Napoleon III reversed his position. Piedmont was allowed to take control of these states and the Emperor was finally rewarded with Savoy and Nice. The real victor, however, was Cavour. He had pushed Piedmont's borders further south than Napoleon III had desired and – to the fury of French Catholics – annexed Papal territory in the process.
- Italian nationalism kicked again. The success of Garibaldi's freelance expedition to Sicily and Naples defied all expectations, and by September had led to the total collapse of Bourbon authority. This development was most unwelcome to Napoleon III. It represented a victory for revolutionary nationalism, whereas the Emperor had always seen himself as the patron of moderate, 'responsible' nationalists – like Cavour. Worse, Garibaldi seemed determined to go on from Naples to attack the Papal States, and make Rome into the capital of a united Italy. The French troops in Rome, who had been the defenders of Papal independence since 1849, would come into conflict with the forces of Italian nationalism.
- Such a collision would be a disaster for Napoleon III. He had no alternative but to sanction Cavour's extraordinary expedition southwards to intercept Garibaldi's army – even though this meant Cavour invading the Papal States! Garibaldi was brought to heel – but as a consequence of these events, Piedmont annexed Sicily and Naples, and all the Pope's territories except Rome itself.

This was not the outcome Napoleon III had planned for in April 1858. He had become the unwitting sponsor of Italian unification. The new state was too big and ambitious to settle for the role of a French satellite – and the presence of the French garrison in Rome, protecting the Pope and an obstacle to full unification, was inevitably a source of antagonism between the two Powers. The impact of unification on

France's domestic politics was largely negative too. The results of the 1863 elections to the Legislative body suggested that Republican enthusiasm for Bonapartism had been short-lived. Worse, many French Catholics were bewildered by the fate of the Papacy in 1860, and deplored the Emperor's betrayal of the Church. The alliance of 'throne and altar', of which the Emperor had helped to lay the foundations with the *Loi Falloux,* was broken. In the Assembly itself, a strongly Catholic deputy demanded: 'are you revolutionary or reactionary? ... It is time to look the Revolution in the face and say to it: you will go no further'. In fact, the whole style of Napoleon III's diplomacy – its secrecy, its wishful thinking, its cloudy objectives, its high risk factor – had startled France's old political *élite.* The question as to how the Emperor might be reined in became increasingly urgent.

KEY ISSUE

Was Napoleon III's intervention in Italy a success?

C *The first instalments of liberalism*

See page 134

Old Orleanists in the Chamber and the Council of State had been concerned by Napoleon III's foreign policy between 1858 and 1860. They were also alarmed by the free trade *coup* of January 1860. Coupled with the free-spending style of government finance, this made many fear that Napoleon III's fiscal and commercial policies needed more careful supervision.

Napoleon III surprised his critics by his response to this developing mood. In November 1860, the Legislative Assembly and the Senate were granted the right to discuss the Emperor's speech (which opened each session). Furthermore, the Emperor promised to arrange for ministers to defend Government policy in the Assembly. An official report of parliamentary debates would now be published. A year later, the Emperor made moves to answer his critics' financial concerns: he publicly acknowledged the dangers of overspending, and appointed Achille Fould, a conservative minded banker, as his Minister of Finance. He also gave the Legislative Body increased powers of control and scrutiny over Government spending.

France was still a long way from becoming a liberal, parliamentary state: ministers were not responsible to the Assembly, and the 1863 election was to be as rigorously managed (although less successfully so) as previous ones had been. But the Emperor's changes did stimulate wider political debate and reduce his freedom of action, in the financial sphere at least. These 'reforms' were followed by further stages of liberalisation: in 1864 the right to strike, in 1867 and 1868 greater freedom of the press, and of public assembly. Finally, in 1870, the Liberal Empire itself proper was inaugurated, with a dramatic overhauling of the Bonapartist constitution.

See pages 145–6

Historians have often debated this trend; since it is unusual for a ruler with semi-dictatorial powers to progressively reduce them. Three explanations have been offered:

● Napoleon III had always intended to liberalise his Government. After all, the Napoleonic legend – of which the Emperor was the most fervent believer – insisted that in 1815 Napoleon I had been planning to give France a truly liberal constitution. When Louis Napoleon had come to power in 1848, France had needed some years of stability and order to purge its destructive passions and begin to grow towards political responsibility. When the Emperor judged the moment right, he would, as he had always intended to, begin to liberalise his regime.

● Liberalisation was a cleverly conceived political strategy, in part a pre-emptive ploy, in part a bid to guarantee the long-term stability of the regime. Sensitive to public criticism, and anxious to defuse it as quickly as possible, Napoleon III's concessions, beginning in 1860, were essentially made from a position of strength. Not the least important aspect of Napoleon III's thinking was dynastic – he was conscious of the relative youth and potential vulnerability of his son (born in 1856), and wanted him to inherit a stable and broadly based regime.

● By contrast, the third interpretation stresses the weaknesses of the regime. By 1860 the threat from the Left had been killed off, and with it the rationale for Napoleon III's 'dictatorship'. Worse, the 'deluge of personal initiatives' [Plessis] which marked the Government's policies between 1858 and 1860 was a deluge of mistakes. According to this interpretation, the Emperor's concessions to liberal opinion marked an increasingly desperate attempt to appease the opposition.

7 ↶ 1861–7: LOSING GROUND

It had been one of the strengths of Bonapartism that it could be 'all things to all men', offering something to every sector of the electorate. But one of the lessons of the confusion into which the Government's foreign and economic policies had fallen between 1858 and 1861 was that some political interest groups would have to be disappointed. For example, committed Catholics and internationalist-minded Republicans were never going to agree about the fate of the Pope's lands in Italy; and the protectionist lobby would always resent free trade. But Napoleon III failed to identify his priorities or follow policies through effectively.

There was a widespread impression that Napoleon III was somehow losing the initiative between 1861 and 1866. The Duke of Morny died in 1865. He had been a versatile operator who, as President of the Assembly, had opened up contacts with liberals and Emile Ollivier, the most talented Republican delegate. Morny's death was a significant blow. The Emperor's own personal health was fragile, gout and gallstones leaving him increasingly depressed and lethargic. The 1863 election results gave him little comfort. Although rural France remained loyal, the opposition vote had increased three-fold since 1857 (it now stood at 1.95 million) and Republicans carried all nine Paris seats. In these circumstances Government policy was likely to come under ever more severe scrutiny. Unfortunately for Napoleon III, a series of foreign policy blunders offered his critics some easy targets to attack. He seemed unable to see the likely consequences of his initia-

See pages 188–97

tives or assess how well they would serve the real interests of France. But it was also his misfortune to come up against Bismarck, who in 1862 began his three decades of making policy in Berlin. Bismarck was to display the ruthlessness, judgement and superabundance of energy which the French Emperor increasingly seemed to lack.

A *Mexico*

In 1861, Napoleon III embarked on an extraordinary expedition to Mexico. What began as a joint debt-collecting exercise with Britain and Spain (a new revolutionary Government in Mexico had suspended all payments to foreign creditors) became a campaign of would-be imperial conquest. This was Napoleon III at his most visionary, and least practical. The idea seemed inspired: Mexico promised to be a land of rich opportunity for French businessmen; French Catholics would warmly support a crusade against the Mexican revolution, which was proving to be viciously anti-clerical; and the successful colonisation of a massive territory in central America would have a dramatic impact on France's standing in the world and on Napoleon III's own prestige. In reality, the affair was a grotesque disaster. By 1866 up to 40 000 French troops were losing the struggle against Mexican guerrillas. At the end of the American Civil War in 1865, the United States made it clear that the Mexicans would enjoy their full backing in clearing the continent of European imperialists. The final humiliation came after the withdrawal of French forces, with the capture and execution of Archduke Maximillian of Austria in May 1867. He had gone to Mexico to rule the colony on Napoleon III's behalf. The Mexican fiasco did immense damage to the French Emperor's reputation: it is the clearest example of his tendency to confuse the verb 'to dream' with the verb 'to think'.

B *Britain*

Friendship with Britain had been one of the key elements of Napoleon III's diplomatic strategy. But after 1859, relations between London and Paris distinctly cooled. The British had been dismayed at the Emperor's intervention in Italy, and especially by the annexation of Saxony and Nice. The French, it seemed, were manoeuvring for their 'national frontiers' and could not be trusted. Their worst suspicions would be confirmed in 1870, when the Prussians cleverly leaked a deal proposed by the French in 1866 involving the annexation of Belgium.

See page 196

C *Austria and Prussia*

However, increasing tensions between Austria and Prussia in 1865 seemed to offer Napoleon III every opportunity of recovering the initiative. Whilst these two Powers, competing together for the mastery of 'Germany', squared up to each other, Napoleon III proceeded to auction his goodwill to the higher bidder. In April 1866, he was instrumental in setting up the Italo-Prussian alliance, by which Italy would be rewarded with Venetia in the case of Austria's defeat. But on the eve of war itself, in reward for the promise of French neutrality, Austria promised to cede Venetia to Italy if Austria won. The Emperor had deviously sold France to both sides! Whichever won the war, Italy would get Venetia, and (Rome notwithstanding), Victor Emmanuel would be deep in Napoleon III's debt. But France could reasonably expect important gains itself. As a consequence of the war, the boundaries of central Europe were likely to be extensively redrawn. France would help to broker the peace at an international conference, and the combatants, victor and vanquished alike, would be too exhausted to object to whatever territorial 'commission' Napoleon III charged for his services. Indeed, at Biarritz in October 1865, the Emperor and Bismarck had already reviewed options for French expansion in the event of Prussian victory.

But the outcome of the war caught the experts by surprise. They had been certain of a long and bloody campaign, and saw Austria as the likely winner. Instead, the Prussian army finally trounced the Austrians at the Battle of Königgrätz in a war that lasted only seven weeks.

Prussia's overwhelming victory caused consternation in Paris, and forced upon the Emperor the single most vital choice of his reign: should France intervene on the side of Austria to restore the balance of power in central Europe, or should he maintain neutrality? After agonised debates, Napoleon III decided France would remain neutral. He had doubts about the readiness of his army, and knew that many of his best troops were in Algeria and Mexico. He had also been kept very closely informed that popular opinion in France was against war. But perhaps most important of all were sentimental and ideological considerations. How could a man whose life had been dedicated to the overthrow of the Vienna settlement and to the support of everything that was progressive in nineteenth century Europe – 'Napoleonic Ideas' embraced nationalism, democracy, even socialism – now side with Austria, the embodiment of everything he loathed?

Bismarck did not give Napoleon III a chance for second thoughts. Quickly offering the Austrians a generous peace, he ended the war. And when the Emperor's representatives arrived to discuss 'compensation' for France, Bismarck indignantly refused. Indeed, he made sure that the still independent states of southwest Germany learnt of France's expansionist ambitions along the Rhine. They were thus persuaded to join a defensive pact with Prussia – a factor of decisive importance in 1870.

See pages 191 and 194

Until early July, Napoleon III had seemed to play his hand in the Austro-Prussian crisis well. There had been every expectation that France would gain in prestige and territory at no risk or expense to itself. But Prussian arms and Bismarck's diplomacy deprived the Emperor of any advantage. The verdict of France's Marshal Randon – 'it is we who were beaten at Königgrätz' – soon became the common view. Thiers gave a sharp warning to the Government. 'I tell you', he told the Assembly, 'there is not a single blunder left to commit'. Napoleon III had stood to one side and allowed a potential superpower to emerge on France's border. The next mistake would spell disaster for the Bonaparte dynasty – and perhaps for France itself.

KEY ISSUE

'There is not a single blunder left to make'. How accurate was Thiers' verdict on French foreign policy?

8 ⌒ 1867–70: DISAPPOINTMENTS, RECOVERY AND CATASTROPHE

In 1867, Napoleon III had two main foreign policy objectives:

● to gain some 'compensation' for France along the Rhine so as to partially restore the power-differential between France and Prussia
● to escape from what was looking like an increasingly dangerous and isolated position in Europe.

Napoleon failed in both objectives.

Details of the Emperor's abortive plans to purchase the Duchy of Luxembourg from the King of Holland can be found on page 195. Whether or not Bismarck consciously led Napoleon III on, only to publicly veto the scheme and so re-establish his own credentials as the hero of German nationalism, is difficult to determine. But it was yet another humiliation for France at the hands of Prussia. In Paris, an appetite for revenge was building up.

A *Austria*

The search for an ally now became urgent. The rise of Prussia presented an unmistakable threat. It seemed likely that Prussia would soon try to absorb the remaining independent states of southwest Germany, thereby completing the process of unification. When the military treaties these states had signed with Prussia in August 1866 became public knowledge, Napoleon III was further embarrassed. It was time to suspend the costly *politique de nationalités*, and explore the potential of an alliance with Austria.

Negotiations between Paris and Vienna began in earnest in November 1868. Right to the eve of the outbreak of the Franco-Prussian War, French diplomats were confident of success. There was a powerful mood in Austria of 'revenge for Königgrätz'. But a Franco-Austrian alliance against Prussia would have been dangerous for both countries. When Gramont, French Foreign Minister in 1870, told the Austrian ambassador on the eve of the Franco-Prussian War that 'Austria [would] march with us if she knew her own interests', Austria decided that its own interests lay in neutrality.

See page 196

B *Domestic stalemate: the politics of army reform*

Napoleon III's search for security was also frustrated at home. The Emperor had long been anxious at the inefficiency and relatively small size (in practice, barely 400 000 men) of the French army. Prussia could now mobilise a force of 750 000. Napoleon instructed his Minister of War, Marshal Niel, to draw up plans of reform. The key features included raising the full fighting force to 1 million by:

- making conscription universal by preventing middle-class parents from buying their sons out of military service by paying for a substitute
- improving the reserve
- creating a new militia.

Niel's scheme provoked a storm of protest. Republicans and ex-Orleanists were suspicious of any plans to increase the size of the peace time army – after all, it was not unknown in recent history for French troops to be turned on French civilians! Taxpayers were dismayed by the expense, and middle class taxpayers by the prospect of their sons' conscription too. Even the generals were suspicious – the vastly expanded numbers would dilute the supposed 'professionalism' of the army. By January 1868 the plans had effectively been dropped. Angry debates in parliament had seen at least one prophetic exchange. A Republican had demanded of the Government: 'Do you want to turn France into a barracks?'. 'Take care', came the reply, 'that you don't turn it into a cemetery'.

This episode offers 'a vivid demonstration of the regime's enfeeblement' [Plessis]. Napoleon was unable to push through a measure vital for the security of the French nation, in contrast to Bismarck's robust handling of the constitutional crisis precipitated by von Roon's plans in Prussia. France resented the rise of Prussia, but was unwilling to make the preparations necessary for a future conflict. Napoleon III's subjects seemed trapped by 'an idea of national grandeur for which [they] no longer wished to pay the price' [Furet]. Yet after the catastrophe of 1870, the French people made Napoleon III, the scapegoat, blaming his incompetence for leading them to such a defeat.

> **KEY ISSUE**
>
> *How well prepared was France to confront Prussia in 1870?*

C Recovery? Emile Ollivier and the birth of the Liberal Empire

The 1869 elections were the most open ever fought in the Second Empire, and they marked a further erosion of Napoleon III's authority: 4.44 million votes for the Government, 3.36 million votes for opposition candidates. In the new Assembly, although the Government faced the irreconcilable opposition of only 25 radical Republicans, it could only count on the unswerving support of (at most) 80 die-hard Bonapartists. Between the two extremes was a spectrum of over 180 deputies, some Bonapartist, some Orleanist, some Republican, but all hoping for a sign that Napoleon III was ready to recast the Second Empire in a more liberal form.

Emile Ollivier took the lead in marshalling support amongst liberals and Bonapartists for an appeal to Napoleon III '[to involve] the country more effectively in the management of its affairs' and to 'form a cabinet responsible to the Emperor and the Chamber'. A total of 116 deputies backed the motion – and Napoleon III responded positively. Between September 1869 and April 1870, the constitution was redesigned along more liberal lines, and in December, the Emperor invited Ollivier 'to indicate the persons who can form a united cabinet faithfully representative of the majority in the Legislative Body'. The new constitution was overwhelmingly approved in a plebiscite held in May 1870 (7.35 million votes for, 1.54 million votes against). Napoleon III was delighted, and looked forward to passing on the crown to his son. The dynasty seemed secure.

The main objective of the creation of the liberal Empire seemed to have been fulfilled. Some historians have argued that the Emperor had succeeded in destroying the mounting opposition: moderate liberals, led by Ollivier, were now on board; more aggressive ones like Thiers had been left stranded; militant Republicans were isolated. Had Napoleon III not been defeated at Sedan, the Second Empire might have survived indefinitely.

However, there are different interpretations. From the start, the Liberal Empire was riddled with tensions and contradictions, which themselves go a long way to account for the blunders of French foreign policy in the summer of 1870:

- Ollivier was a magnificent speaker, and a man of principle and integrity – despite savage criticism from some of his old republican colleagues. But he was infuriatingly conceited and over confident. His tactlessness, inexperience and poor man-management led some observers to predict the rapid fall of his ministry.
- Ollivier's coalition of liberals and Bonapartists was pulling in two very different directions. Hard-line Bonapartists, amongst whom the Empress Eugenie was increasingly prominent, wondered if too many concessions had been made to the Left. They read the May plebiscite as a personal victory for the Emperor himself, and as such the possible starting point of a more authoritarian style of government. But Liberals, in contrast, were not certain that Napoleon III had conceded enough.
- Some features of the Empire did seem liberal. The Legislative Body was to share with the Emperor the power of initiating legislation, and it was also given greater control over taxation. But other elements were at best confusing, and at worst dangerous. The crucial issue of ministerial responsibility was left ambiguous: could the Emperor appoint or keep in office an unpopular minister? Could the Chamber force on the Emperor a minister or a ministry of which he disapproved? There was no clear answer. But the constitution still gave the Emperor considerable personal authority. He remained commander-in-chief of the armed forces, and presided over his ministers' deliberations (Ollivier was not the Prime Minister). He could also veto legislation. All this was a long way from the true liberal's dream of a monarch who 'reigned but did not rule'. Above all, Napoleon III had kept his right to call a plebiscite, thus enabling him to appeal directly to the people over the heads of ministers or deputies. The Second Empire therefore retained its predecessor's potential for '**Caesarism**'.

Therefore liberals, who instinctively distrusted the power of the executive and the people's passions, were still suspicious of the constitution.

Caesarism a style of government combining elements of dictatorship and populism. A leading figure, often backed by the army, overrides the constitution and appeals directly to the people, playing on their irrational fears and longings to whip up mass support

A pessimistic interpretation of the prospects for the Liberal Empire might be that:

● Ollivier was a weak leader
● there was an influential 'court' faction already scheming to restore a more authoritarian regime
● the constitution retained a powerful demagogic element, magnifying the Emperor's power but also leaving him vulnerable to the moods of the 'vile multitude'.

These weaknesses came to the fore in the weeks leading up to the Franco-Prussian War.

KEY ISSUE

What was liberal about the Liberal Empire, and to what extent was Napoleon III strengthened by its creation?

9 ~ THE PATH TO CATASTROPHE: RESPONSIBILITIES

The main focus in this section will be an assessment of responsibility for the declaration of war against Prussia.

● Napoleon III. The events of July revealed that a vacuum existed where the head of the French executive should have been. Illness and premature old age were partly to blame, but there were failures of judgement too (e.g. a lack of realism about the readiness of the army or the likelihood of an Austrian alliance). Napoleon also authorised Gramont's reckless demand that Prussia back down, thereby increasing the unthinking patriotic fervour of French public opinion.
● The Duke of Gramont. The Duke of Gramont was appointed Foreign Minister in May 1870. His passionate concern to defend the honour of France was not matched by a carefully thought through strategy about how this might be achieved. His experience as ambassador in Vienna led him to believe, wrongly, that the anti-Prussian party there would gain the upper hand should war break out between France and Prussia. Instead, France's isolation was to remain complete.

  Gramont also made tactical blunders. For example, his speech to the Legislative Assembly on 6 July was megaphone diplomacy at its worst. If the Hohenzollern candidacy were not withdrawn, he proclaimed, '... we shall know how to do our duty without faltering or weakening'. This very public threat of war delighted the Bonapartist right, but it made the task of negotiating a way out of the crisis more difficult, as well as stirring all the wrong passions in the French press and on the streets of Paris. Another blunder was Gramont's insistence to the French ambassador to Prussia, repeated over 12–13 July, that he secure from Wilhelm I an absolute guarantee that Prussia had no intention of ever again renewing the Hohenzollern candidacy. France had been on the verge of a significant diplomatic victory – Wilhelm had earlier given his personal assurance that the candidacy had been withdrawn – but now the Prussian King felt his honour affronted. He declined, and Bismarck's version of the exchange was published in the 'Ems Telegram'. Gramont's response on receipt of

A full narrative and analysis of the road to war can be found in Chapter 6, pages 193–7

See pages 196–7

For descriptions of the course of the war, culminating in the overwhelming Prussian victory at Sedan (2 September 1870) and the Siege of Paris (September 1870–January 1871) see pages 197–8

TIMELINE

1870: the road to war

February	Bismarck took up the Hohenzollern candidacy – a plan to put a German prince on the vacant Spanish throne
15 May	Gramont became French Foreign Minister
21 June	Madrid was informed that Prince Leopold of Hohenzollern was happy to accept offer of the Spanish throne
2 July	News of the Hohenzollern candidacy was accidentally leaked
6 July	Gramont's speech to the Legislative Body threatened war unless the Hohenzollern candidacy was dropped
9 July	At Bad Ems, Benedetti (the French Ambassador to Prussia) urged Wilhelm I to persuade Leopold to withdraw; although non-committal, the King's response was encouraging
12 July	Leopold's father announced his son's withdrawal
13 July	Gramont instructed Benedetti to extract from Wilhelm I a further promise that the candidacy would not be renewed; Wilhelm I, fearing that further concessions would compromise his honour, politely declined
	Bismarck then received a telegram from Wilhelm I's aide describing this exchange; his edited version, giving the impression that Benedetti had been insolent and duly rebuffed, was published
14 July	Against a background of mounting public indignation in Paris, Gramont, supported by the Empress, and finally with the approval of Ollivier, persuaded Napoleon III to declare war

this was characteristic: 'My dear man', he exclaimed on the morning of 14 July to Ollivier, 'you see before you a man who has just received a slap in the face'. The mood in the Chamber and in Paris was one of fury – Bismarck had indeed shown 'the red rag to the Gallic bull'. War was declared five days later. Gramont had turned triumph to disaster in under a week. Perhaps Bismarck was right to call him 'the stupidest man in Europe'.

● *Emille Ollivier.* Ollivier was one of the least belligerent of French politicians, and he sincerely hoped for friendship with Prussia. But he was acutely sensitive to any slight to France's honour, and, worse, had an exaggerated sense of his own duty to defend it. He was all too conscious of leading a Government which was at last responsible and accountable to the Legislative Assembly and the people of France.

See the bibliography on page 152

KEY ISSUE

Which French politician should bear the greatest responsibility for the outbreak of the Franco-Prussian war?

Neither Ollivier, nor Gramont, nor the Emperor seemed capable of recognising where France's true interests lay or of calculating dispassionately the likely consequences of their actions. As Carr concludes in *The Origins of the Wars of German Unification*, 'that three emotionally unstable people should have been thrown together in positions of power at this crucial juncture was a tragedy for France'.

10 ᭩ EVALUATING NAPOLEON III AND THE SECOND EMPIRE

A *Foreign policy*

Sedan appeared to be the final fruit of the fundamental contradictions and incoherence of the Bonapartist vision in foreign policy. The Emperor desired both to rekindle France's mission to the people of Europe and to reassert the primacy of France, *la grande nation*. The two objectives proved hard to combine, and their simultaneous pursuit produced a string of failures. *La politique des nationalités* did nothing for the Poles, accidentally created a state (and an ungrateful one too) for the Italians, and left France a bewildered bystander as Bismarck began to turn Prussia into Germany. Equally, France's hunger for expansion and glory had led it to Mexico and back; frightened the states of south-west Germany into Prussian embrace; and by 1870, had left Britain disdainful of the fate of the country which had gobbled up Nice and Savoy and greedily eyed Belgium. Isolation; contempt; defeat: Sedan.

See page 198

Such a verdict might be harsh. It was Napoleon III's misfortune to be playing the game of Great Power diplomacy at the same time as Cavour and Bismarck, both cleverer and more unscrupulous than himself. Cavour did Napoleon III comparatively little damage – the Italy created in 1861 was radically different from that envisaged by Plombières, but Napoleon III could live with it, even if Rome were a considerable irritant. But Bismarck was more than an irritant. He showed infinite resourcefulness combined with a total lack of principle, underpinned by a breathtaking capacity for taking risks after carefully calculating the odds. Napoleon III was no fool, but at vital moments he let sentiment, or the pressure of public opinion, shape the course of French foreign policy. The old *Carbonari* in Louis Napoleon compelled him to get involved in 'Italy'; the proponent of *la politique des nationalitiès* could not align himself with Austria in the immediate aftermath of König-grätz; the last Bonaparte could not let Prussia 'get away with it again' in 1870, and look his people in the face. A true cynic would have played every hand differently.

Bismarck only ever claimed to serve the interests of Hohenzollern dynasty; but the French Emperor had to embody the will of the French people. This gave Napoleon III, at least in theory, great freedom of action: he was answerable to no king and no parliament. But this could also be a trap. 'Caesarism' was not a one-way process. When the mob in the streets of Paris screamed 'to Berlin!', was the Emperor following or leading? Unlike Bismarck, he could never dare treat 'the vile multitude' with contempt.

France's underlying problem was to be found in the legacy of the Revolution. Although the appetite of the French people for war can be exaggerated (there was little enthusiasm for it in 1866) and their reluctance to pay for it was clear (as the rejection of Niel's plans in 1867–8 demonstrated) a longing for *la gloire* remained. This explains the contempt in which Louis-Philippe came to be held, and the continued potency of the Republican and Bonapartist traditions. Paris went mad in 1870. Recalling the mood in France on the eve of the Franco-Prussian war, de Tocqueville's former secretary commented, 'No war was ever embarked upon with such a swelling of pride, such an intense delight in going out to inflict harm, or a more absolute certainty in military superiority. ... Blindness had never been pressed to such limits'. Sedan was not just a verdict on Napoleon III, Gramont and Ollivier: it was the price that had to be paid to purge a whole political culture of its arrogance and chauvinism.

The treaties of 1814–15 which constrained France's borders and frustrated her ambitions were widely detested, and not just by Napoleon III. But with hindsight, it is possible to see that the principle of legitimacy they enshrined also gave her security. The Crimean War had undermined the Vienna Settlement and the Concert of Europe, and Bismarck, Cavour and Napoleon III all treated the concept of 'legitimacy' with amused contempt. Perhaps in 1871, with Paris besieged and under bombardment, and Alsace and Lorraine on the point of annexation, even some Frenchmen might have regarded the passing of the Age of Metternich with regret.

B *Domestic achievements*

Some historians, for example Cobban, have concentrated on economic growth as the most positive aspect of the Second Empire. But economic progress should not be exaggerated. The most innovative and dynamic leaders of imperial modernisation – the Pereire brothers and Baron Haussmann – had themselves crashed before the Empire's own collapse. Ollivier's ministry in 1870 had embarked on the restoration of protectionism – a striking reversal of one of Napoleon III's most important personal economic initiatives. In agriculture – and France remained three-quarters rural in 1870 – the peasant population reached its all time peak in the 1860s. In this sector, innovation spread very slowly. These were years of comparative prosperity and security for the peasantry. But this owed less to any revolution in farming methods than to a combination of high prices, good harvests, the exodus of the poorest sections of the rural community to the towns (easing the pressure on soil resources) and the expanding railway network (which meant that any subsistence crises – such as those of 1853–6 – could be readily alleviated). In manufacturing the characteristic site of production, despite striking advances in the key mining, metallurgical and engineering sectors, was still the workshop rather than the factory, and the overall employer – worker ratio remained 1:3. Railways and 'Haussmannisation' notwithstanding, it is difficult to overemphasise the weight of conservatism and tradition in a society where peasants and artisans still predominated.

Napoleon III's domestic record was not one of complete failure. Economic growth, combined with a Government sympathetic to the plight of the workers, was supposed to enable France to escape from the cycle of class war and revolution in which it seemed to be trapped. However, the fate of two imperial initiatives shows their limitations. Large-scale public works, notably the rebuilding of the centre of Paris, had done much in the 1850s to eliminate the chronic urban unemployment. But Fould's appointment as Minister of Finance, coupled with the escalating expense of paying for an overambitious foreign policy, dramatically restricted domestic public spending. Equally, the liberalisation of anti-trade union legislation was not a success. It helped to unleash a torrent of labour militancy. The strikes of 1869 and 1870 were bitter and bloody. Major public order disturbances in Paris were fired by a mixture of class resentment and revolutionary sentiment. Christophe Charle, one of France's leading social historians, has argued that such episodes, provoked 'the rebirth of social fear amongst the bourgeoisie [and] revived memories of June 1848'. The seeds of the Commune can easily be found in the streets of Paris in 1870. Napoleon III had manifestly failed to solve 'the social question'.

For example the law of 1864 – see page 134

See pages 135 and 152

What of the apparently progressive liberalisation of the regime after 1860? Despite high flown talk of 'crowning the edifice of order with liberty', in practice Napoleon III was very reluctant to give up any of his powers. The reforms of 1867 and 1868 seemed grudging: a case of too little too late. The creation of the Liberal Empire in 1869–70 was, arguably, more a concession forced out of a Government whose weaknesses and blunders were manifest on every front (Königgrätz, Mexico, army reform, Haussmann), than a gracious gift made by the Emperor to his people in recognition to their increasing political maturity. Significant weaknesses in the design of the Liberal Empire were soon glaringly obvious too.

Napoleon III must be credited with at least one major achievement. Against all expectation, he survived in power for two decades. Thiers' judgement of the Emperor as a 'cretin' who would easily be managed was misplaced. Critics took his intellectual idiosyncrasies for stupidity, and they completely underestimated his political skills. The Emperor was shrewd, resourceful and difficult to outmanoeuvre – and, as Republicans learnt in December 1851 – he could be ruthless too. With a mixture of sly tenacity, evasiveness and intrigue, he had an annoying habit – in the 1850s at least – of getting his own way. As a friend of Thiers reflected with startled disbelief, 'this idiot is endowed with a rare and powerful faculty of making his own mark on things ... He brings his imagination to bear on the world's affairs, and produces or modifies events according to his fancy'.

Napoleon III left less of a mark on the world, however, than he hoped to. In part this reflected his own personal limitations; in part it reflected the constraints of his political situation, especially the absence of a determined body of Bonapartists to carry out his will. But he never became a prisoner of the old *élites*. Historians like Furet and Zeldin suggest that his support for, and management of, democratic politics might be considered both his greatest achievement and most significant legacy. Of course, many aspects of the democratic process were unsavoury, with bribery, gerrymandering and intimidation rife. Napoleon III showed that democracy could be reconciled to authority and order even if the cost were substantial electoral corruption. Neither Thiers nor any of his successors were able to roll back the popular tide: they would have to work with 'the vile multitude'. From 1851, the political culture of France has been ineradicably democratic. Democracy and railways proved to be Napoleon III's greatest gifts to France. Do they compensate for his greatest failure: his inability to check the rise of Prussia?

11 ➤ BIBLIOGRAPHY

France: Monarchy, Republic and Europe, 1814–70 by K. Randall (Hodder and Stoughton, 1991) is a clear introduction. *Second Empire and Commune: France 1848–1871* by W. Smith (Longman Seminar Studies, 1985) also includes some documents. A more recent and more demanding assessment is *Napoleon III and the Second Empire* by R. Price (Routledge Lancaster Pamphlets, 1997). Broader surveys include *A History of Modern France*, vol. 2, *1799–1871* by A. Cobban (Penguin) and an important study, *France 1814–1914* by R. Tombs (Longman 1996). The best modern biography is *Napoleon III* by J. McMillan (Longman Profiles in Power, 1991). The chapter on 'Bonapartism' in the multi-volume *France 1848–1945* by T. Zeldin (Oxford, 1973, 1979) is also useful. *A Social History of France 1780–1880* by P. McPhee (Routledge, 1992) covers social history; and *The Struggle for Mastery in Europe 1848–1918* by A.J.P Taylor (Oxford, 1954) covers diplomatic history. Three challenging surveys by French historians are *The Republican Experiment 1848–1852* by M. Agulhon (Cambridge, 1983); *The Rise and Fall of the Second Empire 1852–1871* by A. Plessis (Cambridge, 1985); and *Revolutionary France 1770–1880* by F. Furet (Basil Blackwell, 1992).

12 ➤ STRUCTURED QUESTIONS AND ESSAYS

1. (a) Outline the stages by which Louis Napoleon established the Second Empire in France by 1852; (10 marks)
   (b) How do you account for the ease with which Louis Napoleon established himself in power? (15 marks)
2. (a) Outline Napoleon III's domestic policies inside France between 1852 and 1869; (10 marks)
   (b) To what extent did the Second Empire become more liberal before its collapse in 1870? (15 marks)
3. (a) What were the main developments in Napoleon III's foreign policy between 1852 and the outbreak of the Franco-Prussian War; (10 marks)
   (b) How successful was Napoleon III's foreign policy? (15 marks)
4. 'All bluster and no substance.' How valid is this judgement on Napoleon III's reign as Emperor of France? (25 marks)

5. To what extent was Napoleon III responsible for his own downfall? (25 marks)
6. How successful was the development of the French economy during the Second Empire? (25 marks)

13 ⌐ THE SECOND EMPIRE: A SOURCES EXERCISE

Study Sources A–E and answer the questions which follow.

Napoleon III: the Empire means peace?

Some people are saying to themselves, 'the Empire means war'. For me, I say, 'the Empire means peace'. I admit that, as emperor, I have a good many conquests to make. In that role, I want to win over dissident parties to reconciliation and to bring back into the flow of the great popular river those hostile currents which are lost without benefiting anyone.

I want to win over to religion, to morality and to comfortable circumstances that still numerous part of the population who, in the midst of a country of faith and belief, are barely aware of the precepts of Christ; who, in the bosom of the most fertile land in the world, can scarcely enjoy the bare necessities of life.

We have immense tracts of uncultivated land to clear, roads to open, ports to create, rivers to make navigable, canals to finish and our railway network to complete. Facing Marseilles, we have a vast kingdom to assimilate to France. We have all our great western ports to bring closer to the American continent by the speed of those communications which we still lack. Everywhere we have ruins to restore, false gods to cast down and truths to bring to triumph.

That is how I would see the Empire, if the Empire is to be re-established. These are the conquests I am contemplating, and all of you, surrounding me now, who desire, as I do, the good of our nation – you are my soldiers.'

SOURCE A
Napoleon III speaking at Bordeaux – October 1852

SOURCE B (PICTURE 10) *'Napoleon III, the Empress and the Prince Imperial surrounded by their people'. A popular engraving by Flaming (1860?). Note the image of Napoleon I in the background.*

SOURCE C
Napoleon III explains his foreign policy to his ministers, January 1859

If France, while driving the Austrians from Italy, protects the power of the Pope, if it opposes extreme policies and declares that with the exception of Savoy and Nice it is not out for any conquest, then it will have the support of Europe ... Public opinion in Europe will regard the French government not only as the anarchists' ogre [enemy], but as the regime determined to display its strengths at home so as to be able to break its own bonds, to deliver and civilise nations ... On the domestic front, the war will at first awaken great fears; traders and speculators of every stripe will shriek, but national sentiment will put paid to this domestic fright; the nation will be put to the test once more in a struggle that will stir many a heart, recall the memory of heroic times and bring together under the mantle of glory parties that are steadily drifting away from each other day after day.

'[Cavour's record of his negotiations with Napoleon III at Plombières] ... is the refutation of Napoleon's claim that the Empire meant peace. War was never ruled out as a policy option, as he had already demonstrated in the Crimea. Here, too, is the real meaning of the politique des nationalités [policy of nationalities], a pretext for the aggrandisement of France under cover of promoting a limited degree of nationalism. Italy was to be kept divided, not united. France would replace Austria as the dominant influence in northern Italy and reinforce its position as a Mediterranean power. Far from being a contribution to the principle of national self-determination, Plombières was an exercise in the diplomacy of Realpolitik. Napoleon was the true master of the art, with Cavour a mere amateur by comparison. At Plombières he revealed a cynicism, a duplicity, an opportunism and a total absence of any moral sense ... [in a contemporary's phrase] Napoleon III was 'a dreamer, a gambler, a conspirator by taste and habit'.

SOURCE D
James F McMillan, Napoleon III *(Profiles in Power) 1991*

'The fight is, as in 1848, between the Catholic faith, which is both French and Roman, and the revolutionary faith ... But you, who have been imprudent enough to reopen this arena without judging its extent, who are you and what do you want to become? Are you revolutionary? Are you conservative? Step by step, you have retreated before Garibaldi, all the time proclaiming him your greatest enemy ... Come out and tell us just what you are!

'You have asked us to make known all our thoughts, and I will certainly tell you mine. It is time to look the Revolution in the face and say to it: You will go no further!'

SOURCE E
Keller, a Catholic deputy, speaking to the Legislative Body, March 1861

Q

1. *Study Source C. Using this source and your own knowledge explain why Napoleon III argued that France's war against Austria in Italy 'would have the support of Europe'. (6 marks)*
2. *Study Sources A and B. How useful are these two sources to an historian studying the appeal of Napoleon III to the French nation? (6 marks)*
3. *Study Sources A and D. Account for the differences between Source A and Source D as to whether 'the Empire means peace'. (6 marks)*
4. *Using all the Sources A–E, and your own knowledge, assess the validity of the judgement that 'The failure of Napoleon III's foreign policy is rooted in its confused and over-ambitious objectives'. (12 marks)*

Germany
1815–71

The German nation did not exist before 1871. Instead, between 1815 (when it was founded) and 1866 (when it was dissolved), most of German-speaking central Europe was loosely organised in the German Confederation, to which the 38 (39 by 1817) sovereign states of Germany sent their representatives.

This Confederation had little real power, and German nationalists complained bitterly about this. The two main power centres of central Europe were Berlin, capital of Prussia, and Vienna, capital of the Austrian Empire. In 1815, Austria was undoubtedly the more powerful of the two. For the following three decades, through the skilful diplomacy of its Chancellor, Metternich, Austria was mostly able to shape German affairs to its liking. But Metternich, despite his best efforts, was unable to completely stifle the ideas of liberals and nationalists. In the 1848 Revolutions, these liberal and nationalist activists were able to seize power in Prussia and Austria, and all the other German states. Metternich had to flee from Vienna, whilst at Frankfurt, a Parliament was created, aiming to unite all the German people and to guarantee their liberty.

Within a year, a successful counter-revolution had seemingly re-established the old order. But, beneath the surface, important changes were happening. Prussia started to industrialise, and by the 1860s outstripped Austria in wealth. Furthermore, many nationalists, disappointed by the failures of 1848–9, now decided to throw their influence behind Prussia as the Power most likely to unite Germany. Then in 1862, Bismarck became Prussia's Minister President. This ruthless and energetic statesman saw that these developments potentially gave Prussia a decisive advantage. Realising that the Austrians would never recognise Prussia as their equal, he manoeuvred them into war. Prussia's victory in the Seven Weeks War (1866) led to the creation of the (Prussian-dominated) North German Confederation, and to the exclusion of Austrian influence from German affairs. To most nationalists, Bismarck's achievements seemed to be a great step towards unification.

Important states in southern Germany, however, like Bavaria, still remained independent. At first, Bismarck seemed unsure how or when they might be incorporated within his new system. But a diplomatic crisis with France in 1870 – which he had engineered – helped to resolve this problem. When, foolishly, the French declared war on Prussia, all Germans united in a common cause against their traditional enemy. The Prussian army destroyed the French forces at Sedan in

September, and in January 1871, the German *Reich* (Empire) was proclaimed. Germany had been united: not as the consequence of a popular revolution, such as had briefly seemed possible in 1848, but almost as a side effect of Prussia expansionism. Bismarck had effected a 'revolution from above'.

1 ⌐ THE HISTORIOGRAPHY OF GERMAN UNIFICATION

To the first historians of German unification, like Heinrich Treitschke (1834–96), Professor of History at Berlin University, Prussia seemed predestined to play the central role for only Prussia could offer a solution to 'the German Question'.

'The German Question'

'The German Problem' or 'The German Question', is an ambiguous phrase. To nationalists, it identifies the (supposed) anomaly that Germany, had, unlike France, somehow failed to constitute itself as a proper 'nation state'. The problem, therefore, was to identify the means by which unification might be achieved. But it can also identify the problems which 'Germany' has posed for the international order. When disunited, it proved vulnerable to invasion and therefore a source of international conflict. This was the 'German Problem' as perceived by Metternich. However, when united, and especially when fired-up by nationalism, Germany has proved a 'problem' for its neighbours – as the wars of the twentieth century testify.

Treitschke believed that the 'national idea' was innate in the very soul of Germans. It had found in the Prussian state an instrument strong enough to defeat those forces – the Austrians and the French – who opposed its growth. And in Bismarck, it found a statesman of genius whose diplomacy created the circumstances in which Prussia and the cause of the German People could triumph.

To Treitschke, it seemed self-evident that German nationalism was a powerful mass movement, and to him, Prussia's adoption of the national cause was natural and unproblematic. In fact, the popularity and significance of German nationalism is difficult to assess. It has even been suggested (by John Breuilly) that German nationalism, as a mass movement, was as much a consequence as a cause of unification. Many Germans, including many nationalists, were highly suspicious of Prussia. Catholics were wary of Prussia's Protestantism, and liberals wary of its **militarism** and its authoritarian style of politics.

See Bibliography on page 205

militarism a state which gives prominence to the armed forces is militaristic, and may resort quickly to force to solve international or domestic problems

In any case, the first loyalty of most Germans was to their dynastic rulers, their regions, or to their 'home towns'. Rule from Berlin had little obvious appeal. From this perspective, the process which we call German unification can begin to look more like a covert civil war in which Prussia conquered and absorbed her neighbours. Neither should we forget that for many Austrians – who were German speakers under Habsburg rule – the process of 'unification' actually ended in 'disunification' of Germany – that is. in their exclusion from the *Großdeutschland* (Greater Germany) of which many had dreamed.

See page 177

Bismarck's role also needs re-evaluating. Perhaps he was less the servant of the nationalist ideal and more the cynical exponent of *Realpolitik* – a political outlook which is contemptuous of principles and 'sentimentality', believing instead that self-interest dominates politics and diplomacy, and that the end justifies the (nicely calculated) means. Historians are particularly sceptical of the way in which, in his *Memoirs*, Bismarck presented the unification story as if he had every stage mapped out in advance. Instead, they wonder whether Bismarck pursued Prussian expansionism rather than German unification as his objective, and how far his diplomatic genius lay less in the design of any 'master plan', and more in his infinite resourcefulness and capacity for improvisation.

Other historians are unconvinced that Bismarck should be centre stage at all. They suggest that we should give more weight to social and economic forces, rather than be mesmerised by the deeds of 'great men'. Where would Bismarck have been without Prussian industrialisation? The wealth it generated helped to pay for Prussia's army; advanced technology gave that army superior fire power; and Germany's railway network was essential for the army's rapid mobilisation in 1866 and 1870. It has even been suggested that the *Zollverein* (Custom's Union), by simultaneously reinforcing Prussia's economic preponderance within Germany whilst blocking out Austria, tied Prussia's neighbours so closely to it in mutual economic self-interest that they could not have escaped Prussia's pull even if they had wanted too. Thus, political union followed naturally from economic union and would eventually have happened with or without Bismarck.

See page 162

We can summarise these issues as a series of questions:

● has the contribution of nationalism to German unification been exaggerated?
● was German unification really only a by-product of Prussian self-aggrandisement?
● what were Bismarck's objectives?
● did Bismarck have a master plan for unification, or was he an improviser of genius?
● what weight should we give to economic and social factors in our analysis of the unification process?

2 ⌐ RESTORATION GERMANY

A *Germany and Napoleon*

On the map of Germany below it is only possible to pick out some of the 38 sovereign states which made up 'Germany' in 1815. Yet in 1790 it was a medieval patchwork of over 300 assorted states, principalities, bishoprics and free cities. The transformation of central Europe between these two dates was largely the work of Napoleon.

Napoleon was a ruthless rationaliser and moderniser. He abolished the so-called Holy Roman Empire, which for centuries had held the states of Germany together in a loose confederal structure. He abolished hundreds of these states, absorbing some of them directly under French control and forcibly amalgamating many of the others into larger units.

Several states within 'Germany' benefited territorially from Napoleon's generosity, as he rewarded his German allies, like Baden, at the expense of their former neighbours, whose territories they annexed. Such states worked hard to integrate their new territories, and were determined to protect their gains after 1815: therefore they were not natural candidates for absorption themselves within a single unitary German state.

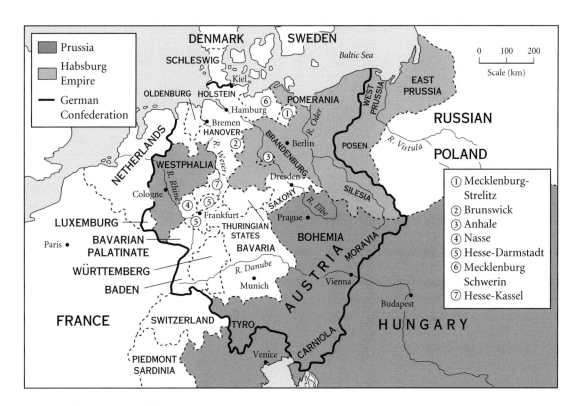

MAP 6 *The German Confederation in 1815*

In other respects, however, Napoleon stimulated German nationalism. His armies had an insatiable appetite for men, money and provisions. Germany seemed in danger of being reduced to semi-colonial status. The response, in some quarters, was strong. An early German nationalist proclaimed: 'I hate all the French without exception in the name of my God and my people'. The defeat of Napoleon in 1813, when he was driven out of Germany, gave nationalism its first great myth. It was remembered as a popular 'War of Liberation', although in fact many Germans fought for Napoleon, and only a fraction of the forces which defeated him were inspired by nationalism. Even so, popular nationalism in the unification era was at its most intense when there was an actual or perceived threat from France.

KEY ISSUE

To what extent did Napoleon help to pave the way for German unification?

Restoration Europe is the name sometimes given to describe the Europe created by the Congress of Vienna. The Congress had tried to **restore** much of Europe's pre-revolutionary political system.

B *Metternich and Restoration Germany*

Metternich was the main architect of Restoration Germany. 'Restoration' is perhaps a misleading term: Metternich discovered that it was impossible and even undesirable to restore Germany completely to its pre-revolutionary condition.

However, Metternich's objectives at the Congress of Vienna were profoundly conservative, even reactionary. They were:

- the new Germany should strengthen the long-term stability of the European states system
- monarchic authority within Germany should be reasserted, and the threat posed by liberals and nationalists be neutralised
- the Great Power interests of Austria itself should be protected and enhanced.

The territorial restructuring of Germany had two main features:

- those states like Bavaria, Württemberg and Baden which had expanded at the expense of their neighbours in the Napoleonic era were allowed to keep the gains
- France, of course, had to give up its conquests in the Rhineland. But these territories were not given back to their former rulers. Several of them were added to Prussia's patchwork of west German lands – which was some compensation for it being denied the right to annex all of Saxony. Prussia's increased power in the west also put it in the front-line against possible future French aggression – a policing role that, at the time, seemed to strengthen the prospects for European stability, but was to have consequences which Metternich could not have foreseen and would not have welcomed.

See page 6

See page 162

The German Confederation was also constructed with the aim of European stability in mind. By giving the sovereign states of German-speaking Europe a formal institutional focus, Metternich hoped to stiffen the European centre against Russia and France, its potential aggressors on the flanks. However, this objective was not easy to reconcile with Metternich's determination to block the progress of German nationalism. The Confederation would have to be structured to make it impossible for it to become an embryonic nation state. But the weaker its central authority, the less effective it would be in its task of organising Germany's diplomacy or armies to keep foreigners at bay.

The main features of the Confederation are identified below:

- it comprised 39 states, most of which were quite small (21 had populations of less than 100 000)
- its central institution was the *Diet* – a sort of standing congress of ambassadors from the member states. Its voting arrangements were carefully weighted so that the smaller states could never effectively 'gang up' to out-number the large ones, but equally the larger ones could never impose their collective will on the others. But these intricate procedures made it hard for the Confederation to achieve anything at all
- the *Diet* was not a parliament. National representatives were not elected, but instead appointed by each state's ruler. Nationalists who might have hoped that the Confederation would grow into a progressive institution sponsoring 'national' policies on defence, tariffs or constitutional reform were disappointed. A 'federal army' existed on paper, but barely in practice, and the development of the *Zollverein* occurred quite independently of the Confederation.

See pages 162–3

In 1815, Metternich must have felt reasonably satisfied with his solution to the German Question, especially as Austria's power *vis-à-vis* its traditional rival Prussia seemed to have been secured by limiting its territorial expansion and winning for Austria the permanent presidency of the Confederation itself. But built into the very structure of the settlement were problems and tensions which were to undermine Metternich's 'Germany' from within.

Metternich had anticipated continuing opposition from liberals and nationalists. He was to fight a long and bitter battle with them in Germany's universities, where (despite censorship and persecution) their ideas would prove very hard to eradicate. But he was also dismayed by developments in some of Germany's most important states. By 1820, the rulers of Bavaria, Württemberg and Baden had each given their subjects liberal constitutions. Anxious to integrate their old and new territories they calculated that the best way to secure the loyalty of their citizens was to give some of them a share in the responsibilities of government.

See page 159

Even more unexpected – and with more serious implications for Metternich's hopes for Germany – were the long-term consequences of Prussia's acquisition in the Rhineland. These territories were eventually to transform Prussia's status in European affairs, although Prussia's leaders had initially regarded the addition of more territories in the Rhineland – 300 miles distant from Berlin – as poor compensation for failing to acquire Saxony:

- the objective of bridging the gap between East and West Prussia became the strongest driving force in Prussia's diplomatic and strategic thinking over the following four decades

- Prussia's possession of a major Rhineland province put it in the front line of possible French expansion: therefore the self-interest of the Prussian state and of the German nation began to converge
- industrialisation was to make this territory, with its massive deposits of coal and iron ore, into one of the wealthiest regions of Germany – to the incalculable benefit of Prussia.

In sum, Prussia's chance expansion in the Rhineland gave it a powerful motive to consolidate and expand its power base in northern Germany; it made it into the power to which nationalists would ultimately look for the defence of the fatherland; and it gave it the economic means to achieve both objectives.

KEY ISSUE

How successfully did Metternich's restructuring of Germany satisfy his objectives?

ANALYSIS

Interpretations of the Zollverein

One of the factors in Prussia's economic development, and its ultimate capacity to challenge Austria for predominance in Germany, was the *Zollverein* – a national custom's union founded in 1834. Sixteen years earlier, Prussia had established its own internal customs' union, abolishing the tariffs which until then had hindered trade between the different regions of Prussia, whilst increasing tariffs on imports entering Prussia from the rest of Germany. The Government's main motives were to increase state revenues (the import tariffs were to be strictly enforced) and to strengthen the links between Prussia's divided territories.

Other German states, resentful of the taxes Prussia was imposing on their exports, tried to set up their own rival Central Customs' Union. But Prussia was too economically powerful, and its highly developed transport system too useful, for any prosperous state to turn its back on it for long, especially after Bavaria and Württemberg joined the *Zollverein* in 1828. The Central Union broke up after 1831, most of its members joining the new, enlarged Prussian-centred 'German Customs Union' in 1834.

Austria, however, was not a member. Influential industrialists in the Empire persuaded the Government to keep their high tariff walls in tact. The resulting economic marginalisation of Austria made Metternich profoundly uneasy. He sensed in the *Zollverein* 'a state within a state', which would increase the prospects of Prussian 'preponderance' within Germany and even, he believed, promoted the 'highly dangerous idea of German unity'.

Metternich's prophecy helped to make the *Zollverein* an important subject for German historical debate. Treitschke praised it as 'the greatest act of national policy' of the Restoration era, and made the *Zollverein* into a decisive instalment of the unification story. However, more recent historians have pointed out that it was not the intention of the founders of the *Zollverein* to lay the framework for unification. It was certainly not the aim of the sovereign states which joined it to undermine their own independence – most simply wanted to increase their customs revenues.

Yet this analysis risks underestimating the strength of the ties which pulled the medium- size states ever more closely into Prussia's orbit. However suspicious the 'middle states' might become of Prussia's intentions towards them, and however desirous they were of bringing Austria into the union to counterbalance Prussian power, they could never contemplate leaving it themselves. Nor were they strong enough to force Prussia to let Austria in, when the latter tried to gain entry in the 1850s and 1860s. By 1860, Prussia's economic predominance, and Austria's economic vulnerability, were unmistakable facts. Some contemporaries were aware of the issues. Friedrich von Motz, the Prussian Finance Minster, argued as early as 1829 that the 'unification of these states in a customs and trading union might well lead to a unification within one and the same political system', and predicted that given Austria's internal divisions and European-wide commitments, only Prussia could assume this role.

Finally, the emotional and ideological impact of the *Zollverein* should not be underestimated. It became a model of what Germans could achieve if they worked together. The contrast between its dynamism, and the stifling inertia of the Confederation, made the latter's political bankruptcy even more obvious.

3 ⌐ GERMANY 1815–40: LIBERALISM AND NATIONALISM, PROTEST AND REPRESSION

Metternich was intensely worried by the spread of liberal and nationalist ideas in post-Napoleonic Germany. To understand why he feared these ideologies, we need to understand what liberals and nationalists stood for, and who they were. But we should also bear in mind the probability that Metternich exaggerated the threat they posed to the established order, and the possibility that the measures he took to suppress them ultimately did the conservative cause more harm than good.

A *German liberalism in theory and practice*

Liberals in the first half of the nineteenth century were not democrats. They believed that the franchise should be limited to *men* of 'education' (who understood politics) and of 'property' (who had a stake in society and the independence to freely exercise their judgement). They did not organise themselves into a Party. This would have been difficult in an age of political censorship and repression, but it also reflected the liberal mentality, which placed a high value on principles and personal integrity – virtues which party politicians often have to sacrifice! Furthermore, they saw their role as critics of authority, not as decision-makers, and their abstract and idealistic cast of mind often made it hard for them to convert their theories into policies. For all the liberals' undoubted talents, these limitations help to explain their ultimately limited impact as a constructive political force (for example, in 1848).

Liberals believed in constitutional government and political rights:

- Liberals generally approved of monarchical government, but insisted that royal authority needed to be constrained not merely by the law (with an independent judiciary to determine if a government had acted illegally) but also by a representative assembly
- the representative assembly should enter into partnership with the king and his ministers: only by acting together could laws be enacted or taxes raised
- the representative assembly would be elected by a propertied and educated *élite*. Liberals did not believe that this attitude was selfish. Ordinary people were not responsible enough to exercise political power wisely, whilst Liberals – rational and public-spirited individuals – would act in the best interests of the community a whole
- basic civil rights were to be guaranteed for all. These included freedom of speech and especially freedom of the press (one of the most sharply contested issues in Restoration Germany), and freedom of religious practice (important in an era marked by sometimes bitter strife between Catholics and Protestants and Christians and Jews).

KEY ISSUE

What were the main beliefs of liberalism?

Why was Metternich so hostile to Liberals? Liberal principles represented a fundamental challenge to Metternich's political philosophy. He stressed the absolute and God-given nature of monarchical authority: the people had no more right to demand a share of a monarch's power than they had to demand a share of his property. Liberal ideas about representative government were merely a self-serving justification for the political ambitions of the middle classes. To Metternich, the middle classes were as stupid as they were presumptuous: they seemed to have forgotten the awful lesson of the French Revolution: that there was no middle way between the monarchical principle and a social revolution which would overturn the rights of all property owners, aristocrats and middle classes alike.

On the whole, the German middle classes were not businessmen or industrialists. The Industrial Revolution probably didn't really 'take-off' in Germany until the 1850s. Instead, the middle classes were largely identified by their level of culture and education (this was why Metternich regarded universities with such suspicion). They were lawyers, doctors, civil servants, journalists and teachers. Given that liberalism and nationalism were rather abstract creeds, it is not surprising that these ideas found their most receptive audience in Germany's educated *élite*.

However, liberalism was not a purely middle class phenomenon. Some of its spokesmen were enlightened aristocrats. At the other end of the social spectrum, self-improving artisans were attracted to liberal principles. More democratic in outlook than the middle class liberals, and more concerned about social problems like poverty and unemployment, they soon constituted a radical wing of the wider movement. The liberal/radical fault-line was to become all important in the revolution of 1848–9.

KEY ISSUE

How serious a threat did liberal ideas pose to Metternich's system?

B *The appeal of German nationalism*

Nationalism appealed to the same sort of people as liberalism. Like liberalism, nationalism challenged traditional ideas about the ultimate source of political authority. 'The people', defined in terms of culture, history, language and/or race were the basic unit of political legitimacy. 'The nation' embodied their collective will and expressed their identity.

Metternich loathed nationalism even more than liberalism. It presented an acute threat to the structure of the Austrian Empire. It asserted the rights of Czechs, Hungarians, Italians and every other race that made up the Austrian Empire to rule themselves. There was no future for Austria as a Great Power in a world where nationalism prevailed. Hence the sense of urgency with which Metternich took up the challenge presented by nationalism in Germany.

However, it seems certain that Metternich exaggerated the scale of the threat posed by nationalism. We cannot know how many Germans in the first half of the nineteenth century were nationalists, but although highly vocal, nationalists probably only constituted a small minority of the population. 'The nation' had many rivals for the loyalty and affection of Germans. However radically the political map of Germany had been redrawn by Napoleon and Metternich, in some regions the ruling dynasty could call on traditions of allegiance that went back many centuries. The Wittelsbach dynasty had ruled Bavaria since 1180! Religious affiliations were also important. The largest single instance of mass mobilisation in nineteenth century Germany happened in 1844, when half a million Catholic pilgrims went to Trier to see the 'Holy Coat' of Jesus. Religion was a political force. Catholics in the Rhineland resented being ruled by Protestants in Berlin, just as Protestants in the Bavarian Palatinate resented being ruled by Catholics in Munich. Thus Germans were divided from Germans.

Other loyalties and animosities could be just as intense. Politics for the peasantry were often dominated by a hatred of feudal oppression and (usually) Jewish moneylenders, whilst the most powerful attachments for many urban craftsmen were towards the communities of their craft guilds and their 'home town'.

There was much more to popular politics and public life than nationalism; equally, there was much more to nationalism than national *politics*.

The most significant father of German nationalism was Johann Gott-fried Herder (1744–1803). Herder was not a politician, but a philosopher and cultural historian. He focused on the role of language and custom in forming human identity. Each people or '*Volk*', he argued, had its own distinct and equally valuable way of living. This was inextricably wrapped up in its collective history and folk memory, which in turn shaped the very language which it spoke. To speak the language was to be immersed in those traditions. Only as part of such an historic language community could any individual find his true identity and fulfil his human potential.

Herder's ideas inspired a generation of linguists, folklorists and historians to explore the roots of the German past. Thereby Germans were helped to escape the cultural inferiority complex which they had used to feel when, in the eighteenth century, they compared themselves with the splendours of French civilisation and the Enlightenment.

Herder's ideas influenced writers everywhere. Throughout Europe, intellectuals compiled dictionaries, collected folk stories, and wrote peoples' histories, so that the national language and the national memory might be preserved and flourish. Some nationalists were therefore furious that their higher education system or civil service were monopolised by speakers of a foreign tongue! In the Austrian Empire for example, cultural discrimination was acute, and resulted in political nationalism. It could be plausibly argued that only in an independent Italian state, for example, would the Italian language be accorded its proper status. In these cases, cultural nationalism inspired political action. But no such institutional discrimination inhibited German speakers in Berlin, Vienna, Munich or Cologne. Therefore, in Germany itself, no obvious political conclusions followed from Herder's ideas. German culture was something of which all educated Germans could be proud, and share in, whilst retaining their political identities as Bavarians or Prussians, and so on.

German nationalism became active against the existing political order in Germany by three routes:

See page 213

- frustrated Liberals tended to become political nationalists. In part, this reflected the intellectual affinity of liberalism and nationalism. But more practically, when German Liberals found their plans for constitutional reform blocked by their local rulers (or indeed by the reactionary German Confederation), they concluded that only by creating a new liberal national political authority could the rights of individual citizens be truly established. Only in a German nation state would citizens be free

- Restoration Germany had more than its fair share of groups or individuals who felt that they had been ill-served by the political and social changes of the post-Napoleonic era. *Ancien Regime* Germany may have seemed to some a medieval backwater, but its intricate social and political networks offered most individuals a sense of security and identity: 'a place for everyone and everyone in their place' was the popular saying. But Napoleon had torn this world apart and Metternich had not been able to patch it together again. Despite the best efforts of their new rulers, many Germans never felt any allegiance to their new states; some, especially religious minorities, actually felt victimised by 'foreign' governments. A German state would confer on the politically homeless and rootless a sense of identity, and its constitution would guarantee them their political, religious and social rights. 'Nationalism' became a sort of blank cheque for the disaffected: in 'Germany', they would be free and happy

- the most important impetus behind the 'politicisation of nationalism', however, came from increasingly widespread anxieties about Germany's strategic vulnerability. From the start, German nationalism had defined itself against France. The separate states which had made up the Holy Roman Empire had proved quite incapable of defending Germany against French aggression in the Napoleonic era, and few Germans were confident that the German Confederation would do any better after 1815. Many Frenchmen still seemed convinced that the Rhine was their 'natural frontier', and during the war scares of 1830–1 and especially 1840, Germans in the Rhineland believed that they were in imminent danger of invasion. Nationalists insisted that only a united Germany could defend itself, and increasingly, they looked to the strength of Prussia rather than to Austria (with its Italian and Balkan preoccupations) to provide the core of the new, strong German state.

See page 19

KEY ISSUE

What was the appeal of German nationalism?

C *Cycles of protest and repression*

Despite Metternich's efforts, liberal and nationalist ideas reached a progressively larger audience between 1815 and 1848. It is not easy to trace this growth, because persecution and censorship drove many activists underground or into organisations like singing clubs, whose propagandist purposes were partially disguised. Nevertheless, by 1848, Liberals and nationalists were numerous and confident enough to take control of the Governments of most of the states of Germany, if only for a few months, and to organise a popular national parliament.

See page 173

NATIONALISM AND REPRESSION 1811–19

Nationalists began to organise amongst the young men of Germany in 1811. Gymnastic clubs were set up, aiming to create a brotherhood of patriots ready to fight to free the Fatherland from Napoleon: their membership ultimately reached 12 000. In the universities, student societies called *Burschenschaften* were established, dedicated to clean living and the ideals of 'Honour, Freedom and Fatherland'. Historians have argued that, together, these movements captured the hearts and minds of a whole generation of students:

- the young nationalists' disappointment at the failure of the Congress of Vienna to create a united Germany was intense. Five hundred of them held a rally at Wartburg Castle in 1817 to rededicate themselves to the cause. Metternich was shocked by this public display of political dissent, and decided to crush the movement

- the assassination of a right-wing spy and propagandist by a militant nationalist in 1819 gave Metternich the excuse he was looking for. At a summit meeting with Frederick William III of Prussia, he convinced the king that all Liberals and nationalists were potential assassins. Frederick William III therefore agreed to cancel some liberal reforms his Government had been considering, and sack nationalist minded teachers and civil servants

- with the Prussian King's backing, Metternich also secured the Confederation's approval for the Carlsbad Decrees (September 1819). These ordered the banning of the *Burschenschaften*, tighter controls over teaching, stricter censorship of books and newspapers, and the dismissal of political troublemakers from public office. At least in the short term, Metternich seemed to have scored a clear victory for the forces of reaction in Germany.

NATIONALISM AND REPRESSION 1830–2

- The 1830 revolution in Paris unsettled public opinion in Germany. It reanimated fears that the German Confederation would be incapable of countering any French moves into the Rhineland, but it also demonstrated that reactionary rulers could be overthrown. It was time for nationalists and liberals to take the initiative. Demonstrators forced constitutions out of the incompetent and sometimes despotic rulers of four of the medium-sized states, and in the liberal-leaning south-west a popular movement against newspaper censorship sprang up. This culminated in the Hambach festival of May 1832, where up to 30 000 nationalists and Liberals gathered to hear inspiring speeches calling for freedom of the press and national regeneration. The scale of the meeting, and the diversity of its social make-up, with professionals, businessmen, and craftsmen now outnumbering students, marked a clear advance for the liberal and national cause. Metternich's attempt to destroy the nationalist movement had failed

- Metternich's response was predictable. In June 1832, he won the Confederation's approval for a new series of repressive laws – the Six Articles. These laid down strict guidelines for the proper workings of the constitutions of individual states, reinforcing the monarchical principle. It was now deemed illegal, for example, for liberals to try and squeeze concessions out of their rulers by blocking a budget. The Articles also established a Central Bureau of Political Investigation to keep enemies of good order under surveillance. The clampdown was particularly severe in Prussia, where anyone discovered belonging to a *Burschenschaften* (these had sometimes survived as secret societies) could now be tried for high treason. Elsewhere, the constitutional concessions which had been made in the wake of the Paris Revolution of 1830 were soon clawed back, and when some liberal academics complained, they were summarily sacked. The brutish king of Hanover, who controlled the university concerned, dismissed the resulting protests with a sneer: 'professors, like whores, can always be had for money'.

Superficially, the 'police-state' style tactics adopted by Metternich hit liberals and nationalists hard. Civil servants and teachers everywhere knew they had to toe the reactionary line. Newspapers were closed down, and 'agitators' were imprisoned. Constitutionally speaking, any chance of the Confederation evolving into a more progressive institution was killed off, while clear limits were imposed on what liberals could achieve in those states which already had constitutions. Metternich seemed to have sent German political life into deep freeze.

But even on its own terms, the effectiveness of Metternich's strategy may be doubted. His 'police-state' was a good deal less terrifying than Hitler's or Stalin's: there were no concentration camps in nineteenth century Germany. Press censorship was applied unevenly; dissident academics or journalists, when sacked or exiled, could usually pursue their careers in other parts of Germany. In fact, Liberals and nationalists were forever finding new means to spread their message. For example, the 1100 men's choral societies which had sprung up by 1848 (estimated membership of over 100 000) might seem innocent enough, but the words of their songs were often pure nationalistic propaganda.

Arguably Metternich's whole strategy was misconceived. In his paranoia, he really did see every nationalist or Liberal as a revolutionary militant. But what he failed to appreciate was that the very oppressiveness of his own policies was likely to turn Liberals and nationalists – usually men of property with a socially conservative outlook – into enemies of the established order. The Confederation's interference in the constitutional affairs of the liberal states taught progressives that the reform of the Confederation was an essential precondition of any progress at regional level. But Metternich had made it impossible for the Confederation to reform itself. Most Liberals and nationalists were unlikely revolutionaries. They sought a share in political power, not to overthrow the state; they wanted to build, not barricades, but a Germany that enjoyed a secure and dignified place amongst the nations of Europe. But by making it impossible for the institutional life of Restoration Germany to evolve so as to begin to accommodate those aspirations, Metternich ensured that Liberals and nationalists became revolutionaries. Metternich's policies were paradoxically those most likely to produce the catastrophe he dreaded.

> **KEY ISSUE**
>
> *How successful was Metternich's strategy of repression?*

4 ⌐ GERMANY 1840–9: EXPECTATIONS AND FRUSTRATIONS

Although industrialisation only 'took off' there in the 1850s, Germany already had a sizeable, prosperous and self-confident middle class before the 1848 Revolution. Its leaders were lawyers, doctors, teachers and civil servants. This social *élite*, proud of its education and culture, was the natural carrier of liberal and nationalist ideas. They bought books and liberal-leaning newspapers, reflecting the revolution in literacy and communications which had transformed public life in Germany in the first half of the nineteenth century. 'Public opinion' had become an important political factor: it might be ignored, but it wouldn't go away. There was a growth in clubs and societies: chambers of commerce, literary discussion groups, and, most popular of all, choral and gymnastics societies. The clubs discussed political and social issues. Businessmen increasingly complained about bureaucratic interference and red-tape; lovers of literature eagerly discussed radical poetry; the choirs sang about freedom and unity for the German people; and the gymnasts trained for greater fitness and strength, the better to serve the nation. Political parties might be banned in Restoration Germany, but the public realm was full of political life and political organisations.

Political life was also taking on an increasingly national dimension, aided by the expanding railway network. 'All-German' congresses and festivals became a regular feature of patriotic self-expression; for example, choral societies from all over Germany descended on Würzburg (1845) Cologne (1846) and Lubeck (1847).

Railways in particular came to symbolise the march of modernity and progress. In 1840, Germany had only 462 kilometres of track; by 1850, it had almost 6000 kilometres. Railways were far from politically neutral. Together with the *Zollverein* – whose goods it increasingly carried – the railway was an instrument of national integration and proof of what the German people were capable, when they broke free of Restoration Germany's political restrictions.

A *Frederick William IV: a romantic reactionary?*

See page 19

The events of 1840 gave a double impetus to the expanding currents of liberalism and nationalism. The French war-scare of that year marked a new peak of patriotic sentiment, whilst the new Prussian King Frederick William IV shared many of the emotions of German nationalists.

Frederick William IV was an unusual product of the Hohenzollern dynasty. More happy discussing grand architectural projects than reviewing troops, he was acutely aware of the challenges monarchy faced in an era of industrialisation, liberalism and revolution. Unlike Metternich, however, he did not believe that bureaucratic absolutism, dependent for security on soldiers and spies, could guarantee stability.

Romantic dreamer that Frederick William IV was, he wanted to come before his people as a sacred father figure, as he believed his medieval ancestors had done. To cement the natural bond between King and people, he planned to call together the Estates of the Realm – nobles, townsmen and peasants – so that the people would pay homage to him, and he would redress their grievances. He believed that this would appease the widespread desire for increased popular political participation – without him having to grant a constitution or a representative assembly, modern concepts which the King completely loathed.

PICTURE 11 *A nineteenth-century German cartoon showing Frederick William IV caught between the government and the military*

Frederick William IV therefore had no affinity with German liberalism, however easily Liberals confused his ideas with their hopes for representative government. But he did support German nationalism. He saw himself as the potential War Lord of a regenerated Holy Roman Empire, loyally following his feudal master, the Habsburg Emperor, in the service of the national cause. Not surprisingly, he was widely misunderstood.

The first political crisis of Frederick William IV's reign was in the mid 1840s. Prussia could only raise the necessary capital to expand its railways if a full state parliament approved the loan. The King decided that this was the perfect opportunity to implement his plans for calling together an assembly of the Estates of the realm, based on the already existing semi-feudal regional *diets*. So, he called a 'United *Diet*', consisting of separate deputations from the nobility, the towns and the peasantry. At first, Prussian Liberals thought that this was the national assembly which they had long dreamed of: Frederick William IV seemed to be taking Prussia down the constitutional path, thus making Prussia fit to take the lead in national regeneration.

They could not have been more mistaken. When Frederick William IV opened the United *Diet* in April 1847 he proclaimed that: 'No power on earth will succeed in moving me to transform that natural relationship between ruler and people ... into a legalistic or constitutional

KEY ISSUE

How did the accession of Frederick William IV help to destabilise Prussian and German politics?

one; and I will never ever allow a written piece of paper to come between Our Lord God in Heaven and this country ... to rule us with paragraphs as a substitute for our old sacred loyalty. The Christian people, that simple, true, loyal people of Prussia does not want representatives to share in government ... or to see the genuine power of its kings broken'.

The *Diet* refused to approve the loans, so the King abandoned his railway project and closed the assembly down. The gap between the state and society in Prussia was now wider than ever: the events of March 1848 would reveal just how isolated and vulnerable Frederick William IV's Government was.

B *The social crisis 1844–7*

What made Frederick William IV's experiments particularly dangerous was that they coincided with an unusually severe social crisis. This had been brewing for many years, and it affected not just Prussia but most of Europe. It will be examined in more detail in Chapter 7, but the main features in Germany were:

- the root of the crisis was demographic. Between 1815 and 1848, the population of Germany grew by over 50 per cent, from 22 million to 35 million, outstripping the rate of economic development
- widespread and persistent poverty resulted. 'The proletariat' came to be the word used to describe the rootless, property-less class which drifted in and out of work, and in and out of crime. 'Impoverished, unskilled, politically and socially volatile, the proletariat was ready for anything – the raw material of outlaw bands, urban mobs and revolutionary movements' (Sheehan)
- these ongoing structural crises were compounded in the mid-1840s by a series of appalling harvest failures. Starvation and resulting epidemics carried off 50 000 in Silesia alone. With those in work spending almost all their wages on food, consumer manufacturing was badly hit too. A vicious downward spiral set in.

See the bibliography on page 205

The political consequences were dramatic. Starving workers, who would not have built barricades to defend the beliefs of nationalists and Liberals, began to long for a social order which might bring them their daily bread. Liberals and nationalists saw in the popular plight further confirmation of the rottenness of Restoration Germany. But the Liberals were also aware of the potential of the 'mob' for uncontrollable violence and political anarchy. The success and failure of the Revolutions of 1848–9 would in large part be determined by the working out of these contrasting feelings of despair, anger, hope and fear.

5 ∽ GERMANY IN REVOLUTION

A *Springtime in Germany*

When news of the February Revolution in Paris reached the Rhineland, the impact was dramatic. A radical, drinking in a Karlsruhe inn, remembers 'people [leaping] from their seats, [embracing] each other, [raising] their glasses in jubilation, and shouting, "Let us quickly work for Germany's liberation, let us act now!"'. Liberals and radicals quickly organised petitions, deputations and demonstrations. The Governments of most of the important states of Germany soon found themselves confronting a seemingly irresistible tide of public opinion.

Demoralised by the news from Paris, crippled by self-doubt as to their own legitimacy, loathe to turn their (unreliable?) troops on their own citizens, one by one Germany's princes gave in to the liberal demands. These included an end to press censorship, the introduction of trial by jury, and the establishment of ministerial responsibility. Liberal-dominated 'March ministries' were appointed to implement these measures. In mid-March, the startling news from Vienna, where revolution had forced Metternich into exile, and Berlin, where Frederick William IV seemed to have thrown in his lot with the Revolution, confirmed the hopelessness of reaction. By the end of the month, most of Germany's states boasted new constitutions, and their Governments were committed to support the idea of unification.

Preparations were made for the election of a National Assembly, to meet in Frankfurt. Its task would be to work out the political structure of the new German state. All 'mature, independent' citizens were given a vote – in practice, about three-quarters of all German males. The representatives selected were overwhelmingly from the ranks of local 'notables' (breakdown of these 'notables' is given Table 4 in the margin).

Although these men were principled and politically progressive, they were also socially conservative, and rather unresponsive to the needs of ordinary Germans.

For all the euphoria which marked the Parliament's opening in May, one major problem soon overshadowed its proceedings: how was the Parliament to enforce its decisions? The Parliament needed to create its own executive. In late June Archduke John of Austria was nominated as the 'Imperial Vicar' – a sort of emergency head of state. He was a Habsburg prince with longstanding links to the German movement, and he led a non-aristocratic style of life. It seemed an inspired choice. But Archduke John had no real power: no money, no bureaucracy, no subordinate authorities in the country, and, above all, no army. The executive was dependent on the goodwill of the individual states to implement its policies. Above all it was dependent on the goodwill of Austria and Prussia.

B *Springtime in Austria and Prussia*

The prospects for the German Revolution looked promising. Within the span of seven days in mid-March, Vienna and Berlin – previously

Civil servants, judges, etc.	312
University lecturers and teachers	124
Lawyers	106
Doctors	23
Writers, journalists	20
Clergymen	39
Merchants	35
Manufacturers	14
Publishers	7
Landowners, farmers	46
Craftsmen	4
Other professionals	38
Details unknown	44
Total	**812**

TABLE 4
Representatives selected for the election of a National Assembly

Q
How representative was this assembly of the German nation?

An outline of the cause of the Austrian Revolution, which culminated in the fall of Metternich, can be found on pages 218–19

Q

Compare and contrast this table with the one identifying the occupations of delegates to the Frankfurt Parliament.

Workers and proletarians	52
Apprentices	13
Journeymen (e.g. joiners, tailors and shoemakers)	115
Masters	29
Servants, small traders	34
'Educated classes'	15
Non-working women	7
Non-working youths	4
Unidentified	33
Identified, no profession given	1
Total	303

TABLE 5

Survey of the 303 people who were killed in March 1848 in Berlin, or who subsequently died of their wounds

two bastions of reaction – had fallen to liberal/nationalist inspired revolution. The Frankfurt Parliament, and Germany's March Ministries, could flourish in the resulting power vacuum.

When news of the Austrian Revolution reached Berlin on 16 March, the impact was dramatic. The city and Government were already in turmoil. Demonstrators had been protesting about widespread unemployment and the absence of political reform for weeks, and Frederick William IV and his advisors were uncertain how to respond. They were also preoccupied with the birth of the new French Republic, which was widely expected to try and export its revolution by invading the Rhineland.

On the evening of 17 March, the King decided to grant a constitution. This move was designed not simply to appease the forces of revolution in Berlin, but to position Prussia for leadership of the national/liberal cause in Germany. When the constitution was announced the following day, the demonstrators were at first jubilant. But the King and his advisors grew increasingly worried that the crowd was still potentially dangerous. In the absence of an adequate police force, cavalry were ordered to clear the square, supposedly using minimum force. The result was a disaster: shots were fired, and several citizens were killed. Thinking they had been tricked, the citizens of Berlin rushed to put up barricades. The city was soon out of control. Three hundred citizens died in the fighting – a survey of people killed is given in Table 5.

The general responsible for Berlin was uncertain whether his troops could re-establish order. He recommended that the army and Government evacuate the city, surround it and bombard it into submission This was too much for the King, who instead issued an appeal to his 'beloved Berliners', asking them to clear the barricades, in exchange for which he gave his word 'that all the streets and squares will be immediately evacuated by the troops'. But this unexpected concession appalled Frederick William IV's more conservative advisers. In the confusion which reigned at court, the King's orders seem to have been misinterpreted, and **all** armed forces – even those guarding the palace – were withdrawn to their barracks, out of the city.

Frederick William IV was now effectively in the hands of his 'beloved Berliners'. On 19 March, he paid homage to the corpses of the Revolution's dead. Even more extraordinary scenes followed on 21 March, as the King, bedecked in the black-red-gold tricolour of the German national movement, rode in procession through the thronged streets of Berlin, expressing to popular acclaim his support for the nationalist cause. The King made another proclamation: 'To my people and the German Nation':

> With confidence I speak today, when the Fatherland is in the greatest danger, to the German nation, among whose noblest tribes my people may proudly count itself. Germany is in a state of internal ferment and can be threatened by external danger from more than one side. It can be saved from this double, urgent danger only by the most intimate unity of the German princes and peoples under one leadership.

> Today I take over this leadership for the days of danger. My people, which does not shirk danger, will not desert me, and Germany, will follow me with confidence. I have today taken the old German colours and put Myself and My people under the venerable banner of the German Reich. Prussia henceforth merges in Germany …

Q

Why might liberals and nationalists have welcomed Frederick William IV's statement?

How can Frederick William IV's behaviour in March be explained?

The Prussian Revolution seemed complete on 29 March with the appointment of the leading Rhenish liberal businessmen, Camphausen and Hansemann, to head a new ministry. They arranged for the election of a new, essentially democratic Prussian assembly. When it first meet on 22 May (with barely a landowner in its ranks), the King assured it that the 'unity of Germany is my fixed goal'. But it was soon to become apparent that Frederick William IV was temperamentally incapable of pursuing a 'fixed goal'.

KEY ISSUE

Why did revolution triumph in Berlin in March 1848?

C *Berlin: from summer to winter*

The course of the Prussian Revolution would be bedevilled by two problems:

- the extremely sensitive constitutional issue of whether the King or his parliament should have ultimate control of the army
- the growing pressure from radicals in the Assembly and militants on the streets of Berlin for a second revolution, that would accelerate the process of political and social change begun in March.

Prussian civilians had long feared the army. With inadequate police forces (Berlin, with its population of around 400 000, had a grand total of 160 'sergeants' and 'gendarmes' in 1848), Prussian Governments often had little option but to put the army into the front line of crowd control duties.. The soldiers all-too-readily reached for their rifles; and the *Junker*-dominated officer class, a byword for intolerance and arrogance, actually seemed to delight in shedding civilian blood. To ordinary Prussians, getting the army under proper control was a matter of justice and safety; to liberal politicians, alert to the dangers of counter-revolution, it was a matter of political survival.

These issues were brought into focus on 26 July, with the publication of the 'Waldeck Charter' – the Assembly's blue-print for a liberal Prussia. Proposals like the abolition (without compensation) of remaining feudal rights were controversial enough. But plans to limit the King's power of veto over legislation, and to strengthen the popular militia at the expense of the army, infuriated conservatives. Worst of all were demands that the King give up his powers as supreme commander. The more Frederick William IV was pushed, the more persuasive he found the arguments of the reactionary group which was urging him to launch a counter-revolutionary *coup*.

See pages 223–5

The mood in Berlin had anyway begun to turn against the forces of liberalism and radicalism. Conflicts between militant Republicans, strikers and demonstrators, and the Berlin militia – one clash in mid-October left 11 dead – increasingly made property owners long for the restoration of order.

Frederick William IV finally authorised his army to move against the liberal Prussian Assembly in November. He had been emboldened by the overwhelming success of Habsburg counter-revolution in Vienna. Prussian troops encountered no opposition: any resistance to the 13 000 strong army would have been suicidal. Plans for a taxpayers' strike collapsed: the middle classes had had enough of revolution. But the King's advisers were also disappointed. They had expected that counter-revolution would mean the restoration of absolutism. Instead, although the Assembly was dissolved on 5 December, on the same day Frederick William IV proclaimed a new constitution. It was much more conservative than the Waldeck Charter. For example the crown was to have an absolute veto over legislation. Furthermore, the new legislature's lower house was soon given a special voting system, which reserved two-thirds of the seats for the top two-thirds of Prussia's tax-payers – that is less than 20 per cent of the electorate. But the fact that Prussia had kept any constitution at all was potentially highly significant. It pleased moderate Liberals, isolated the radical Left, and consolidated monarchical authority; and it kept Prussia and the *Kleindeutsch* option (see below) in play at Frankfurt. Although the Revolution in Prussia was over, the hopes of Liberals and nationalists in Frankfurt were still alive.

KEY ISSUE

How and why did Prussian conservatives regain the political initiative after Spring 1848?

D *Frankfurt: from spring 1848 to spring 1849*

The delegates who had met at Frankfurt on 18 May faced a daunting task. They aimed at nothing less than bringing freedom and unity to the German people. They took as their first job the definition of the basic rights of German citizens. After all, Liberals had spent most of the previous three decades calling for political rights like free speech, and being persecuted for their pains. A formal proclamation of the rights to be enjoyed by **all** Germans would signal victory after years of reaction and would itself constitute a powerful statement of national unity.

However, Parliament acted slowly. The list of Basic Rights was not published until 27 December. Their limited nature provoked criticism. There was nothing in the document which addressed the demands for social and economic reform being made by radicals on behalf of the poor and unemployed. Worse, during the months of debate in Frankfurt, the political initiative was allowed to slip away. In the spring and summer of 1848, Habsburg authority seemed to have been broken, and in Berlin, the Liberals were still in the ascendancy. This was the time to deal with difficult questions like the future relationship of Austria with Germany, or the issue of who might be made king of the new state. But these problems were postponed; and by the time the delegates came to deal with them, they found their room for manoeuvre much circumscribed.

Großdeutsch or Kleindeutsch: two rival visions of Germany

A major problem was to decide where the boundaries of the 'Germany' should be. The *Großdeutsch* (Big German) solution envisaged the inclusion of the German speaking part of the Austrian Empire (including Prague as well as Vienna) within the new state, but the exclusion of all Austria's non-German regions. The *Kleindeutsch* solution envisaged the exclusion of all of the Austrian Empire, leaving a 'little Germany' centred on Prussia.

Most delegates favoured the *Großdeutsch* solution. Austrians were Germans, and Vienna was one of the great centres of German political life. But there could be no place for the Empire's Italians, Hungarians and so on in the new state: that would make a nonsense of the basic principle of nationalism. Therefore, the Empire would have to be institutionally broken up, and the Habsburg dynasty bound to its non-German lands by personal union alone.

For most of the summer of 1848, this was regarded as a practicable solution to the problem, largely because the Austrian Empire seemed on the verge of disintegration anyway. But the recovery of Habsburg power, beginning with Radetzky's victory at Custozza, transformed the terms of the debate. The revitalised Government in Vienna was hardly likely to agree to the *Großdeutsch* solution. For this would entail the destruction of the structures by which the Empire was held together just when, miraculously, the Empire seemed to have survived perhaps the greatest challenge to its survival in its long history. Once Windischgrätz had retaken Vienna, clearing a path for the energetic and ruthless Prince Schwarzenburg to become Austria's Minister President, it was made clear that Vienna would veto any plans for *Großdeutsch* Germany. 'The maintenance of Austria's political unity,' he proclaimed, 'was a German and a European necessity'.

See page 366

Attention thus came to be focused on the *Kleindeutsch* (Little German) answer to the question. Although this was to be the form which, under Bismarck, German unification finally took, the *Kleindeutsch* advocates of 1848 looked instead to a liberal Prussia that was ready to **merge** into, rather than **conquer** Germany – the sort of Prussia which seemed to have been created in March of that year.

See page 180

The *Kleindeutsch* solution, however, faced significant obstacles. By no means all German nationalists welcomed it, and many liberal-minded, Catholic southerners were still suspicious of Prussia's Protestant, militaristic and absolutist traditions. But far more significant were the views of the new Habsburg Government. Austria's exclusion from Germany would mean the definitive victory of Berlin over Vienna in the century-long struggle between these two capitals for predominance within the German sphere.

Late in March 1849 the Assembly decided, without great enthusiasm, to offer the crown of Germany to Frederick William IV. 'Better to have a small Germany than no Germany at all', it was said. But the Prussian King was never seriously tempted, and on 3 April, he rejected the offer. Partly he was being realistic: acceptance might well have provoked conflict with Austria and Russia. More fundamentally, he was revolted by Frankfurt's offer. Their crown, he privately remarked was 'an imaginary trinket baked from dirt and clay', tainted by the 'whorish smell of revolution'; 'the dog collar with which people want to chain me to the 1848 revolution'. Fixated romantic that he was, Frederick William IV could only dream of kingship 'by grace of God': the idea of becoming *Kaiser* (Emperor) 'by grace of the German people' was an appalling travesty of tradition and legitimacy.

This rejection of the crown should have marked the end of the revolution. The Prussian Government demanded the return of their delegates from Frankfurt; the Austrians had already gone. But the Left was determined to fight on: a rump parliament reconvened itself at Stuttgart, and the radical Central March Association – boasting a membership of over 100 000 – mobilised its supporters behind the 1848 constitution. Saxony, the Palatinate and Baden became the centres of this 'second' revolution. But between May and July, Prussian troops – acting throughout Germany as the enforcers of reaction – crushed the rebellions one by one.

> **KEY ISSUE**
>
> *What were the strengths and weaknesses of the Frankfurt Parliament?*

E *The failure of the 1848 Revolution in Germany*

The Revolution was not a total failure: most of the peasantry's remaining feudal dues had been abolished; and Prussia now had a constitution. But, compared with the hopes of Spring 1848, these gains were small. To some historians, 1848–9 marks a decisive turning point in German history; a definitive defeat for liberalism which left the way open for an ominous fusion of nationalism, conservatism and militarism in future generations.

The following factors should be considered in any explanation of the Revolution's defeat:

● the 'social fear' of the Liberals, which led them to exaggerate the threat of a second, left-wing revolution, and to underestimate the potential for counter-revolution from the Right
● the weaknesses of the Frankfurt Parliament: its tendency to talk too much; its failure to respond to the problem of poverty and unemployment; above all, its over-reliance on moral as opposed to physical authority
● above all, the Parliament had no troops of its own. Instead, as the painful events of September 1848 demonstrated, it was dependent

See page 223

on the armies of Germany's separate states to enforce its policies and to protect itself. But it was difficult to bend these forces to the will of the Revolution

● in retrospect, it is possible to argue that the revolutions were doomed from the start. The 'conflicting expectations' which had driven it were always going to be hard to satisfy; and as the course of the Revolution unfolded, it became apparent that 'there were too many and too great a variety of confusing interconnected problems that needed to be solved at once' (Nipperdey).

See page 222

See the bibliography on page 205

6 ⤙ PRUSSIA, AUSTRIA AND GERMANY

Before 1848, although the growth of the *Zollverein* had given Metternich some anxiety, Austria and Prussia had usually co-operated in their approach to German affairs. After the revolutions, however, the 'dualism' or rivalry which had characterised Austro-Prussian relations for most of the eighteenth century returned. The 1850s began with a humiliating set-back for Prussian ambitions, but the rest of the decade was marked by a sequence of dramatic reversals for Austria, and an explosive growth in Prussia's economic power, single-mindedly exploited so as to keep Austria out of the *Zollverein*.

Bismarck, who had observed Austria closely whilst Prussia's representative to the *Diet* of the German Confederation, realised how wide the gap was between Austria's pretensions as a Great Power and its actual strength. His appointment as Prussian Prime Minister in 1862 not only led to the resolution of a domestic political crisis which had threatened to paralyse the country; it effectively gave him control of Prussian foreign policy. He was to display immense skill, energy, resourcefulness and ruthlessness in his determination to increase the power of the Prussian state.

See page 183

TIMELINE

Events in German unification between 1848 and 1870

1848	Uprising in Berlin
	German National Assembly met in Frankfurt
1849	National Assembly offered German crown to Frederick William IV
1850	Prussia given a 'liberal' constitution
	Erfurt Union
	Treaty of Olmütz
1858	William becomes Regent of Prussia (King from 1861)
1862	Bismarck became Prussian Minister President
1864	Prusso-Danish War
1865	Convention of Gastein
	Bismarck met Napoleon III at Biarritz
1866	Austro-Prussian War
	Treaty of Prague
1867	North German Confederation set up
1870	Outbreak of Franco-Prussian War

A *Prussian and Austrian foreign policy in the 1850s: a shifting balance of power*

Although Frederick William IV had refused the German crown, he retained some spirit of romantic nationalism, and worked out a scheme by which he hoped to reconcile the objective of German unification with his belief in divine right monarchy. Prussia would take the lead in a League of Kings, which could fill the vacuum left by the collapse of the German Confederation.

At first this new 'German Union' had the reluctant support of most of the German states. However, the German Union's chances for success depended almost completely on Austria's military fortunes. By September 1849, having finally crushed the Hungarian rebels, Austria was ready to give its full attention to German affairs – and this meant putting Prussia in its place. Encouraged by Austria's recovery, the larger German states began to break away from the Union. Schwarzenberg, Austria's dynamic new Chancellor, re-established the old *Diet* at Frankfurt under Austria's presidency. Prussia boycotted the meeting and tried to press on with its *Kleindeutsch* plans. The resulting standoff very nearly ended in war. A domestic crisis in the strategically sensitive state of Hesse-Kassel led to the Confederation sending in troops to restore its ruler's authority – troops which could also be used to cut the vital road links between east and west Prussia which ran through this little state. The thought of conflict between Austria and Prussia appalled the more cautious advisers around Frederick William IV, not least because Prussia seemed certain to lose, and Russia was siding with Austria.

At Olmütz in November 1850, Prussia agreed to abandon its Union project and to rejoin the restored Confederation. These terms represented a total humiliation for Prussia, and the end for over a decade of its *Kleindeutsch* dreams.

But Olmütz did not lead to a clear restoration of Austrian primacy within Germany, nor reopen an era of Austro-Prussian co-operation. In fact, it was Austria's last foreign policy success for almost three decades. Austrian diplomacy began to go awry with the Crimean War. Russia was trying to expand its influence over the Ottoman Empire, a move strongly resisted by Britain and France. The Tsar confidently expected Austria to contribute at least diplomatic support to his cause: after all, he had come to the Habsburgs' assistance in 1849. Instead, Austria supported the British and French, even mobilising its army along the Danube frontier in a gesture of hostility to the Russians. The Tsar denounced Austria's 'shameful ingratitude'. In alienating Russia, Austria had lost its most powerful and consistent ally. Austria's dangerous diplomatic isolation was confirmed in 1859, when it went to war with France and Piedmont to try and defend its Italian possessions. This time, Russia offered no assistance in Austria's hour of need, and the Prussians did little to help either – at least until Austria had suffered some significant reversals. This calculated reluctance provoked Emperor Franz Joseph to denounce the Prussians – in private – as 'despicable scum'. It was all too clear that the Government in Berlin had outgrown

See pages 28 and 221

See page 103

the role of honoured junior partner in which Metternich had usually been able to cast it.

B *Liberals and nationalists in the 1850s: a shifting conception of power*

Whilst diplomats in Berlin and Vienna dramatically re-evaluated their mutual relationship, German Liberals and nationalists were re-thinking their strategy. They were to discover **Realpolitik** – the politics of realism.

According to proponents of *Realpolitik*, the men of 1848 had been too idealistic and unworldly. Liberal principles and nationalist theories were admirable in their way, but the business of politics was to get things done. This entailed the need for compromise, and a frank recognition that beliefs had to be harnessed to power, especially the power of the state.

This analysis encouraged Liberals and nationalists to look anew at what Prussia might contribute to their cause. Prussia was not their most obvious ally. As German Liberals had finally realised, Frederick William IV was emphatically not a Liberal, and the traditions of the Prussian state were profoundly militaristic and authoritarian. But it was not easy to find alternatives to Prussia for the role of nationalist battering ram. Austria, as the Crimean and Italian Wars had demonstrated, had an exhausting range of commitments which pulled it into conflicts in which 'Germany' had no interests at stake, whilst the multi-ethnic nature of its empire made it a most unlikely patron of nationalism. Prussia at least had liberal-national potential. Its Rhineland province made it the natural defender of the fatherland; and the *Zollverein* was a Prussian success, already knitting *Kleindeutschland* together in a web of trade, industry and transport.

In 1858, it even seemed possible that Prussian politics was about to take a liberal turn. Frederick William IV had a stroke and was forced to abdicate. His younger brother, finally crowned as Wilhelm I in 1861, became Regent. Wilhelm had no time for the medieval claptrap of his predecessor, or for the reactionary clique around him at court. The old order seemed distinctly out of favour. Furthermore, the Liberals did remarkably well in the 1858 *Landtag* elections, winning a majority over the conservatives of more than 150 seats. A 'New Era' seemed to have opened.

This was the context in which the National Society was founded in 1859. Partly in imitation of the Italian Nation Society, which was then helping to pave the way for Piedmontese-led Italian unification, this National Society looked to Prussia to take the lead in Germany. It was not a mass movement, but its membership of 25 000 represented much of the professional and propertied *élite* of Germany, and not just of Prussia. Alongside it, the choral societies and gymnasts clubs continued to grow, their nationalist-minded forces now augmented by a new 'rifle-men movement', whose annual festivals were attracting up to 100 000 participants in the early 1860s.

KEY ISSUE

To what extent did Prussia's position vis-à-vis Austria improve or deteriorate between 1850 and 1856?

Realpolitik is one of the most important concepts of nineteenth and twentieth century politics and diplomacy. Because it has no precise English equivalent, historians usually leave it in its original form

See pages 162–3

See pages 106–8

KEY ISSUE

How did liberal nationalists rethink their strategy in the 1850s?

Bismarck saw much potential in these developments. They suggested to him that the programme of Prussian expansionism which he had been advocating since 1852 might actually – in its nationalist guise – enjoy widespread popular support, and thus also more easily win international approval.

C New era, old habits: Wilhelm I, army reform and constitutional crisis

These hopes and calculations made the political crisis which paralysed Prussia between 1859 and 1862 terribly disappointing for the national-liberal movement. The lesson was painful: if a nationalist solution to the German question were not possible with Austria, a liberal solution was not possible with Prussia.

The New Era of liberal dreams, according to which a forward-looking Prussia, led by Wilhelm I, would take up the banner of 'freedom and unity' on behalf of the German people, turned out to be wishful thinking. Wilhelm I was no progressive: he was unimaginative, dutiful and deeply conservative. Above all, he was a Prussian soldier. The army was his life and love, and Wilhelm I was determined to expand its numbers and improve its efficiency. When the *Landtag* first queried and then blocked the reform schemes which von Roon (Wilhelm I's Minister of Defence) proposed, it was not just a challenge to the King's authority: it seemed to him like an attack on the traditions and well-being of the Prussian state.

Liberals in the *Landtag* did not object to the planned increase in the size of the army. It was the downgrading of the *Landwehr* – a sort of National Guard – which made them uneasy. Here, they rightly detected an underlying political agenda. Neither the King nor the Defence Minister had a high opinion of the *Landwehr*. To them, this militia was not just militarily inefficient; these 'soldiers' were merely citizens in uniform. Wilhelm I believed in a totally professional army quite separate from society, officered by aristocrats, whose loyalty to the monarchical order was beyond question, and whose troops had had instilled into them a spirit of total obedience; in other words, an army that could be relied on to shoot dead not just *Frenchmen*, but, if revolution reared its head, *Prussians*.

The liberal majority in the *Landtag* wanted to negotiate with the Government. Perhaps a larger role for the semi-civilian *Landwehr* could be preserved? Perhaps – and this was initially their underlying agenda – the aristocratic arrogance with which army officers often treated 'mere' civilians could be reduced?

Wilhelm I refused to concede an inch. Immediately, the issue took on ominous constitutional significance. Parliamentarians feared that, if they capitulated, reactionaries would begin to push them around all the time; more aggressive Liberals wanted to seize the opportunity to teach the King a lesson and assert their right to control the military budget. For Wilhelm I, it then became a question of 'King's army or parliament's army', and ultimately a question of 'monarchy or revolution'. 'If Prussia goes red', von Roon exclaimed, 'the crown will roll in the mud'.

There seemed to be only one way out of the crisis: new elections might secure Wilhelm I's conservative ministers the anti-liberal majority they needed to get the Army Bill through. But the more elections Wilhelm I called, the larger and more defiant the Liberal majority became. By March 1862, 285 of the parliament's 352 delegates were Liberal.

The promise of the New Era had totally evaporated. Civil war was a possibility, with prominent generals advocating counter-revolution and military dictatorship. Wilhelm I considered abdicating. Either way, disaster beckoned for Prussia. It was at this dramatic point of crisis that Bismarck was called to Berlin.

OTTO VON BISMARCK

PROFILE

Bismarck (1815–98) was born to be a servant of the Prussian state. His father was a *Junker* (an aristocratic landowner) who had served in the Prussian army, and his mother came from a family of distinguished civil servants. Although he loved the countryside, Bismarck was too adventurous to accept the life of the provincial nobleman. Elected to the United *Diet* in 1847, Bismarck soon won notoriety for his forceful speeches defending the Prussian monarchy against its critics, and he became a member of the circle around Frederick William IV which urged the need for counter-revolution. He increased his reactionary reputation with a defence of the capitulation of Olmütz, in which he expressed relief that Prussia had turned its back on a liberal-national foreign policy, and looked forward instead to an era of close co-operation between Berlin and Vienna. His appointment (1851) as Prussia's representative at the Frankfurt *Diet* was both a reward for his services and a chance to put his hopes for collaboration with Austria into practice.

However, he soon reassessed his views of Austro-Prussian dualism. Vienna, Bismarck became convinced, was simply disguising the promotion of its own national self-interest beneath talk of Austro-Prussian monarchical solidarity. Bismarck became convinced that Prussia deserved parity with Austria in German affairs. He judged that Austria's relative economic backwardness and the burdensome range of its imperial commitments made it unrealistic for Austria to claim the right to lead. But Austria refused to yield, leaving Bismarck to conclude that 'Germany is clearly too small for us both; as long as an honourable arrangement concerning the influence of each cannot be concluded, we will both plough the same disputed acre. In the not too distant future we shall have to fight for our existence against Austria.'

PICTURE 12 *Bismarck in the North German Reichstag. 'Decisive he is and a powerful speaker – that has to be conceded' (Figaro, Vienna, 5 March, 1870)*

This conclusion, combined with Bismarck's recommendation that Prussia pursue its struggle against Austria through an alliance with Napoleon III – illegitimacy personified to German conservatives – shocked his more cautious friends in Berlin. Bismarck's reputation for unprincipled adventurism was confirmed when he went on to argue that Prussian interests might best be advanced if the Government adopted the Liberals' own programme of *kleindeutsch* nationalism, thereby neutralising its domestic critics and drawing them into the service of the Prussian state.

Bismarck's readiness to follow through the unsentimental logic of *Realpolitik* to its natural conclusion had led him a long way from the orthodox conservatism of 1848–50.

When Bismarck was transferred to the post of ambassador to St Petersburg in 1859, he was probably right to express the view that he was being put 'in cold storage'. It was an indication of the depth of the political crisis that convulsed Prussia in 1862 that Wilhelm I felt that he had no alternative but to turn to him to save the monarchy. Bismarck was to remain at the centre of Prussian life for the next quarter century. With his powerful and sceptical intelligence, and ruthless will to dominate, he was to revolutionise the face of German and European politics.

Wilhelm I was considering abdicating when he interviewed his future Minister-President. But Bismarck, as he recalled in his *Memoirs*, was able to reassure Wilhelm I that all was not lost:

I succeeded in convincing him that … it was … a question of monarchical rule or parliamentary government, and that the latter must be avoided at all costs, if even by a period of dictatorship. I said: 'In this situation I shall, even if your Majesty command me to do things which I do not consider right, tell you my opinion quite openly; but if you finally persist in yours, I will rather perish with the King than forsake your Majesty in the contest with parliamentary government.' This view was at that time strong and absolute in me, because I regarded the negotiations and phrases of the Opposition of that day as politically disastrous in face of the national task of Prussia, and because I cherished such strong feelings of devotion and affection for William I, that the thought of perishing with him appeared to me, under the circumstances, a natural and congenial conclusion to my life.

This meeting laid for a successful working relationship that would last until Wilhelm I's death in 1888. The partnership was not without its strains. The King had uncomplicated beliefs about right and wrong which were sometimes upset by Bismarck's unorthodox approach. As a consequence, Bismarck admitted, it could be 'hard work to bring the old man round'. 'But', he added, 'once you had won him for something, he held fast to what had been decided'. Wilhelm I was the rock on whom Bismarck built his quarter-century long dominance of German politics.

1. *What made Bismarck's appeal to Wilhelm I so effective?*
2. *What are the strengths and weaknesses of Bismarck's Memoirs for the historian?*

D *Austro-Prussian rivalry resolved*

LAYING THE GROUNDWORK

Bismarck is often presented – not least by himself in his *Memoirs* – as a political genius who rarely, if ever, made a mistake, and who followed a grand programme leading inexorably to German unification under Prussian control. However, it should be noted:

- in domestic politics, he made tactical blunders in his first three years in office in his attempts to get an understanding with the Liberals. By 1865 he seemed to have failed
- in foreign policy, his diplomatic outmanoeuvring of Denmark in 1863–4, culminating in a total victory for Prussia, owed much to Danish miscalculation
- the war which Bismarck and Prussia fought against Austria in 1866 was essentially a German civil war, and initially made Bismarck a villain, not a hero, in the eyes of many German nationalists. Furthermore, the war was a terrible gamble whose ultimate success owed much to Austrian incompetence
- although the war was a decisive defeat for Austrian ambitions in Germany, it was by no means clear to Bismarck how, how far, or at what pace, Prussia might move thereafter towards the unification of the rest of Germany.

Bismarck's first priority on becoming Chief-minister was to resolve the domestic crisis over the military budget. Many on the right of Prussian politics expected him to resort to a royalist *coup*, dismissing the *Landtag* (Parliament) and establishing a dictatorship. But Bismarck disliked the thought of ruling 'at the point of bayonets': he doubted whether an effective, energetic government could be established on the basis of crude military power. Instead, he attempted an altogether subtler strategy. He tried to reconcile Liberals and nationalists to his Government by implying that the Prussian state might take up the banner of nationalism. In a speech to the Prussian *Landtag* on 29 September 1862 Bismarck declared:

KEY ISSUE
Which aspects of his speech did Bismarck hope would appeal to Prussian supporters of German nationalism?

Germany doesn't look to Prussia's liberalism, but to its power: Bavaria, Württemberg, Baden can indulge in liberalism, but no one will expect them to undertake Prussia's role; Prussia must gather and consolidate her strength in readiness for the favourable moment, which has already been missed several times; ... not by means of speeches and majority verdicts will be the great decisions of the time be made – that was the great mistake of 1848 and 1849 – but by iron and blood ...

The Prussian Liberals and nationalists were not to be bought off yet. The historian and nationalist Heinrich von Treitschke – later one of Bismark's greatest admirers – wrote to his brother-in-law: 'You know how passionately I love Prussia, but when I hear this shallow country squire Bismarck bragging about the 'iron and blood' with which he intends to subdue Germany, the ugliness of it seems to me only exceeded by the absurdity'.

Bismarck had no alternative but to impose his budget and push through von Roon's reforms without parliamentary approval. Outraged by Bismarck's bullying tactics, his opponents were convinced, mistakenly, that his fall was inevitable.

WAR AGAINST DENMARK

The Austro-Prussian War against Denmark over the Schleswig–Holstein question was a triumph for Bismarck, as much for the skill with which he subordinated Austria's foreign policy to Prussia's needs, as for the finesse with which he manoeuvred through the labyrinth of the 'Schleswig–Holstein' question itself. This 'question' was complex:

See Map 6 on page 159

● The Duchies of Schleswig and Holstein were located between Denmark and Prussia. Although ruled by the King of Denmark since 1460, they were not part of the Danish state. The King ruled them as their Duke.
● Holstein was part of the German Confederation, and its population was predominantly German. The population of Schleswig was mixed: predominantly German to the south, Danish in the north.

German nationalists dreamed of incorporating both Duchies within a united Germany; Danish nationalists wanted Schleswig fully absorbed within the Danish state.

- In March 1848, a German nationalist rebellion had broken out in the Duchies, aided by Prussian troops. The Great Powers forced Prussia to back down, and the Treaty of London (1852) restored the pre-war arrangements.
- The accession of Christian IX as King of Denmark in 1863 reopened the question. Germans in the Duchies disputed his right to inherit (he was only the cousin of the childless, deceased Danish King); they claimed that the Duke of Augustenburg, a German, was their rightful ruler. Augustenburg promptly became the hero of German nationalists. But Danish nationalists forced their new King, Christian IX, to try to absorb Schleswig completely within the Danish state.
- This was a decisive blunder which not only outraged German nationalist sentiment but broke the Treaty of London, and thus gave Bismarck a chance to intervene in the crisis as the defender of international law.

Looking back, Bismarck believed that his handling of the ensuing crisis was perhaps his greatest single achievement. The individual actions, he mused, were, in themselves, mere trifles: 'to see that they dovetailed was the difficulty'.

Bismarck's ultimate success in bringing both Duchies under Prussian control was both startling and unexpected. By-passing the claims of the Duke of Augustenburg, he secured Austrian co-operation for a joint invasion of Schleswig in February 1864, with the public objective of forcing Denmark to respect its treaty obligations. The Danes were soon defeated at the Battle of Düppel, but, hoping for British intervention, they rejected a compromise settlement at a peace conference in London. They badly miscalculated: British help failed to materialise, and by the Treaty of Vienna (August 1864), Denmark had to hand over Schleswig and Holstein to Austria and Prussia.

A BREATHING SPACE

Bismarck had reason to be satisfied. The German Confederation, which he regarded as a useless pro-Austrian and anti-Prussian talking shop, had largely been ignored in the crisis, further diminishing any claim it might have to be a national forum. Neither had he allowed Prussian foreign policy to be subordinated to the cause of German nationalism – Augustenberg had been sidelined. The Prussian army had given the Danes a beating. But the ultimate fate of Schleswig-Holstein had to be settled. And how were Austro-Prussian relations to develop?

The Austrian Emperor Franz Josef hoped for a return to the fruitful Austro-Prussian partnership of the Metternich era of 1815–48. The victory over Denmark was, by these lights, a victory for international law and established rights in European diplomacy. Bismarck appeared to agree, stating to Vienna that he '[regarded] the Danish conflict as being in essence an episode in the struggle of the monarchical principle against the European revolution …'.

See page 28

However, negotiations in August 1864 between Prussia and Austria to plan future policy got nowhere. One proposal involved Prussian support for the Austrian re-conquest of Lombardy, in return for Austria conceding to Prussia a controlling influence in the affairs of northern Germany, including the annexation of Schleswig-Holstein. But Wilhelm I expressed unease at grabbing the Duchies, and Franz Josef proved reluctant to give up Austria's traditional claims to the leadership of the German Confederation. Neither would the Prussians agree to Austrian membership of the *Zollverein*. Anti-Prussian influences prevailed in Vienna, and to Prussia's annoyance, Austria began to encourage Augustenburg's supporters to reassert their hero's claims to the Duchies.

War between Austria and Prussia could have come in 1865, but it was postponed by the Convention of Gastein (August). This divided the administration of the duchies: Schleswig to Prussia, Holstein to Austria. There was no doubt as to who held the upper hand. Holstein, bordering on Prussia, was militarily indefensible. A bankrupt Austria was reluctant to fight anyway. But Bismarck was merely biding his time. As long as Austria refused to concede parity to Prussia within the German sphere – this, and not the quest for German unification, was the deeper issue at stake – war, sooner or later, was inevitable.

Frantic diplomatic activity followed the signing of the Convention . The international position favoured Prussia. Austria was isolated. Russia had still not forgiven Austria's betrayal during the Crimean War. Neither could Austria realistically hope for help from France. Napoleon III regarded Austria as the upholder of the 'detested' treaties of 1815; in particular Austrian retention of Venetia had left the unification of Italy (a project undertaken in 1859 under French patronage) tantalisingly incomplete. The British were entering an era of semi-isolationism in their dealings with continental Europe. Furthermore, London saw Napoleon III as the greatest threat to the European balance of power. In that respect, a stronger Prussia might be better able to contain French adventurism.

Bismarck made two moves between 1865–6 to consolidate Prussia's diplomatic advantage. In October 1865, he sounded out Napoleon III, and in April 1866 he signed a military alliance with Italy. Both helped to clear the way for war against Austria.

Bismarck's so-called 'conversation at Biarritz' with the French Emperor was inconclusive and remains rather mysterious. In the 1850s, Bismarck had shocked his friends by talking of Prussia's need for an alliance with France against Austria and he may still have hoped for one. But in the end, Bismarck seemed happy enough with an understanding that France would most likely remain neutral in any forthcoming Austro-Prussian conflict. It was evident to Bismarck that Napoleon III's opposition to the Habsburg system in general, and Habsburg rule over Venetia in particular, was so strong as to make any *rapprochement* between Vienna and Paris most unlikely. As an extra inducement to Napoleon III to remain neutral, Bismarck seems to have given a highly general gesture of approval for France's future expansion

– not in the German speaking Rhineland, but 'anywhere [for example Belgium or Luxembourg, perhaps] where French is spoken in the world'. Whatever actually happened at Biarritz, Bismarck could return to Berlin reasonably confident that his plans for Prussian expansion would not meet with French opposition.

Bismarck's confidence could only be increased by the assistance Napoleon III gave in brokering the military alliance with Italy. By this treaty, Italy was committed to join Prussia in any attack on Austria launched within a three-month period, with Venetia to be its reward in the event of Austria's defeat. The prospect of a two-front war compelled the Austrians to divide their forces; a possibly decisive factor in their ultimate defeat by the Prussians at Königgrätz.

See page 185

The negotiation of the Italian alliance was therefore a significant achievement for Bismarck. It was also a characteristic one. Old-fashioned Prussian conservatives were shocked at the course of Bismarck's diplomacy over 1865–6. The mutual understanding that had been achieved with the upstart 'Emperor' Napoleon III was distasteful enough, but the alliance with Italy was worse: this was a brazen conspiracy with Victor Emmanuel, which aimed at war with Emperor Franz Josef – a fellow sovereign and a brother German! Where was legitimacy or monarchical solidarity now?

Bismarck's energetic and unorthodox *Realpolitik* continued. Abroad, his agents were liaising secretly with Hungarian and Balkan revolutionaries, apparently aiming to subvert the Austrian Empire. Within Germany, he startled friends and enemies alike in March 1866 by announcing plans to replace the Federal Assembly with a German Parliament elected according to universal manhood suffrage. Prussia, Bismarck was convinced, now had to make common cause with the German national movement, whose natural leader he argued it was. On the eve of war itself, Wilhelm I's proclamation 'To the German People' made Bismarck's strategy even clearer. It announced Prussia's 'decision to take up the struggle for the unity of Germany hitherto thwarted by the self-interest of the individual states'. Well might Bismarck exclaim: 'they accuse me of being reactionary … but I would march if need be even with revolution'.

Bismarck had not gone mad. He had recognised since the late 1850s that German nationalism was a political force which could be turned to Prussia's advantage. Playing the nationalist card should unite the Prussians, Liberals and conservatives alike, behind the Hohenzollern dynasty. Beyond this, it could be used to justify and accelerate a programme of Prussian expansionism, with the smaller German states being swept away in nationalist fervour. It would also help to resolve the Austro-Prussian duel in the latter's favour, for Austria could never play the nationalist card: Austria's multi-national Empire could have no role in the new, Prussian-led German state.

But, on the eve of the Austro-Prussian War, not everything had gone according to plan. Prussian Liberals mostly remained unconvinced. Certainly no one had taken seriously Bismarck's plans for a German parliament. Many nationalists bitterly resented the 'war of brothers'

KEY ISSUE

What were the long term and short-term causes of the Austro-Prussian War?

which was set to divide the German people. Within the Confederation, all the other significant German states were allied with Austria, whilst abroad France and Austria were in last minute negotiations. Bismarck had staked absolutely everything on a single throw of the dice. For once, there was no way out. The clash of armies would decide all.

WAR AGAINST AUSTRIA AND ITS CONSEQUENCES

In the coming conflict, Bismarck's had the advantage that General von Moltke, Chief of the Prussian General Staff, was a military strategist of genius, whilst his Austrian counterpart, General Benedek, was incompetent. Moltke revolutionised military thinking in the nineteenth century in three ways:

- he recognised that the sheer size of conscripted armies (a total of 500 000 troops fought at Königgrätz) meant that new, devolved command structures had to be created
- he appreciated that the coming of the railway and the telegraph would make it possible to move armies relatively quickly over great distances, and that very careful planning would be needed to do this effectively
- he realised that rapid developments in military technology – the advent of the breech-loading rifle and (especially after 1866) of the steel breech-loading cannons – would revolutionise battlefield tactics too.

The Seven Weeks War against Austria was a triumphant vindication of Moltke's approach. The key to his success was the Prussian General Staff. Working under von Moltke's calm and meticulous direction, this bureaucratic military *élite* planned the mobilisation, deployment and provisioning of Prussia's forces. By exploiting Prussia's superior railway network (five lines led down towards the likely Bohemian war zone, compared with one line serving Austrian needs), the Prussian army could mobilise in half the time that would be taken by the enemy. By splitting his army into three units along a front 200 miles long, Moltke greatly increased its speed of movement and flexibility. Tactically, the breech-loading rifle gave the Prussian troops a crucial advantage too: soldiers could fire it lying down and at five times the rate of the Austrians' much more primitive muzzle-loading musket.

But the Austrian cause was far from hopeless. On the morning of the battle of Königgrätz, two-fifths of the Prussian army failed to appear! At midday, William I exclaimed anxiously, 'Moltke, Moltke … we are losing this battle'. But Benedek, over-cautious and over-pessimistic, missed the opportunity to smash the Prussian centre, and in the early afternoon, the Prussian Second Army finally arrived. From thereon, Austria's defeat was inevitable.

Bismarck displayed his diplomatic and political genius after the war:

- he managed the international repercussions of Königgrätz by quickly making peace with Austria, and minimising French interference in the peace process

KEY ISSUE

Why did Prussia win the Seven Weeks' War?

- he reconstructed 'Germany'. The old Confederation was dead, and Austrian influence within Germany too. Bismarck had to consolidate Prussia's ascendancy
- he helped to refashion the internal political life of Prussia.

Bismarck's methods were distinctly unorthodox, bewildering some old-fashioned Prussian conservatives. But his hardheaded approach served the long-term interests of the Prussian state.

The briefness of the Seven Weeks' War had frustrated Napoleon III. He had been anticipating a long drawn out struggle, resulting in the exhaustion of both participants and only ending with a European peace congress at which France would be able to assert its power. After Königgrätz, the Emperor was under considerable domestic pressure to intervene on the Austrian side, to check Prussia's all too rapid ascendancy and stake France's claim for territorial 'compensation'.

Bismarck had to act quickly: a generous peace treaty was the key. He explained his thinking to his wife:

> If we are not excessive in our demands and do not believe that we have conquered the world, we will attain a peace that is worth our effort. I have the thankless task of pouring water into the bubbling wine and making it clear that we do not live alone in Europe but with three other Powers that hate and envy us.

The terms of Treaty of Prague (23 August) reflected these anxieties. Austria was to pay an indemnity, but, with the exception of Venetia, (at last acquired by Italy, even though its only contribution to the campaign itself had been two defeats), it was to suffer no losses of territory.

Bismarck struggled to get these terms accepted, not by Austria or France – which both appreciated that the terms were the best Austria was likely to get – but by Wilhelm I and General von Moltke. Bismarck had only been able to persuade the old King to proclaim war in the first place by convincing him that Prussia had been the victim of Austrian aggression. But the King now could not understand why a defeated aggressor should not be decisively punished. Bismarck, however, knew that the Prussian victory had been decisive. Austria was forced to turn its back on Germany. In practice, this meant the dismantling of the old Austrian-led Confederation, its replacement with a new North German Confederation of Bismarck's design, and significant additions to Prussian territory itself – albeit not at Austria's expense. For almost 150 years, Prussia and Austria had manoeuvred and fought against each other for ascendancy within the German sphere. That struggle was now over.

Bismarck's ruthlessness was evident in the annexation of Holstein, and of those territories in North Germany which had dared to oppose Prussia: Schleswig, Hanover, Hesse and Nassau. This was more like conquest than unification. To principled Prussian conservatives, such acts marked the awful triumph of 'Godless and lawless greed'. But most

Prussians took pleasure in the fruits of a great military victory, especially as these gains finally filled out the strategic gap between the Prussia's Rhineland provinces and old Prussia in the east.

The constitution of the new North German Confederation (February 1867) ensured that Prussian control extended beyond its new borders. Superficially, the Confederation's federal structure preserved some independence for the still sovereign states (like Saxony) included within it. These kept their own legal and administrative systems, and their own parliaments (as, of course, did Prussia). But key features of its constitution were tailored to meet Prussia's, and Bismarck's needs:

- the King of Prussia was to be the President of North German Confederation, and the commander-in-chief of its army, with the power of making war and peace. He also had the power of appointment or dismissing the Chancellor
- the Chancellor – that is Bismarck – was responsible only to the President. He did not need the support of a majority in the *Reichstag* (see below), nor could the *Reichstag* dismiss him
- the *Reichstag* was to be elected by universal manhood suffrage (Bismarck was gambling here on German peasants being essentially conservative and patriotic in outlook). But its powers were limited – for example it had no control over the Chancellor (see above) and very little over military spending
- there was an upper chamber – the *Bundesrat* (Federal Council) – which consisted of 43 delegates from the Confederation's member states. Seventeen of these were from Prussia; not surprisingly, Prussia was never outvoted and its bloc vote gave it an absolute veto over constitutional changes, for which a two-thirds majority was needed.

The smooth running of the new Confederation's *Reichstag* seemed unlikely to pose too many problems for Bismarck, given the political revolution he had already effected within Prussia. Here, the central problem was the long-standing rupture between the executive and the *Landtag* – that is between Bismarck and the Liberals. To Prussian reactionaries, Königgrätz had seemed a wonderful opportunity. Liberalism could be damned as unpatriotic and politically bankrupt; Wilhelm, Bismarck and the victorious army could tear up the constitution with popular approval. But to the dismay and incredulity of the hard-liners, Bismarck's strategy was the very opposite: he used Königgrätz to negotiate, from a position of strength, a political alliance with the Liberals. The key to this realignment was the passage of an Indemnity Bill in September 1866.

In this Bill, the Prussian executive explicitly recognised that its four years rule without a budget had been without 'legal foundation', and sought Parliament's assurance that no action would be taken against it. Some Liberals suspected a Bismarckian trick; some conservatives felt betrayed by the Government's readiness to compromise with the old liberal enemy: but out of the resulting parliamentary confusion the Indemnity Bill became law and the National Liberal Party was born.

This party was committed to consolidating and completing the drive towards unification which had been so dramatically begun, and to supporting Bismarck.

It is possible to see the majority decision of the Prussian Liberals as a sell-out: overwhelmed by the speed with which Bismarck was achieving their *Kleindeutsch* dreams, they agreed to forget the persecuting authoritarianism of the preceding years. They wilfully ignored how far Königgrätz was itself a victory for the traditions of Prussian militarism which they abhorred. But such an analysis underestimates both the concession Bismarck had to make to secure the compromise – he had had to seek indemnification from parliament – and his desire to work constructively with the forces of liberal nationalism in the future. Even Bismarck knew that he could not build the *Reich* by himself.

7 ⌐ BISMARCK VERSUS NAPOLEON III: THE TWISTING ROAD TO SEDAN

Unlike his new liberal allies, Bismarck was not in a hurry to complete the process of unification. And yet, less than five years after the Battle of Königgrätz, the *Reich* was proclaimed in the Hall of Mirrors at Versailles, Bavaria, Wurttemberg and Baden were absorbed within its federal structure, and King Wilhelm I added 'German Emperor' to his titles.

A *Background to war*

Unification was to be forged in war against France, the traditional foe. This did not come about by accident. But how far Bismarck planned the events – a boast to be found in his *Memoirs* – is questionable. In February 1869, Bismarck wrote to his representative in Munich:

> That German unity could be promoted by actions involving force, I think is self-evident. But there is a quite different question, and that has to do with the precipitation of a powerful catastrophe and the responsibility of choosing the time for it. A voluntary intervention in the evolution of history, which is determined by purely subjective factors, results only in the shaking down of unripe fruit, and that German unity is no ripe fruit at this time leaps, in my opinion, to the eye. If the time that lies ahead works in the interest of unity as much as the period since 1840, the year in which a national movement was perceptible for the first time since the war of liberation [i.e. 1813–14] then we can look to the future calmly and leave the rest to our successors.

KEY ISSUE

How did Bismarck consolidate his victory over Austria abroad and exploit it at home?

1. Explain
   (a) 'the shaking down of unripe fruit', *and*
   (b) 'if the time that lies ahead … the war of liberation'.
2. When you have read pages 195–7, contrast Bismarck's attitudes towards 'actions involving force' in this document with his actions in 1870.

See page 143

The Hohenzollern candidacy

In September 1868, Queen Isabella of Spain was overthrown in a military *coup*. Madrid's generals, however, did not want to turn Spain into a Republic (which would have had radical connotations) and so began headhunting amongst the royal houses of Europe for a likely candidate to ascend the Spanish throne. Leopold of Hohenzollern-Sigmaringen, a Catholic prince who had married into the Portuguese royal family and was a distant relative of the King of Prussia, seemed to be the front-runner.

Even ardent German nationalists would not have dared to predict that a war between France and Prussia was near, that a war would result in the total defeat of France, or that Germany would be united as a result of victory. This was because immediately after Königgrätz, the cause of unification had seemed to be going *backwards*. Bismarck's approach to the 'problem' of the south German states was cautious. He knew very well how distinctive and different their political cultures were. Their Catholic, liberal traditions put them at the opposite end of the religious and political spectrum to Prussia. He wondered how easily they would be digested, and worried that their absorption would dilute the *Junker* values of aristocracy, authoritarianism and militarism which he cherished. But he could hardly leave the south German states in vulnerable isolation. Only a few days after Königgrätz, Napoleon III began to talk about 'compensation' along the Rhine. Bismarck increased their security – and Prussian influence over them – by negotiating a secret offensive/defensive military alliance with them in August 1866.

Bismarck then drew these states deeper into Prussia's gravitational field by creating a national *Zollparlament* (Custom's Parliament) in 1867. By having the citizens of all the *Zollverein* states – which included Bavaria, Baden and Württemberg – elect representatives to the *Zollparlament*, Bismarck hoped that all Germans might get into the habit of thinking and voting nationally. Anti-Prussian prejudice would be eroded by the *Zollparlament's* common purpose, and neutralised by its members' common prosperity.

However, the opposite happened. Elections to the *Zollparlament* in 1868 became the forum for the denunciation of Prussia's designs to dominate what was left of free Germany. The National Liberals' slogan, *Von Zollparlament zu Vollparlament* ('from Custom's Parliament to Full (National) Parliament') struck all the wrong notes with the voters of the south German states. To them, union with Prussia meant higher taxes, conscription, and an authoritarian style of government. The 1868 elections were a disaster for the Chancellor's schemes. In Württemberg, pro-national candidates failed to win a single seat! Parliamentary elections in Bavaria the following year proved even more ominous. There, the Catholic clergy had taken the lead in organising a 'Patriotic Party' which bitterly opposed the pro-Bismarck government in Munich. A major political crisis followed, with Bismarck even contemplating sending in the Prussian army to help restore the authority of his southern political allies.

Neither was Bismarck comfortable with developments in the North German Confederation. The National Liberals were growing increasingly frustrated at the setbacks to the *Kleindeutsch* project. Some demanded a revision of the 1867 constitution; for example, for the introduction of the principle of ministerial responsibility to Parliament, and for proper parliamentary control over military spending. Bismarck had no intention, however, of diluting the powers of the Prussian crown or of the Chancellor. Conflict loomed.

It was at this point that Bismarck took a serious interest in **the Hohenzollern candidacy**. Bismarck knew Paris would be severely provoked by the thought of a German prince on the Spanish throne. Confident of winning any showdown – diplomatic or military – Bismarck calculated that with a triumph over Napoleon III, he could kick-start the national project back into life and simultaneously wrest the political initiative back from those tiresome and fractious parliamentarians in Berlin and Munich.

Franco-Prussian relations had been deteriorating since 1866. The French public soon realised that Königgrätz had been a major defeat for France as well as Austria and Napoleon III began a desperate search for 'compensation'. The Emperor settled on the acquisition of Luxembourg as a means of restoring French prestige. Its owner, King William III of Holland, wanted to sell it to clear his debts! But Luxembourg had been a member of the German Confederation, and was still garrisoned by Prussian troops. Prussia would obviously have to give its approval. At first, Bismarck seemed to raise no objections. But in April 1867, a storm blew up in the *Reichstag*, probably secretly prompted by Bismarck, with nationalist deputies insisting that the future of Luxembourg was a matter of German honour. Von Moltke was eager to turn the affair into a pretext for war. A conference in London defused the crisis: Prussia withdrew its garrison, but Napoleon III had to abandon his planned take-over, leaving the French feeling humiliated. Any lingering beliefs that Bismarck was a man with whom they might do business, were abandoned. In its place, the opinion in Paris grew that Prussia would have to be contained, and, if possible, put firmly in its place.

Bismarck knew that the next Franco-Prussian crisis would be played for very high stakes; and in February 1870 he decided to precipitate it. When the issue of the Hohenzollern candidature first emerged in 1869, Bismarck took little notice, and seemed perfectly content when Leopold turned down the idea. Yet now (the Spanish having renewed the offer), Bismarck launched an intensive campaign to encourage the young man to put his name forward, and to persuade King Wilhelm I to give the scheme his own full backing. What had changed since April 1869 was the marked deterioration of Bismarck's domestic situation and, in January 1870, the emergence of Emile Ollivier – a man who displayed 'extraordinary sensitivity to any slight … to the honour of France' (Carr) – as Napoleon III's Chief Minister.

Bismarck decided that it was time to stir up an international crisis. He could not be certain of its outcome. It might be war; it might lead to a diplomatic humiliation for France; it might precipitate the collapse of the Second Empire. In brief, there was no 'master-plan'. It was difficult to persuade Wilhelm I to endorse the candidature (he only agreed after more cajoling in June). Neither could Bismarck have predicted the way in which the scheme accidentally leaked out in early July, or the self-defeating hysteria with which the French responded. Like a gambler calculating the odds in a poker game, Bismarck had, throughout, to rely on intuition and improvisation. But he also knew he held some very good cards in his hand.

The best card was Prussia's undoubted diplomatic advantage. Bismarck preferred to confront his enemies when they were isolated, and in this

KEY ISSUE

What setbacks did Bismarck's plans suffer in 1868–9?

See pages 145–6

KEY ISSUE

Why did Bismarck promote the Hohenzollern candidature?

Königgrätz
Austria's defeat at
Königgrätz had had
dramatic domestic
consequences. The
whole constitution of
the Empire was
redesigned, its new
name – the Austro-
Hungarian Empire –
indicating the equality
of status now accorded
the Empire's two
leading parts.

respect France was to suffer the same fate as Denmark had in 1864 and
Austria in 1866. A Franco-Austrian alliance was unlikely. However much
Vienna wished to avenge Königgrätz, renewed war against Prussia ran
directly counter to the needs of the Austro-Hungarian Empire. The
Hungarians were appalled by the prospect of any attempt to restore the
Empire's Germanic orientation; and with Austrian ambitions focused
on the Balkans, Russia loomed as a possible future enemy. An alliance
with France would be at best a distraction; at worst it might precipitate
a ruinous Russo-Prussian counter-alliance, threatening disaster on
every front. Neither could France look to Italy or Britain for help.
Napoleon III had kept a French garrison in Rome, preventing Italy
from claiming it as the Italian capital. In doing so, he may have sustained the support of the French Catholics for his regime; but he made
a Franco-Italian alliance very unlikely. Finally Britain, isolationist anyway, regarded the expansionist adventurer Napoleon III with distaste –
particularly in July 1870 when Bismarck leaked to the London press
details of proposals Napoleon III had made to him (whilst searching for
'compensation') for Prussian gains.

By allowing themselves to be manoeuvred into war in these circumstances, the French blundered badly. The Duke of Gramont, Napoleon
III's new Foreign Secretary, was mainly responsible. Gramont's task was
to restore the prestige of France abroad. He was inclined to posture,
and he overestimated France's strength. When he could have settled for
a pleasing diplomatic victory over Prussia, he decided to attempt its
complete humiliation instead. But he overplayed his hand.

B *The Ems Telegram*

Secret negotiations between Berlin and Madrid to put Leopold on the
Spanish throne were almost complete when details of the plot accidentally came out. The revelation horrified the French Government, but it
also offered Gramont a splendid opportunity. However vehemently Bismarck denied his involvement, it was generally and rightly assumed
that he was the architect of this devious scheme which, in its blatant
provocation of France, threatened the peace of Europe. Wilhelm I, holi-
daying in the spa town of Ems, was deeply embarrassed. He had never
liked Bismarck's plan, and when (in response to international pressure)
Leopold's father withdrew his candidacy, the Prussian king offered his
'entire and unreserved' endorsement of the retreat. Paris exulted, and
Bismarck considered resignation. But Gramont snatched defeat from
the jaws of victory. He told Benedetti, his ambassador in Germany, to
try to extract from King Wilhelm a public declaration that the candidacy would never be renewed. There was even talk of demanding an apology. Wilhelm I was displeased. His sense of honour ruled out an
apology; equally, the idea of a formal declaration seemed to imply that
his earlier endorsement of the termination of the Hohenzollern candidacy was somehow not trustworthy. The French should take him at his
word, and everybody could then forget about the wretched business.
Believing that his earlier concession had defused the crisis, but main-

taining the dignity of his station, he firmly but politely refused any further discussion of the matter with Benedetti.

Bismarck had been deeply worried as these events had unfolded. His policy seemed to have resulted in a humiliating climb-down, not for France but for Prussia. But he saw a way to recover the initiative. By skilfully editing the telegram he received from Ems describing the final exchanges between Wilhelm I and Benedetti, he down-played the King's readiness to seek accommodation and instead implied that Benedetti had been sent packing.

Bismarck released this statement:

> After the news of the renunciation of the Prince of Hohenzollern had been communicated to the Imperial French Government by the Royal Spanish Government the French ambassador made a further demand of His Majesty the King at Bad Ems that he should authorise him to send a telegram to Paris to the effect that His Majesty undertook in perpetuity never again to give his consent should the Hohenzollerns once more renew the candidature. His Majesty the King thereupon refused to receive the ambassador again and through his adjutant informed the ambassador that he had nothing further to say.

When this text was published in the Paris newspapers, French public opinion was outraged. Napoleon III, Gramont and Olliver would have been incapable of resisting the cry of 'to Berlin!' even if they had wanted to. So France declared war. It thereby put itself in the wrong in the eyes of all Europe – and, more importantly, in the eyes of all Germany too.

C *The Franco-Prussian War*

The campaign which followed was as disastrous for the French as the diplomacy which preceded it. French mobilisation was chaotic, making a nonsense of any plans to fight the war on German soil. By contrast, 380 000 German troops were quickly mobilised and were soon advancing into France, an operation masterminded by von Moltke and his supremely professional General Staff. The French had to look to the Emperor himself and to Marshal Bazaine, for leadership, and neither was capable of giving it. Napoleon III had never shown any aptitude for military affairs, and was now old and suffering from an agonising bladder complaint which made it torture for him to ride. Bazaine was personally courageous and a popular hero. But he was hopeless as a strategist, allowing his army to become besieged in the fortress town of Metz. His performance was so feeble that he was tried after the war for treason, and found guilty.

The Emperor's own army, attempting to come to Bazaine's rescue, instead found itself trapped at Sedan. As the Prussian artillery took position on the hills surrounding their fortress-town, a French general declared: 'we are in a chamber pot, and we are going to be shat on'. He was right. On 1 September, Krupp's steel breech-loading

Q

Identify the phrases in Bismarck's description of the exchanges between Benedetti and Wilhelm I which were calculated to inflame:
1. *German, and*
2. *French opinion.*

KEY ISSUE

How far was Bismarck responsible for the outbreak of the Franco-Prussian War?

field-pieces opened fire on the French below. Despite heroic attempts to break through, the position was hopeless. Napoleon III and his 100 000 soldiers surrendered.

PICTURE 13 *Anton von Werner's famous depiction of* The Proclamation of the Empire *in the Hall of Mirrors at Versailles*

The Proclamation of the Empire *in the Hall of Mirrors at Versailles*

Anton von Werner's famous depiction of *The Proclamation of the Empire* in the Hall of Mirrors at Versailles repays careful attention. It became an icon of German nationalism, symbolising the centrality of Bismarck (standing out in white – he had, in fact, worn a dark uniform on the day); the glory of Germany's noble warrior caste (there is not a civilian in sight) and (standing together on dias), the pre-eminence of *Kaiser* Wilhelm I, and the heads of Germany's other princely houses. The venue itself, as Wilhelm's adjutant general explained, was chosen as a 'symbol of revenge taken by Germany for centuries of [French] injustice … a symbol of the victories by which we regained the city of Strasbourg that Louis XIV stole from us'. Authoritarianism, militarism, monarchism, vengeance and conquest: the spirit in which *Kleindeutsch* unification celebrated its founding movement was very different from the spirit in which Liberals and radicals, civil servants, lawyers and teachers, had gathered together in Frankfurt barely two decades earlier.

The war was effectively over, but peace itself proved elusive. When news of the catastrophe of Sedan reached Paris, the Government collapsed, and the Second Empire was replaced by the Third Republic. To the surprise and increasing dismay of Bismarck and von Moltke, the new Government decided to fight on. This had tragic consequences. The conflict became warped by deepening hatreds on both sides. Paris was besieged, starved and bombarded, and 'Resistance' fighters in occupied France launched attacks on German troops which in turn provoked savage retaliation on the local civilian population. When Paris surrendered in January 1871, and peace negotiations finally began, reconciliation was on nobody's agenda.

The new German *Reich* was proclaimed at Versailles in January 1871. The French aggression of July 1870 had not only activated the 1866 military alliance between Prussia and the south German states; it had also precipitated a torrent of national feeling throughout Germany. This had swept away the doubts of most Liberals and Catholics in the south-west about the dangers of being ruled from Berlin. Even the few who were still attached to the idea of independence had to admit that its price would be political impotence, economic decline and escalating defence budgets. Bismarck still had to channel the new national will into formal structures, and this required some delicate negotiations. King Ludwig II of Bavaria in particular had to be handled carefully, being very conscious of the ancient dignity of the Wittelsbach dynasty. A large bribe helped King Ludwig make up his mind, along with the concession of the Bavaria's right to run its own railway, postal and telegraph systems, and levy taxes on beer and spirits. In most other respects, however, the new federal *Reich* was just an expanded version of the existing North German Confederation. Any concessions Bismarck made were minor.

8 ᖰ INTERPRETATIONS OF UNIFICATION

A *The economic dimension*

Not all historians have accepted the traditional Bismarck-centred account of German unification. As early as the 1920s, the British economist J.M. Keynes suggested that 'the German Empire was not founded on blood and iron, but on coal and iron'. In the 1960s, the German historian H. Böhme even seemed to imply that unification, in its *Kleindeutsch* form, would have happened with or without Bismarck:

> the history of the Empire's foundation can no longer be written as part of the biography of Otto von Bismarck: neither can the years 1859 or 1864 be regarded as the beginning of the movement for unity … [between 1849 and 1864], Prussia succeeded in manoeuvring Austria out of the German area in economic matters … From 1865 onwards, German unity was a question of time.

The two maps overleaf might suggest that Böhme's argument has much to commend it. The borders of the *Zollverein* – from which

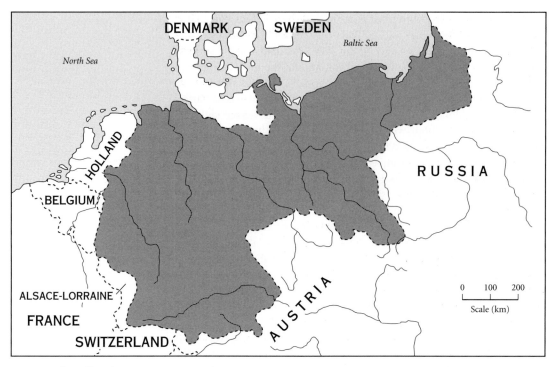

MAP 7 *The Zollverein*

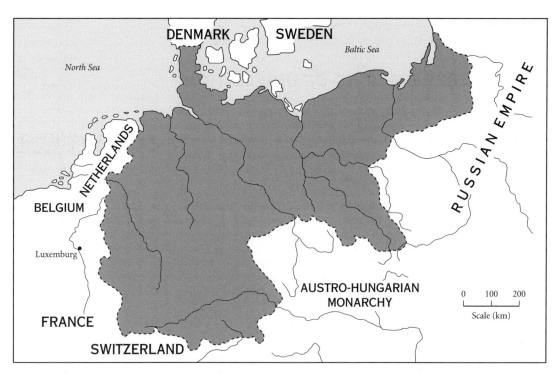

MAP 8 *The German Empire 1871*

Austria had been successfully and repeatedly excluded by Prussia before Bismarck's ascendancy – prefigure the borders of *Kleindeutsch* Germany very closely. Economic necessity had locked the smaller states of Germany firmly into Prussia's embrace before the 1860s.

However, it was by no means inevitable that Prussia would have been able to convert these economic ties into political ones. Much depended on the fortunes of diplomacy and war. Indeed, in 1866, almost all of the medium-sized and smaller German states sided with Austria against Prussia in the Seven Weeks' War. Had Austria actually defeated Prussia at Königgrätz – not an impossible scenario – the *Kleindeutsch* programme would have suffered a dramatic reversal. Böhme's claim that, by 1865, 'German unity was a question of time', should be treated with caution.

See page 191

Keynes' analysis is perhaps more persuasive: the roots of Prussia's ascendancy, he implies, lay in its industrial wealth. Prussian economic growth was indeed phenomenal. The expansion of Germany's railway network – focused on Berlin – offers one index: 4000 miles of track in 1852; 24 000 miles in 1873. Or consider Alfred Krupps' arms factory in the Ruhr: in 1836, he employed 60 men; by 1873, over 16 000. Industrialisation had 'taken off' in Prussia, and had thereby created the tax-base which made von Roon's army reforms affordable. And of course, Krupps' cannons, and the rapid military mobilisation facilitated by the rail network, themselves had large roles to play in the victories of Prussia's armies.

But it would be wrong to imagine that economic factors gave Prussia a **decisive** advantage over Austria and France. Whilst Austria lagged behind Prussia in all the important indices, incompetent diplomacy and generalship contributed more to the defeat at Königgrätz than economic backwardness. France's defeat was even less economically determined. Economic historians calculate that in 1870 France's gross national product was still greater than Germany's (albeit only slightly). France's crucial failure lay in its inability to effectively convert that wealth into military might. The failure of Niel's army reforms can be contrasted with the earlier, hard-won success of von Roon's schemes in Prussia. The key to France's defeat in 1870 was a total failure of leadership, first in diplomacy, then in politics, and finally on the battlefield.

See pages 144–5 and 182–3

KEY ISSUE

What are the strengths and weaknesses of the economic interpretation of German unification?

B *Militarism and diplomacy*

Industrial take-off, and a revolution in transport and military technology, put the Prussians in a powerful position. But it still required the genius of specific individuals – men of vision, judgement, energy and will power – to convert potential into performance. Bismarck and von Moltke are the key individuals in the history of German unification. Bismarck's role was crucial, but so was von Moltke's meticulous planning and cool direction of resources.

Bismarck was a supremely resourceful diplomat, but he was lucky, especially in his enemies. Danish foreign policy in 1863–4 was amateurish; Austrian foreign policy between 1864 and 1866 was confused and naïve; French foreign policy from 1866 onwards, but above all in 1870, was disastrous. He was also lucky in his circumstances. The relationships of the European Powers in the 1860s ideally suited Prussian expansionism. Crucially, Britain and Russia, the two flanking Powers, accepted it. Arguably, Britain did not have much choice in the matter: when Palmerston had blustered, threatening possible intervention in Denmark, Bismarck had privately joked that he would have to send the Prussian police to *arrest* the (tiny) British army if it tried to invade. Britain, essentially a naval Power, could not compete with the continental heavyweights and their large conscript armies. But anyway, the British had no inclination to assist Prussia's enemies: the Austrians, repressive and illiberal, won little sympathy in London; the French, expansionist and untrustworthy, even less. In theory, Russia did have the capacity to intervene: its reputed 800 000 strong army could not be ignored. But defeat in the Crimean War had turned Russia inwards, as it embarked on a programme of internal reform. More important still, Russia's Crimean experience had made it hostile towards Austria. Britain and Russia were two of the most important pieces in the European diplomatic jigsaw – and, without any real effort on Bismarck's part, they simply fell into place.

See pages 28 and 237–9

It was Bismarck's genius to sense and ruthlessly exploit the opportunities created by this uniquely favourable diplomatic constellation. But the image of Bismarck the master-planner, with every move worked out in advance, should not be taken seriously. Bismarck himself explicitly denied that there was a 'science of politics', capable of generating laws or clear predictions. Instead, he remarked, 'I could never foresee exactly whether my plans would succeed … politics is a thankless job, chiefly because everything depends on chance and conjecture. One has to reckon with a series of probabilities and improbabilities, and base one's plans upon this reckoning … there are no rules and formulas with which to sum up the results in advance'.

What Bismarck did cultivate were the skills of intuition, judgement, and improvisation, calculating the odds and the variations. He was always ready to seize any opportunity, and to drive home his advantage. What made him such a devastating opponent, however, was not just his capacity to think harder than anybody else, or his readiness to take better informed risks – it was his startling reassessment of the relationship between means and ends in diplomacy and politics. His aims remained fundamentally conservative. He wanted to serve the Hohenzollern dynasty by increasing the power of the Prussian state, whilst preserving the distinctive identity of Prussia and its monarchy. But the means he used to achieve these traditional objectives were startlingly unorthodox. In domestic politics, he sought a working relationship with the Liberals. In foreign affairs, the values of legitimacy and monarchical solidarity were nothing to him (except when it suited his purposes to pretend otherwise). For example – an alliance with the upstart Italians; a war against Austrian brothers; the expropriation of princely territories – such was the work of 1866 alone!

The following letter, written by the Austrian Foreign Minister Rechberg to Emperor Franz Josef in October 1864, illustrates the difficulties contemporaries had in getting to grips with Bismarck:

It increases to a more than ordinary degree the difficulties of conducting business ... when one is dealing with a man who so openly professes political cynicism as to reply to the passage in my letter where I say that we must make the maintenance of the Confederation and of the legitimately acquired rights of the German princes the foundation of our policy ... with the outrageous piece of claptrap that 'we must not allow the situation to be obscured for us by fogs emanating from the doctrines of German political sentimentalism'. This is language worthy of a Cavour (the architect of Italian unity). Holding fast to what is lawful is 'foggy sentimentalism!' The task of keeping this gentleman in check and talking him out of his megalomaniac utilitarian politics ... is one that exceeds human powers.

Rechberg displayed a 'traditional' attitude totally at odds with Bismarck's combination of unprincipled improvisation and shattering drive. Franz Josef later confessed: 'we were very honourable but very stupid'. Napoleon III fared even worse. As Pflanze concludes: 'Napoleon lacked Bismarck's acute sense of timing, certainty of purpose, and suppleness in manoeuvre'. Bismarck had sensed as much: the French Emperor, he reflected in his *Memoirs* 'was not so shrewd as the world thinks him'.

C *Bismarck, German nationalism and geopolitics*

Nationalism was one of Bismarck's most potent weapons. His relationship with German nationalism is complex. When he claimed in 1879 that 'from the beginning of my career I have had but a single guiding purpose: to bring about the unity of Germany, whatever the means and whichever the way', he was indulging in oversimplification and myth-making. He never allowed Prussia to become the servant of the national idea. Some historians have argued that German nationalism was, for Bismarck, no more than a cloak used to disguise Prussian ambition, and that unification was a by-product of the growth of Prussian power.

Bismarck certainly retained a profound allegiance to the Hohenzollern dynasty, and to his Prussian fatherland. 'My country is Prussia, and I have never left my country, and I shall never leave it', he declared in the *Landtag* in 1849. In private, he commented: 'we do not wish to see the Kingdom of Prussia obliterated in the putrid brew of cosy south-German sentimentality'. Bismarck used the weapon of nationalism on the condition that Prussia's identity would survive, and its power be strengthened within the new German nation. The constitution of the North German Confederation was designed to ensure this. Equally, Bismarck's suspicions of 'south German sentimentality' explain his cautious approach to this region in the aftermath of 1866.

Bismarck's strategy was certainly bold. It was based on the recognition that nationalism – until 1848–9 feared by conservatives across Europe as a revolutionary idealogy – might in fact be used as an instrument of state building. But Bismarck's relation with nationalism was not purely manipulative: the interests of Prussia, and of *Kleindeutsch* nationalism converged.

In the 1850s, Bismarck was to redefine his understanding of how the Prussian state might best be served. From his experiences as the leader of Prussia's delegation at Frankfurt, he concluded that Austria and Prussia were condemned by geography and history to compete for predominance within the German sphere, and that as long as Austria refused to concede equality of status to its rival, war – sooner or later – was inevitable. But Prussia would need allies for such a war. He was prepared to search anywhere. Abroad, Bismarck looked to France; at home, he noted the significance of the *Nationalverein*. This society looked to Prussia to impose a *Kleindeutsch* solution on the question of German unity. In 1859, the *Nationalverein's* leaders confided in Bismarck that they 'would be sincerely happy to see [him] appointed Minister of Foreign Affairs. Now more than ever Prussia needs a clear, firm, bold policy. The bolder it is, the less risky it will be, relatively speaking'. Such sentiments paralleled Bismarck's own thoughts.

Thus, even before Bismarck came to power in 1862, the main elements of his strategy were evident: a conviction that Prussian national self-interest required a contest with Austria, and that in such a contest, German liberal/national opinions might be an invaluable ally.

The fusion of Bismarckian power politics with German nationalism was completed in 1866. Thus, despite the furore over Bismarck's 'Blood and Iron' speech, his contemptuous disregard of the claims of Augustenburg, and the widespread perception that the Seven Weeks War was a civil war which Bismarck had forced upon the German people, Bismarck's assertion in 1858 proved accurate: 'there is nothing more German than the development of Prussia's special interests as properly understood'.

Prussia's geography explains this statement. The Prussian state, as defined by the 1815 Congress of Vienna, was divided into two unequal portions. How were the two Prussias to be united? The *Zollverein* was initially designed to strengthen the bonds between Berlin and Rhenish Prussia; but the Hesse-Kassel crisis of 1849 was an uncomfortable reminder of how vulnerable the links between east and west might be. Only territorial expansionism would make Prussia whole. Austria, however, set its face against Prussian hegemony 'north of the Main'. Vienna's rejection of parity with Berlin eventually brought it war, and defeat. By 1867, via a ruthless strategy of annexation, and the establishment of the North German Confederation, Prussia had won control of all it had wanted. But Bismarck's triumphs also made a conflict with France – sooner or later – all but certain. And in France, the Prussian state and the German people had a **common** enemy. German nationalists had looked to Prussia to defend them against French aggression since at least 1840. This was why Bismarck could claim that the growth of Prussian power and the advance of the

See page 180 and
Map 6 on page 159

German idea were effectively one and the same. After 1866, Napoleon's insistent talk of 'compensation' now put the south German states in the front line. Pflanze argues, 'the south was a political vacuum predestined to be filled by the power of France, Prussia or a resurgent Austria'. It was, in part, Bismarck's fear that this framework was collapsing which prompted him to take up the Hohenzollern candidacy – and thus to embark on the path which led from Ems, via Sedan, to the Hall of Mirrors at Versailles. Whatever Bismarck's doubts about plucking the 'unripe fruit', when the moment of decision came in 1870, there was to be no hesitation.

Prussia's strategic requirements had encouraged Bismarck to adopt the cause of German nationalism. The resultant rivalry with France had forced Bismarck to complete the nationalist agenda. The history of Germany in the five decades after unification would in the large part be shaped by the difficulties its statesmen experienced in digesting that 'unripe fruit', and in containing the aggressive spirit of nationalism which the events of the years between 1864 and 1871 had done so much to excite.

See bibliography below

See page 194

9 ⤸ BIBLIOGRAPHY

Two relatively brief and very useful books are *The Unification of Germany 1815–1870* by A. Stiles (Hodder and Stoughton) and *Bismarck and Germany 1862–1890* by D. Williamson (Longman Seminar Studies in History, 1986). *The Formation of the First German Nation-State 1800–1871* by J. Breuilly (Macmillan, 1996) is a more recent and more demanding analysis. *A History of Germany 1815–1990* by W. Carr (1991) is an outstanding textbook with comprehensive coverage. Useful collections of documents include *From Confederation to Empire* by C. Lodge (Hodder and Stoughton, 1997) and *The Unification of Germany* by M. Gorman (CUP, 1989). Vital insights into the pre-Bismarck era can be found in *The Struggle for Mastery in Germany 1779–1850* by B. Simms (Macmillan, 1998). Biographies of Bismarck, in ascending order of difficulty, include those by A.J.P. Taylor (Hamish Hamilton, 1955), O. Pflanze (Princeton University Press, 1990) and L. Gall (Allen and Unwin, 1986). The following are also recommended: *German History 1770–1866* by Sheehan (OUP, 1989), *The Origins of the Wars of German Unification* by Carr (Longman, 1991), *The Course of German Nationalism* by Schulze (CUP, 1991), and *Germany 1780–1918* by Blackbourn (Fontana, 1997) Difficult but rewarding is *Germany from Napoleon to Bismarck* by T. Nipperdey (Gill and Macmillan, 1996).

10 ⤸ STRUCTURED QUESTIONS
AND ESSAYS

1. (a) What factors worked in favour of German unification between 1815 and 1848? (10 marks)
   (b) Why did the 1848 Revolutions fail in the German states? (15 marks)

2. (a) What were the differences between the *Kleindeutsch* and *Gross-deutsch* solutions to the problem of German unification? (10 marks)

  (b) Why did Prussia rather than Austria become the leader of German unification? (15 marks)

3. (a) What were the main provisions of the *Zollverein*? (10 marks)

  (b) How important was the *Zollverein* in the economic and political history of 'Germany'? (15 marks)

4. (a) Outline Bismarck's career in politics until 1862; (10 marks)

  (b) Why was Germany able to emerge as the dominant power in Germany between 1862 and 1871? (15 marks)

5. Was Germany unified by 'blood' or 'iron'? (25 marks)

6. Why did Prussia and not Austria succeed in unifying Germany? (25 marks)

11 ✍ BISMARCK'S DIPLOMACY — THE ART OF *REALPOLITIK*: A SOURCES EXERCISE

Study Sources A–F and answer the questions which follow.

Opinions may differ as to whether or not a close alliance with Austria be desirable. But experience permits no doubt that pliancy and assurances of friendship are not the means by which Prussia can succeed in living upon endurable, not to mention secure, terms with Austria. Gratitude for favours received, patriotic sympathies — in a word, feelings of any description, do not guide the policy of Austria. Her interests constrain her to fight against and detract from Prussia's prestige and influence in Germany to the best of her ability. If Prussia takes up a position independent of the Confederation, she will become, by virtue of her intrinsic force, the natural centre of crystallisation for those connections of which her neighbours stand in as urgent need as herself. In such connections she will be backed up by the weight of her greatness and speciality as a purely German state, as well as by the similarity of her requirements and developments to those of the German people at large.

SOURCE A

A memorandum from Bismarck to his superiors, 1858

Even if, as I believe, the military reorganisation [i.e. the army reforms of 1860–2] was itself a good thing and in any event cannot be suspended now in view of the great dangers from abroad and in spite of all the many serious shortcomings of the army, that does not make Bismarck, etc. any less intolerable. It is nothing short of revolting that this group should use this measure which is correct in itself to cover up its passage by arbitrary force. From the very beginning there has been a group who desire this measure not because it was good but because it was to cloak the way it was to be forced through. I do not know whether this brutality or that of the extreme Left will win the day in the end. In any case the Prussian state and freedom are finished.

SOURCE B
A letter from J. Droysen, a liberal and nationalist, to H. von Sybel (October 1863)

If we are not excessive in our demands and do not believe that we have conquered the world, we will attain a peace that is worth our effort. But we are just as quickly intoxicated as we are plunged into dejection, and I have the thankless task of pouring water into the bubbling wine and making it clear that we do not live alone in Europe but with three other Powers that hate and envy us.

SOURCE C
Bismarck writing to his wife on 9 July, six days after the Battle of Sadowa

Regarding the negotiations with Austria to find a basis for peace, I respectfully beg your Majesty to allow me to lay before you the following considerations:

It seems to me of greatest importance that the present favourable moment should not be missed. [*Marginal note by Wilhelm I:* Agreed.] By Your Majesty's declared acceptance en bloc of the proposals of His Majesty the Emperor of the French, the danger of France's taking sides against Prussia, which by diplomatic pressure could easily turn into active participation, has been eliminated.

The double declaration of Austria that it will withdraw from the German Bund and agree to a reconstruction of it under Prussia's leadership without Austrian participation, and that it will recognise everything that Your Majesty thinks fit to do in N. Germany, provides all the essentials that Prussia demands of her. The preservation of the Kingdom of Saxony is the wish of both Austria and France. [*Wilhelm I:* That besides the preservation of the Kingdom of Saxony its integrity will also be guaranteed, bears very hard on me, as Saxony was the chief instigator of the war and has come out of it unimpaired]…

If this goal can be assured on this basis by a rapid conclusion of the preliminaries, then in my humble opinion it would be a political blunder to put the whole outcome in jeopardy by attempting to wrest from Austria a few more square miles of territory or a few more millions of war payments, and expose it to the risk of a prolonged war or negotiations in which foreign intervention could not be excluded. [*Wilhelm I*: Agreed, but it depends on how much money or land can be acquired without risking everything in one throw] ...

Any hindering of a speedy settlement with Austria by seeking to obtain secondary advantages, will be contrary to my respectful counsel and suggestions. [*Wilhelm I*: If in spite of what we apparently have the right to expect of the defeated power it is not possible to demand what the army and the country have a right to expect, namely heavy indemnities from Austria as the main enemy or territorial gain to a really visible extent, without endangering the main object [*see above*], then the victor will have to bite into this sour apple at the gates of Vienna and leave it to posterity to judge. Nikolsberg, 25.7.66 Wilhelm.].

SOURCE D
Bismarck writing to Wilhelm I, 24 July 1866 (the 'Nikolsberg' Memorandum)

There is no longer any getting away from the fact that Count Bismarck has a rare capacity for statesmanship which it would be unfair to judge according to so-called principles ... this man, glowing coldly, passionately moderate, heedless of friend and foe, of parties and principles, entirely rooted in the facts, in the reality of this state, can act. If the nation had more understanding than indolence, more sincerity than deception, more recognition of its weaknesses and its misery, than comfortable, lazy complacency in its humble and humiliating position, it would thank God that at last a Hercules has arrived to clean out the Augean stables that it has fouled. But many of them, above all our German brothers in the south, go on preferring to roll about in their own filth.

SOURCE E
A letter from J. Droysen to R. Ehmek, 14 October 1866

According to Liberal and national public opinion, [Bismarck] stood for the counter-revolution. He was the tool of the army and of super-conservatism with the task of ending by every means at his disposal the constitutional conflict between the crown and the Liberal majority in the Chamber over the army budget, and of forcing parliamentary Liberalism to its knees. To start off with, King William I and his military camarilla viewed him in the same way. However, all sides had judged Bismarck wrongly in their assumptions about his motives for his policy. He did not consider the Prussian Prime Minstership as an end in itself, but as a means of achieving a higher purpose. He was concerned with broadening Prussia's power base and consolidating her position in a revolutionary Europe, a road which he was convinced could only be followed by establishing Prussian hegemony in Germany at Austria's expense, but in unison with the other European powers' interests. His means were revolutionary, but his aim was conservative... On top of this, there was his readiness to go to extremes, and his passion for taking every crisis to the limit.

SOURCE F
From The Course of German Nationalism (1991) *by H. Schulze*

1. *Study Source A*
   Using the evidence of Source A, and your own knowledge, explain the significance of the phrase 'Gratitude ... does not guide the policy of Austria'. (4 marks)
2. *Study Sources B and E, and use your own knowledge.*
   Compare the views of Bismarck and his policies expressed in these two sources, and account for the differences between them. (8 marks)
3. *Study Sources C and D and use your own knowledge.*
   How useful are these sources for an historian assessing Bismarck's skills as a diplomat in the aftermath of the Prussian victory at Sadowa in 1866? (8 marks)
4. *Study this collection of Sources A–F and use your own knowledge.*
   With reference to Bismarck's foreign policy, evaluate Schulze's claim in Source F that '[Bismarck's] means were revolutionary, but his aim was conservative'. (10 marks)

The 1848 Revolutions

7

See page 93

See pages 63–4
and 218

INTRODUCTION

THE REVOLUTIONS OF 1848: AN OVERVIEW AND SOME THEMES

The scale and complexity of the Revolutions which swept Europe in 1848 were unprecedented. With the important exception of Russia, most of continental Europe's capitals and major cities saw bloody confrontations between soldiers and civilians which, more often than not, resulted in the retreat of the old order and the establishment of new regimes. The sheer speed with which the Revolution spread and the cumulative impact which the news of these dramatic events had, is indicated by Table 6.

The Revolutions were like a series of chain reactions. In Italy, the overthrow of Bourbon rule in Palermo encouraged Liberals in Naples to pressurise Ferdinand II, King of the Two Sicilies, into granting a constitution for the mainland. His agreement encouraged Liberals and nationalists across the rest of the peninsula to press their demands, and by the end of March, political life in Florence, Turin, Rome, Milan and Venice had been transformed out of all recognition.

The final stages of this revolutionary shockwave were given even greater impetus by the news from Paris and Vienna. The overthrow of Louis-Philippe and the creation of a French Republic must rank as the single most important event of the 'spring time of the peoples'. In Vienna, Metternich saw in Louis-Philippe's fall his own political death knell, and he was soon forced into exile himself. News of the Austrian Chancellor's flight precipitated demonstrations in Berlin, shortly fol-

TABLE 6

The Springtime of the Peoples: the 1848 Revolutions

12 January	Revolt in Sicily
10 February	Constitution proclaimed in Naples
17 February	Constitution announced in Florence
22 February	Outbreak of revolution in Paris
24 February	Flight of Louis-Philippe
4 March	Constitution proclaimed in Piedmont
12 March	Outbreak of revolution in Vienna
13 March	Flight of Metternich
14 March	Pius IX granted constitution in Rome
17 March	Manin led revolution in Venice
18 March	Revolution in Berlin. Frederick William IV granted constitution March Uprising in Milan

lowed by the capitulation of Frederick William IV to his people's demands. Metternich's exit was also the signal for a revolutionary chain reaction to spread across the Habsburg Empire, with mass demonstrations in Prague, Budapest, Zagreb and beyond.

See page 174

The 1848 Revolutions were unique in their geographical breadth, the scale of their mass mobilisation and their overwhelming early success. But from the summer of 1848 onwards, Europe experienced a chain reaction of counter-revolution, as conservatives recovered their nerve, drawing mutual inspiration from their early successes, and ultimately re-established their authority. As early as May 1848, Ferdinand II was again the master of Naples. The 'June Days' smashed the hopes of the Reds and Radicals in Paris: France was to be a *conservative* Republic. Habsburg armies knocked the heart out of the Italian Revolution in July, and crushed the militants in Vienna in October. In November, Frederick William IV finally authorised a (bloodless) counter-revolutionary *coup* in Berlin. Although the Revolutions in Hungary and Venice were finally defeated only in August 1849, their fates had been sealed months earlier.

See page 122

Three questions suggest themselves:

● why was so much of Europe convulsed by Revolutions in 1848, and why were they initially successful?
● why were Europe's conservatives able so quickly to re-establish their power?
● what long-term difference, if any, did these abortive Revolutions make to the course of European history?

1 ⤳ THE CAUSES OF THE 1848 REVOLUTIONS

A *Economic and social preconditions*

The roots of many of the social problems which fuelled the Revolutions of 1848 can be traced back to the dramatic growth in population (see Table 7) which Europe experienced over the first half of the nineteenth century. 'How could these extra mouths be fed, these extra backs be clothed, these extra hands be given work to do?' (Sperber). When considering this problem, the counter-example of Britain is crucial to understanding what happened in continental Europe. Table 7 overleaf might suggest that Britain's population explosion threatened to produce the gravest crisis of all. But Table 8 indicates an important reason why British society was able to absorb its massive growth in population without experiencing a political revolution. Between 1800 and 1850, Britain took giant strides down the road to industrialisation: its textile factories, mines and foundries constituted dynamic sources of employment and wealth. But continental Europe – with the exception of a few centres of production (see below) – was much slower to industrialise.

Revolutions
Revolutions are complicated events to analyse: one helpful way to go about this is to distinguish between pre-conditions (long-term causes); precipitants (medium-term causes); and triggers (short-term causes). See page 60 for a further explanation of these terms.

See the bibliography on page 228

Country	1800	1850
Holland	2.2	3.1
Belgium	3.0	4.3
Great Britain	10.9	20.9
Italy	18.1	23.9
Austria-Hungary	23.3	31.3
The German States	24.5	31.7
France	26.9	36.5

TABLE 7

Estimated populations of various European countries from 1800 to 1850 (in millions). Source : Carlo M. Cipolla, The Fontana Economic History of Europe: Vol. 3, The Industrial Revolution (London), 1973, p. 29

Country	1800	1850
Great Britain	620	1290
German States	40	260
France	90	270
Austria	20	100
Belgium	40	70
Russia	20	70
Italy	10	20
Spain	10	20
Europe	860	2240

TABLE 8

Manufacturing capacity throughout Europe (thousands of horsepower of steam power)

Until at least 1850, manufacturing there was almost always done in workshops rather than factories, or by outworkers in the countryside.

The social and economic consequences of this relative backwardness were highly significant. Continental Europe's 30 per cent population increase swelled the ranks of the peasantry and the hand-workers: not the ranks of any factory workers. It therefore increased rural land-hunger and poverty, increasing urban immigration. But the supply of labour and craft-products in the towns already exceeded demand.

Sperber concludes that 'in the quarter century before 1850 ... the living standards of the majority of the population seemed to be in decline'.

In the 1840s, where there were isolated pockets of industrialisation – for example, in the Ruhr and in Saxony, and in the suburbs of Paris, Berlin, Vienna and Prague. But these tended to *worsen* social and political discontent rather than to *alleviate* it:

● industrialisation in these areas brought to the fore a new class of factory-owning capitalists who added their voices to the demands for political change which merchants and middle-class professionals had been making

● industrialisation threatened certain traditional crafts and labour practices with 'technological unemployment': for example, weavers were undercut by cheaper factory-produced textiles; bargemen along the Rhine by competition from steam tugs. Such 'losers' in the process of technological change were amongst the most militant protesters in 1848

● the sheer size, as well as the volatility of the working classes as they congregated in the rapidly expanding cities was another worry. Paris, Berlin and Vienna were each the capitals of Great Powers: risings there might neutralise the nerve centres of government. As early as 1830, Louis Philippe had been warned by a conservative adviser that the factories and industrial workers of the suburbs of Paris 'will be the cord that one day wrings our necks'.

Two other social problems added to the unstable mix:

● about 80 per cent of Europe's population were peasants. Life was rarely comfortable for this class, but in many regions of central and especially eastern Europe, a variety of feudal dues made it intolerable. In most of the Habsburg Empire, peasants were still required to work for nothing for a set number of days on their lords' lands a

TABLE 9

Population of major European cities

City	1800	1850
London	900 000–1 000 000	2 363 000
Paris	547 000 (1801)	1 053 000 (1851)
Vienna	247 000	444 000
Naples	350 000	415 000 (1871)
St. Petersburg	200 000	485 000
Moscow	200 000	365 000
Berlin	172 000	419 000

system harshly enforced with whip and stick. It has been calculated that up to 70 per cent of a peasant's income might be taken up by feudal dues

● unemployed university graduates doubtless suffered less, but the political consequences of their dissatisfaction could be serious. In the first half of the nineteenth century, an over-expansion in higher education had led to a surplus of educated men. As a French conservative warned, 'it isn't the workers one should fear, it is the doctors without patients, lawyers without briefs, all the misunderstood, the discontented, who, finding no place at the banquet table, try to overturn it'. Liberalism and nationalism – with their promises of a dramatic reshaping of Europe's political order – were particularly attractive to these people, who provided many of the radical leaders of 1848.

KEY ISSUE

What long-term economic and social factors contributed to political instability in Europe between 1825 and 1850?

B *Ideological preconditions*

Liberalism and **nationalism** presented serious challenges to the reactionary autocracies which dominated central Europe as refashioned by the Congress of Vienna.

The Austrian Chancellor Metternich devoted much time to stifling the growth of these subversive ideas through measures such as the Carlsbad Decrees [1819] and the Six Articles [1832]. The outbreak of Revolutions across the length and breadth of Germany and Italy in 1848 suggests that, in the long run, these tactics failed. Indeed, they may even have been counterproductive. Liberals wanted a share of political power; they rarely aimed to overthrow existing Governments, having little taste for revolutionary upheaval and none at all for social equality. But, consistently spurned by Metternich and other conservatives, they found themselves amongst the opposition. The meetings and campaigns they organised in the run up to the 1848 Revolutions mobilised the masses and undermined the self-confidence of Europe's old rulers.

See pages 167–9

liberals wanted to replace autocracies with constitutional monarchies, where political rights (for example, free speech) would be guaranteed for all citizens; **nationalists** believed that the different peoples of Europe – for example. Italians and Germans – had the right to rule themselves in their own states, and not be divided between themselves or ruled by foreigners

C *Economic and social precipitants*

It was not easy for Liberal and nationalist activists to gain a hearing in rural, predominantly illiterate societies. But a sharp downturn in the (already strained) economic circumstances of the workers and peasants of Europe fuelled popular despair and anger, creating a demand for change. In these circumstances, Liberals and nationalists were able to give form, content and direction – albeit briefly – to discontents whose roots were more often economic and social than political.

Three overlapping and mutually reinforcing economic crises had, by the beginning of 1848, left millions of workers and peasants across Europe apparently trapped in acute, intolerable poverty:

● the potato crop – the staple diet of the poor in northern Europe – was almost completely wiped out by disease (potato blight) in 1845

PROFILE

KARL MARX, THE COMMUNIST MANIFESTO AND THE 1848 REVOLUTIONS

'A spectre is haunting Europe – the spectre of Communism'. This was the opening sentence of Karl Marx's *Communist Manifesto*, written in the weeks before the outbreak of the 1848 Revolutions. Fear of Communism had a significant impact on the direction taken by the Revolutions of that year. But its impact was largely negative. The communist 'spectre' was an important factor in ultimately driving anxious middle-class property owners towards conservatism and reaction.

See the bibliography on page 228

They probably worried too much. The *Manifesto* itself 'went virtually unnoticed' (McLellan), and the Communist Party, which was later to adopt it as its defining creed, did not yet exist. There **was** a Communist network, linking activists in Brussels, London, Paris and Cologne, but the collection of expatriate German workers and political exiles who mostly constituted it had no significant popular following. In fact, the early Communists seemed to spend as much time in acrimonious internal debate as in agitating the cause of revolution.

Marx was at the centre of these arguments. He combined hard-headed political realism and rigorous intellectual inquiry. Under his influence, the old Communist slogan 'All men are Brothers' was replaced by a fiercer call to class war: 'Working men of all countries, unite!'.

Marx was a great scholar, and he poured all of his learning into his journalism and theorising. His expertise in economics and German philosophy (especially Hegel), and his knowledge of world history (especially the French Revolution) were each brought into play. Marx concluded that 'class struggle' was the driving force of history; that human progress had been accelerated by the victory of the middle class (*bourgeoisie*) over the aristocracy (a process already completed, Marx believed, in Britain and France); that the next stage would be a successful *bourgeois* revolution in Germany, and a victory over the *bourgeoisie* by the proletariat (the factory-based working class) in Britain and France. In the long run, the victory of the proletariat was everywhere ultimately inevitable (the growth of modern industry made the factory-owning *bourgeoisie* its own grave-diggers), and with it would come to an end all social oppression and exploitation. It was the mission of the Communists to open the eyes of the proletariat to its role in history, and to organise it for the struggle ahead.

The *Communist Manifesto* was a brilliant mixture of history, propaganda and prophecy. But it was less useful as a guide to political action in 1848. It expected too much of the French proletariat. It was a very small percentage of the workforce, even in Paris, where

Republican militants were crushed in the June Days. Marx spent most of 1848 in the Rhineland, agitating amongst the workers and founding and editing an ultra-radical newspaper. He hoped to persuade the workers to support the *bourgeoisie* in their revolutionary challenge to aristocratic and absolutist rule. But his programme – Marx called for a democratic German Republic – was too radical to win any middle class approval, yet too tame for some of Marx's Communist allies, who had no desire to collaborate with the middle classes. Marx could therefore do little to affect the course of the revolution, and with its defeat, went into exile in London. The great days of Marxism as a mass political movement only came after 1870.

● the cereal harvest of 1845 was poor too, and the harvest of 1846 a disaster – the worst for three decades. The cumulative effect of this was to double – sometimes quadruple – the cost of basic foodstuffs

● the soaring cost of living depressed the manufacturing sector – the more people spent on food, the less they had available for clothes, shoes, and so on. By 1847 manufacturing was anyway in a crisis of its own. In France, for example, a speculative boom in railway construction had crashed, with knock-on effects in engineering, iron and steel and construction. So, even though the harvest of 1847 was very good (and food prices had returned to normal by 1848), unemployment remained high

● a banking and debt crisis was the consequence of these combined problems in agriculture and industry. Individuals and families had had to borrow money to pay for food; businesses closed down, often owing money to banks – which themselves went bankrupt; Governments, forced to subsidise and/or import food, had to borrow heavily themselves. Public confidence in the whole system neared collapse; the economic and financial structure of 'Restoration Europe' seemed doomed.

D *Political precipitants*

Crucially, leading figures in the Restoration regimes shared some of these feelings. Confusion and self-doubt characterised Court politics in France, Prussia and Austria. In Paris, the elderly Louis Philippe had become increasingly out of touch with politics and was still depressed at the death of his eldest son in 1842. In Berlin, Frederick William IV's eccentric political ideas and unstable personality were already breeding disappointment and uncertainty. Metternich was tired and depressed in Vienna, and the Habsburg Emperor – 'Ferdy the Loony': – was mentally subnormal. When the Revolutions of 1848 broke out, the revolutionaries were helped by the fact that the leadership of Restoration Europe was so weak and so plagued by self-doubt.

See pages 62–3, 94 and 170

By contrast, those who wanted change were dynamic and confident. Italian nationalists and Liberals had been inspired by the election of an (apparently) sympathetic Pope; their German equivalents were busier than ever with their congresses, newspapers and manifestos; whilst in France, parliamentary reformers were mounting an increasingly popular and sophisticated campaign against the Government. Although Liberals and nationalists were as surprised as anybody by the rapidity of the old order's collapse in 1848, they believed that they were the voice of the future.

E *Triggers: short-term political and military factors*

See the bibliography on page 228

It is not easy to explain the speed of the old regime's collapse. Europe's rulers might have used force, but they opted to negotiate – and usually, to capitulate. According to Anderson, 'there is no more astonishing series of events in the history of modern Europe than this collective and cumulative failure of nerve on the part of monarchies and governments which were, in a physical sense, fully able to control events and repress the sometimes almost trivial movements before which they hastened to abase themselves'. He argues that 'timidity', 'defeatism', 'an unwillingness to shed blood', and 'a simple loss of nerve' characterised the leaders of Europe's pre-Revolutionary order in its moment of crisis.

However, the following should also be emphasised:

- the loyalty of the old order's armed forces could not always be taken for granted: Louis Philippe was profoundly demoralised by the desertion to the revolutionary ranks of the National Guard; and in Italy, the Austrian commander Radetzky always had to bear in mind that a high percentage of his soldiers were Italian
- using soldiers against civilians in cities was anyway a highly problematic business: crucial turning points in each of the big revolutions (Paris, Vienna, Berlin) came when troops, frightened, belligerent or simply inexperienced in the art of crowd control, opened fire on demonstrators. The martyrs this created infuriated the people, and the level of violence escalated
- the citizens of Paris, Vienna and Berlin responded to these massacres by building hundreds of barricades aiming to protect themselves from further attacks and to paralyse the Government. These obstacles were surprisingly hard to deal with. Soldiers attempting to storm them would come under fire from the upper floors of adjacent houses; units could easily find themselves trapped and cut off in the warrens of streets which characterised the city centres of these ancient capitals. The whole experience of having to turn guns on civilians was anyway often demoralising enough
- militarily, the best strategy in the face of these urban insurrections would probably have been a temporary withdrawal of troops, followed by a large-scale artillery bombardment and then a full-scale infantry assault – a plan recommended to (but rejected by)

Frederick William IV in Berlin in March, but one followed through (with variations) in Paris and Prague (June) and in Vienna (October). Such action required great ruthlessness – and it is perhaps not surprising that, faced with these alternatives, the old order often preferred major concessions to mass bloodshed.

It could be argued that, in the long run, a strategy of concession proved surprisingly effective. Only France became a Republic in 1848: elsewhere, the revolution 'stopped at the base of the throne'. Furthermore, the new constitutions which emerged in March were in many ways conservative, leaving rulers with much of their executive powers in place – notably their command of the armed forces. And crucially, the latter were still very much intact; perhaps humiliated, but undefeated. The potential remained, therefore, for them to be put to counter-revolutionary use. In brief, the old order was 'down', but not 'out'.

A detailed analysis of the causes of the French, German and Italian Revolutions can be found on pages 59–64, 172–5 and 87–8, respectively. The causes of the Austrian Revolution are analysed on pages 218–19

KEY ISSUE

Why did the old order make such a feeble attempt to assert its authority in the face of revolution?

2 ✍ EUROPE IN REVOLUTION

A *Economic dislocation and social tension*

The main impact of the Revolutions was to actually worsen the social crises which had helped to bring them about, and undermine the prospects of economic recovery. Hopes that new Governments would achieve prosperity and alleviate social injustice proved utopian. The Revolutions damaged business confidence, disrupted trade, and threatened property. Stock exchanges crashed, bankruptcies multiplied and unemployment rose. Political and economic stability proved elusive. The Frankfurt Parliament and the Republican Government in Paris both set up elaborate commissions to examine the causes of the depression and explore new ways of organising work, but found no solutions. The National Workshops in Paris disappointed hopes, and their cost outraged France's taxpayers. The workshops' closure in June precipitated a rising in Paris, which was ruthlessly crushed.

See pages 121–2

The 'June Days' could be seen as the first stage by which the forces of order reasserted themselves. They certainly revealed the intensity of the 'social fear' with which property owners regarded the poor. The Revolution of 1848 has been described as 'a revolution of conflicting expectations'. 'What does freedom of the press mean for us? Freedom to eat is what we want!', demanded a Badenese peasant. A Neapolitan Liberal and landowner had a different perspective, however: 'freedom was [not] a banquet at which everyone was to sit and have his fill'. The more the workers and peasants of Europe demanded 'their fill', the more Europe's property-owning Liberals were likely to be driven back into the arms of conservatism.

ANALYSIS

The causes of the Austrian Revolution

The causes of the Austrian Revolution, which culminated in the fall of Metternich on 13 March, were complex:

- The Austrian Empire suffered from major structural weaknesses. Despite having an absolutist Government, its ruler from 1835 was the mentally retarded Ferdinand I. Decision-making at the Habsburg court was drawn out and marked by bitter infighting between Metternich and his rivals. Shortage of funds made it almost impossible to sustain numerous military commitments across central and eastern Europe. The spread of liberal and nationalist ideas outside Austria (with Hungarians, Czechs and Italians pressing – at the very least – for greater autonomy) and of liberalism within Austria (with the Austrian middle classes frustrated by the Government's total lack of public accountability), presented a set of drastic challenges to the authority of the Habsburg dynasty.

The fragility of Habsburg rule was cruelly exposed by the events of 1846–8, which helped to precipitate Revolution:

- harvest failure and the threat of starvation were added to the burden of feudal dues
- an industrial recession coincided with the harvest failure, and hit politically sensitive areas of the Empire hard: unemployed Bohemian factory workers flooded into Prague; lay-offs blighted the working class quarters of Vienna, too
- in Budapest, Lajos Kossuth had emerged as the charismatic spokesman of Hungarian nationalism.

See pages 220–1

Other sparks threatened to set all this combustible material alight:

See page 94

- mounting unrest in Italy convinced many Austrians that war there was likely – a war which the Austrian exchequer could not afford, and which would have a disastrous impact on taxes and savings
- news of Louis-Philippe's abdication detonated the crisis, prompting mass demonstrations, calls for political reform and the sacking of Metternich
- Kossuth's demand for greater independence for Hungary was greeted ecstatically in Budapest, and further encouraged the radicals in Vienna
- Metternich wanted to stay and fight but his rivals were happy for him to depart; the decision swung against the Chancellor after an unplanned exchange of fire between troops and demonstrators left several dead, and led to barricades and fires being raised across Vienna. Metternich fled Vienna on 13 March

● Metternich's dismissal (and the promise of a constitution) had seemed to be a price worth paying to appease the radicals and re-establish calm. But his downfall was the signal for further revolutionary surges, notably in Hungary and Italy. With Metternich gone, what might not be possible?

B *The unravelling of ideological alliances*

Social tensions were reflected in increasingly painful ideological divisions. During the first days and weeks of Revolution Liberals and radicals had fought alongside each other on a victorious, united front. But even then, differences were not far beneath the surface. Liberals advocated constitutional monarchies, in which kings shared power with ministers, who were to be responsible to a representative assembly, itself elected by an educated and propertied *élite*. The radical vision was much more democratic, entailing a wider franchise, greater sensitivity to the economic needs of the masses, and, on the radical Left, embracing outright Republicanism.

If the united front of Liberals and radicals was fragile, the rivalries and antagonisms of competing nationalisms were even more divisive. 1848 revealed that nationalists had very different evaluations of the respective merits of their own and of other nations, and of how and where the boundaries between different nations might be drawn.

This was particularly true of the Habsburg and German lands. German nationalists themselves were split into *Großdeutsch* and *Kleindeutsch* camps, but their divisions were as nothing to the bitter rivalries of the eastern half of the Habsburg Empire, involving Hungarians, Czechs, Slovaks, Croats, Serbs, Romanians and Poles. These different peoples were often inextricably intermingled; with a variety of competing linguistic, cultural and historic claims sometimes focusing on the same region. Germans felt that they possessed a more distinguished history and cultural tradition which gave them the right to 'lord it' over Poles and Czechs. Similarly, Magyars felt superior to Croats. Not surprisingly, Poles, Czechs and Croats disagreed.

See page 117

As a consequence, the 'springtime of the peoples' soon descended into a conflict of 'people' against 'people'. The only clear beneficiary of these divisions were the Habsburgs, who skilfully and cynically promoted them, endorsing, for example, the campaign of Croat and Romanian nationalists against their would-be masters in Budapest. German nationalists actually welcomed the successful bombardment of Prague by the Habsburg General Windischgrätz (a definitive defeat for Czech nationalism) and the victory of the Habsburg General Radetzky at Custozza (a massive blow against Italian nationalism). They were oblivious to the fact that these victories laid the foundation for the recovery of Habsburg authority everywhere and so ultimately enabled Vienna

Lajos Kossuth (1802–1894) and Hungarian nationalism

Vienna had long regarded Hungary as the least manageable region of the Austrian Empire. It was unique in that its *Diet* (Parliament) had to give its approval before any taxes could be levied. As the ill-tempered sessions of 1825–7 and 1832–6 displayed, it was not afraid to defy the Habsburgs. Furthermore, Hungarian nationalism was a potent force. Fearing that German-speaking bureaucrats from Vienna and the Slav-speaking population of the south and east (Croats, Serbs and Romanians) would between them submerge Hungarian culture, the *Diets* had won for the Hungarian language a privileged position in government and education. The fact that Hungarian speakers manifestly regarded themselves as culturally superior to the non-German races of the Empire added to the ethnic friction.

Lajos Kossuth did little to dampen such tensions. The son of an impoverished nobleman he trained as a lawyer and, thanks to his fluent journalism and inspiring speeches, he had established himself by the mid-1840s as the leading figure in opposition politics. Seizing the initiative after Metternich's fall, he persuaded the Hungarian parliament to present a series of demands to Vienna, insisting on liberal political reforms and national autonomy (although Hungarians would still recognise the ultimate authority of the Habsburg crown). Early in April, the Liberal Government in Vienna, reeling in the wake of its own Revolution, accepted these demands.

The new situation was, however, fraught with difficulties. Constitutionally speaking, vital aspects of the settlement were ill defined: could Budapest pursue a different foreign policy to Vienna? What financial obligations did Hungary have towards the Empire? Who had the right to control the Hungarian units of the multi-ethnic Imperial army? With Vienna near bankruptcy, and struggling to contain armed revolts in Lombardy and Venetia, such questions were crucial. Just as problematic was the new Budapest Government's relationship with its ethnic minorities (Magyars, the ethnic Hungarians, constituted less than 40 per cent of the population of Hungary). Nationalism had captured the imagination of Croats, Serbs and Romanians too (all races within the Austrian Empire but now, mostly – in theory at least – under Budapest's control), and they feared and resented Magyar arrogance.

In the summer of 1848, the constitutional and national problems combined to force Budapest to repudiate its links with Vienna (although it would be April 1849 before Hungary declared itself to be a Republic). Initially, the loss of Milan and Venice had seemed to cripple Austrian power. Kossuth blocked Vienna's calls for assistance against the Italian nationalists, and many in

Budapest were predicting the complete break up of the Austrian Empire. But the Battle of Custozza changed everything. With the Piedmontese threat neutralised, conservatives in the Habsburg court could begin to contemplate reclaiming some of the power they had lost in Budapest. Vienna gave its backing to General Jelacic, the leader of a predominantly Croatian army, and who had been itching to strike a blow against Magyar chauvinism and to prove his loyalty to his Emperor. His forces invaded Hungary on 11 September.

Kossuth rose to the crisis. The Hungarian Parliament appointed a National Defence Committee, which he soon dominated, to organise resistance. The Croatian assault was repulsed, and Kossuth began to raise the *Honved* – Home Army. At its peak in June 1849, it was 170 000 strong. Kossuth's oratory, charm and sincerity mesmerised the peasant masses, and made him politically invincible. He became, in effect, Hungary's dictator.

The armed struggle lasted until August 1849. Kossuth organised a major munitions industry out of nothing. Inspired by his passionate nationalism and conviction that destiny was on the Magyars' side, his government survived the loss of Budapest in January 1849. General Arthur Görgey's brilliant victories against over-confident Austrian forces in April even briefly left open the road to Vienna, but the opportunity was missed, and relations between Görgey and Kossuth became embittered. The latter vainly hoped for intervention from France or Britain to save the day. By contrast, the young Emperor Franz Josef in May 1849 successfully begged Tsar Nicholas I to send in 200 000 Russians on an anti-revolutionary crusade. Their arrival made the Hungarian cause hopeless. Hungarian forces surrendered in August to face the savage retribution of the Austrians. Kossuth himself escaped into exile, where he was to spend the last 45 years of his life.

Divisions within the nationalist ranks had cost Kossuth dear: his armies had had to confront Croats, Romanians and Serbs as well as Austrians and Russians. But the recovery of the Austrian cause, as in Germany, can be traced back to Custozza. The Hungarian Revolution was really defeated in northern Italy.

to frustrate *German* nationalists' hopes for national unity. The old imperial maxim of 'divide and rule' had rarely been more strikingly demonstrated than in the crisis years of 1848–9. As a consequence, as Sperber concludes, 'rather than a crescendo of nationalist demands tearing the Austrian Empire to pieces, the different national movements fought each other, and cancelled each other out'.

KEY ISSUE

How significant was the rivalry of the competing national movements in the defeat of the 1848 Revolutions?

C *The question of authority: kings, generals and armies*

By 'stopping at the base of the throne' (see page 217), the Revolutions ultimately left themselves at the mercy of their sovereign's goodwill and armies. The armies were the bastions of counter-revolution. The upper ranks of the Habsburg and Hohenzollern armies were mostly drawn from the traditionally highly conservative land-owning and noble classes, who had an arrogant contempt for civilians – especially any members of the middle class with political pretensions. Furthermore, great care had been taken with ordinary soldiers to keep them separate from the civilian world, and any subversive political ideas that might be found there.

See pages 175–6

The new ministries found it difficult to control the armies. Attempts to bring them to heel, as in Prussia in the summer of 1848, only accelerated counter-revolution. Only in Hungary was a serious, sustained attempt made to create a new force loyal to the Revolution – and it is surely significant that the Hungarian Revolution proved by far the most difficult to overturn.

Elsewhere, the Liberals' situation became ever more vulnerable, with the practical autonomy of the King, his court and his courtiers a major problem. Rulers were unaccustomed to playing the role of constitutional monarchs, sharing power with ministers and parliament, and they proved disinclined to learn the new rules. The Austrian court, based for much of 1848 not in Vienna but in Innsbruck or Olmütz, retained considerable freedom of action – especially in its dealings with the generals

See pages 223–4

of the Habsburg army. In Prussia, Frederick William IV turned increasingly for advice to a clique of courtiers. These reactionary aristocrats, outraged by the Liberal assault on their traditions and privileges, were soon plotting *coups* and counter-revolutions, and the King listened with increasing sympathy.

Just as the outbreak of Revolution in February–March 1848 was marked by a domino-effect, as rulers in successive European capitals, seeing the downfall of brother monarchs, tended to lose heart and capitulate, so counter-revolution was characterised by a chain reaction too. The process started with the June Days in Paris. Here events showed that even the 'reddest' capital city could be tamed. But the most important victory for European counter-revolution was won by Radetzky at Custozza. At a time when the Viennese Government had been on

See pages 122–3

See page 95

the brink of negotiating away Lombardy and even Venetia to Piedmont, Sperber rates this victory as 'the most decisive military triumph of the embattled (Austrian) empire, responsible more than anything else for its survival'. A little over three months later, Windischgrätz subdued Vienna with the same mixture of artillery bombardment followed by infantry assault which had been unleashed on Paris in June. Encouraged by these successes in December, Frederick William IV finally made his move on Berlin: its citizens sensibly declined to resist.

KEY ISSUE

Why did the Liberal ministries established by the 1848 Revolutions prove to be so vulnerable militarily?

The lessons of Malmö and Frankfurt

The most striking example of the powerlessness of the Revolutions was the Frankfurt Parliament. In September 1848, without consulting Frankfurt, the Prussians pulled their forces out of Schleswig-Holstein, where they had been defending German nationalists against Danish aggression. This betrayal outraged the delegates in the National Assembly. But after bitter debates, they reluctantly voted to recognise the Prusso-Danish armistice: they had no power to demand that the Prussians continue fighting This, in turn, infuriated radicals on the streets of Frankfurt who murdered two leading conservative delegates and attempted to storm the Assembly building. To protect themselves, the parliamentarians called in Prussian troops, and the insurgents were beaten off with heavy casualties. But the lesson was clear to reactionaries in Vienna and Berlin: the Parliament not only lacked the authority to pursue its own foreign policy – it even lacked the power to defend itself.

ANALYSIS

See pages 186–7

1848: Vienna's roller-coaster ride

No other European city experienced as much political turmoil as Vienna did in 1848, and nowhere was the final triumph of counter-revolution so emphatic. Metternich's flight on 13 March not only detonated demonstrations and risings throughout the Habsburg lands but created tremendous expectations of change in Vienna itself. Initially, the court failed to match these: some liberal reforms were effected, but the new ministers were mostly old faces, and the proposed constitution which finally emerged on 25 April was rather conservative (a powerful House of Lords, a high franchise, and so on). Violent protests followed, and, with crowds besieging the Palace, the beleaguered Government made a series of concessions ultimately agreeing to the calling of a National Assembly (with only one chamber and a very wide franchise) which would work out a new constitution. The radicals seemed to have triumphed.

But the next months brought a series of crises which exposed deep divisions amongst the revolutionaries. On 17 May, the Habsburgs and their court, fearing for their lives, fled to the safety of the ultra-loyalist city of Innsbruck. This increased their freedom of action, and greatly complicated the tasks of the ministry in Vienna which was trying to make constitutional monarchy work. An attempt by the Government to rein in the radicals by closing down the university and disbanding its Academic Legion (see below) backfired: workers and students, helped by members of

ANALYSIS

the militia, forced the Government to back down, and set up a Committee of Security – which became a major power in Vienna. Although the court returned in July, social tensions were growing all the time. Inflation and unemployment were taking their toll, with up to 50 000 workers employed on public relief works. Taxpayers resented this dole, and the Government attempted to reduce it. Demonstrations and riots followed; the resulting clashes with Government troops left hundreds dead and wounded. The university was finally forced to close, the Ministry of Public Works was dissolved and the Committee of Security wound up.

The militants were getting desperate, and a Government order in early October to send in troops against the Hungarian Revolution gave them a final opportunity. The troops mutinied, and a mob lynched the Minister of War. The court again moved out, this time to Olmütz, the Emperor calling 'all men who loved Austria and freedom' to rally round him.

This was the signal Windischgrätz, one of the Habsburgs' leading generals, had been waiting for. In June, he had subdued a revolt by Czech nationalists in Prague with an artillery bombardment; he now set out for Vienna. A Hungarian relief force was defeated, and in late October Windischgrätz surrounded the city and began to bombard it. Two thousand were killed in the assault; 25 were executed after the city fell. It was indicative of the mood in the capital that, in late November, representatives of the middle classes formally expressed their gratitude to Windischgrätz for having 'liberated all men of goodwill from the night of anarchy, the chains of terror and the rule of a party which had sworn the destruction of all good citizens'.

The fate of the Viennese Revolution was vitally important. Robert Blum, one of the leading radicals in the Frankfurt Parliament, had travelled there in late October to give it his support. From Vienna, he wrote to his wife that 'if the revolution is victorious here, it can regain its momentum, but if the revolution is defeated, then Germany will be ... as quiet as a tomb'. For Blum himself, these words were to prove all too true: the new Austrian Prime Minister Schwarzenburg had him executed in the aftermath of Vienna's fall. His wider prophecy was true, too; indeed, the prospects for the European Revolutions in general now looked grim.

The subjugation of Vienna inevitably transformed the terms of debate at Frankfurt. Schwarzenburg effectively vetoed any ideas of a *Großdeutschland* solution to the German question, but it was made equally clear that a resurgent Austria would try and check Prussian Liberals' hopes for a *Kleindeutsch* solution too. In Italy, Austria's vice-like grip of Venice soon tightened; in the east, a drive towards Budapest was launched in December. Victory over the Hungarians would prove surprisingly difficult: but Custozza

See page 177

and the recapture of Vienna made it inevitable. The Habsburgs were back in business.

Three factors help to explain this decisive victory:

● the militancy of the Viennese Revolution was self-defeating: its large, student population, with its own 5000 strong Academic Legion, combined with a reservoir of working class discontent, together constituted a powerful vanguard, pushing the Revolution down radical paths in May and October 1848. But the majority of middle class Viennese were left behind and became increasingly frightened, whilst the upper classes – following the court – literally deserted the capital

● the Viennese radicals' also failed to mobilise provincial Austria behind them. Not only did the prominence of students and proletarians in their ranks make them untypical of Austrian society as a whole; their anti-clericalism and (suspected) re-publicanism offended many outside the city. Furthermore, the peasantry, whose grievances made them potential allies of the Revolution, was effectively neutralised by one of the great concessions won by the Revolution in its early days, the abolition of feudalism in the Austrian Empire

● the revolutionaries in Vienna never wrested control of the army from the Habsburg dynasty, or established an effective fighting force of their own. Radetzky, Windischgrätz and Jelacic had a habit of ignoring orders from their constitutional superiors: their loyalty to the Emperor and to the values of the army itself ('the army is our Fatherland') tended to short-circuit such liberal niceties. And in a showdown, the Academic Legion was no match for Windischgrätz's cannon.

See page 226

See page 222

By Christmas 1848, counter-revolution was not yet finally triumphant: the defeat of the Hungarian Revolution was to be difficult, and the Frankfurt Parliament still had some moves to make. But with Habsburgs and Hohenzollerns firmly re-established in Vienna and Berlin, the conservative ascendancy was clear. The heroism of Dresden and Baden, and of Venice and Rome was to prove, inevitably, futile. The old order was back in charge. But the experience of 1848–9 did not leave Europe unchanged.

See pages 96 and 178

3 ⌒ THE CONSEQUENCES OF REVOLUTION

Ostensibly, the gains made by the Revolution were slight: the ending of most feudal dues within 'Germany'; the abolition of feudal labour

See page 217

ANALYSIS

The peasants and the 1848 revolutions

Of all the peoples of Europe, the peasants arguably had the most acute grievances. But it was very hard to predict how – if at all – they would convert their despair and antagonisms into political activity. Rural illiteracy made it difficult for Liberals or nationalists to take their message into the countryside. In any case 'Freedom to eat' mattered more than 'freedom to speak', whilst appeals to the 'national unity' must have been incomprehensible to villagers whose idea of 'foreigners' might often begin with the inhabitants of the neighbouring valley. The confused mixture of modern political slogans and more ancient prejudices was evident in the demands of the peasants of rural Baden for 'Freedom, equality and the murder of the Jews'. The fact that liberal and nationalist ideas often came from the towns and/or local landowners did not add to their appeal.

Peasant rejection of alien ideologies was evident in the massacre of Polish nobles by Galician peasants in 1846. Polish nationalists, some based in Paris, had convinced themselves that the time was ripe for another attempt to overthrow Russian and Austrian control of their country. But their plans were leaked, and backfired horribly. The regional peasantry, far from feeling sympathy with the national cause, rose instead against their Polish feudal lords, slaughtering them by the thousand. They proclaimed themselves the '[Austrian] Emperor's loyal peasants': some seemed to believe that their Emperor had somehow suspended the Ten Commandments, and had even set a price on the head of any Polish nobleman – whose corpses were accordingly delivered to local officials by the cartload.

Metternich was both appalled and reassured by the massacres. Peasant blood lust revolted him, but he believed that these events were 'extraordinarily significant'. The masses had risen to smash a nationalist revolution: 'the democrats', he wrote, 'have mistaken their base; a democracy without the people is an illusion'. But the peasantry could just as easily show a radical face. In 1848, in southwestern Germany, peasants were often in the vanguard of the Revolution. Tax collectors, forest-wardens, estate agents and moneylenders (often Jewish) – all, hated figures of authority – would be lucky to escape a rural mob with just a beating up. Often, a nobleman's castle would be stormed, and the legal documents recording feudal obligations be burned – and sometimes the castle along with it. Faced with such a capacity for violence, the March ministries of Germany quickly abolished Germany's remaining feudal obligations. Vienna shortly followed this example. Perhaps the only achievement of the Austrian *Reichstag* (formally opened in July 1848) was its approval of the motion, proposed by Hans Kudlich, son of a Silesian serf, that 'from now on the subservient [feudal] relationships, together with all the rights and obligations which spring from it, will be abolished'. After lengthy debate some compensation to the nobility was agreed, and the Emperor ratified the law in September. As in Germany, the effect was to neutralise the peasantry as a political force: 'for them the revolution was over, and their interest in the Reichstag began to wane'. (Siemann.) Perhaps liberals and conservatives alike sensed that it was safer to remove such unpredictable, and potentially violent players, from the political arena.

See the bibliography on page 228

services within the Austrian Empire; and the establishment of constitutional monarchies in Prussia and Piedmont. Elsewhere, not least in Vienna, reactionaries seemed to be reversing any political changes that had been made in 1848–9.

In fact, across Europe, thoughtful conservatives were reassessing their strategies. 'The old times are gone, and cannot return,' remarked a Prussian minister: 'to return to the decaying conditions of the past is like scooping water with a sieve'. In Piedmont and Prussia, the more intelligent politicians on the right had begun to see that constitutional government was compatible with monarchical and aristocratic power. After all, the way events had unfolded over 1848–9 had given Liberals a disturbing insight into the destructive potential of radicalism and republicanism – and made them into the potential allies of conservatism.

Nationalists were rethinking their strategies too. The lessons they drew from the failures of 1848–9 was that idealism – marked by an attempt to cling to principles and a disdain for power politics – was crippling. Instead *Realpolitik* – a readiness to face up to 'power realities' and to do deals with the men who controlled the armies – was the way forward. Nationalists soon discovered they could do business with statesmen like Cavour and Bismarck, who had the necessary flexibility and imagination.

The lessons for revolutionaries, however, were less encouraging. In 1848, Europe's old order seemed destroyed; yet within a year, counter-revolution had triumphed everywhere. Utopian ideals, social grievances and mass revolutionary mobilisation had ultimately proved unable to spike the cannons of Cavaignac, Windischgrätz and Wrangel. Perhaps revolutions could only succeed if the armies of the old regime could be subverted and turned against their masters. But how might this be achieved? It would take the cataclysmic defeats inflicted on Russian, Austrian and German forces in World War I and their consequent total demoralisation before the imperial dynasties of central and eastern Europe would be finally overthrown. In 1848, by contrast, the great imperial armies remained loyal to their Habsburg and Hohenzollern rulers. This above all was the key to these dynasties' survival.

4 ⤳ BIBLIOGRAPHY

Helpful overviews of the Revolutions can be found in the following: *The Ascendancy of Europe 1815–1914* by M. Anderson (Longman, 1985); *Barricades and Borders: Europe 1800–1914* by R. Gildea (Oxford, 1987); *A History of Modern Europe*, Vol. 2 by J. Merriman (W.W. Norton, 1996); and *European History 1848–1945* by T. Morris (Unwin Hyman, 1985). Two short surveys concentrating on the Revolutions are: *The 1848 Revolutions* by P. Jones (Longman Seminar Studies, 1981); and *The Revolutions of 1848* by R. Price (Macmillan, 1998). A demanding synthesis is *The European Revolutions, 1848–1851* by J. Sperber (Cambridge, 1994).

Suggested reading for the study of individual Revolutions includes: *The German Revolution of 1848–9* by W. Siemann (Macmillan, 1998), which also includes material on Austria; *The Decline and Fall of the Habsburg Empire 1815–1918* by A. Sked (Longman, 1989); and *The Habsburg Empire 1790–1918* by C. Macartney (Macmillan, 1969). An excellent biography of the hero of the Hungarian Revolution, is *The Lawful Revolution: Louis Kossuth and the Hungarians 1848–49* by I. Deak (1979). *The Revolutions in Europe 1848–49: From Reform to Reaction* by R. Evans and H. Pogge von Strandmann (Oxford, 2000) is also useful.

5 ⤳ STRUCTURED QUESTIONS AND ESSAYS

1. (a) Outline the main causes of the 1848 Revolutions; (10 marks)
   (b) Explain why the Revolution was unsuccessful in any **one** country. (15 marks)
2. Was nationalism or liberalism primarily responsible for the 1848 Revolutions? (25 marks)
3. Why was revolution so widespread in Europe in 1848? (25 marks)

6 ⤳ THE DYNAMICS AND DIVISIONS OF NATIONALISM IN 1848–9: A SOURCES EXERCISE

Read the following collection of Sources A–E and answer the questions which follow:

… the nation was to be the object of everyone's highest loyalty and devotion. All religions, social classes, regions, dynasties were to be subsumed under the nation. As August Hoffmann von Fallersleben's *Deutschlandlied* (written in 1840) proclaims, 'Deutschland, Deutschland über alles/Über alles in der Welt' – Germany, Germany, above everything/Above everything in the world. For truly convinced nationalists, the nation stood above all mundane considerations; it was transcendent, an object of almost religious devotion, indeed, often a substitute for such devotion.

… In a sense, nationalism was the feeling of unity with other participants while taking part in a mass meeting … [like] the 1832 National Festival of the Germans in Hambach or the feeling that emerged from attending a public lecture or theatrical performance in which the Rumanian or Czech language was used for the first time. Nationalist feelings emerged from working closely with other conspirators in a secret society. Newspapers, offering reports from everywhere a common language was spoken, helped to build this feeling. In Germany, between 1815 and 1850 there developed the three organisations that became the bearers of nationalist ideas, not just in the German-speaking world, but in much of continental Europe: the choral, gymnastics and sharpshooting societies. Nationalism was cultivated in such groups, in the experience of choral singing; in the unison movements practised in gymnastics societies (in contrast to the floor exercises or apparatus work of today's gymnastics); in the sharpshooters marching behind a flag – and, of course, in being part of the crowd witnessing these spectacles.

**SOURCE A:
THE APPEAL OF
NATIONALISM**
J. Sperber, Revolutionary Europe *1780–1850 (2000)*

Modern nationalism in Hungary began, as everywhere else in Central and Eastern Europe, in the form of a cultural and linguistic revival, soon to be turned into a political and social reform movement. Almost from the beginning, the positive elements of hope and faith in progress were juxtaposed with elements of fear and hopelessness. The nation on the rise was also a nation threatened by extinction. Expanding and dynamic Hungary was seen as menaced by German and Slavic expansion. Fear became the dominant motive of Hungarian nationalism: a fear powerfully nourished by the German writer, Johann Gottfried Herder. Instead of identifying nation and language with the state. Herder investigated the spiritual roots of nationality. He saw language as the repository of a people's tradition, culture, history, religion, wisdom, heart and soul. Turning to Central Europe, Herder predicted that the Magyar language, and hence the Magyar people, would soon disappear in the sea of Slavic peoples. His prophecies caused the Magyar leaders to advocate the spreading by law of the Magyar culture. … they believed that by teaching Hungarian in the schools, they would achieve the universal acceptance of Magyar as the state language. After all, they argued, Hungarians had founded the state; they had consistently proved themselves the leaders in the Carpathian Basin, and they possessed the superior warlike qualities that alone entitled a nation to lead others.

**SOURCE B:
HUNGARIAN
NATIONALISM**
From I. Deak, The Lawful Revolution: Louis Kossuth and the Hungarians 1848–49 *(1979)*

SOURCE C:
KOSSUTH'S DEMANDS
Kossuth writing in his newspaper Pesti Hirlap *in 1842*

In Hungary, Magyar must become the language of public administration, whether civil or ecclesiastic, of the legislative and the executive, of the government, of justice, of public security, of the police, of direct and indirect taxation and of the economy. To accept less, would be cowardice; to insist on more would be tyranny; both would mean suicide on our part.

Rise, Magyar! Is the country's call!
The time has come, say one all:
Shall we be slaves, shall we be free?
This is the question, now agree!
For by the Magyar's God above
We truly swear,
We truly swear the tyrant's yoke
No more to bear!

Alas! Till now we were but slaves;
Our fathers resting in their graves
Sleep not in freedom's soil. In vain
They fought and died free homes to gain.
But by the Magyar's God above
We truly swear,
We truly swear the tyrant's yoke
No more to bear!

5. The Magyar's name will soon once more
   Be honoured as it was before!
   The shame and dust of ages past
   Our valor shall wipe out at last.
   For by the Magyar's God above
   We truly swear,
   We truly swear the tyrant's yoke
   No more to bear!

SOURCE D:
HUNGARIAN
NATIONLISM
The National Song of Hungary, written on the eve of the 1848 revolution by Sandor Petöfi (1823–49) poet and militant radical and nationalist. He died fighting for Hungary in 1849

6. And where our graves in verdure rise,
   Our children's children to the skies
   Shall speak the grateful joy they feel,
   And bless our names the while they kneel.
   For by the Magyar's God above
   We truly swear,
   We truly swear the tyrant's yoke
   No more to bear!

I am a Czech of Slav descent and with all the little I own and possess I have devoted myself wholly and forever to the service of my nation. That nation is small, it is true, but from time immemorial it has been an independent nation with its own character; its rulers have participated since old times in the federation of German princes, but the nation never regarded itself nor was it regarded by others throughout all the centuries, as part of the German nation …

The second reason which prevents me from participating in your deliberations is the fact that from all that has been so far publicly announced of your aims and purposes you irrevocably are, and will be, aiming to undermine Austria forever as an independent empire and to make its existence impossible – an empire whose preservation, integrity and consolidation is, and must be, a great and important matter not only for my own nation but for the whole of Europe, indeed for mankind and civilisation itself. Allow me kindly to explain myself briefly on this point …

You know that in south-east Europe, along the frontiers of the Russian empire, there live many nations widely different in origin, language, history and habits – Slavs, Rumanians, Magyars and Germans, not to speak of Greeks, Turks and Albanians – none of whom is strong enough by itself to be able to resist successfully for all time the superior neighbour to the east [i.e. Russia]; they could do it only if a close and firm tie bound them all together. Certainly, if the Austrian state had not existed for ages, we would be obliged in the interests of Europe and even of mankind to endeavour to create it as fast as possible …

And if Hungary, following its instincts severs its connections with the [Austrian] state or – will then Hungary which does not wish to hear of national equality within its borders be able to maintain itself free and strong in the future? Only the just is truly free and strong. A voluntary union of the Danubian Slavs and Rumanians, or even of the Poles themselves, with such a state which declares that a man must first be a Magyar before he can be a human being is entirely out of the question; and even less thinkable would be a compulsory union of this kind …

SOURCE E:
THE PROBLEMS OF
NATIONALISM IN
THE HABSBURG
EMPIRE
František Palacký, a leading
Czech nationalist, wrote to
the German National Assembly
in April 1848 rejecting an
invitation to join the Frankfurt
Parliament

Q

1. What does Source A suggest about the mass appeal of nationalism? (5 marks)
2. To what extent does Source B present a more negative view of nationalism? (5 marks)
3. Identify the elements of propaganda in Sources C and D. How useful are these two sources to an historian of the 1848 Revolutions? (8 marks)
4. What does Source E reveal about the complexities of nationalism in the Habsburg Empire? (8 marks)
5. Using this collection of Sources A–E, and your own knowledge, assess the validity of the judgement that 'nationalist feeling was both the great strength and the great weakness of the movement for revolutionary change in 1848–9'. (14 marks)

Russia
1855–81

8

INTRODUCTION

THE REIGN OF ALEXANDER II, 1855–81

The 1860s were a crucial decade for Russia. There were important reforms affecting the fabric of a still rural society. Tsar Alexander II ascended the throne during the Crimean War. His father Nicholas I had been well aware of the need for change, particularly to the institution of serfdom, but had been unwilling to face the unpredictable consequences. However, Russia's defeat in war highlighted the issues more starkly. Consequently Alexander took up the challenge. The most significant reform was the emancipation of the serfs, which brought him the epithet 'The Tsar Liberator'. However, Alexander discovered, like most reformers, that trying to implement change created stresses and opposition. These prompted a much more conservative approach, particularly after revolt in Poland and an attempt on the Tsar's life in the mid 1860s. Some historians have therefore drawn a clear distinction between the two periods in his reign, although this distinction can be exaggerated. Alexander implemented more reforms than any previous Tsar since Peter the Great; but his reign also saw opposition to the tsarist regime develop in new and ultimately more threatening directions, as the fundamentals of the tsarist system remained unchanged.

1 ⌁ POLITICAL HISTORY

A *The emancipation of the serfs*

Alexander was committed to reform from the start. His aunt, the Grand Duchess Helen, and his brother Grand Duke Constantine, both supported him, along with a group of reforming bureaucrats active in the administration since the 1840s. Reforming ministers included Nicholai Milyutin, Dmitrii Milyutin (Minister of War 1861–81) and Michael Reitern (Minister of Finance 1862–78). Alexander had practical motives for change:

- failure to change might lead to the eventual dissolution of the autocracy. Alexander recognised that serfdom was an insecure

TIMELINE

Events in Russia 1855–81
(foreign affairs in italics)

1855 Accession of
Alexander II
1856 Treaty of Paris
1858 *Amur acquired from
China*
1859 Length of army service
reduced
1861 Emancipation of the
serfs began
1863 Polish Revolt
1863 Educational reforms
begun
1864 *Zemstvos* set up
Reform of local
government
Legal reforms
1865 Censorship relaxed
1866 Attempted assassination
of Tsar
1870 Municipal reforms
1871 Censorship tightened up
Straits Convention
1873 *Dreikaiserbund*
1874 Universal military
conscription
1876 Formation of 'Land and
Liberty'
1877 *Russo-Turkish War
Treaty of San Stefano*
1878 *Congress of Berlin*
Trial of Vera Zasulich
1880 Commission into unrest
1881 Assassination of
Alexander II

foundation for a Great Power anxious to regain its reputation and influence after military defeat

● although serfs were the backbone of the army and paid most of the taxes, their number was rapidly expanding without a rise in productivity; whilst the Tsar's traditional supporters, the nobility, were increasingly in debt. At the time of Alexander's accession, 60 per cent of private serfs and 50 per cent of land values were mortgaged to the state.

It was a system that could not safely continue unchanged. Yet as an autocrat, how could the Tsar make concessions without avoiding on the one hand the backlash of entrenched opposition, and on the other hand raising unrealistic expectation? He was determined not to open the floodgates to more radical reforms which might be equally threatening to the long-term stability or even survival of the autocracy.

PICTURE 14
Cartoon from Punch *showing Tsar Alexander II succeeding to his throne*

THE YOUNG CZAR COMING INTO HIS PROPERTY.

TSAR ALEXANDER II (1818–81)

Alexander came to the throne at the age of 37, well prepared for the task of governing. He had extensive experience already as a member of the Council of State and several committees. Like his father Nicholas I, he was conservative, patriotic and religious by nature, but unlike him he also enjoyed the worldly pleasures of the court. Alexander was more adaptable, partly because he had received a liberal education. However, he was prone to bouts of apathy, pessimism and indecision. He appointed both reforming ministers like Nicholai Milyutin, who pushed through emancipation, but also appointed reactionaries like Shuvalov.

Historians sometimes divide Alexander's reign into two periods: one of reform from 1855 to the early 1860s, then a period of reaction as dissatisfaction with his policies grew. For example, H. Seton Watson wrote that 'The reign of Alexander II which began with bright promise, and changed to dreary stagnation, ended in tragedy. The Tsar-liberator was a victim of the unsolved conflict between social reform and the dogma of political autocracy' (*The Decline of Imperial Russia*, 1964). However, a simplistic chronological division is not helpful, since throughout his reign Alexander never intended reform to touch his personal power, and there was not necessarily a contradiction in his own mind between autocracy and his ability to grant limited reform from above. Other critical assessments include J. Grenville: 'He was indecisive and throughout his reign alternated between reforming impulses and reaction ... the degree of discontent was raised more by the hope of reform than satisfied by their application' (*Europe Reshaped 1848–1878*, 1976). W. Mosse wrote: 'Alexander proved himself not only a disappointing 'liberal', if indeed that term can be applied to him, but ... an inefficient autocrat ... He merely succeeded in proving that a pseudo-liberal autocrat is an unhappy hybrid unlikely to achieve political success' (*Alexander II and the Modernisation of Russia*, 1992). Balanced assessments take account of the context in which Alexander came to the throne and the difficulties facing anybody trying to do more than uphold the *status quo*. M. Lynch concluded that 'He was convinced that he had to remain in charge of events if Russia was to avoid revolution. An autocrat's task is a difficult one. The task of a reforming autocrat is the most difficult of all' (*Russia 1815–81*, 1991). S Lee emphasised elements of continuity during Alexander's reign: the fact that there was evidence of reform and reaction throughout; there was continuity in some of the personnel; and the fact that military and fiscal concerns were always at the core of the Tsar's thinking – he 'realised that effective autocracy must depend ultimately on sound financial management and military strength. This was a traditional Romanov approach and had as much to do with Alexander's reforms as any enlightened theories' (*Aspects of European History 1789–1980*, 1982).

Alexander was considering further reform at the time of his assassination in 1881.

KEY ISSUE

What were the motives for the 1860s reforms?

Whatever Alexander's approach, the process of reform was bound to be complex in Russia. Like all Tsars, Alexander was effectively his own Prime Minister. Government ministers never discussed policy as a group, but were individuals who reported briefly and individually to the Tsar, and were often not aware of what their colleagues were doing. The State Council was an advisory body which had no independence, and its advice could be ignored. When decisions were taken, the lack of an efficient network of local government in far-flung provinces made co-ordinated implementation of policy difficult. In such a system, much depended upon the Tsar's determination and hard work. This made Alexander II's efforts to tackle major issues like serfdom the more commendable. Despite the fact that the Tsar was an autocrat with few theoretical limits on his power, the practical difficulties of governing nineteenth century Russia should always be borne in mind when assessing the practical impact of reforms.

Alexander wanted to satisfy both the peasantry and the nobility. He told the latter in 1856 that 'the existing system of serf owning cannot remain unchanged. It is better to begin abolishing serfdom from above than to wait for it to begin to abolish itself from below.' How could he satisfy both the serfs and their owners? The committee set up in 1856 to consider the issue first met in secret to avoid the spread of rumour. The Government felt it important that freed serfs stayed on the land, rather than drift to the towns where they might become a large discontented working class of the kind which frightened European Governments in 1848. Therefore Alexander insisted that the serfs, if freed, must be given property rights, even if the land belonged to the nobility.

In 1857 the Tsar and his ministers produced a plan of action to be considered in each province. Consultation began in earnest in 1858 when provincial assemblies of nobles were invited to make proposals for reform. It was immediately evident that opinion was divided: some liberal nobles were willing to give the serfs both full personal liberty and full property rights. This was far too radical for most nobles, who wanted to retain extensive powers over the peasantry. Those nobles who relied upon serfs to farm their land were afraid that they would lose this power if peasants were free to uproot themselves. Differences amongst the nobility allowed the Government to take the initiative and insist on the more radical proposal that freed serfs must be allowed land. Representatives from the provinces which were most supportive of change were invited to Moscow in 1859, and their opponents in 1860. The administration itself wanted to preserve the *mir* or village commune, since it managed taxes and acted as an adjunct to the bureaucracy. Nevertheless, as the debates dragged on and peasant discontent grew, the Government decided that the peasants must be granted land if serious unrest were to be averted.

The great Emancipation Decree was issued on 19 February 1861. It was a complex decree made up of 22 separate Acts. The first abolished the institution of serfdom, and there were to be three main stages, outlined in the analysis box.

KEY ISSUE

Why did proposals to emancipate the serfs create such debate?

ANALYSIS

The stages of the emancipation of the serfs

Stage 1. *1861–3.* Landlords' serfs were declared free, allowing them to own land and marry. But other than the land on which their households were established, which was declared to belong to the peasants, the rest belonged to the nobility and had to be bought from it. In return for the right to farm, the peasants had to continue paying existing feudal dues. Therefore their true status was little altered.

Stage 2. This was to begin in *1863.* Ties between the ex-serfs and landlords were further loosened, with landlords losing their judicial rights over the peasants. Feudal dues would continue but agreements had to be negotiated obliging the peasant to buy, and the landlord to sell, a certain amount of land. The transfer of land was not compulsory until 1881. The Government regulated prices and the amount that had to be bought and sold. Household serfs were also freed, but received no land.

Stage 3. This would begin *after the negotiations were completed.* The Government paid landlords most of the price of the land; peasants had 49 years in which to reimburse the Government in 'redemption payments'. The *mir* continued to allot shares of land to the peasants. So some 23 million peasants would still have obligations – but to the *mir* and the Government rather than to private landlords. This was a significant change in the status of peasants, although economically their position was little altered.

B *The results of emancipation*

The peasants saw little benefits from the reforms, and were confused about their implications:

- they now had to pay for land they regarded as theirs anyway
- they received relatively little land, at high prices. Land distribution was unequal: peasants in the more fertile regions received less land than in the less fertile areas, often less than the amount they had previously worked. In some areas, like the central and southern provinces, peasants lost up to one-quarter of their land. Over 1 500 000 serfs received no land at all, and by the end of Alexander's reign, over 60 per cent of peasants had less than the minimum land that the Government itself considered necessary for subsistence
- the redemption costs varied from area to area: they were very high for example in Poland. Many peasants tried to buy more land and fell into more debt. Those peasants without land often found alternative work hard to come by.

The number of peasant disturbances increased in the two years after 1861. Although the unrest did die down, the peasants' situation steadily worsened as the considerable growth in population (from 74 million to 125 million between 1858 and 1897) put pressure on the land. The *mir*, traditionally the protector of the peasants' interests, still allocated land, but had no particular interest in improving farming methods. Consequently Russia fell further behind other European Powers in crop yields, and failure to revitalise the rural economy meant that much more drastic measures were necessary in the future in order to provide a basis for industrialisation.

Most nobles also resented the changes. Those that had been serf owners lost their control over the peasantry, and much of their influence generally. Many nobles were themselves in debt, and over half their land had been sold off by 1911. Many abandoned farming and took up other professions.

KEY ISSUE

What was the reaction of the peasants and nobility to emancipation?

C *Other reforms*

Alexander II implemented other reforms which had important social implications. Destroying the old relationship between serf and noble affected more than land ownership, since the nobility had played a significant role in local government and administering justice. Who would now exercise these powers? In 1864 *zemstva* were created. These were elected local government assemblies with responsibility for education, public health, transport and the prison system. The Prussian three-class voting system was adopted which meant that although all classes could elect *zemstva* members, they were dominated by the nobility. However, more liberal members of these councils began to press for more powers, whilst other interest groups were set up representing professional or social groups. The central Government retained control of the police, whilst provincial governors could overturn *zemstva* decisions. The reform was therefore less radical in practice than it appeared on paper.

This was also true of the judicial reforms of 1864. For the first time all Russians were declared equal before the law. Justice was to be open, with independent judges and trial by jury in most cases. However, the Government retained the right to hold closed trials in 'political cases'; special courts continued to try cases involving ex-serfs; and it was still possible to exert pressure on judges.

There were other reforms in the 1860s:

- from 1862 Government finances were determined by a public budget
- the tax system was modernised
- in 1863 universities were given powers to run their own affairs
- censorship was partially relaxed in 1865
- military reform, very necessary following Russia's performance in the Crimean War, ended exemption from conscription for the privileged in 1874 and reduced the lengthy period of active service to six years, with nine years in the reserves. However, the modernisation of military technology and tactics was a slow process.

KEY ISSUE

How significant were the 1860s reforms?

Alexander II's reforms were linked with each other in at least one important respect. Recovering Russia's international standing depended upon economic progress and having a modern army, which depended on abolishing serfdom, incompatible with maintaining a well-trained reserve. The *zemstva* and other reforms were more designed to appease the nobility. The reforms certainly had a cumulative effect overall. They increased the power of the professional bureaucracy, but at the expense of the nobility, not the Government.

Superficially the reforms appeared to be in line with earlier developments in more liberal Western European states, but in reality the tsarist regime remained autocratic, subject to few real restraints. After the mid 1860s, Alexander, troubled by the Polish Revolt and attempted assassination, abandoned reform. He removed all the reforming ministers except for Dmitrii Milyutin and Reitern.

How significant were Alexander's reforms? They raised expectations of change without satisfying the aspirations of many Russians. The nobility could no longer rely upon the compulsory labour of serfs and had lost its judicial and police powers. Government officials now performed many of the old duties. Receiving payment from the Government for land they were forced to sell, and having the right to serve in the *zemstva*, did not seem adequate compensation to nobles for the loss of status and real power. However, for the first time in Russia elected representatives had a part in government, albeit at the local level through local councils. Some prominent Russians even advocated extending this principle to central government, possibly through a consultative assembly: they included Valuev, Minister of the Interior between 1861–8, the Tsar's brother and P. Shuvalov, head of the political police during the 1870s.

The Tsar was too much the autocrat to consider any proposals for sharing power at the top. He voiced approval of his father's policies and declared that his reign would see a continuation of them. Yet ironically, he did consider further change shortly before his assassination. In 1878 the young radical Vera Zasulich was acquitted despite shooting and wounding the unpopular Governor of St. Petersburg, General Trepov. Alexander established a commission to investigate the causes of unrest, and he agreed in February 1881 that local councils should elect members to serve on commissions, alongside appointed experts, to advise on legislation. However, his assassination in the following month effectively put an end to serious discussion of reform for more than a generation.

D *The growth of opposition*

Although the autocracy had achieved success in the short term, reinforcing its authority and appearing to implement some necessary reforms, trouble was also being stored up for the future. The regime could rely to a large extent on the traditional loyalty of the peasantry towards the Tsar, the 'Little Father', but not when economic pressures became too great. The nobility had once been the Tsar's natural allies, but its powers had been increasingly handed over to bureaucrats. The nobility might be less willing to support the Tsar in all circumstances in the future. Educated and liberal Russians, both nobles and from other classes, were increasingly frustrated by what they regarded as the unwillingness of a regime to introduce more modern, western-style practices into what remained, in European terms, a semi-feudal state.

Disillusion with the impact of Alexander II's reforms also created movements for change of a type new to Russia. Before there had been serf uprisings and plots by disaffected nobles. But, for example, Russia had been relatively untouched by the European Revolutions of 1848. Now there were new forces of dissent. Some belonged to Liberals, who, in the tradition of the American and French Revolutions of the eighteenth century, believed in individual liberty and the rule of law. Many of the more radical thinkers became socialists: they went further than Liberals in their insistence that guarantees of individual rights and freedoms meant little if those who were landless in a society based on private property could be exploited by those who owned the land. In other words, true equality and freedom could only exist in a society based upon collective ownership of land and the means of production. The reforms of the 1860s also appeared to socialists to confirm that legal freedom for ex-serfs meant little if they were weighed down by debts and poverty.

Radical reformers were almost bound to become revolutionaries, since in an autocratic society like Russia, with police and censorship to buttress the system and no national parliament in which to debate change, there were few legitimate means to openly pursue an organised political programme. Revolutionaries came from a variety of backgrounds, but they were usually well-educated. Two influential figures who inspired the revolutionary movement were the journalist Nicholas Chernyshevskii (1828–9) and the nobleman Alexander Herzen (1812–70). Herzen's newspaper, *The Bell*, was published in London in the 1850s and 1860s. Herzen looked to the Russian peasant for salvation, and saw the *mir* as a socialist organisation which would lead Russia into a utopia in which inequalities of wealth and status would disappear. It was a vision which inspired other radicals, known as Populists because of their belief in the Russian people as the instrument of change. Most Populists were scarcely interested in Western Liberal ideas of liberty, equality and fraternity. Rather they were 'Slavophils' who put their faith in the particular virtues of the Russian peasant. Recognising the low level of industrial development, they believed that Russia could avoid the capitalist development of Western Europe and move directly to peasant socialism.

The Polish Revolt of 1863 fanned the flames of discontent. Polish peasants were treated relatively generously under emancipation. However, the Tsar followed a policy of *Russification*, enforcing the dominant status of the Russian language. In 1863 200 000 Poles took up arms against Russian control and a National Government was proclaimed. Russian armies commanded by the Tsar's brother suppressed the rising. Although the Revolt failed, nationalist feeling inside Poland continued to grow.

KEY ISSUE

Why was there growing opposition to Alexander II and what forms did the opposition take?

Following an assassination attempt in 1866 Alexander, already alarmed by the Polish Revolt, abandoned further attempts at reform. Student Populists had already fomented discontent in St. Petersburg and other cities from 1862. They now responded with more plots and underground newspapers. In the early 1870s students responding to the clarion call 'To the people!', descended on the Russian countryside in order to spread the message of revolution to the peasants. The students involved probably numbered only about 2000. Most peasants mistrusted these outsiders and were uncooperative, sometimes even turning Populists over to the authorities.

Disillusioned with the failure of the direct appeal to the people, some radicals began to argue for the formation of more secretive, organised groups which would work for revolution underground. Their methods were a foretaste of the Bolshevik organisation later in the century, without the Bolsheviks' discipline and ideology. Some groups employed terrorist tactics. One such, *Narodnaya Volya* or 'People's Will', with about 500 members, succeeded in blowing up Alexander II in March 1881. The brief era of reform had already ended several years before, but the Tsar's death nevertheless was to mark a new stage in the underground war between the autocracy, bolstered by the secret police and the censors, and the small groups of violent and determined revolutionaries.

2 ⌁ ECONOMIC HISTORY

The basics of the Russian economy in the mid-nineteenth century are outlined in Chapter 12. During Alexander II's reign the textile and sugar industries were well developed, but the once prosperous iron industry was lagging behind competitors in Western Europe. As the Government implemented major reforms in the 1860s, so it also became much more interventionist in the economy than it had been during the reigns of Alexander's two predecessors, although not as extensively as later in the nineteenth century. Some measures were not beneficial. A liberal approach to reducing tariffs in the 1850s and 1860s reduced Government revenue and the import of cheap goods into Russia was a disincentive to indigenous enterprises. So tariffs had to be increased again in the late 1870s and 1880s. On the other hand, the railway network expanded by 400 per cent between 1868 and 1878, mostly as a result of private enterprise. There were over 14 000 miles of track by 1881. Urban expansion continued.

> **KEY ISSUE**
>
> *What economic progress did Russia make in the period 1855–81?*

The abolition of serfdom in theory made industrial development more feasible. The population became less tied to the land and more mobile. The potential labour force was enlarged. Therefore M. Falkus asserted that 'the year 1861 can in many respects be taken as marking the beginning of Russia's modernisation' (M. Falkus, *The Industrialisation of Russia 1700–1914*). However, it was only the basis for further development: although both heavy industry and consumer-goods industries began to expand at an average rate of probably 5 per cent a year, industrial growth in most sectors only became really significant from the

1880s. Production in mining, wool, sugar and paper actually declined in the 1860s, mainly due to the difficulties of adapting after emancipation. Although production picked up, there was a serious depression in the early 1870s before another upturn towards the end of the decade.

Russian economic development was assisted by the development of financial institutions. There were few banks in 1855, but over 300 in 1881, and 566 joint-stock companies. Restrictions on the settlement of Jews were relaxed, enabling them to better utilise their traditional financial and commercial skills.

3 ⇌ FOREIGN POLICY

A *Russia and Europe*

See pages 26–8

Russia's defeat in the Crimean War considerably weakened its international position, as confirmed in the Treaty of Paris. Russia lost control of the mouth of the Danube and its use for navigation. It could no longer intervene in the Danubian Principalities. Above all there was the neutralisation of the Black Sea. Britain, France and Austria were pledged to uphold the terms of the Treaty.

Russian foreign policy in Europe faced a dilemma. Traditionally, as a great conservative supporter of the status quo after 1815, Russia had wanted to preserve the balance of power and the existing state system – which seemed the best guarantee against revolutionary upheaval. Yet in 1855 a defeated Russia became a revisionist Power, keen to drive a wedge between its former enemies. Alexander II and Prince Alexander Gorchakov, Foreign Minister between 1856 and 1882, wanted to revise the Treaty of Paris, but it would not be easy.

During the 1860s Russia avoided significant involvement in Europe, concentrating instead on internal affairs. This detachment allowed Prussia to strengthen its position in central Europe. However, The Straits issue was raised by Gorchakov when the situation seemed favourable – notably during the Franco-Prussian War of 1870–1, when Russia insisted that its participation in a European Congress depended on a revision of the Treaty. British refusal to support Russia's demands led Alexander II to unilaterally repudiate the clauses neutralising the Black Sea in October 1870. Gorchakov worked hard to placate other Powers: for example he emphasised to Britain Russia's desire to preserve the Turkish Empire, and also promised France to stand up for it in defeat. He declared that the Tsar 'has no intention of reopening the Eastern Question ... He desires only to preserve and strengthen peace'. Gorchakov succeeded: a Conference in London in March 1871 gave international agreement to Russia's action over the Black Sea.

Russian policy was important in making the unification of Germany possible. Russia's neutralisation of Austria helped to keep the Franco-Prussian War a localised affair, as recognised by Kaiser Wilhelm's expression of gratitude to the Tsar in March 1871, and despite French influence inside Russia. Russia tolerated a German state because it saw

KEY ISSUE

What principles underpinned Alexander II's foreign policy?

the German Empire as a force for conservatism. However, it indirectly helped Germany become the strongest Power in Europe. Russia welcomed the Three Emperors' League (*Dreikaiserbund*) because it wanted to remain on good terms with Germany, particularly since Russia was concerned about British policy in Asia. The agreement to join the League, more a statement of intent than an alliance, signified Russia's return to the centre of European events on an equal basis. In 1873 Russia also signed a defensive alliance with Germany. However, Russia did not secure its principal aim – a free hand in the Balkans and Turkish Empire.

Towards the end of his reign, Alexander became more actively involved in the Balkans, encouraged by Pan-Slavs in Russia who saw themselves as protectors of Slavs in the region. Turkish policy, combined with Russian ambition and dreams of expansion towards Constantinople, led to the Russo-Turkish War of 1877–8 and Russian gains at the Treaty of San Stefano. Even after the Treaty was reversed at the Congress of Berlin, which outraged Pan-Slavs, Russia had regained the mouth of the Danube, although Russia's ambassador to Turkey, the Panslav Nikolai Ignatev, wanted a much more forward policy than his Government adopted.

KEY ISSUE

How successful was Alexander II's foreign policy in Europe?

See pages 390–1

B *Russia and Asia*

Despite his desire to improve Russia's international standing, Alexander II's policy in Europe was generally cautious. However, during his reign there was considerable Russian expansion particularly in Central Asia. The Khanates of Khiva, Khokand and Bukhara were absorbed. Although Alaska was sold to the United States, cessions were won from China, enabling the Russians to establish themselves on the Pacific Coast. The future Vladivostok was reached in 1859. Sakhalin was acquired from Japan. The Caucasus was brought more firmly under Russian control. During the 1850s and 1860s the Russians moved South, conquering Uzbek lands. Partly the motives for expansion were to do with prestige: Russia could demonstrate its Great Power status in Asian lands without the risks involved in expansion in Europe. Partly the Government absorbed territory after following up initiatives begun by traders and explorers, who were carving out their own trails across Asia. Interests of trade, security, and a missionary, civilising impulse were all combined. Gorchakov explained Russia's situation as

the same as the position of any civilised state which comes into contact with a semi-barbarous people ... In such cases the interests of frontier security and of trade relations always require that the more civilised state acquires a certain power over its neighbours.

Subject peoples did not appreciate Russian motives. Nationalist groups expanded in Finland, despite tolerant treatment by the Tsar which included allowing a Finnish parliament to meet. Nationalist

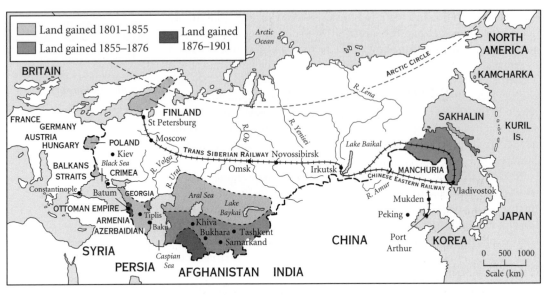

MAP 9   *Russian territorial expansion in the nineteenth century*

feeling also developed in the Baltic States and the Ukraine, in addition to exploding into revolt in Poland.

Assessments of Alexander II's success in foreign policy have varied:

● he did avoid a major conflict whilst giving Russia the opportunity to reform itself internally. Russia was a Great Power again, had emphasised its interests in the Balkans and enlarged the Russian Empire in Asia, bringing access to oil and mineral wealth. Shortly after Alexander's death the *Dreikaiserbund* was renewed, assuaging Russia's fear of having to fight several enemies if it were at war with a fourth Power

● however, Russia's longer-term ambitions had been thwarted at the Congress of Berlin: it was no nearer fulfilling the dream of controlling Constantinople and the Straits. Some Russians thought that Alexander had not promoted Russia's interests with sufficient energy, and Russia had allowed Germany to consolidate its position as the strongest Power in Europe, with serious implications in the long term.

KEY ISSUE

How significant was Russian expansion into Asia?

4 ⌒ BIBLIOGRAPHY

Useful books for this period of Russian history are *Russia 1815–81* by M. Lynch (Hodder and Stoughton, 1991), which is written for the 16–19 age group and includes essay and source material; *Tsarist Russia 1901–1917* by J. Hite (Causeway Press, 1989); *The Emergence of Modern Russia 1801–1917* by S. Pushkarev (Pica Press, 1986); and *Russia in the Age of Reaction and Reform 1801–1881* by D. Saunders (Longman, 1992). Useful specialised studies of Alexander II's reign include *Alexander II and the Modernisation of Russia* by W. Mosse (I.B. Tauris, 1992) and *Alexander II, Emancipation and Reform in Russia, 1855–1881* by M. Perrie (Historical Association, 1989). A detailed study of the reforms is *Russia's Great Reforms 1855–1881* edited by B. Eklof, J. Bushnell and L. Zakharova (Indiana University Press, 1994).

5 ↬ STRUCTURED QUESTIONS AND ESSAYS

1. (a) Briefly outline the main terms of the emancipation of the serfs in Russia in 1861; (10 marks)

   (b To what extent did the emancipation fulfil the aims of its supporters? (15 marks)

2. (a) Outline the reforms made in local government, education, the law and the army during the reign of Alexander II; (10 marks)

   (b) Why did opposition to Alexander II's regime increase during his reign? (15 marks)

3. Does Alexander II deserve the title 'the reforming Tsar'? (25 marks)

4. (a) Outline the main steps of Alexander II's foreign policy in Europe; (10 marks)

   (b) To what extent did Alexander succeed in reversing the setback to Russia's prestige suffered during the Crimean War? (15 marks)

6 ↬ DOCUMENTARY EXERCISE ON REFORM AND OPPOSITION IN ALEXANDER II'S REIGN

Study the collection of Sources A–G below and answer the questions which follow:

The *first opinion* is held by those who have shown little sympathy for the liberation of the serfs and are motivated by the personal and material interests of the estate owner ... The majority of them, brought up on the concept of serfdom, cannot understand the urgent need for reform and expect it to bring irreparable losses. In their fright they imagine approaching ruin and poverty for themselves and their descendants ... The initial act of the opponents of emancipation was to attempt to stop any action in the peasant question by trying to frighten the government with predictions of revolt ...

Second opinion ... This is the trend of *class interest* ... among the rich and prominent estate owners. Placing in the forefront the class interests of the nobility, they wish to establish a landed aristocracy, like that of England ... In exchange for giving the peasants homesteads and the use of arable lands, the estate owners would retain special rights ...

The *third opinion* is subscribed to by those desiring the complete abolition of serfdom. They comprise a substantial section of the Russian nobility, though by no means the majority.

SOURCE A
Memorandum to the Tsar by Sergei Lanskoi, Minister of the Interior, August 1859, summarising reports on the proposed emancipation of the serfs sent in by provincial committees of the nobility

For four years it [the emancipation issue] has dragged on and has been arousing various fears and anticipations among both the estate owners and the peasants. Any further delay could be disastrous to the state ... My late father was continuously occupied with the thought of freeing the serfs. Sympathising completely with this thought, already in 1856, I called the attention of the leaders of the nobility...to the necessity for them to occupy themselves with improving the life of the serfs, adding that serfdom could not continue forever and that it would therefore be better if the transformation took place from above rather than from below.

SOURCE B
Alexander II's address in the State Council, 28 January 1861

Enthusiasm was in the streets. Crowds of peasants and educated men stood in front of the palace, shouting hurrahs, and the Tsar could not appear without being followed by demonstrative crowds running after his carriage ... . If anything could have provoked revolts, it was precisely the perplexing vagueness of the conditions created by the new law ...And yet ... Russia remained quiet – more quiet than ever. With their usual good sense, the peasants had understood that serfdom was done away with, that 'freedom had come' and they accepted the conditions imposed upon them, although these conditions were very heavy ...They knew perfectly well how difficult it would be to pay the redemption tax for the land ... But they so much valued the abolition of their personal enslavement that they accepted the ruinous charges – not without murmuring, but as a hard necessity.

SOURCE C: THE POPULAR RESPONSE TO EMANCIPATION
Peter Kropotkin Memoirs of a Revolutionist *(1930). Prince Kropotkin (1842–1921) was a student at a select military school in St Petersburg in 1861*

The sovereign has betrayed the hopes of the people; the freedom he has given them is not real ...We do not need a tsar, or an emperor, or the Lord's anointed, or a robe of ermine covering up hereditary incompetence ... If we have to slaughter a hundred thousand landowners in order to realise our aspirations – the distribution of the land among the common people – we would not be afraid of that either ... We want the authority that governs us to be an intelligent authority which understands the needs of the country and acts in the interests of the people. And in order to be such, it must come from our own midst; it must be elective and limited. We want freedom of speech ... We want all citizens of Russia to enjoy equal rights; we do not want privileged classes to exist ...We want the land to belong to the nation and not to individuals ... We want to preserve communal possession of the land, with periodic redistribution at long intervals.

SOURCE D: REVOLUTIONARIES' DISSATISFACTION WITH EMANCIPATION
From a revolutionary proclamation of 1861, published by the novelist M. Mikhalov, who was exiled to Siberia

Year	Disturbances	Year	Disturbances
1861	1859	1866	91
1862	844	1867	68
1863	509	1868	60
1864	156	1869	65
1865	135		

SOURCE E
Number of peasant disturbances in Russia after emancipation

We are socialists and populists ... The people is in a state of complete economic and political slavery...Accordingly this is our goal: to seize power from the existing government and transfer it to a [universally elected] constituent assembly ... [our] programme is as follows:

1. A permanent national representative body ...
2. Broad regional self-government, guaranteed by the elective character of all officers ...
3. The self-determination of the village commune as an economic and administrative unit.
4. The ownership of the land by the people.
5. ... transferring all industrial plants and factories to the workers.
6. Complete freedom of conscience, of speech, of the press, of assembly ...
7. Universal suffrage ...
8. The replacement of the standing army by a territorial militia.

SOURCE F: THE 'PEOPLE'S WILL' REVOLUTIONARY PROGRAMME
From the programme of People's Will, January 1880. It was this group which assassinated Alexander II

15 April 1876 ... The sovereign often displays a fine trait of character; he magnanimously makes concessions, sacrificing his own pride, when he recognises that this is necessary for the welfare of the state. There is a great deal of gentleness and flexibility in his character and behaviour.

20 April 1879 ... It must be acknowledged that our entire governmental structure demands basic reform from top to bottom. The structure of rural self-government, of the *zemstvo* ... as well as of institutions on the central and national level – all of them have outlived their time ... Most regrettably, such a colossal task is beyond the powers of our present statesmen, who are incapable of rising above the viewpoint of a chief of police or even of a city constable. The higher echelons of government are intimidated by the impudent displays of socialist propaganda of the past few years and think only of protective police measures, instead of acting against the root of the evil. The disease appears and the government imposes a quarantine, without undertaking anything aimed at healing the disease itself.

22 January 1880 ... It is hardly possible to put an end to the revolutionary underground activity, which has already assumed such considerable proportions, by these police measures, terror, and violence alone. It is hard to root out the evil when not in a single layer of society does the government encounter either sympathy or true support.

SOURCE G: A MINISTERIAL VIEW OF ALEXANDER II'S GOVERNMENT
Excerpts from the diary of Minister of War, D. Miliutin

Q

1. *Using your own knowledge, explain the reference in Source C to the 'conditions' imposed upon the Russian peasants in 1861. (3 marks)*
2. *To what extent does Source A suggest that opinions on the proposed emancipation of the serfs were divided? (6 marks)*
3. *Using Source B, and your own knowledge, summarise Alexander II's reasons for proposing emancipation of the serfs. (6 marks)*
4. *Compare Sources C, D and E as evidence of the response of Russians to emancipation. (7 marks)*
5. *Assess the uses and limitations of Sources E and G as evidence of the impact of Alexander II's reforms. Which has the most value? (8 marks)*
6. *Using your own knowledge, comment on the extent to which the demands of the revolutionaries in Source F had been met by Alexander II's reforms. (10 marks)*
7. *Using this collection of Sources A–G, and your own knowledge, comment upon the validity of the judgement that 'Alexander II's reforms made little fundamental difference to Russian society'. (12 marks)*

France
1871–1914

9

THE THIRD REPUBLIC

The history of the Third Republic presents a considerable paradox. It was born in the ashes of France's defeat in the Franco-Prussian War of 1870–1, hardly an auspicious start. It was some years before the existence of the Republic was confirmed. During the following decades, the Republic faced, and survived, several crises and scandals. The challenge of a possible Royalist or Bonapartist restoration had to be met. There was other opposition to a Republic on the Right, for example from elements in the army and the strongly conservative Catholic Church. There were financial and other scandals. There was opposition to a moderate Republic from Socialists and extremists on the Left. Governments came and went with apparently alarming regularity.

And yet under the surface much of the apparent instability was deceptive. Although Governments fell, the efficient bureaucracy continued to administer France as it had done since the days of Napoleon I. The majority of peasants, the most numerous class in France, were conservative by nature and not interested in political arguments in Paris. Although France underwent economic and social development, it was spared most of the pressures which affected some other Great Powers like Russia and Italy. Following its recovery from the Franco-Prussian War, France took its place again on the European and world stage as a Great Power, and pursued a vigorous imperialist policy. By the end of the nineteenth century it had escaped the German attempt to keep it diplomatically isolated, by allying with Russia. Although there were quarrels with Britain, these were resolved early in the new century. By 1914, many Frenchmen were confident that France, the only Great Power to be a Republic, could once again be the leader of Europe.

World War I was to be a shattering experience for France. Although it emerged on the winning side, victory was achieved at tremendous economic, human and psychological cost. The experience scarred France for the next generation, since it was clear, despite Germany's defeat, that it was Germany, not France, that was potentially the power-house of Europe. And yet, ironically, the Third Republic, for all its initial problems and periodic crises, was the only one of pre-1914 continental

MAP 10 *France after 1871*

Great Powers whose regime and institutions survived World War I, not succumbing to fundamental change until the trauma of defeat by Germany in the next World War in 1940.

1 ～ POLITICAL HISTORY

A *The Commune*

Defeat in the Franco-Prussian War was a traumatic experience for France. The Treaty of Frankfurt of May 1871 forced France to concede Alsace-Lorraine to Germany, pay reparations of 5000 million francs and suffer temporary occupation by German troops. On top of this, there was the psychological humiliation of an established and proud Power, France, losing face to a new nation on the European scene. Even before the Treaty had been signed the collapse of Napoleon III's regime after the Battle of Sedan had complicated matters. A new Republic was

TIMELINE

(Foreign affairs in italics)

1871	Defeat against Prussia
	Elections for National Assembly
	Paris Commune
	Treaty of Frankfurt
	Thiers elected President
1873	MacMahon elected President
1875	Adoption of Republican Constitution
1877	Crisis in relations between President and Chamber
1879	MacMahon replaced by Grévy
1880	Anti-clerical legislation
1881	*Occupation of Tunis*
1882	Free, compulsory primary education introduced
1883	*Protectorate over Indo-China declared*
1887	Beginning of Boulanger crisis
1889	Flight of Boulanger
1892	*Franco-Russian Military Convention*
	Panama scandal
1893	*Franco-Russian Alliance*
1894	Assassination of President Carnot
	Conviction of Dreyfus
1896	*Annexation of Madagascar*
1898	Acquittal of Esterhazy and Zola's J'Accuse
	Fashoda crisis
1899	Waldeck-Rousseau Ministry
	Retrial of Dreyfus case. Eventual pardon
1900	*Secret Franco-Italian Agreement*
1901	Religious Associations Law
1902	*Franco-Italian Entente*
1903	Dissolution of religious orders in France
1904	*Entente Cordiale*
1905	Separation of Church and State
	Moroccan crisis
	Foundation of United Socialist Party
1906	*Algeçiras Conference*
	Exoneration of Dreyfus
1909–10	Major strikes
1911	*Agadir Incident*
1912	Poincaré Ministry
	Morocco became French protectorate
	Anglo-French Naval Convention
1913	Three-year military service introduced
1914	Assassination of Jaurès
	Outbreak of World War I

proclaimed and General Trochu formed a Provisional Government of National Defence in Paris. Paris endured siege by the Prussians and starvation. Meanwhile rapidly-organised elections in February 1871 resulted in a conservative Assembly, which met at Bordeaux. The mood of the nation was for peace. Under the leadership of the ageing Adolphe Thiers, this Government, containing ministers of several different shades of party opinion, signed the peace treaty with the German Empire.

Thiers had been a minister during the July Monarchy and an opponent of the Second Empire, but he also distrusted democracy. Therefore at this time he represented the middle ground in French politics between monarchy and radical republicanism. But Thiers' Government was faced with serious opposition from within France.

The new Assembly in Bordeaux contained only 30 Bonapartists. Its conservative majority made a restoration of the monarchy a strong possibility, although consideration of a new constitution was put on hold. The prospect of a restoration alarmed Republican Paris, which was already smarting from defeat by the Prussians. Traditionally Paris had played a major part in initiating revolution in France. There were many revolutionaries in Paris, of various shades of opinion, but all distrustful of the government and with their own political demands for direct democracy. They had a formidable instrument of power available in the form of the National Guard, an armed militia of some 360 000 men.

In March 1871 republican-minded citizens prevented French troops requisitioning artillery from the National Guard in Paris. The troops were withdrawn and Republican, Socialist and revolutionary activists set up a Commune to exploit the power vacuum and run the city. There were several aspects to the Commune:

- it was protesting against surrender to the Prussians
- it was a protest against the deprivations of war and the siege
- it was a protest against the conservative Government
- it was a call for decentralised, vigorous local government, as part of a federal structure, and the Communards hoped for similar communes to be established throughout France.

KEY ISSUE

Why did the Commune come about?

The Commune introduced radical legislation, for example passing laws to promote education and the status of women.

Thiers was concerned to crush this radical force and to preserve French unity. Historians debate as to whether he was deliberately trying to 'teach radical Paris a lesson' or simply respond to a specific situation in which large numbers of weapons and armed men were outside the control of the Government. With a decisiveness which surprised many contemporaries, French troops were ordered to fight their way into Paris in May 1871. Whilst the Prussians looked on, Frenchman killed Frenchman in a bloody civil war of revenge. Over 25 000 Parisians died; many more were captured and imprisoned before the Commune fell. Atrocities were widespread on both sides. The effects of the Commune were long-lasting:

- Paris had long been renowned for its radicalism and leadership of change in France, certainly since the 1789 Revolution. However, the crushing of the Commune marked the end of Paris's reputation as the centre of radical politics, at least until 1968
- change was seen by moderates as suspect. Conservative elements in France were frightened that even moderate reform might degenerate into violent revolution. Politics were polarised and social bitterness

between classes increased, although many on the Left were temporarily silenced by the crushing of the Commune

- the events surrounding the Commune had a considerable influence on Karl Marx and European Socialism generally, and they were frequently part of the debate on the Left about the advantages and disadvantages of reformism versus revolution, although of course the Commune itself had nothing to do with Communism. Later attempts to portray the Commune as an expression of international proletarian revolution are simplistic. They ignore the strong element of 'looking backwards', with many of the participants strongly influenced by the myths and realities of the revolutionary struggles in Paris in the 1790s.

> **KEY ISSUE**
>
> *What was the short-term and long-term significance of the Commune?*

> **ANALYSIS**

History as propaganda: a Marxist interpretation of the Commune

Earlier in this chapter an interpretation of the causes of the crisis of the Commune and its significance was outlined, drawing on various sources. The Commune became enshrined in left-wing folklore, and influenced generations of would-be revolutionaries, who tried to draw lessons from its failure and relate it to their own contemporary situations. This was certainly true of Marxists. Marx himself lived through the Commune; in the next generation, Lenin put his own particular interpretation on events:

Extracts from a plan drawn up by Lenin for a lecture to Russian political exiles in Geneva, 1905:

Growth of proletariat after June 1848 ... Its persecution by Napoleon III ... Proclamation of republic on September 4, 1870. Artful liberals seize power. Liberal lawyers and double-faced monarchists: Thiers.

Government of national defence = government of national betrayal. Trochu: 'plan' for defending Paris ... Capitulation on January 28, 1871.

Bismarck imposes conditions for convocation of the National Assembly ... Thiers' intrigues with the monarchists ... National Assembly moved to Versailles; suppression of republican newspapers and so on. Making the poor pay for the war. Armed Paris workers and – a monarchist assembly. Conflict inevitable ...

Last act of provocation. Seizure of the guns from the National Guard ... Thiers' fraudulent pretexts ...

Revolutionary instinct of the working class asserts itself despite fallacious theories ...

Crash. Deficiencies of organisation ... Thiers-Bismarck deal (role of Bismarck = hired assassin) ...

Bloody week, May 21–28, 1871. Its horrors, exile, etc. Slanders ...

20 000 killed in streets, 3000 died in prisons ... 13 700 persons sentenced ...

Lessons: Bourgeoisie will stop at nothing. Today liberals, radicals, republicans, tomorrow betrayal, shootings.

In Memory of the Commune An article written by Lenin in April 1911:

The Commune sprang up spontaneously. No one consciously prepared it in an organised way. The unsuccessful war with Germany, the privations suffered during the siege, the unemployment among the proletariat and the ruin among the lower middle classes; the indignation of the masses against the upper classes and against authorities who had displayed utter incompetence, the vague unrest among the working class, which was discontented with its lot and was striving for a different social system; the reactionary composition of the National Assembly, which roused apprehensions as to the fate of the republic – all this and many other factors combined to drive the population of Paris to revolution ...

After the revolution of March 18, when M. Thiers' government had fled from Paris with its troops, its police and its officials, the people became masters of the situation and power passed into the hands of the proletariat. But in modern society, the proletariat, economically enslaved by capital, cannot dominate politically unless it breaks the chains which fetter it to capital. That is why the movement of the Commune was bound to take on a socialist tinge, i.e. to strive to overthrow the rule of the bourgeoisie ...

At first this movement was extremely indefinite and confused. It was joined by patriots who hoped that the Commune would renew the war with the Germans ... It enjoyed the support of the small shopkeepers who were threatened with ruin ... Finally, it enjoyed, at first, the sympathy of bourgeois republicans who feared that the reactionary National Assembly (the 'rustics', the savage landlords) would restore the monarchy. But it was of course the workers ... who played the principal part in this movement.

Only the workers remained loyal to the Commune to the end. The bourgeois republicans and the petty bourgeoisie soon broke away from it: the former were frightened off by the revolutionary-socialist, proletarian character of the movement; the latter broke away when they saw that it was doomed to inevitable defeat. Only the French proletarians supported their government fearlessly and untiringly, they alone fought and died for it ...

Deserted by its former allies and left without support, the Commune was doomed to defeat ... Two conditions, at least, are necessary for a victorious social revolution – highly – developed productive forces and a proletariat adequately prepared for it. But in

1871 both of these conditions were lacking. French capitalism was still poorly developed, and France was at that time mainly a petty-bourgeois country ... There was no serious political organisation of the proletariat ...

But the chief thing which the Commune lacked was time ... The Commune had to concentrate primarily on self-defence ... However, in spite of these unfavourable conditions, in spite of its brief existence, the Commune managed to promulgate a few measures which sufficiently characterise its real significance and aims [e.g. abolishing the standing army, proclaiming the separation of church and state, improving working conditions] ... bourgeois society could not feel at ease as long as the Red Flag of the proletariat waved over the Hotel de Ville in Paris. And when the organised forces of the government finally succeeded in gaining the upper hand over the poorly organised forces of the revolution, the Bonapartist generals, who had been beaten by the Germans and who showed courage only in fighting their defeated countrymen ... organised such a slaughter as Paris had never known...

The bourgeoisie were satisfied. 'Now we have finished with socialism for a long time,' said their leader, the bloodthirsty dwarf Thiers, after he and his generals had drowned the proletariat of Paris in blood. But these bourgeois crows croaked in vain ... the thunder of the cannon in Paris awakened the most backward sections of the proletariat from their deep slumber, and everywhere gave impetus to the growth of revolutionary socialist propaganda ...

The cause of the Commune is the cause of the social revolution ... It is the cause of the proletariat of the whole world. And in this sense it is immortal.

> **KEY ISSUE**
>
> *Identify which parts of these two documents are propaganda and which are accurate in their interpretation of the Commune*

B *Birth of the Republic*

THE MONARCHIST CHALLENGE

After the dust had settled Thiers worked for a consolidation of the Republic until his death in 1877. He was declared Head of the Executive power and decided that a restoration of the monarchy was impossible. Numerous by-elections in July 1871 returned mostly Republican deputies. Also there were competing claimants to the throne, and the Assembly could not decide which one to champion:

- Henri, Comte de Chambord, was the grandson of Charles X, and to his Bourbon or Legitimist supporters was already known as Henri V
- Phillipe Albert, the Comte de Paris, was the grandson of Louis Phillippe, and therefore supported by the Orleanists
- Napoleon III's son, the Prince Imperial, was also in the frame until his death in 1879, and his claims were supported by the relatively few Bonapartists.

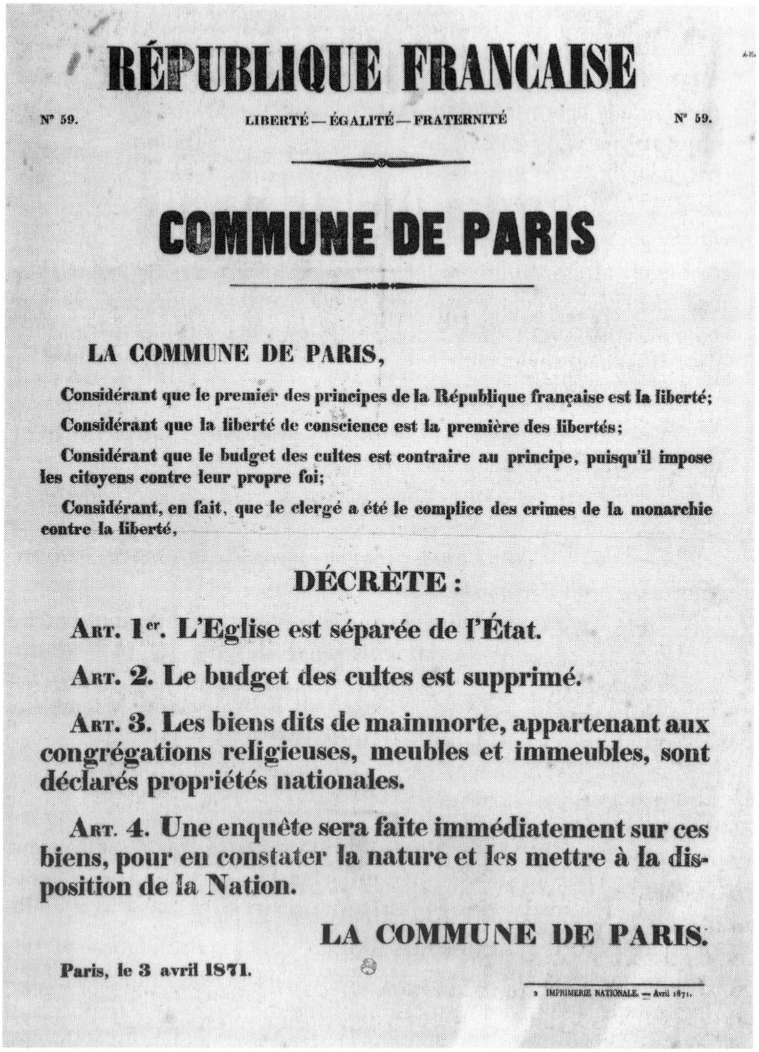

RÉPUBLIQUE FRANCAISE

Nº 59. LIBERTÉ — ÉGALITÉ — FRATERNITÉ Nº 59.

COMMUNE DE PARIS

LA COMMUNE DE PARIS,

Considérant que le premier des principes de la République française est la liberté;

Considérant que la liberté de conscience est la première des libertés;

Considérant que le budget des cultes est contraire au principe, puisqu'il impose les citoyens contre leur propre foi;

Considérant, en fait, que le clergé a été le complice des crimes de la monarchie contre la liberté,

DÉCRÈTE :

Art. 1er. L'Eglise est séparée de l'État.

Art. 2. Le budget des cultes est supprimé.

Art. 3. Les biens dits de mainmorte, appartenant aux congrégations religieuses, meubles et immeubles, sont déclarés propriétés nationales.

Art. 4. Une enquête sera faite immédiatement sur ces biens, pour en constater la nature et les mettre à la disposition de la Nation.

LA COMMUNE DE PARIS.

Paris, le 3 avril 1871.

IMPRIMERIE NATIONALE. — Avril 1871.

PICTURE 15 *'Decree of the Commune on the Separation of Church and State, 3 April 1871'*

PICTURE 16   *The last struggle between French troops and Communards in the Pere Lachaise Cemetery, Paris*

PICTURE 17   *The Wall of the Communards. Monument at the spot in the Pere Lachaise Cemetery where the last Communard fighters were executed on the spot as the Government forces retook Paris*

KEY ISSUE

Why did the monarchist challenge to the Republic fail?

Chambord had potentially the most support, but he alienated many potential monarchists by his determination to restore monarchical power, symbolised by his declaration that the old Bourbon flag should replace the Republican tricolour. Even most royalist-minded politicians wanted a parliamentary, constitutional monarchy, not the 'traditional' authoritarian one which Chambord espoused.

Thiers infuriated the monarchist majority in the Chamber by declaring himself in favour of a Republic in November 1872, having already been elected President of the Republic by the National Assembly. Thiers achieved several successes: a New Army Law in 1872 reorganised the French army on the Prussian model; reparations to Germany were paid off; and a programme of railway and building construction repaired the damage of the war. But hostility to Thiers led to his parliamentary defeat and he resigned in 1873. His successor Marshall Patrice MacMahon was a monarchist although without much personal ambition. His Prime Minister was the leading Orleanist supporter, the Duc de Broglie.

De Broglie tried but failed to arrange a compromise by which Chambord would become king on acceptable terms. In the hope of effecting a restoration at some future date, Macmahon's term as President was extended in 1875 for another seven years, 'to keep the King's place warm.' Meanwhile the issue of the Constitution had to be resolved.

THE CONSTITUTION

The Constitution of the Third Republic was voted into being as a series of laws in 1875. France was committed to a Republic by one vote when the Wallon amendment was passed. It included the phrase 'the President of the Republic'. The main provisions of the Constitution were:

- the National Assembly comprised a Chamber of Deputies, elected for four years by adult manhood suffrage in single-member constituencies. By 1914 it had 586 members
- the Senate had 75 life members chosen by the Assembly, and 255 members elected for nine years by an electoral college (which eventually elected all the members) of mayors and local councillors. The Senate had limited power, but did stand as a bulwark against the possibility of extremist measures
- the deputies and senators elected a President for seven years. Direct popular election of the President was avoided to preclude the possibility of a charismatic Bonapartist-type candidate being swept to power. The President chose the ministers, negotiated treaties, could suggest laws and dissolve the Chamber with the consent of the Senate
- elections to the Chamber were to be held regularly at four-year intervals
- a Council of Ministers ran the Government. The President of the Council was appointed by the President and he then selected members of the Council, so in effect he was the Prime Minister, although this was not a technical term in the Constitution.

A. Thiers	1871–3	resigned
P. MacMahon	1873–9	resigned
J. Grévy	1879–87	resigned over Wilson scandal
S. Carnot	1887–94	assassinated
J. Casimir-Perier	1894–5	resigned
F. Faure	1895–9	died in office
E. Loubet	1899–1906	served full term
A. Fallières	1906–13	served full term
R. Poincaré	1913–20	served full term

TABLE 10
Presidents of the Third Republic 1871–1920

Ministries were responsible to parliament and needed a majority of Republican deputies in order to survive.

CONSOLIDATION

The Senate was dominated by the Right, but Republicans dominated the Chamber after elections in 1876. MacMahon found it difficult to work effectively with Republican political leaders such as Gambetta, and appointed conservative ministers. A crisis took place in 1877. MacMahon dismissed his Republican Ministers and replaced them with Orleanists and Bonapartists led by de Broglie. This was legal, but the Chamber would not support Government measures. Therefore MacMahon dissolved the Chamber. In the ensuing election, in which the Government put up 'official' candidates, the Republicans won, albeit with a reduced majority. MacMahon accepted the verdict: de Broglie was dismissed and ministers acceptable to the Chamber were appointed.

MacMahon resigned, and the monarchist cause was effectively dead. The first Republican President, elected in 1879, was Jules Grèvy. It was now accepted that although the President chose the Prime Minister, the latter should be someone who commanded majority support in Parliament.

The reality of parliamentary life in the Third Republic was that party politics were very fluid. Party groupings were not fixed and one man might belong to several factions, so it was impossible to forecast voting patterns. Deputies were often more loyal to their constituency interests than a party, and many were also members of their local councils. Most deputies, despite political differences, came from a similar background – at least half were from the professions, and many were repeatedly elected to parliament, which made for stability. Because the fall of a Government did not automatically mean a general election and all the complications that involved, deputies were willing to vote against Governments and therefore there were frequent changes of ministry. The resignation of a Prime Minister simply led to the search for a new one. On average Governments lasted less than one year. Political practice was very similar to that of the new Italy after 1870. However, of crucial importance was the fact that a professional and long-established structure of civil service and administration, including the Prefects running the *departements*, ensured that orderly life went on, and therefore the

KEY ISSUE

*How stable was
political life in the
Third Republic?*

impression that political life was unstable is misleading. The Third Republic lasted until 1940, despite serious crises and divisions which sometimes brought Governments down.

The monarchists ceased to be a serious threat after the mid 1870s, and in 1884 laws were passed to prevent a Republican form of government ever being revised and disbarring members of royal families from the presidency. However, the Republicans were split into Radicals and more conservative elements, sometimes called Opportunists, led by Leon Gambetta and Jules Ferry. The Radicals were anti-clerical, wanted to abolish the Senate and advocated social and economic reform. Groups on the Right of politics, although divided amongst themselves, supported the power and status of the Catholic Church.

Internal political divisions were not the only major area of controversy in the early years of the Republic. There were also strong differences of opinion over:

- the relationship between the State and the Church, which had long been a thorny issue in France
- the extent to which France should pursue an ambitious colonial policy
- the stance France should adopt towards its recent enemy, Germany. Strident nationalists demanded priority be given to exacting revenge. The most prominent nationalist group was Paul Déroulède's *Ligue des Patriotes*, formed in 1882.

Grévy was cautious in his approach and helped create a political climate in which the fears of many anti-Republicans of extreme left-wing measures were allayed. Ferry was the leading Government minister between 1879 and 1885 and implemented some reforms:

- education in state schools was removed from clerical control, although church-run schools remained
- state-run education was improved, and primary education became compulsory in 1881–2
- the Jesuits were expelled from France
- the system of life membership in the Senate was progressively abolished
- local government was made more representative by having all the mayors, except in Paris, elected. This was a significant step because the mayors were important agents of the central government
- various civil liberties were assured: freedom of the press was guaranteed, divorce and trade unions were legalised
- competitive examinations were introduced into the civil service.

Ferry also pursued an active colonial policy. His time in office seemed to many to be productive, although his attack on the influence of the Church reinforced the hostility of the clerical establishment towards Republicanism.

C *The years of crisis*

The Republic appeared to have achieved stability after difficult beginnings. However, the Right made a strong comeback in the 1885 election and a series of crises and scandals emerged to threaten the existence of the Republic or at the very least highlighted the bitter political and social divisions that separated those who supported the Republic and those who wished for its overthrow.

THE BOULANGER CRISIS

General Georges Boulanger was briefly a reforming Minister of War in 1886. He improved conditions for the soldiers and sacked some monarchist officers. His dashing image brought him public attention. After losing office, he attracted the hostility of Bismarck and the support of French nationalists for his strident support for the idea of *revanche* or revenge against Germany for the defeat of 1871. Disgust at revelations of the involvement of President Grévy's son-in-law Daniel Wilson in financial scandals added to Boulanger's appeal as the new man to restore France's pride and good name.

Boulanger had many supporters of different shades of opinion. He resigned from the army and stood in several by-elections to the Chamber, winning all of them. His original left-wing Republican supporters became increasingly disenchanted and alarmed by Boulanger's apparent swing to the Right. In 1889 he even won a traditionally Republican seat in Paris. There were rumours of an impending *coup*. But the Government held its nerve. Right-wing organisations were prosecuted. Frightened of being arrested for treason, Boulanger fled to Brussels in April 1889, committing suicide two years later. The Government banned multi-constituency candidatures. Boulangist deputies still won 40 seats in the general election of November 1889, but the bubble had been burst. Boulanger proved to be a broken reed. Although the affair showed how feelings against the Republic could still be easily whipped up, some Frenchmen who were traditionally anti-republican, including churchmen, now declared that French citizens should rally to the support of the Republic – the so-called *Ralliément*.

THE PANAMA SCANDAL

The *Ralliément* was not a long-term success. It was never accepted by die-hard monarchists and clericals; and only some moderate Radicals or Opportunists were prepared to concede concessions to the Church in return. The Republic still appeared to be under threat and its integrity was again threatened a few years later, this time by a major financial scandal. In the 1880s the Government had backed the building of the Panama Canal. The canal company went bankrupt in 1889. It was alleged early in the 1890s that members of the government had been bribed by the company in order to get its backing. A Jewish financier, Baron Jacques de Reinach, committed suicide and another financier, Cornelius Herz, was accused of blackmail. A Government Commission investigated several politicians, including five ministers and ex-ministers. The Radical

---

KEY ISSUE

What was the significance of the Boulanger and Panama crises?

politician Georges Clemenceau was implicated and had his career temporarily checked. The Finance Minister, Rouvier, resigned, declaring 'What I have done all politicians worthy of the name have done before me.' The crisis stimulated anti-semitism. It also furthered a popular perception that the Republic existed for corrupt individuals to feather their nests. 30 per cent of the electorate did not vote in the 1893 election.

THE DREYFUS AFFAIR

The Dreyfus Affair began in 1894 and was even more serious in its implications than the Panama scandal. Captain Alfred Dreyfus, a French army officer of Jewish descent, was convicted in 1894 of selling military secrets to Germany. He was disgraced and sent to the notorious Devil's Island penal settlement for life. There was some suspicion that an unpopular officer had been made a scapegoat in the hope that a quick conviction would prevent the French army suffering too much embarrassment at a time when relations with Germany were tense. There was also a strong element of anti-semitism in the case. These were the feelings of Colonel Georges Picquart of the French Intelligence Service: his investigation of the incriminating evidence proved that a Major Esterhazy was the guilty party. The army, still trying to sweep the affair under the carpet, tried to quieten Picquart by posting him to Tunisia. Picquart communicated his views to the press. Public interest forced the army to try Esterhazy. A secret court-martial acquitted Esterhazy and confirmed Dreyfus's guilt. Picquart was dismissed from the army.

The Dreyfus affair began to arouse widespread passion in some quarters in France and was made a great public issue by intellectuals, although it also confirmed and widened the split between Republicans and anti-republicans:

> ### KEY ISSUE
>
> *Why was the Dreyfus Affair so divisive?*

- against Dreyfus were the army and the Establishment, claiming that the controversy was a plot to undermine the Republic and insisting that the honour and reputation of the army and the good of the State must be upheld, and that this was more important than the fate of one individual. There was also a strong strain of anti-semitism
- on the other hand radicals, anti-clericals and anti-militarists were critical of the Establishment. They were concerned that justice should be seen to prevail for all individuals, regardless of race or creed, or what were perceived as interests of state. However, some Republican politicians were reluctant to support Dreyfus for fear of falling foul of popular anti-semitic prejudice in France.

The great French novelist Emile Zola, in a public letter *J'Accuse*, published in Clemenceau's paper *L'Aurore*, openly accused the army of wrongfully clearing Esterhazy and convicting Dreyfus. Zola was fined and sentenced to imprisonment for libel. He fled to London. The case dragged on. In 1898 the Minister of War Cavaignac tried to produce new proof against Dreyfus. But the evidence was found to be faulty. Colonel Henry of Military Intelligence and a leading figure in the case against Dreyfus, committed suicide. Esterhazy fled to England. Yet there was still official reluctance to exonerate Dreyfus. He was re-tried in 1899 and received the absurd verdict that he was guilty 'with extenuating circumstances' and his sentence was reduced. Either Dreyfus was guilty or he was not. President Loubet pardoned Dreyfus, but he was only fully cleared and restored to his rank in 1906. For years the case continued to divide sections of society.

D *Consolidation and the last years of peace*

STATE AND CHURCH

The Dreyfus affair convinced reformers that they must redouble their efforts and not take the Republican regime for granted, and in particular there must be a challenge to the power of the Church and a more positive attitude towards social reform. Many Radicals and Socialists formed an alliance called the *Bloc des Gauches* in defence of the Republic.

The radical coalition of René Waldeck-Rousseau was unusual in surviving for more than a few months. It tackled the age-old problem of the relationship between the Church and the State, not resolved by the 1882 educational reforms. The Church establishment was still monarchist in sympathy and opposed to the extension of democracy. Churchmen had made inflammatory statements during the Dreyfus affair. The Church was still closely connected to the State, principally through the appointment and payment of bishops and priests by the Government. Anti-clerical measures were introduced: for example civil marriage and divorce were permitted. Although Pope Leo XIII appeared relatively complacent and acquiescent in these measures, the Church Establishment within France was reinforced in its hostility towards the Left and was seen in some quarters as increasingly intolerant.

The anti-clerical Prime Minister Emile Combes began a series of initiatives to lessen the influence of the Church in French life. The Law of Associations of 1901 gave freedom to virtually all associations except religious ones. Monastic orders were also restricted. Only five religious orders were to remain in being. Others lost their property. Pius X, Pope from 1903, was less tolerant than his predecessor. Continued clashes finally led the Government to annul Napoleon's *Concordat* of 1801. The 1905 Law of Separation disestablished the Church:

● Catholicism was no longer the established religion and was no longer financially supported by the state
● clergy had to negotiate the use of churches
● all monastic orders were dissolved.

Essentially the Church lost its political influence and was put in a difficult position by the Pope's refusal to recognise the anti-clerical legislation. The Church's efforts now went into retaining its hold on people's minds.

The attack on the Church was paralleled by changes to the army to restrict its independence and political interference by the officer class. In 1905 the period of military service was reduced from three to two years and exemptions were forbidden.

THE CHALLENGE FROM THE LEFT

Not all the Republic's problems came from the Right. The militant Left was also an increasing threat to political stability. Radicals were disappointed by the failure of the Republic to implement measures such as a progressive income tax, and the fact that most Presidents were anxious not to give office to Radicals, preferring moderate 'consensus' politics. The growth of left-wing militancy was also partly the result of economic depression which affected both rural and industrial areas from the 1870s. Economic discontent was sometimes channelled into Marxist agitation. Some discontents became anarchists. In 1894 President Carnot was assassinated at Lyons by an Italian anarchist. Some Socialists remained reformists, prepared to work for change within the system.

There were three main Socialist organisations in France by the turn of the century, and several local federations. All Socialist groups joined in 1896 to form the *Fédération des Socialistes Independants de France.* The first Socialist Minister was Alexandre Millerand, appointed to Waldeck-Rousseau's Government in 1899 as Minister of Commerce. Jean-Leon Jaurès, who first became a deputy in 1885, led those Socialists who worked within the parliamentary system to change economic and social conditions. Amongst his followers were the future Prime Ministers Aristide Briand (who became a minister in 1906) and Leon Blum. Jaures was a popular figure who never entered government. He founded the left-wing paper *L'Humanité*, but was assassinated in 1914.

In 1901 the Socialists reorganised into two parties: the PSDF (*Parti Socialiste de France*); and the PSF (*Parti Socialiste Française*). The PSDF were Marxists who believed that extra-parliamentary methods and even revolution were necessary to achieve their goals of a radically different society. Their leader was Jules Guesde, elected a deputy in 1893. He eventually accepted a government post in the First World War when patriotism proved stronger than Marxist internationalism. When the Second international (representing all Socialist parties throughout the world) voted against reformism, Jaures accepted the decision and a new united party, the SFIO (*Section Française de L'Internationale*) adopted a revolutionary programme. It became the second largest party in the Chamber of Deputies by 1914.

Relatively little Socialist legislation was introduced. A Ten-hour Factory Act was passed in 1900 and factory inspectors were appointed. Old age pensions were introduced in 1910. Income tax was planned but was postponed by the outbreak of war in 1914.

Militant trade unions were also active in seeking better conditions. In 1895 they formed themselves into the CCT (*Confédération Générale du Travail*). It represented half of France's trade unions. Militant unionists were syndicalists, believing that the working class should use industrial action, including the general strike, as a political weapon to get to power. The chief Syndicalist philosopher was George Sorel, who published *Reflections on Violence* in 1908.

There were many strikes in the 1900s, often accompanied by violence, but no general strike. The Government was ruthless in suppressing industrial violence and sometimes the army intervened, and strikers were drafted into the army, as during a rail strike in 1910.

French Socialism was less united and less influential than its German counterpart. Nevertheless reform and industrial unrest went hand-in-hand together. Tension, symbolised by Jaurès' assassination, was still high in 1914. Some Frenchmen welcomed World War I as a cathartic force which might heal the divisions between Right, Left and Centre in France.

	Urban	Rural
1851	25.0	75.0
1891	37.4	62.6
1911	44.2	55.8

TABLE 11

Distribution of total population between urban and rural areas in France (in percentages)

2 ⌒ ECONOMIC HISTORY

A *Rural France*

In the context of European economic development generally, the French economy during the period 1870–1914 presents a picture of stability and moderate growth. France remained predominantly a country of small farms, almost half of which were owner-occupied. An agricultural depression hit French farmers in the 1880s, and in the same period the wine industry suffered badly from destruction by greenfly, although it rapidly recovered. Competition in agricultural produce from Russia and the USA, possible through improved communications, reduced the prices for farm produce and therefore the value of land. However, the tariffs on imports imposed as part of a protectionist policy isolated France from the worse problems and technical improvements increased agricultural productivity. The wages of agricultural labourers actually rose. Economic and social historians argue about the extent to which the rural population was passive and content during this period. There were examples of strikes and unrest, but also of peasants forming cooperatives and trying to better themselves economically and socially. Most rural communities were Republican, despite the influence of the Church, but also conservative, and rural life continued without major upheaval. Throughout France as a whole the middle class or *petite bourgeoisie* was numerous, and the nobility remained an important social force, although its political influence had long been destroyed.

B *Industry*

Industrial development was slow compared to Germany and Britain; on the other hand, in some respects the French economy compared favourably to the economic development of other European Powers such as Russia, Italy and Austria-Hungary. France's industrial population, of which almost 40 per cent was female by 1914, remained smaller than its rural workforce. It was supplemented by one million immigrant workers. Many workers were 'rural proletarians', moving back to their village of origin for the harvest, or working on small plots of land.

An important reason for France losing its once dominant position in Europe to Germany during this period was not just the creation of the

> **KEY ISSUE**
>
> *To what extent did the French economy develop and prosper between 1871 and 1914?*

1870–4	15
1875–9	17
1880–4	20
1885–9	22
1890–4	26
1895–9	31
1900–4	33
1905–9	36
1910–14	40

TABLE 12

Output of coal and lignite 1870–1914 (annual averages for five-year periods in million metric tons)

1880	0.4
1890	0.7
1900	1.6
1910	3.4

TABLE 13

Output of steel 1880–1910 (annual production in million metric tons)

1860	9 167
1880	23 089
1900	38 109
1913	40 770

TABLE 14

Railway mileage open 1860–1913 (kilometres)

German Empire in 1871 and its defeat of France, but the fact that the German economy grew at a much faster rate than France's in the four decades before the First World War. This was evident in the production of vital materials such as iron and steel, engineering products and chemicals. The British economy also expanded at a faster rate, reaping the rewards of earlier industrialisation. French industrial growth was hampered by a comparative lack of raw materials, compounded by the loss of Alsace-Lorraine in 1871, of particular importance for iron ore resources. During this period 60 per cent of French imports were raw materials. France lacked other raw materials such as copper, zinc and lead.

France also lagged behind Germany and Britain in other ways important for industrial expansion:

● France did not have the same amount of capital investment available for industrial development. France did invest, but much French capital went into Russia, France's ally in the 1890s. Ironically, to a large extent the Russian economic boom of the late nineteenth century was largely funded by French capital – much of it confiscated by the Communists when they came to power in 1917

● France also invested capital in overseas colonies and in foreign projects. Much was allocated – and lost – in the Panama Canal project. Money was also lent – and sometimes lost for good – to South American Governments

● there was less of a tradition in France, compared to Germany and Britain, of applying invention and science to industry to stimulate more efficient production

● French industry was mostly organised on a smaller basis than its European competitors. Family businesses were the norm: the majority of firms had an average workforce of less than three by 1906. France avoided some of the social problems associated with massive industrialisation, but on the other hand it also missed out on economies of scale and some of the other advantages

● the entrepreneurial impulse was perhaps less developed in France than in Britain and Germany. Many Frenchmen distrusted banks. Thousands of ordinary Frenchmen lost their savings through investing in the failed Panama Canal project and were distrustful of speculation. Less money was available for future investment.

Life was hard for industrial workers, especially women, who were paid considerably less than men. The law of 1892 which imposed an 11-hour maximum working day was widely ignored. Trade unions were not well developed in national terms: for example, attempts to organise a nationwide miners' strike in 1902 failed.

It should be emphasised that despite these qualifications, the French economy did expand after 1895 at a rate of 9 per cent a year, which was impressive although far less than the German average of over 30 per cent. French steel production trebled between 1890 and 1900, and doubled between 1900 and 1920, and the growth rate in some new industries such as the car industry was impressive.

3 ↶ FOREIGN POLICY

A *European policy*

France's foreign policy between 1871 and 1914 was dominated by memories of the humiliating defeat of 1871 and the creation of the German Empire, events which reshaped the balance of power in Europe. France found it difficult to come to terms with the fact that it was no longer the dominant power in Europe. Some French people were *revanchists*, obsessed with wanting revenge for 1871 and the return of Alsace-Lorraine. Wiser counsels recognised that France could not take on a powerful Germany alone. However, finding European allies was not easy, and Bismarck's foreign policy aimed at perpetuating French isolation:

- colonial expansion sometimes brought about strained relationships with other Powers
- there was a history of Anglo-French suspicion, and in any case, Britain's small army seemed of doubtful value in a continental context
- Russian autocracy seemed at odds with French Republicanism
- Austria-Hungary was firmly tied into the German alliance.

However, France and Russia had significant financial ties, French capital being behind much of Russia's economic expansion. By the 1890s, with the restraining hand of Bismarck gone from the reins of German foreign policy, both Russia and France felt more insecure. The two countries signed a military convention in 1893, and this was soon turned into a formal, although secret, alliance between France and Russia. Each promised the other help in the event of an attack by Germany or Austria supported by Germany. France at last felt a sense of security. The agreements were confirmed in 1899 and supplemented by a naval convention in 1912. A 1913 military protocol committed both Powers to mobilise if either were attacked by Germany 'without there being need for preliminary agreement.'

> **KEY ISSUE**
>
> *How successfully had France overcome its isolation in Europe by 1900?*

Relations between France and Italy became strained over the French occupation of Tunis, and Italy became a member of the Triple Alliance. However, a commercial treaty in 1898 ended a long-standing tariff war between the two countries. In 1900 Italy recognised France's interests in Morocco in return for French recognition of Italian claims to Tripoli.

Relations between France and Britain were frequently strained. France was upset when its influence in Egypt was reduced following the British occupation of it in 1882. Politicians of several different persuasions set up a Committee of French Africa to pursue colonial goals, which were likely to create new tensions. Relations with Britain became particularly tense in 1896 over the Fashoda incident. A French expedition led by Captain Jean-Baptiste Marchand set out from French Equatorial Africa and ran into a British force, led by Lord Kitchener, at Fashoda, on the Upper Nile in the Sudan. The French were forced to back down and concede territorial claims in the area to Britain.

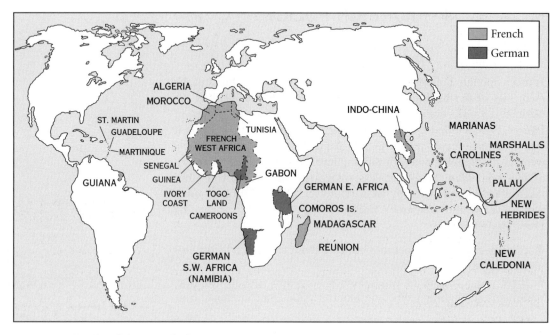

MAP 11   *French and German colonies*

However, anti-English feeling receded in the face of a perceived bigger threat from Germany. French Foreign Minister Delcassé was keen to avert the possibility of an Anglo-German alliance. Britain and France agreed to the *Entente Cordiale* in 1904. It was an agreement, not an alliance. It resolved some outstanding issues over colonial territories in Newfoundland, West and Central Africa, Madagascar, Siam and the New Hebrides. More significantly, France agreed to recognise British interests in Egypt, in return for Britain agreeing to French interests in Morocco. Relations were further strengthened by military conversations and co-operative military planning in 1906, and a naval convention in 1912 following the Agadir Crisis of the previous year. The French took responsibility for patrolling the Mediterranean, whilst Britain took responsibility for the North Sea, implying a British commitment to the defence of France's Northern coastline.

The final years of peace saw renewed feelings of French confidence and nationalist outrage against Germany. The French army was over-hauled and in 1913 the term of conscription was extended from two to three years. Prime Minister Raymond Poincaré was perceived as being anti-German, although claims that he actually wanted war were probably exaggerated.

B   *Colonial policy*

Jules Ferry began an ambitious colonial policy in the 1880s, one which led to the creation of an extensive French Empire overseas, despite the fact that many politicians on the Left and Right disliked the expense involved. In 1881 France occupied Tunisia and confirmed a protectorate there by the Treaty of Bardo. French influence was also extended in Algeria and Morocco. By 1904 France had secured British, Italian and Spanish consent to its ambitions in Morocco, but Germany's provocative declaration in support of Moroccan independence provoked the crisis of 1905. The ensuing 1906 Algeçiras Conference prevented France from annexing Morocco, although it was given a share with Spain of the control of Morocco's customs and police. Foreign Minister Delcassé was forced to resign over the crisis. In 1909 Germany did recognise French 'special political interests' in Morocco, but a crisis blew up again when in 1911 French troops quelled anti-foreign riots in Fez and Germany responded by sending the gunboat *Panther* to Agadir. In the ensuing compromise, Germany agreed to a French protectorate in Morocco in return for part of the French Congo. Therefore French interests were further extended in North Africa, but the process became inextricably bound up with and complicated by the Great Power posturings involving Germany, France, Britain and other countries in the years preceding the outbreak of war in 1914.

> **KEY ISSUE**
>
> *How extensive and successful was French colonial policy 1870–1914?*

Elsewhere in Africa French colonialism proceeded rapidly. In West Africa protectorates were established in French Guinea (1893), the Ivory Coast (1893) and Dahomey (1894). In 1904 French West Africa became a single entity, comprising these three territories plus Senegal, Upper Senegal and Niger. Having extended control over a large area of the Congo since an expedition to the Northern Congo in 1880, France began to dream of a continuous belt of French colonies from West Africa to French Somaliland on the East coast. This would require the acquisition of the Southern Sudan, but the Fashoda crisis prevented this. Nevertheless, the colony of French Equatorial Africa was consolidated out of Gabon, Ubanghi-Shari and the Middle Congo in 1910. France's huge Empire in North, Central and West Africa made it one of the leading colonial Powers, although large areas such as the Sahara Desert were of little use economically, and France invested far more in Russia than it ever did in its Empire.

The French were also active in the Far East. A French protectorate over Tonkin was recognised by China in the Treaty of Tientsin (1885), although an earlier French defeat there brought down Jules Ferry. In 1898 the French were granted a 99-year lease on Kwangchowan, and so France was able to play a significant role in the economic exploitation of China.

4 ⤶ BIBLIOGRAPHY

Useful surveys of the Third Republic include *France: The Third Republic 1870–1914* by K. Randell (Hodder and Stoughton, 1986), which includes advice on note-taking and essays; *The Third Republic From 1870 to 1914* by R. Gildea (Longman Seminar Studies in History, 1988) which considers various interpretations and includes some documents;

and *France, 1870–1914* by R. Anderson (Routledge and Kegan Paul, 1977). Detailed but rewarding is *The Third Republic of France: The First Phase, 1871–1894* by G. Chapman (Macmillan, 1962).

There are several studies of the Commune, but *The Paris Commune of 1871* by E. Schulkind (Historical Association, 1971) remains a succinct summary. There are other studies of specific crises: for example *The Boulanger Affair* by F. Seager (Cornell University Press, 1969), *The Dreyfus Affair* by H. Kedward (Longman, 1969) and *France and the Dreyfus Affair* by D. Johnson (Blandford Press, 1966). There are many political biographies. Clemenceau's career spanned the whole period of this chapter and is covered in *Georges Clemenceau. A Political Biography* by D. Watson (Eyre Methuen, 1974). French foreign policy is covered in *France and the Origins of the First World War* by J. Keiger (1983).

5 ↩ STRUCTURED QUESTIONS AND ESSAYS

1. (a) Give reasons for the formation of the Paris Commune in 1871; (10 marks)
   (b) Why was the Commune unsuccessful? (15 marks)
2. (a) Outline the stages by which the Third Republic was established in the 1870s; (10 marks)
   (b) How significant were the actions of Adolphe Thiers and Marshal MacMahon in its establishment? (15 marks)
3. (a) Outline the main events of any **two** of the following three crises: the Boulanger affair; the Panama scandal; the Dreyfus affair; (10 marks)
   (b) For each of your two choices, consider the extent to which they threatened the stability of the Republic. (15 marks)
4. To what extent was the existence of the Third Republic under threat from the Left and the Right during the period from the 1880s to 1914? (25 marks)
5 Why did the Dreyfus affair arouse so much controversy in France? (25 marks)
6. Consider the extent to which any **one** of the following posed a threat to the stability or existence of the Third Republic in the period 1870–1914: monarchism; the Church; Socialism. (25 marks)
7. (a) Outline the main developments in the French economy in the period 1870–1914; (10 marks)
   (b) To what extent did France undergo an 'economic revolution' during this period? (15 marks)
8. (a) Outline the stages by which France reached agreements with Russia and Britain in the 20 years before the outbreak of war in 1914; (10 marks)
   (b) To what extent did France regain its Great Power status between 1871 and 1914? (15 marks)
9. How successful was French colonial policy during the period 1871–1914? (25 marks)

6 ⌐ INTERPRETING CARTOONS: A SOURCES EXERCISE

Many of the points that need to be considered when analysing cartoons as a source of historical evidence are similar to those involved in evaluating photographs. However, it is also important to consider the specific implications of analysing cartoons.

See page 327

Cartoons are often used to illustrate an event or topic in a satirical way. They may have either a humorous element or an obviously serious one. They usually employ one or more of several techniques – often exaggeration, sarcasm, irony or outright ridicule – in order to make a telling point. Some historical cartoons have achieved a fame which survives long after the event itself has faded in the memory: a classic example is the *Punch* cartoon of the German *Kaiser* Wilhelm II 'dropping the pilot', his Chancellor Bismarck, in 1890.

Usually the cartoonist is trying to make a particular point, and in order to do so, exaggeration or caricature may be more important to the cartoonist than the literal truth. Cartoons can be a valuable source of historical evidence if interpreted with care, When faced with one to analyse, start with the 'simple' questions:

● what event or topic is being represented? Can any individuals be identified, or are the representations symbolic? If the latter, of what are they symbolic?
● there is often a caption or attribution. If so, what information does it give?

Having worked out the message of the cartoon, consider these points:

● what point is the cartoonist trying to make? Has the cartoonist got a particular point of view?
● is the cartoon a reliable source of evidence about the topic? Is it just the point of view of the cartoonist? Why was the cartoon produced? What was the likely intended audience?
● does the message represent a widely-held view at the time?
● what are the uses and limitations of the cartoon as evidence? Does it give any historical insights?

As with photographs, you must make your analysis of cartoons specific to the particular example, and not make generalised comments about cartoons without any particular context.

Bearing these points in mind, study the following collection of cartoons showing aspects of the Third Republic in its domestic and foreign policies. For each cartoon, answer the questions above as well as you can, and also compare the cartoons from different countries. Is there any difference in their approach according to the country of origin? To what extent, if any, do the cartoons add to our understanding of the events or issues involved?

PICTURE 18

A Punch cartoon published after the Treaty of Frankfurt which ended the Franco-Prussian War

"AU REVOIR!"

GERMANY. "FAREWELL, MADAME, AND IF——"
FRANCE. "HA! WE SHALL MEET AGAIN!"

"ANY PORT IN A STORM!"

(FRANCE, IN TERROR OF THE IMPERIAL EAGLE, WHOSE SHADOW LOOMS DARK OVERHEAD, THROWS
HERSELF INTO THE ARMS OF THE CONSERVATIVE REPUBLIC.)

PICTURE 19

A Punch *cartoon from*
6 March 1875

A DECIDED PREFERENCE.

FRANCE (*surveying herself in a Looking-glass*). "AFTER ALL, THIS STILL SUITS ME BEST, AND I MEAN TO WEAR IT."

PICTURE 20

A Punch cartoon from the late 1870s

PICTURE 21
A French anti-Dreyfusard cartoon. Left to right: Scheurer-Kestner, Picquart, Reinach, Loubet, Dreyfus, Zola

PICTURE 22
From the cover of a French anti-clerical journal

PICTURE 23
*German cartoon showing
France, watched by Britain,
washing her dirty linen*

PICTURE 24
*British cartoon of
the* Entente Cordiale.
'Let Germany be careful now'

Germany
1871–1914

10

INTRODUCTION

THE SECOND *REICH*

The unification of Germany had not been the result of a popular revolution but was the result of the activities of Prussia in extending its power and influence over other German states, a situation consolidated by Prussia's victory over France in the war of 1870–1. Prussia's dominance was to be reflected in the structure of the German Empire created in the euphoria of victory. Many Prussian practices were institutionalised in the new Germany. Prussia's Emperor and Chancellor, now in charge of the German Empire, were determined to maintain Prussian dominance in Germany, and to maintain Germany's strong position in Europe. In this respect Germany was a force for conservatism on the international scene at least until 1890.

The arrival of the German Empire as a Great Power was of great significance not just for 'Germans' but for Europe as a whole. In so far as there had been a 'balance of power' in Europe before 1871, it had been seriously upset by Prussia's victory. French pretensions to the leadership of Europe had been shattered in the Franco-Prussian War. Austrian weakness had already been highlighted by defeat against Prussia in 1866 and by its need to make the compromise of the *Ausgleich* with Hungary in 1867. Russia was something of an unknown quantity, but still smarting from defeat in the Crimea. British policy was still that of avoiding definite commitments to other Great Powers. Britain was prepared to intervene if it felt its interests under serious threat, but it was a naval Power, not a force to reckoned with militarily on the continent.

The new Germany upset any previous calculations. Bismarck, the dominant force in German politics for 20 years after Prussia's victory, was not an expansionist. He wanted to consolidate Germany's new position in Europe, and his main preoccupation in European politics was to isolate France, so as to avoid the possibility of a recent enemy seeking revenge for defeat in 1871, perhaps by allying with other Great Powers. However, for all Germany's conservatism, the very existence of Germany in the heart of Europe was a potentially unsettling force on the international scene: simply because a united Germany quickly became the economic powerhouse of Europe. And since military power was increasingly dependent upon a powerful industrial base, Germany was well on the way to becoming the strongest military power in Europe also, if it were not so already.

MAP 12 *The German empire after 1871*

This is not to say that Bismarck had a smooth ride inside Germany. There were political alliances to be made and broken in order to maintain his position and implement his policies, and not all these were successful. Bismarck's attempts to crush what he perceived as the growing threat of Socialism failed in the long run. However, whilst Wilhelm I was Emperor, Bismarck's position was reasonably secure. The accession of Wilhelm II and Bismarck's fall from power created a very different situation. The new *Kaiser* proved to be a destabilising influence in European affairs. He portrayed himself as the 'People's *Kaiser*'. He did not significantly change the course of Germany's domestic policy, but he did not allow his Chancellors as much leeway as Bismarck had enjoyed under his grandfather's regime.

What was significantly different from 1890 was the *Kaiser*'s aggressive nationalism, his determination that Germany should play a major role in world affairs and be a powerful military force. Although some of the *Kaiser*'s activities were only posturing, the fact that the most powerful nation in Europe appeared to be adopting a more aggressive stance and upsetting the balance of power was bound to be a disturbing factor for other Great Powers. Whilst historians have debated the precise degree of responsibility that can be attributed to Germany for World War I, and some commentators have even identified a trend in German policy leading from the Second Empire to Hitler's Third *Reich*, there is general agreement that the impression created by Germany that it was a 'dissatisfied' power contributed to whatever sense of instability there was in international affairs. There was certainly a concern as to whether the rulers in Berlin were capable of conducting foreign policy with the tact and wisdom that would avoid a sense of unease in other European capitals.

1 ↪ POLITICAL HISTORY

A *The Constitution*

The German Empire created during the Franco-Prussian War was a federal structure comprising 25 states which had been part of the old North German Confederation, plus the South German states. Prussia made up two-thirds of the Empire's territory. Its dominance in the process of German unification was reflected in the 1871 Constitution, which was partly based upon the 1850 Prussian one:

> **KEY ISSUE**
>
> *To what extent did the German Constitution provide for democratic or representative government?*

● individual state governments appointed the 58 members of the *Bundesrat* or Federal Council. Most states had one member, but the larger states had more: Prussia had 17 members. Although not significant in terms of day-to-day government, and acting essentially as a rubber stamp for legislation, the *Bundesrat* was the guardian of the Constitution. Its members were also the representatives of their state legislatures and followed their instructions. Since only 14 out of the *Bundestag*'s 58 votes were necessary to block any constitutional

TIMELINE

Events 1871–90 (foreign affairs in italics)

1871	Proclamation of Wilhelm I as German Kaiser
	German Constitution adopted
	Treaty of Frankfurt with France
1872	Anti-clerical measures
	Dreikaiserbund with Austria and Russia
1873	Falk Laws on education and the clergy
1875	Formation of SDP
	'Kulturkampf' at its height
	Foundation of Reichsbank
	War scare with France
1878	Bismarck's break with National Liberals
	Anti-Socialist legislation
1879	Introduction of general tariffs
	Exceptional Law against SDP
	Some of anti-clerical legislation repealed
	Dual Alliance signed with Austria
1881	New *Alliance of the Three Emperors*
1882	*Triple Alliance with Austria and Italy*
1883	Act providing medical treatment for workers
1884	Accident Insurance Act
	German occupation of Southwest Africa, Togoland and Cameroons
1885	*German protectorates over Tanganyika and Zanzibar*
	German annexation of Northern New Guinea and Bismarck Archipelago
1886	Extension of accident and sickness insurance
1887	*Reinsurance Treaty with Russia*
1888	Crown Prince Frederick succeeded to the throne
	Death of Frederick and accession of Wilhelm II
1890	Reichstag rejected anti-Socialist bill
	Resignation of Bismarck
	Erfurt Congress committed SDP to Marxist policy
	Reinsurance Treaty with Russia lapsed
	German occupation of Rwanda-Urundi
	Acquisition of Heligoland from Britain in return for Zanzibar

change, and Prussia alone had 17 votes, Prussian supremacy was enshrined in the Constitution. A majority vote was needed for other decisions, but in practice Prussia was never outvoted

● the lower house or *Reichstag* was the major parliamentary body. It was elected every five years by all men over 25. It debated and approved legislation, and could amend Government bills, but it could also be dissolved at any time by the *Kaiser*, with the consent of the *Bundesrat*

● the Chancellor was not a member of the *Reichstag* and was not accountable to it, only to the *Kaiser*. The *Kaiser* was therefore one of the most powerful rulers in Europe. The Chancellor was not dependent upon the *Reichstag*, but he was on the Emperor, which made him vulnerable. Bismarck was a strong Chancellor; but as soon as Wilhelm II asserted himself at the end of the 1880s, Bismarck was forced to give way, and his years of experience counted for nothing.

Nevertheless the constitution was the creation of Bismarck. It lasted from 1871 to 1918, and along with political life generally, had several features which meant that Germany did not have an all-powerful parliamentary system of government, although neither could Germany be classified as an autocracy like the Russian Empire:

● the *Kaiser* was not responsible to parliament. He had considerable power, particularly in determining foreign policy and commanding the army. The Constitution stated that Germany had been united 'from above', not by the people. In a situation of political stalemate, the *Kaiser* had the right to effectively stage a *coup* by the army and suspend the Constitution. Bismarck frequently considered invoking such a move when there were difficulties in parliament
● individual state governments controlled education, health and the police. There was no national system of income tax, and the Federal Government was short of money, relying on income from tariffs and internal duties. The states collected their own revenues. The Federal Government's shortage of money became an increasing problem
● Prussia was by far the dominant state. Its own parliament was elected on an indirect system of voting designed to ensure the dominance of the conservative upper and middle classes. Prussia not only dominated the *Bundesrat* but largely ran foreign policy and the army. Nevertheless some historians have argued that the extent of Prussian dominance has been exaggerated, and that Prussia gradually became absorbed into 'Germany'; and also that the *Reichstag* won increasing importance for itself by the 1900s
● the Chancellor was a powerful figure. He was also Prime Minister of Prussia and responsible to the Kaiser
● the system had inbuilt checks and balances: the *Reichstag* could not dictate policy, but the Chancellor needed support in the *Reichstag* to get his own policies passed into law
● organised political parties were still in their infancy in 1871
● the army had great prestige in Germany and was subject to few external controls. Its needs were always given priority. Bismarck and the *Kaiser* wore military uniform to symbolise the army's importance. After 1893 the *Reichstag* could approve the army's budget only every five years, giving it a considerable degree of independence, and the army chiefs advised the *Kaiser* directly. Because the majority of officers were Prussian, the army's structure was another factor in ensuring Prussian dominance within Germany. Over 50 per cent of officers were titled, and therefore were closely bound up with the powerful Prussian aristocracy, the *Junkers*
● the Constitution did not catalogue basic civil rights.

KEY ISSUE

How important were the respective roles of the Kaiser and the Chancellor in the Constitution and in practice?

Bismarck was determined to maintain Prussian dominance at the expense of the Federal Government. He also despised political factions, distrusted opposition to Government measures as almost treasonable, and used political parties to gain support for particular policies, only to discard them when it suited him. Bismarck was able to act thus because he kept the goodwill of *Kaiser* Wilhelm I. The political system

The political parties in Germany

In 1871 these were little more than electoral associations, very loosely organised. They gradually became more organised and 'professional' although deputies were not paid until 1906.

The Right

There were two main political groupings on the Right:

(i)   *The Conservatives (DKP).* These were the mouthpiece of the landowning classes, particularly in Prussia. They were loyal to the *Kaiser* and believed in military and nationalist virtues. Their biggest power base was in the Prussian parliament or *landtag.*

(ii)   *The Independent or Free Conservatives.* As well as landowners, they included some industrialists. Whilst sharing many of the views of the DKP, they also favoured economic protectionism.

The Centre

The Catholic Centre Party (Z or Zentrum). Founded in 1871 to represent the interests of Catholics, it opposed Prussian dominance. It was conservative in that it opposed the growth of Socialism, but the Centre Party was in favour of some social reform and therefore balanced Right and Left.

The Liberal parties

(i)   *The National Liberal Party.* Dominant in the 1870s, it was conservative by instinct and represented the growing middle class. It was in favour of free enterprise and supported constitutional government.

(ii)   *The DFP or Liberal Progressives.* These were slightly more to the Left, and were more critical of the Government and the influence of the military.

The Left

The Social Democratic Party (SPD) was founded in 1869 by Wilhelm Liebknecht and August Bebel. Despite restrictions on its activities in the 1870s and 1880s, it steadily grew in strength, becoming the largest party in the *Reichstag* by 1912. It was also more professional in approach than other parties. In 1891 the SPD adopted the Erfurt Programme, which committed it to Marxism. In 1900 the Party explicitly rejected a reformist approach, the belief that Social Democrats should work for economic and social change through the existing political system. Nevertheless in practice the Party was less radical, and many members did get elected to the *Reichstag* and provincial parliaments.

Others
There were other minority parties: splinter left-wing groups; some anti-Semitic deputies from 1890; and representatives in the *Reichstag* of minority nationalities, including Poles, Danes and Alsace-Lorrainers.

In addition to political parties, other organisations exerted varying amounts of influence. There were various lobbies such as the Federation of German Employers' Associations; trade unions and professional organisations; agricultural pressure groups such as the Agrarian League; and nationalist organisations like the Pan-German League, the Navy League and the German Colonial Society.

was resistant to reform, but after 1890 was subject to pressures in two directions: from those who favoured an even more absolutist system of government, and from those favouring a more democratic parliamentary system to take account of changing social and economic conditions in Germany. Some historians like Wehler claim that the Constitution became increasingly unworkable, and that the *Kaiser* became a shadow Emperor whilst real power was fought over by other powerful forces like the army and industry.

B *Bismarck's ascendancy*

THE NATIONAL LIBERALS AND PROTECTIONISM
Bismarck dominated Germany's Government until 1890. He rarely held a collective meeting of the secretaries of state who ran the Government departments. He did not solve the problem of friction between the Imperial Government and the various state governments, but his own position was never seriously under threat whilst Wilhelm I ruled.

Bismarck's first priority was to consolidate the unification of Germany. Although the states retained many powers, a universal system of currency and a unified railway system were created. This, together with a policy of free trade, helped the German economy to prosper. Bismarck was supported in parliament by the National Liberals, although he distrusted their championing of parliamentary rights.

THE *KULTURKAMPF*
Bismarck's manipulation of the political system was demonstrated clearly in his treatment of Roman Catholics. These were a large minority, including French and Polish subjects and Germans in those South German states most opposed to Prussian dominance. Bismarck decided to move against the Catholics because:

- the Catholic Centre Party had quickly established a substantial presence in the *Reichstag* (winning 57 seats in the party's first year of existence). Bismarck distrusted its programme of religious freedom, personal liberty and moderate social reform and he feared that it would act as a focus for national minorities which were also Catholic, for example the Poles
- Bismarck regarded the Catholics as owing allegiance to a foreign Pope, who was trying to establish his hold over followers through measures such as the Decree of Papal Infallibility
- Catholics seemed more likely than other groups to resist the expansion of Prussian power.

Bismarck's measures against the Roman Catholics became known as the *Kulturkampf*, or 'struggle between two cultures'. The measures were applied most strongly in Prussia and started with a Government press campaign, criticising the Church. Various measures were then taken:

- the expulsion of the Jesuit order from Germany
- diplomatic relations with the papacy were severed in 1872
- the passing of the 1873 May Laws (or Falk Laws, named after the Prussian Minister of Religion and Education) which effectively brought the Catholic Church under state control by insisting upon civil marriage, examinations for priests, and the ending of financial aid to the Church
- the withdrawal of the rights of the Church over its own schools
- Prussian Catholics lost their legal and civil rights.

Bismarck was aware that some German Catholics were unhappy with the Pope's policies and he supported this particular group when it was criticised by the Catholic establishment. However, Bismarck had not anticipated the unifying effect which his persecution had on most Catholics, nor the unease which many Protestants also felt about the State attacking citizens' rights. He certainly did not expect the Centre Party to increase its electoral support to 91 seats in 1874.

Bismarck, ever the realist, abandoned his policy against the Catholics when aware of its failure. The *Kulturkampf* had not brought unity, rather the reverse. Pope Leo XIII, elected in 1878, showed a willingness to compromise. Bismarck wanted allies against the new perceived threat of Socialism, and could no longer count upon the support of the National Liberals. Falk was forced to resign and several of the May Laws were repealed in 1880.

In the late 1870s Bismarck changed to a protectionist policy of imposing tariffs. His main motives were:

- to boost trade and raise more revenue for the central Government
- to get the support of conservative groups, especially industrialists and landowners, and also the Centre Party. By doing so Bismarck could end his dependence on the National Liberals.

Tariffs were imposed on agricultural and manufactured imports in July 1879.

> **KEY ISSUE**
>
> *Why did Bismarck introduce the Kulturkampf and how successful was it?*

> **KEY ISSUE**
>
> *Why did Bismarck introduce protectionism and abandon the Liberals?*

| PROFILE | # OTTO VON BISMARCK (1815–98) |

There have been many assessments of Bismarck's career for its importance both for Germany and Europe after 1871, which is hardly surprising. He was an influential figure, and there was a lot of evidence about Bismarck left behind by the man himself and his contemporaries. However, there is no agreement about his significance. Bismarck himself made contradictory statements about his policies. Most historians are in broad agreement about his motivation after 1871 – to keep himself and Prussia pre-eminent in Germany and guarantee the *status quo* and French isolation in Europe. But there is a wide variety of opinions about the degree of success of these policies and Bismarck's overall significance. Some historians see him above all as a planner or schemer. Others see him as an opportunist, seizing the moment to Prussia's advantage and his own. Most historians now regard him as a realist and often refer to Bismarcks's statement about the importance of 'blood and iron' in determining the issues of the day.

A.J.P. Taylor belonged to the school of historians which preferred to deflate the image of the calculating, arch-manipulator of events. He described Bismarck as 'nervous and highly-strung, given to hysterical weeping and racked with sleeplessness'; a man who 'despised his supporters even more than he hated his enemies.' (*Europe: Grandeur and Decline* Penguin, 1967, pages 87–8.) Taylor played down Bismarck's achievements by claiming that he tried to resist nationalism and Socialism in Germany, but ended up by making them stronger; whilst his diplomacy, far from giving Germany security, eventually gave more security to other Powers. Taylor conceded that Bismarck had a range of qualities: he 'was dealing with Germans. The personal spite; the raucous evocation of Power; the irritation at opposition – these were qualities which he shared with other German politicians. The restraint; the ability to see into the minds of others; the readiness to risk his own prestige for the sake of peace and moderation; these were things that Bismarck added' (*ibid*, page 95).

Taylor's comments were perhaps coloured by the fact that they were written soon after World War II when anti-German feeling still ran high. Assessments by later historians were often more generous. Some historians were anxious to exonerate Bismarck from earlier charges that somehow he was the precursor of Wilhelm II or even Hitler, both of whom were certainly less moderate. Even historians who partially blamed Bismarck for the legacy he left – for example the fact that he did not cultivate a suitable successor, refusing to accept that he was dispensable – conceded the political skill he displayed over a long period.

Ultimately any assessment of Bismarck's career after 1871 will be strongly coloured by your interpretation of the Germany which he governed. You may argue that the Constitution which he gave to Germany was only a façade, with the trappings but not the reality of democracy. On the other hand Bismarck did need to secure parliamentary majorities in order to govern, and a higher proportion of the population could vote in Germany than in most other countries with more liberal traditions.

Germany was a hierarchical society, and critics sometimes point to the powerful aristocracy and the army as a 'state within the state' – yet most Germans were satisfied with their place in Europe and did not seek expansion, so it is dangerous to talk of a warlike *élite* during Bismarck's lifetime. There were increasing social and political pressures inside Germany after Bismarck, and the men who followed him into Government were not of the same stature. But whether you decide that Bismarck was a statesman of genius or an opportunistic manipulator, it is difficult to assign all the responsibility to Bismarck for the relative decline in Germany's international position after 1890 and the fact that parliamentary government was ultimately to prove so fragile within Germany.

SOCIALISM

Whereas Bismarck had underestimated the affect his anti-Catholic measures would provoke, he probably overestimated the perceived threat of Socialism to his Prussianised state. The Universal German Workingman's Association, a revolutionary group, had merged with the more moderate and larger Social Democratic Party in 1875. Bismarck distrusted the professed internationalism of the SDP, its programme of social equality, and its gradual increase in parliamentary strength. In 1876 Bismarck failed to get a bill aimed at suppressing Socialist propaganda through the *Reichstag*, and in 1877 the SDP increased its electoral support. However, attempted assassination attempts on the *Kaiser* in 1878 were used as the pretext for an Anti-Socialist Law passed in that year with the support of Conservatives and National Liberals:

- Socialist organisations and meetings were banned
- the police were given powers to imprison or deport Socialists. About 1500 were imprisoned and others chose to emigrate.

However, the Socialists continued to gain electoral support until the laws were repealed in 1890.

During the 1880s Bismarck embarked upon a new tactic. He tried to woo working-class support away from the Social Democrats. He introduced a system of state welfare which was well ahead of its time in Europe. It involved:

- sickness insurance for three million low-paid workers and their families. They received medical treatment and sick pay. Workers paid two-thirds of the contributions, and employers one-third
- accident insurance in 1884, extended to agricultural workers in 1886, and paid for by employers
- old age and disability pensions in 1889, paid for by workers, employers and the state, and given to citizens over 70.

KEY ISSUE

How do you account for the growth of Socialism and how did Bismarck respond to it?

TABLE 15

Reichstag election results 1871–1890 (in thousands)

	1871 Votes	1871 %	1871 Seats	1874 Votes	1874 %	1874 Seats	1877 Votes	1877 %	1877 Seats
SDP	124	3.2	2	352	6.8	9	493	9.1	12
Centre	742	18.6	63	1446	27.8	91	1341	24.8	93
Left Lib	361	9.3	47	470	9.0	50	463	8.5	39
Nat Lib/Lib	1453	37.2	155	1597	30.7	158	1605	29.7	141
Free Cons	346	8.9	37	376	7.2	33	427	8.0	38
Conservat	549	14.1	57	360	6.9	22	526	9.7	40
Minorities (Poles, Danzes, Guelphs, Alsatians)	255	6.6	21	462	10.5	34	519	9.6	34
Splinter groups	76	2.0	–	46	0.9	–	28	0.5	–

	1878 Votes	1878 %	1878 Seats	1884 Votes	1884 %	1884 Seats	1884 Votes	1884 %	1884 Seats
SDP	437	7.5	9	312	6.1	12	550	9.7	24
Centre	1328	23.1	94	1183	23.2	100	1282	22.6	99
Left Lib	451	7.8	29	1181	23.1	115	1093	19.3	74
Nat Lib	1487	28.5	109	747	14.6	47	997	17.6	51
Free Cons	786	13.6	57	379	7.4	28	388	6.8	28
Conservat	750	13.0	59	831	16.3	50	861	15.2	78
Minorities	505	8.7	40	449	8.8	35	479	8.5	43
Splinter groups	17	0.3	–	15	0.3	–	13	0.2	–

	1887 Votes	1887 %	1887 Seats	1890 Votes	1890 %	1890 Seats
SDP	763	7.1	11	1427	19.7	35
Centre	1516	22.1	98	1342	18.6	106
Left Lib	1062	14.1	32	1308	18.0	76
Nat Lib	1678	22.3	99	1178	16.3	42
Free Cons	736	9.8	41	482	6.7	20
Conservat	1147	15.2	80	895	12.4	73
Minorities	579	7.6	33	475	6.6	38
Splinter groups	48	0.6	2	75	1.0	2

The measures were novel by European standards and controversial. Employers disliked the costs, whilst many workers were suspicious of the Government's motives. Support for the SDP continued to grow. It is difficult to judge the extent to which Bismarck succeeded in his efforts to mould a compliant population – the SDP was becoming a more moderate force and German Socialism might have developed so without Bismarck's measures. The essentially patriotic loyalty of the working class to the national cause was demonstrated in 1914 when German Social Democrats fell in behind the German war effort.

C *The fall of Bismarck*

Bismarck's political skills could not prevent him facing an increasingly difficult *Reichstag* in which Conservatives, Liberals, Socialists and the Centre were all competing for influence. He manufactured a crisis atmosphere in 1887 at the time of the Boulanger affair in France, for example calling up reservists, and he called an election. A victorious coalition of Conservatives, Free Conservatives and National Liberals, between them controlling 220 seats, gave Bismarck the majority he needed to pass an act submitting the military budget to scrutiny only once every seven years.

However, Wilhelm I's death in 1888 meant the loss of Bismarck's chief ally, one who had allowed the Chancellor a free hand. Wilhelm's son Frederick reigned for only three months before his own death, and he was succeeded by his son Wilhelm II. The new young *Kaiser* had his own ideas on government, which included more social reform and personal direction of foreign policy. Bismarck thought him inexperienced and foolish, and probably underestimated him. He soon faced problems. Bismarck decided to abandon the recent electoral alliance, desert the Liberals and seek a new alliance of the Centre and Conservatives as the basis for a renewed attack on the Socialists. The February 1890 election produced big gains for the SDP. But Bismarck failed to persuade the *Kaiser* of the need for new anti-Socialist laws, and also upset him by trying to insist that ministers went through him before the *Kaiser*. Wilhelm II stood firm and Bismarck resigned. Until his death in 1898, Bismarck remained critical of the *Kaiser* and tried to justify his own career.

> There is an assessment of Bismarck on pages 184 and 286–7

> **KEY ISSUE**
>
> *How do you account for Bismarck's fall from power?*

D *Wilhelmine Germany 1890–1914*

The new *Kaiser* was determined to be his own ruler, and boasted that he had never read the Constitution. That Constitution gave him considerable influence to appoint and listen to whom he chose. Historians such as Rohl have emphasised the selective nature of the *Kaiser*'s rule, surrounding himself as he did with friends and flatterers who did little to temper his pretensions to grandeur. None of his Chancellors were of the calibre of Bismarck.

DROPPING THE PILOT.

PICTURE 25 Punch*'s comments on Bismarck's resignation*

TABLE 16
German Chancellors 1871–1917

O. von Bismarck	1871–1890
L. von Caprivi	1890–1894
Prince von Hohenlohe-Schillingsfurst	1894–1900
Baron von Bülow	1900–1909
T. Bethmann-Hollweg	1909–1917

KAISER WILHELM II (1859–1941)

Wilhelm II was the son of Friedrich III, who reigned as Emperor for only 99 days before his death in 1888, and Victoria, eldest daughter of Queen Victoria of Britain. Throughout his rule Wilhelm was to maintain a love-hate relationship with Britain. A complex character, who had a difficult relationship with his parents, he adopted aggressive attitudes partly to disguise his insecurity and physical disabilities (which included a paralysed left arm damaged during a difficult birth). Wilhelm has always interested psychologists as well as historians. His mother, referring to her son, wrote to Queen Victoria that 'I feel like a hen that has hatched ducklings.' Although not experiencing active army service, Wilhelm loved his military training and always retained enthusiasm for uniforms and all the trappings of military life.

He was certainly capable of great bluster, did not take criticism well, lacked consistent application, and was capable of considerable self-delusion and behaviour which was dangerously unsettling in the ruler of the most powerful country in Europe. Wilhelm retained a firm belief in the principle of absolute monarchy, regretting – and sometimes forgetting – that there were some restrictions on his power; and also retained a belief in a strong army and Germany's destiny to be a world Power.

Of particular interest to historians is Wilhelm's role in government and influence over German policy. Some historians like Rohl have emphasised the personal nature of his rule. He surrounded himself with personal friends, especially Count Philip Eulenburg, who flattered Wilhelm. Other historians have criticised this emphasis, arguing that it plays down the importance of powerful political and economic forces which inevitably influenced German policy. The *Kaiser's* role was important, but difficult to assess, because he was erratic and inconsistent: for example he changed his mind completely on important issues such as moderation towards Socialists and protectionist policies. He was capable of major gaffes as over the *Daily Telegraph* affair in 1908, when he gave an interview full of tactless remarks on the theme that he was friendly towards Britain, unlike most Germans.

Balanced interpretations of Wilhelm tend to go behind the bluster and look at what he actually did. One of his biographers claims that the decision to expand the German navy was 'the only major German policy for which prime responsibility must be laid at the Kaiser's door' (*The Kaiser and his Times* by M. Balfour, Penguin, 1975, page 433). On the other hand, Balfour concedes that he 'was a distracting rather than a steadying influence ... holding a position in which he could have done much to counteract the tendencies around him, he instead gave them added emphasis ... William's story demonstrates clearly that good intentions and intelligence are not enough in a ruler. Energy unaccompanied by steadying qualities is a menace rather than an advantage ... His nervousness and impetuosity doomed him to be a lightweight, jostled along by the forces among which he found himself ... The simple truth about the Kaiser is that, for all his undoubted gifts, he was not up to the out-size job which destiny had assigned to him' (*ibid*, pages 433–4). This was particularly true in the war crisis of July 1914, when despite growing doubts about the seriousness of the situation, the *Kaiser* allowed his doubts to be pushed aside and acquiesced in the arguments of the generals that the die had been cast and Germany had to go all the way.

TIMELINE

Events 1890–1914 (foreign affairs in italics)

1892	Schlieffen Plan devised
	Reichstag rejected Army Bill to increase size of army and length of service
	Anglo-German agreement over Cameroons
1893	Army Bill passed
	Foundation of Agrarian League and Pan-German League
	Resignation of Caprivi
1894	*German protectorate established over Togoland*
1897	*German occupation of Kiao-Chow*
1898	Foundation of Navy League
	Navy Bill passed
	Anglo-German agreement over Portugese African colonies
1899	End of laws to repress Socialism
1900	Second Navy Bill passed
1903	Extension of sickness insurance and laws against child labour
1905	*Moroccan crisis*
1908	'Daily Telegraph affair'
1909	Bethmann-Hollweg appointed Chancellor
1911	*Agadir incident*
1912	SDP became largest party in *Reichstag*
1913	Naval Bill passed and army enlarged
	Zabern affair
1914	*Outbreak of World War I*

PICTURE 26   *A portrait of the Kaiser as he liked himself to be shown.*
(A French General commented: 'That is not a portrait, it is a declaration of war'.)

CAPRIVI

Wilhelm appointed Leo von Caprivi to succeed Bismarck as Chancellor. Caprivi differed from Bismarck in being more prepared initially to cooperate with the *Reichstag*. He pleased the *Kaiser* by strengthening the army, although this involved a struggle with the *Reichstag* which was only won by agreeing to reduce the period of conscript service from three years to two and allowing parliament to debate the military budget every five years instead of seven.

Caprivi favoured limited reform, allowing the laws against Socialism to lapse and restricting the working hours of women and children. Industrial courts to arbitrate wage claims were set up, factory inspec-

TABLE 17

Reichstag election results 1893–1912 (in thousands)

	1893		1898		1903	
	Votes	Seats	Votes	Seats	Votes	Seats
SDP	1787	44	2107	56	3011	81
Centre	1469	96	1455	102	1875	100
Left Lib	1092	48	863	49	872	26
Nat Lib	997	53	971	46	1317	51
Free Cons	438	28	344	23	333	21
Conservat	1038	72	859	56	949	54
Right-wing splinter groups	264	16	284	13	245	11
Minorities (Poles, Danes, Guelphs, Alsatians)	461	35	471	34	559	32
Other splinter groups	129	5	397	18	334	11

	1907		1912	
	Votes	Seats	Votes	Seats
SDP	3259	43	4250	110
Centre	2180	105	1997	91
Left Lib	1234	49	1497	42
Nat Lib	1631	54	1663	45
Free Cons	472	24	367	14
Conservat	1060	60	1126	43
Right-wing splinter groups	249	16	52	3
Minorities	651	29	706	33
Other splinter groups	528	17	550	16

tion was made more rigorous and workers were allowed to elect committees to negotiate with employers about working conditions. Caprivi also reduced tariffs in an attempt to stimulate foreign trade. This was not a policy to endear him to conservative interests, although it proved beneficial to the German people by reducing the costs of food imports. Wilhelm was also concerned about the continued growth in support for the SDP. Caprivi was unable to sustain the support of a stable coalition. He resigned over his refusal to draft anti-Socialist legislation in 1894, having initially been given the brief of conciliating the SDP. After a long stopgap chancellorship under Prince Chlodwig zu Hohenloe-Schillings-furst, who had no influence over the *Kaiser*, the Government was taken over by Count Bernhard von Bülow, who was Foreign Minister from 1897–1900 before acting as Chancellor 1900–9.

PICTURE 27 *The growing threat of Socialism*

BÜLOW AND TIRPITZ

Bülow and other prominent colleagues like Navy Secretary Admiral Alfred von Tirpitz believed in *sammlungspolitik* – a governing coalition of patriotic forces. But Bülow's main concern was to pander to Wilhelm's wishes. The campaign against Socialism was allowed to lapse, and more attention was paid to foreign and colonial affairs. Domestic issues were left to Interior Minister Count Arthur von Posadowski. Some more concessions were made to the working class: in 1900 accident insurance was extended and pensions increased. In 1901 industrial courts to settle disputes were made compulsory in large towns. In 1903 sickness benefits were extended and in 1908 there were additional restrictions on the employment of children.

Tirpitz was an able politician and propagandist, and got his Navy Laws passed in 1897, 1900 and 1906, providing for a much larger German navy and the widening of the Kiel Canal. However, there were also arguments about tariffs, Socialism and social reform. Bülow was secure whilst he had the *Kaiser*'s support, and together with Tirpitz and senior Foreign Office official Friedrich von Holstein had a significant influence upon policy. However, in 1906 Bülow's Government was attacked in the *Reichstag* over complaints about misrule by officials in German South West Africa. The Government found it increasingly difficult to manipulate parliament. Then in 1908 the *Kaiser* caused a minor diplomatic incident by claiming in a *Daily Telegraph* interview that he was pro-British, unlike most Germans. Bülow did not support the *Kaiser* when he was criticised for this gaffe. Wilhelm II was annoyed, and Bülow also had to take responsibility for heavy financial debts incurred in expanding the armed forces and Germany's colonial empire. There was controversy over attempts, resisted by Conservatives, to increase taxes and the contributions by individual states to the federal budget. Bülow, now lacking the *Kaiser*'s confidence, was forced out of office in favour of Germany's last pre-war Chancellor, Theobald von Bethmann-Hollweg, a hard-working but relatively inexperienced and uninspiring politician.

BETHMANN-HOLLWEG

The Government's relations with the *Reichstag* proved increasingly difficult. The *Kaiser*'s Governments traditionally relied for support on the right-wing parties – the Conservatives, Free Conservatives and National Liberals. However, these parties were losing electoral ground to the SDP, the Left Liberals and the Centre, all of which were more critical of the Government. Although politicians on the Left were themselves divided between reformists and radicals, the balance of opinion between those wanting little or no change and those seeking a more genuine parliamentary democracy was slowly shifting towards the latter. This was bound to cause difficulties with an imperial regime which still tried to behave autocratically.

Bethmann-Hollweg's Government was cautious: it reduced expenditure and raised taxes in 1912. Moderate proposals to democratise the Prussian voting system were dropped after opposition. Even so, the

Government upset Conservatives by the rise in taxes, and support for the SDP continued to grow.

Divisions in politics and society were highlighted by the Zabern Affair in 1913. After disturbances in this Alsatian town, army officers arrested some local civilians without going through the legal authority. The affair seemed to highlight the virtually independent status of the army in Germany. The army claimed it was responsible to the *Kaiser* alone. Although the *Kaiser* supported the army, Bethmann-Hollweg was criticised and defeated in the *Reichstag* – although he was able to stay on as Chancellor.

Some historians have even claimed that elements within the Government and ruling class favoured war in 1914 as a means of resolving perceived social tensions in Germany. This view has been hotly disputed by others. It is true that the contradictions created by Bismarck's 1871 Constitution were not resolved: the *Reichstag* never controlled the Government, and there were frequent political disagreements between them, whilst the Government needed the *Reichstag* in order to pass legislation. However, such disagreements between the legislature and executive are common in many parliamentary systems.

E *Germany in World War I*

The war was to prove a traumatic event for Germany as for all participating nations. Germany entered the war on a patriotic wave, with political parties declaring an internal truce in the interests of unity. Enthusiasm was eventually dimmed by the failure to achieve quick victory, but discontent was muted. The *Kaiser*'s confidence was destroyed by the outbreak of war and he ceased to exert major influence over political or military affairs. Germany's generals and the War Ministry increasingly ran the economy and internal affairs. In 1916 Generals Hindenburg and Ludendorff were effectively put in charge of the country, and Bethmann-Hollweg was forced out of office in 1917. The war wrecked Germany's economy and political system, and caused major social tensions by the time of the armistice and the November Revolution in 1918. And yet, ironically, by handing over power to a new civilian regime, the German army escaped most of the blame which many civilians later attached to the politicians for supposedly losing the war; and the new regime, the Weimar Republic, was never fully able to live down the stigma of having being born amidst defeat and despair.

> **KEY ISSUE**
>
> *How was the German Government affected during World War I?*

2 ⁓ ECONOMIC HISTORY

By 1914 Germany was the most economically prosperous country in Europe, and its military power was in large part based upon its industrial strength.

The signs of economic progress were already evident in the 1860s and early 1870s:

ANALYSIS

Change and continuity in the Second Empire

German historians trying to explain the course of German history, and especially the conditions which gave rise to the traumatic and destructive period of Nazism, have long studied the history of the period 1870–1914 to discover whether there were elements of continuity in the German experience throughout this period, or whether developments after 1918 can be explained purely in terms of what happened in the war years and their immediate aftermath. For example, historians debated whether the nationalism of Wilhelm II's Germany was the precursor of something more sinister under the Nazis or a phenomenon which was very much part of the general European experience in the years before 1914. In other words, were the Germans fundamentally 'different' from other peoples or were they in the mainstream of European politics, different only in so far as they became a nation late in the day?

There was also the question of continuity before and after 1890. Was there a fundamental difference between the Germany of Bismarck and that of Wilhelm II? In the past this argument often focussed on the supposedly very different policies and methods of Bismarck, who dominated German politics between 1871 and 1890, and those of Wilhelm II, who tried to become his own master. Clearly Bismarck was more cautious in his approach, and less prone to unpredictable outbursts. However, the danger of emphasising this interpretation is that it can exaggerate the impact of these individuals on events – neither had quite as much influence as is sometimes assumed. It also ignores the important social and economic changes taking place in Germany, changes which created their own pressures.

The German historian Fritz Fischer caused a sensation in the 1960s by rejecting the arguments of earlier historians who were reluctant to trace the roots of Nazism back beyond the defeat of 1918. Fischer professed to find a link between the aggressive expansionism and nationalism of the Hitler period and that of the Germany of Bismarck and Wilhelm II. Proponents of this view also studied the tensions created by massive industrialisation and social dislocation, and argued that the leaders of an inflexible political structure created in 1871 deliberately channelled these pressures into an aggressive foreign policy and desire for European domination, thereby creating a safety valve. By implication, Germany became responsible for World War I.

In the 1970s the 'Bielefelder' school of German historians (named after the University of Bielefeld), represented particularly by Hans-Ulrich Wehler, developed the Fischer thesis, highlighting the political immaturity and authoritarianism of post-1871 politics and the militarism they identified in German society. Wehler

See the bibliography on page 309

assumed that Bismarck was alarmed by a perceived threat of social revolution in Germany and tried to deflect it by pursuing peace in Europe and consolidating imperial rule at home. Later he introduced welfare policies. Criticisms of this school of thought emerged in the same decade, based on several grounds. It was claimed in particular that historians like Wehler exaggerated the importance of domestic forces in influencing international relations and exaggerated the degree of social control supposedly exercised by the Establishment. Historians like Hillgruber and Hildebrand argued that foreign policy had its own dynamics and was not just an extension of domestic politics – in effect an 'old-fashioned' view of history.

Historians since the 1970s have studied in detail many different aspects of Germany history in this period to demonstrate that it was a rapidly developing society and not some monolithic entity controlled by either Bismarck or his successors. This 'revisionist' view was developed by some British historians (for example Eley and Blackbourn in *The Peculiarities of German History*, Oxford 1985). The emphasis on Germany's diversity was developed: for example the considerable divisions based on geography (the diversity of the states has sometimes been underestimated), different ethnic groups, religion, class and gender. This approach emphasises the growing pluralisation of German society by 1914. Historians in recent years with a broad approach to German history have therefore become less interested in the question of why Hitler came to power in 1933, as if this were something inherent in German history since 1871. They have concentrated instead on explaining why an increasingly complex and maturing society, subject to pressures and opportunities present to a greater or lesser extent in all developing societies at this time, should have had a Government which appeared to have made such a crass decision or miscalculated risk to go to war in 1914. In the words of G. Layton 'Imperial Germany on the eve of World War I was a land of contrasts – a complex mixture of forces for change and forces for conservatism. However, it was an essentially civilised nation. It enjoyed a highly sophisticated cultural tradition and an advanced education system. And despite the authoritarian constitution, the values of the *Kaiserreich* were squarely in the tradition of what the Germans call the *Rechtsstaat* (the constitutional state)...in 1914 Germany could have evolved along any one of several different lines of historical development and ... in the long-term, genuine parliamentary democracy was just as feasible as authoritarian dictatorship' (G. Layton *From Bismarck to Hitler: Germany 1890–1933*, Hodder and Stoughton, 1995, page 152).

- the iron, steel, coal, textile and railway industries expanded, funded by credit which was increasingly available from a rapidly expanding banking system
- French reparations were used to pay for public works and to pay off debts
- Germany benefited from an expanding and relatively young population; extensive natural resources including coal from the Ruhr, Silesia and the Saar and iron from Alsace-Lorraine and the Ruhr; and navigable rivers and an extensive railway network
- the last quarter of the nineteenth century saw the expansion of powerful enterprises like Krupps and Thyssen, whilst the urban population outgrew the rural one. Huge industrial cartels or trusts were encouraged as a means of bringing economies of scale. There were over 350 cartels by 1905
- Germany had the best system of elementary and higher education in Europe.

> **KEY ISSUE**
>
> *To what extent and why did Germany become the dominant economic power in Europe during this period?*

Progress was not consistently smooth. Germany was affected by the European financial crash of 1873, brought on by unwise speculation. From the 1870s there was increasing competition in agricultural markets from the USA and Russia. Nevertheless the German economy performed relatively better than its European competitors, and during this period the foundations of Germany's later economic supremacy were firmly laid. Already by 1914 Germany's expanding population (rising from 50 million in 1890 to 65 million in 1910) was producing half of Europe's coal and two thirds of its steel. German agricultural output also increased, although not to the same extent.

Powerful interest groups promoted their economic goals. In addition to the formation of cartels, there was a campaign against free trade in the 1870s by industrialists, the Prussian landowning aristocracy and bankers, all concerned at foreign competition and afraid of working class discontent should the economy slump. Powerful pressure groups like the League of German Iron and Steel Industrialists were formed. Bismarck was aware of these pressures, and he also became involved in the tariff issue because of his own political manoeuvrings. Support from the Centre Party allowed him to introduce tariffs on iron goods and grain in 1879. Tariffs were reduced after 1890, and this stimulated trade. Despite a relative slump in the 1890s, the German economy was in full swing again after 1895, apart from short downturns in 1900–2 and 1907–8. The period from the 1890s has sometimes been termed Germany's second industrial revolution, with an average growth rate of 4.5 per cent per year and further major developments in the electrical and petro-chemical industries, which came to rival the contribution of the older staple industries to Germany's prosperity. Germany's population grew apace, increasing the supply of workers and soldiers and providing bigger markets. By 1914 Germany was indisputably the economic powerhouse of Europe.

More controversial for historians has been the social impact of these economic developments. Sections of the German population suffered as the economy as a whole progressed or at least feared that they would do so. Certainly the agricultural labourers and smallholders who still made up 15 per cent of Germany's population in 1913 did not share in the growing prosperity. Agricultural labourers in the East actually suffered wage cuts. The landowning *Junkers* class of East Prussia feared foreign competition. The urban working class suffered some of the strains of rapid industrialisation such as housing shortages. There were also regional disparities: the more industrialised Western areas of Germany prospered more than the East. Not all workers did benefit from the industrial advances, and this partly accounts for the rise in support for the SPD. Real wages fluctuated: for example they fell between 1895 and 1900. However, in the overall period between 1895 and 1913 real wages rose by over 30 per cent, whilst during the same period the working week was reduced and unemployment was as low as 3 per cent. The paradox is that higher wages sometimes went hand-in-hand with worsening living conditions in overcrowded cities. Some Germans rightly perceived that disparities in wealth increased, with the upper and middle classes improving their lot more quickly. However, attempts to picture pre-1914 Germany as riven with social divisions, so much so that some in the military and civilian establishments supposedly sought social peace through a unifying war of conquest, have been unconvincing. The most telling fact is that the population explosion was successfully absorbed into the labour market at the same time as living standards for the majority improved.

3 ↪ FOREIGN POLICY

A *Bismarck and European politics*

Germany's role in international relations in the years leading up to World War I is dealt with in Chapters 14 and 15. In this section there will be an overview of German foreign and imperial policy under Bismarck and his successors.

It is apt to refer to 'Bismarck's policy' throughout the period 1871–88, because with the support of Wilhelm I, he did conduct foreign affairs. Victory for Prussia in 1871 left Germany dominant in Europe. Bismarck's subsequent strategy was centred on the need to preserve the new status quo. It was therefore a defensive strategy, assuming that Germany had no territorial demands in Europe. It meant isolating France, which it was assumed would wish for revenge for the defeat of 1871. It also meant keeping Austria, Germany and Russia on good terms with each other, or at least in such a situation that Germany's security was guaranteed. This necessitated, according to Bismarck, 'trying to be one of three as long as the world is governed by the unstable equilibrium of five great powers'.

Ultimately Bismarck was unsuccessful, and there has been considerable debate as to how much Bismarck actually 'planned' events. The main landmarks of Bismarck's foreign policy were:

TABLE 18

Germany's economic and social development 1870–1914

(i) Population of the German Empire and its five largest states (in thousands)

	1871	1880	1890	1900	1910
German Empire	40 997				64 568
Prussia	24 689	27 279	29 957	34 473	40 165
Bavaria	4 863	5 285	5 595	6 176	6 887
Saxony	2 556	2 973	3 503	4 202	4 807
Wurttemburg	1 819	1 971	2 037	2 169	2 438
Baden	1 462	1 570	1 658	1 868	2 143

From census figures.

(ii) Growth of some major cities 1850–1910 (in thousands)

City	1850	1871	1880	1900	1910
Berlin	412	826	1122	1889	2071
Hamburg	175	290	290	706	931
Munich	107	169	230	500	596
Leipzig	63	107	149	456	679
Dresden	97	177	221	396	548
Cologne	97	129	145	373	517
Breslau	111	208	273	423	512
Frankfurt/Main	65	91	137	289	415
Dusseldorf	27	69	95	214	359
Nuremberg	54	83	100	261	333
Hanover	28	88	123	236	302

From census figures.

(iii) Structure of the labour force in occupational groups 1875–1913 (in thousands)

Sector	1875	1885	1895	1905	1913
Agriculture	9 230	9 700	9 788	9 926	10 701
Mining	286	345	432	665	863
Industry and handicraft	5 153	6 005	7 524	9 572	10 857
Transport	349	461	620	901	1 174
Commerce/ banking	1 116	1 457	1 970	2 806	3 474
Insurance/hotels/ domestic services	1 490	1 488	1 571	1 541	1 542
Other services	589	659	894	1 159	1 493
Defence	430	462	606	651	864
Total	18 643	20 577	23 405	27 221	30 968

Source: W.G. Hoffmann *Das Wachstum der Deutschen Wirtschaft seit der Mitte des 19 Jahrhunderts* (Berlin, 1965).

(iv) Births, deaths and marriages in Germany 1871–1910 (in thousands)

TABLE 18 (CONT.)
Germany's economic and social development 1870–1914

	Births	Deaths	Marriages
1871	1414	1213	337
1880	1696	1173	337
1890	1759	1199	395
1900	1996	1236	476
1910	1925	1046	496

From census figures.

(v) Deaths of infants per 1000 live births 1871–1910

1871	330
1880	240
1890	226
1900	229
1910	162

From census figures.

(vi) Railway mileage open 1840–1913 (kilometres)

1840	1860	1880	1900	1913
469	11 089	33 838	51 678	63 378

(vii) Net agricultural production at current prices 1870–1913 (millions of marks)

Year	Cereals and vegetables	Meat	Milk, Eggs, etc.	Total
1870	1698	976	1406	4 080
1875	2073	1417	1579	5 069
1880	2316	1426	1677	5 419
1885	2085	1653	1558	5 296
1890	2451	2019	2042	6 512
1895	2287	2119	1787	6 193
1900	2842	2647	2115	7 604
1905	3082	3275	2675	9 032
1910	3168	3986	3545	10 699
1913	3540	4593	3607	11 740

Source: Hoffmann *ibid.*

TABLE 18 (CONT.)
Germany's economic and social development 1870–1914

(viii) Livestock 1861–1913 (in thousands)

Year	Horses	Cattle	Pigs	Sheep
1861	3194	14 999	6 463	28 017
1873	3552	15 777	7 124	24 999
1883	3523	15 787	9 206	19 190
1892	3836	17 556	13 174	13 590
1900	4195	18 946	16 807	9 693
1913	4558	20 994	25 659	5 521

Source: H. Aubin and W. Zorn eds, *Handbuch zur Deutschen Wirtschafts- und Sozialgeschichte*, vol. 2 (Stuttgart, 1976).

(ix) Pig iron production 1870–1913 annual averages (in thousands)

1870–4	1579	1895–1899	5 974
1875–9	1770	1900–1904	7 925
1880–4	2893	1905–1909	10 666
1885–9	3541	1910–1913	14 836
1890–4	4335		

Source: W. Grutter and G. Lottes, *Die Industrielle Revolution* (Paderborn, 1982).

(x) Production indices of key industries 1870–1913

Year	Coal	Lignite	Iron	Steel	Shipbuilding	Cars	Chemicals
1870	13.9	8.7	7.2	6.0	–	–	–
1875	19.7	11.9	10.5	8.8	–	–	–
1880	24.7	13.9	14.1	10.9	–	–	–
1885	30.7	17.7	14.1	13.4	–	–	–
1890	36.9	21.9	24.1	18.0	–	–	–
1895	41.7	28.4	28.3	22.4	–	–	–
1900	57.5	46.4	43.6	33.4	–	–	–
1905	63.8	60.2	56.9	47.0	–	–	–
1910	80.4	77.5	76.6	75.8	63.8	51.1	80.5
1913	100.0	100.0	100.0	100.0	100.0	100.0	100.0

Source: Hoffmann *ibid*.

(xi) Balance of external trade with leading Powers 1880–1910 (millions of marks) (I = Imports, E = Exports)

	France		Russia		UK		USA	
	I	E	I	E	I	E	I	E
1880	246	285	336	213	351	438	–	–
1890	258	231	542	206	601	690	397	417
1900	303	277	717	325	719	862	1004	440
1910	509	543	1387	547	767	102	1188	633

(xii) Growth of Government expenditure 1872–1913 (millions of marks). 1872–1900 five-year averages

TABLE 18 (CONT.)
Germany's economic and social development 1870–1914

Year	Armaments		Administration		Social Insurance subsidy		Totals
	mill.	%	mill.	%	mill.	%	
1872–5	822.1	98.3	14.0	1.7	–	–	836.1
1876–80	583.0	94.4	34.2	5.6	–	–	617.2
1881–5	460.8	95.0	24.0	5.0	–	–	484.8
1886–90	818.1	95.3	32.8	3.8	7.5	0.9	858.4
1891–5	882.9	93.9	40.1	4.3	17.3	1.8	940.3
1896–1900	841.1	90.8	62.4	6.7	22.8	2.5	926.3
1901	1162.9	90.4	94.8	7.4	28.1	2.4	1286.6
1902	1122.8	88.7	112.2	8.8	30.4	2.5	1265.9
1903	1105.7	85.6	109.1	8.4	33.7	2.6	1292.1
1904	1152.2	87.9	117.6	9.0	40.6	3.1	1310.4
1905	1233.5	88.4	116.9	8.4	42.0	3.2	1394.6
1906	1358.2	88.4	131.6	8.5	45.8	3.1	1535.6
1907	1631.1	88.4	121.7	6.6	90.7	5.0	1843.5
1908	1463.7	89.2	122.1	7.5	54.1	3.3	1639.9
1909	1593.6	89.2	134.6	7.6	58.2	3.2	1786.7
1910	1771.3	89.5	146.8	7.4	61.9	3.1	1980.0
1911	1707.5	88.6	152.4	7.9	66.8	3.5	1926.7
1912	1781.3	89.4	146.2	7.3	65.2	3.3	1992.9
1913	2406.4	90.1	176.0	6.6	87.9	3.3	2670.3

Source: P.-C. Witt, *Die Finanzpolitik des Deutschen Reiches von 1903 bis 1913* (Lubeck, 1970).

- the 1873 *Dreikaiserbund*: or Three Emperors League: an agreement by Germany, Austria and Russia to resist revolutionary threats to the map of Europe. Initially it was designed as much allay Austro-Russian distrust as to isolate France
- a series of German 'threats' against France in 1875 when it seemed that France was recovering rapidly from defeat and might seek revenge. This incident showed Bismarck that he must act with care, because other Powers expressed their concern that Germany might initiate military action
- the 1879 Dual Alliance with Austria-Hungary. Bismarck tried to deflect international tension, especially between Austria and Russia, during the Near Eastern crisis resolved at the 1878 Berlin Congress. But Bismarck felt committed to forming an alliance with Austria, without getting Austria's support against France
- in an attempt to keep Russia within the fold, Germany signed a renewed version of the Three Emperors' Alliance in 1881 – without solving the problem of Russia's growing estrangement from its former allies
- the 1882 Triple Alliance: Italy was added to the Dual Alliance without significantly increasing German security
- the 1887 Reinsurance Treaty: a last attempt by Bismarck to keep Russia friendly without alarming Austria.

Ultimately Bismarck's foreign policy was a failure, and was probably bound to be so. It was really based upon the proposition that France would be permanently isolated in diplomatic terms, and this was never likely. Austro-Russian rivalry, especially in the Balkans, meant that international tensions were never far beneath the surface. Consequently whilst some historians, especially from earlier generations, praised Bismarck for statesmanship, moderation and skill on the European stage, others have been less charitable. Some have suggested that peace was more due to the moderation and caution of others than Bismarck, and that he had no clear-cut strategy at all. Fundamentally, if Bismarck's policy did rest essentially on the isolation of France, it was always likely to fail in the long-run, particularly since little was done to eliminate the basic causes of suspicion and antagonism between Austria and Russia, and therefore the possibility of either of them allying with France was always a strong one.

B *Bismarck and colonies*

Bismarck had never expressed an interest in acquiring overseas colonies, but appeared to have been suddenly converted in 1884–5 when Germany gained the Cameroons, Togo, South West Africa and East Africa. His reasons have been variously analysed as carefully thought-out or opportunistic. Possible reasons for his change of heart were:

KEY ISSUE

Why did Bismarck pursue a colonial policy?

● Bismarck was bowing to powerful pressure groups at home, demanding colonies for economic reasons and as a matter of national pride. This is the argument of some historians such as Craig
● to divert attention from difficult issues at home and assist social stability – the argument of historians such as Wehler.

Bismarck soon lost interest in the colonies when they did not prove profitable, but rather became an administrative and financial burden on Germany.

C *Weltpolitik*

There was a clear sea-change in German foreign policy after Bismarck, and Germany's international position steadily declined for two principal reasons:

See page 416

● French reconciliation with Russia, culminating in the 1894 alliance which ended France's isolation – which in turn had been the cornerstone of Bismarck's policy
● growing antagonism with Britain. This eventually pushed Britain into the French and Russian camps, producing two large, hostile alliances in Europe.

The first development was probably inevitable and was already occurring during Bismarck's chancellorship, and therefore it would be simplistic to view German foreign policy going into a dramatic decline after Bismarck. The second development was largely due to the unpredictable and provocative *Weltpolitik* of Wilhelm II. This was a vague concept, a mishmash of ideas of European domination, colonial expansion, nationalist expansion, and even the notion of earning respect as a Great Power. Historians such as Fischer have argued that by embarking on this policy in 1897, Germany was in fact seeking to establish world hegemony. The counter-argument is that, if this were the case, the policy was remarkably incoherent and uncoordinated for such an ambitious one. Hence the more moderate assessment is that, far from being a grandiose attempt at expansionism, German foreign policy was the product of a somewhat vague feeling that Germany, as a new Power, had been unfairly left behind in the colonial and prestige stakes, and was made to feel an inferiority complex by long-established Powers like Britain.

Whatever *Weltpolitik* did mean precisely, it was unsettling, largely due to *Kaiser* Wilhelm II's behaviour. It involved Germany in unnecessary confrontations with France and Britain over the Moroccan crisis, and an ultimately fatal commitment to Austria during the Balkan crisis of 1908.

It led Germany into a 'naval race' with Britain which Britain could not lose: Germany, with a large army also to maintain, increased its naval spending by 105 per cent between 1905 and 1914; in the same period, whilst staying ahead, Britain increased its naval spending by only 28 per cent. A few extra colonial gains like Kiaochow from China in 1897, some Pacific islands in 1899 and part of the French Congo in 1911, did not compensate for Germany's increasingly isolated position. This position, and Germany's growing awareness of it, has led some historians to accuse the *Kaiser's* Government of deliberately manufacturing a war crisis in 1914 to enable Germany to break out of 'encirclement' whilst there was still time. If so, it was a fairly rapid development. Even in 1911 when Germany provoked the Agadir crisis in Morocco, it backed down when there seemed a real risk of war. Historians of the Fischer school argue that German humiliation was such that in 1911 Germany became committed to eventual war; that Germany was concerned that its ally Austria was increasingly threatened by a resurgent Serbia; and that Germany was in danger of being dragged into a Balkan conflict with Russia.

Because war plans existed by 1914, including the notorious Schlieffen Plan which assumed a two-front war with both Russia and France, some have argued that the German generals were pushing for a preventive war, believing that it was better to come sooner than later, and that this affected German behaviour in the crisis of 1914. Most historians accept that Germany bears some of the responsibility for the escalation into war, but there is no unanimity as to the exact degree of responsibility or even whether Germany was the prime culprit.

> **KEY ISSUE**
>
> *What was* Weltpolitik *and what was its significance?*

See pages 445–6

> **KEY ISSUE**
>
> *What responsibility does Germany bear for World War I?*

L'ENFANT TERRIBLE!

CHORUS IN THE STERN. "DON'T GO ON LIKE THAT—OR YOU'LL UPSET US ALL!!"

PICTURE 28 *Wilhelm II was an unsettling influence in international relations*

4 ～ SUMMARY: GERMANY 1871–1914

Kaiser Wilhelm II's Germany of 1914 was different in several ways from Bismarck's Germany of 1871–90:

● Germany was more powerful militarily and had the second greatest navy in the world
● Germany was the greatest economic power on the continent
● Germany's domestic and foreign policies were led much less effectively by the Kaiser and a succession of Chancellors than had been the case under Bismarck
● there had been advances in living and working conditions, but also some social tensions
● there was a growing belief in German ruling circles that Germany was the greatest European Power by right
● despite political strains and conflicts, Germany had developed a more mature parliamentary system, and a more complex, modern society.

Most of the gains that had occurred were shattered by World War I. Although a brief experiment with democratic government followed in the 1920s, Germany then experienced a more sinister authoritarian regime in the shape of Nazism.

5 ⌐ BIBLIOGRAPHY

There are several useful books on this period of German history. Two books in the Longmans *Seminar Studies* series, *Bismarck and Germany 1862–1890* by D. Williamson (Longman, 1986) and *Imperial Germany 1890–1918* by I. Porter and I. Armour (Longman, 1991) provide extensive analyses plus some documents. The latter part of *The Unification of Germany 1815–1890* by A. Stiles (Hodder and Stoughton *Access to History*, 1989) covers the Bismarck period; and *From Bismarck to Hitler: Germany 1890–1933* by G. Layton (Hodder and Stoughton *Access to History*, 1995) covers the period from 1890. Both books include advice on note-making and essays. A variety of sources, along with analyses and exercises, will be found in *Imperial and Weimar Germany 1890–1933* by J. Laver (Hodder and Stoughton, 1992). *The Second Reich* by W. Simpson (Cambridge University Press, 1995) contains a lot of documents. *Bismarck* by B. Waller (Historical Association, Blackwell, 1985) is a brief biography. Also useful is *Bismarck* by E. Crankshaw (Macmillan, 1981). *The Kaiser and his Court* by J. Rohl (Cambridge, 1994) is a detailed biography. *Germany in the Age of Kaiser Wilhelm II* by J. Retallack (Macmillan, 1996) is a useful survey of different interpretations. *The German Empire, 1871–1918* by H.-U. Wehler (Berg Publishers, 1985) is not easy but is an important German contribution, as is *Germany Without Bismarck: The Crisis of Government in the Second Reich* by J. Rohl (Batsford, 1967). Various political, economic, social and cultural perspectives are covered in detail in *Imperial Germany 1871–1914* by V. Berghahn (Berghahn Books, 1994). In foreign policy, the most accessible introduction to Fritz Fischer's ideas is his *From Kaiserreich to Third Reich* (Unwin Hyman, 1986). A detailed study of foreign policy is *Germany and the Approach of War* by R. Berghahn (Macmillan, 1993).

6 ⌐ STRUCTURED QUESTIONS AND ESSAYS

1. (a) Outline the main features of the Constitution established in Germany in 1871; (10 marks)
   (b) Why was Bismarck able to keep himself in power for so long after 1871? (15 marks)
2. (a) Describe the fortunes of any **two** of the following political parties in Germany 1871–1914: National Liberals, Centre Party; Social Democrats; (10 marks)
   (b) How do you account for any changes in their situation between the beginning and the end of this period? (15 marks)
3. Why, and with what success, did Bismarck take on the forces of Roman Catholicism and Socialism in the German Empire? (25 marks)
4. (a) Outline the main features of Bismarck's domestic policy 1871–90; (10 marks)

(b) To what extent was his domestic policy consistent? (15 marks)

5. Why was Bismarck successful for so long in German politics after 1871, and why did he eventually lose power? (25 marks)

6. (a) Outline the main developments in German domestic politics between 1890 and 1914; (10 marks)

   (b) To what extent did Wilhelm II bring a new direction to German domestic politics in this period? (15 marks)

7. (a) Outline the main developments in the German economy 1871–1914; (10 marks)

   (b) Why was Germany able to become the dominant economic power in Europe during this period? (15 marks)

8. 'Bismarck's achievements have been overestimated.' How valid is this assessment in relation to **either** Bismarck's domestic policy **or** foreign policy? (25 marks)

9. (a) Outline Bismarck's dealings with Austria and Russia in the period 1871–90; (10 marks)

   (b) How successful was Bismarck's foreign policy? (15 marks)

10. (a) What was *Weltpolitik*? (10 marks)

    (b) Why did Kaiser Wilhelm II embark on an ambitious foreign policy? (15 marks)

11. (a) Outline Germany's role in the Moroccan crises before World War I; (10 marks)

    (b) To what extent did German foreign policy contribute to the outbreak of World War I? (15 marks)

7 ⌐ DOCUMENTARY EXERCISE ON GOVERNMENT IN THE GERMAN EMPIRE, 1871–1914

Study the following collection of Sources A–E and answer the questions which follow:

> In my [Bülow's] presence and in the bosom of the family, he expressed some violent opinions of his domestic enemies. He did not want in the least to govern autocratically, he said, although the reproach was daily levelled against him. Real autocracy would be very different from the present government in Germany. He was perfectly well aware that, in Germany, in the second half of the nineteenth century, absolutism and autocracy would be impossible, apart from the fact that such government had never been one of his ideals. But a parliamentary regime seemed to him just impossible. Our parties possessed neither the patriotism of the French nor the sound common sense of the English. Under the circumstances he did not understand what benefits the German Liberals promised themselves from the 'inauguration of responsible ministries of the realm', which they had lately adopted as part of their programme. As long as he remained in office

he would never countenance such a thing. Considering the political incapacity of the average German, the intellectual parliamentary system would lead to conditions such as had prevailed in 1848, that is to say, to weakness and incompetence on the top, and to bumptiousness and ever new demands from below.

SOURCE A:
BISMARCK'S VIEWS OF POLITICAL PARTIES
From the Memoirs of Prince von Bülow, *a professional diplomat between 1873 and 1898 before becoming Foreign Minister and then Chancellor*

By and large, Prince Bismarck represents for me the incarnation of the state. I do not always like his methods. Sometimes – I have in mind particularly universal and equal suffrage – he has gone too far in the direction of liberalism for my taste, at other times he has regrettable tendencies towards conservatism, at yet other times he encourages interest-group politics which appeals to egoism and therefore slights the nobler motives in political life and must have a confusing and even corrupting effect. But in the face of all this I remind myself that nobody else has such a lively regard for the idea of making the young empire vital, permanent and resilient, and that he is untiringly and successfully at work to realise this ideal with sensible realism according to circumstances.

SOURCE B:
THE VIEWS OF A NATIONAL LIBERAL
The notes for a speech in February 1881, by Rudolf Haym, an historian and National Liberal deputy in the Reichstag

What is at stake is the defence of the state, it is a matter of delimiting the scope of domination of priests and kings, and this limitation must be drawn so that the state can maintain itself, for in the realm of this world the state has the paramount power ... If this programme had been realised we would therefore have had, instead of the unitary Prussian state, instead of the German Empire which was in the course of development, two political organisms running in parallel: one with its general staff in the Centre Party, the other with its general staff in the government and person of His majesty the Emperor. This situation was a totally unacceptable one for the government; and it was its duty to defend the state against this danger.

SOURCE C:
BISMARCK AND THE CATHOLICS
A speech by Bismarck in the Prussian Landtag, 10 March 1873

(i) The French axiom that 'the King rules but does not govern' is basically false and revolutionary. I do not wish to rule in a merely nominal way and I will not do so, but instead intend to be the actual sovereign of my people.

A letter from Wilhelm II to Tsar Nicholas II of Russia, 25 October 1895

(ii) Democratic principles can only create weak and often corrupt pillars of society. A society is only strong if it recognises the fact of natural superiorities, in particular that of birth.

The Kaiser, quoted in the Boston Transcript, 1882

SOURCE D:
KAISER WILHELM II'S VIEWS ON GOVERNING
Extracts from letters and reports

(iii) Public opinion didn't concern him. He knew that people didn't love him, and cursed him; but that wouldn't deter him. I then reminded the Emperor of the difference between Prussia and the Empire; said that in Prussia he had old rights which continued to exist, so far as the Prussian Constitution had not limited them. In the Empire the Emperor had only the rights which the Reichstag conceded to him. The Emperor interjected 'the Emperor hardly has any rights', which I attempted to refute. Besides, this was quite unimportant, said HM: the South German democratic states didn't worry him. He had 18 army corps and would make short work of the South Germans.

Report by Hohenlohe, March 1897

(iv) The soldier and the army, not parliamentary majorities and decisions, have welded the German Empire together. I put my trust in the army.

Speech by the Kaiser 18 April 1891

(v) You recruits have sworn loyalty to me. You have only one enemy and that is my enemy. In the present social confusion it may come about that I order you to shoot down your own relatives, brothers or parents but even then you must follow my orders without a murmur.

Speech by the Kaiser 23 November 1891

**SOURCE E:
AN AMERICAN ASSESS-
MENT OF THE KAISER**
*Letter by Theodore Roosevelt to
Sir G. Trevelyan, 1 October
1911*

Down at the bottom of his heart, the Kaiser knew perfectly well that he himself was not an absolute sovereign. He had never had a chance to try ... on the contrary, when Germany made up its mind to go in a given direction, he could only stay at the head of affairs by scampering to take the lead in going in that direction. Down at the bottom he realised this and he also knew that even this rather shorn power which he possessed was not shared by the great majority of his fellow-sovereigns. But together with this underlying consciousness of the real facts of the situation went a curious make-believe to himself that each sovereign did represent his country in the sense that would have been true two or three centuries ago.

Q

1. *Summarise Bismarck's views on government as revealed in Sources A and C. (6 marks)*
2. *Compare and contrast Bismarck's views on government with those of Kaiser Wilhelm II in Source D. (7 marks)*
3. *To what extent does the author of Source B admire or dislike Bismarck's political methods and attitudes? How can you account for the author's views? (7 marks)*
4. *(i) How accurate and reliable were the Kaiser's views of his powers as revealed in Source D? (6 marks)*
   (ii) How accurate was Roosevelt's view of the Kaiser in Source E? (6 marks)
5. *Assess the uses and limitations of Sources B and E as evidence for an understanding of the nature of German government during the Second Reich. (6 marks)*
6. *'Germany under the Second Reich was a constitutional state, but not a parliamentary or a democratic one.' Using this collection of Sources A–E, and your own knowledge, assess the validity of this statement. (12 marks)*

8 ⌐ USING STATISTICS

Statistics can be a valuable source of evidence for historians, provided that they are used with care. Clearly it is important to establish their accuracy and reliability.

Look at the collection of statistics on pages 302–5, covering a range of political, economic and social aspects of the Second *Reich*. Consider what information can be gleaned from them, what are their uses and limitations as evidence, and what they can add overall to our understanding of Germany in this period.

Italy
1870–1914

INTRODUCTION

FROM UNIFICATION TO WORLD WAR

Despite the proclamation of the Italian State in 1861, 'Italy' was far from being a united country. Venetia and Rome were brought under Italian rule during the next decade, but other areas claimed by the Italians remained under Habsburg rule. There were great differences in wealth, culture and tradition within the Italian peninsula, particularly between North and South, and these differences remained throughout the period of this book. In what had been the Papal States and the Kingdom of the Two Sicilies, poor agricultural land and a lack of industry contributed to poverty and a poor peasantry unable to pay taxes. There was little enthusiasm for unification in these regions. The North contained fertile farming land and more industry, but even here many people lived at subsistence level and there was no meaningful concept of 'Italianness'. Italy remained an artificial creation. Some of the problems evident in 1861 were even magnified during the next half century. The new State wanted Great Power status but, as Bismarck observed, Italy had 'a large appetite and poor teeth' in comparison with neighbouring, more established Powers. For much of the period Italian politics was regarded as corrupt and not relevant by much of the population. This was particularly true of those Catholics who were told to have nothing to do with a State which had deprived the papacy of its territory in Italy. Lack of stability and Great Power clout hindered Italy's military performance when it eventually entered World War I in 1915.

See page 86

1 ～ POLITICAL HISTORY

A *The problems of unification*

Modern Italy became more or less complete in 1870 when Rome became part of the nation. However, the reality of unification was that Italy faced serious problems from the beginning, chief among them:

● many Italians resented the new central Government, which threatened to interfere with established practices and imposed new taxes and laws. Most Italians had not taken part in the struggle for unification, and did not see it as their affair

MAP 13 *Italy in 1890*

- many Italians lived in the *Italia Irredenta*, the unredeemed territories, such as the Tyrol, Trentino and Istria, all part of the Habsburg Empire
- Pope Pius IX told Catholics not to recognise the Italian State which had deprived the papacy of its lands in Italy, despite the 1871 Law of Guarantees which offered the Pope a privileged position in the Vatican, which would be owned by the State. The papal policy of non-recognition was continued by his successor Leo XIII (1878–1903). Committed Catholics played no part in political life
- economic problems – poverty, unemployment, low wages, a relatively undeveloped economic sector generally – helped increase instability, as did widespread crime in the South
- many Italians could not vote, had little interest in national politics, and certainly had nothing in common with the Liberal politicians who governed from Rome

TIMELINE

(Foreign affairs in italics)

1861	Formation of Kingdom of Italy
1870	Rome incorporated into Italy
1871	Pope rejected new Italian State
1874	Pope forbade Catholics to participate in political life
1876	Liberals came to power
1877	Primary education made compulsory
1878	Umberto I succeeded Victor Emmanuel II
	Pope Leo XIII succeeded Pius IX
	Tariff war against France begun
1882	Franchise extended
	Italy joined Triple Alliance
	Depretis announced 'Trasformismo'
1885	*Italy occupied Massawa*
1886	Reform of working conditions for children
1887	*Triple Alliance renewed*
	Mediterranean Agreements
1890	*Eritrea declared an Italian colony*
1893	Crispi Prime Minister
1895	Italian Socialist Party formed
	Socialist newspaper 'Avanti' published
1896	*Italians defeated at Adowa in Ethiopia*
	Fall of Crispi
	Franco-Italian Convention
1900	Assassination of Umberto I.
	Accession of Victor Emmanuel III
	Franco-Italian colonial agreement
1903	Death of Leo XIII
1904	General strike
1908	Italian Socialist Party adopted reformist programme
1911	*Invasion of Tripoli (Libya)*
1912	Universal manhood suffrage introduced
1914	General strike and disorder
	Giolitti resigned
	Salandra became Prime Minister
1915	Entry of Italy into World War I

KEY ISSUE

What problems faced the new State of Italy in 1870?

- the lack of a concept of 'Italianness' was emphasised by the fact that in 1870 only about one per cent of the population spoke Italian – the rest spoke regional dialects. There was no compulsory education but there was widespread illiteracy.

B *The Constitution and political practice*

Italy's new Constitution was based upon the Piedmontese–Sardinian model. It was a parliamentary system, with a constitutional monarch, Victor Emmanuel II. He could appoint and dismiss the Prime Minister but otherwise kept out of politics, except when it came to major decisions in foreign affairs. Members of the Senate were appointed by the Government for life. More important than the Senate was the Chamber of Deputies, elected every five years. The deputies came mostly from a middle-class professional or landed background and generally held similar views. Whilst wanting to cement unification and believing in progress they were also conservative by temperament. They doubted whether the majority of the population was politically mature enough to be given a major say in determining its future – hence the limited franchise. The Liberals had other concerns also:

● they distrusted Radicals and Republicans on the Left, who might exert a dangerous influence over the politically uneducated peasants and workers
● they distrusted the Catholic Church, because it would not recognise the new Italian State.

Prime Ministers needed support in parliament in order to govern. Unfortunately there was no clearly-defined party system. Politicians formed factions around prominent individuals, but they might change their allegiance and stance towards the Government of the day at any time. Political practice bore similarities to France under the Third Republic. Government defeats did not necessarily result in a general election. Between 1870 and 1922 there were 22 changes of Prime Minister, and individual politicians spent much of their political life bargaining or even bribing in order to fashion a Government with a working majority. This situation was probably inevitable because:

● parties were not well organised
● a property qualification restricted the franchise to a small percentage of the population, and consequently the opportunities for patronage and bribery were all the greater and more tempting.

The franchise was restricted to about 600 000 voters until 1882 when it was extended to two million, male voters over 21 being required to pay taxes of 19 lire and pass a literacy test. The requirements were relaxed in 1912 to extend the electorate to 8.6 million – still less than 25 per cent of the population. The Government used the Prefects in charge of Italy's 69 provinces to manipulate election results through bribery and other methods. According to Mussolini's father, 50 cows were registered by name to vote in one constituency.

No politician of Cavour's stature came forward for some time, and political leaders found it difficult to command support throughout the country. Prime Ministers Ricasoli and Farini helped to begin the process of unifying institutions and developing the economy in the 1870s, but succeeding Governments were as much concerned with extending Italian influence abroad as carrying out reforms at home.

> **KEY ISSUE**
>
> *What were the key features of Italy's Constitution?*

C *Depretis and Trasformismo 1876–87*

Between 1870 and 1876 the Right was the most influential political grouping. Governments concentrated on trying to restore order in the South and balance the budget. However, in 1876 Tuscan deputies, angered by the decision to make Rome rather than Florence the national capital, brought down the Government. The Liberal Agostino

1881	Agostino Depretis
1887	Francesco Crispi
1891	Antonio di Rudini
1892	Giovanni Giolitti
1893	Francesco Crispi
1896	Antonio di Rudini
1898	Luigi Pelloux
1900	Giuseppe Saracco
1901	Giuseppe Zanardelli
1903	Giovanni Giolitti
1905	Alessandro Fortis
1906	Sidney Sonnino
1906	Giovanni Giolitti
1909	Sidney Sonnino
1910	Luigi Luzzatti
1911	Giovanni Giolitti
1914	Antonio Salandra

TABLE 19

*Italy's Prime Ministers
1880–1914*

Depretis came to power and dominated politics for the next ten years. His policy of *Trasformismo* meant building consensus in Italy by appealing to all Italians except those of the extreme Left and Right. In his phrase, 'we will accept the help of all honest men,' whilst carrying out moderate reform:

- free, compulsory primary education was introduced in 1877
- the tax on bread was reduced, to help the poor
- the franchise was extended fourfold in 1882 to 2 million, although the literacy qualification still excluded most peasants.

Depretis benefited from an industrial boom in the early 1880s but was criticised for his modest foreign policy and lack of further reform at home. His Government was seen as too cautious and concerned for consensus.

D *Crispi 1887–96*

Depretis died in 1887. His successor was his critic the Sicilian Francesco Crispi, Prime Minister between 1887 and 1891 and 1893 and 1896, and simultaneously Foreign Minister and Minister of the Interior. He was unfortunate in coming to power as an economic boom was ending. Crispi had once been a revolutionary supporter of Garibaldi; now he was more moderate, regarding himself as the Italian Bismarck, but without a specific programme. He responded to pressures for protection created by Northern industrialists and Southern landowners, raising tariffs in 1887 in order to protect Italy against foreign competition, but this meant higher prices for the poor. In 1894 Sicily was put under martial law following riots by Sicilian workers, upset by harvest failures and the effects of tariffs. Crispi suspended parliament for six months to prevent criticism there of his policies. For all his self-confidence, Crispi's reputation was fatally damaged in three particular respects:

- there were revelations in 1893 that banks had been lending money interest-free to politicians in return for favours. Politicians accused of corruption included Crispi himself and Giolitti
- the failure of his colonial policy in Africa
- Crispi did not manage to come to terms with increased Socialist activity on the Left. His only answer was the traditional Italian one of trying to manipulate elections, ban Socialist groups and resort to other authoritarian practices judged necessary to control Italians who were not yet ready to be good Liberals. Martial law was declared in Sicily.

> **KEY ISSUE**
>
> *How successful were the ministries of Depretis and Crispi?*

E *Giolitti and reconciliation*

ORDER AND REFORM

After Crispi's fall internal violence and repression increased, in response to nationwide riots after the poor harvest of 1897 and rises in prices. At least 80 rioters were killed by the army in riots in Milan and there was martial law in 30 provinces. The Government believed that Socialists were orchestrating the discontent and many were jailed. The army was preoccupied in maintaining internal order. The Government lost support for its apparent failure to maintain control, and in the 1900 election 200 opposition candidates were elected. In the same year an anarchist assassinated King Umberto I.

The Liberal Giovanni Giolitti became Minister of the Interior in 1901, and Prime Minister in 1903., having already briefly held that office in 1892–3. He dominated the period from 1903–14. He recognised that repression was not the long-term answer to Italy's problems, and was determined to attract people of various persuasions into his Government, including moderate Socialists. He also wanted to keep the Government out of industrial unrest as far as possible, so as not to give the appearance of taking sides. He largely achieved this: although the number of strikes grew in the 1900s, they were mostly economic disputes about wages and working conditions rather than being overtly political. The Government was forced to intervene sometimes, and there were fatal clashes between strikers and police. However, Giolitti's policy bore fruit. After a general strike in 1904, the Government increased its support at the following general election at the expense of the opposition on the Left.

Giolitti's reforms included:

- Government spending on public works such as roads
- improved working conditions
- laws to protect adult workers and prevent children under 12 from working
- a reduction in food taxes
- the franchise was extended
- where local councils approved, religious instruction was permitted in schools, so improving relations with the papacy
- the railway system was nationalised in 1904–5.

MOUNTING PROBLEMS

Giolitti even succeeded in winning the support of some moderate Catholics. However, like Crispi he eventually suffered from unsuccessful involvement in foreign adventures. The Libyan War of 1911 caused the Socialists to leave his Government.

In the 1913 election the Liberals won 318 out of 511 seats. Although Radicals (mostly anti-clerical Liberals) won only 70 seats, and the Socialists 78. The Liberals had to do a deal with the Catholics to ensure a secure majority. Although many Catholics would have nothing to do with politics, the Pope was alarmed by the growth of the Left and in 1905 he gave bishops the right to consider allowing Catholics in their diocese to vote, so politicians began competing for their favours. However, politics were increasingly divided. Extremists on the Left advocated violence. The Right did not approve of Giolitti's wooing of the Liberals. Giolitti never managed to get the Nationalists on board. They became more organised during the 1900s, particularly under the influence of Alfredo Rocco. The Nationalists pushed for a more aggressive foreign policy, a clampdown on strikes at home, more spending on defence and economic protectionism. The Socialists wanted reforms to make welfare conditions more comparable with those of Western Europe, and disliked expenditure on arms and foreign policy. Catholics were divided amongst themselves over the desirability of social reform. Giolitti himself continued to rely upon traditional methods of patronage and manipulation. But his vulnerability was demonstrated in 1914 when the Radicals withdrew from his Government. Italian politics was increasingly polarised. Antonio Salandra formed a Government in March 1914 which moved to the Right.

A general strike in 1914 was held in protest at high taxes. During the 'Red Week' in June 1914 there were strikes and protests in parts of Italy: several towns even declared their independence from the State.

This was dangerous for Italy's fragile democracy. Italy entered World War I increasingly divided: Salandra did not even consult parliament or the army leadership when he made the decision to join the war, and his decision was based as much on his own political ambitions to keep his rival Giolitti out of power as national considerations. The fruits of Italy's political divisions became evident after the war when Italy became a battleground between the forces of Communism and Socialism on the Left and the new Fascist movement on the Right, which eventually triumphed.

> **KEY ISSUE**
>
> *How successful was Giolitti in strengthening Italian democracy and stability?*

2 ↳ ECONOMIC HISTORY

Economic backwardness compared to other European Great Powers was a crucial factor in Italy's difficulty in translating its foreign and imperialist ambitions into effective action. Economic differences between the regions of Italy widened after political unification: the North became more industrialised, whilst the agricultural, malaria-ridden South remained poor and lacked investment by absentee landlords. Agriculture was hampered by infertile soil. Poverty was widespread in the South: many of the peasants had no land and hired themselves out on a day-by-day basis, and had lost old feudal rights. The economy in the South suffered from competition with the North after the 1860s. Sixty per cent of Italy's population worked on the land, although two-thirds of the country was hilly or infertile. The most fertile area was the Northern plains.

Although industrialisation increased in the North, most industry remained on a small scale. The absence of natural resources like coal and iron ore hindered progress, although coal imports doubled between 1879 and 1885. Most industry was domestic and small-scale. The relatively few factories, often producing textiles, were mostly worked by women and children. After 1880 Italian agriculture was hit further by world recession. In contrast, there was an increase in industrial activity, in industries such as iron and steel and the railways, partly

> **KEY ISSUE**
>
> *What economic problems confronted Italy in the late nineteenth century and to what extent were they resolved by 1914?*

TABLE 20
*Some economic and
social statistics*

% of population in agriculture	
1871 – 68%	1913 – 57% (cf. 15% in Britain)

% of population in industry	
1871 – 13%	1913 – 23%

Death rate per 1000 inhabitants	Northern Italy	Southern Italy
1881–5	26.1	29.4
1921–5	16	19.6

Adult illiteracy as % of adult population	Northern Italy	Southern Italy
1871	42.3	88
1911	11	65.3

Emigration from Italy 1870–1920 (in thousands)				
1871–80	1881–90	1891–900	1901–10	1911–20
168	992	1580	3615	2194

Railway mileage open 1840–1913 (in kilometres)				
1840	1860	1880	1900	1913
20	2404	9290	16 429	18 873

because Italy had a low-wage competitive economy. Government subsidies and contracts benefited the railway industry.

Economic problems fed social ones. Governments were reluctant to introduce higher taxes, and in any case prevailing liberal principles discouraged active intervention in the economy. Economic poverty was reflected in social problems such as poor health and a low level of literacy. Working class discontent fuelled the growth of Socialism in the later nineteenth century. Thousands of Italians emigrated each year, hoping for a better life, whilst the *Mafia* prospered in the South. Emigration to the USA alone was running at over 200 000 a year by 1888.

The picture was not uniformly bleak: an economic boom in the 1880s saw significant progress in the iron, steel and engineering industries. However, overall progress was halted by competition from cheaper American grain and textiles from the Far East, which challenged Italy's traditional silk industry. Crispi's response in 1887 was to raise tariffs, but this provoked a trade war with France and led to higher prices for the poor. A crisis of confidence led to the collapse of several banks.

Italian socialism

Politically and economically inspired violence was a feature of Italian life even before unification. Anarchist movements were suppressed with difficulty in the 1870s and 1880s. Then more organised Left wing political movements began to develop. The growth of Socialism was a notable feature of the decades before World War I. It was born out of poor industrial and living conditions and a growing awareness that a large majority of the population was effectively excluded from political life, despite a gradual extension of the franchise. Some Socialists were not prepared to work within the system: they held politics in contempt and saw extra-parliamentary activity as more likely to achieve radical change than a corrupt and narrow political framework. Others were more moderate or 'reformist'.

KEY ISSUE

To what extent was Socialism a major force in Italian politics by 1914?

Italy's trade unions were mostly militantly Socialist and grew in size as large companies like Fiat, founded in 1899, expanded their workforces in the early 1900s. In 1908 the General Confederation of Labour (CGL) was formed to coordinate union activity, but the union movement was divided in its loyalties.

The Socialist movement really took off politically in the 1890s. In 1891 Filippo Turati organised an Italian Workers' Conference. In 1892 his workers' movement split into a minority anarchist-syndicalist group which preached revolutionary strikes as a means of achieving political power; whilst the majority Socialist group worked for reforms within the existing political structure. Its economic programme included the eight hour day and the introduction of income tax. Despite a Government ban on the Socialists in 1894, they got 15 deputies, mostly middle class intellectuals, into parliament in the 1895 general election. In that year the Italian Socialist Party (PSI) was formed. Giolitti's programme of moderate social reform was designed partly to win over Socialists and prevent the growth of their Party.

In 1900 the Left tried to resolve the differences between the revolutionaries and the reformists, those who were prepared to work within the existing political system. The Socialist Party Congress in Rome agreed on a long-term programme and a more moderate short-term one, including universal suffrage and the eight-hour day. Turati was invited to join Giolitti's Government in 1903 but rejected the offer for fear of renewing the split in his Party. Opposing the more moderate leadership were:

- Enrico Ferri, editor of the Socialist newspaper *Avanti* from 1903
- the Syndicalists, who believed in the industrial strike and violence to achieve Socialism and a workers' state. They had some influence in Northern industrial cities and led the general strike of 1904.

PICTURE 29 *Congress of the Italian Socialist Party in Firenza, September 1908. Turati is in the second row from the front, second from the left*

From 1908 the reformists dominated the Party, and their more moderate programme was adopted at the Florence Party Congress in 1908. The leaders, Turati and Bissolati, supported Giolitti, although they again refused to join his Government in 1911. The extreme Left continued to protest – amongst the opposition were those from the South who felt neglected and the fiery young Socialist Benito Mussolini. The Left's revival was marked by its domination of the 1914 Congress in Ancona, followed by a general strike and widespread disorder.

Although Turati declared that 'the emancipation of the proletariat is not to be achieved by outbursts of disorganised mobs', many on the Left remained unreconciled to Italy's political system, conscious that Italian wages, working conditions and welfare benefits were much inferior to those in other Western economies. A sense of economic and political injustice accompanied Italy into World War I and was to continue afterwards.

The economy made much more rapid progress after the mid 1890s. There was a shift towards heavy industry such as engineering, steel and chemicals, although historians debate as to whether this progress was due to technological innovation or the increasingly protectionist policies of the Government. Most of the progress was in the North, and in 1911 almost 60 per cent of Italy's population was still employed in agriculture. Government attempts to help the South by introducing public works and tax concessions were only partially successful: the 1911 census showed that income per head in the South was only half that of the North. There were still major economic problems in 1914.

3 ↩ FOREIGN POLICY

A *European relationships*

Italy, like other States with Great Power pretensions, harboured ambitions to extend its power and influence. However, there were disagreements about whether this should be to the North or overseas, particularly in North Africa, an area with which Italians had historic connections. However, Italy suffered three great disadvantages in trying to extend its influence:

- as a new State, there was little worthwhile territory to exploit outside Europe that was not already within the orbit of other Powers
- lacking a strong industrial and military base, for Italy to compete with established Great Powers was fraught with risks
- it was expensive. Between 1870 and 1913 a quarter of State expenditure went on the army and navy (although the army was as much used for suppressing internal disorder as for protecting national security).

KEY ISSUE

What factors hampered Italy's aspirations to be a Great Power?

See pages 394–5

Italy's weakness was illustrated, for example, by the fact that the Government could do little about the fate of Italians living within the Habsburg Empire, although individual Italian adventurers did stir up trouble in Trieste and the South Tyrol.

Italy needed allies. Ironically, given past conflicts with the Austrians and past friendly associations with Britain and France, Italy joined Germany and Austria-Hungary in the Triple Alliance of 1882. It offered protection to Italy against a French attack: an unlikely prospect, although in 1881 France had annexed Tunis, an area which Italy coveted. Crispi saw a strong foreign policy as essential to his own success and tried to strengthen Italy's links with the Triple Alliance, and also began a tariff war against France. However, once Italian passions over Tunis had cooled, the Triple Alliance had little logic for Italy other than conferring Great Power status. Italy and France swallowed some of their differences in a Convention in 1896 by which Italy recognised the French protectorate over Tunis. A commercial agreement in 1898 ended the tariff war; and in 1900 Italy secretly recognised French ambitions in Morocco in return for recognition of Italian aims in Tripoli. Then in

1902 Italy secretly promised not to become involved in any war which also involved France – effectively making a nonsense of the Triple Alliance.

Italy also maintained good relations with Britain. Italy told its allies that it would not fight Britain, and in the 1887 Mediterranean Agreements Italy joined with Britain and Austria in agreeing to maintain the *status quo* in the Near East, the Straits and the Balkans. In a contradictory action, in 1909 Italy agreed to support Russian plans to open the Straits in return for complicity in Italy's North African ambitions.

Italy's commitment to the Triple Alliance remained lukewarm, and it was little surprise when Italy stayed neutral in 1914 rather than join Germany and Austria-Hungary in World War I. In return for a promise of French and British help in obtaining territory from Austria, Italy joined the Allies in 1915 to fight Austria, which many Italians regarded as their natural enemy. Italy was courted for its support once war had started, but before the war it had not proved a particularly worthwhile ally, being of doubtful strength and prone to making conflicting obligations to different Powers.

KEY ISSUE

In what ways, and why, was Italy not fully committed to the Triple Alliance?

B *Colonial adventures*

Like other 'new' Powers, notably Germany, Italian Governments felt the urge to acquire an overseas empire, for economic reasons but above all for national prestige. But Italy's colonial ventures brought more problems than gains. Depretis's Government joined the scramble for territory in 1885 by seizing Massawa on the Red Sea coast and beginning the building of a great navy. But the first disaster was Crispi's. Italy had already been exploiting Ethiopia, acquired Eritrea in 1890, and began to penetrate the future territory of Italian Somaliland. Crispi supported Menelek, who became sole ruler of Ethiopia in 1899 and signed a treaty with Italy. But Menelek was alarmed at Italian penetration, and confronted Italian troops after the Italian occupation of Tigre Province in 1895. An Italian army invaded Ethiopia from Eritrea. At the battle of Adowa in 1896, 5000 Italians were killed – the first defeat in modern times of a European army by non-European forces. This defeat forced Crispi's resignation and was to rankle with Italy until Mussolini's invasion of Abyssinia (or Ethiopia) in 1935.

Giolitti adopted a forward imperialist policy, partly in response to the demands of extreme Nationalists like Gabriele D'Annunzio. Italy invaded Tripoli (modern-day Libya) in September 1911, having acquired the consent of the other Great Powers. After a difficult and costly campaign Italy acquired its cession from Turkey in 1912. Italy also occupied the Dodecanese islands, including Rhodes, but evacuated them under the Treaty of Ouchy. Italy's victory aroused controversy at home. The venture into colonialism had proved expensive in terms of money and manpower, far from glorious, and helped to confirm the shallowness of Italy's pretensions to be a Great Power.

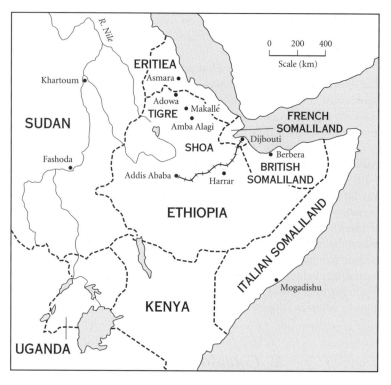

MAP 14   *Italian East Africa*

4 ⤸ BIBLIOGRAPHY

There are few accessible books which deal exclusively with this period of Italian history, But there are useful books which include coverage of the period 1870–1914. Particularly useful for students are *Italy: Liberalism and Fascism 1870–1945* by M. Robson (Hodder and Stoughton, 1992), which includes advice on note-taking and essays, and *Modern Italy 1871–1982* by M. Clark (Longman, 1984). Detailed coverage of this period is in *Italy, A Modern History* by D. Mack Smith (University of Michigan, 1959). *Italy From Liberalism to Fascism: 1870–1925* by C. Seton-Watson (Methuen, 1967) is also useful.

5 ⤸ STRUCTURED QUESTIONS AND ESSAYS

1. (a) Outline the main political and economic problems which faced Italy at the time of its unification; (10 marks)
   (b) To what extent were these problems overcome in the years before World War I? (15 marks)
2. (a) Outline the domestic policies of Crispi and Giolitti; (10 marks)

(b) To what extent did they achieve stability in Italian political life? (15 marks)

3. To what extent did the Catholic Church and Socialism cause problems to the Italian State between 1870 and 1914? (25 marks)

4. 'Politically weak and economically immature'. How valid is this assessment of Italy in the period 1870 to 1914? (25 marks)

5. (a) Outline the main features of Italian foreign and colonial policy during the period 1870–1914; (10 marks)

   (b) How true is it to say that Italy 'failed to achieve Great Power status in the 25 years before World War I'? (15 marks)

6 ⌐ INTERPRETING PHOTOGRAPHS: A PHOTOGRAPHIC EXERCISE ON LIFE IN ITALY AT THE TURN OF THE TWENTIETH CENTURY

Photographs can be a useful source of evidence for a student of modern history. They can show details of everyday life and also of significant individuals and events, or at least a moment of time during those events. Although photographs have been around for a long time, they can still be effective in recreating atmosphere or capturing a particular moment not always as evident in moving film or other sources. In so doing, they can bring us as close as possible to an event which we did not experience directly ourselves.

Nevertheless, like all forms of evidence available to historians, photographs have to be treated with care. Photographs may be posed or actually faked in order to achieve a desired effect. Even 'everyday' photographs not taken with an ulterior motive in mind need careful consideration if they are to be of use to an historian. Various questions should be asked of the photograph: apart from the content, which may or may not be obvious, what were the motives of the photographer? To what use might the photograph have been put? How valuable is the photograph as evidence?

Ask yourselves these specific questions about the photographs which follow:

1. What does each photograph actually show (obviously the captions will be of help here)? Is there any reason to doubt its authenticity?

2. Is it likely that the photograph was taken for a particular purpose? For information? For propaganda? For other reasons?

3. Is the photograph reliable as evidence? Reliable for what?

4. How might the photograph or series of photographs affect our interpretation of events? Can we learn anything of significance from this evidence?

5. What are the uses and limitations of the photograph as evidence?

Do ensure that you relate your analysis to the context of the particular photograph, and avoid making generalised comments about the value of *any* photograph.

PICTURE 30 *Inside a Milan Labour Exchange, about 1891*

PICTURE 31 *Distribution of bread and flour during the disorders in Bari, 1898*

PICTURE 32 *Dismounted cavalrymen destroying a barricade in Milan, 1898*

PICTURE 34 *Emigrants at Genoa, about 1894*

PICTURE 35 *A schoolroom in Rome in the early twentieth century*

7 ～ AN EXERCISE IN INTERPRETING LIBERAL ITALY: HOW SUCCESSFUL WAS LIBERAL ITALY?

The history of Italy in the period 1870–1914 has sometimes been neglected, falling as it does between the dramatic periods of the *Risorgimento* before 1870 and the rapid rise of Fascism in the 1920s. And yet it was in the period surveyed in this chapter that the new Italian state had to find its feet. Because many of the problems evident at the beginning of the period were not resolved, because Italy's performance as a Great Power and specifically during World War I was not particularly glorious, and because Italy appeared to fall relatively easily to the Fascist movement after 1918, there has sometimes been a tendency to dismiss Liberal Italy as a 'failure'. Is this fair?

'Liberal' historians, sympathetic to the new Italian state and the liberal ideas of many of its politicians, tended to praise the Italian State post-1861, emphasising the achievements of individuals and the ideals of men like Giolitti who tried to unite individuals with a range of political prejudices. Benedetto Croce was a prominent example of such an influential and committed 'Liberal' Italian historian. Other Italian historians included those of Catholic or Nationalist persuasions. Others, often foreign, have sometimes been critical of certain aspects of the new Italian State. For example Denis Mack Smith emphasised the lack of popular support for Liberal Governments, and the fact that politicians with liberal ideas were quite prepared to indulge in electoral manipulation to maintain themselves in power. Certainly the 'pessimists' appear to have a strong case. Italy's attempts to demonstrate Great Power status were not convincing: the colonial adventure in Abyssinia ended in humiliation, and Italy was not regarded as being in the first rank of Great Powers in Europe. At home, although there was economic progress, it was uneven and the South lagged seriously behind. In political life, more and more Italians were drawn into the political process, and 'Italy' became something more tangible than a name; but there were large sections of society on the Right and Left which were discontented with the system, and Governments rarely felt secure. Whilst Giolitti was commended in some quarters for attempting to unite different factions, others condemned him for cynical 'political fixing'. On the other hand, Liberal Italy could not realistically be blamed for not solving all the problems that faced a divided new State in 1870. Whilst Liberalism was killed off in the 1920s for more than a generation to come, Italy was not the only country to succumb at this time to Right-wing extremism, and World War I, exacerbating as it did the problems outlined above, had much to do with the collapse of Italy's fragile democracy in the following years.

Study Sources A–D and answer the questions which follow:

SOURCE A

From a letter by Mazzini in 1871

The Italy which we represent today is a living lie ... Italians are now a vassal people; a narrow franchise means that we are governed by a few rich men who are powerless for good. Our army is not popularly based and is used for internal repression. Rights of the press and free association are fettered and a corrupt political system is bringing a slow but growing financial collapse.

SOURCE B

The Italian Communist Antonio Gramsci, writing after World War I

The leaders of the Risorgimento said they were aiming at the creation of a modern state in Italy, and they in fact produced a bastard. They aimed at stimulating the formation of an extensive and energetic ruling class and they did not succeed; at integrating the people into the framework of the new state, and they did not succeed. The paltry political life from 1870 to 1900, the fundamental rebelliousness of the Italian popular classes, the narrow existence of a cowardly ruling stratum, they are all consequences of that failure.

SOURCE C

Vincenzo Morello in 1910 (quoted in P Arcari: La Coscienza Nazionale in Italia, Milan 1911)

In Italy a really extraordinary thing has happened. There is no religious sentiment, yet a clerical party has been set up; there is no class hatred, yet a large Socialist party has been organised; but although there is a mature State, equipped with Army, Navy, Civil Service and Foreign Office, nobody has ever been able to create even the glimmering of a State party. In the struggle for existence, only the State has no membership, no ideology, no strategy, no tactics. Contemporary history is all about the State's enemies; but the State itself does not exist.

SOURCE D

From Garibaldi and the Making of Italy *by the British historian G.M. Trevelyan (1911)*

Nothing is more remarkable – though to believers in nationality and ordered liberty nothing is more natural – than the stability of the Italian Kingdom...The foundations of human liberty and social order exist there on a firm basis. The growing difficulties of the social problem, common to all Europe, find at least mitigation in the free political institutions of a nation so recently created by the common efforts of all classes ... In Italy the traditions of the Risorgimento unite and elevate her children. All classes from the king to the workman, all provinces from Piedmont to Sicily are bound together by these memories of a history so recent yet so poetical and so profound.

1. Summarise the criticisms of the new Italian State made by the authors of Sources A and B. *(6 marks)*
2. To what extent do the authors of Sources C and D agree with these criticisms? *(9 marks)*
3. Which, judging by your own knowledge, is the most accurate of the four interpretations, and in what ways? *(6 marks)*
4. How do you account for any differences of interpretation between the authors of the four sources? *(7 marks)*
5. How useful and reliable is this collection of four sources for an historian studying the successes and failures of Liberal Italy in the period 1870–1914? *(12 marks)*

Russia
1881–1914

THE REIGNS OF ALEXANDER III AND NICHOLAS II

There is sometimes a temptation when studying Russian history between the late nineteenth century and 1914 to analyse the period mainly as a prelude to the Bolshevik Revolution of 1917. Within a few years of that Revolution Russia, or the Soviet Union as it was to become, was radically transformed politically and economically and emerged as a major Power on the world stage. Marxist historians who analysed history in class terms assumed an inevitable transition in society from feudalism (represented by tsarist Russia) to capitalism and then socialism. Marx himself had based his political philosophy on developments in industrialised Western Europe. Russia did not fit this orthodox model of a capitalist economy. Nevertheless, once the Russian Revolution had broken out, Russian Communists accepted Lenin's modification of classical Marxist theory. This allowed for a rapid development from feudalism through state capitalism, by which he meant Soviet control of the economy, to Socialism, thereby justifying the Communists in establishing a ruthless dictatorship in Russia. The kernel of Lenin's argument was that in many respects Russia at the turn of the twentieth century was still a feudal society, with capitalist development in its infancy. However, with a disciplined Marxist party leading the small working class or proletariat, which lacked a developed 'political consciousness' in Marxist terms, Lenin argued that it was possible to compress the period of capitalist development and move much more quickly to a Socialist stage of society than Marx had anticipated. Looking back at Russia's history before 1914 with the benefit of hindsight, Marxist historians then proposed a determinist argument that the Revolution of 1917 was inevitable, something that lay 'in the logic of history'. The question was not **why** there should be a revolution but **when**?

The danger of this approach is that it leads to simplistic interpretations of Russian history in the two generations before 1914. It should be emphasised that in 1914 itself very few Russians, including the revolutionaries themselves, expected a revolution to break out in the near future. The Tsarist regime survived revolutionary disturbances in 1905, following a humiliating defeat in war against Japan. The regime granted a few concessions after 1905, in particular the establishment of a parliament with very limited powers. However, the fundamentals of the autocracy remained. The regime regained most of its confidence, and like the other Great Powers of Europe, entered World War I on a wave of optimism and patriotic fervour. It was Russia's disastrous performance in that war which brought down the Tsarist regime in March 1917 (February by the old Russian calendar). The way was then open for a small group of committed revolutionaries led by Lenin to carry out a *coup* in November 1917 (October by the old calendar), dashing the hopes of non-Marxist radicals and Liberals for a democratic Russia in the wake of Tsarism's collapse.

None of this was 'inevitable'. Events were due to a combination of circumstances and the actions of individuals. Therefore the period of Russian history from 1881 to 1914 is certainly worthy of study in its own right and not just as the prelude to revolution. There were important developments in Russia during this period. Tsars Alexander III and Nicholas II were determined to maintain the principle of autocracy. This meant the continued suppression of opposition to the regime from isolated dissenters and the relatively small revolutionary or terrorist groups dedicated to its overthrow. It also meant continued frustration of the hopes of liberal intellectuals seeking constitutional reform, moderate by Western European standards but viewed as dangerous by the autocracy.

The defeat in war against Japan in 1904–5 did prompt changes: the setting up of a parliament and reforms in the countryside being the most obvious examples. Constitutional Liberals and Marxist revolutionaries continued to be frustrated. However, important social and economic developments were taking place, and they influenced attitudes. Notable developments were industrial expansion and the accompanying growth of an urban working class. An increasing population put more pressure on the land. Meanwhile the Russian Empire consolidated its expansion Eastwards into Asia towards the Pacific. In foreign affairs Russia's commitment to Bismarck's Three Emperors' League weakened as Russian support for pan-Slavism and rivalry with Austria in the Balkans increased. Defeat in war against Japan focussed Russia's attention firmly on Europe again. Russia played a crucial role in the events leading to World War I.

There had long been a pulling in different directions in Russian history between inward-looking isolationism and a desire to extend links with Europe in the West. Those influences were still in opposition, but for the immediate future, Russia was very much at the centre of European affairs.

1 ⌐ POLITICAL HISTORY

A *Alexander III and Pobedonostsev*

The assassination of Alexander II in 1881 shocked the Russian Empire and had a profound effect upon the next two rulers. The dead Tsar's son, Alexander III, was even more determined to maintain the autocracy.

Alexander II's grandson, the future Nicholas II, was only a child when he witnessed the bloody assassination, and the experience accentuated his own reluctance to assume the crown in 1894.

Alexander III had no intention of continuing the reforms of his father. Instead he took his inspiration from Nicholas I's belief in autocracy and orthodoxy as the pillars of government. Ironically, the assassination set the hopes of radicals back for more than a generation. A 'state of emergency' was declared, suspending the normal rule of law, and this was to last for years in many provinces. Under the 1881 Act Concerning Measures for the Protection of State Security and the Social Order, special courts were set up and the Government reserved the right to remove elected officials and to arrest critics. A new secret police, the *Okhrana*, was created. Ideas of democracy and socialism were more suspect to the Government than ever before.

The new Tsar had been tutored from 1861 by Konstantin Pobedonostsev, created Director of the Holy Synod in 1880. Pobedonostsev was a strong advocate of divine-right, absolute monarchy. He was also fiercely nationalistic, suspicious of Western influences and deeply anti-semitic. He called democracy 'the greatest falsehood of our time', believing that

TIMELINE

Events in Russia 1881–1914 (foreign affairs are in italics)

1881	Accession of Alexander III
1882	Restrictive press laws introduced
1884	Universities lost their autonomy
1887	Lenin's brother involved in assassination attempt against Alexander III
1891	Construction of Trans-Siberian railway began
	Beginning of severe famine in Russia
1892	Witte appointed Minister of Finance
1894	*Defensive Franco-Russian alliance signed*
	Accession of Nicholas II
1898	Formation of Social Democratic Labour Party
1901	Formation of Socialist Revolutionary Party
1903	Social Democratic Party split into Bolshevik and Menshevik factions
1904	*Outbreak of Russo-Japanese War*
1905	Bloody Sunday in St Petersburg
	Potemkin mutiny
	War ended by Treaty of Portsmouth
	Formation of Constitutional Democratic Party (Kadets)
	October Manifesto issued
1906	First Duma met
	Stolypin became Prime Minister
	Beginning of Stolypin's land reforms
1907	Second Duma met
	Election of Third Duma
	Anglo-Russian Entente signed
1911	Assassination of Stolypin
1912	Lena goldfields massacre
1913	Election of Fourth Duma
1914	Germany declared war on Russia

KONSTANTIN POBEDONOSTSEV

Pobedonostsev's reactionary views can be seen from these letters he wrote to Alexander III, before and after he became Tsar.

Ah! to my misfortune, I see about me and hear all those men who at present hold the fortunes of the state in their hands, I cannot express the pity and bitter sadness they arouse. I can see no one who knows what he wants, who desires anything with an ardent spirit, who could resolve to act with a firm will, who sees the truth, who speaks the truth firmly. They are all like eunuchs, rather than men; the best of them vacillate, shrink from danger, are of two minds on everything, and as a result merely talk but do not act; they are divided among themselves, and there is not a single resolute will which would unite and direct them. [May 17, 1879]

Your Imperial Highness.
In the present time of troubles all good Russian men are full of apprehension and sick at heart.
I see a great many people of various rank and station. All the officials and learned men here sicken my heart, as if I were in the company of half-wits or perverted baboons. I hear from all sides that trite, deceitful, and accursed word: constitution. I fear that this word has already made its way into high circles and is taking root. [December 14, 1879]

If they sing to you those old sirens' songs – that you should remain calm, that you must continue on a liberal path, that it is necessary to make concessions to so-called public opinion – oh, for God's sake, do not believe them...This will mean ruin, Russia's ruin and yours, that is as clear as day to me. This will not bring you safety but only lessen it still more. The mad villains who killed your father will not be satisfied by any concession and will only burst into a frenzy. They can be repressed, the evil seed can be uprooted, only by a battle to the death with them, by blood and iron...A new policy must be proclaimed immediately and resolutely. This is just the time to put an end, once and for all, to all talk about freedom of the press, freedom of assembly, and a representative assembly. All this is the deceit of vacuous and flabby men, and it must be spurned for the sake of the integrity and welfare of the people. [March 6, 1881, five days after the assassination of Alexander II]

Q

1. Summarise Pobedonostsev's advice to Alexander III.
2. What evidence do you have that the advice was carried out in Alexander III's reign?

the people needed to be protected against their own wickedness. Pobedonostsev was also convinced that a free press would destroy moral values. He referred to Alexander II's reforms as 'criminal acts', and one of his first deeds in the new reign was to persuade his ex-pupil to reject Loris-Melikov's reform proposals. Pobedonostsev advised Alexander to introduce reactionary legislation and to champion the

KEY ISSUE

What influence did Pobedonostsev have on Alexander III's policies?

Orthodox Church as a buttress of conservatism in education and in society as a whole. Whilst he did not directly determine Government policy, the 'Grand Inquisitor' Pobedonostsev undoubtedly reinforced the already conservative tendencies of Alexander, and also those of the less confident and impressionable Nicholas II in his perceived duty to maintain the autocracy.

B *Reaction and reform*

Alexander III's reign was marked by several measures which reversed the 'liberal' trends of his father:

- qualifications for entry to secondary and higher education were tightened up in order to confine access to the *élite*. In 1884 universities lost rights of self-government granted in 1863. Student organisations were suppressed. By 1904 less than 30 per cent of Russian children of school age received formal schooling
- in 1890 the powers of the *zemstvos* in local government were reduced
- in order to reinforce aristocratic control over rural areas, land captains, usually chosen from the gentry, were appointed in 1889 with extensive powers over the peasantry. These included the right to inflict corporal punishment, and land captains could also overrule the *mir*
- judges lost security of tenure and the Government increasingly interfered in the courts. Justices of the peace were abolished
- censorship was extended
- nationalistic decrees were passed, particularly aimed at Jews. They were denied voting rights and entry to education, and restrictions were placed on their movement. The authorities encouraged or turned a blind eye to vicious *pogroms* against Jewish people and property. Further attempts were made to Russify national groups such as Finns, Ukrainians and Poles. For example, Russian replaced Polish as the language of instruction in Polish provinces, and many Muslim Tartars were forcibly converted to Christian Orthodoxy.

KEY ISSUE

What was the impact of Alexander III's domestic policies?

Not all was reaction. There were some reforms during Alexander III's reign:

- land redemption payments were reduced
- the Peasants' Land Bank was set up in 1883 to provide cheap loans to help peasants buy land
- the employment of women and children in factories was restricted, and a factory inspectorate was created.

However, these limited reforms did not detract from the overall atmosphere of reaction and the determination to enforce autocratic government. A facade of stability was preserved, and revolutionary activity declined, but long-term problems were not addressed. Leon Trotsky wrote that 'Alexander III bequeathed Nicholas II a Revolution.'

C *Nicholas II and reaction*

Alexander III died suddenly and unexpectedly in 1894, thrusting his son Nicholas II into the spotlight. An unwilling Tsar, but forced by the dictates of conscience and duty to assume the role, Nicholas tried to continue his father's political line. Like Alexander, he was influenced by Pobedonostsev, but being a much weaker character, also relied on advisers of varied ability. Nicholas distrusted many of his ministers but was incapable of resolving the disputes and intrigues which affected ministers, advisers and the bureaucracy.

The coronation ceremony was marked by a disaster in which over 1000 subjects were killed in a stampede for gifts. Nicholas of course regretted such incidents but continued repressive policies, reinforced by the advice of his beloved German wife the Empress Alexandra:

- Nicholas rejected requests by *zemstvo* representatives for more say in government. He labelled such requests 'senseless dreams', a phrase given to him by Pobedonostsev
- Alexander III's emergency decrees continued in force. The universities were temporarily closed after student protests and strikes
- **pogroms** against Jews continued, as did Russification. For example, Finland lost its constitutional rights in 1899
- rather than concede reform, the regime adopted repressive tactics such as destroying what remained of local self-government and increasing police activity. For example, it tried to take over leadership of the trade union movement. These policies were particularly associated with Interior Minister Viacheslav Phleve.

> **pogrom** a racially inspired attack

> **KEY ISSUE**
>
> *What was the impact of Nicholas II's domestic policies?*

D *Growing opposition to the regime*

Opposition had been muted after the assassination of Alexander II. However, by the 1890s dissatisfaction with the Government was increasing again, and took varying forms.

LIBERALS AND THE *ZEMSTVOS*

Liberals from the small, educated, professional middle class wanted 'western' style policies that would enable Russia to compete with the Great Powers of Europe. They supported economic development but also admired Western European constitutional Governments which granted political influence to people like themselves. Many Liberals became politicised for the first time in response to the famine of 1891–2, which was ineffectively dealt with by the authorities and led many intellectuals and professional people to question the competence of the regime. Many Liberals were active in the *zemstvos*, which began to debate reformist views. The first annual Congress of *Zemstvos* Presidents was held in 1896, and proposed a national assembly. The second Congress was banned, and Liberals were increasingly dissatisfied by what they regarded as a reactionary Government. A group of intellectuals led by Peter Struve published an illegal newspaper *Liberation* in

1902, and this led to the *Liberation League* of 1903, which proposed constitutional government and civil liberties.

POPULISTS AND MARXISTS

Populist groups had become increasingly diversified in the 1870s and 1880s, but many of their members were still active. Some continued terrorist tactics. Five terrorists, including Lenin's older brother, were hanged in 1887 for being members of a plot to assassinate Alexander III. Others became convinced of the need to 'educate' the Russian people and have more detailed policies. A group called the Emancipation of Labour was founded in 1883 by several ex-Populists, including George Plekhanov, Vera Zasulich and Paul Axelrod. Under Plekhanov's direction, they took a Marxist line, which meant concentrating upon the industrial workforce or proletariat rather than the peasantry as the revolutionary force. Plekhanov believed that Russia would develop according to the same economic and social laws as the rest of Europe. Whilst particular historical phases of development might be shortened, they could not be by-passed altogether. Plekhanov believed that Russian capitalism was creating a potentially revolutionary proletariat, but that a socialist society was still a long way off. Nevertheless for people like Plekhanov, Marxism appealed because it appeared to offer a 'scientific' explanation of social and economic development and a certainty that, however limited Russian industrial development was, it would continue, and that the regime would be unable to control the social consequences which one day would lead to revolution and a just society. 'Scientific Socialism' held out more prospect of success than terror, and its intellectual followers held evening classes and study groups for factory workers, although many of the latter were more interested in achieving better conditions than transforming society.

> **KEY ISSUE**
>
> *What were the aims and motives of the various opposition groups in Nicholas II's Russia?*

There were still Populists who followed a different line. Populism revived in the 1890s following the 1891 famine. Those who still saw the peasantry as the key to revolution formed themselves into the Socialist Revolutionary Party in 1901, led by Victor Chernov. The SRs were not a tightly-knit group, but they did have more support than other left-wing parties. They carried out terrorist acts such as the assassinations of Phleve in 1904 and the Tsar's uncle Grand Duke Sergei, Governor of Moscow, in 1905.

In 1898 in Minsk, a group of Marxists such as those influenced by Plekhanov formed the Russian Social Democratic Party. Although designed to unify Marxists, the Party was immediately engulfed in arguments about whether to work for revolutionary change or accept 'economism', a policy of seeking better working conditions by trade unionism, legal means, or even by supporting the Liberals' constitutional campaign. Such a policy was strongly attacked by Vladimir Ulyanov or Lenin, who believed that a mass political movement of workers was impractical in Russian conditions. Lenin, having qualified as a lawyer, joined a St. Petersburg Marxist group in 1893. He favoured an *élite*, secret party of full-time revolutionaries, to act as a vanguard of the proletariat.

The Marxist view of economic and social development

Marx and his followers assumed a pattern of historical development that in essence had gone through three stages and was destined to progress through two more.

THE FIRST STAGE: PRIMITIVE COMMUNISM
In early times Marx identified a primitive economic system in which there was no organised government or class structure. People scratched a living mainly from the land.

THE SECOND STAGE: FEUDALISM
Class differences had developed, leading to societies dominated by aristocracies and absolute monarchies; the mass of the population were peasants. As trade and commerce expanded, the rising middle class would extract power, or a share of it, in order to further its own economic interests.

THE THIRD STAGE: CAPITALISM
In developing industrial societies the middle classes, particularly represented by industrialists and financial interests, would exercise power, often through parliaments. The majority of the population would be the proletariat or industrial working class. Workers would be deprived of the rightful fruits of their labour in order to maximise the profits of bosses. Eventually workers would develop revolutionary ambitions and overwhelm the rich, but numerically much smaller, ruling class.

THE FOURTH STAGE: SOCIALISM
Workers would take over the state and run it in the interests of their class – the 'dictatorship of the proletariat'. Goods and services would be distributed fairly in a more equal society, and gradually the organs of state, with their repressive functions no longer necessary, would begin to 'wither away'.

THE FIFTH STAGE: COMMUNISM
All would be equal in a community without an organised state power. All would work gladly for the benefit of the community – 'From each according to his ability, to each according to his needs'.

Since late nineteenth century Russia was still a peasant society without a developed industrial base, in classical Marxist terms it was still in the second stage of feudalism, only beginning to emerge into a capitalist stage. One of Lenin's contributions to Marxist thought was the idea that a revolutionary socialist consciousness could still be inculcated in a small proletariat if a disciplined. An *élite* revolutionary party was developed. This party would help to seize power in the name of the workers and institute 'state socialism', rather than wait for capitalist development to take its 'natural' Marxist course.

Doctrinal disputes dogged the small Social Democratic Party. Its second Congress, which opened in Brussels in 1903 but then moved to London to escape police surveillance, was marked by a split. The minority of delegates, or *Mensheviks*, favoured a more open party. Lenin's supporters, the *Bolsheviks* or majority delegates, favoured an *élite* and secret party. The Bolsheviks dominated the Party's Central Committee and the board of *Iskra*, the Party newspaper.

In 1905 the split in the Party became permanent. For a long time both Mensheviks and Bolsheviks remained relatively insignificant: they had limited support and most of their leaders were in prison or exile abroad.

E *The 1905 Revolution*

When Revolution did break out in 1905 it was not due to the activities of Marxists but was the result of growing discontent:

- serious outbreaks of peasant discontent had already occurred in the Southern provinces since 1902. Leading Government minister Sergei Witte was convinced that land reform was necessary, but Nicholas refused. Serious famines had occurred in 1891, 1897, 1898 and 1901
- there was an increasing number of strikes, especially in St Petersburg, where over 100 000 workers had downed tools by January 1905. There were growing demands for reduced hours and higher wages
- Russia's failure in the war against Japan angered Russians. However, the 1905 Revolution was not an organised *coup* against the regime but a series of often loosely-connected events
- on Bloody Sunday, 22 January 1905, thousands of St. Petersburg citizens marched to the Tsar's Winter Palace with a petition calling for reforms, civil liberties and a constitution. The march was led by Father Gapon, a double agent. The Tsar was not at home, but nervous troops opened fire and hundreds were killed. For the first time many Russians lost faith in the Tsar, the 'Little Father'. The author Maxim Gorky wrote 'I believe that this is the beginning of the end of the bloodthirsty Tsar'
- trade unions were formed and were coordinated into a 'Union of Unions'
- the crew of the battleship *Potemkin*, in the Black Sea, mutinied, in protest against poor conditions. Some army regiments also mutinied
- there was a general strike in St. Petersburg and an armed uprising in Moscow
- workers in St. Petersburg elected a *soviet* or council, with Leon Trotsky as its chairman.

KEY ISSUE

What were the causes and significance of the 1905 Revolution?

Although uncoordinated, such a series of events presented a major threat to the regime, particularly since Liberal moderates, revolutionaries, workers, peasants, and some members of the armed forces were all thrown together on the same side, a new phenomenon. Witte advocated a mixture of concessions and repression. For once Nicholas listened. In

October 1905 he issued a manifesto promising individual freedoms and a state parliament or *duma*, both entirely novel in Russian history. However, the Tsar retained most of his powers and kept his financial independence from the *duma*, as he emphasised in his Fundamental Law which he issued after the Revolution.

The promises of reform worked. Moderates were won back to the Tsar's side, and importantly, the bulk of the army remained loyal. The Government moved to arrest the leaders of the *soviet* and suppress further outbreaks of discontent. The revolutionaries for their part had learned something about tactics and organisation, but for the time being the Tsar had emerged relatively unscathed from the crisis. Lenin justified the failed Revolution as a 'dress rehearsal' for the real thing.

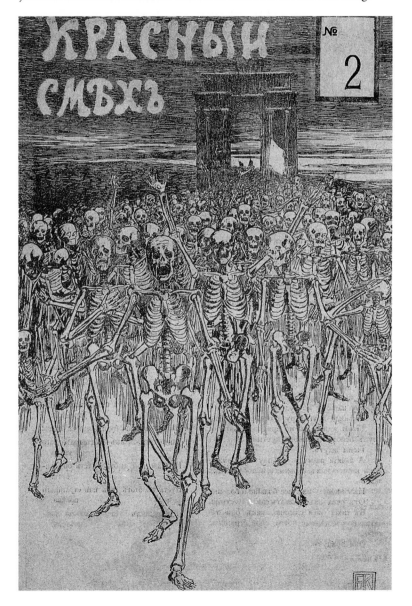

> ### KEY ISSUE
>
> *Why did the 1905 Revolution fail to overthrow the Tsarist regime?*

PICTURE 36 *Cover of a satirical magazine* Red Laughter, *1906, commemorating the first anniversary of* 'Bloody Sunday'

F *Stolypin and the Dumas*

THE *DUMAS*

The new state assembly was announced in May 1906:

● it had two chambers, the Imperial Council and the *duma*
● half the Council was appointed by the Tsar, and the other half by representatives of the wealthier classes
● the *duma* was elected by an electoral college, whose members were chosen according to social class. One member was chosen for every 2000 landowners, but only one for every 90 000 urban workers
● the Council of Ministers remained responsible only to the Tsar.

Nicholas decided to sack Witte, who had advised concessions, and replaced him as chief minister with the conservative Ivan Goremykin. The first *duma* met in May 1906. It contained loose-knit groups rather than political parties, chiefly:

● the **United Nobility**. These were members of the nobility who wanted some reform but also looked to preserve the status of the aristocracy
● the **Octobrists**. These looked to the Tsar's October Manifesto for inspiration. They wanted a constitutional monarchy, supported by a wealthy peasantry, but did not regard themselves as an organised party
● the more radical **Kadets** (Constitutional Democrats). Formed by Paul Milyukov in October 1905, they included *zemstvo* Liberals and radicals seeking universal suffrage, land redistribution to benefit the peasants, self-determination for the nationalities, full civil rights and free and universal primary education. The Kadets were relatively organised, with a network of branches and congresses, although they were never officially recognised because they would not condemn terrorism
● representatives of **national groups**
● a small number of **Social Democrats**, mostly Mensheviks. Other Social Democrats boycotted the elections
● **peasant deputies**. A high proportion of the peasants voted, and peasant deputies played a prominent role in the *duma*.

When the *duma* demanded that ministers be responsible to it, and also demanded reforms such as land redistribution, Nicholas II dissolved it in July. He wrote that 'private property *must* remain inviolable.' In protest at the dissolution. 200 *duma* members, mostly Kadets, crossed into Finland and issued the Viborg Manifesto, calling for reforms.

In February 1907 the second *duma* met. It contained 50 Social Democrats. Although the Kadets decided to cooperate with the Government, other deputies pressed for reform, so the *duma* was dissolved after three months.

The Tsar (illegally) manipulated the ensuing elections, increasing the representation of large landowners at the expense of workers and the

KEY ISSUE

To what extent were the dumas a successful experiment?

national minorities. The resulting third *duma*, which met from 1907 to 1912, was much more compliant, as was the fourth, which met from 1912 to 1917. These *dumas* had conservative majorities, and in any case, had too little power to seriously embarrass the Tsarist regime.

REACTION AND REFORM UNDER STOLYPIN

During the period of the *dumas*, the regime tried to maintain its authority by a mixture of repression and concession. The able Peter Stolypin became Prime Minister in June 1906. He ruthlessly hunted down those involved in the 1905 Revolution. Summary trials and executions of hundreds of Russians took place across Russia; the gallows were known as 'Stolypin's neckties.' However, Stolypin was an intelligent man who realised that the Tsar needed a more secure and broader base of support if long-term stability were to be achieved. He favoured building up a class of wealthy peasants who would be conservative and loyal, and whose purchasing power would benefit the economy. A series of Agricultural Reform Acts between 1906 and 1911 abolished land captains and gave peasants more individual freedom. An emergency decree of November 1906 gave the heads of peasant households the right to claim land held communally as their own. Peasants were freed from the authority of the *mir* and could consolidate their holdings rather than farm them as separate strips. Half a million peasants were resettled in the East, with Government assistance. Redemption payments were ended in 1907. Model farms and agricultural colleges were set up.

> ## KEY ISSUE
>
> *How significant were Stolypin's reforms?*

Historians debate the effectiveness of these reforms. The majority of peasant deputies in the *duma* actually voted against some of them, regarding the reforms as inadequate. After some initial enthusiasm, applications from households to separate from the commune fell off after 1909, outside the more fertile areas of South Russia and the Ukraine. Those who did break away were often treated with resentment by other peasants. Nobles' land was untouched. A rising population continued to put pressure on the land, and crop yields remained low. However, by 1916 about 24 per cent of the peasantry did own its own land.

Stolypin adopted a nationalistic policy of trying to integrate the Empire more closely, for example abolishing Finland's special status. He manipulated the electoral system in the West so as to restrict Polish influence. However, when he attempted reforms he faced resistance from the Tsar and groups in the *duma*, the Church and the Government. Attempts to introduce universal primary education and give full civil rights to the Jews failed. Nicholas was grateful to Stolypin for helping to suppress revolution, but now regarded Stolypin's reforming zeal as a threat to his autocracy, already considering the *dumas* and the Council of Ministers as rival centres of power. Nevertheless the Tsar was shocked when Stolypin was assassinated in a Kiev theatre in 1911.

The years from 1906 to 1914 were relatively peaceful, but there were underlying forces which threatened ultimate stability. There were

The debate about the state of Russia by 1914

There is considerable debate about how secure the Tsarist regime was by 1914, and how successfully Russia was developing as an economic power.

Many of the revolutionaries were not confident that their message was getting across. This article was written in the newspaper *Vpered* (*Forward*) by a group of Bolsheviks in 1910:

'Our party is in a very serious condition. In the two and one-half years since the time of the 1907 London Congress ... our organisations have grown much smaller: where there were thousands of members before, there are only hundreds now; where there were hundreds, there are only scores; and many local groups have disintegrated altogether. To the same degree, or still more, all local activity has been curtailed. Because of countless arrests and banishments, and also because of the desertion of the intelligentsia, there is an enormous shortage of forces for leadership and propaganda ... The ties between organisations have become extremely weak ... the party has no success in guiding the activity of its Duma faction in any systematic way, or making any serious use of it. Work in the armed forces and among the peasantry has died down altogether ... After thousands of comrades were thrown out of the ranks of the party, and the unstable intelligentsia took flight along with those circles of social-democratic workers less imbued with class consciousness, there remained a firm and steady proletarian nucleus of party organisations. It bears the entire burden of reaction, makes innumerable sacrifices for the party cause, and carries it on, over all the difficulties and obstacles, with hardly any help and support.'

Statistics suggest that the Russian economy was undergoing considerable development, as the following examples show.

Index of economic growth

	Total ind.	Total agric.	Urban pop.	Railways length	Iron revenue	Govt
1861	1.00	1.00	1.00	1.00	1.00	1.00
1901	7.50	1.81		25.64	9.67	4.41
1906	8.10	1.89		28.91	9.00	5.57
1913	11.65	3.09	6.96	31.91	14.00	8.38

Comparative production of major industries in million tons, 1914

	Russia	France	Germany	USA	Britain	Russian ranking
Coal	36	40	190	517	292	5
Oil	9.1	0	0	33.1	0	2
Iron	4.6	5.2	16.8	31	10.4	5
Steel	4.8	4.6	18.3	31.8	7.8	4

Contribution of industry to gross national product in 1910

Russia	30%
Austria-Hungary	47%
Germany	70%
Britain	73%

Value of foreign trade in 1913, in £million

Britain	1223
Germany	1030
France	424
Austria-Hungary	199
Russia	190
Turkey	67

Russia's international situation in 1914 was considered precarious by member of the State Council Peter Durnovo, who wrote a memorandum to the Tsar in February 1914, a few months before the outbreak of World War I. The following extracts are an adaptation:

The central factor of the period of world history through which we are now passing is the rivalry between England and Germany. This rivalry must inevitably lead to an armed struggle between them. The future Anglo-German war will be transformed into an armed conflict between two groups of powers. The Russo-Japanese War radically changed the relations among the great powers and brought England out of her isolation. After the war our diplomacy faced abruptly about and definitely started along the road towards rapprochement with England. We find it difficult to perceive any practical advantages gained by us in this. It inevitably threatens us with an armed clash with Germany. The fundamental groupings in a future war are self-evident: Russia, France, and England, on one side; Germany, Austria, and Turkey, on the other. The main burden of the war will fall on Russia, since England is hardly capable of large-scale participation in a continental war, while France will probably confine itself to strictly defensive tactics. Are we prepared for so stubborn a struggle? We must note the insufficiency of our military supplies, and our excessive dependence upon foreign industry. The vital interests of Russia and Germany do not conflict anywhere. Germany's future lies on the sea, where Russia has no interests. We have no surplus population which would require territorial expansion. What can we gain from a victory over Germany? Also there is good reason to believe that the Germans would agree sooner than the English to let us have the Straits. It is to England's advantage to destroy Germany's industry and maritime trade. It is to our advantage for Germany to develop them, and to open her domestic market to our products. Even after the victorious conclusion of a war we would fall into financial and economic bondage to our creditors. Also a struggle between Germany and Russia is profoundly undesirable for both sides, as it would undoubtedly lead to a weakening of the conservative monarchical principle of which they are the only two reliable bulwarks. Also there must inevitably break out in the defeated country a social revolution which would spread to the country of the victor. In Russia any revolutionary movement will inevitably degenerate into a socialist movement. Russia will be flung into anarchy such as she suffered in 1905–6. It will start with all disasters being attributed to the government, resulting in revolutionary agitation. The defeated army will prove to be too demoralised to serve as a bulwark of law and order. The legislative institutions, lacking real authority, will be powerless to stem the rising popular tide, which they themselves had aroused, and Russia will be flung into hopeless anarchy, the outcome of which cannot even be foreseen.

Using this and other information you can find, consider the extent to which Russia was more stable and developed by 1914 in comparison with the start of Nicholas II's reign in 1894, and also how accurate were Durnovo's analysis and predictions regarding Russia's position.

Would Tsarism have survived but for World War I?

limited reforms: notably resulting in an increase in literacy as education was extended. Justices of the peace replaced the hated land captains. But many of the new trade unions were suppressed, and censorship continued, Stolypin launched a new repression of the universities in 1910 and emergency laws stayed in force. Employers clawed back some of the concessions on wages and hours forced on them in 1905. In 1912 270 strikers were killed by troops in the Lena goldfield strike. There was an increasing number of strikes classified as 'political', culminating in a general strike in St. Petersburg in July 1914. The Bolsheviks made some headway in increasing their influence amongst the proletariat.

However, most Russians were not actively working for the overthrow of the regime. The declaration of war in August 1914 actually united most of the nation behind the Tsar. The *duma* agreed to suspend its sitting indefinitely.

KEY ISSUE

How stable was the Tsarist regime in 1914?

G *World War I*

Whatever the debate about how stable Russia was in 1914, there is general agreement that ultimately it was World War I that brought down the regime. Russia was militarily unprepared for a long war against Germany. Continuing and heavy defeats brought staggering military losses, economic problems and disillusionment at home. By the spring of 1915 cooperation between the *élites* and the regime had broken down. Rival centres of power developed, such as the *Union of Zemstvos* and the Progressive Bloc in the *duma*, with its own programme of reform. The Tsar was increasingly discredited by his family's association with the hated Rasputin, the notorious faith healer and unofficial adviser, and by his own decision to take command of the army in 1915. The Tsar continued to refuse concessions and increasingly lost the support of influential Russians. The war dragged on, and desperation turned into a *coup*. Demonstrations in February 1917 became a Revolution as soldiers joined the demonstrators in the capital. The Tsar finally abdicated and soon disappeared into oblivion. A Provisional Government of *duma* deputies took power.

The Provisional Government's failure to end the war and carry out fundamental reforms weakened its position. The Bolsheviks led by Lenin stepped into the power vacuum and seized power in October, with remarkably little bloodshed. The Communist Revolution had begun.

2 ↜ ECONOMIC HISTORY

A *Witte and industrialisation*

The late nineteenth century saw significant economic developments in Russia, due mainly to the policies of two Ministers of Finance, Ivan Vyshnegradskii (1887–92) and Sergei Witte (1892–1903). The most notable feature was an industrial boom in the 1890s. Witte in particular was convinced that the state must intervene to promote industrial growth if Russia were to compete with other Great Powers, particularly at a time of world economic depression in the 1890s. The chief planks of Witte's programme were:

● substantial railway development, which not only improved communications but acted as a spur to other industrial development. For example, the Trans-Siberian Railway was begun in 1891 and largely completed by 1904. Two thirds of Russia's railways were owned and operated by the state

- putting up tariffs, both to raise revenue and protect Russia's domestic industries. Raised substantially in 1891 and again later, tariffs soon accounted for one third of the value of all imports
- achieving a favourable balance of payments by encouraging exports of grain
- putting Russia on the gold standard in 1897 and then encouraging foreign investment in Russia. Between 1890 and 1915 the proportion of foreign capital, mainly from Western Europe and particularly France, which was invested in Russian industry rose from 26 per cent to 41 per cent of the total. This was also due to low international interest rates as well as to Witte's policies
- paying off some foreign loans
- encouraging the growth of a class of dynamic entrepreneurs.

KEY ISSUE
What was the impact of Witte's economic strategy?

Historians debate the long-term success of Witte's strategy. Industrial growth increased by over 8 per cent a year in the 1890s. Railway construction expanded from about 30 000 kilometres to about 53 000 kilometres between 1890 and 1900, increasing Russia's ranking from fifth in the world to second only to the USA in the size of the network. After 1900 industrial expansion was as much self-generated as state-sponsored. The rate of industrial growth fell off rapidly between the late 1890s and 1905, with several crises involving bankruptcies, falling prices and falling output. There were rising interest rates and declining international investment. Industries which had expanded most rapidly in the late 1890s were worst hit. However, there was another boom between 1906 and 1913, less dependent on the state. The factory workforce expanded by one million between 1910 and 1914. Industrial growth was at 6 per cent a year after 1906, largely due to the benefits of earlier investment, improving conditions for the rural population, and better terms of trade. Textiles remained the dominant industry, and large enterprises were the norm in cities. Between 1900 and 1914 bank deposits more than doubled and the number of banks mushroomed.

However, by 1914 Russia was also Europe's largest debtor nation. The state debt was already 6.5 thousand million gold roubles by 1904, with little prospect of it being paid off. Industrial progress was rapid partly because Russia was expanding from a primitive industrial base. Expansion put a strain on a country with poorly developed technological and communications systems. Government expenditure was dangerously high, partly because of the Russo-Japanese War. Russian industrial output continued to lag behind that of other Great Powers, and Russia actually fell down the industrial ranking of major powers: by 1913 it was behind Italy in tenth position. Industry made up only 20 per cent of national income, whilst only 18 per cent of the population lived in towns. It was not until Stalin's brutal industrialisation drive of the late 1920s and early 1930s that Russia could seriously compete with other Great Powers economically, and then in quantity rather than quality.

B *Economic and social pressures*

These economic developments did not benefit many ordinary Russians. Much of the new industrial workforce was recruited from the peasantry: many peasants migrated back and forth between town and country according to the season. In 1910 almost 70 per cent of the inhabitants of Moscow and St. Petersburg were still classified as 'peasants'. Living and working conditions in the rapidly expanding industrial cities of Moscow and St. Petersburg were terrible. Despite new employment laws passed from 1897 onwards, the working day in factories was long, conditions difficult and inspection ineffectual. Real wages rose slowly. The right to strike for economic reasons was granted in December 1905, and the right to form trade unions in March 1906. But by 1907 fresh restrictions were imposed on unions. Nevertheless wildcat strikes did take place, and the Bolsheviks gained dominant influence in some unions by 1914.

Russia remained an agricultural economy, and rural conditions were poor in most areas. Emancipation had not improved the lot of most peasants. Taxes were increased to raise revenue. A quarter of state revenue came from the Government's monopoly on alcohol sales. Grain prices were depressed. Above all the rising population put more pressure on the land. The population rose from 74 million to 155 million between 1858 and 1914. There were outbreaks of famine and rural unrest. Many peasants migrated, often assisted by the government, to the undeveloped lands beyond the Urals, or else into the cities. Stolypin's reforms helped create a class of richer peasants or *kulaks*, but they were a small proportion of the total.

Many wealthy landowners amongst the gentry and aristocracy also suffered. They were often in debt, and farmed inefficiently. The landowning nobility lost 40 per cent of its land between 1861 and 1905. Consequently this class could no longer be counted upon as a buttress of support for the Tsarist regime. The bureaucracy quadrupled in size between 1861 and 1914, and the Tsar increasingly depended upon bureaucrats and soldiers to maintain his authority rather than the nobility.

> **KEY ISSUE**
>
> *How developed was the Russian economy by 1914?*

TABLE 21

Concentration in Russian industry 1901–14

Size of plant	Enterprises	%	Workers	%
		1901		
Under 100 workers	15 168	83.9	414 785	24.4
101–500 workers	2 288	12.6	492 095	28.9
501–1000 workers	403	2.2	269 133	15.8
Over 1000 workers	243	1.3	525 637	30.9
		1914		
Under 100 workers	11 117	78.4	348 876	17.8
101–500 workers	2 253	16.1	504 440	25.7
501–1000 workers	432	3.1	296 347	15.1
Over 1000 workers	344	2.4	811 197	41.4

Many industrial workers, peasants and even aristocrats failed to benefit from economic development. The small urban middle class did benefit, but even members of this class were dissatisfied by the fact that their political influence did not reflect any economic gains they made.

3 ⌐ FOREIGN POLICY

A *Europe*

Russian foreign policy in the lead-up to World War I is dealt with in detail in Chapters 14 and 15. During Alexander III's reign Russia was effectively isolated in Europe, mainly because Austrian and Russian interests in the Balkans were increasingly at odds, and Germany was committed to Austria. Relations with Britain were strained by mutual concerns over the Eastern Mediterranean and the approaches to India. Russia retained its strong interest in the Balkans. It acted as the patron of Serbia and was also keen to extend its influence over Bulgaria. There was also the long-term Russian ambition of gaining control of Constantinople and the Straits, thereby securing access to and from the Black Sea.

Despite the differences in the political systems of Republican France and Imperial Russia, the two countries were increasingly drawn together. This was partly due to French investment and loans to Russia, and partly due to common concern at German power. The Reinsurance Treaty between Germany and Russia, originally signed in 1887, was not renewed in 1890, chiefly because it conflicted with the Austro-German alliance. A defensive alliance between Russia and France was eventually ratified in 1894, having been preceded by a military convention in 1892.

A possible agreement between Germany and Russia was still being discussed in 1904, when the German *Kaiser* Wilhelm II suggested a Franco-Russo-German alliance against Britain. However, Nicholas II was reluctant to sign up before getting French agreement. In July 1905 Wilhelm II did persuade Nicholas to sign the secret Treaty of Björko, by which Germany and Russia pledged full mutual support in the event of war. The alliance was clearly at odds with existing alliances, was disliked by ministers in both countries, and the Treaty was not ratified. Thereafter Russo-German relations deteriorated. The 1908 Bosnian crisis ended any possibility of an agreement between Russia and Austria.

However, since France had an *Entente* with Britain, and Russia was weakened after the Russo-Japanese war, Russia moved closer to Britain. An Anglo-Russian *Entente* was signed in 1907, based on settling colonial issues. Persia was divided into three zones of influence, one Russian, one British and one neutral; Afghanistan and Tibet were secured from direct Russian or British interference.

The Balkans remained the most sensitive area. Russian patronage of Serbia was confirmed by a military agreement between the two Powers in 1902, and there was a similar agreement with Bulgaria. However, Russian ambition in the Balkans was checked by Austria's annexation of

KEY ISSUE

What was the significance of the Franco-Russian alliance?

Bosnia-Herzegovina in 1908. Still weak from the events of 1904–5, Russia felt unable to back Serbia. Following Serbia's victory in the Balkan Wars of 1912–13, Russia was unable to prevent the Great Powers blocking Serbian attempts to gain territory on the Adriatic coastline. Russia's other ally Bulgaria was defeated in the Second Balkan War. These setbacks help to explain Russia's behaviour in the war crisis of 1914. Nicholas II felt obliged to back Serbia after the Sarajevo crisis despite Germany's backing of Austria. He would have preferred for Russia to have mobilised against Austria alone, but was swept along by events. Russia rejected German demands to suspend its mobilisation and hence Germany's declaration of war on Russia on 1 August 1914. The war eventually brought down the Romanov dynasty.

> **KEY ISSUE**
>
> *How did Russia become involved in World War I?*

B *The Far East*

Nicholas II did not add any territory to the Russian Empire beyond that gained by his predecessors. But his Government did harbour ambitions in the Far East. In the 1850s Russia had acquired the island of Sakhalin and the Kurile Archipelago. The Treaty of Peking, signed with China in 1860, settled the frontier between the two countries. Further adjustments in territory were made: in 1867 Russia sold Alaska to the United States, and in 1875 Russia gave the Kurile Archipelago to Japan in return for Japanese recognition of the Russian occupation of Sakhalin. However, Russia lacked an ice-free port on the Pacific, and China controlled Manchuria, which was a salient into Russian territory. Russia was concerned by Japan's victory over China in a war in 1895, which led to Japan acquiring the Pescadores Islands, Formosa and the Liaotung Peninsula. Russia, with German backing, sought to consolidate its own position in the region by:

- persuading Japan to leave the Liaotung Peninsula to China in 1896, following Russian loans to China and a treaty of protection
- persuading China to allow Russia to build a railway across Manchuria
- in 1898, securing a 25-year lease on the Liaotung Peninsula, including the ice-free Port Arthur
- securing international recognition of Korean neutrality despite Japanese control of Korea
- occupying the cities of Northern Manchuria following the 1900 Boxer Rebellion.

> **KEY ISSUE**
>
> *What were the causes of the Russo-Japanese War?*

Nicholas was keen to exploit the resources of Manchuria and possibly North Korea. Russian activities in the region alarmed the Japanese, who offered a free hand for Russia in Manchuria in return for a free hand in Korea. Russia would not assent, and after long and fruitless negotiations, the Japanese attacked Port Arthur in February 1904. The Russian Government welcomed the prospect of a short victorious war to boost its prestige and stop unrest. Despite Witte's opposition and poor preparation for fighting a war so far from European Russia, the Government determined on a full-scale war. It proved disastrous for Russia. After an

MAP 15   *The Far East*

11 month siege, Port Arthur fell to the Japanese in January 1905, by which time the Russians had lost 100 000 men. In May 1905 came the final humiliation when Russia's Baltic fleet, having sailed halfway round the world, was sunk by the Japanese fleet at Tsushima.

Defeat at the hands of a non-European power in a major war was unprecedented and was a major spark for the 1905 Revolution. After the War, with Russia increasingly preoccupied with European affairs, it came to an agreement with Japan. Russian rights in Northern China were settled by a treaty in 1907, and Russia secretly acknowledged Japanese rights in Korea and Southern Manchuria, whilst Japan acknowledged Russian interests in Mongolia and Northern Manchuria. Japan was able to formally annex Korea in 1910. Although Russian influence was still important in the Far East, the setback of the 1904 war concentrated Russian attentions back on the Balkans, heightening Great Power tension there and contributing to the outbreak of World War I.

4 ⤚ BIBLIOGRAPHY

There are several books covering this period of Russian history. A brief survey is *The End of Imperial Russia, 1855–1917* by P. Waldron

(Macmillan, 1997). Parts One and Two of *A People's Tragedy: The Russian Revolution 1891–1924* by O. Figes (Jonathan Cape, 1996) provide a readable introduction. Also useful is *Reaction and Revolutions: Russia 1881–1924* by M. Lynch (Hodder and Stoughton, 1992). More detailed is *Russia in the Age of Modernisation and Revolution* by H. Rogger (Longmans, 1983). *Late Imperial Russia 1890–1917* by J. Hutchinson (Longmans, 1999) is a description and analysis of the period complemented by documentary sources; as is *Nineteenth-century Russia: Opposition to Autocracy* by D. Offord (Longmans, 1999). Detailed biographies include *Nicholas II, Emperor of all the Russias* by D. Lieven (John Murray, 1993) and *Sergei Witte and the Industrialisation of Russia* by T. von Laue (Columbia UP, 1963). Russian foreign policy is dealt with in *Russia and the Origins of the First World War* by D. Lieven (St. Martin's Press, 1984).

5 ↬ STRUCTURED QUESTIONS AND ESSAYS

1. (a) Outline the main domestic policies of Alexander III in Russia, 1881–1894; (10 marks)
   (b) To what extent did Alexander III reverse the reforming trend of his father, Alexander II? (15 marks)
2. (a) Outline the main features of Tsarist government under Nicholas II before 1905; (10 marks)
   (b) How important was the role of the *dumas* between 1906 and 1914? (15 marks)
3. Compare and contrast the policies of Alexander III and Nicholas II as rulers of Russia between 1881 and 1914; (25 marks)
4. (a) Outline the domestic policies of Witte and Stolypin; (10 marks)
   (b) How successful were they in reforming the Russian political and economic systems? (15 marks)
5. (a) Outline the causes of the 1905 Revolution in Russia; (10 marks)
   (b) Why did the Tsarist regime manage to survive the 1905 Revolution? (15 marks)
6. How valid is the judgement that 'The Russian Empire underwent a remarkable economic transformation between the 1880s and the outbreak of World War I in 1914'? (25 marks)
7. (a) What were the main objectives of revolutionary political groups in Russia during the reign of Nicholas II, between 1894 and 1914? (10 marks)
   (b) Why had they not achieved their objectives by 1914? (15 marks)
8. Analyse the strengths and weaknesses of the Tsarist regime on the eve of war in 1914. (25 marks)
9. (a) What were Russia's main objectives in foreign policy in the period 1881–1914? (10 marks)
   (b) To what extent were those objectives realised during this period? (15 marks)
10. (a) Outline the causes of the Russo-Japanese War; (10 marks)

(b) Why did Russia lose the war and what was the outcome of the defeat for Russia? (15 marks)

11. 'Politically and economically backward, but stable.' To what extent is this an accurate assessment of the Russian Empire in 1914? (25 marks)

6 ∽ DOCUMENTARY EXERCISE ON THE PERIOD OF THE *DUMAS*, 1906–14

Study Sources A–D below and answer the questions which follow:

(i) The first place among these representatives of the people was occupied by a tall man, dressed in a worker's blouse and high, oiled boots, who examined the throne and those about it with a derisive and insolent air. I could not take my eyes off him. Near me stood Stolypin, the new minister of internal affairs, who turned to me and said: 'We both seem to be engrossed in the same spectacle. I even have the feeling that this man might be carrying a bomb'.

adapted from *The Memoirs of Count Kokovtsov: Out of My Past* (1935)

(ii) The hostility of the majority of the First Duma toward the throne was clearly shown on the first day of its sessions. All the Duma members attended the Imperial reception in the throne room of the Winter Palace dressed in a deliberately careless fashion. Be it said, however, that there was a certain lack of tact on both sides. The court had decided that this reception was to be particularly solemn and brilliant ...The contrast was striking. The court and the government, flourishing gold-laced uniforms and numerous decorations, was set opposite the grey, almost rustic group representing the people of Russia. Naively believing that the people's representatives, many of whom were peasants, would be awed by the splendour of the Imperial court, the ladies of the Imperial family had worn nearly all their jewels; they were literally covered with pearls and diamonds. But the effect was altogether different. This Oriental method of impressing upon spectators a reverence for the bearers of supreme power was quite unsuited to the occasion. What it did achieve was to set in juxtaposition the boundless Imperial luxury and the poverty of the people. The demagogues did not fail to comment upon this ominous contrast. Nor did the Tsar's address of welcome improve matters.

Vladimir Gurko *Features and Figures of the Past: Government and Opinion in the Reign of Nicholas II* (1939). Gurko was a high official in the Ministry of Internal Affairs.

(iii) As silence falls, the tsar reads the speech handed to him. He reads very distinctly. Immediately after the speech a military band breaks into the national anthem, 'God save the Tsar' and the right-thinking part of the assembly begins to shout 'hurrah!'. The procession slowly returns to the inner chambers. The entire ceremony was conducted with extraordinary decorum and success. To be sure, this success was assisted by the fine weather, warm and sunny, and by the great number of troops stationed in the squares and the streets surrounding the palace.

adapted from the private diary of A Polovtsev, a member of the State Council

SOURCE A
Accounts of the opening of the First Duma, April 27 1906

The State Duma will submit for Your Majesty's approval a law concerning popular representation, based upon universal suffrage. The State Duma is united in the fervent desire to reinvigorate Russia and to create a government based on the peaceful coexistence of all classes and nationalities and on civil freedom. All ministers must be made responsible to the people's representatives. There must be laws assuring personal freedom, freedom of conscience, freedom of speech, of the press and of assembly. There must be equality before the law. The acute land needs of the toiling peasantry must be met, and the peasants must be given equality. There must be a law concerning universal free education. The tax burden must be made fairer. Local government must be based on universal suffrage. The demands of individual nationalities must be satisfied. The Duma awaits from you a full amnesty for all actions prompted by religious or political causes as well as to all agrarian offences.

SOURCE B
The First Duma's Address to the Tsar, May 5 1906

Instead of legislative work, the people's elected representatives have digressed into an area outside their competence, undertaking to investigate the actions of the local authorities appointed by us, to point out to us faults in the Fundamental Laws, which may be changed only at the instance of our sovereign will, and engaging in such clearly illegal actions as an appeal to the people in the name of the Duma.

Stirred up by such improper actions and expecting no legal improvement in its condition, the peasantry has turned ... to open looting, appropriation of other people's property, and disobedience of the law and of legal authorities.

But let our subjects remember that lasting improvement in the life of the people is possible only under conditions of complete order and tranquillity. Let it be known that we shall not tolerate any insubordination or lawlessness and shall employ every power of the state to bring those who disobey the law to submission to our imperial will.

SOURCE C
The Manifesto on the Dissolution of the Duma, *July 9 1906*

(i) Although the Emperor dreamed only of reducing as far as possible all liberties granted the people, Stolypin was of an entirely different opinion. He had set himself the task of reconciling public and government. He believed steadfastly that even the most malevolent representatives of the public were opposed to the government because of its continuation of certain out-of-date practices of the past. He was thoroughly convinced that as soon as the government proved its sincere desire to heed the voice of the people by effecting certain liberal reforms and by repealing certain regulations which caused the most exasperation, the opposition would be disarmed and public sympathy would be his. In particular, he believed that the government would have to make certain important concessions to the Duma's demands concerning the land question.

V Gurko *Features and Figures of the Past: Government and Opinion in the Reign of Nicholas II* (1939).

(ii) M Stolypin's agrarian reforms met with extraordinary success, surpassing the most optimistic expectations. The Russian peasant is possessed of a keen intelligence. He was not slow in finding means of acquiring additional land by proper and legal methods. The new legislation, reinforced by a considerable extension of the activity and power of the 'Peasants' Bank,' produced widespread results in a surprisingly short time. The results were so satisfactory that, on the eve of the revolution of 1917, it is safe to say that the entire agrarian problem was in a way to be definitely solved. The upheaval caused by the revolution destroyed, alas, those magnificent results.

adapted from A. Isvolsky *The Memoirs of Alexander Isvolsky* (1920).

(iii) The position of the government, and of Stolypin in particular, was truly tragic. He openly and honestly desired to attract into the government men who had popular support. Yet he also recognised that the Emperor was unsympathetic to this idea, and, further, that such public men as he had in mind were less than frank in their dealings with him and were far from anxious to exchange the freedom of opposition for responsibility. Deep in his heart Stolypin certainly craved power, loved it, and was loath to let it slip from his hands. But he was unquestionably an honourable and honest man, and he perceived that the problem was either to safeguard public order in the form in which it had recently been established or to take the easy road of making concessions which might lead to the destruction of the entire regime.

adapted from Kokovtsov *Memoirs of Count Kokovtsov* (1935).

SOURCE D
Opinions of Stolypin

1. Explain the reference to the 'Fundamental Laws' in
   Source C. (3 marks)
2. What indications are there in Sources A (i), (ii), (iii) and Source C
   of the real and potential difficulties in the relationship between the
   First Duma and the Tsar's government? (8 marks)
3. (i)   Using Source B and your own knowledge of Russian history,
         explain the extent to which the Duma's demands for reform
         were radical. (8 marks)
   (ii) To what extent had the demands been met by 1914? (6 marks)
4. Compare and contrast the evaluation of Stolypin's character and
   nature in Sources D(i), (ii) and (iii). (8 marks)
5. Using your own knowledge, assess the accuracy of Izvolsky's claim
   in Source D (ii) about Stolypin's success. (6 marks)
6. Assess the value and reliability of any one of the sources in this
   collection as evidence of the problems of governing Russia in the
   period 1905–1914. (7 marks)
7. Using this collection of Sources A–D, and your own knowledge,
   assess the validity of the judgement that 'the so-called period of
   political and economic reform in Russia 1905–14 was little more
   than a sham'. (14 marks)

The Habsburg Empire 1801–1914

AN EMPIRE IN DECLINE?

The Habsburg Empire in the eighteenth century was one of the Great Powers of Europe. At the end of the century it was defeated in the French Revolutionary Wars, and again in the struggle against Napoleon's attempts to dominate Europe. However, after France's defeat in 1815, Austria became one of the guarantors of the 1815 peace settlement, and a force for conservatism in post-Napoleonic Europe as part of the Holy Alliance. Under the influence particularly of Metternich, Austria gained the reputation of being a reactionary standard-bearer against reform and revolution.

The Habsburgs ruled a multinational Empire, and as such were influenced by the growth of nationalist tensions in nineteenth-century Europe. The Habsburg monarchy survived the 1848 Revolutions with difficulty. Thereafter Austria fought a long and ultimately unsuccessful battle on several fronts: to maintain the territorial integrity of the Empire and its influence in Italy; to maintain its leadership of the German States; to combat Russian influence in South Eastern Europe; and to maintain control of a large multinational Empire. In 1914, although Austrian actions played a large part in provoking World War I, the Empire entered that war very much as the junior partner of Germany. The war was unsuccessful on the military front, and before it had ended the once-great Empire had broken up into various constituent parts, a situation confirmed by the peace treaties of 1918–19.

Some historians have tended to analyse the history of the Habsburg Empire in the nineteenth century as one of almost continuous decline and failure, with the implication that its ultimate demise was inevitable: a question not of 'whether' but 'when'? Other historians have been less convinced. They have pointed to facts such as Austria's emergence from the Napoleonic wars in a territorially more consolidated state than before, and with the leadership of Germany and Italy. They point to Metternich's considerable influence, and the fact that Austria did recover from the crisis of 1848.

It is certainly dangerous to assume that the Empire was in continuous and terminal decline. It showed itself capable of compromise in 1867, by the creation of the Dual Monarchy. Despite internal conflicts

MAP 16 *The Habsburg monarchy 1866–1914*

between the peoples of the Empire, very few people actually wanted the Empire to break up, and not everybody was pessimistic about its future even in the years immediately prior to World War I.

1 ➥ POLITICAL HISTORY

A *The Metternich period*

In 1809, following its defeat by Napoleon, Austria was virtually a client state of France. During the next few years, largely due to Metternich, Austria restored its reputation and its influence. The Emperor Francis I and his Chancellor Metternich agreed on most policies. Although

TIMELINE

1809	Metternich appointed Foreign Minister
1821	Metternich appointed State Chancellor
1835	Accession of Ferdinand I
1848	Revolutions in Europe
	Resignation of Metternich
1849	Austrian, Hungarian and Italian Revolutions defeated
	Schwarzenberg became Austrian Prime Minister
1850	Treaty of Olmütz
1851	Sylvester Patent Constitution
1861	February Constitution
1866	Austro-Prussian War
	Austria expelled from Germany
1867	*Ausgleich*
1878	Occupation of Bosnia-Herzegovina
1879	Dual Alliance of Austria-Hungary and Germany
1907	Universal suffrage in Austria
1908	Universal suffrage, with literacy qualifications, in Hungary
	Annexation of Bosnia-Herzegovina
1914	World War I broke out
1916	Death of Franz Josef

Francis was frequently indecisive and disorganised in his approach to government, Metternich had a clear belief that Austrian power depended upon the maintenance of the principle of 'legitimacy' – established dynastic and territorial arrangements were sacrosanct. Insistence upon this principle enabled Austria to win back its central European territories, secure the leadership of the German Confederation, and secure control of most of Italy. Metternich genuinely believed in monarchical power, but favoured an efficient system of government, based upon a centralised monarchy with ministers and a consultative council responsible to it. Some historians like Alan Sked believe that Metternich only paid lip-service to the principle of constitutional government. Evidence for this viewpoint would be the extensive 'system' of police, agents and censorship by which Metternich attempted to keep Liberal ideas at bay not just in the Empire but throughout Europe.

Metternich's policy of upholding tradition and established dynastic rights worked in the short term. However, by identifying the State with the interests of the Habsburg dynasty, the Empire was personalised and lacked the national identity that might have encouraged the development of the popular patriotism which took place in some other European states. Given the fact that there was no one dominant ethnic grouping, this was probably inevitable. It made the Empire vulnerable to nationalist discontent as the century wore on.

One of the ironies of Metternich's career is that he often seemed to exercise more influence over foreign policy than domestic affairs:

● his influence in Austria was challenged after 1828 by Count Franz Anton Kolowrat, a Czech and head of the *Staatsrat* or Council. Unlike Metternich, Kolowrat wanted to reduce expenditure on the

---

KEY ISSUE

What were Metternich's basic political principles?

THE HABSBURG EMPERORS

FRANCIS II (1792–1835). On the dissolution of the Holy Roman Empire he became **Francis I** of Austria, in 1804. Francis was conscientious but hesitant when it came to making important decisions.

FERDINAND I (1835–48) has been described as an 'amiable but epileptic half-wit'. During his reign the governing State Council comprised Metternich, Kolowrat, the Archduke Louis and Franz Josef's father, Francis Charles.

FRANZ JOSEF (1848–1916) became Emperor of Austria-Hungary in 1867. Born in 1830, he endured a rigorous education and training, learning to love the army. He was widely regarded as conscientious, with a strong sense of duty. He was not an intellectual, but he was obstinate. Conservative by nature, Franz Josef was opposed to liberalism and constitutional principles, partly due to Metternich's influence on him, and partly due to his mother's belief in divine right monarchy. Metternich taught him that foreign policy was his most important responsibility. Despite his principles, Franz Josef adapted with difficulty to the role of constitutional monarch after 1867. He suffered personal tragedy when his son Crown Prince Rudolph committed suicide in 1889, the Empress Elizabeth was assassinated by an Italian anarchist in 1898, and Archduke Franz Ferdinand was assassinated in 1914.

Critical historians like Steven Beller claim that Franz Joseph paid more attention to maintaining his personal position and the Empire's status than on necessary internal reforms, and that, although a decent individual, he was an anachronism. Alan Sked goes further in his criticism, claiming that Franz Josef was so afraid of the growth of Serbian power that 'the monarchy deliberately started a world war rather than compromise internally or externally on the South Slav question.' (A. Sked, *The Decline and Fall of the Habsburg Empire 1815–1918*, page 269). He retained considerable influence until the army assumed power during World War I. Steven Beller emphasises both the paradoxes of his reign and its symbolic importance, given its length:

He was the monarch who reneged on constitutional government, only to have it forced back on him. He was the monarch who tried to completely subjugate Hungary, only to be forced to become Hungary's constitutional monarch. He was also the monarch who lost the Habsburg's position in both Italy and Germany ... He was a staunch Catholic, who signed a Concordat with the Papacy, yet was forced to accept essentially anti-clerical legislation, and became almost a symbol of religious toleration and pluralism even before his death. He was a man with absolute convictions and aristocratic preferences, who nevertheless became a supporter of universal male suffrage. Above all, after the calamity of 1866–7, he came to pride himself as the 'peace emperor', only to go down in history as the man who started the war ... He ruled over the transition from a largely feudal and traditional society, to an increasingly urban, modern one, which saw mass industrialisation and mass politics, and which produced Sigmund Freud, Ludwig Wittgenstein, Franz Kafka, George Lukacs and Adolf Hitler. His reign also saw the further development of mass nationalism, with all its pressures and problems, especially for a dynastic, multi-national state such as the Habsburg Monarchy. He presided over the decline of that Monarchy from one of the leading great powers of Europe to, by his death, a clearly subordinate status to its ally ... the German Empire. (S. Beller, *Francis Joseph*, Longman, 1996, pages 2–3.)

PROFILE

METTERNICH (1773–1859)

Prince Clemens Metternich was born into an aristocratic Rhineland family and experienced the effects of revolution at first hand when his family moved to Vienna in 1794 to escape the invading French armies.

In 1801 Metternich followed his father's footsteps into the diplomatic service. His background, his contacts, and his belief in his own ability soon made Metternich one of the leading diplomats of his time, and hence his importance in Habsburg and European affairs for almost 40 years, as Austrian State Chancellor (1821–48) and Foreign Minister (1809–48).

Metternich's historical reputation has been affected by the climate in which historians have worked. Those welcoming the development of nation states and the triumph of liberal political principles tended to emphasise Metternich as the reactionary enemy of progress, harking back to an era before the 'terrible social catastrophe' of the French Revolution. Later generations showed more appreciation of his diplomatic skills, particularly in the context of the post-1945 Cold War when the West was intent on resisting Communist subversion, real or imagined, and parallels were drawn with Metternich's struggle against revolutionary change. There were debates as to whether Metternich was an opportunist or had a long-term strategy; and whether he had more influence in the Habsburg Empire or in Europe as a whole.

The Duke of Wellington described Metternich as 'a society hero and nothing more.' Later historians could be equally dismissive. A.J.P. Taylor called him a 'very silly man ... Vain and complacent ... His thoughts, like those of most conservatives, were banal and obvious ... He was good at his job, though it was not so difficult a job as is often supposed ... In the usual way of statesmen who rule over a decaying empire, he urged others to preserve the Austrian monarchy for their own good ... His only answer to either liberalism or radicalism was, in fact, repression ... Since he had no genuine conservative ideas himself, he denied that radical ideas were genuine; and solemnly maintained that discontent everywhere was the result of "a conspiracy". (A.J.P. Taylor, *Europe: Grandeur and Decline*, Penguin, 1967, pages 23–6.)

There have been kinder assessments, for example this one written in 1966: 'he represents the mellow autumn of the diplomacy of the ancien regime, rational, calculating, opposed to all over-weening ambitions...he was genuinely 'European-minded', preoccupied with equilibrium, intelligent enough to see that Austria could only survive in a world where all the checks and balances were set to preserve peace' (J. McManners, *Lectures on European History 1789–1914*, Blackwell, 1966, page 121.) Alan Sked emphasises the limits within which Metternich had to work: despite Metternich's frequently voiced pessimism, 'he had a genuine conviction in the value of his work ... he did believe that strong, central government was necessary in post-revolutionary Europe and he was convinced that concessions to liberal reform were the surest recipe for revolution ... there is no reason to believe that he lacked genuine conviction in the essential benevolence of his system' (Sked, pages 36–7.)

KEY ISSUE

What limitations were there on Metternich's power inside the Habsburg Empire?

army and police. Whilst Metternich controlled the police, defence and foreign affairs, Kolowrat controlled finance. Hostile to Metternich, Kolowrat secured his resignation in 1848. Metternich complained that he had never been able to govern Austria effectively

● Ferdinand I was incapable of effective leadership and Metternich found it difficult to influence him

● Hungary had its own constitution and the right to pass laws. The Hungarian *diet* would only accept measures to raise more revenue in return for concessions. Metternich tried to alter this, since it was an obstruction to his own belief in centralised government, but he failed and so Vienna did not exert full control over the provinces.

B *The 1848 revolutions*

By 1848 Metternich's 'system' was under threat from revolutions in Germany and Italy and opposition to autocratic rule within Austria itself.

These developments are dealt with in Chapter 7 in more detail. The key stages in the restoration of order and normality within the Empire were:

● the defeat of the Italians by Radetsky
● the defeat of the Hungarian revolutionaries

Metternich	1809–48
von Kalowrat	1848
von Schwarzenberg	1848–52
Bach	1852–9
von Schmerling	1861–5
Beust	1867–70
von Taaffe	1870–1
von Auersperg	1871–8
Taaffe	1879–93
Windischgrätz	1893–95
Badeni	1895–97
von Beck	1906–8
von Biernerth	1908–11
von Sturgkh	1912–16

TABLE 22
Principal ministers in the Empire

- the defeat of revolutionaries in Vienna who failed to secure control of the army
- Liberals and nationalists in the Austrian parliament supported the army in restoring order, whilst the new Prime Minister Prince Felix Schwarzenberg advised that Ferdinand abdicate in favour of Franz Josef
- a diplomatic struggle with Prussia over the leadership of the German states. This culminated in the Prussians backing down at the Treaty of Olmütz in November 1850 and the re-creation of a German Confederation.

C *From revolution to dual monarchy*

Franz Josef succeeded to the throne in December 1848. He rejected a liberal constitution which would have forced the Emperor to share power with parliament, guarantee the rights of nationalities and Liberals, and disestablish the Church. The Emperor and Schwarzenberg also did not put into practice the more moderate Stadion Constitution. The 1851 'Sylvester Patent' Constitution allowed an advisory council or *Reichsrat*, but otherwise no checks on the Emperor's powers. The Empire's domestic affairs were run after the 1848 Revolutions by Schwarzenberg and Minister of the Interior Count Franz Stadion. Like Metternich, Schwarzenberg wanted to strengthen the Empire, but lacked a definite blueprint other than supporting imperial power. Although he failed to get the Empire as a whole into the Confederation or the *Zollverein*, he did manage to retain influence within the Confederation through Austrian possession of the presidency.

After the deaths of Stadion and Schwarzenberg in 1852 the most influential Minister (of the Interior) was Alexander Bach. He centralised the administration of the Empire, working towards his ideal of a unified, German-speaking bureaucracy. Bach believed that in a modern, economically prosperous state with an educated people, all equal underneath the Emperor, the issue of political rights would die away. The authority of the Government, and thereby the Emperor, was upheld by enforcing the control of the Catholic Church over education, in return for the absolute loyalty of the Church to the State – formalised in a *concordat* signed in 1855. Representative institutions, including those in Hungary, were abolished. Feudal dues were also abolished, although this did not significantly decrease the power of the landed magnates.

Franz Josef's autocracy seemed secure, until it was undermined by defeat in Italy in 1858–9. Then there was growing dissatisfaction with the autocracy from German Liberals and nationalistic Hungarians and Czechs. Franz Josef responded with a series of constitutional experiments, none of which fundamentally reduced imperial power:

- under the 1860 *October Diploma*, the Austrians made an agreement with Hungarian conservatives and the Austro-Bohemian nobility to set up a federal structure which had an assembly with limited

---

KEY ISSUE

What changes were made in the administration of the Empire between 1848 and the Ausgleich of 1867?

powers and the Emperor very much still the dominant figure. This plan foundered on middle-class opposition

- the 1861 *February Constitution*. This operated until 1865. It provided for a centralised system of administration, with an imperial parliament elected indirectly by the provincial *diets*, but so designed as to ensure German dominance. The Emperor retained control of foreign and military policy
- after opposition from the Hungarians, the February Constitution was amended, then restored in 1867, and lasted until the *Ausgleich*.

Some historians consider that the Habsburg Empire played into Prussia's hands by refusing to give it concessions within the Confederation, and not giving constructive leadership within that body, thereby enabling Bismarck to utilise anti-Austrian feelings. Nevertheless most German states still supported Austria in the crisis of 1866.

See pages 190–1

D *The Ausgleich*

Austria's defeat in the 1866 war was due to a variety of factors, including deficiencies in the army and Franz Josef's interference with his commanders' management of the campaign. The defeat not only expelled Austria from Germany but forced the Habsburgs into concessions to Hungary, whose *élites* had been upset by the centralised nature of Bach's administration. Franz Josef was persuaded that concessions were necessary to retain any influence in Southern Germany. He unwillingly accepted the proposals of the Hungarians Francis Deak and Count Julius Andrassy for constitutional change as the price for restoring Hungarian support. The 1867 *Ausgleich*, which established the Dual Monarchy, was not popular in many quarters, especially amongst Germans. It represented a compromise:

- the monarchy comprised (a) the Kingdom of Hungary and (b) Cisleithania (officially Austria from 1915), of which over half the population was non-German
- the Emperor of Austria was separately crowned King of Hungary
- there were joint ministries for defence, foreign affairs and finance. They were subordinate to the Emperor but were also accountable to delegations from the former Hungarian *Diet* and Austrian *Reichsrat*, which met annually in the same city, alternately Vienna and Budapest, but without any joint deliberation
- the Emperor was assisted by a Joint Ministerial Council, or Crown Council, which operated informally as his personal cabinet.

The *Ausgleich* was a compromise and contained anomalies:

- the Austrians and Hungarians retained separate laws, and the Hungarian parliament assumed that it now represented a separate state, which was not the perception of the Austrians
- although Hungary had internal independence, its Government had to submit proposals for laws to the Emperor, who had a veto, before putting them before Hungary's own parliament

What were the main provisions of the Ausgleich, and what potential problems did it create?

- matters of common interest were discussed between the Emperor and the two Governments concerned, and did not directly involve the parliaments
- Hungary was not independent in the normal meaning of the term. It had no influence over the unified German-speaking army, which was under the Emperor's control. Originally 70 per cent of the army was to be Austrian, and 30 per cent Hungarian
- the Emperor was left in a powerful position. His was the most influential voice, and his will usually prevailed if there were internal disputes over jurisdiction. However, he also had to accept compromises which he disliked. For example earlier concessions to the Church were reversed: the State reasserted control over education and the Church hierarchy, and the *Concordat* was abolished in 1870
- the Slavs in particular regarded themselves as the losers by this arrangement. Their leaders felt that they had been given over to domination by more powerful nationalities, particularly the Magyars in Hungary. Foreign Minister Friedrich Beust declared frankly in February 1867: 'I am quite aware that the Slav peoples of the Monarchy will view the new policy with mistrust; but the government cannot always be fair to all the nations. Therefore we have to rely on the support of those with the most viability...and those are the Germans and the Hungarians.'

E *The growth of nationalism – from 1867 onwards*

AUSTRIA

From 1867 to 1879 the German liberals were a strong force in Austria. They introduced several reforms, notably the introduction of compulsory primary education and a new criminal code. They lost favour with Franz Josef in 1878 by opposing the occupation of Bosnia Herzegovina. Thereafter the Emperor relied upon Count Edward Taaffe to govern through a coalition of disparate anti-Liberal groups containing Czechs, Poles, German Conservatives, Slovenes, Croats and Romanians. After the 1879 election in Austria this coalition had 168 seats out of 353 (the German Liberals and their allies had 174). To maintain his coalition, Taaffe skilfully made some concessions to various national groups: for example in 1880 Czechs were allowed to conduct Government business in their own language. However, this in turn alarmed many Germans. Taaffe also passed social legislation, putting limits on child and female labour and on working hours, and introducing sickness and accident insurance. He fell from power in 1893 when he proposed extending the franchise. Universal male suffrage was eventually introduced in 1907.

Taaffe was succeeded by a coalition of German Liberals, Conservatives and Poles under Prince Alfred Windischgrätz, until in turn he was succeeded in 1895 by Count Casimir Badeni. In 1897 Badeni was forced to accept a right-wing coalition of Clericals, Christian Socials, Poles and

Slavs	15.5
Germans	7.0
Magyars	3.3
Romanians	1.0
Italians	0.3
Total	29.1

Source: F. Schuselka, *Ist Osterreich Deutsch?* (Leipzig, 1843).

TABLE 23
The population of the Habsburg Empire in 1843 (millions)

Racial group	Austrian half	Hungarian half
Germans	9 950 266	2 037 435
Magyars	10 974	10 050 575
Czechs	6 435 983	
Poles	4 967 984	
Ruthenes	3 518 854	472 587
Italians	768 422	
Romanians	275 115	2 949 032
Slovaks		1 967 970
Slovenes		1 252 940
Serbs	783 334	1 106 471
Croats		1 833 162
Others		469 255
Approximate total	28 000 000	21 000 000

TABLE 24
The principal nationalities of the Habsburg Empire – the 1910 census

Note. 'Others' included Jews and Muslims. Jews were concentrated in cities, especially Vienna. Most Muslims were in Bosnia-Herzegovina.

Czechs. He tried to make more language concessions to the Czechs, but in so doing upset both Slovenes and Germans. Increasing arguments inside and outside parliament led to rule by decree under Badeni's successor, Ernst von Körber. Social Democrats and Christian Socialists vied for influence, but politics were complicated by the activities of nationalist groups and bargaining between parties. There were four Prime Ministers between 1897 and 1900, and parliamentary government gave way to rule by the Emperor's officials, despite the presence of about 30 political parties.

KEY ISSUE

To what extent did the Germans and Magyars retain their influence in Austria and Hungary?

HUNGARY

In Hungary the liberals were in power for three decades from the 1870s, under Count Koloman Tisza and then his son, Stephen. The Liberals were a Magyar party, and indeed the Magyars dominated parliament, in which other nationalities were virtually unrepresented by means of a limited and manipulated electoral system designed to retain Magyar superiority. Although comprising about half the population of Hungary, the Magyars dominated the bureaucracy and professions, discriminating against non-Magyar speakers. Education Acts between 1879 and 1891 made the teaching of Magyar compulsory. At the same time Tisza pursued liberal trade policies. The Hungarian Liberals wanted to maintain the connection with Austria, but extorted concessions such as favourable trading terms from Vienna. Attempts to set up a separate Hungarian-speaking army were resisted by Franz Josef, who set up a Government, effectively suspending the Hungarian parliament. Relations were smoothed somewhat when Tisza became Prime Minister again: Franz Josef backed down from his threat to challenge the Hungarian *élite* by extending universal suffrage to Hungary. The principal threat to the Liberals came from the rising Independence Party but a Magyar *élite* remained in power.

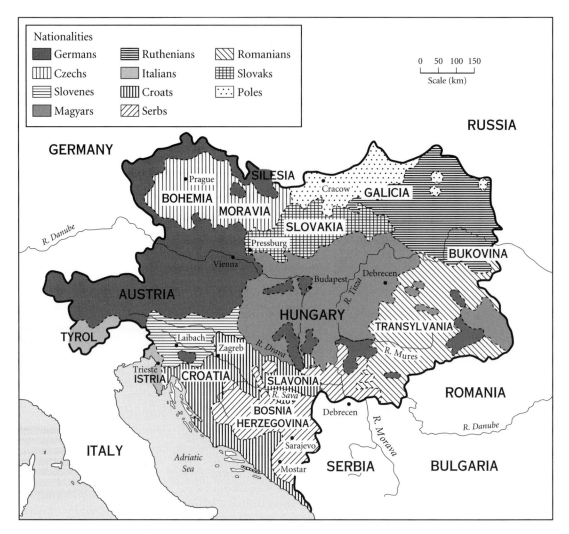

MAP 17   *Nationalities of the Habsburg monarchy*

THE CHALLENGE OF NATIONALISM

Historians dispute whether growing dissatisfaction with their lot by the various nationalities of the multinational Empire was the major factor in its ultimate collapse. Certainly nationalism raised complex issues:

● Magyar nationalism provoked dissatisfaction within Hungary as much as Austrian attempts to exert their influence throughout the Empire. A compromise agreement between Croatia and Hungary in 1868 had similar features to the *Ausgleich*: Croatia retained a *Diet* to manage Croatian affairs and was represented in the Hungarian parliament when matters of joint interest to Hungary and Croatia were discussed

- however, Magyarisation or the extension of Hungarian influence proceeded at all levels. For example, although an 1868 law made concessions to the use of other languages inside Hungary, various Education Acts made Magyar compulsory in schools
- the Magyars had most representation in the electorate, and had over 90 per cent of the seats in the Hungarian parliament
- internal quarrels and a slower rate of development amongst other nationalities hindered their political development. For example, rivalry between the Croats and the Serbs played into Hungarian hands. The South Slavs were divided between Hungary and Cisleithania. The Austrians found more difficulty in dampening down the political demands of 'their' Slavs
- the Czechs wanted a federal solution to their nationalistic claims. The Czechs disagreed with the Germans on issues like parliamentary representation and language rights. Many Czechs wanted an *Ausgleich* giving them similar privileges to the Hungarians. An increasingly articulate Czech middle class won concessions: in 1897 the Czech language was given equal status with German in the internal administration of Bohemia and Moravia, a concession withdrawn after German civil servants objected to the requirement that they be bilingual. However, the Czechs were only given equality in areas which indisputably had a Czech majority. Other nationalities were afraid that the Czechs wanted dominance over them
- Italians wanted their own assembly: but ironically within the Empire they already had more parliamentary representatives in relation to their numbers than any other nationality
- Germans increasingly had their own grievances, and some advocated union with Germany as a means of guaranteeing their long-term dominance. Union was the aim of Georg von Schonerer's anti-semitic, anti-Slav and pan-German movement.

Despite real and perceived grievances, there were relatively few demands for a break-up of the Empire. Most Czechs, despite their dissatisfaction, preferred to stay within some sort of federation; an independent state might be at the mercy of a powerful German neighbour. Many Magyars recognised that on their own, they might fall prey to Russian expansionism. Most Poles, despite later demands for a separate state, were content to stay within the protection of the Austrian State, particularly since they were allowed to dominate Galicia, which contained a large Ruthenian minority. Despite the pessimism of many about the prospects for the Empire as the nineteenth century drew to a close, a number of compromises were worked out.

> ### KEY ISSUE
>
> *What problems did nationalist discontent pose for the Habsburg Empire?*

F *War and dissolution of Empire*

The declaration of war in 1914 brought temporary unity to quarrelling factions within the Empire. This did not last long. Franz Josef lost much of his control as power was concentrated in the army high command. Military defeats highlighted and exacerbated long-standing problems. The principal features of the war years were:

● inadequate military planning
● increasing national divisions, often reflected within the army
● increasing economic problems and shortages
● the accession of Franz Josef's inexperienced and indecisive great-nephew Karl in 1916.

Austria fell increasingly under German control, and in 1916 had to agree to a Joint High Command, with the Germans controlling Habsburg forces. Even before the end of the War, national groups were breaking away from the control of Vienna and Budapest. Ironically, although the dissolution of the Empire had not been a war aim of the Allies in 1914, and indeed Powers like Britain saw the Empire as a force for stability, the results of the War included the creation of new states like Poland, Czechoslovakia and Yugoslavia. These had been beyond the dreams of most nationalists in the years immediately preceding the war.

2 ꞁ ECONOMIC HISTORY

Economic progress in the Empire was variable after 1815. Dynamic industrial growth took place in the 1830s and 1840s, in parts of Austria, Bohemia and Moravia. Bohemia had extensive deposits of coal and iron ore, and almost a third of its population worked in industry by 1890. There were patches of urbanisation and a development of manufacturing industry, sometimes on aristocratic estates. Vienna was a centre of light industry. However, industrial development was slower than in many German States, and was held back by a shortage of credit and the regime's attempt to encourage self-sufficiency. Hungary remained essentially agricultural. Harvest failures after 1845, growing unemployment, social problems and high costs of administration helped to create the social and economic problems which contributed to the crisis of 1848–9 in the Empire.

After 1848 Austria's economy was affected by relations with the other German States. A treaty of 1853 excluded Austria from the *Zollverein* until at least 1860, but it granted most of the benefits of membership such as free access to German markets for Austria's most important exports, grain and wool. The economy also benefited from other measures: for example the abolition of tariffs between Austria and Hungary; further railway building; and the establishment of the *Creditanstalt* Bank in 1855. Historians debate as to how significant economic progress was, because development was variable. The foundations of a more modern economy were laid, although resources were not enough to adequately support the Empire's foreign and defence ambitions.

There appears to have been significant economic growth in the years immediately after the *Ausgleich*; then a depression between 1873 and

KEY ISSUE

What were the main characteristics of economic development in the Habsburg Empire?

	1835–44	1855–64	1885–94	1905–14
Austria	49.4	60.0	66.2	85.9
Hungary	51.0	68.1	102.6	131.7

TABLE 25
Output of grain crops 1835–1914 (annual averages in million quintals)

1840	1860	1880	1900	1913
144	4543	18 507	36 330	44 748

TABLE 26
Railway mileage open in the Habsburg Empire 1840–1913 (kilometres)

1830	1850	1870	1900	1913
297	554	1663	3638	6177

TABLE 27
Value of the Habsburg Empire's external trade 1830–1913 (million kronen)

1879; moderate growth until the mid 1890s; then a period of substantial growth before World War I. The Austrian economy grew steadily overall during the nineteenth century, although at a slower rate than the industrial regions of Western Europe, and the internal political divisions of the Empire probably had a less significant economic effect than was sometimes imagined. Hungary's economic development was amongst the fastest in the Empire, but in 1890, 95 per cent of Magyars, either the aristocratic *élite* or the peasantry, still made their living from agriculture. Grain was Hungary's largest export.

3 ～ FOREIGN POLICY

A *The Metternich period*

Metternich was influential not just in Habsburg affairs but in Europe as a whole. He helped to preserve the Empire after 1809, despite its weakness in the wake of Napoleon's victories. After 1815 he sought continued co-operation between the victorious Allies to preserve the Vienna peace settlement and to avert the threat of revolution: hence his so-called 'system' of Congresses. In several respects Metternich was successful:

- the Congresses enabled Metternich to exert some influence over the monarchs and diplomats of other Great Powers, although the extent of this influence is debated by historians
- he secured Austrian control over the post-war German Confederation
- he restored Habsburg control in Italy.

In the long run, Metternich failed. Austria lost control of Italy and Germany. He could not avert revolution. He never had a 'system' which controlled Europe – although his conservative strategy worked for a long time.

See Chapter 1 for European diplomacy in the period 1815–48

KEY ISSUE

What were the main principles of Metternich's foreign policy?

B *Post-Metternich*

Franz Josef controlled Habsburg foreign policy after 1848, but until 1859 largely relied upon the advice of Foreign Minister Count Karl Buol. During this period Austria abandoned its alliance with Russia, partly because of concern at possible Russian designs on Turkey, and joined Britain and France in imposing a peace treaty on Russia after the Crimean War. However, Austria did not have a close relationship with the Western Powers, and was therefore effectively neutral. Austria was isolated in its struggle with Piedmont over Austrian control in Northern Italy. Austrian military deficiencies and financial weaknesses were exposed in this war, as they were to be later. Buol was sacked after the Italian fiasco, and Franz Josef relied more upon his own resources.

One of the factors which helped to keep the Habsburg Empire together after Metternich's fall was the acknowledged desirability of a common foreign policy. Whatever grievances particular nationalities had against their neighbours within the Empire, the prospects for small independent states in a Europe dominated by Great Powers sometimes seemed less attractive. However, different parts of the Empire sometimes had their own priorities. Despite Austria's defeat by Prussia in 1866, Austria maintained a close relationship with the Prussian-dominated German Empire after 1870. German friendship became increasingly important in the face of Austro-Russian rivalry in the Balkans. The Hungarians also feared Russia and therefore had a common interest with Austria in maintaining friendship with Germany. However, the Czechs were both anti-German and pro-Russian by inclination. The Serbs favoured their Russian Slav neighbour, although they had no particular cause to be anti-German. Poles were both anti-German and anti-Russian by inclination, which was scarcely surprising given their past treatment by the Great Powers.

From 1867 the Dual Monarchy operated a joint foreign policy, with a common Foreign Minister. He required the agreement of both Prime Ministers for his policies. Count Andrassy became Foreign Minister in 1871 and was very influential in the role. Having helped to negotiate the 1867 constitutional arrangement, he then negotiated both the Three Emperors Alliance and the Dual Alliance of 1879.

Andrassy feared the encroachment of Pan Slavism and Russian expansionism. The Empire became increasingly obsessed with the Balkans, particularly after the Bosnian Revolt of 1875. A weak Turkey threatened a dangerous power vacuum close to the Empire's Dalmatian territories. But Austria's own encroachments there created complications. Having been given the right to occupy Bosnia-Herzegovina after the Congress of Berlin, there was a reluctance to incorporate it within the Empire since it would have significantly increased the Slav population. It was put within the administration of the common Foreign Minister.

The Habsburgs were prepared sometimes to cooperate with Russia in the interests of stability in the Balkans. In 1881 Austria rejected a Turkish proposal of an alliance against Russia. But renewed Russian interest

See page 28

See page 103

KEY ISSUE

How successful was Habsburg foreign policy after Metternich?

in Europe after the defeat of 1905 threatened confrontation, particularly after the 1908 Bosnian crisis. Count Alois von Aehrenthal, Foreign Minister from 1906, was forceful in his policy of making Austria an independent force in Great Power politics. He wanted to maintain the *status quo* but was also determined to prevent Serbian expansionism towards the sea. Franz Josef too was unwilling to allow his prestige to be challenged by the Serbs. This attitude was reinforced when Austria helped to enforce the settlement after the Balkan Wars of 1912–13. One of Austria's main concerns was that Germany might not back it to the hilt: once Austria was assured of German support in 1914, it was prepared to declare war on Serbia. Austrian Chief of Staff Conrad wanted war. Alan Sked believes that Franz Josef's fear of Serbian nationalism was a major cause of the war and that 'the Monarchy deliberately started a world war rather than compromise internally or externally on the South Slav question' (Sked, page 269). An equally big mistake was to assume that other Great Powers would consent to Habsburg policy towards the Serbs.

See pages 446–7

4 ∽ BIBLIOGRAPHY

There are a number of useful and accessible studies on the history of the Empire during this period. Somewhat dated now but still useful is *The Habsburg Monarchy, 1809–1918* by A.J.P. Taylor (Hamish Hamilton, 1960). Also useful are *The Decline and Fall of the Habsburg Empire 1815–1918* by A. Sked (Longman, 1989) and *The Habsburg Empire 1815–1918* by N. Pelling (Hodder and Stoughton, Access to History 1996), both of which consider a range of interpretations. *The Dissolution of the Austro-Hungarian Empire 1867–1918* by J. Mason (Longmans Seminar Studies, 1986) contains documents as well as analysis. *Francis Joseph* by S. Beller (Longman Profiles in Power, 1996) is not just a biography but is a useful analysis of the whole period. *Austria-Hungary and the Origins of the First World War* by S. Williamson (Macmillan, 1991) is a detailed study of foreign policy issues.

5 ∽ STRUCTURED QUESTIONS AND ESSAYS

1. (a) Outline the main features of Metternich's domestic and foreign policies; (10 marks)
   (b) Which was more successful, and why? (15 marks)
2. (a) What were the main problems facing the Habsburg Empire between 1815 and 1848? (10 marks)
   (b) How successfully did the Empire deal with these problems? (15 marks)
3. To what extent, and why, have historians disagreed about the importance of Metternich in Austrian and European politics? (25 marks)

4. (a) What were the main terms of the *Ausgleich* of 1867? (10 marks)
   (b) How was the government of the Dual Monarchy after 1867 different from that of the Habsburg Empire between 1815 and 1867? (15 marks)
5. In what ways did nationalism pose a significant threat to the Austro-Hungarian Empire after 1867? (25 marks)
6. In what ways, and why, was Magyar nationalism a threat to the Habsburg Empire in the nineteenth century? (25 marks)
7. (a) What were the main grievances of the various nationalities in the Habsburg Empire after 1815? (10 marks)
   (b) To what extent were these grievances resolved by 1914? (15 marks)
8. (a) What were the main principles of Austro-Hungarian foreign policy after 1867? (10 marks)
   (b) How successful was that foreign policy in practice? (15 marks)
9. How responsible was Austria-Hungary for World War I? (25 marks)
10. To what extent was the dissolution of the Austro-Hungarian Empire inevitable by 1918? (25 marks)

6 ⌐ AN EXERCISE IN HISTORICAL PERSPECTIVE: TO WHAT EXTENT WAS THE DISSOLUTION OF THE HABSBURG EMPIRE INEVITABLE AFTER 1867?

With the benefit of hindsight there is a temptation to think that, with all the internal problems there were in the Habsburg Empire in the nineteenth century, and the complications of foreign policy before World War I, that its eventual dissolution was inevitable. Did 'nationalism' have to triumph? Such an approach is actually dangerously unhistorical: there was nothing 'inevitable' about such a development. Might the Empire actually have survived for much longer but for World War I and Austria's defeat? Some commentators after World War I positively welcomed the break-up of the Empire, feeling that successor states like Czechoslovakia were more progressive in outlook. Some later commentators felt that a strong Austria would actually be a better counterweight to other Great Powers, especially Germany and Russia. However, A.J.P. Taylor, whilst sympathetic to the idea of a strong central European power bloc, concluded that the Habsburgs had been unable to provide it. Others were less certain: Edward Crankshaw (*The Fall of the House of Habsburg*, 1983) thought that Franz Josef's regime might have developed into a genuinely constitutional monarchy but for World War I, which he did not specifically blame on Austria. This latter idea was taken up by the German historian Fritz Fischer, who as part of his argument that Germany was the main instigator of war in 1914, preferred to see Austria as manipulated by Berlin, rather than being one of the prime movers in bringing about war.

Historians have tackled the question of 'inevitability' as the following extracts show. Read them and then answer the questions which follow.

Many expert observers in the years before 1914 believed that the internal problems of the Habsburg Monarchy could and would be solved. Almost until it was on its deathbed in 1918 most of the nationalities under its rule continued to seek satisfaction for their grievances within the empire rather than outside it. Supported by the army and bureaucracy and by the still powerful feeling of loyalty to the dynasty, aided above all by the complete lack of unity between the subject-nationalities, which sometimes disliked each other more than they did their German or Hungarian rulers, the Habsburg regime showed surprising vitality. It successfully surmounted the crises of the later 1890s ... and in the decade before the First World War it seemed if anything to be gaining strength. What doomed it was not the strength of national feeling in its territories but its foreign policy, its inability and unwillingness to adopt the strict neutrality in international affairs which alone might have saved it. The way to its collapse was opened above all by the determination of the emperor and his ministers to maintain the fiction that it was a great power.

SOURCE A
M. Anderson, The Ascendancy of Europe 1815–1914 *(Longman, 1972), pages 162–3*

There seems little doubt that the Ausgleich of 1867, which gave the Magyars an effective veto over any future amendments to the constitution, had effectively petrified the political system. It is therefore tempting to argue that the Ausgleich of 1867 finally sealed the fate of the Habsburgs.

But possibly the problem went even deeper than that. The real reason the nationalities problem found no political solution is perhaps that the dynasty did not put much effort into looking for one. He [Franz Josef] did not conceive of the Empire as a device for allowing a community of national groups to live together in peace and harmony: he thought of it simply as the territorial possessions of the house of Habsburg. He was only genuinely interested in short-term political fixes which would enable him to retain, defend and possibly enlarge these territories, which in turn meant that he demanded the right to control foreign policy. In this sense the Ausgleich gave him all that he wanted ... the interpretation that sees the nationalities problem as condemning the Empire to self-destruction is slightly too simplistic: only the addition of the Emperor's lack of political initiative ensured the eventual disintegration of his Empire.

SOURCE B
N. Pelling, The Habsburg Empire 1815–1918 *(Hodder and Stoughton, 1996) pages 117–18*

SOURCE C
S. *Beller,* Francis Joseph
(Longman, 1996) page 179

One of the most popular presentations of the emperor in his final years would like to suggest, the old man, beset by wicked fate, betrayed by feuding nationalities, nobly soldiering on as the last remaining link of an empire which would fall apart as soon as he left the saddle of command ... he himself, as ruler of the empire for over sixty years, had had a large a role as any in bringing this rather sorry state of affairs about. He was not so much a victim, let alone part of the solution, as one of the main causes of the problem. Indeed the very fact that the empire seemed to depend on Francis Joseph's personal survival for its continuation was a measure of the emperor's failure as a dynast, let alone a head of state.

SOURCE D
A. *Sked,* The Decline and Fall
of the Habsburg Empire
1815–1918 *(Longman, 1989)*
pages 187 and 231

almost nobody inside the Monarchy was working for a republic during this period and practically no one wanted to see the Monarchy break up ... It was only defeat in war, therefore, which was to precipitate collapse ... had the Central Powers actually won the First World War, the Habsburg Monarchy would have survived not merely intact, but almost certainly expanded ... At no point between 1867 and 1914 did the Monarchy even vaguely face the sort of challenge to its existence that it faced in 1848–9 ... economic growth was continuing and the Monarchy was becoming more and more integrated in terms of living standards, infrastructure and finance.

Q

1. *Identify any similarities and differences in interpretations of the causes of the break-up of the Habsburg Empire given in Sources A–D (10 marks)*
2. *Explain why interpretations of the break-up have differed (10 marks)*
3. *Using the information in these extracts and the chapter as a whole, analyse what evidence can be used for and against each of the following statements:*
   (i)   Mistakes in foreign policy led to the break-up of the Empire.
   (ii) The multinational character of the Empire made its eventual dissolution inevitable.
   (iii) The nature of the monarchy caused the break-up of the Empire.
   (iv) Economic weakness contributed seriously to the weakness of the Empire. (20 marks)

The Age of *Realpolitik*: European Diplomacy, 1870–90

14

See Map 18 on
page 380

INTRODUCTION

THE EMERGENCE OF GERMANY ON TO THE INTERNATIONAL SCENE

When studying the complicated and involved course of European diplomacy during this period, it is helpful to keep in mind the following key developments:

- The creation of the German Empire and the Treaty of Frankfurt marked a real shift in the balance of power in Europe. Germany had emerged as the strongest military force in Europe. Disraeli, the leader of the Conservative Party in Britain, went so far as to argue in the House of Commons that:

> 'This war represents the German revolution, a greater political event than the French revolution of the last century ... . You have a new world, new influences at work, new and unknown objects and dangers with which to cope ... The balance of power has been entirely destroyed ...'.

- On the other hand Germany would not be able to defend its newly won superiority if the other Powers combined against it. France, humiliated by defeat and the loss of Alsace-Lorraine, would sooner or later seek to challenge it either by building up an anti-German alliance or by exploiting to Germany's disadvantage a major international crisis. In the early 1870s, as A.J.P. Taylor has written, 'the prospect of French recovery was the dynamic factor in European politics'.
- Over the next 20 years the principal aim of German foreign policy was therefore to contain France either by isolating it or by appeasing it in areas where its policy represented no threat to Germany.
- But French revisionism was not the only source of unrest in Europe. The accelerating decline of the Turkish Empire led to acute Austro-Russian rivalry in the Balkans. Austrian hostility was reinforced by

---

Reparations
After the fall of Paris in January 1871 a preliminary peace was negotiated. Then on 10 May the Treaty of Frankfurt was concluded. France ceded the whole of Alsace and most of Lorraine and had to pay Germany the sum of five billion Francs in reparations. German troops occupied Eastern France until 1873 when the reparations were paid in full.

KEY ISSUE

What was the impact on Europe of German unification?

MAP 18 *The European States in 1879 after the Franco-Prussian War*

the British, who feared Russian expansion into the Mediterranean
and the extension of Russian power up to the borders of
Afghanistan.

● Given Germany's position at the centre of the European continent
every crisis involving the European Powers had potentially important consequences for its security. Bismarck above all feared that a

ANALYSIS

Differing views on Bismarck's foreign policy

The American historian, William Langer, in his comprehensive study, *European Alliances and Alignments, 1871–90* argued that 'no other statesman of [Bismarck's] standing had ever before shown the same great moderation and sound political sense of the possible and desirable'. He saw Bismarck after 1871 as a great statesman constantly striving for peace. This view has by no means been accepted uncritically by other historians. A.J.P. Taylor portrayed Bismarck's foreign policy as essentially **opportunist**. Bruce Waller has pointed out that Langer's views on German foreign policy 'were strongly coloured by the effort to take a fair-minded view after the excesses of First World War propaganda'. He argues that Bismarck 'created and preserved tension' by encouraging rivalry in the colonies and the Balkans and even suggests that at times 'Bismarck's actions would have led to war had it not been for the good sense of other European statesmen'. Bismarck was a statesman of genius, but it would be a mistake to ignore the negative side of his policies.

opportunist a policy adapted to circumstance and opportunities with no long-term aims

major war over the Balkans would give France the chance to escape from isolation and revise the Treaty of Frankfurt. He was thus forced out of self preservation into pursuing what amounted to a European rather than German foreign policy.

1 ↜ THE PERIOD OF ADJUSTMENT, 1871–5

Langer described the four years after the Treaty of Frankfurt as a 'formative period during which the European states were attempting to adjust themselves to changed circumstances'. Bismarck managed so successfully to reassure the eastern European Powers that Germany was a '**saturated power**' and had not the slightest ambition to extend its frontiers any further that by the end of 1873 Berlin was the centre of an informal grouping of states, which was known as the League of the Three Emperors or *Dreikaiserbund*.

A *The League of the Three Emperors*

By 1872 the Austrians had come to terms with their defeat of 1866 and were anxious to persuade Germany to sign an alliance aimed at stopping Russian expansion into the Balkans and Turkey. Tsar Alexander II was determined to prevent such an alliance and thus insisted on visiting Berlin at the very time the Austrian Emperor, Franz Josef, was there in

TIMELINE

May 1871 The Treaty of Frankfurt

May 1873 Fall of the Thiers Government in France

June and October 1873 The League of the Three Emperors created

April 1875 The *Is War in Sight?* Crisis

'**saturated power**' a state which has enough land and economic resources

Naming of Austria-Hungary
Since the *Ausgleich* of 1867 Austria had officially been transformed into Austria-Hungary

See page 11

September 1872. As both powers were seeking Germany's friendship, Bismarck was skilfully able to paper over the differences between Russia and Austria and represent the meeting of the three Emperors as a sign of mutual friendship and unity against revolutionary republican threats and so ensure the isolation of France. The following year further negotiations resulted in the **League of the Three Emperors** with which Italy later became associated. In some ways the League appeared to be a return to the politics of the old Holy Alliance of 1815 in that its leaders were pledged to defend the monarchical principle against revolutionary threats, but in reality each of its members wanted something different out of it:

- the Austrians were determined to use the League to build up a close relationship with Berlin to ensure that the Germans did not in the future ally with Russia to divide up their Empire
- the Russians were equally determined to use the League to stop the development of close Austro-German ties at the expense of their own influence in eastern Europe
- Italy hoped that an association with the League would guarantee its annexation of Rome and prevent the Pope from enlisting international help to restore his control of the city
- to Bismarck the League demonstrated the isolation of France. It brought together Russia and Austria and enabled Germany to avoid making a choice between them, which might result in driving the Power, with which Berlin was not allied, into the arms of France.

KEY ISSUE

Why was the League of the Three Emperors formed and how important was it?

The **League of the Three Emperors** was negotiated On 6 June 1873 at Schönbrunn when the Emperors of Austria-Hungary and Russia agreed to 'consult together' in the event of a crisis and 'to impose the maintenance of peace in Europe against all attempts to destroy it from whatever quarter they come'. If joint military action were needed, a fresh agreement would have to be concluded. The German Emperor joined the League on 22 October.

Franco-Italian relations since 1871

In September 1870 the Italians occupied Rome once the French garrison there had been withdrawn to fight the Prussians. The Pope remained determined to regain control of the city and hoped that a French Government would support him. The Italians felt particularly threatened when the French sent a war ship to cruise off the Italian coast in case the Pope needed help and therefore sought protection by looking to the predominantly Protestant state of Germany.

B *The 'Is War In Sight' crisis*

To break out of isolation France needed a defensive treaty with Russia, but at this stage Russia had no quarrel with Germany. Anglo-French relations were good, but this was no substitute for a Russian alliance, as Britain had only a small army and anyway had no quarrel with Germany. Officially the French talked of revenge, but in reality the Thiers Government, which was in power from 1871–3, was primarily concerned with paying off the indemnity and ending the German occupation of eastern France. The next Government under Macmahon was more aggressive and pursued the high risk policy of attempting to provoke Bismarck into some hostile action which would unite the European states against Germany. It also supported the Catholic Church in its struggle with the Prussian state and accelerated the modernisation of the French army.

Bismarck did become sufficiently worried by France's recovery to make a serious diplomatic blunder. He inspired an aggressive article in the newspaper, the *Berliner Post*, on 8 April, entitled *Is War in Sight?*, which suggested that Germany was about to declare war on France. This impression was further strengthened when a high ranking German diplomat in Berlin openly defended the idea of a preventive war against France. Most likely Bismarck was bluffing and attempting to slow up France's military recovery, but the reaction of Britain and Russia indicated the underlying changes in the European balance of power brought about by German unification. It was made clear to Bismarck that neither country wanted to see the destruction of France. They accepted the settlement of 1871, but could not tolerate any further extension of German power. The crisis underlined the potential weakness of Germany's position in Europe and showed that the threat of further German expansion in Europe at the expense of France would eventually create a hostile coalition. Bismarck, however, rapidly managed to reassure St Petersburg and London that he had no intention of attacking France and the crisis blew over.

> **KEY ISSUE**
>
> *What was the significance of the* Is War in Sight *crisis?*

2 ↜ THE EASTERN CRISIS OF 1875–8

A *The attitude of the Great Powers to the Eastern Question*

All the Great Powers with the exception of Germany had vital but conflicting interests in the Balkans and the Straits :

- the Straits of the Bosphorus and the Dardanelles were of great strategic and economic importance for the Russians as they provided access to the Mediterranean, but since they were still controlled by the Turks who could close them any time, the Russians felt, in Langer's words, that 'the very key to their house was in the hands of a foreigner'. The influential Russian Pan-Slav movement to which

See Map 19 on page 384

TIMELINE

July 1875	Revolt against Turkish rule in Bosnia and Herzegovina
April 1876	Bulgarian revolt broke out
June	Serbia and Montenegro declared war on Turkey
July	The Reichstadt Agreement between Russia and Austria
October	Turks advanced on Belgrade
Dec–Jan 1876–7	Constantinople Conference
March 1877	Budapest Convention
April 1877–Jan 1878	Russo-Turkish War
March 1878	The Treaty of San Stefano
June–July 1878	The Congress of Berlin

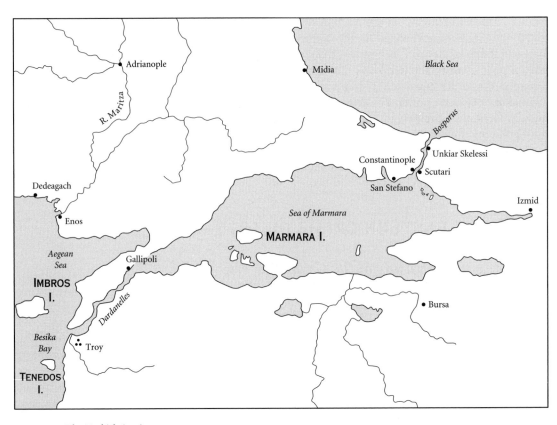

MAP 19 *The Turkish Straits*

General Ignatiev, the Russian ambassador at Constantinople belonged, also believed that Russia was the natural protector of the Balkan Slavs from both the Turks and the Austrians

- the Austrians were economically dependent on the Danube, which carried most of their trade with the outside world. They did not therefore want the collapse of Turkish rule in the Balkans and the emergence of a strong pro-Russian Serbia which would block any future extension of their influence to the south east and also act as a magnet for the Slavs in Hungary. To prevent this they were ready to intervene in the Balkans and annex Bosnia and Herzegovina. As Austria had ceased to have any influence in Germany after its defeat in 1866, the future of Balkans became a matter of increasing concern
- Britain even more than Austria wished to preserve the Turkish Empire as it prevented the extension of Russian power into the eastern Mediterranean, which had become an area of great strategic importance for the British Empire since the opening of the Suez Canal in 1869 as the shortest route to India
- the French, too, wished to maintain Turkish power in the Balkans as they had large sums of money invested in the Turkish Empire.

Pan-Slav Movement
The Pan-Slav movement was set up in 1858 when the Slavic Welfare Society was established. The 'Bible' of the Panslavs was N. Danilevski's book, *Russia and Europe* which argued that Russia's main enemies were Turkey and Austria

See page 396

B *The Balkan uprisings, 1875–6*

What was left of the unity of the League of the Three Emperors was further shaken by the revolts which broke out in the Balkans in July 1875 and rapidly escalated into a major European crisis. In July 1875 the Slav peasants of Herzegovina and Bosnia rose up against Turkish rule. At first the League with some backing from Britain unsuccessfully tried to mediate between the rebels and the Turkish Government. In December the Austrians managed to persuade the Sultan to accept a programme of reforms aimed at improving the conditions in the two provinces only to have them rejected by the rebels as insufficient. By the Spring of 1876 the unity of the League was beginning to come under considerable pressure. The Russians were openly arguing for intervention and a possible partition of the Balkans while the Austrians still clung to the idea of forcing Turkey to accept the reform programme. In May Russia grudgingly consented to present the Turks with yet another package of reforms (outlined in a document called the *Berlin Memorandum*) coupled with a demand for a cease-fire in the fighting. The Russians and Austrians also agreed that if the Turkish Empire collapsed, Austria would occupy a part of Bosnia, while Russia would take southern Bessarabia in Romania, which it had lost in 1856. This initiative failed for two reasons:

See Map 20 on page 386

- it was rejected by the British, who were anxious to keep the Russians out of the Balkans
- it met with violent opposition in Constantinople, which resulted in the overthrow of Sultan Abdul Aziz and his replacement by Murad V.

MAP 20

The Balkans and the Congress of Berlin, 1878

Meanwhile the crisis deepened: the revolts spread into Bulgaria and briefly it looked as if the whole of the Ottoman Empire was about to collapse, which naturally encouraged Serbia and Montenegro to come to the help of the rebels and declare war on Turkey. Russia was swept by a wave of popular support for the Balkan rebellions. Several thousand volunteers flocked to help the Serbs. The Russians, confident of a Serb victory, managed to persuade the Austrians at Reichstadt in July 1876 to agree to an ambitious programme of territorial changes in the Balkans which would safeguard each Power's vital interests there. Then, contrary to all expectations, the Turks managed to inflict a decisive defeat on the Serb forces in September.

The Eastern crisis now entered a new and potentially more danger-ous phase, as the Russian Government could not simply sit back and allow Turkey to re-establish itself in the Balkans. Gorchakov, the Russ-ian foreign Minister, therefore launched a diplomatic campaign to win over the Powers to support a policy of Russian intervention on behalf of Serbia and Bulgaria. In this he was enormously helped by the impact of the news of Turkish atrocities in Bulgaria on British public opinion in early September, which effectively forced Disraeli, if only temporari-ly, to abandon his support for Turkey.

> **KEY ISSUE**
>
> *Why did Gorchakov gain support for Russian intervention in the Balkans?*

ANALYSIS

The Bulgarian massacres

When the Bulgarian uprising first started at the end of April 1876 the Turkish authorities did not have enough regular troops at their disposal and therefore armed the local Muslim population. Angered by the murders of unarmed Turks carried out by the rebels, they effectively put down the uprising with great brutality. At the lowest estimate some 60 villages were destroyed and 12 000 killed. Gladstone seized the chance to attack Disraeli's foreign pol-icy and on 6 September published his famous pamphlet, the *Bul-garian Horrors and the Question of the East*. He called upon Britain to give up its dislike of 'the standing hobgoblin of Russia ... and emulate Russia by sharing in her good deeds ...'.

C *Germany's attitude to the Eastern Question, 1875–7*

Yet despite the strong humanitarian case for intervention it was clear that both in London and Vienna there were considerable suspicions about Russia's motives. Increasingly Berlin was seen as the key to the situation by all three Powers. Both the British and Russians wanted Bismarck to seize the initiative and call a conference to sort the prob-lem out. The Tsar actually sounded out the Berlin Government in October 1876 to see whether it would support Russia in the event of war with Austria. This was the one question which Bismarck dreaded because he did not want to have to choose between the two Empires. This would upset the balance of power and so give France a chance to regain its influence. Not surprisingly Bismarck's reply was ambiguous. He stressed that Germany wanted to see neither Power weakened and hoped that Austria and Russia would be able to agree on a joint policy. At the end of 1876 he did not see the Eastern Question in itself as a problem for Germany, as he remarked in a speech to the German *Reichstag* on 5 December:

> I will not advise the active participation of Germany in these things [the Eastern Crisis] as long as I see no interest for Germany in it which – forgive the blunt expression – would be worth the healthy bones of a single Pomeranian musketeer. I have sought to emphasise that we must be more sparing with the blood of our people when it is a question of deliberately embarking on a policy in which no interest of ours is involved ...

'Nevertheless he was worried about the effect of the crisis on the international situation and thus on Germany's own security. Essentially, as Waller has pointed out, he wanted to create 'a political constellation in which all Powers except France needed Germany and were kept from forming an opposing coalition'. Thus he was quite happy to see the Ottoman Empire partitioned in such a way that it would encourage better relations between Britain, Austria and Russia without quite removing all rivalries and frictions. In the famous Kissingen memorandum of 15 June 1877 he suggested that Britain should have Egypt and Turkey, while Russia be given the Black Sea:

status quo existing situation

> Both would be in a position to be satisfied for a long time ahead with the **status quo**, and yet in their most important interests would be involved in a rivalry which would hardly allow them to take part in coalitions against us ...

D *Russia prepares for intervention, October–April, 1876–7*

By the end of October 1876 the Turks were advancing rapidly on Belgrade, which was only saved by a Russian ultimatum demanding a temporary armistice. The British used this pause to propose that the Great Powers should call a conference at Constantinople to work out yet another programme of reforms to be imposed on the Turks. As Disraeli cynically remarked, 'its purpose was to keep the Russians out of Constantinople, not to create an ideal existence for Turkish Christians'. The Conference opened in December, but the Sultan skilfully found a pretext to reject the proposed reform programme by introducing a new western style parliamentary constitution. He argued that now, as all Turkish subjects lived under a constitutional monarch with civil liberties, the intervention of the Powers was unnecessary. The conference broke up on 20 January 1877 and Turkey was isolated. The way for Russian intervention was made easier by two important agreements:

● the London Protocol which committed the Great Powers again to make a further attempt to enforce reform on the Turks. If this failed the assumption was that there would be fresh talks between the Powers before any action was to be taken

- if however, as seemed very likely, the Turks rejected the London Protocol, the Russians prepared the way for intervention by negotiating with Austria the Convention of Budapest in March 1877. Austria's neutrality was secured in return for its right to occupy Bosnia and Herzegovina. Serbia and Montenegro would remain neutral 'buffer states' between areas occupied by the Russian and Austrian armies, while Russia would regain southern Besserabia. If the Turkish empire collapsed, the situation in the Balkans would be regulated by an international conference. Both sides agreed in advance that no large independent Slav state would be created in the Balkans.

E *The Russo-Turkish War and its consequences*

When the Turkish Government rejected the London Protocol on 9 April, Russia ignored the provisions it contained for further talks. Once the snows had melted on the Balkan mountain passes, Russian troops moved into Turkish territory. As the advance gathered momentum, the prospect of a Russian victory revived British and Austrian suspicions of Russia's real intentions. But an immediate crisis was averted by Osman Pasha's heroic defence of Plevna, which delayed the Russian forces for five months. When the fortress fell on 11 December the Russian advance resumed, and by 20 January Tsarist troops were just outside Constantinople. The Turks had little option but to sue for peace.

The terms, which were first outlined in an armistice on 31 January and then confirmed by the Treaty of San Stefano in March, fuelled British and Austrian suspicions of Russia's real motives in the Balkans. They were negotiated by the Russian Ambassador at Constantinople, the Pan-Slav Ignatiev, who seized the chance decisively to strengthen Russian's position in the Balkans. In the words of M.S. Anderson, San Stefano was 'the fullest practical expression ever given in Russian foreign policy to the Panslav ideal':

See Map 20 on page 386

- Montenegro and Serbia were to be given their independence
- Romania would also become independent, but would give up southern Besserabia to Russia in exchange for the Dobrudja
- Bosnia and Herzegovina were to be united under a Turkish governor whose appointment would be approved by the Great Powers
- contrary to what had been agreed at Budapest in March 1877 a large self-governing pro-Russian Bulgaria under an elected prince was to be created, which would stretch from the Danube to the Aegean, thus potentially giving Russia access to the Mediterranean. It was to be occupied for two years by Russian troops.

Not surprisingly these terms provoked the British to sending the fleet to Constantinople and to strengthening their garrison in Malta. For a short time it really looked as if war might break out between Britain and Russia.

KEY ISSUE

Why were the British and Austrians so hostile to the Treaty of San Stefano?

ANALYSIS

How near to a general war was Europe in 1878?

War could easily have broken out by accident in January and February 1878. On 8 February the British fleet was ordered to sail up the Straits to Constantinople, but it made itself look ridiculous when it turned round after entering the Straits because it had not received permission from the Sultan to proceed to Constantinople. This made Disraeli all the more determined to defend British prestige. On 15 February the fleet actually reached Constantinople. The Russian Commander in Chief, Grand Duke Nicholas, meanwhile, was told that he had a free hand to occupy the city. If he had, war would probably have resulted. Fortunately Nicholas believed that the Turkish defences were too strong and did not therefore advance, but his army remained encamped just outside Constantinople until the Berlin Congress was finished. This ensured that the British fleet also remained anchored off Constantinople. The smallest incident could have caused a war. As the British Admiral, Lord Charles Beresford observed, 'if even a midshipman (junior naval officer) had lost his temper, he might have run the country into war'.

In an attempt to defuse the crisis the Powers agreed at Austria's suggestion to discuss the whole problem at a congress in Berlin, a sign in itself that Berlin and not Paris was now the political centre of Europe. Before the congress met the Powers attempted to safeguard their key interests through a series of secret agreements. Ominously for Russia it was the British and Austrians who had the greatest success:

- Britain managed to persuade Russia to agree to divert the proposed frontier of the new Bulgaria away from the Aegean. Turkey therefore retained Macedonia
- Britain also negotiated a secret treaty with Turkey which would in exchange for a British guarantee of its Asiatic territories allow the British to use Cyprus as a military base
- Austria also won British support for the break-up of Bulgaria.

F *The Berlin Congress*

The Berlin Congress was to prove to be one of the great peace conferences of the nineteenth century even though many important preliminary decisions had already been taken. Bismarck in his role as 'honest broker' dominated the negotiations. Yet however hard he tried to be neutral, the very fact that he presided over a Congress that stripped

Russia of many of its gains from the Turkish war made the Russians bitterly resentful of Germany's 'false friendship'. Under Bismarck's skilful chairmanship the Congress managed to find at least temporary solutions to some of the intractable problems of the Eastern Question. The large Bulgaria of San Stefano was broken up into three parts:

- the largest of these sections was the core state of Bulgaria, which officially became a self-governing principality under ultimate Turkish suzerainty or overlordship. The Russians were to control its administration for nine months. In April 1879 Alexander of Battenberg, the nephew of the Tsar, was elected Prince of Bulgaria
- the second section was called Eastern Rumelia and placed under a Turkish governor although a European commission was to draw up a programme of reforms for him to introduce
- the rest of 'big Bulgaria' which included the strategically important territory on the Aegean Sea was back under direct Turkish control.

The three Balkan states of Serbia, Montenegro and Romania gained complete independence but lost some of the land given to them at Stefano. Austria was given the right to occupy, but not annex, Bosnia and Herzegovina and to station troops in the **Sanjak** of Novibazar, while Britain's occupation of Cyprus was confirmed, and France was encouraged to occupy the self-governing Turkish territory of Tunis.

Most historians argue that the Congress was a defeat for Russia. Langer wrote, for example, that 'Russia could hardly have been more effectively checked even by war': 'Big' Bulgaria was divided into three, the Turkish Empire still survived and British power in the eastern Mediterranean was enormously increased. Yet, as another American historian, Jelavich, has stressed, it was in reality far from being as great a defeat as the Panslavs argued. Turkey was in fact seriously weakened and although it survived, it lost control of huge areas of its Empire. Even in Bulgaria Russia had saved something from the disaster of the Congress. It was seen as a liberating power by the population, and *provided* it remained popular, there was no reason why in time it should not be able to increase its influence, and possibly even establish a permanent military base there. One Russian official, A.H. Jomini, went so far as to write:

> My God! Would we not have treated as mad anyone who would have dreamed of such a result two years ago? And all with the sanction of Europe.

However, to the majority of the Russians the Congress remained a humiliation for which Bismarck was to a great extent responsible.

See Map 20 on page 386

Sanjak was an administrative area like a county in the Turkish Empire. The Sanjak of Novibazar is the mountainous area between Serbia and Montenegro

KEY ISSUE

What did the Berlin Congress achieve?

3 ∽ BISMARCK'S WEB OF ALLIANCES, 1879–83

A *The Austro-German Dual Alliance, 1879*

A major consequence of the Berlin Congress was the destruction of the Three Emperors' League. At first Bismarck attempted to revive it, but by the winter of 1878 it was clear that Russia's resentment at Germany's role in the Congress made this impossible and Bismarck began to consider a defensive alliance with Austria alone. Russo-German relations continued to deteriorate. On the commissions set up to carry out the decisions of the Berlin Congress the German representatives usually voted with their British and Austrian counterparts. Then in July 1879 Berlin further antagonised Russia when tariffs were introduced, severely damaging its grain exports to Germany.

In August the Tsar warned Wilhelm in what became known as the 'Box on the ears letter' of 'the sad consequences [of Bismarck's policies] ... to our good neighbourly relations by embittering our two nations against each other ... '. Wilhelm was inclined to agree with the Tsar, but Bismarck by threatening to resign, eventually succeeded in convincing him of the case for an Austrian alliance. This was signed on 7 October 1879 and its terms were:

> *Russian grain exports*
> About 75 per cent of Russian exports consisted of grain, much of which went to Germany

● should one Power be attacked by Russia, the other would come to its rescue with 'the whole war strength' of its Empire
● if one of the two Empires were attacked by a third Power, the other would adopt a neutral but friendly attitude
● the Treaty was in the first instance to last five years but could be renewed
● it was secret, but in the event of Russian threats its gist would be leaked to the Tsar to deter him from taking any further action.

B *The Alliance of the Three Emperors*

The Russians viewed with increasing alarm the growing co-operation between Austria, Germany and Britain. Their obvious move was to negotiate an alliance with France, but France could provide Russia with little effective help in the Balkans. Influential officials in St. Petersburg, such as Saburov and Giers, consequently advised the Tsar urgently to

ANALYSIS

Why did Bismarck negotiate this treaty?

The Dual Alliance was, in Gordon Craig's words, a 'landmark in European History'. In 1854 Bismarck had been highly critical of the Prussian Government when it renewed its alliance with Austria and accused it of 'tying the trim Prussian frigate to the worm eaten Austrian galleon' Why then did he do exactly this in 1879? Some German historians, such as Bohme and Gall, believe that Bismarck wanted to create a large Central European bloc (*Mitteleuropa*) which would be able to hold its own with the Russian and British Empires. Langer too saw the alliance as re-establishing close relations between Vienna and Berlin and as 'the logical completion of German unification begun in the 1860s'. This was certainly part of Bismarck's thinking, but he had also come to the conclusion that it was in Germany's interests to see Austria survive as a Great Power to balance Russia. The Dual Alliance gave Germany considerable influence over Austrian foreign policy, which would enable Bismarck in a crisis to moderate it so that it did not provoke an unnecessary war with Russia.

KEY ISSUE

What was the significance of the Dual Alliance?

improve Russo-German relations. In the Autumn of 1879 Saburov was sent to Berlin to discuss a possible agreement. Bismarck was ready to consider some sort of revival of the Three Emperors' League which would open the way up to better relations between Vienna and St. Petersburg and continue to keep France isolated. Once Disraeli had been defeated in the general election of April 1880 British foreign policy became less aggressive and the prospect of joint Anglo-Austrian action against Russia seemed less likely. The Austrians therefore came round to Bismarck's proposal for an agreement with Russia and the Three Emperors' Alliance was signed on 18 June 1881. Its main terms were:

- Austria and Germany agreed that the Straits should be closed to the warships of all nations. This stopped the threat of Britain sending its navy into the Black Sea and greatly strengthened Russia's position
- Austria conceded the eventual reunification of Bulgaria, while Russia agreed that at some time in the future Austria would be able to annex Bosnia and Herzegovina
- if a member of the Alliance found itself at war with a fourth Power, unless it were Turkey, the other two Powers would remain neutral
- there were to be no further territorial changes in the European possessions of the Turkish Empire without the consent of the three Empires
- the Treaty was in the first instance to last three years.

KEY ISSUE

How did the Alliance of the Three Emperors differ from the League of the Three Emperors?

See page 385

Although Medlicott and Coveney have called it 'little more than an armistice', as it provided no long-term solution to Austro-Russian rivalry in the Balkans, it did at least temporarily reduce the friction between Austria and Russia.

C THE TRIPLE ALLIANCE, 1882

Despite the Three Emperors Alliance Russian foreign policy, particularly towards Germany, remained unpredictable. The new Tsar, Alexander III, received conflicting advice. The professional diplomats in the Russian Foreign Office wanted good relations with Germany, while the Pan-Slav leaders tried to convince him that a struggle between the German and Slav races was inevitable. What particularly alarmed Bismarck was that the Pan-Slavs were beginning to establish contact with Russian sympathisers in the French army and media. He responded by trying to strengthen the German and Austrian position so that it would put off even the most fanatical Pan-Slav from running the risk of war, yet at the same time he wanted to encourage the peace party in

PICTURE 37 *A French view of the Triple Alliance*

Russia led by the new Foreign Minister, Giers. Consequently when Italy, angered by the French occupation of Tunis, which it regarded as being in its own sphere of interest, proposed in 1882 an alliance with Austria, Bismarck immediately suggested extending it into a triple alliance, and agreed to the following terms:

● both Austria and Germany were now committed to support Italy in the unlikely chance of an attack from France
● Italy in its turn would help them only if they were attacked by two other Powers (say France and Russia).

The real gain for Germany from this agreement was that Austria was now freed from the threat of an Italian attack in its rear should war break out with Russia. Austria's position was further strengthened by an alliance with Serbia in June 1882 and with Romania in 1883 which Germany joined and turned it into a defensive alliance against Russia. At the same time by both refusing demands from German farmers for further rises in tariffs which would damage Russian trade and by encouraging German banks to finance Russian loans he also successfully managed to strengthen the hand of the pro-German group in St. Petersburg. As a result in 1884 it was able to persuade the Tsar to renew the Three Emperors' Treaty.

> **KEY ISSUES**
>
> *What was the role of the alliances in Bismarck's foreign policy?*

4 ↶ THE ANGLO-FRENCH QUARREL OVER EGYPT

A *Should France follow a colonial or continental policy?*

Bismarck made no secret of the fact that he wished to encourage France to seek compensation for the loss of Alsace Lorraine by building up a colonial empire. This would both distract France from seeking revenge against Germany and create tension with the other colonial Powers. Not surprisingly he fully backed the French occupation of Tunis and ignored Italian protests. Yet in France colonial expansion was viewed with mixed feeling precisely because Bismarck backed it. The 'colonialists' were opposed by the 'continental school' which argued that an imperial policy would only make enemies of Britain and Italy and thus

TIMELINE

1869	Suez Canal opened
1875	Britain bought the Khedive's shares in the Canal
November 1876	Anglo-French joint control over Egyptian finances established
February 1882	Nationalists seized power in Egypt
July 1882	British forces landed in Egypt
September	The battle of Tel el Kebir

See page 269

play into Bismarck's hands. Gambetta, the leader of French resistance to the Prussians in 1870 was, for instance, highly critical of the Tunisian adventure, and when he formed a short-lived Government in November 1881, he attempted to cooperate with Britain in Egypt and cultivate closer relations with the Russians.

B   *The Egyptian Question*

Gambetta's aim of forging closer links with Britain was thwarted for nearly a generation by the intense bitterness in France caused by the British occupation of Egypt in 1882. This was supposed to be only a temporary measure until order had been restored, but the area was of such strategic importance that British troops did not finally quit Egypt until 1956. This inevitably led to growing tension between London and Paris which had important consequences for the European balance of power:

ANALYSIS

Anglo-French rivalry in Egypt

Egypt was nominally under the control of Turkey. France had taken great interest in Egypt ever since Napoleon had led a military expedition there in 1798. It was a French engineer, Ferdinand de Lesseps, who had built the Suez Canal, which was opened in 1869. The British initially opposed the canal's construction as they feared that it would weaken Turkey's hold on Egypt still further and strengthen French influence. However, once the canal was built, British shipping increasingly used it to shorten the route to India and the Far East. It therefore became a very important link in Imperial communications. Disraeli seized the chance in 1875 to buy the majority of the shares when Ismail Pasha, the Khedive, or Turkish Viceroy of Egypt, went bankrupt and had to sell them. Even the profits from this sale were insufficient to pay off Egypt's debts, and in November 1876 Britain and France took over control of its finances to ensure that interest was paid on the loans lent to Egypt by European investors. In February 1882 the Egyptian nationalist movement led by a small group of army officers seized power and set up a Government which attempted to regain control of the country's finances. Britain and France responded by sending gun boats to Alexandria to force its resignation. After a wave of anti-western riots in Alexandria, British troops landed to restore order. No French troops accompanied them because permission was refused by the French parliament. Egyptian forces were defeated at Tel el-Kebir and the British gained effective control of Egypt.

KEY ISSUES

What were the consequences of the Anglo-French quarrel over Egypt?

- up to this point the two states had formed a loose western European block as a balance to the League of the Three Emperors. Its break up greatly reinforced Germany's position in Europe and gave Bismarck a powerful lever against Britain just at the time he was moving towards creating a German colonial empire
- Bismarck could either extract concessions from Britain in return for German diplomatic support and isolate France completely, or, if no concessions were forthcoming, he could cooperate with France and thus in effect create a Continental alliance against Britain.

His policy was made very clear in a letter he sent the German Ambassador in London:

Owing to her geographical position England is in no serious danger from any Power except from France in Europe, and in Asia from Russia. France, however, should she adopt a menacing attitude towards England, would require at the very least the certainty of German neutrality, and Russia must also have an eye to the attitude of Germany, should she really wish to move against England, whether in India or Constantinople. We believe, therefore, that our attitude – I will not say towards England herself, with whom we should not think of quarrelling – but our attitude to her enemies or rivals is of more importance to British policy than the possession of Heligoland and all the trade rivalry of German and British firms in distant seas. England can secure for herself the continuance of our active support for her political interests through sacrifices, which she would hardly feel.

Bismarck and Britain Bismarck wanted to gain control of the island of Heligoland in the North Sea, just off the Schleswig coast, which had been British since 1815, as it was of strategic importance to Germany in view of plans to build the Kiel Canal

Thus when Bismarck found Britain uncooperative in his efforts to protect Germany's growing trade interests in the Pacific and South West Africa, he did not hesitate to exploit its problems in Egypt. In 1884 the British were particularly anxious to strengthen Egypt's finances by cutting the rate of interest paid to the European **bondholders** so that the Egyptians could contribute more towards the costs of the military occupation. To do this, Britain needed the backing of the other European Powers, who were all represented on the International Debt Commission in Cairo. Bismarck, however, supported French objections and effectively vetoed the plan. Relations improved dramatically between France and Germany, and, as the French Prime Minister, Jules Ferry said, France was no longer 'the Cinderella of European politics'.

bond is a certificate issued by a government to an individual promising to pay back a financial loan or investment at a fixed rate of interest

5 ⌐ GERMANY ACQUIRES A COLONIAL EMPIRE

A *The reasons for Bismarck's change of policy*

In 1884–5 Bismarck acquired a colonial empire five times the size of the German *Reich*. Bismarck's sudden enthusiasm has puzzled historians

TIMELINE

Feb 1884	Anglo-Portuguese Treaty
1884–5	Foundations of German colonial empire laid
Nov 1884–	
Feb 1885	Berlin West Africa Conference

since he had always scornfully dismissed colonies as an expensive luxury for a new state like Germany rather like 'a poverty stricken Polish nobleman providing himself with silks and sables [furs] when he needed shirts'. A.J.P. Taylor argued that Bismarck set out to acquire colonies so that he that he could pick a quarrel with Britain in order to strengthen the developing **Entente** with France. This may well have been *one* of Bismarck's motives, but there were others as well:

- he needed to protect German trade in South West Africa and the South Seas
- British isolation made it an easy task to move into areas which Britain regarded as its own sphere of interest
- German public opinion, particularly as expressed by the National Liberal Party and the newly founded *Kolonialverein* (Colonial League), was pressing for colonies, and an election was coming up in the Autumn of 1884
- Bismarck like other European leaders also realised that an exciting colonial policy with easy conquests could unite the German people behind him and make them forget the shortcomings of his Government. One eminent German historian, H-U. Wehler, has called this 'manipulated social imperialism'.

See pages 289–9

B *The Annexations*

In the Spring of 1884 the German Government granted formal protection to German trading stations in South West Africa, the Cameroons, Togoland and New Guinea to forestall British claims to the area. Bismarck hoped that the trading companies themselves would be responsible for administering the new colonies, while the *Reich* would simply provide external protection. In fact, once having intervened in Africa, Bismarck found that he could not run Germany's colonial empire on the cheap. In West and East Africa the chartered companies proved so incompetent that Berlin was landed with responsibility for both internal administration and defence.

See the maps on pages 399 and 400

German trading stations For instance the East African Company drove the African population into open revolt in 1888 and was only saved by the despatch of German troops, while the South-West African Company was so inefficient that Berlin had to send out an Imperial Commissioner to take control. In 1889 the New Guinea Company went bankrupt

C *The Berlin West Africa Conference, 1884–5*

Bismarck exploited British isolation to ensure that Germany's interests were protected in the Congo and West Africa. Both France and the trading company, the International Association of the Congo, whose president was King Leopold of Belgium, were suspicious of British intentions when the Anglo-Portuguese Treaty was signed in February 1884. They suspected that Britain was exploiting Portugal's weakness to increase its own influence in the Congo and the Portuguese colonies of Angola and Mozambique. Leopold skilfully managed to mobilise international opinion against the Treaty and win Bismarck's support. The Portuguese were pushed into proposing an international conference, which Bismarck with French backing suggested should meet in Berlin.

See Map 21 on page 399

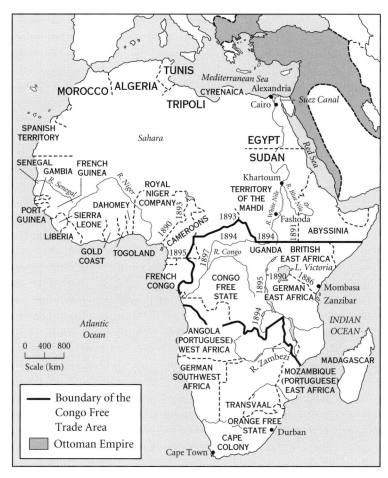

MAP 21 *The partition of Africa*

The Conference opened on 15 November and was attended by representatives of all the great European Powers, the United States, Turkey, Portugal, Spain, Belgium, Denmark and Holland. It was as Rich has stressed 'a noteworthy sign of the times that the Africans themselves were [not] invited to attend'! When the Conference ended in February 1885 it was clear that Britain's ambition to control the Congo Basin indirectly through Portugal had failed. Yet Britain was not as isolated as Russia had been during the previous Berlin Conference. The British and German Governments had the shared aim of keeping the Congo region open to free trade and increasingly made common cause against the **protectionist** French. The Conference agreed on a treaty which laid down some important ground rules for a huge belt of Central African territory stretching from the Atlantic to the Indian Ocean:

protectionist supporting a policy aimed at protecting a country's trade through high tariffs which keep out the imports of other states

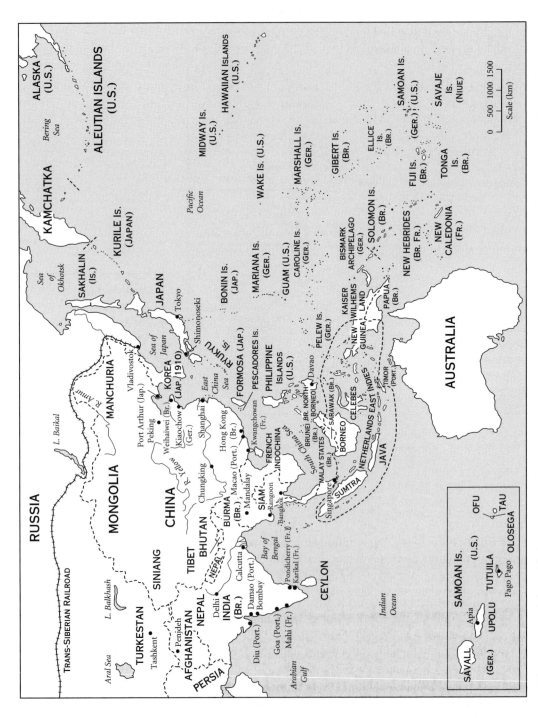

MAP 22 *The Far East and the Pacific in 1912*

- all states were to have free access to the rivers and ports of this region for their trade
- the entire area was to be a free trade zone
- religious missions and scientific research were to be protected
- the slave trade was to be forbidden in the area and the Powers committed themselves 'to bring home the blessings of civilization' to the local African population.

The actual division of the area amongst the Powers was not part of the Berlin Treaty but was negotiated behind the scenes in Berlin. Portuguese sovereignty was limited to Angola, while the Congo Association cleverly managed to play on German and British fears of French protectionism to gain recognition of their control over the huge central area which became known as the Congo Free State. French influence was confined to a bloc of land to the north of the Congo.

See Map 21 on page 399

KEY ISSUE

Why did Bismarck create a German colonial empire?

6 ↝ RENEWED THREAT OF AN ANGLO-RUSSIAN CONFLICT

Despite the improvement in Anglo-German relations in the Spring of 1885 Britain still remained isolated in Europe. Russia, on the other hand, thanks to the Three Emperors' Treaty, could rely on German diplomatic support in any clash with Britain.

Ever since the Crimean War the Russians had been moving southwards towards the frontiers of Afghanistan and British India. Their aim was to be in a position where they could threaten India if the British again tried to send a fleet through the Straits as they did in 1878. In June 1884 Giers, the Russian Foreign Minister, wrote:

See page 393

See Map 22 on page 400

> Our movements in Central Asia have been commanded by our own interests, as well as by the necessity of securing a defensive position against the hostility displayed by the English government towards us since the Crimean War and more recently during the war with Turkey. At present we have, through great sacrifices, reached the stage where we can consider our security fully guaranteed.

The reality of the Russian threat was brought home to London when Russian troops defeated an Afghan army at Penjdeh on the borders of Afghanistan in March 1885. Although troops were mobilised in India and the British fleet threatened Vladivostock, Bismarck with the backing of Austria, Italy and France insisted that the Sultan of Turkey should not allow British ships through the Straits, thereby depriving London of the most effective way to put pressure on Russia. Britain thus had little option but to climb down and suggest that the dispute should be solved through arbitration.

KEY ISSUE

Why was Britain so vulnerable?

7 ∽ THE END OF THE FRANCO-GERMAN *ENTENTE* AND THE DISINTEGRATION OF THE THREE EMPERORS' ALLIANCE, 1885–7

Briefly the Continental Powers had established what was in effect a coalition against the British Empire, and as long as this lasted Britain was forced onto the defensive. However in the course of 1885 this new found solidarity was wrecked by events in France and in the Balkans.

A *The consequences of the fall of Jules Ferry for the Franco-German entente*

Ferry faced growing opposition in France to the colonial war in Indo-China. When the news came through that the French had been pushed out of Lang-Son, riots broke out in Paris and Ferry's Government fell. The new Government gradually reverted to a more anti-German policy over the course of the summer. In January 1886 Prime Minister Freycinet was forced to accept as Minister of War, General Boulanger, who believed that his mission was to prepare for war against Germany. He rapidly became a cult figure for the French League of Patriots and for a time it seemed, much to the alarm of Bismarck, that he might even seize power and become a dictator. The German army was confident that it could again defeat the French, but gone were the days when France could be dealt with in isolation. In the winter of 1886–7 there was talk in both Moscow and Paris of a Franco-Russian alliance.

> **KEY ISSUE**
>
> *What destroyed the Franco-German Entente?*

TIMELINE

30 March 1885	The fall of the Ferry Government
Sept	Bulgaria and Eastern Rumelia united
January 1886	Boulanger appointed War Minister
February 1887	First Mediterranean Agreement
April	The Schnaebele incident
May	Resignation of General Boulanger
June	The Russo-German Reinsurance Treaty
December	Second Mediterranean Agreement

B *The Bulgarian crisis, 1885–7*

French attempts to establish closer relations with Russia were powerfully helped by the eruption of the Bulgarian crisis. In the Autumn of 1886 for a brief period of time it looked as if a Franco-Russian alliance directed against Germany might become a reality. The crisis, which destroyed the Three Emperors' Alliance and brought Europe close to war, was triggered by a successful revolt in Eastern Rumelia in favour of unity with Bulgaria under Prince Alexander in September 1885. Initially the Russians tried to reassure the British and Austrians that, despite their bad relations with Alexander, they had no intention of intervening, but the crisis began to escalate dangerously. Serbia launched an attack on the Bulgarians in November 1885 in an effort to gain territory which would compensate it for the increase in Bulgarian strength brought about by unification. When its troops were decisively defeated at Slivnitza, the Austrians made it clear that they would protect Serbia if the Bulgarians invaded. The Russians, alarmed by the prospect of an Austrian occupation of Serbia, protested strongly, and behind the scenes Bismarck firmly vetoed all Austrian plans for assisting Serbia. A compromise was suggested by Britain whereby the two Bulgarian states would remain technically separated but Alexander would become the Governor-General of Rumelia. Temporarily tension subsided, but the Russians, quite contrary to their earlier intentions, were determined to stop a unified Bulgaria under Alexander, whom they now considered to be an outright enemy. In August 1886 they had him kidnapped and he was forced to abdicate a month later. Inevitably these events fuelled British and Austrian fears of Russia's intervention in Bulgaria. The Austrian Foreign Minister announced in November 1886 that

> ...even a temporary single-handed occupation of Bulgaria by foreign troops [meaning, of course, Russia], without the previous consent of Turkey and the other powers would be a violation of the treaties, which in our opinion is not admissable.

Meanwhile in Berlin the Russian Ambassador told Bismarck that

> It is absolutely necessary that we should make Austria disappear from the map of Europe.

The Alliance of the Three Emperors had collapsed and both Austria and Britain looked to Berlin to take the lead against Russia, but Bismarck was determined not to be pushed into confrontation at the very time that Boulanger was urging a war of revenge against Germany. He therefore adopted a dual strategy towards Russia:

- he attempted desperately to restrain both Austria and Russia, whom he described as 'two savage dogs'. He tried to persuade both Powers to divide the Balkans into spheres of influence and made it again very clear to his Austrian allies that he would not be dragged into war against Russia
- on the other hand he was not prepared to stand back and see Austria defeated by Russia. Consequently he encouraged Britain, Italy and

Developments in Bulgaria, 1879–84

In 1879 the Russians were determined to maximise their influence in Bulgaria and eventually unite it with Eastern Rumelia. Thus before they pulled their troops out, they ensured that the administration was effectively under control of Russian officials. At first the Russians had been seen as liberators, but the officials treated Bulgaria as a colony and rapidly lost the Bulgarians' support. The Russians were also determined to link Bulgaria by rail to Russia. When the new Bulgarian parliament refused to find the funds for this, the Russian Government became increasingly annoyed with Prince Alexander. In September 1883 Alexander, determined to assert Bulgarian independence, formed a new coalition Government and expelled two key Russian officials, Generals Kaulbars and Sobolev.

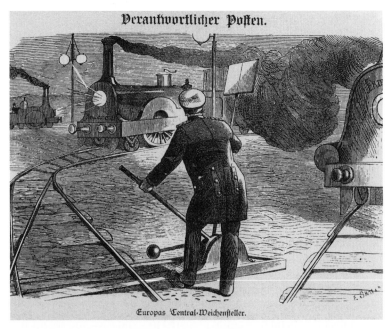

PICTURE 38 *A German cartoonist's view of Bismarck's role in the 1887 crisis*

ENTER BISMARCK.

"I SPEAK OF PEACE, WHILE COVERT ENMITY,
UNDER THE SMILE OF SAFETY, WOUNDS THE WORLD;
AND WHO BUT 'BISMARCK,' WHO BUT ONLY I,
MAKE FEARFUL MUSTERS AND PREPARED DEFENCE."
Henry the Fourth, Part II. (Induction).

PICTURE 39 *The English view of Bismarck*

Austria to negotiate secretly the first Mediterranean Agreement in
February 1887 to contain Russia in the Balkans and at the Straits.
He hoped that the Agreement would encourage these Powers to
stand up to Russia and convince Tsar Alexander that only through
negotiations with Berlin could a compromise over Bulgaria be
arranged.

C *Improvement in Franco-German relations*

During the Bulgarian crisis Bismarck also took steps to isolate France in
Western Europe so as to deter its Government from supporting Russia.
The Triple Alliance was renewed in February 1887 and an Italian-

> **KEY ISSUE**
>
> *What was the
> significance of the
> Bulgarian crisis and
> how did Bismarck try
> to defuse it?*

ANALYSIS

The Schnaebele Incident

Schnaebele was a French frontier official originally from Alsace. He used his position to set up an espionage system in Alsace-Lorraine. On 2 April 1887 the Germans arrested him after a struggle which allegedly took place just inside the French frontier. There was an immediate outcry in the press of both countries and the French were convinced that Bismarck was hoping to provoke them into war. However Bismarck ordered Schnaebele's release when it was discovered that he had been invited across the frontier to discuss official matters and given a safe-conduct note.

Spanish Agreement was signed aimed at preventing French colonial expansion in North Africa. By 1887 France, as Langer observed, was 'completely hedged about'. This network of agreements combined with a formidable increase in German military strength had a considerable impact on Paris, and, despite the Schnaebele incident, the threat of an anti-German Franco-Russian agreement did, for the time being at least, recede. Franco-German relations improved considerably when Boulanger was forced to resign as War Minister in May.

See page 261

D *The Reinsurance Treaty, 18 June 1887*

Any improvement in Germany's relations with Russia was dependent on the outcome of the struggle to influence the Tsar which was bitterly waged between the Pan-Slavs and the traditionally pro-German Russian Foreign Office. In March 1887 Tsar Alexander finally lost his patience with the increasingly more outspoken attempts of the Pan-Slavs to influence his foreign policy, and rejected their demands for a break with Germany. He refused, however, to follow the advice of his Foreign Minister, to renew the Three Emperors' Treaty, but he did agree to negotiate a secret three year agreement with Germany, which was signed on 18 June 1887. Its terms were:

KEY ISSUE

What was the role of the Reinsurance Treaty in Bismarck's alliance system?

● both Empires were pledged to be neutral in a war fought against a third Power unless Germany attacked France or Russia
● Germany recognised the rights 'historically acquired' by Russia in the Balkans – particularly in Bulgaria and Eastern Rumelia
● Turkey was not to open the Straits to the navy of a Power hostile to Russia. If it did, Germany and Russia would regard it as a hostile act towards themselves.

Why was the Reinsurance Treaty so controversial?

Otto Pflanze has written that '[n]o treaty concluded by Bismarck has been subjected to greater scrutiny and more controversy'. Ever since the text of the treaty was published in 1918 historians have disagreed about whether it contradicted the Dual Alliance with Austria by recognising Russia's 'right historically acquired' in the Balkans. Pflanze, Taylor and Langer all argued that it did not, as Bismarck had always urged that the Balkans should be divided into Austrian and Russian spheres of influence. Yet Lowe points out that it conflicted with the spirit, if not the letter, of the Dual Alliance of 1879'. Lothar Gall even goes so far as to add that '[h]ad it come to notice of the other side it would have shattered the credibility of German policy, almost certainly brought about the collapse of Bismarck's intricate system of alliances and left Germany largely isolated'. It undoubtedly contradicted the Mediterranean Agreement, the whole point of which was to stop Russia expanding into the Balkans. Although Germany had not signed this Agreement, Bismarck had encouraged its negotiation.

Historians also question the overall importance of the Treaty. To Langer it marked the completion of an 'intricate system of checks and balances which was intended to preserve the peace of Europe', but Taylor, for instance, viewed the Treaty 'at best' as a temporary and not very effective means for dealing with the crisis of 1885–7. Gall, too, felt that the importance of the Treaty was exaggerated and argues that it was aimed at preventing the immediate danger of a war over Bulgaria. In other words it was an exercise in crisis management.

KEY ISSUE

Did Bismarck manage to reconcile in the Reinsurance Treaty his support for Austria with his desire for good relations with Russia?

8 ᪥ THE END OF THE BISMARCKIAN SYSTEM

The Reinsurance Treaty failed to calm the tension in the Balkans. The Bulgarian Parliament stubbornly refused to accept a Russian candidate, General Erenroth, as its ruler, and voted instead in July 1887 for Prince Ferdinand of Coburg, who was born in Vienna and had served in the Austrian army. Inevitably this was regarded by the Russians as an Austrian conspiracy. Once again the Pan-Slavs whipped up a press campaign against Germany which was accused of secretly supporting Austria. In the Autumn the Russians carried out large scale troop manoeuvres on Germany's eastern borders and, so it seemed, began to prepare to advance into Bulgaria. To stop this Bismarck very effectively used financial pressure. In November 1887 the German Government

KEY ISSUE

Why did Russia oppose a unified Bulgaria under Prince Alexander and distrust Ferdinand?

Russian bonds
The bonds acted as guarantee or 'collateral' that the Russian Government would repay loans raised in Germany

See page 414

stopped the *Reichsbank*, the National Bank of Germany, from accepting Russian bonds as collateral security for loans raised in Germany. This had very serious economic consequences for the Russians as Germany was the source of most of its foreign loans. Russia was therefore plunged into financial chaos which effectively prevented it from occupying Bulgaria or risking war with Austria. In December Bismarck, again quite contrary to the spirit of the Reinsurance Treaty, further strengthened the position of Austria by persuading Britain and Italy to conclude with it a second Mediterranean Agreement aimed at keeping Russia out of Bulgaria and Turkey.

Although these measures did deter the Tsar from sending troops into Bulgaria, the Russians continued to do everything they could to undermine Ferdinand. They also turned to France for the loans which the Germans were no longer ready to raise. Inevitably this strengthened Franco-Russian relations, but neither side was yet ready to conclude an alliance. When Wilhelm II came to the German throne in June 1888, and began to urge on Bismarck a British alliance, the Tsar rapidly became more appreciative of Bismarck's policy and offered to renew the Reinsurance Treaty permanently. Bismarck, however, was dismissed in March 1890 before negotiations could begin and his successor, General von Caprivi, convinced that the Treaty contradicted the Triple Alliance and would complicate Germany's relations with Britain, did not renew it. This effectively signalled the end of the Bismarckian alliance system.

9 ⤳ CONCLUSION

The period from 1871–90 was a period of transition from a European to a global political system. Although Great Power rivalries were acute and in the Balkans brought Austria, Russia and Britain to the verge of war in 1878, the two decades were also a time of profound peace and growing economic integration. Taylor argued that ' [m]en were too busy growing rich to have time for war'. Yet public opinion could all too often be jingoistic and aggressive. Mass education, the emergence of a popular press and more representative parliaments ensured that public opinion was increasingly influencing foreign policy. One reason why the violent outbreaks of nationalist sentiment did not lead to war was that Bismarck was determined to safeguard the newly won unity of Germany by preventing the formation of any hostile coalitions. He used Germany's pivotal position at the centre of Europe to build up, as Langer has put it, 'the most complicated system of alliances that Europe had ever known in peace times'. He was determined that Germany should never be isolated, and should be one amongst three in a Europe of five Great Powers. He may not have been quite the benign peacemaker Langer made him out to be, as his alliance system often deliberately created tensions between both friends and potential enemies, yet it was essentially one of restraint which tried to avoid or at least postpone war. That Germany remained a 'saturated' power, except for a brief period in Africa, is surely one of the main reasons for European peace during the period 1871–90.

KEY ISSUE

How strong was the impact of public opinion on the foreign policies of the Great European Powers?

10 ↝ BIBLIOGRAPHY

A good introduction to this period is in the first part of *Rivalry and Accord: International Relations, 1870–1914* by J. Lowe (Hodder, 1990). The most thorough survey is still *European Alliances and Alignments* by W. Langer (Knopf, 1931). *The Struggle For Mastery of Power in Europe* by A.J.P. Taylor (OUP, 1954) contains several informative and provocative chapters covering the years 1870–90. A more recent study, particularly for great power rivalry in Egypt and elsewhere in Africa, is *Great Power Diplomacy, 1814–1914* by N. Rich (McGraw-Hill, 1992). *The Great Powers and the German Problem, 1865–1925* by J. Lowe gives a clear account of the reaction of the great European powers to Bismarck's foreign policy. Most biographies and general studies of Bismarckian Germany contain useful accounts of Bismarck's foreign policy. A compact study of his foreign policy, 1871–90, is in *Bismarck and Germany, 1862–1890* by D.G. Williamson (Longman, second edition, 1998). *Bismarck* by B. Waller (Blackwell, 1997, second edition) has a chapter on foreign policy which is a good introduction to the historiography of the topic. There are sections on foreign policy in *Bismarck and the Development of Germany, vols. II & III* by O. Pflanze (Princeton University Press, 1990). *Bismarck at the Crossroads, the Restoration of German Foreign Policy after the Congress of Berlin* by B. Waller (Athlone Press, 1974) is a detailed guide to Bismarck's foreign policy after 1879. A good introduction to the crisis in the Balkans is *The Eastern Question, 1774–1923* by A.L. Macfie (Longman, second edition 1996). The same ground is covered in more detail in *The Eastern Question 1774–1923* by M.S. Anderson (Macmillan, 1966). More specialised studies are *Tsarist Russia and Balkan Nationalism* by C. Jelavich (University of California Press, 1958) and the *Congress of Berlin and After* by W.N. Medlicott (Frank Cass, 1963). Franco-German relations are dealt with in *Bismarck and the French Nation* by A. Mitchell (Bobbs-Merrill, 1971). A short guide to European rivalry in Africa is the *Scramble for Africa* by M.E. Chamberlain (Longman, 1974). German colonial policy is covered in *The German Colonial Empire* by W. Smith (University of North Carolina Press, 1978) and 'Bismarck's Imperialism, 1862–1890' by H.U. Wehler in *Past and Present*, vol. 48, 1970. The best document collection covering this period is *Bismarck and Europe* by W.N. Medlicott and D. Coveney (Arnold, 1971).

11 ↝ STRUCTURED QUESTIONS AND ESSAYS

1. (a) Outline the stages by which Bismarck attempted to isolate France, 1871–5; (10 marks).
   (b) Explain how successful these attempts were. (15 marks).
2. (a) Outline the main developments in the Eastern Crisis, 1875–8; (10 marks)
   (b) Explain why this crisis did not lead to a European war; (15 marks).

3. (a) Outline the development of Bismarck's alliance policy between 1879 and 1883; (10 marks)

   (b) Explain why the Dual Alliance of 1879 has been called 'a landmark in European history', while the three Emperors' Alliance of 1881 has been described as 'little more than an armistice'; (15 marks)

4. (a) Outline the nature of the threats to the British Empire from rival European Powers, 1882–5; (10 marks)

   (b) Explain why Bismarck tried to exploit the Anglo-French quarrel over Egypt and why he failed to bring about a lasting improvement in Franco-German relations; (15 marks)

5. (a) Outline the main developments in the Bulgarian Crisis, 1885–7; (10 marks)

   (b) Explain its impact on Bismarck's alliance system; (15 marks)

6. (a) Outline Bismarck's policy towards Russia, 1887–90; (10 marks)

   (b) Explain why the Reinsurance Treaty of 1887 has caused so much controversy; (15 marks)

7. How successfully did Bismarck achieve his aim of isolating France in the 20 years following the Franco-Prussian War of 1870–71? (25 marks)

8. To what extent has the impact of Bismarck on European Great Power politics in the years 1870–98 been exaggerated? (25 marks)

12 ⌁ DOCUMENTARY EXERCISE ON BISMARCK'S ALLIANCE SYSTEM

There follow a number of documentary extracts which deal with Bismarck's alliance system. Most of these sources are diplomatic documents. These are sometimes memoranda advising the Government on what direction a country's foreign policy should take, records of confidential discussions between Governments or reports from ambassadors. Sometimes they can be very revealing and full of insights, but do not assume, just because they are secret, that they can be accepted at face value. Ambassadors' dispatches [reports to their Governments], for instance, are often records of conversations where one side is trying to mislead the other or at best merely hinting at the truth.

Study Sources A–E and attempt the questions that follow:

SOURCE A

The historian Bruce Waller writes about Bismarck's alliance system

This network of treaties and agreements is what most historians mean when they refer to the Bismarck system ... Perhaps the network was not the essence of his foreign policy, but merely one aspect. Indeed the key to understanding his foreign policy after 1871 is his desire for balanced tension. He seemed to believe that German security and manoeuvrability would be most strongly guaranteed by creating and perpetuating tension between other powers. The alliance system – if such we may call it – was the creation or perpetuation of a fluid state of affairs in which tension was finely balanced and friends as well as opponents were immobilized.

I wish that without making it too noticeable, we should encourage the English with any designs they may have on Egypt; I consider it in our interest, and useful for us in the future, to promote an arrangement between England and Russia giving the prospect of good relations between them ... and shortly afterwards of both of them with us ... If England and Russia could agree on the basis that the former would have Turkey and the latter the Black Sea, both would be in a position to be satisfied for a long time ahead with the *status quo* [the existing situation], and yet in their most important interests would be involved in a rivalry which would hardly allow them to take part in coalitions against us ... .

SOURCE B
Bismarck dictated the following note on his policy at Kissingen on 15 June 1877

... the advanced position of Russian cavalry at our frontier, the raving language of the Petersburg and Moscow press, have convinced the Chancellor that he can no longer rely on Russia nor even on its rulers to the same extent as before: hence for the sake of a doubtful friendship with Russia one could not afford to have a breach with the other Powers, particularly not with England or Austria. On the contrary, with the latter one should strive for a closer tie ... .

SOURCE C
General von Schweinitz, the German Ambassador at St. Petersburg, recalled in his memoirs that Bismarck made the following points in a conversation on 5 April 1879

You too often lose sight of the importance of being one of three on a European chess board-board. That is the invariable objective of all the cabinets and mine above all others. Nobody wishes to be in a minority. All politics reduce themselves to this formula: to try to be one of three, so long as the world is governed by the unstable equilibrium of five great powers. That is the true preservative against coalitions.

SOURCE D
In a series of discussions with the Russian Ambassador, P.A. Saburov, in Berlin, 31 January–7 February 1880 Bismarck is reported as saying the following

... Austria, as well as Germany and the England of today, belongs to the number of satisfied nations, 'saturated' in the words of the late Prince Metternich [Austrian Chancellor, 1821–48], and hence pacific and conservative Austria and England have loyally accepted the *status quo* of the German Empire, and have no interest in seeing it weakened. France and Russia on the other hand seem to be threatening us ... .

... Given this state of affairs we must regard as permanent the danger that our peace will be disturbed by France and Russia ... war against France and Russia allied ... would always be a sufficiently great calamity for our country for us to try to avoid it by an amicable arrangement with Russia ... Thus we shall avoid a Russian war as long as this is compatible with our honour and security, and as long as the independence of Austria-Hungary, whose existence as a great power is of paramount importance for us is not called into question.

SOURCE E
A private letter from Bismarck to the British Prime Minister, Lord Salisbury, 22 November 1887

Q

1. *Using your own knowledge, explain briefly what is meant by 'the raving language of the Petersburg and Moscow press' in Source C, lines 1–2 (3 marks)*
2. *To what extent does Source B support Source A concerning Bismarck's desire for 'balanced tension' (Source A, line 4) (6 marks)*
3. *How useful is Source C in helping the historian to understand why the Dual Alliance with Austria was signed? (8 marks)*
4. *In what ways do Sources D and E help us understand Bismarck's policy towards Russia after 1879? (8 marks)?*
5. *Using this collection of Sources A–E, and your own knowledge, explain why Bismarck constructed so complex an alliance system after 1871. (15 marks)*

The Clash of Empires: The Origins of World War I

15

ARGUMENTS ABOUT RESPONSIBILITY

The causes of World War I are one of the most controversial debates in modern history. Ever since 1919 historians and politicians have bitterly argued about who should take the blame for triggering that terrible struggle that did so much damage to Europe. At the Paris Peace Conference the Allied Powers had little doubt that 'this responsibility rests first on Germany and Austria', but in the 1920s and 1930s this view was rejected by historians not only in Germany but in America, Britain and even France. They insisted that the real causes of the war were far more complex and were a result of the European 'system' that came into existence in 1871. In their opinion the key causes were:

● the alliance system
● nationalism
● militarism
● imperialism
● economic rivalry.

In his *War Memoirs* Lloyd George summed up this view when he wrote that 'the nations in 1914 slithered over the brink into the boiling cauldron of war'. Right up to the 1960s it was generally agreed that all the Great Powers were responsible for the War but then this consensus was challenged by a new generation of German historians led by Fritz Fischer. He argued in two key books that the German leadership by 1912 was more than ready to risk war both to make Germany into a world power and to consolidate its position at home, which was threatened by the rise of democracy and socialism. Despite bitter criticism from many of his fellow historians Fischer's arguments are now accepted, although there is still considerable disagreement about whether Germany was really aiming at 'world power' or merely wishing to consolidate its position in central Europe. By concentrating on Germany Fischer played down the widespread war mentality that existed throughout Europe. War was, as Ruth Henig stressed, 'regarded not just in Germany but in Britain, France and Russia as offering a colourful escape from the dull existence, as giving opportunities for individual heroism and acts of bravery'.

See page 298

KEY ISSUE

*What were the
long-term causes of
World War I?*

As you read this chapter, you must make up your own mind what you think were the real causes of World War I. Are they primarily long-term, dating perhaps as far back as 1870, or were they a consequence of the intense imperialist and nationalist rivalries after 1890 and the clumsy and aggressive policies of Bismarck's successors?

TIMELINE

15 Mar 1890	Bismarck's dismissal
18 June	Reinsurance Treaty lapsed
1 July	Anglo-German Colonial Agreement
27 Aug 1891	Franco-Russian Political Agreement
17 Jan 1892	Franco-Russian Military Convention ratified
July 1893	Siam Crisis
4 Jan 1894	Franco-Russian Alliance signed
4 March	Russo-German trade Treaty
9 July	Austro-British talks abandoned.

See Map 18, page 380

1 ∼ THE NEW COURSE IN GERMAN FOREIGN POLICY, 1890–4

A *The break with Russia and the attempt to secure alliance with Britain*

Once Bismarck was dismissed by *Kaiser* Wilhelm, German Foreign Office officials advised his successor, General Leo von Caprivi, not to renew the Reinsurance Treaty with Russia. They argued with some justification that it conflicted with the Triple Alliance and the Mediterranean Agreements. It was feared that Russia would be able to blackmail Germany by threatening to reveal these contradictions to Britain and Austria. The *Kaiser* agreed, and decided to work for a new alliance system or 'New Course', which would associate Britain with Germany's two allies, Italy and Austria, and so hold in check both Russia and France. He felt that Germany was now strong enough to give up Bismarck's complicated system of checks and balances and could ally with states with which it had apparently a common interest. Even before the Reinsurance Treaty had officially ended, the German Government had already approached the British Government with a proposal to settle any outstanding colonial disagreements. The British drove a hard bargain. In return for Germany giving up its claims to Zanzibar and extensive areas of East Africa, they ceded Heligoland, a strategically important island, which dominated the mouths of the Elbe and the Weser rivers. The Agreement was seen in both Paris and St. Petersburg as the prelude to an Anglo-German alliance.

The end of the Reinsurance Treaty was a turning point in European history. It terminated most of Germany's links with Russia and so brought to an end the Bismarckian diplomatic system. It marked the beginning of a period of increasing international instability which ultimately resulted in the outbreak of World War I. The Germans became more dependent on their partners in the Triple Alliance, and could no longer frighten them with the threat of co-operating with Russia. Consequently the Austrians were in a position to put pressure on the Germans to back them more firmly in the Balkans.

KEY ISSUE

*What were the
consequences of
the non-renewal of the
Reinsurance Treaty?*

The Siam Crisis

In 1893 the French were completing their occupation of Indo-China. Siam had now become a buffer state between the British in Burma and the French. On 30 July a report reached London that the French had ordered British gunboats to leave Siamese territorial waters. Briefly the British Government thought that war was about to break out and appealed to the *Kaiser*, who was visiting his grandmother (Queen Victoria) in Britain, for help, but before he could decide what to do, it emerged that the report was inaccurate and that France was happy to leave Siam as a neutral buffer state.

The Germans were puzzled by Britain's refusal to join the Triple Alliance, and believed that ultimately it would be forced into an alliance with Germany by Franco-Russian pressure. In July 1893 this momentarily seemed possible when it looked as if Britain and France would go to war over Siam (Thailand), but the crisis was rapidly resolved without any need for intervention from Germany. The British Government therefore remained convinced that there was no need to commit itself to joining the Triple Alliance. It was also aware that a firm alliance with Germany would increase Berlin's power enormously and enable it to exert intense pressure on both the French and the Russians, which would upset the balance of power in Europe. The Germans, however, optimistically remained convinced that sooner or later Britain would have to turn to them to help. Commenting later on the Siam Crisis Caprivi wrote:

> For us the best opening of the next great war is for the first shot to be fired from a British ship. Then we can be certain of expanding the Triple into a Quadruple alliance.

B *The Franco-Russian Alliance and its consequences, 1892–4*

Potentially the Germans were in danger of isolation. The 'New Course' had not led to an alliance with Britain, but it did drive France and Russia together. The Anglo-German Colonial Agreement and then the *Kaiser*'s state visit in July 1891 to London convinced the Russians – wrongly of course – that Britain and Germany had signed a secret alliance. Giers therefore suggested to the French that the two states should begin to negotiate an **Entente**. Talks began almost immediately, and the French fleet visited the Russian base of Kronstadt as a symbolic act of friendship. Within a month the two states had already agreed to 'to take counsel together upon every question of a nature to jeopardise the general peace'. A year later this was backed up with a military convention or agreement which was finally approved by both Governments in January 1894. Its terms were as follows:

- Russia would assist France with 'all her available forces' if it were attacked by Germany or Italy supported by Germany
- France would do the same for Russia if it were attacked by Germany or Austria backed by Germany
- the Treaty was to last as long as the Triple Alliance.

The Treaty was a considerable triumph for the French as it marked the end of their diplomatic isolation in Europe. However, both Russia and France each wanted different things from it. Paris was determined to turn it primarily into an anti-German alliance, while the Russians saw it more as an alliance directed against Austria and hoped, too, that it could be used against Britain in Asia. The Treaty confirmed German fears that in any future war France and Russia would be allies. Consequently von Schlieffen, the Chief of the Prussian General Staff, drew the logical conclusion and began to prepare the German army for a war on two fronts, but Caprivi also tried rather belatedly to revive Bismarck's policy of re-establishing good relations with Russia by negotiating a trade treaty which made considerable economic concessions to Russia.

See page 438

The British Government, too, was alarmed by the Franco-Russian agreement. Its potential as an anti-British alliance was shown when the Russian Fleet visited the French naval base in Toulon in October 1893. It realised that it might in any future crisis in the Eastern Mediterranean have to deal with the combined fleets of both France and Russia. Inevitably then it looked to the Triple Alliance for assistance. Unofficial talks opened with the Austrians but by July 1894 it was clear that no agreement was possible because Britain was unwilling to accept the commitment of a formal defensive alliance which bound it to defend Austia and Germany against a *land* attack from Russia or France in Europe. This in Taylor's words effectively 'marked the end of Anglo-Austrian cooperation against Russia' in the Balkans and eastern Mediterranean.

Temporarily the isolated and therefore potentially dangerous situation in which Germany found itself in, was partly obscured by the shift of European rivalries in the 1890s from Europe and the Near East to Africa and Asia. For a time Germany still remained confident that Britain, whose huge and vulnerable empire was coming under intense pressure, would be forced into an agreement on Germany's terms with the Triple Alliance, but this too was to be a miscalculation.

KEY ISSUE

What was the Impact of the Dual Alliance on the European balance of power?

2 ∽ THE BALKANS 1890–1905

Although during most of this period the interest of the Great Powers, with the exception of Austria, lay in Africa and Asia, the continued weakness of the Turkish Empire and the fierce nationalisms and rivalries of the Balkan peoples ensured that a series of potentially dangerous crises and problems continued to erupt.

See Map 23 on page 418

A *The Armenian Question*

The Armenian Nationalists, inspired by the success of other similar Balkan movements, set up in 1890 the Armenian Revolutionary Federation with the ultimate aim of creating an Armenian national state. They set out through terrorist campaigns to provoke the Turks into taking brutal reprisals which would, they hoped, lead to international intervention. When the Turks reacted with their usual toughness, the Powers professed shock but were deeply suspicious of each other's motives when intervention was discussed. The British took the lead in 1894 and suggested joint action to impose a reform programme on the Sultan, but the Germans refused to join and the Russians ruled out any use of force because they did not want to risk international control over Constantinople if Turkey collapsed.

In 1896, after a group of Armenian revolutionaries had occupied the Ottoman bank in Constantinople, the Turks massacred the city's Armenian population. The Great Powers again drew up a reform programme, but there was still no agreement on how to enforce it and it was quietly shelved when their attention was taken up by events in China and the revolution in Crete.

Armenian Nationalists
The Armenians were not a compact ethnic group, but spread out over three different states: Russia, Persia and Turkey. Their aim of achieving a national state was therefore almost impossible to bring about.

B *The Austro-Russian Treaty of 1897*

In January 1897 the British Government broke with its traditional foreign policy when it decided that it could protect its interests in the Eastern Mediterranean from bases in Egypt. Consequently it no longer minded whether the Russians occupied the Straits. At a stroke this removed the one factor that could still bring together London and Vienna. Austria had little option but to turn directly to Russia in an effort to stabilise the Balkans. As Russia wished to concentrate on the Far East, in May 1897 both states agreed to do as little as possible to disturb the existing situation in the Balkans and Near East. Austria accepted that Russia had the right to insist on the closure of the Straits to foreign warships, but also revealed its long-term ambitions in the Balkans:

See page 427

MAP 23   *The growth of Balkan independence 1822–1913*

- the annexation of Bosnia–Herzegovina and the Sanjak of Novibazar
- the creation of an independent Albania
- the division of the rest of the Turkish occupied Balkans between the small states that were already independent in such a way that a balance of power could be achieved which would prevent any one state from becoming dominant.

This programme raised major issues about the future of the Balkans and not surprisingly the Russians refused to commit themselves to it.

C *The Cretan and Macedonian problems*

The Austro-Russian agreement was partly a response to the crises in Crete and Macedonia. In Crete Greek Nationalists, convinced that the Turkish empire was about to collapse, had revolted and demanded union with Greece. The Greek Government responded by sending warships to Crete and attacking Turkey in the North where their troops were decisively defeated. Although the Great Powers wished to preserve the Turkish Empire, they nevertheless forced the Sultan in September 1897 to grant Crete internal independence under Turkish **suzerainty**. The fragility of the cooperation between the Powers was shown by the fact that Austria and Germany not only opposed the appointment of Prince George of Greece as Governor of the island, since this could be seen as an attempt to strengthen Greek influence there at the cost of Turkey, but also withdrew their forces from the international army of occupation, which remained on the island until 1909.

In their brief war with Turkey the Greeks had tried to seize Macedonia. Although Macedonia was the birth place of Alexander the Great, it was in fact a complete jumble of ethnic groups and religions, and both Bulgaria and Serbia also had claims to it. Only the decisive defeat of the Greeks by Turkish forces and joint diplomatic pressure from Austria and Russia prevented a full-scale Balkan war. In 1903 a revolt started by the Macedonian Revolutionary Organization, which aimed at an independent Macedonia, was crushed, only then to be followed by virtual civil war between the various ethnic groups. Again Austria and Russia, agreed in October 1903 to draw up a program of reforms, but these was difficult to enforce effectively, and as Norman Rich has put it, 'Macedonia remained a dangerous repository in the notorious Balkan powder keg'.

> **suzerainty** ultimate control over another state which has internal self-government

> **KEY ISSUE**
>
> *Did the Austro-Russian Agreement of 1897 make a solution to the Balkan problem possible?*

D *The Bagdad Railway*

Another potential threat to peace in the Near East was the growing German economic and military involvement in Turkey. Ever since the end of the Russo-Turkish war of 1877–8 German officers had been re-organising the Turkish army. When the Sultan decided to build a network of railways, an important part of which was the proposed trunk route from Constantinople via Bagdad to the Persian Gulf, he also looked to Germany for financial help. In 1888 the *Deutsche Bank* set up the Anatolian Railway Company. Its Plans ran into fierce opposition from both Britain and Russia which were worried about the strategic implications of the Bagdad Railway. The Russians wanted to keep Turkey weak and feared that the railway would enable the Sultan to rush troops to Constantinople in a time of crisis, while the British feared that it could be used to transport Russian troops down to the Middle East and so threaten British bases there. They also feared its economic impact on the Suez Canal and the shipping lines to India as the Germans were anxious to capture the Indian freight and passenger traffic which went on British ships via the Suez Canal. The combined

ANALYSIS

See pages 413 and 440

The Bagdad Railway as a factor in international relations, 1908–14

M.S. Anderson has argued that the history of the Bagdad railway particularly after 1908 shows that '[m]ore than any other strand in the events of the years before 1914 … the unwillingness of the great Powers to quarrel really seriously about interests which were mainly economic'. Once it became clear that a German dominated company was going to construct the line, the other powers accepted the inevitable and began to negotiate with Berlin agreements which respected their key interests. Thus Russia gained recognition of its intentions to build railways in northern Persia, the French similarly in Syria, while the British were able to protect their position in the South. The Turkish Government agreed not to allow the railway to be extended to the Persian Gulf without British agreement and Germany recognised the monopoly of the Anglo-Persian Oil Company in Southern Mesopotamia and Central and Southern Persia.

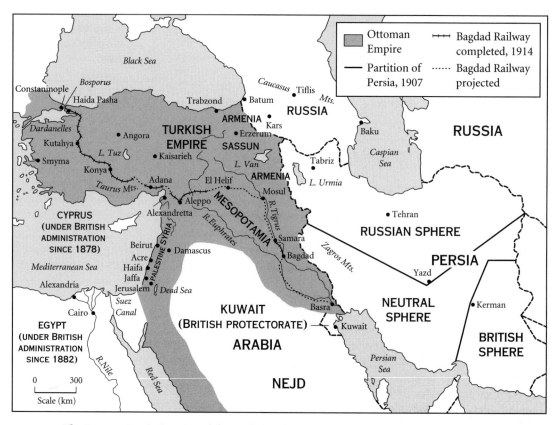

MAP 24 *The Ottoman Empire in Asia and the Bagdad Railway*

opposition of the Russian and British Governments in 1903 slowed up but did not stop the finalisation of plans for construction. The German Bagdad Railway Company managed to raise money from investors in Austria, Switzerland and France.

KEY ISSUE

Does the history of the Bagdad railway show that economic rivalry as a cause of the Great War can be exaggerated?

3 ∽ WORLD-WIDE IMPERIAL RIVALRIES

A *Introduction*

We have seen that already in the 1880s the Continental states were beginning to build up their own empires outside Europe, which inevitably brought them onto a collision course with Britain. Ten years later an even more intense scramble for territory broke out. France, Russia and Germany redoubled their efforts to carve out colonial empires, while they were joined by two new Powers, the United States and Japan. Britain as the largest and most vulnerable imperial Power was thrown onto the defensive, and Powers which were rivals in Europe often found common ground in opposing British influence in China or Africa. What caused this sudden burst of expansionism that has often been called the 'new imperialism'?

TIMELINE

May 1894	British Treaty with Congo Free State
August	Outbreak of Sino-Japanese War
April 1895	Treaty of Shimonoseki
May	Far Eastern 'Triplice' forced its re-negotiation
January 1896	Kruger Telegram
March	Italian defeat at Adowa
June	Russo-Japanese Treaty on Korea
November 1897	German missionaries murdered in Shantung
December	German forces occupied Kiao-Chow
March 1898	Russia granted lease of Liaotung peninsular
July	Marchand reached Fashoda
	Britain granted lease of Weihaiwei
August	Anglo-German Treaty over the Portuguese Colonies
September	Battle of Omdurman.
November	French ordered Marchand to evacuate Fashoda
March 1899	Anglo-French Agreement on Nile basin
September	First American note on the 'Open Door'
October	Boer War broke out
June 1900	Boxer uprising
July	Russian troops occupied Manchuria
October	Anglo-German Yangtzee Agreement
January 1902	Anglo-Japanese Alliance
May	Treaty of Vereeniging: Boer War ended
February 1904	Japan attacked Port Arthur
September 1905	Treaty of Portsmouth

ANALYSIS

How new was the 'New Imperialism'?

Imperialism, that is control or influence of one power over another, has existed as long as there have been states and peoples. The expansion in the last two decades of the nineteenth century is usually regarded as 'new' in that the European powers instead of controlling territories in Africa and Asia indirectly through economic influence and trade began to take over direct responsibility for their administration and defence. Yet in reality the difference between old and new imperialism is far from clear cut. Ever since 1815 the British had been steadily extending direct rule over the Indian and Malay states, and the French too in Algeria and Tahiti. The Russians also conquered huge areas in Central and Eastern Asia, while European settlers steadily populated North America, Australia and New Zealand.

Initially historians and political scientists, such as J.A. Hobson, H.N. Brailsford and V.I. Lenin were convinced that 'new imperialism' was caused by economic factors, which can be divided into two main groups:

capital is money invested in businesses to make a profit

- the existence of so much surplus **capital** in the European states that businessmen and investors wanted to invest it in new profitable enterprises in the colonies
- economic competition between the industrialised states of the world for markets and raw materials, which they thought that they could find in the colonies.

Right up to the 1950s these arguments were accepted as an 'orthodoxy', but closer analysis has shown up the inconsistencies in some of the economic arguments. For instance Germany and Italy, two countries with great colonial ambitions, actually suffered from a shortage of capital and needed it at home, Similarly detailed research on colonial companies, such as Cecil Rhodes' South Africa Company, has shown that in reality they were not very profitable and often paid no dividends. It can also be argued that the new colonies, particularly in tropical Africa, could hardly provide large markets for European manufactures. In view of these objections it is not surprising that some historians have argued that the New Imperialism was triggered by political rather than economic causes. Robinson and Gallagher, for instance, argued that it was Britain's occupation of Egypt which was carried out to safeguard the Suez Canal as the route to India that set off a chain reaction that led to the partition of Africa. Similarly A.J.P. Taylor interpreted Bismarck's colonial policy as a means to strengthen the short-lived Franco-German *Entente*. Fieldhouse sees the New Imperialism primarily as 'the extension into the periphery of the political struggle in Europe'. In other words, once it became clear that the frontiers of the major European states

See page 398

could not easily be changed without war, the rivalry of the Great Powers shifted to Africa and Asia.

Nevertheless it would be a mistake to down play economic factors too much. Economic factors *were* very important. Increasingly as more and more powers introduced tariffs, the possession of a large colonial empire was seen as the only way to guarantee access to vital raw materials needed by modern industrial economies. Businessmen in Marseilles, Liverpool and Hamburg were constantly pushing their Governments into annexing areas where they had important trading interests. There was also often an exaggerated and wildly inaccurate belief in the potential wealth of new colonies. In the early twentieth century, for instance, German public opinion believed that Morocco was fabulously wealthy and bitterly resented the growth of French influence there.

See page 437

Increasingly in the last two decades of the nineteenth century European Governments, backed by public opinion, began to believe that their states could remain great nations only if they had colonial empires which would provide trade, raw materials and opportunities for settlement. Thus a French political economist, Paul Lerroy-Beaulieu, stressed, for instance, that it was 'a matter of life and death' for France to become a 'great African power or in a century or two she will be no more than a secondary European power and will count for about as much in the world as Greece or Romania'. By 1900 imperialism had in Norman Rich's words developed into a 'mass cult. Colonies became symbols of national greatness and prestige, desired by nationalists of every economic and social class. The imperial idea, like nationalism itself, had been stirred into flames by visionaries, theorists, and prophets; it was subsequently nourished by the systematic propaganda of interest groups, patriotic and colonial societies and the nationalist press. But, again like nationalism, imperialism appears to have met some profound psychological need for **vicarious** excitement, to feel oneself the member of a national team that was making its mark in the world and proving its superiority over other peoples and races ...'.

vicarious something delegated or experienced only in the imagination

The struggle for empire was at its most intense in

- the Upper Nile
- South Africa
- China.

As the rivalry of the Great Powers in these areas is analysed, you should make up your mind on what you think were the main causes of the New Imperialism.

KEY ISSUE

What were the causes of the New Imperialism?

See page 396

See Map 21 on page 399

Cape-to-Cairo Railroad This was the dream of Cecil Rhodes, the Prime Minister of Cape Colony until 1896. It would open up Africa to British imperial and commercial interests

See page 427

B *The Upper Nile and Fashoda Crisis*

When the British took control of Egypt in 1882, they did not think that the Sudan, which the Egyptians had conquered earlier on in the century, was worth the cost of occupying. A few years later, however, its strategic importance dramatically increased in the eyes of the colonial powers when it was argued that any state which could control the upper waters of the Nile, would be able to dam or divert them before they flowed into Egypt, and consequently be in a position be to ruin the Egyptian economy and so dictate to the British administration in Cairo. To stop the Sudan falling into the hands of a rival Power became a major aim of British foreign policy. The French, bitterly resentful of Britain's position in Egypt, were the main threat, and their intention was to seize a wide strip of territory right across central Africa from the Indian Ocean to the Atlantic.

To prevent this the British acknowledged in November 1893 German claims to a large area in West Africa, which would block any French advance from the Congo into the Nile valley, but the Germans, pursuing their aim of putting pressure on Britain so as to force it to join the Triple Alliance, handed over this territory to the French in March 1894. The British then resorted to leasing to King Leopold of the Belgians, the head of the Congo Free State, large areas of territory of British claimed but unoccupied territory to the west of the Nile. They were promised in return a 25 kilometre wide corridor through which they would eventually be able to extend the Cape-to-Cairo railway. Again the Germans intervened and in combination with the French forced Leopold to drop the whole agreement.

The British Government now had little alternative but to occupy the area itself. Consequently it sent an Anglo-Egyptian force under Kitchener down the Nile to re-establish complete control over the area. The *Kaiser* was convinced that this force would be defeated and that 'the English will yet come to us crawling on their knees if only we let them struggle long enough'. What developed next was a race to control the Upper Nile. The French had dispatched a small military mission which moved along the Congo River from the West and the Belgians and Abyssinians prompted by French and Russian agents also organised similar expeditions. Marchand reached the Upper Nile first and hoisted the French flag at Fashoda, but he was confronted on 18 September by Kitchener's army, which had just annihilated the Sudanese forces at Omdurman. An immediate confrontation that could have led to war between Britain and France was avoided, when Kitchener decided not use force to eject Marchand. Instead it was left to the two Governments to find a diplomatic solution. Britain was in a very strong position to compel the French to back down and refused to compromise. Public opinion and the press were violently anti-French, and the British navy, which was ostentatiously mobilised, was in a position to stop the French from sending reinforcements to Africa. Germany, despite its earlier hostility, had just signed yet another colonial agreement with Britain in August, and Russia was resentful that France had not been of more assistance in the Balkans; and so neither power wished to be dragged into a confrontation with Britain in Africa. France therefore had little option but concede totally to British demands in the Sudan.

Fashoda has been called by J. Keiger, 'the worst crisis in Franco-British relations since Waterloo'. Yet, it also led to an improvement in Anglo-French relations, as influential voices in Paris particularly in the Colonial party, began to argue that France should cut its losses, write off Egypt and gain British backing for the annexation of Morocco.

See page 435

KEY ISSUE

How serious was the Fashoda Crisis?

C *South Africa*

In South Africa the British faced similar threats to their colonial ambitions and were anxious to ensure that their scope for expanding northwards was not blocked by rival Powers moving in and seizing strategically important territory. Above all British officials and businessmen feared that the Germans would try to extend their power eastwards from their colony in South West Africa through uncolonised territory to the semi-independent state of the Transvaal. Under pressure, particularly from Cecil Rhodes, the Prime Minister of Cape Colony in 1890, steps were taken to fill this vacuum. Rhodes set up the British South Africa Company, to which the British Government gave the right to colonise and govern the whole area north of the Transvaal and between Mozambique, German Southwest Africa and Angola.

See Map 21 on page 399

Developments in Southern Africa up to 1881

ANALYSIS

In 1814 Cape Colony was given to the British by the Treaty of Paris. The Dutch settlers there, the Boers, deeply resented both the abolition of the slave trade throughout the British Empire in 1834, as it deprived them of cheap farm labour, and the efforts of the new Colonial Government to protect the native Africans from exploitation by the settlers. Between 1836 and 1840 a large number of Boers migrated (the 'Great Trek') to found new colonies in what later became called the Orange Free State and Transvaal. In 1877 both states, which were threatened by Zulu military power, agreed to annexation by the British. However, once the Zulus were defeated at the battle of Ulundi, they began to agitate for independence. This led in 1880 to the first Boer War. The British Liberal Government under Gladstone sympathised with their demands and by the Convention of Pretoria, August 1881, recognised their freedom to run their own affairs, although London was still theoretically responsible for their foreign policy.

GERMANY AND THE TRANSVAAL

The economic significance of the Transvaal was transformed by the discovery of gold there in 1886. Foreign prospectors and adventurers, a large number of whom were British, poured in. Inevitably this posed a challenge to the supremacy of the Boer population, and Paul Kruger, the President of the Transvaal, began to look to Germany for support against the growing pressure from Rhodes. By the mid-nineties the Germans dominated the Transvaal economy: they controlled the National Bank, held the whisky and dynamite monopolies and supplied the state's water. Consequently when Cecil Rhodes on his own initiative launched a badly planned and unsuccessful attempt to overthrow Kruger, the so called Jameson raid, the Germans could hardly remain indifferent to it, but the way they reacted, revealed, as Gordon Craig has written, 'all the faults of German diplomacy in the most glaring light'. The *Kaiser* at first wanted to declare the Transvaal a German protectorate, send military aid to Kruger and then summon a Congress in Berlin, which would redraw the map of South Africa, but in the end he was persuaded that because of British sea power, these were just empty threats. Instead he sent the following telegram to Kruger:

> I wish to express my sincere congratulations that you and your people without asking the help of friendly powers, have succeeded in restoring peace through your own actions against armed bands, which broke into your country as disturbers of the peace, and in preserving the independence of your country against attack from without.

However illegal the raid had been, this telegram was a diplomatic blunder. It triggered a wave of anger amongst the British public and 'a flying squadron' of warships was specially set up by the Admiralty ready to be sent at short notice to anywhere in the world. The telegram did much to turn British public opinion against Germany, and failed to win any support from either France or Russia.

THE BOER WAR AND THE ABSENCE OF
A CONTINENTAL LEAGUE

The Jameson crisis strengthened Kruger, who was able to negotiate an alliance with the Orange Free State, and persuaded the British that he could only be removed by war. Skilfully Rhode's successor, Alfred Milner, managed to provoke him into sending the British an ultimatum in October 1899. Kruger, who had rebuilt the Boer army and equipped it with more modern artillery than the British themselves possessed, believed that it would be able to seize the port of Durban and prevent British troops from landing, thereby encouraging the intervention of France, Germany and Russia. The Boers never reached Durban, but the British did fear the possibilities of foreign intervention, particularly in the early months when they were thrown on the defensive by brilliantly led republican troops. ' There could never be', as A.J.P. Taylor has written, 'a more favourable opportunity, in theory, for the Continental powers to exploit British difficulties'. Public opinion in France, Russia and Germany was decidedly pro Boer, and Delcassé, the French Foreign Minister, attempted to secure a joint intervention by these three Powers. Why was he not successful? Again to quote Taylor 'the British navy decided the issue' in that it made military intervention physically impossible. Yet if the three Powers had set up a Continental League or alliance, they might have been able eventually to force Britain to agree to mediation or a Congress. Tsar Nicholas II wrote to his sister:

> 'I do like knowing that it lies entirely with me to decide the ultimate course of the war in South Africa ... all I need to do is to telegraph orders to all troops in Turkestan to mobilize and advance to the frontier [of Afghanistan].

See Map 22 on page 400

In practice, however, neither France nor Russia were ready to intervene against Britain unless they had German backing, but the Germans would only intervene if all three Powers guaranteed each other's European territory. France was unwilling to agree to this as it refused to recognise German control of Alsace-Lorraine and Russia was fully absorbed by the situation in the Far East. The British had also managed to buy off the Germans with a cynical deal over the Portuguese colonies in August 1898. It was agreed that British and German banks would both participate in any future loans to be made to Portugal. The Portuguese colonies would serve as security to be divided up between Britain and Germany in case Portugal was unable to repay the loan. In reality the British, of course had no intention of ever letting this happen. In October 1899 they signed a secret treaty with Portugal, which was positively Bismarckian in its double dealing, as it promised British protection for its colonies and so contradicted the agreement with Germany. The British were therefore able to defeat the Boers in isolation even though the war dragged on to March 1902.

See page 430

KEY ISSUE

Why were the Continental Powers unable to intervene on the side of the Boers?

D *China*

As in Africa Great Power rivalry in China was determined by a mixture of political, economic and strategic factors. In 1860 Russia had become a Pacific power by expanding into the Chinese Amur and Maritime provinces. It wished to round off these gains by annexing Manchuria, opening up its market to Russian imports and acquiring an ice free Port in Korea, over which China still theoretically had suzerainity. The Trans-Siberian railway, the construction of which started in 1891, would eventually enable the Tsar to move troops from Europe to the Far East in a fortnight and so realise his ambitions in Northern China. The French, too, were exploiting China's weakness to extend the frontiers of their Indo-Chinese colony further into Chinese territory. Inevitably these moves were opposed by Britain, which up to this point

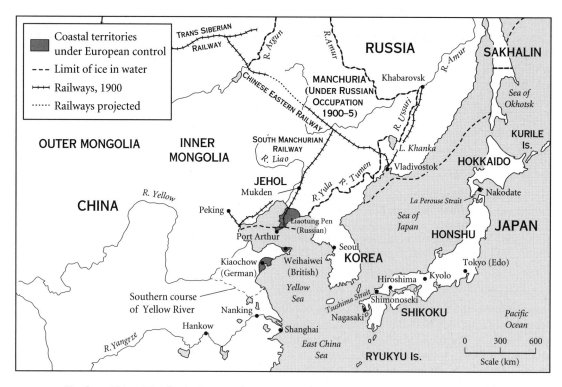

MAP 25 *Northern China, Manchuria, Korea and Japan*

had been able dominate China's foreign trade and through its superior sea power block any attempts at partition. Inevitably the construction of the Trans-Siberian Railway would change this, as Russia would be able to back up its demands with troops. In China, unlike Africa, Britain therefore faced the prospect of a challenge to its commercial position from a major military land power. Russia could usually rely on the backing of France and Germany, while it became gradually clear that Britain's only potential ally was Japan.

THE CHINESE–JAPANESE WAR OF 1895 AND ITS CONSEQUENCES

Like Britain, Japan was opposed to the growth of Russian influence in Manchuria and Korea. Its chance to strengthen its position in Korea came in 1894 when a rebellion broke out against the Korean Government. Both the Chinese and Japanese sent troops which rapidly crushed the revolt. However, when it became clear that Tokyo was not going to withdraw its forces, China declared war on Japan but was quickly defeated. Japan then dictated a very tough peace, the Treaty of Shimonoseki. By this China was forced to

See Map 25 above

● recognise the independence of Korea, which became in effect a Japanese protectorate

China and Japan: two contrasting histories

Both empires were in 1800 isolationist and hostile to Western contacts. Japan, however, was able to adapt to westernisation and to emerge as an important regional power by 1900, while China seemed to be on the verge of being divided up between the Great Powers, like Africa. A major step in opening up China to Western influence was the Treaty of Nanking of August 1842. The British forced the Chinese not only to import opium from India, but also to cede them the island of Hong Kong and to open up five coastal cities to foreign traders. Over the next 50 years further concessions were forced out of the Chinese. For instance by the Peking treaties of October 1860, 11 more treaty ports were opened up. On the periphery of the Empire Chinese territory was also taken over by Britain and France in Burma and Indo-China respectively, while Russia annexed the Amur province. Chinese opposition to Western imperialism was also hampered by internal rebellions and a series of natural catastrophes.

Japan's isolation ended when the Americans sent a fleet in 1854 and persuaded its Government to open up two ports for trade and the use of the American navy. Gradually similar privileges were extended to the other European Powers. In 1868 a political revolution took place in Japan, the so called Meijii Restoration, which gave greater power to the Emperor. This marked the victory of the westernisers and modernisers, who then rapidly transformed Japan into a modern state.

- hand over to Japan Formosa (Taiwan) and the Pescadores as well as the Liaotung Peninsula with the important port of Port Arthur
- pay both a large indemnity and grant Japan significant commercial privileges.

See Map 22 on page 400

Britain welcomed the Treaty as it created a buffer between its interests in Southern China and Russia's expanding sphere of influence in the North. To the Russians, however, it was a serious blow to their ambitions for acquiring an ice-free port in Korea and terminating the Trans-Siberian railway at Port Arthur. They therefore organised a joint European protest to force the Japanese to renegotiate the Treaty. Not surprisingly the British remained aloof, but the Germans, even though they had no major interests in China, were the first Power to support the Russians. They calculated that if they backed Russia they would strengthen their position in Europe because

- it would encourage Russia to become involved in China rather than the Balkans
- it would also make a Russo-British war more likely and both sides would then look to Germany for support

● it would force France to support Russia in China even though the French Government wanted to refocus Russian interest away from China back to Europe.

As the Germans foresaw, the French supported the Russians to form what the diplomats called the 'Far Eastern Triplice' or 'Triple *Entente*', which successfully forced the Japanese to return the Liaotung Peninsula to China. Apart from fuelling Russia's ambitions in China, Germany, gained very little from its membership of the 'Triplice'. The Russians, however, were able significantly to strengthen their position. In 1896 they forced Japan to agree to setting up a joint Russo-Japanese protectorate over Korea. They also signed a treaty with China promising assistance in the event of an attack, and in return were given permission to extend the Trans-Siberian railway across Manchuria to Vladivistock.

THE GERMAN SEIZURE OF KIAOCHOW
AND THE BOXER REVOLT

Germany was not prepared to play a passive role in China. Like the other European Powers it was attracted by the potential of the huge Chinese market of 450 million people. Consequently the murder of two German missionaries in Shantung in 1897 provided Berlin with a convenient pretext to seize Kiachow as a site for a coaling station and naval base. This then triggered a chain reaction from the other European Powers and it looked as if the partition of China was about to begin:

● the Russians led the way by seizing the Liaotung peninsular in December 1897 and forcing the Chinese to grant them a 25 year lease
● the French then demanded a 99 year lease on the Kwangchowan peninsular in southern China
● while the British insisted on similar lease on the Kowloon Peninsula opposite Hong Kong and in a second treaty with the Chinese Government secured a lease on Wei-hai-wei which was to run as long as the Russian lease on Liaotung.

The Boxers
The Boxers were a secret Chinese nationalist organisation the literal translation of which is the 'Society of the Harmonious Fists'

Not surprisingly these demands led to an anti-Western backlash in China. In the summer of 1900 the Boxer revolt broke out. In Peking European property was destroyed and the German Ambassador shot. In response to this the European Powers were forced to work together and an international force under a German general was sent. The Boxer movement was rapidly defeated, but it provided Russia with an excellent excuse to send an army into Manchuria to occupy the main cities and strengthen its grip on the railway corridor.

BRITAIN'S OPEN DOOR POLICY AND
THE ANGLO-JAPANESE TREATY OF 1902

Both Britain and Japan viewed Russia's advance into Manchuria as a major threat to their interests in China. Although Britain had occupied Wei-hai-wei in 1897, essentially its policy was still to preserve a united China as a market for its exports. In this it was backed up by the Americans who in two notes to the European states with interests in

PICTURE 40 *'The Germans to the front'. A painting by Carl Röchling in 1900. The title refers to a remark by a British Admiral. The picture was very popular and often hung in the more nationalistically inclined households in Germany before the War*

China called for the policy of 'the open door', by which was meant that there should be free trade and no tariffs in any part of the Chinese Empire. The British also sought German support, and in October 1900 negotiated with Berlin the Yangtze Agreement, which backed the 'open door policy' and declared that neither Britain nor Germany were interested in annexing any Chinese territory. Britain was convinced that Germany had come round to supporting the *status quo* in China, but in fact the Germans had not the slightest intention of risking war with Russia over Manchuria. Inevitably then as soon as Britain called on Germany to put pressure on Russia to withdraw from Manchuria, the German Chancellor announced his 'absolute indifference' to the Manchurian question.

The collapse of the Yangtzee Agreement did very serious harm to Anglo-German relations. A.J.P. Taylor has called it 'the moment of decision in Anglo-German relations'. For a few months Britain was dangerously isolated, but then in the Autumn the Japanese came up with a proposal for an anti-Russian alliance in Asia, which in effect amounted to Britain holding the ring to ensure that neither French nor German assistance was forthcoming while Japan defeated Russia. Japan recognised Britain's interests in China, while Britain recognised that Japan was 'in a peculiar degree politically as well as commercially and industrially' interested in Korea. Both powers then went on to agree in January 1902 that if these interests were threatened, each power should be free to take the necessary action to protect them. The last two articles of the agreement then defined what would happen:

KEY ISSUES

How significant were economic factors in European involvement in China?

ANALYSIS

Was an Anglo-German alliance possible?

Intermittently between 1898 and 1901 there were alliance negotiations conducted at various levels between London and Berlin, but they never came to anything. After World War I Baron von Eckardstein, who had close links with both the British and German Governments, claimed that this was a missed opportunity of major proportions. Yet in reality both sides wanted something different. The Germans remembered the British alliance with Frederick the Great of Prussia in the mid-eighteenth century when they were left to do most of the fighting on the Continent while Britain was able to seize territory in India and Canada. They were only ready to settle for a formal treaty which firmly tied Britain to the Triple Alliance. Thus in 1901 the Germans offered a defensive alliance covering the whole of the British Empire and all three countries of the Triple Alliance, which would come into effect if one or more of the states signing the treaty were attacked by two or more Great Powers. The British were not tempted because, as Lord Salisbury observed, 'the liability of having to defend the German and Austrian frontiers against Russia is heavier than that of having to defend the British isles against France'.

II. 'If either Great Britain or Japan, in the defence of their respective interests ... should become involved in war with another Power, the other High Contracting Party will maintain a strict neutrality, and use its efforts to prevent other powers from joining in hostilities against its ally.

III. If, in the above event, any other Power, or Powers should join in hostilities against that ally, the other High contracting party will come to its assistance, and will conduct the war in common, and make peace in mutual agreement with it.

THE RUSSO-JAPANESE WAR, 1904–5

The Anglo-Japanese Treaty significantly strengthened Japan's position and should logically have led to a settlement with Russia. The Russians at first seemed conciliatory and agreed in April 1902 to withdraw their troops from Manchuria in three stages over an eighteen month period, but then a year later delayed completing the second stage. The Japanese responded by seeking to negotiate a general settlement with Russia, the gist of which was that Japan would recognise Russia's control of the railway in Manchuria, while Russia would cede Japan the dominant position in Korea. The Russian Foreign Minister was anxious to do a deal with Japan, but his efforts were sabotaged by the powerful Manchurian lobby led by Bezobrazov, whom one historian has called a 'hare brained schemer'. Under his influence any compromise with Japan became impossible. Russia insisted on the fullest rights for itself in Manchuria while attempting to reduce Japanese influence in Korea to the barest minimum.

In February 1904 the Japanese finally decided that they could not afford to wait until Russia had built up its power in the Far East and launched a pre-emptive attack on Port Arthur. The war was fought in isolation. Germany and France were not ready to help Russia in the Far East. Neither wanted to fight Britain and each feared that its involvement in a Far Eastern War would make it vulnerable to an attack in Europe from its neighbour across the Rhine. After the defeat of the Russian fleet at Tsushima and of the Russian army at Mukden, the Russians, paralysed by revolution at home, agreed to mediation by the American President in August 1905. By the terms of the Treaty of Portsmouth (New Hampshire) Russia ceased to be an immediate threat to either Britain or Japan in the Far East:

● Russia recognised Japan's leading role in Korea
● its lease on the Liaotung peninsula was handed over to Japan
● both powers agreed to withdraw from Manchuria.

4 ⌐ THE DIPLOMATIC REVOLUTION, 1897–1907

At the end of the nineteenth century it was the British Empire that was under pressure and a war between Britain and Russia over China seemed imminent. Although Germany faced a potentially hostile Franco-Russian alliance in Europe, in Africa and the Far East it was often able to cooperate with these two Powers against Britain. By 1907, however, the international situation had undergone a sea change. It was Germany that was isolated and Britain had settled its most acute disagreements with both Russia and France. It can therefore with some justification be said that a 'diplomatic revolution' had taken place. The main causes of this revolution are as follows:

● the construction of the German fleet combined with an aggressive or clumsy **Weltpolitik** forced Britain into taking action to preserve its position as a Great Power
● the Anglo-Japanese alliance of 1902 made Britain independent of Germany in the Far East
● the Franco-British Agreement of April 1904 at last marked the end of Anglo-French hostility over Egypt
● Germany's violent reaction to French claims to Morocco in 1905 only cemented the Franco-British *Entente* even more
● Russia's defeat by Japan in 1905 made Russia less of a threat to British interests in China and made possible the Anglo-Russian Agreement of 1907.

TIMELINE

1898	First German Naval law
1900	Second German Naval law
1902	Anglo-Japanese Alliance
April 1904	Anglo-French Entente
2 Jan 1905	Bloody Sunday in St. Petersburg
31 Mar	The Kaiser visited Tangier. First Moroccan Crisis started
June	Delcassé resigned
July	Treaty of Björkö
5 Sept	Treaty of Portsmouth
Jan 1906	Algeçiras Conference opened Anglo-French staff talks began
June	Third German Naval Law
Aug 1907	Anglo-Russian Agreement

A *German Weltpolitik and the construction of a battle fleet*

Weltpolitik is the German for a global policy

The ultimate aim of **Weltpolitik** was to create a large German colonial empire which would give Germany its 'place in the sun'. Fritz Fischer has argued that the German Government was trying to carry out a programme to create a large empire in Central Africa. In practice, however, German colonial expansion during the decade 1897–1907 was more erratic, but it was not totally unsuccessful – it gained Kiaochow, Britain's share in Samoa and several of the Spanish islands in the Pacific as well as economic concessions in the Turkish Empire, all of which pleased German public opinion. By 1900 the British, reluctantly perhaps, had come to live with the Germans as rather an awkward if, as yet, minor colonial power, which was considerably less threatening than either France or Russia; even though they had been irritated by the collapse of the Yangtzee agreement.

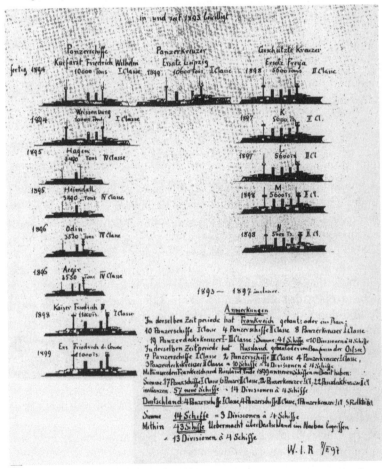

PICTURE 41 *A naval chart drawn by Wilhelm II. The Kaiser heads the chart with the title in his handwriting: 'Germany's new ships built in and since 1893'. At the bottom of the page he comes to the conclusion that France and Russia have a lead of 43 ships together over Germany*

It was, however, the launching of the German naval programme in 1898 that caused real alarm in Britain, and led to growing tension and an arms race between the two states, which by 1912 in the words of the Austrian Foreign Minister had become the 'dominant element of the international situation'. The German Government intended to build within 20 years a German fleet of 60 battleships. This fleet was from the very beginning to be aimed against Britain in the North Sea. Admiral Tirpitz, the Secretary of State of the Imperial Navy Office, made this crystal clear when he told *Kaiser* Wilhelm that

> For Germany, the most dangerous enemy at the present time is England.. It is also an enemy against which we most urgently require a certain measure of naval force as a political power factor ... Our fleet must be constructed so that it can unfold its greatest military potential between Heligoland and the Thames ... The military situation against England demands battleships in as great a number as possible.

Tirpitz believed that ultimately a strong fleet stationed in the North Sea would force Britain to make major colonial concessions to Germany. The naval programme was an important part of *Weltpolitik*. By 1902 the British Government was beginning to respond to the challenge. The navy was modernised, more of its ships concentrated in home waters and three years later a programme was drawn up for launching four new capital ships per year. By 1905, especially as the Japanese had destroyed most of the Russian fleet, the British were reasonably confident that they could maintain their **two power standard**, although this attitude was to change radically three years later.

> **two power standard** a fleet larger than the combination of any two other

> **KEY ISSUE**
>
> *What role did Anglo-German naval rivalry play in the causes of World War I?*

B *The Franco-British Entente*

Delcassé, smarting from France's diplomatic defeat at Fashoda, had initially attempted to improve relations with Germany. Above all he wanted to secure support for French control of Morocco. When it was clear in 1901 that the Germans wished to keep a free hand in case they could still persuade Britain to join the Triple Alliance, Delcassé began to look to London. Britain had initially been hostile to the prospect of a French **protectorate** in Morocco, as it might threaten Gibraltar, but by 1902 Morocco was on the verge of civil war and the restoration of order by the French seemed the better option. It was the French Ambassador in London, Paul Cambon, who first floated the idea of an Egyptian-Moroccan deal, while the successful state visit of Edward VII to Paris in May 1903 and the return visit by President Loubet in July created a favourable atmosphere for the talks. These were a series of complex negotiations aimed at resolving the clash of global British and French interests. The looming war in the Far East between Japan and Russia also played an important part in pushing the states into agreement as both feared what Lowe has called the 'nightmare scenario of Britain

See Map 21 on page 399

> **protectorate** a territory or state that is controlled or 'protected' by another state

and France having to fight each other as the 'seconds' of their allies'. Ultimately Delcassé and Cambon hoped to associate Britain with the Franco-Russian Dual Alliance, while Landsdowne, the British Foreign Secretary, hoped that the Anglo-French colonial agreement would set the pattern for a similar agreement with Russia, that would ease the pressure on the British Empire. The Agreement was signed on 8 April 1904 and settled colonial problems in three main areas:

- the French exchanged their fishing rights around Newfoundland for territorial compensation in West Africa
- Siam was divided into two zones of influence and a **condominium** was set up in the New Hebrides
- France agreed not to block British plans for financial reform in Egypt, provided Britain recognised France's right to maintain law and order in Morocco. Secret clauses then made provision for the establishment of a protectorate at some future date by France over Morocco and by Britain over Egypt.

condominium joint control of a territory by two states

This agreement certainly improved Anglo-French relations, but it was not an alliance since both countries retained full freedom of action. Indeed it can be argued that together with the Japanese alliance it made Britain even more independent of Continental entanglements and that it was only Germany's violent reaction to its provisions for the French control of Morocco that turned it into a virtual Franco-British alliance against Germany.

KEY ISSUE

Why was the Anglo-French Entente agreement negotiated?

C The German reaction: the first Moroccan Crisis, 1905–6

The German Government assumed that when the Russo-Japanese war broke out France's new *Entente* with Britain, an ally of Japan, would make the Franco-Russian alliance almost impossible to maintain, but in fact Delcassé by skilfully defusing the Dogger Bank incident managed

ANALYSIS

The Dogger Bank incident

The 'nightmare scenario' of an Anglo-Russian war appeared to come close to realisation when on 21 October 1904 the Russian fleet which was sailing to the Far East fired on a fleet of British trawlers fishing on the Dogger Bank in the North Sea sinking one trawler and killing two men. The Russians assumed that the trawlers were Japanese torpedo boats! Briefly it looked as if war might break out between Britain and Russia, but the British Government appealed to the French Government to mediate and the whole problem was submitted to the Hague Tribunal, the International court of Arbitration, which had been set up in 1901.

to avoid having to make any choice between Britain and Russia. Terrified that the *Entente cordiale* would in time lead to an Anglo-French Russian realignment against Germany, Chancellor Bülow decided to challenge the right of the French to control Morocco. According to the Madrid Convention of 1880 the Germans ought to have been consulted. He was sure that neither Britain nor Russia, which had not only been defeated by the Japanese, but also faced growing internal unrest, would support the French. Thus optimistically he was convinced that both the Dual Alliance and the *Entente cordiale* would be destroyed, a new Russo-German alliance would emerge and that France would in effect be forced into becoming a German satellite.

In early 1905 the French Government ignored all warnings from Berlin and sent a mission to Fez with instructions to start reforming the Moroccan administration. The *Kaiser* interrupted his Mediterranean cruise to land at Tangier and greeted the Sultan of Morocco as an independent ruler. The Germans then demanded a conference on the future of Morocco and the resignation of Delcassé. At first it seemed that Berlin really would win a significant success. The French Cabinet agreed to a conference and, bowing to massive German pressure, forced Delcassé to resign in June 1905. Then in July the *Kaiser* and Nicholas II met at Björkö and signed a defensive alliance to operate against any Power in Europe. Nicholas was assured that the Moroccan crisis was a 'stepping stone' to better Franco-German relations. Yet all these successes were purely temporary and by April 1906 Germany had suffered a crushing defeat. Berlin failed to break up the Dual Alliance as the Russian Government refused to abandon it and in November 1905 let the Björkö Agreement lapse. The *Entente* was significantly strengthened when the British Government came down firmly on the side of the French and even authorised secret military staff talks between the British and French armies on the the subject of sending an expeditionary force to France in the event of war with Germany.

When the Conference opened at Algeçiras in January 1906 Germany secured the backing of only Austria and Morocco. The other nine states agreed that France had a special interest in Morocco. Together with the Spanish the French were therefore entrusted with the supervision of the Moroccan Police, while France was also given control of the state bank. However the Germans did win the important concession that all the Powers should enjoy equal economic rights within Morocco.

Germany had suffered this major diplomatic set-back partly because Bülow's aggressive and provocative policy, which continued even after the fall of Delcassé, persuaded the British Government firmly to back France. The Germans also by insisting on calling a conference and defending the independence of Morocco, excluded the possibility of negotiating a separate deal with France. Finally their leadership was divided and it also failed to plan its tactics at the Algeçiras Conference effectively and so was easily outmanoeuvred by the French.

KEY ISSUE

What did Germany intend to achieve during the Moroccan Crisis and why did it fail?

ANALYSIS

See page 383

How near to war did Europe come in 1905–6?

The Moroccan incident was, as Taylor has stressed, 'a true crisis, a turning point in European history'. For the first time since 1875 a Franco-German war was a real possibility. There were no armies or fleets mobilised, but the senior official in the German Foreign Ministry, von Holstein, and the German Military High Command were certainly ready to risk war, as Russia was weak and the French army was inadequately equipped. In December 1905 von Schlieffen perfected his plans for a two front war, while the British and French military staffs began seriously to discuss what action should be taken if Germany invaded France.

D *The Anglo-Russian Colonial Agreement*

Essentially the Anglo-Russian Colonial Agreement of 1907, like the Anglo-French Agreement, was not in the first instance aimed against Germany. The British had long wished to negotiate a compromise with Russia that would take the pressure off Afghanistan and northern India. On the Russian side the Anglo-French *Entente* and Japan's victory in the Far East made an agreement with Britain increasingly necessary. It had little option but to improve its relations with London if it were to maintain its alliance with France. In the Far East peace seemed dangerously precarious. The Japanese felt cheated by the Treaty of Portsmouth and were building up their armed forces very quickly. A good understanding with Britain would however almost certainly act as a brake on their ambitions. Consequently the new Russian Foreign Minister Izvolsky was ready to negotiate a colonial agreement with Britain. He was quite ready to renounce any action that might threaten the security of India as Russia was hardly in the position to risk war with Britain. Besides he was convinced that in view of the failures in the Far East Russia should from now on concentrate on gaining control of the Turkish Straits. To neutralise possible Austrian opposition British support would be needed.

KEY ISSUE

Why did Britain and Russia sign the 1907 Agreement?

The Anglo-Russian Agreement was signed in August 1907. Like the Anglo-French Agreement it was concerned only with colonial matters:

See Map 24 page 420

● the Russians gave up all claims to Afghanistan and recognised British interests in Tibet
● Persia was divided into zones of influence: the North went to Russia, the South to Britain with a neutral zone in between.
● both Empires recognised Chinese sovereignty over Tibet.

E *Conclusion: was Germany encircled?*

The Triple *Entente* was not a formal alliance system, but it did mark a shift in the balance of power in Europe. No longer could the Germans assume that an Anglo-Russian war would break out, which would enable them to force Britain – or Russia – into becoming a subordinate ally. The *éntentes* did not completely remove all friction between their members. Anglo-Russian friction continued, for instance, in Persia. Nor did they necessarily mean that Germany would be isolated and encircled. There were influential voices in France in 1909 arguing for a settlement with Germany. It was, however, the aggressive and frequently clumsy policy of Germany, which was first displayed in 1905–6 and then repeated in the Bosnian and Second Moroccan Crises, that was to turn the Triple *Entente* into an anti-German re-alignment.

5 ~ BRITAIN, FRANCE AND GERMANY, 1907–12

A *Franco-German relations 1907–10*

In the aftermath of the First Moroccan Crisis Franco-German relations temporarily improved. In 1906 a settlement of sorts had been reached in Morocco which guaranteed German economic interests there. Increasingly over the next five years German and French financiers and businessmen began to cooperate more closely, indicating that economic factors far from dividing the two countries had the potential to bring them together. The real driving force to improve Franco-German relations came from the French Ambassador in Berlin, Jules Cambon, the brother of Paul, the French Ambassador in London. He believed strongly that through colonial and economic concessions German pressure on France could be eased. Thus he managed skilfully to play down the Casablanca Deserters Affair in September 1908, which was caused by the local German Consul giving refuge to six French Foreign Legion deserters, and did much to support the negotiation of the Franco-German Moroccan Agreement of February 1909. By this Germany recognised France's special political interests in Morocco as long as both countries were able to share equally in its economic development. Cambon hoped that this would lead on to further cooperation with Berlin. Privately he realised that:

> The Alsace-Lorraine question is untouchable for Germany, like Rome for Italy; it is the cornerstone of the Empire and the **complicity** of all the confederated states is after all the link that has united them.

Consequently he believed that Paris should recognise its final loss. Historical research has shown that potentially some compromise there was possible. Public opinion in Alsace-Lorraine was increasingly less pro French and more interested in gaining independence from both Germany and France.

TIMELINE

June 1908	Fourth German Navy Law
Oct	Bosnia and Herzegovina annexed by Austria
Feb 1909	Franco-German Agreement on Morocco
March	British Naval bill passed for 8 Dreadnoughts
July	Bethmann Hollweg appointed German Chancellor
May 1911	French troops occupied Fez
1 July	Panther arrived at Agadir
21 July	Lloyd George's Mansion House speech
4 Nov	Franco-German agreement on Morocco
Jan 1912	Poincaré appointed French Prime Minister
Feb	Haldane Mission
Sept	Italy invaded Libya

complicity the German states all agreed that Prussia should annexe Alsace-Lorraine in 1871

ANALYSIS

The Franco-German economic Entente

French businessmen and financiers were already co-operating in Turkey, Serbia, Romania, Bulgaria and South America, but from 1907 onwards big German firms were setting up subsidiaries or buying up firms in France. For instance German steel makers like Thyssen, and Krupp, in order to guarantee long term supplies of ore began to buy up French firms in French Lorraine and Normandy. Similarly French firms like Schneider and Saint-Gobain increased their investments in Lorraine and the Ruhr coal firms. There was then an element of 'economic inter-penetration of interests', to quote J.V. Keiger, between 1906 and 1910, even though German exports to France were increasing more quickly than the latter's exports to the former.

It seems therefore that there was at least some scope for an improvement in Franco-German relations. Yet the chance was missed and by the end of 1910 relations were rapidly worsening:

- local French officials in Morocco were breaking the Algeçiras Agreement by steadily increasing their powers in administrative, economic and financial affairs
- the French Foreign Minister, who had listened to Jules Cambon, was replaced by a more aggressive politician, Jean Cruppi, who blocked plans for economic cooperation between France and Germany in Morocco
- in Germany a new Foreign Secretary had been appointed, Kiderlen-Wächter, who was determined to pursue a more decisive and aggressive foreign policy.

KEY ISSUE

Could it be argued that economic rivalry was not a major cause of World War I?

B *The Second Moroccan Crisis*

Kiderlen-Wächter's opportunity came when French troops were sent to keep order after riots against the Sultan of Morocco had broken out in Fez in April 1911. Fez was occupied in May, and it was clear that the French were not going to withdraw and had every intention of turning Morocco into a protectorate. Inevitably this broke the 1906 and 1909 agreements and played into Germany's hands. Kiderlen-Wächter warned the French that if they remained in Morocco, Germany would insist on some form of territorial compensation. As they made no move, the German Government sent on I July the *Panther*, a gun-boat, to the south Moroccan port of Agadir. The hope was, as Kiderlen-Wächter expressed it, that

'By seizing a [territorial] pawn, the Imperial Government will be placed in a position to give the Moroccan affair a turn which should cause the earlier set backs of 1905 to pass into oblivion .... .

The Germans initially demanded the whole of the French Congo. At first it looked as if they might score a major success. The French army was in no position to fight as it had not sufficient heavy artillery, and the Russians, still resenting the lack of French help during the Bosnian Crisis, refused to give the French any diplomatic backing. But then on 21 July Britain intervened decisively. The Chancellor of the Exchequer, Lloyd George, voiced the Government's policy when he stated at a dinner at the Mansion House that:

See page 445

> If a situation were to be forced upon us in which peace could only be preserved by the surrender of the great and beneficent position Britain has won by centuries of heroism and achievement, by allowing Britain to be treated where her interests were vitally affected as if she were of no account in the Cabinet of Nations, then I say emphatically that peace at that price could be humiliation, intolerable for a great country like ours to endure … .

The British were anxious to prevent a German diplomatic success, which they feared would destroy the *Entente*, but they were also signalling to the French that Britain must not be ignored in any new Moroccan agreement. In fact the warning was seen as an ultimatum against Germany and it made a Franco-German compromise much more difficult to achieve. In the end through secret negotiations Caillaux, the French Prime Minister, reached a compromise with the Germans in November 1911, which allowed France to establish a protectorate over Morocco, provided that Germany was given part of the French Congo and its economic interests in Morocco respected.

The crisis had very serious consequences for the peace of Europe. It increased tension between Germany and the *Entente* powers, which fuelled the arms race. The French occupation of Morocco persuaded the Italians in 1912 to invade Tripoli in case the French moved in there too. This caused a war with the Turkish Empire, to which Tripoli theoretically still belonged, and encouraged the Balkan states to seize what was left of European Turkey, whilst the Turks were fighting the Italians.

KEY ISSUE

Did Germany over-react during the second Moroccan Crisis?

See Map 21, page 399

C *Anglo-German naval rivalry*

In the second Moroccan Crisis the real antagonists were Britain and Germany. The accelerating rate of the construction of the German battle fleet had continued to poison relations between the two states and ensured that London increasingly saw the Triple *Entente* as a key means of containing Germany.

In 1906 battleship construction had been revolutionised by the invention of the *Dreadnought*, which inevitably made every other ship afloat obsolete. By 1909 Britain had already constructed ten of these. Paradoxically, however, the creation of this new super ship made it easier for the Germans to catch up, as it inevitably reduced Britain's overwhelming lead. Thus when in 1908 the Germans announced a supplementary

Invention of the Dreadnought *HMS Dreadnought* was 17 900 tons compared to the conventional battleship of 16 000, her speed was 21 knots rather than 16 and she was much better armed than her predecessors

programme consisting of four capital ships per year for the next four years, often hysterical demands in the British popular press and skilfully orchestrated campaigns by the Navy League pressure group pushed the British Government into agreeing to build eight new battleships in 1909 and a further ten over the next two years.

Inevitably the sheer cost of these construction programmes made Britain put out feelers to see if a naval agreement were possible. There was, too, a group of ministers in the Cabinet, the so called 'Potsdam Party', which wished for a political settlement with Germany. Similarly in Germany Bülow's successor, Bethmann Hollweg, wanted to improve Anglo-German relations. In 1909–10 and then again in 1912 after the second Moroccan Crisis attempts were made to find a formula which could defuse the dangerous tensions generated by the naval race, but each time there were insuperable objections to a settlement:

<table>
<tr><td>

KEY ISSUE

Why did Germany try to challenge British naval supremacy?

</td></tr>
</table>

● in 1909–10 the British wanted to negotiate a fixed ratio for capital ships between the two Powers which would guarantee British naval superiority, while the Germans wanted a cast iron assurance that Britain would not join a coalition directed against the *Reich*. The *Kaiser* and Tirpitz were determined to press on with the expansion of the fleet, while the British rejected the German attempt to prise them out of the Triple *Entente*. Sir Edward Grey, the British Foreign Secretary, observed:

> An entente with Germany such as M. Kiderlen [Wachter] sketches would serve to establish German hegemony [control] in Europe and would not last long after it had served that purpose

● in 1912 shaken by Britain's policy during the Second Moroccan Crisis, Bethmann Hollweg put out feelers to the British Government, which then sent out Lord Haldane with a set of more modest proposals. Provided the Germans agreed not to increase their exist-

<table>
<tr><td>

ANALYSIS

</td><td>

Popular opinion and Anglo-German naval rivalry

In both Britain and Germany pressure groups, as Paul Kennedy has argued, both 'fed off and contributed to, the tensions generated by Anglo-German naval rivalry'. In Germany the *Flottenverein* [the Fleet league] had close links to the Navy Office and was financed by Krupp, the big armaments concern. The construction of the fleet was genuinely popular in Germany as it was perceived, unlike the Army, which was still Prussian in spirit, to be national and middle class. In Britain the navy was regarded as the fundamental basis of the country's existence as a Great Power.

</td></tr>
</table>

ing naval programme, Britain would be ready to make some colonial concessions and sign a mutual declaration debarring 'either power from joining in **aggressive** designs or combinations against the other'. Again the German Government, very much on Tirpitz's advice and contrary to Bethmann Hollweg's wishes, insisted that a new naval law providing for the construction of six extra battleships, should be included in the German total, and that Britain should agree to remain neutral in the event of Germany becoming involved in a European war. These extra ships clearly changed the whole picture. Neither could the British Government commit itself to remaining neutral if Germany fought in a Continental war, which might involve an invasion of France. Negotiations therefore collapsed.

> This formula using the word **aggressive** would enable Britain to maintain the *Ententes* with France and Russia as they were arguable **defensive** and not obviously aimed at Germany

Anglo-German relations reached their lowest point in 1911–12, but over the next two years they improved despite the absence of a naval agreement. Britain and Germany were for instance able to cooperate during the London Conference of 1913 on the Balkans. Nevertheless the root of Anglo-German rivalry lay in the fact that Britain was a Power in slow decline. It had to retain its existing control of the seas in order to preserve its Empire, while Germany ultimately rejected this claim. As long as Germany continued to build up its navy, Britain would ultimately be numbered amongst Germany's enemies.

See page 447

D *Poincaré and the Triple Entente*

When Poincaré became French Prime Minister in 1912, French foreign policy became much more coherent. He believed that a clear balance of power would have the best chance of containing Germany and so keep the peace of Europe. He was even convinced that attempts to break up the Triple Alliance would only destabilise the European situation and provoke Germany into some rash act. One of his officials summed up his thinking when he wrote in 1912:

> The penetration of the alliances, in fact corrupts and dissolves them. By upsetting the balance and by obscuring the clarity of the situation, in reality it leads to ambiguity and instability... it eventually weakens the guarantees for peace.

In the Spring of 1912 Poincaré was concerned by the state of Franco-Russian relations. In the Bosnian crisis of 1908, France had not helped Russia, while Russia had signed in 1909 a secret agreement with Italy at Racconigi supporting Italian ambitions in Tripoli in return for backing in the Straits without telling Paris at all. Poincaré therefore set about tightening up links with Russia. The Franco-Russian Naval Convention was signed in July 1912 in which both navies agreed to work out joint tactics in the event of war. The Military Chiefs of Staff also met and

See page 445

decided that should war break out with Germany both the Russian and French armies would immediately attack.

Poincaré also wanted to strengthen the *Entente* with Britain. He was relieved by the failure of the Haldane Mission, which, had it been successful, might have threatened the unity of the *Entente*. In July talks between the British and French naval staffs took place about the part each navy would play in the event of war in the Mediterranean and Channel. In November the two Governments exchanged letters defining the *Entente*. In essence they stated that the naval and military agreements between the two countries did not constitute a proper alliance, but if either state were attacked by a third Power, they would immediately meet to discuss whether they would take any joint measures. This was as far as the British Cabinet was willing to go.

By the end of 1912 both the Dual Alliance and the Anglo-French *Entente* had been greatly strengthened. Germany, facing isolation, was consequently all the more determined to cling to its alliance with Austria. It was this that was to make the Balkan crises of 1908–14 so dangerous.

KEY ISSUE

To what extent did Poincaré restore close cooperation between the three Entente Powers?

TIMELINE

Oct 1908	Bosnia and Herzegovina annexed by Austria-Hungary
Aug 1911	Potsdam Agreement
Mar 1912	Bulgarian-Serbian alliance
29 May	Greece, Bulgaria and Serbia formed Balkan League
8 Oct	First Balkan War began
31 May 1913	Treaty of London ended the First Balkan War
29 June	Second Balkan War broke out.
11 Aug	Treaty of Bucharest ended Second Balkan War
December	Liman von Sanders arrived in Constantinople

See Maps 20 and 23 on pages 386 and 418

---

6 ⌐ THE BALKANS AND THE GREAT POWERS, 1906–14

Weakened by defeat in the Far East and the subsequent turmoil at home, the Russian Government at first hoped to maintain the agreement negotiated with Austria in 1897 (see page 417) which was aimed at keeping the *status quo* in the Balkans. However it was Russia's very weakness that upset the balance of power in the Balkans and tempted Austria to take advantage of it to defend its interests against the growing Serb threat.

A *Growing Austrian–Serbian friction*

In 1903 the Serbian King, Alexander Obrenovich, was assassinated by Serbian nationalists and replaced by Peter, a member of the rival Karageorgevich dynasty. Peter followed a fiercely anti-Austrian and strongly nationalist policy, which he hoped would attract Russian support. The Austrian Government attempted to force him to follow a more friendly policy by suspending all Serb trade with the Habsburg Empire, but this backfired as the Serbs found markets elsewhere and became even more determined to secure access to ports in the Adriatic and Aegean seas. Aehrenthal, the Austrian Foreign Minister, hoped to strengthen Austria's position in the Balkans by annexing Bosnia-Herzegovina and eventually partitioning Serbia. As a first step towards this, the Austrians decided to construct a railway through the Sanjak of Novibazar to link up with the existing line to Salonika. This would not only drive a wedge between Serbia and Montenegro, and so stop these two ethnically related territories from ever unifying, but it would also help Austria to extend its economic and political influence southwards.

B *The Bosnian Crisis, 1908–9*

Inevitably this drew sharp protests from both the Serbs and the Russians who argued that the proposed railway threatened the *status quo* in the Balkans, but anxiety about the consequences of the Young Turk revolution temporarily revived Austro-Russian co-operation. The Russians had over the last year been playing with the idea of doing a deal with Austria whereby Russian warships would be able to pass through the Straits while this right would still be denied to the other Powers. In exchange Austria would be able formally to annex Bosnia and Herzegovina, which she had in fact administered since 1878. The deal was approved by Aehrenthal and Izvolsky, the Russian Foreign Secretary, at a meeting at Buchlau in September. The latter apparently insisted that any Austrian move would have to be confirmed later by a European conference, but this was never put down on paper, a fact that explains much of what was to follow.

See page 391

The Young Turk Revolution

This was started by a group of army officers in Macedonia in July 1908. They wanted parliamentary government and political representation in a Turkish parliament for all the ethnic groups in the empire, including those in Bosnia, Herzegovina and Bulgaria. This challenged the settlement of 1878 and appeared to foreshadow a revival of Turkish power in the Balkans at the expense of Austria and Russia.

ANALYSIS

The Austrians went ahead and annexed Bosnia-Herzegovina in October, while the Russians found little international support for their plans at the Straits. The annexation was, however, met with a storm of complaint throughout Europe. In Russia and Serbia, which eventually hoped to make these provinces part of a Greater Serb state, there were demonstrations calling for war against Austria. Facing strong criticism in the Russian press and *Duma* for finally giving Slav provinces to the Austrians, Isvolsky decided to pose as the champion of the Slavs and demand the calling of the European conference, to which he insisted the Austrians had in principle agreed. Austria immediately vetoed this proposal, as it feared a repetition of what had happened at Algeçiras where the Central Powers were heavily outvoted. What made the crisis so dangerous was that Austria, which had the unconditional backing of Germany, was ready to fight Serbia even if supported by Russia. Bülow had given Aehrenthal a 'blank check' when he informed him on October 30 that 'I shall regard whatever decision you come to as the appropriate one'. He was aiming to isolate Russia and force her out of the Triple *Entente*. The Russians received backing from neither the French, who were busy negotiating the Moroccan Agreement with Germany, nor the British. Russian attempts to persuade the Germans to mediate, were ruthlessly brushed aside and the Russian Government had no option but accept the annexation.

See page 437

See page 439

KEY ISSUE

Why did the Bosnian crisis not start a major war?

The dangerous consequences of this crisis were that it did long-term and serious damage to Russia's relations with Germany and Austria, and made cooperation in the Balkans much more difficult, whilst at the same time bringing Russia and Serbia together. It is, of course true that in 1911 Germany and Russia were still able to come to an agreement over the Bagdad railway – the so-called Potsdam agreement, but the fact remains, as D.C. Lieven has stressed, that German behaviour during the Bosnian crisis 'exerted a real influence over the way in which the Russian government handled the crisis of July 1914'.

ANALYSIS

See page 420

> ### The Potsdam Agreement of 1910
>
> The Germans managed to exploit growing Anglo-Russian tension in Persia by offering to recognise Russia's sphere of influence there, if in return it abandoned opposition to the construction of the Bagdad railway. Eventually Russia agreed to this but rejected attempts to persuade it to leave the *Triple Entente*.

C *The Balkan Wars, 1912–13*

See page 441

See Map 23 on page 418

With the Turkish army busy in Tripoli the Balkan states overcame their internal rivalries and by late summer had formed a hostile coalition against Turkey. Despite appeals from the Great Powers, which with the exception of Italy, were all acutely aware of the dangers that would result from the collapse of what remained of the Turkish Empire in Europe. Montenegro declared war on Turkey on 8 October to be followed a few days later by Bulgaria, Greece and Serbia. Within three weeks the Bulgarians had occupied Thrace and were advancing on Constantinople, the Serbs had advanced to the Adriatic and the Greeks had taken Thessaly and southern Macedonia. The Turkish Empire in Europe had collapsed, which, to quote Lieven, was 'a giant stride towards the outbreak of European war in 1914'.

The sheer speed and scale of the victory created an acute crisis for the Great Powers. As Izvolsky himself said, the situation was

palliative something which alleviates or eases

> the most fraught with threatening consequences for the general peace; it would bring forward, in its full historical development, the question of the struggle of Slavdom not only with Islam but also with Germanism. In this event one can scarcely set one's hopes on any **palliative** measures and must prepare for a great and decisive European war.

What made the situation so tense was that:

● Austria faced a greatly strengthened Serbia which had occupied part of Albania. Austria, however, was determined to make Albania an independent state so as to deny Serbia access to the Adriatic. At first Russia supported Serbian claims and Austria began to concentrate troops near the Russian frontier

- Russia was equally determined to stop Constantinople falling to Bulgaria as the Straits were becoming increasingly vital for its economic development. Between 1903 and 1912, for instance, 37 per cent of its exports and over 75 per cent of its grain exports passed through

- the crisis also threatened to activate 'the alliance system'. Behind Austria stood Germany and behind Russia stood France. Although neither wanted war in the Balkans both Powers made clear that they would stand by their ally if it were attacked

- the German declaration on 2 December promising help to Austria if attacked by a 'third party' was answered by a statement from London stressing that Britain would not remain neutral in a major conflict

- partly in response to this on 8 December the *Kaiser* called a conference of his service chiefs. Von Moltke, Chief of the General Staff, argued for 'War – the sooner, the better'.

The immediate danger to Russia passed when Bulgaria failed to take Constantinople and the Balkan States signed an armistice with Turkey on 3 December. The Great Powers then agreed to call a peace conference in London to settle the territorial problem in the Balkans. By the Treaty of London of 30 May 1913 the Turks gave up all their territory in the Balkans except for a small zone around the Dardanelles and Bosporous which satisfied Russia, while Austria's demand that an independent Albania be set up was also agreed to. Yet at the end of June the Second Balkan War broke out when Bulgaria, which felt cheated of its just share of territory, attacked Serbia. The Greeks, the Romanians and the Turks all supported Serbia and within a month Bulgaria was defeated. The subsequent Treaty of Bucharest increased the territories of Serbia, Greece and Romania, while Turkey through the Treaty of Constantinople regained some of the territory it had lost to Bulgaria.

The clear loser in the Second Balkan War was Austria. Serbia had emerged stronger and in M.S. Anderson's words was 'for the first time in her history, in a position to resist effectively pressure from either the Habsburg Empire or Russia'.

> **KEY ISSUE**
>
> *In what ways did the outcome of the Balkan Wars threaten Austria's position in the Balkans?*

D *Germany and Turkey, 1913–14*

As the Straits were of such economic importance to Russia, the sending of a German military mission under General Liman von Sanders on the invitation of the Turkish Government to Constantinople to take over responsibility for training the Turkish army both infuriated and alarmed the Russians. Sazonov, the Russian Foreign Minister, told a German journalist:

> You know what interests we have at the Bosporous, how sensitive we are at that point. All southern Russia depends on it, and now you stick a Prussian garrison under our noses .... the state which possesses the Straits will hold in its hands not only the key to the Black Sea and the Mediterranean, but also ... for the penetration of Asia Minor and the sure means to establish its hegemony over the Balkans

The Liman von Sanders affair galvanised the Russians into increasing the size of their army, attempting to rebuild a Balkan alliance against the Central Powers and competing with both the Germans and Austrians for the favour of the Poles. Germany's new interest in the Straits put Berlin on collision course with Russia. In February 1914 the volatile Wilhelm II observed: 'Russo-Prussian relations are dead once and for all'.

7 ✍ THE OUTBREAK OF WORLD WAR I

The series of major international crises stretching from the First Moroccan incident up to the Balkan wars had all in their turn been at least temporarily defused. Why then did the Sarajevo assassinations lead to the outbreak of hostilities?

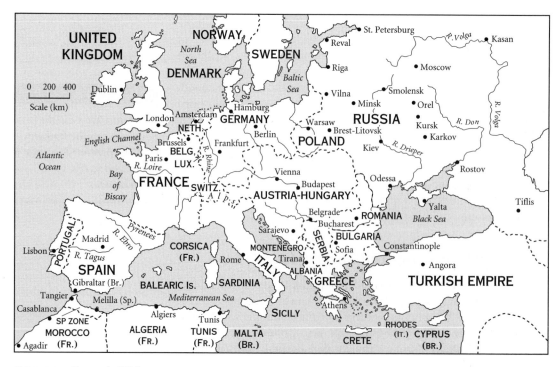

MAP 26 *Europe in 1914*

A *The assassination of Franz Ferdinand*

By 1914 Austria had every reason to fear the growing power of Serbia backed by Russia. The Serbian Government's desire to create a Greater Serbia which would include Bosnia and Herzegovina was an open challenge to Vienna. Austria's position in the Balkans was further threatened by Italy and Romania which were both hoping to make territorial gains if the Habsburg Empire collapsed.

On 28 June Archduke Francis Ferdinand, the heir to the Austrian throne, and his wife were assassinated at Sarajevo by Gavrilo Princip, who was closely associated with the Serb terrorist group, the Black Hand. The significance of the assassination was that it confirmed Austrian suspicions of Serbia, and at last provided an excuse to eliminate the Serb 'menace' To succeed, however, Vienna needed to gain German backing in case of Russian intervention and also to move quickly while the horror of the assassination was still fresh in the minds of the European Governments. On 3 July Count Hoyos was sent to Berlin with a general memorandum on Austria's position in the Balkans and a letter from the Emperor, which openly stated that Austrian policy was to eliminate Serbia as 'a political factor in the Balkans'. After discussions with the *Kaiser* and Bethmann Hollweg he got the crucial backing necessary – the so-called 'blank cheque', as it was later called. In 1928 Sidney Fay wrote:

> The Kaiser and his advisors on July 5 and 6 were not criminals plotting the World War; they were simpletons putting 'a noose about their necks' and handing the other end of the rope to a stupid and clumsy adventurer who now felt free to go as far as he liked.

In fact more detailed research by Fritz Fischer and Volker Berghahn has shown that the Germans thought they knew what they were doing. Bethmann Hollweg believed that decisive action against Serbia could be kept localised as Russia would not in the end intervene. Subsequently he hoped that Germany could exploit Austria's success to improve relations with the *Entente* Powers from a position of strength. However this plan, if it ever had any chance of working, was spoilt by the long time the Austrians took to send the ultimatum and then the reaction of Russia and France. Sazonov informed Poincaré, who was paying a state visit to St. Petersburg, 20–23 July, that Russia would not tolerate the destruction of Serbia. Poincaré, while determined to maintain the Dual Alliance and the existing balance of power, was initially more cautious. He proposed that Britain and France should urge Austria to adopt a more conciliatory policy.

TIMELINE

28 June 1914	Franz Ferdinand and his wife assassinated at Sarajevo
5 July	Kaiser gave Austria-Hungary a 'blank cheque'
20–23 July	Poincaré's visited to St. Petersburg
23 July	Austria sent ultimatum to Serbia
26 July	Grey proposed Conference of Ambassadors in London
28 July	Austria declared war on Serbia
30 July	Russia ordered general mobilisation
31 July	Germany sent ultimatum to Russia
1 Aug	Germany declared war on Russia
3 Aug	Germany declared war on France
4 Aug	German troops invaded Belgium
4 Aug	Britain declared war on Germany.

KEY ISSUE

Why did Germany give Serbia a 'blank cheque'?

The Black Hand and the Assassination

The Black Hand was founded in May 1911 and by 1914 probably had about 2500 members. They included a considerable number of the army officers who had taken part in the Serbian revolution of 1903. The Serbian Government feared the Black Hand but did not dare ban it because of the backing it had from the army. The Black Hand targeted the Austrian Crown Prince because it thought that his plans for giving the South Slavs in the Empire autonomy might win them over to Austrian rule. The murder was planned by Colonel Dragutin Dimitrievich, the head of the Intelligence Department of the Serbian General Staff, and the group of assassins was helped to cross the frontier by Serb customs officials. Nevertheless when the Serb Prime Minister, Pashich, heard of these plans, he did try to stop them and alerted the Austrian authorities in Bosnia-Herzegovina, and Dimitrievich himself ordered the assassins to return home, but Princip refused. Austrian security was very lax and the Archduke's visit to Sarajevo was in itself provocative as it was the anniversary of Serbia's National Day which mourned the destruction of the Serbo-Bosnian state and the beginning of Turkish rule at the Battle of Kossovo in 1389.

B The Austrian ultimatum and the Serb reply

The Austrian ultimatum was at last sent to Belgrade on 23 July. Its despatch was delayed so long because Vienna had to overcome the opposition of the Hungarian Cabinet to possible military action and 50 per cent of its army was on harvest leave. Care had also to be taken to avoid it arriving at Belgrade just when Poincaré was making his state visit to St. Petersburg for fear that he might influence Russia's reaction.. The crucial part of the ultimatum insisted that Serbia should carry out under the supervision of Austrian officials a whole series of anti-terrorist measures. The Austrians doubted whether Belgrade would be able to accept this demand, as it would force Serbia to root out terrorism and enable Austria to gain control of its internal affairs. The Serb reply to the ultimatum was skilfully drafted. It rejected, as Vienna expected, and indeed hoped, the crucial demand that Austrian officials should supervise the anti-terrorist measures, yet its tone was so conciliatory that it cunningly appeared to offer Austria most of what it wanted. The Austrians were not fooled by this 'masterpiece of public relations'. They broke off diplomatic relations and then on 28 July declared war on Serbia.

KEY ISSUE

Why was Austria determined to smash Serbia?

C The reaction of the Great Powers

On 27 July the British put forward a plan for a Conference of Ambassadors to meet in London to discuss the crisis. The Italians and the French backed it but the Germans by now aware of the threatening scale of the crisis, believed that direct Austro-Russians talks would be more effective. For Berlin the priority was, as Bethmann Hollweg told his Ambassador in Vienna:

> solely one of finding a way to realise Austria's desired aim, that of cutting the vital chord of Greater Serbia propaganda without it at the same time bringing on a world war, and if the latter cannot be avoided in the end, of improving the conditions under which we have to wage it where possible.

On 28 July there were further attempts at a settlement. Both the *Kaiser* and Sir Edward Grey separately urged Austria to restrict its occupation of Serbia to Belgrade, but Emperor Franz Josef dismissed this suggestion outright:

> From a mere occupation of Belgrade we should gain absolutely nothing, even if Russia should give her consent to it. All this would be mere tinsel. Russia would come forward as the saviour of Serbia, and especially of the Serbian army. The latter would remain intact, and in two or three years we should again have to look forward to the attack of Serbia under far more unfavourable conditions.

The Russians, too, were anxious to defuse the crisis, yet determined not to tolerate the destruction of Serbia. The Tsar was advised by his ministers that Belgrade should be told to

> show a desire for conciliation and fulfil the Austrian Government's requirements in so far as they did not jeopardise the independence of the Serbian state.

Perhaps given more time the deadlock could have been broken, but in both Russia, Germany and even Britain the military planners were desperate to get their forces mobilised before hostilities broke out. As soon as the Austrians declared war on Serbia and began to bombard Belgrade the Russian Government issued orders for a partial mobilisation of the army on 28 July. Two days later this was changed to full mobilisation despite the initial reservations of the Tsar and a personal appeal from the *Kaiser*. Russian mobilisation made German mobilisation inevitable given the Schlieffen Plan which depended on defeating the French *before* the Russian army was fully ready. Germany therefore had little option but to act quickly. On 31 July it despatched an ultimatum to Russia warning its Government that unless it stopped mobilisation within 12

Total Russian mobilisation
The reason for this was that the Russians had a rule that military units should be composed of 75 per cent Slav and 25 per cent non Slav personnel so that they would prove reliable and loyal to the Tsar. To get this balance *total* mobilisation was essential

KEY ISSUES

Can the decision by the Russians to proceed to full mobilisation be seen as the point when World War I became inevitable?

hours, Germany would fully mobilise its armed forces. France was also asked how it would react to a war between Russia and Germany. The Germans assumed that France would immediately support Russia *but* if the totally unexpected happened and France decided to remain neutral, the German Ambassador in Paris was instructed to demand the surrender of the two fortresses of Toul and Verdun to Germany as a pledge of its good faith. Obviously the French could never have agreed to this! The Russians attempted unsuccessfully to persuade the Germans that their mobilisation plans did not mean war, while the French Government informed Berlin that it would 'act in accordance to her interests'. The count down to war had begun:

- 1 August both France and Russia ordered full mobilisation
- at 7 o'clock that evening Germany declared war on Russia
- 2 August an ultimatum was dispatched to Brussels declaring that, as Germany had accurate knowledge that France was planning to occupy Belgium, it demanded the right of free passage for its troops through Belgian territory
- the Belgians rejected this ultimatum and on 3 August the Germans declared war on France
- on 4 August the Germans invaded Belgium, an action which threatened Britain directly. This enabled Grey and the 'War party' to overcome the waverers in the Cabinet, who clung to the hope that Britain could still keep out of the war
- the British then sent an ultimatum demanding that Germany pull out of Belgium, the neutrality of which both Britain and Prussia had guaranteed in 1839
- when this failed to happen Britain declared war at midnight on 4 August.

8 ∽ WAS WAR INEVITABLE?

See page 413

An analysis of events in late July 1914 does indicate that Germany, France, Britain and Russia all hoped that a general European war could be avoided. Does this mean that Lloyd George was right that they 'slithered' into war? In many ways this view is a simplification of history. The war was after all fought about real international issues of the sort which had in previous centuries led to conflict:

- the tension caused by the sudden rise of a Great Power, Germany, which as a consequence of its economic and military strength was inevitably a threat to the more established powers like Britain, France and Russia
- Austro-Russian rivalry in the Balkans caused by the decline of Turkey
- imperial rivalries outside Europe.

Paul Schroeder has argued that:

> The search for the fundamental cause of World War I is futile, while the argument that the War simply happened is unhelpful. Is there no exit from the cul de sac [dead end]? A different question may help: not why World War I? but why not? ... War was a normal development in international relations.

Thus a case can possibly be made out that war was inevitable, but if that was so why did it break out in 1914 and not earlier? Was it really inevitable that Germany and Austria should be confronted by the Triple *Entente*? Up to the end of the nineteenth century war between Britain and Russia or France seemed much more likely, yet ultimately these states managed to compose their differences. It can be argued that the developing power of Germany brought about this 'diplomatic revolution'. Certainly the growth of the German fleet antagonised Britain as later German ambitions in the Turkish Empire did Russia. German policy seemed at times calculated to alienate its neighbours as the two Moroccan and Bosnian crises showed. This undoubtedly tightened the links of the Triple *Entente* and made Germany more dependent on its one remaining ally, Austria-Hungary. Certain groups in Germany – the *Junkers* and the Army, for example, did, as Fischer has shown, press for war, which if victorious would enable Germany to break out of its encirclement and at the same time save the Bismarckian constitution of 1871, yet without the ongoing crisis caused by the decline of the Turkish Empire and the growth of nationalism in the Balkans, World War I might never have broken out. The emergence of a greatly strengthened Serbia in 1913 with its claims on Bosnia and Herzegovina was a deadly threat to the Habsburg Empire. Austria went to war in 1914 to preserve its position as a Great Power. The American historian Joachim Remark has observed:

> Turkey was dying and now Austria was: 1914–18 was the longest but by no means the only war of the Turkish succession. It was the third Balkan War.

It was of course, much more than a Balkan war. The Sarajevo assassinations brought together all the explosive tensions in Europe. Germany could not allow its only reliable ally to be humiliated by Serbia and Russia. Once Germany declared war on Russia, France could not stand back and see Russia defeated, while Britain, despite initial hesitations, could not afford to run the risk of a German victory. The decisions of the statesmen were backed for the most part by their people who saw the war as a struggle and a matter of honour and principle to preserve their nations' and empires' independence, greatness and future potential.

9 ⌒ BIBLIOGRAPHY

Rivalry and Accord: International Relations, 1870–1914, 2nd edition by John Lowe (Hodder, 1998) is a good, accessible introduction to both the long and short-term causes of World War I. *The Struggle For Mastery in Europe* by A.J.P. Taylor (OUP, 1954) and *Great Power Diplomacy, 1814–1914* by N. Rich (McGraw-Hill, 1992) contain excellent analyses of the two decades before 1914 as does *The Great powers, Imperialism and the German Problem, 1865–1925* by J. Lowe (Routledge, 1994). A concise guide to the theories on and historical development of Imperialism is *The New Imperialism* by M.E. Chamberlain (Historical Association (reprinted 1975). Events in Africa are well covered in *The Scramble For Africa* also by Chamberlain (Longman, 1974). The classic study of Great Power colonial rivalry is *The Diplomacy of Imperialism, 1890–1902* by W.L. Langer (revised edition Knopf, 1951). There is an enormous literature on the causes of World War I. There are the immensely detailed 'classics', *The Origins of the World War* by S.B. Fay (Macmillan, 1930) and *The Origins of the War of 1914* (3 vols) by L. Albertini (translated, OUP, 1952–7). A clear, concise and well-written account is in *The Origins of The First World War* by G. Martel (2nd edition, Longman,1996). A more detailed account that also covers Imperialism, Militarism and the domestic causes of the War is *The Origins of The First World War* by J. Joll (2nd edition, Longman, 1992). A good guide to the historiography and conflicting arguments about the causes of the war are in *The Origins of The First World War* by R. Henig (2nd edition, Routledge, 1993). Key extracts from the work of some of the most important historians can be found in *The Outbreak of the First World War. Causes and Responsibilities* edited by D.E. Lee (D.C. Heath, 1975) and in *The Outbreak of World War I* by H.H. Herwig (Houghton Mifflin, 1997). There is of course much on Germany's part in the causes of the war. A detailed, but readable analysis of German policy can be found in *Germany and the Approach of War in 1914* by V.R. Berghahn (Macmillan, 1973), and *Germany's Aims in the First World War by* Fritz Fischer (Norton/Chatto and Windus, 1967) presents the Fischer thesis. *France and the Origins of the First World War* by J.V. Keiger (Macmillan, 1993) is a useful guide to French policy, *while Russia and the Origins of the First World War* by D.C. Lieven, (Macmillan, 1983) is a very good survey of Russian policy. In the same series *Austria-Hungary and the Origins of the First World War* by S.R.Williamson (Macmillan, 1994) and *Britain and the Origins of the First World War* by Z.S. Steiner (Macmillan, 1978) are indispensable guides to Austrian and British foreign policy, respectively. The complicated problem of Anglo-German relations is dealt with in the *Rise of Anglo-German Antagonism, 1860–1914* by P. Kennedy (Allen and Unwin, 1980).

10 ⌇ ESSAYS AND STRUCTURED QUESTIONS

1. (a) Outline the aims and contents of the 'New Course' in foreign affairs, which Germany followed after the fall of Bismarck; (10 marks)
   (b) Explain why the 'New Course' failed;(15 marks)
2. (a) Outline the main crises in the Balkans, 1890–1908; (10 marks)
   (b) How successfully did the Great Powers deal with these crises? (15 marks)
3. (a) What were the causes of the new imperialism? (10 marks)
   (b) Explain how Britain managed to avoid war with both Russia and France; (15 marks).
4. (a) Outline the stages by which the 'diplomatic revolution' came about between 1898 and 1907; (10 marks)
   (b) Explain how and why the first Moroccan crisis strengthened the Anglo-French *Entente*; (15 marks).
5. (a) Outline the main developments in relations between the *Entente* powers and the Central Powers, 1907–12; (10 marks)
   (b) Explain why relations between Britain and Germany, 1907–12, were often worse than between France and Germany; (15 marks).
6. (a) Outline the main threats to Austria's influence in the Balkans, 1903–14; (10 marks)
   (b) Explain the reasons why the assassinations at Sarajevo led to a general European war; (15 marks).
7. To what extent was the alliance system responsible for the outbreak of war in 1914? (25 marks)

11 ⌇ DOCUMENTARY EXERCISE ON THE CAUSES OF WORLD WAR I

Study Sources A–E and attempt the quest;ions that follow:

... the Royal Government finds itself obliged to demand from the Serbian Government an official assurance that it condemns the propaganda directed against Austria-Hungary and in their entirety the dealings whose ultimate aim is to disjoin [detach] parts of the territory belonging to the Monarchy and that it pledges itself to suppress with all the means in its power this criminal and terrorist propaganda ...

The Royal Serbian government will moreover pledge itself to the following:
... to consent that Imp[erial] and Royal officials assist in Serbia in the suppressing of the subversive movement directed against the territorial integrity [unity] of the Monarchy ...

SOURCE A
Extracts from the Austrian ultimatum sent to Serbia on 23 July

SOURCE B

The Russian Foreign Minister, Sazonov, told the Tsar on 25 July that the demands of the Austrian ultimatum:

bear no relation either in form or in content to those omissions for which a measure of blame might possibly be imputed [attributed] to the Serbian Government ... . The clear aim of this procedure – which is apparently supported by Germany – is the total annihilation of Serbia and the disturbances of the political equilibrium in the Balkans.

SOURCE C

The American historian Samuel R. Williamson, in 1983

In 1914 Austria-Hungary was not an innocent, middle level government pressured into war by its more aggressive, ambitious northern ally. Rather those in power in Vienna were determined to control and fulfil the only international mission left to the Habsburgs: benevolent supervision of the Balkans. To do so effectively ... required, so they believed, the reduction or elimination of the most potent internal danger to the monarchy – the south Slav problem.

SOURCE D

On 18 July the German Foreign Secretary, von Jagow informed the German Ambassador in London, Prince Lichnowsky, of his government's support for Austria

The maintenance of Austria, and, in fact, of the most powerful Austria possible, is a necessity for us both for internal and external reasons. That she cannot be maintained forever, I will willingly admit. But in the meantime we may perhaps be able to arrange other combinations.

We must attempt to localise the conflict between Austria and Serbia. Whether we shall succeed ... will depend first on Russia and secondly on the moderating influence of Russia's allies. The more determined Austria shows herself, the more energetically we support her, so much the more quiet will Russia remain.

THE BOILING POINT.

PICTURE 42 *Cartoon in the British magazine* Punch, *2 October, 1912*

Q

1. *To what extent does Source E accurately sum up the attitude of the powers in 1912 towards the Balkans? (3 marks)*
2. *To what extent do Sources A and C show that source B is an accurate assessment of Austria's policy towards Serbia? (8 marks)*
3. *How useful is Source D as a guide to German policy in July 1914? (6 marks)*
4. *To what extent does source B indicate that Jagow's hopes for limiting the Balkan conflict (Source D) are too optimistic? (8 marks)*
5. *Using this collection of Sources A–E, and your own knowledge, explain why the assassinations at Sarejevo led to the outbreak of World War I. (15 marks)*

Glossary

Index